SKILLS For SUCCESS

with Office for
Mac 2011

VOLUME 1

TOWNSEND | FERRETT | HAIN | VARGAS | HAYES

PEARSON

Boston   Columbus   Indianapolis   New York   San Francisco   Upper Saddle River
Amsterdam   Cape Town   Dubai   London   Madrid   Milan   Munich   Paris   Montréal   Toronto
Delhi   Mexico City   São Paulo   Sydney   Hong Kong   Seoul   Singapore   Taipei   Tokyo

Editor in Chief: *Michael Payne*
Executive Editor: *Jenifer Niles*
Product Development Manager: *Laura Burgess*
Editorial Assistant: *Andra Skaalrud*
Development Editor: *Nancy Lamm*
Marketing Coordinator: *Susan Osterlitz*
Marketing Assistant: *Darshika Vyas*
Managing Editor: *Camille Trentacoste*
Senior Production Project Manager: *Rhonda Aversa*
IT Procurement Lead: *Natacha Moore*
Operations Specialist: *Maura Zaldivar-Garcia*

Senior Art Director: *Jonathan Boylan*
Text and Cover Designer: *Jonathan Boylan*
Digial Media & Assessment Editor: *Eric Hakanson*
Media Project Manager, Production: *John Cassar*
Project Coordination, Editorial Services, and Text Design: *Electronic Publishing Services Inc., NYC*
Full-Service Project Manager: *Melinda Durham*
Art Rendering and Electronic Page Makeup: *Jouve*
Printer/Binder: *Quad Graphics/Eusey Press Inc.*
Cover Printer: *Lehigh-Phoenix Color/Hagerstown*
Typeface: *Minion Pro Regular 10.5/12.5*

Credits and acknowledgments borrowed from other sources and reproduced, with permission, in this textbook appear on appropriate page within text.

Apple screen shot(s) reprinted with permission from Apple Inc. © 2009 Apple Inc. All rights reserved.

Snagit Icon reprinted with permission from TechSmith Corporation.

Library of Congress Cataloging-in-Publication Data

Hayes, Darren Richard.
  Skills for success with Office for Mac 2011 / [Darren Richard] Hayes [and four others].
    pages cm
  Includes index.
  ISBN-13: 978-0-13-310990-0
  ISBN-10: 0-13-310990-9
1. Microsoft Office.   2. Macintosh (Computer)   3. Apple computer.   4. Business—Computer programs.   I. Title.
  HF5548.4.M525H39 2014
  005.5—dc23

2012041872

10 9 8 7 6 5 4 3 2 1
ISBN-10: 0-13-310990-9
ISBN-13: 978-0-13-310990-0

Contents in Brief

Common Features

Chapter 1   Common Features of Office 2011   2

Word

Chapter 1   Create Documents with Word 2011   28

Chapter 2   Format and Organize Text   60

Chapter 3   Work with Graphics, Tabs, and Tables   92

Chapter 4   Apply Special Text, Paragraph, and Document Formats   124

Excel

Chapter 1   Create Workbooks with Excel 2011   156

Chapter 2   Create Charts   188

Chapter 3   Manage Multiple Worksheets   220

Chapter 4   Use Excel Functions and Tables   252

PowerPoint

Chapter 1   Getting Started with PowerPoint 2011   284

Chapter 2   Format a Presentation   316

Chapter 3   Enhance Presentations with Graphics   348

Chapter 4   Present Data Using Tables, Charts, and Animation   380

Glossary   412

Index   418

Table of Contents

Common Features

Chapter 1   Common Features of Office 2011   2

Skill 1   Start Word and Navigate the Word Window   4
Skill 2   Start Excel and PowerPoint and Work with Multiple Windows   6
Skill 3   Save Files in New Folders   8
Skill 4   Print and Save Documents   10
Skill 5   Open Student Data Files and Save Copies Using Save As   12
Skill 6   Type and Edit Text   14
Skill 7   Cut, Copy, and Paste Text   16
Skill 8   Format Text and Paragraphs   18
Skill 9   Use the Ribbon   20
Skill 10   Use Shortcut Menus and Dialogs   22

More Skills

More Skills 12   Use Microsoft Office Help   24
More Skills 13   Organize Files   24

Word

Chapter 1   Create Documents with Word 2011   28

Skill 1   Create New Documents and Enter Text   30
Skill 2   Edit Text and Use Keyboard Shortcuts   32
Skill 3   Select Text   34
Skill 4   Insert Text from Other Documents   36
Skill 5   Change Fonts, Font Sizes, and Font Styles   38
Skill 6   Insert and Work with Graphics   40
Skill 7   Check Spelling and Grammar   42
Skill 8   Use the Thesaurus and Set Proofing Options   44
Skill 9   Create Document Footers   46
Skill 10   Work with the Print Page Function and Save Documents in Other Formats   48

More Skills

More Skills 11   Split and Arrange Windows   50
More Skills 12   Insert Symbols   50

Chapter 2   Format and Organize Text   60

Skill 1   Set Document Margins   62
Skill 2   Align Text and Set Indents   64
Skill 3   Modify Line and Paragraph Spacing   66
Skill 4   Format Text Using Format Painter   68
Skill 5   Find and Replace Text   70
Skill 6   Create Bulleted and Numbered Lists   72
Skill 7   Insert and Format Headers and Footers   74
Skill 8   Insert and Modify Footnotes   76
Skill 9   Add Citations   78
Skill 10   Create Bibliographies   80

More Skills

More Skills 11   Record AutoCorrect Entries   82
More Skills 12   Use AutoFormat to Create Numbered Lists   82
More Skills 13   Format and Customize Lists   82
More Skills 14   Manage Document Properties   82

Chapter 3   Work with Graphics, Tabs, and Tables   92

Skill 1   Insert Pictures from Files   94
Skill 2   Resize and Move Pictures   96
Skill 3   Format Pictures Using Styles and Artistic Effects   98
Skill 4   Set Tab Stops   100
Skill 5   Enter Text with Tab Stops   102
Skill 6   Apply Table Styles   104
Skill 7   Create Tables   106
Skill 8   Add Rows and Columns to Tables   108
Skill 9   Format Text in Table Cells   110
Skill 10   Format Tables   112

More Skills

More Skills 11   Insert Text Boxes   114
More Skills 12   Format with WordArt   114
More Skills 13   Create Tables from Existing Lists   114
More Skills 14   Insert Drop Caps   114

Chapter 4   Apply Special Text, Paragraph, and Document Formats   124

Skill 1	Create Multiple-Column Text	126
Skill 2	Insert a Column Break	128
Skill 3	Apply and Format Text Effects	130
Skill 4	Use Quick Styles	132
Skill 5	Add Borders and Shading to Paragraphs and Pages	134
Skill 6	Insert and Format Clip Art Graphics	136
Skill 7	Insert SmartArt Graphics	138
Skill 8	Format SmartArt Graphics	140
Skill 9	Create Labels Using Mail Merge	142
Skill 10	Preview and Print Mail Merge Documents	144

More Skills

| More Skills 11 | Create Resumes from Templates | 146 |

Excel

Chapter 1   Create Workbooks with Excel 2011   156

Skill 1	Create and Save New Workbooks	158
Skill 2	Enter Worksheet Data and Merge and Center Titles	160
Skill 3	Construct Addition and Subtraction Formulas	162
Skill 4	Construct Multiplication and Division Formulas	164
Skill 5	Adjust Column Widths and Apply Cell Styles	166
Skill 6	Use the SUM Function	168
Skill 7	Copy Formulas and Functions Using the Fill Handle	170
Skill 8	Format, Edit, and Check the Spelling of Data	172
Skill 9	Create Footers and Change Page Settings	174
Skill 10	Display and Print Formulas and Scale Worksheets for Printing	176

More Skills

More Skills 11	Create New Workbooks from Templates	178
More Skills 12	Use Range Names in Formulas	178
More Skills 13	Change Themes	178
More Skills 14	Manage Document Properties	178

Chapter 2   Create Charts   188

Skill 1	Open Existing Workbooks and Align Text	190
Skill 2	Construct and Copy Formulas Containing Absolute Cell References	192
Skill 3	Format Numbers	194
Skill 4	Create Column Charts	196
Skill 5	Format Column Charts	198
Skill 6	Create Pie Charts and Chart Sheets	200
Skill 7	Apply 3-D Effects and Rotate Pie Chart Slices	202
Skill 8	Explode and Color Pie Slices and Insert Text Boxes	204
Skill 9	Update Charts and Insert WordArt	206
Skill 10	Prepare Chart Sheets for Printing	208

More Skills

More Skills 11	Insert and Edit Comments	210
More Skills 12	Change Chart Types	210
More Skills 13	Copy Excel Data to Word Documents	210
More Skills 14	Fill Series Data into Worksheet Cells	210

Chapter 3   Manage Multiple Worksheets   220

Skill 1	Work with Sheet Tabs	222
Skill 2	Enter and Format Dates	224
Skill 3	Clear Cell Contents and Formats	226
Skill 4	Use Move, Copy, Paste, and Paste Options	228
Skill 5	Work with Grouped Worksheets	230
Skill 6	Use Multiple Math Operators in a Formula	232
Skill 7	Format Grouped Worksheets	234
Skill 8	Insert and Move Worksheets	236
Skill 9	Construct Formulas That Refer to Cells in Other Worksheets	238
Skill 10	Create Clustered Bar Charts	240

More Skills

More Skills 11	Create Organization Charts	242
More Skills 12	Create Line Charts	242
More Skills 13	Set and Clear Print Areas	242
More Skills 14	Insert Hyperlinks	242

Chapter 4   Use Excel Functions and Tables   252

Skill 1	Use the SUM and AVERAGE Functions	254
Skill 2	Use the MIN and MAX Functions	256
Skill 3	Move Ranges with Functions, Add Borders, and Rotate Text	258
Skill 4	Use the IF Function	260
Skill 5	Apply Conditional Formatting with Custom Formats, Data Bars, and Sparklines	262
Skill 6	Use Find and Replace and Insert the NOW Function	264
Skill 7	Freeze and Unfreeze Panes	266
Skill 8	Create and Sort Excel Tables	268
Skill 9	Use the Search Filter in Excel Tables	270
Skill 10	Convert Tables to Ranges, Hide Rows and Columns, and Format Large Worksheets	272

More Skills

More Skills 11	Apply Conditional Color Scales with Top and Bottom Rules	274
More Skills 12	Use the Payment (PMT) Function	274
More Skills 13	Create PivotTable Reports	274
More Skills 14	Use Goal Seek	274

PowerPoint

Chapter 1   Getting Started with PowerPoint 2011   284

Skill 1	Open, View, and Save Presentations	286
Skill 2	Edit and Replace Text in Normal View	288
Skill 3	Format Slide Text	290
Skill 4	Check Spelling and Use the Thesaurus	292
Skill 5	Insert Slides and Modify Slide Layouts	294
Skill 6	Insert and Format Pictures	296
Skill 7	Organize Slides Using Slide Sorter View	298
Skill 8	Apply Slide Transitions and View Slide Shows	300
Skill 9	Insert Headers and Footers and Print Presentation Handouts	302
Skill 10	Add Notes Pages and Print Notes	304

More Skills

More Skills 11	Type Text in the Outline Tab	306
More Skills 12	Use Keyboard Shortcuts	306

More Skills 13	Move and Delete Slides in Normal View	306
More Skills 14	Design Presentations for Audience and Location	306

Chapter 2   Format a Presentation   316

Skill 1	Create New Presentations	318
Skill 2	Change Presentation Themes	320
Skill 3	Apply Font and Color Themes	322
Skill 4	Format Slide Backgrounds with Styles	324
Skill 5	Format Slide Backgrounds with Pictures and Textures	326
Skill 6	Format Text with WordArt	328
Skill 7	Change Character Spacing and Font Color	330
Skill 8	Modify Bulleted and Numbered Lists	332
Skill 9	Move and Copy Text and Objects	334
Skill 10	Use Format Painter and Clear All Formatting	336

More Skills

More Skills 11	Edit Slide Masters	338
More Skills 12	Save and Apply Presentation Templates	338
More Skills 14	Design Presentations with Contrast	338

Chapter 3   Enhance Presentations with Graphics   348

Skill 1	Insert Slides from Other Presentations	350
Skill 2	Insert, Size, and Move Clip Art	352
Skill 3	Modify Picture Shapes, Borders, and Effects	354
Skill 4	Insert, Size, and Move Shapes	356
Skill 5	Add Text to Shapes and Insert Text Boxes	358
Skill 6	Apply Gradient Fills and Group and Align Graphics	360
Skill 7	Convert Text to SmartArt Graphics and Add Shapes	362
Skill 8	Modify SmartArt Layouts, Colors, and Styles	364
Skill 9	Insert Video Files	366
Skill 10	Apply Video Styles and Adjust Videos	368

More Skills

More Skills 11	Compress Pictures	370
More Skills 12	Save Groups as Picture Files	370
More Skills 13	Change Object Order	370
More Skills 14	Design Presentations Using Appropriate Graphics	370

Chapter 4 Present Data Using Tables, Charts, and Animation   380

Skill 1	Insert Tables	382
Skill 2	Modify Table Layouts	384
Skill 3	Apply Table Styles	386
Skill 4	Insert Column Charts	388
Skill 5	Edit and Format Charts	390
Skill 6	Insert Pie Charts	392

Skill 7	Apply Animation Entrance and Emphasis Effects	394
Skill 8	Modify Animation Timing and Use Animation Painter	396
Skill 9	Remove Animation and Modify Duration	398
Skill 10	Navigate Slide Shows	400

More Skills

More Skills 12	Insert Hyperlinks in a Presentation	402
More Skills 14	Design Presentations with Appropriate Animation	402

Glossary   412

Index   418

Contributors

We would like to thank the following people for their work on Skills for Success:

Instructor Resource Authors

Julie Boyles
Stacy Everly
Jennifer Lynn
Tony Nowakowski
Joyce Thompson

Technical Editors

Julie Boyles
Lisa Bucki
Dennis Cohen
Mara Zebest
Susan Samuels

Reviewers

Darrell Abbey	*Cascadia Community College*	Lennie Coper	*Miami Dade College*
Bridget I. Archer	*Oakton Community College*	Tara Cipriano	*Gateway Technical College*
Laura Aagard	*Sierra College*	Paulette Comet	*Community College of Baltimore County—Catonsville*
John Alcorcha	*MTI College*		
Barry Andrews	*Miami Dade College*	Gail W. Cope	*Sinclair Community College*
Natalie Andrews	*Miami Dade College*	Susana Contreras de Finch	*College of Southern Nevada*
Wilma Andrews	*Virginia Commonwealth University School of Business*	Chris Corbin	*Miami Dade College*
		Janis Cox	*Tri-County Technical College*
Bridget Archer	*Oakton Community College*	Tomi Crawford	*Miami Dade College*
Tahir Aziz	*J. Sargeant Reynolds*	Martin Cronlund	*Anne Arundel Community College*
Greg Balinger	*Miami Dade College*	Jennifer Day	*Sinclair Community College*
Terry Bass	*University of Massachusetts, Lowell*	Ralph DeArazoza	*Miami Dade College*
Lisa Beach	*Santa Rosa Junior College*	Carol Decker	*Montgomery College*
Rocky Belcher	*Sinclair Community College*	Loorna DeDuluc	*Miami Dade College*
Nannette Biby	*Miami Dade College*	Caroline Delcourt	*Black Hawk College*
David Billings	*Guilford Technical Community College*	Michael Discello	*Pittsburgh Technical Institute*
Brenda K. Britt	*Fayetteville Technical Community College*	Kevin Duggan	*Midlands Technical Community College*
Alisa Brown	*Pulaski Technical College*	Barbara Edington	*St. Francis College*
Eric Cameron	*Passaic Community College*	Donna Ehrhart	*Genesee Community College*
Gene Carbonaro	*Long Beach City College*	Hilda Wirth Federico	*Jacksonville University*
Trey Cherry	*Edgecombe Community College*	Tushnelda Fernandez	*Miami Dade College*
Kim Childs	*Bethany University*	Arlene Flerchinger	*Chattanooga State Tech Community College*
Pualine Chohonis	*Miami Dade College*	Hedy Fossenkemper	*Paradise Valley Community College*

Contributors continued

Kent Foster	*Withrop University*	Jean Lacoste	*Virginia Tech*
Penny Foster-Shiver	*Anne Arundel Community College*	Gene Laughrey	*Northern Oklahoma College*
Arlene Franklin	*Bucks County Community College*	David LeBron	*Miami Dade College*
George Gabb	*Miami Dade College*	Kaiyang Liang	*Miami Dade College*
Barbara Garrell	*Delaware County Community College*	Linda Lindaman	*Black Hawk College*
Deb Geoghan	*Bucks County Community College*	Felix Lopez	*Miami Dade College*
Jessica Gilmore	*Highline Community College*	Nicki Maines	*Mesa Community College*
Victor Giol	*Miami Dade College*	Cindy Manning	*Big Sandy Community and*
Melinda Glander	*Northmetro Technical College*		*Technical College*
Linda Glassburn	*Cuyahoga Community College, West*	Patri Mays	*Paradise Valley Community College*
Deb Gross	*Ohio State University*	Norma McKenzie	*El Paso Community College*
Rachelle Hall	*Glendale Community College*	Lee McKinley	*GA Perimeter*
Marie Hartlein	*Montgomery County Community College*	Sandy McCormack	*Monroe Community College*
Diane Hartman	*Utah Valley State College*	Eric Meyer	*Miami Dade College*
Betsy Headrick	*Chattanooga State*	Kathryn Miller	*Big Sandy Community and Technical*
Patrick Healy	*Northern Virginia Community*		*College, Pike Ville Campus*
	College—Woodbridge	Gloria A. Morgan	*Monroe Community College*
Lindsay Henning	*Yavapai College*	Kathy Morris	*University of Alabama, Tuscaloosa*
Kermelle Hensley	*Columbus Technical College*	Linda Moulton	*Montgomery County Community College*
Diana Hill	*Chesapeake College*	Ryan Murphy	*Sinclair Community College*
Rachel Hinton	*Broome Community College*	Stephanie Murre Wolf	*Moraine Park Technical College*
Mary Carole Hollingsworth	*GA Perimeter*	Jackie Myers	*Sinclair Community College*
Stacey Gee Hollins	*St. Louis Community College—Meramec*	Dell Najera	*El Paso Community College, Valle Verde*
Bill Holmes	*Chandler-Gilbert Community College*		*Campus*
Steve Holtz	*University of Minnesota Duluth*	Scott Nason	*Rowan Cabarrus Community College*
Margaret M. Hvatum	*St. Louis Community College*	Paula Neal	*Sinclair Community College*
Joan Ivey	*Lanier Technical College*	Bethanne Newman	*Paradise Valley Community College*
Dr. Dianna D. Johnson	*North Metro Technical College*	Eloise Newsome	*Northern Virginia Community*
Kay Johnston	*Columbia Basin College*		*College—Woodbridge*
Warren T. Jones, Sr.	*University of Alabama at Birmingham*	Karen Nunan	*Northeast State Technical Community College*
Sally Kaskocsak	*Sinclair Community College*	Ellen Orr	*Seminole Community College*
Renuka Kumar	*Community College of Baltimore County*	Carol Ottaway	*Chemeketa Community College*
Kathy McKee	*North Metro Technical College*	Denise Passero	*Fulton-Montgomery Community College*
Hazel Kates	*Miami Dade College*	Americus Pavese	*Community College of Baltimore County*
Gerald Kearns	*Forsyth Technical Community College*	James Gordon Patterson	*Paradise Valley Community College*
Charles Kellermann	*Northern Virginia Community*	Cindra Phillips	*Clark State CC*
	College—Woodbridge	Janet Pickard	*Chattanooga State Tech Community College*
John Kidd	*Tarrant County Community College*	Floyd Pittman	*Miami Dade College*
Chris Kinnard	*Miami Dade College*	Melissa Prinzing	*Sierra College*
Kelli Kleindorfer	*American Institute of Business*	Pat Rahmlow	*Montgomery County Community College*
Kurt Kominek	*NE State Tech Community College*	Mary Rasley	*Lehigh Carbon Community College*
Dianne Kotokoff	*Lanier Technical College*	Scott Rosen	*Santa Rosa Junior College*
Cynthia Krebs	*Utah Valley University*	Ann Rowlette	*Liberty University*

Contributors continued

Kamaljeet Sanghera	*George Mason University*
June Scott	*County College of Morris*
Janet Sebesy	*Cuyahoga Community College*
Jennifer Sedelmeyer	*Broome Community College*
Kelly SellAnne	*Arundel Community College*
Teresa Sept	*College of Southern Idaho*
Pat Serrano	*Scottsdale Community College*
Amanda Shelton	*J. Sargeant Reynolds*
Gary Sibbits	*St. Louis Community College—Meramec*
Janet Siert	*Ellsworth Community College*
Robert Sindt	*Johnson County Community College*
Karen Smith	*Technical College of the Lowcountry*
Robert Smolenski	*Delaware County Community College*
Robert Sindt	*Johnson County Community College*
Gary R. Smith	*Paradise Valley Community College*
Patricia Snyder	*Midlands Technical College*
Pamela Sorensen	*Santa Rosa Junior College*
Eric Stadnik	*Santa Rosa Junior College*
Mark Stanchfield	*Rochester Community and Technical College*
Diane Stark	*Phoenix College*
Neil Stenlund	*Northern Virginia Community College*
Linda Stoudemayer	*Lamar Institute of Technology*
Pamela Stovall	*Forsyth Technical Community College*
Linda Switzer	*Highline Community College*
Margaret Taylor	*College of Southern Nevada*
Martha Taylor	*Sinclair Community College*
Michael M. Taylor	*Seattle Central Community College*
Roseann Thomas	*Fayetteville Tech Community College*
Ingrid Thompson-Sellers	*GA Perimeter*
Daniel Thomson	*Keiser University*
Astrid Hoy Todd	*Guilford Technical Community College*
Barb Tollinger	*Sinclair Community College*
Cathy Urbanski	*Chandler Gilbert Community College*
Sue Van Boven	*Paradise Valley Community College*
Philip Vavalides	*Guildford Technical Community College*
Pete Vetere	*Montgomery County Community College—West Campus*
Asteria Villegas	*Monroe College*
Michael Walton	*Miami Dade College*
Teri Weston	*Harford Community College*
Julie Wheeler	*Sinclair Community College*
Debbie Wood	*Western Piedmont Community College*
Thomas Yip	*Passaic Community College*
Lindy Young	*Sierra Community College*
Matt Zullo	*Wake Technical Community College*

About the Book

Skills for Success with Office for Mac 2011 is based on the Mac version of Microsoft Office 2011, and therefore only covers the features that are available in the Mac version of the Office software.

This book is intended for courses using Macintosh computers. MyITLab and all related media are based on Microsoft Office 2010 for PCs. If your course uses MyITLab, you will need to download the MyITLab Mac Compatibility Solution.

The MyITLab Mac Compatibility Solution uses a remote desktop client to run MyITLab in a virtual Windows environment. Two installations are necessary. The first is one time only. The second must be done each time you access MyITLab. Visit http://wps.prenhall.com/bp_myitlab2010_macuser for instructions on how to download the MyITLab Mac Compatibility Solution.

Note the following:

You must be running Mac OS 10.5 to 10.7.
Training Simulations are based on the Windows/PC version of Microsoft Office.
This solution is not intended for MyITLab Grader Project activities. If you need to complete any of the MyITLab Grader Project activities for your course, you will need to complete these on a PC.
This solution is only supported for customers in the United States and Canada.

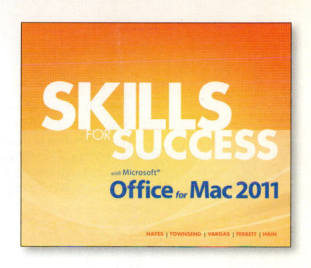

A Microsoft® Office textbook that recognizes how students learn today

Skills for Success

with **Office for Mac 2011**, Volume 1

- **10 x 8.5 Format –** Easy for students to read and type at the same time by simply propping the book up on the desk in front of their monitor
- **Clearly Outlined Skills –** Each skill is presented in a single two–page spread so that students can easily follow along
- **Numbered Steps and Bulleted Text –** Students don't read long paragraphs of text, but they will read information presented concisely

Chapter Introduction – Briefs students on what is important and sets the stage for the project the student will create

File Summary – A quick summary of the files the students need to open and the names of the files they will turn in

Clock – Tells how much time students need to complete the chapter

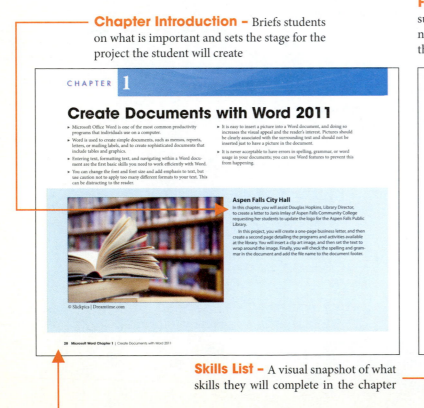

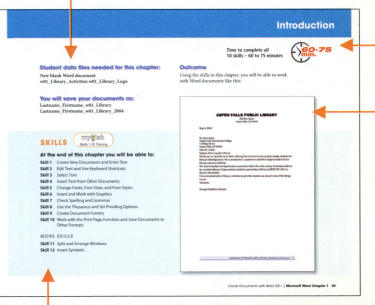

Skills List – A visual snapshot of what skills they will complete in the chapter

Outcome – Shows students up front what their completed project will look like

Sequential Pagination – Saves you and your students time in locating topics and assignments

Skills for Success

Written for Today's Students – Skills are taught with numbered steps and bulleted text so students are less likely to skip valuable information

Two-Page Spreads – Each skill is presented on a two–page spread to help students keep up their momentum

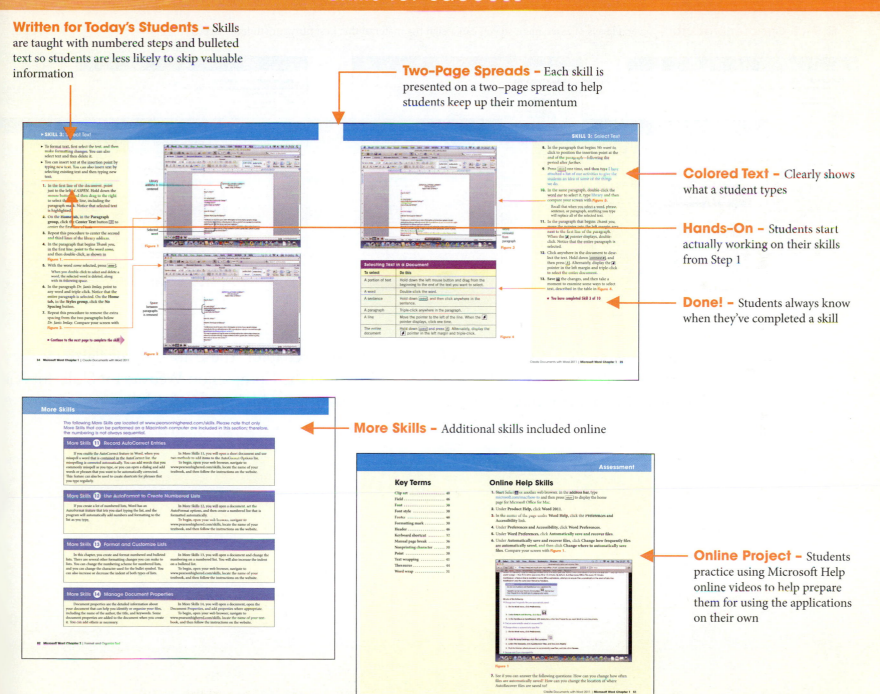

Colored Text – Clearly shows what a student types

Hands-On – Students start actually working on their skills from Step 1

Done! – Students always know when they've completed a skill

More Skills – Additional skills included online

Online Project – Students practice using Microsoft Help online videos to help prepare them for using the applications on their own

Skills for Success

End-of-Chapter Material – Several levels of assessment so you can assign the material that best fits your students' needs

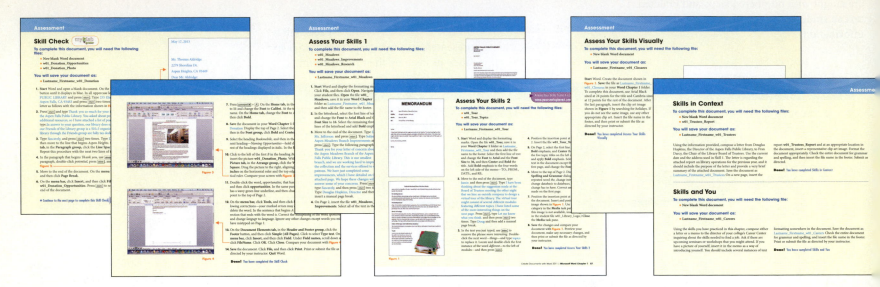

Videos! –
A visual and audio walk-through of each skill within a chapter. These are only available for the Windows version of Office. To view these videos, visit the Companion Website for Success with Microsoft Office 2011, Volume 1, at www.pearsonhighered.com/skills.

All Videos and Instructor materials available on the IRC

Instructor Materials

Assignment Sheets – Lists all the assignments for the chapter, you just add in the course information, due dates, and points. Providing these to students ensures they will know what is due and when

Scripted Lectures – Classroom lectures prepared for you

Annotated Solution Files – Coupled with the scoring rubrics, these create a grading and scoring system that makes grading so much easier for you

PowerPoint Lectures – PowerPoint presentations for each chapter

Prepared Exams – Exams for each chapter and for each application

Scoring Rubrics – Can be used either by students to check their work or by you as a quick check–off for the items that need to be corrected

Syllabus Templates – For 8–week, 12–week, and 16–week courses

Test Bank – Includes a variety of test questions for each chapter

Companion Website – Online content such as the More Skills Projects, Online Study Guide, Glossary, and Student Data Files are all at www.pearsonhighered.com/skills

About the Authors

 **Kris Townsend** is an Information Systems instructor at Spokane Falls Community College in Spokane, Washington. Kris earned a bachelor's degree in both Education and Business, and a master's degree in Education. He has also worked as a public school teacher and as a systems analyst. Kris enjoys working with wood, snowboarding, and camping. He commutes to work by bike and enjoys long road rides in the Palouse country south of Spokane.

 **Robert L. Ferrett** recently retired as the Director of the Center for Instructional Computing at Eastern Michigan University, where he provided computer training and support to faculty. He has authored or coauthored more than 70 books on Access, PowerPoint, Excel, Publisher, WordPerfect, Windows, and Word. He has been designing, developing, and delivering computer workshops for more than two decades.

 **Catherine Hain** is an instructor at Central New Mexico Community College in Albuquerque, New Mexico. She teaches computer applications classes in the Business and Information Technology School, both in the classroom and through the distance learning office. Catherine holds a bachelor's degree in Management and Marketing and a master's degree in Business Administration.

 **Alicia Vargas** is an Associate Professor of Business Information Technology at Pasadena City College in California. She holds a bachelor's and a master's degree in Business Education from California State University, Los Angeles, and has authored numerous textbooks and training materials on Microsoft Word, Microsoft Excel, and Microsoft PowerPoint.

Darren R. Hayes is CIS program Chair and Lecturer at Pace University. He is also a consultant for the Department of Education in New York City, where he provides high school teachers with training in computer forensics. He is passionate about computer forensics, works closely with law enforcement, and believes that the field of study is a great way to get students interested in computing. He's not a native of New York but shares the same birthplace as Oscar Wilde, Bram Stoker, James Joyce, and Bono. On his breaks from university life, he likes to travel home to Ireland or to his wife's native Trinidad. In the summertime, you might see him and his children trekking along the magnificent bike paths of Harwich, Massachusetts.

A Special Thank You

Pearson Prentice Hall gratefully acknowledges the contribution made by Shelley Gaskin to the first edition publication of this series—*Skills for Success with Office 2007*. The series has truly benefited from her dedication toward developing a textbook that aims to help students and instructors. We thank her for her continued support of this series.

Common Features of Office 2011

SKILLS
For SUCCESS

with Office for
Mac 2011

VOLUME 1

Common Features of Office 2011

- ► Microsoft Office is a suite of several programs—Word, PowerPoint, Excel, and others.
- ► Each Office program is used to create different types of personal and business documents.
- ► The programs in Office 2011 share common tools that you use in a consistent, easy-to-learn manner.

- ► Common tasks include opening and saving files, entering and formatting text, and printing your work.
- ► Because of its consistent design and layout, when you learn to use one Microsoft Office program, you can use most of those skills when working with the other Microsoft Office programs.

© Lipik | Dreamtime.com

Aspen Falls City Hall

In this project, you will create documents for the Aspen Falls City Ha which provides essential services for the citizens and visitors of Asp Falls, California. You will assist Todd Austin, Tourism Director, to crea a flyer promoting tourism.

You will work with documents, spreadsheets, and presentations practice skills common to all Microsoft Office 2011 programs. You w also practice opening student data files and saving them with new names.

Time to complete all
10 skills – 60 to 90 minutes

60-90 min.

Student data files needed for this chapter:

cf01_Visit
cf01_Visit_River
cf01_Visit_Events

You will save your files as:

Lastname_Firstname_cf01_Visit1
Lastname_Firstname_cf01_Visit2
Lastname_Firstname_cf01_Visit3

SKILLS

Skills 1-10 Training

At the end of this chapter you will be able to:

Skill 1 Start Word and Navigate the Word Window
Skill 2 Start Excel and PowerPoint and Work with Multiple Windows
Skill 3 Save Files in New Folders
Skill 4 Print and Save Documents
Skill 5 Open Student Data Files and Save Copies Using Save As
Skill 6 Type and Edit Text
Skill 7 Cut, Copy, and Paste Text
Skill 8 Format Text and Paragraphs
Skill 9 Use the Ribbon
Skill 10 Use Shortcut Menus and Dialogs

MORE SKILLS

Skill 12 Use Microsoft Office Help
Skill 13 Organize Files

Outcome

Using the skills in this chapter, you will be able to work with Office documents like this:

Visit Aspen Falls!

Aspen Falls overlooks the Pacific Ocean and is surrounded by many vineyards and wineries. Ocean recreation is accessed primarily at Durango County Park. The Aspen Lake Recreation Area provides year round fresh water recreation and is the city's largest park.

Local Attractions
- Wine Country
  - o Wine Tasting Tours
  - o Wineries
- Wordsworth Fellowship Museum of Art
- Durango County Museum of History
- Convention Center
- Art Galleries
- Glider Tours

Aspen Falls Annual Events
- Annual Starving Artists Sidewalk Sale
- Annual Wine Festival
- Cinco de Mayo
- Vintage Car Show
- Heritage Day Parade
- Harvest Days
- Amateur Bike Races
- Farmer's Market
- Aspen Lake Nature Cruises
- Aspen Falls Triathlon
- Taste of Aspen Falls
- Winter Blues Festival

Contact Your Name for more information.

► The Word 2011 program can be launched by clicking the Word icon, on the Dock.

► When you start Word, a dialog will display where you can select a blank document or choose a template.

1. At the bottom of your screen, on the **Dock**, click the **Microsoft Word** icon 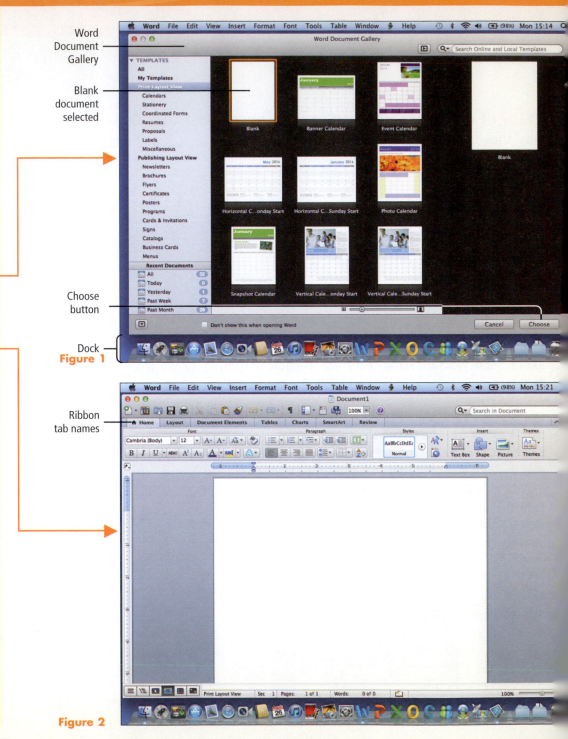.

   A Word Document Gallery displays with a list of template categories. You can also access recently used Word documents from here.

2. In the displayed **Word Document Gallery**, make sure that **Blank** is selected, and then compare your screen with **Figure 1**.

   A variety of templates are available to choose from or you can select a blank document.

3. Click the **Choose** button, and then compare your screen with **Figure 2**.

   A blank Word document displays. The layout of the window is quite similar to Office 2010 for Windows, although there are some notable differences in terms of different icons, placement of various operations, and the tools available.

   ■ **Continue to the next page to complete the skill**

Word Document Gallery

Blank document selected

Choose button

Dock

Figure 1

Ribbon tab names

Figure 2

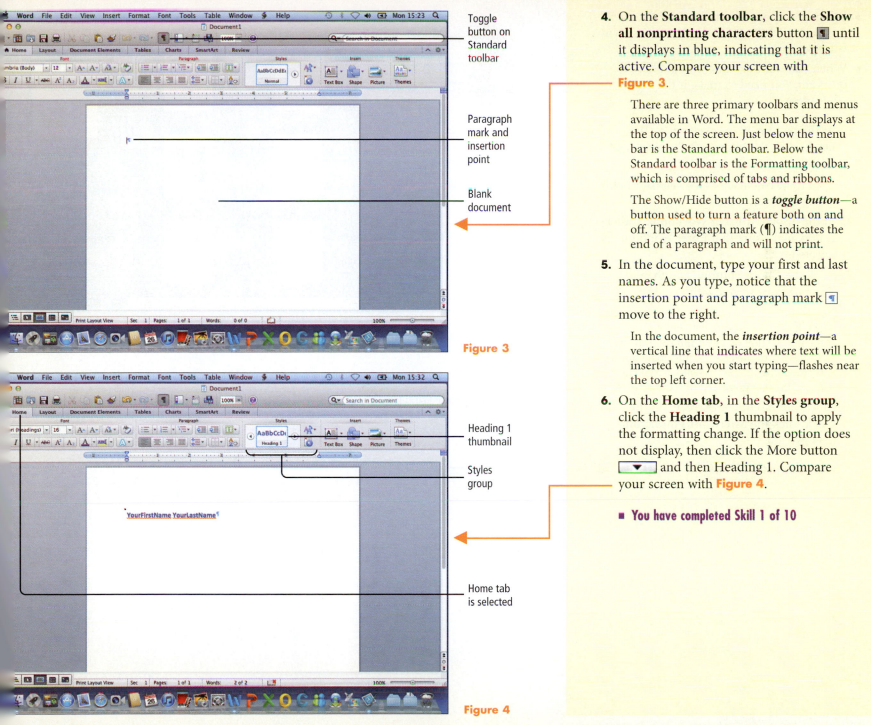

Toggle button on Standard toolbar

Paragraph mark and insertion point

Blank document

Figure 3

Heading 1 thumbnail

Styles group

Home tab is selected

Figure 4

4. On the **Standard toolbar**, click the **Show all nonprinting characters** button ¶ until it displays in blue, indicating that it is active. Compare your screen with **Figure 3**.

There are three primary toolbars and menus available in Word. The menu bar displays at the top of the screen. Just below the menu bar is the Standard toolbar. Below the Standard toolbar is the Formatting toolbar, which is comprised of tabs and ribbons.

The Show/Hide button is a *toggle button*—a button used to turn a feature both on and off. The paragraph mark (¶) indicates the end of a paragraph and will not print.

5. In the document, type your first and last names. As you type, notice that the insertion point and paragraph mark ¶ move to the right.

In the document, the *insertion point*—a vertical line that indicates where text will be inserted when you start typing—flashes near the top left corner.

6. On the **Home tab**, in the **Styles group**, click the **Heading 1** thumbnail to apply the formatting change. If the option does not display, then click the More button ▼ and then Heading 1. Compare your screen with **Figure 4**.

■ **You have completed Skill 1 of 10**

▶ When you open more than one Office program, each program displays in its own window.

▶ When you want to work with a different program, you need to make it the active application.

1. At the bottom of your screen, on the **Dock**, click the **Microsoft Excel** icon ⊠. Compare your screen with **Figure 1**.

An Excel Workbook Gallery displays with a list of template categories.

2. In the displayed **Excel Workbook Gallery** dialog, make sure that Excel Workbook is selected.

3. Click the **Choose** button, and then compare your screen with **Figure 2**.

A new blank worksheet displays in a new window. The first *cell*—the box formed by the intersection of a row and column—is active as indicated by the thick blue border surrounding the cell. When you type in Excel, the text is entered into the active cell.

4. At the bottom of your screen, on the **Dock**, click the **Microsoft PowerPoint** icon ⊡.

■ **Continue to the next page to complete the skill**

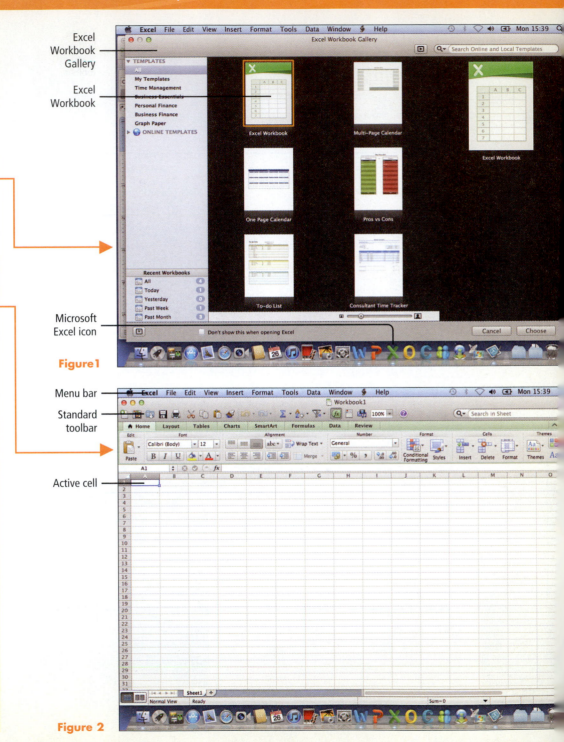

Excel Workbook Gallery

Excel Workbook

Microsoft Excel icon

Figure 1

Menu bar

Standard toolbar

Active cell

Figure 2

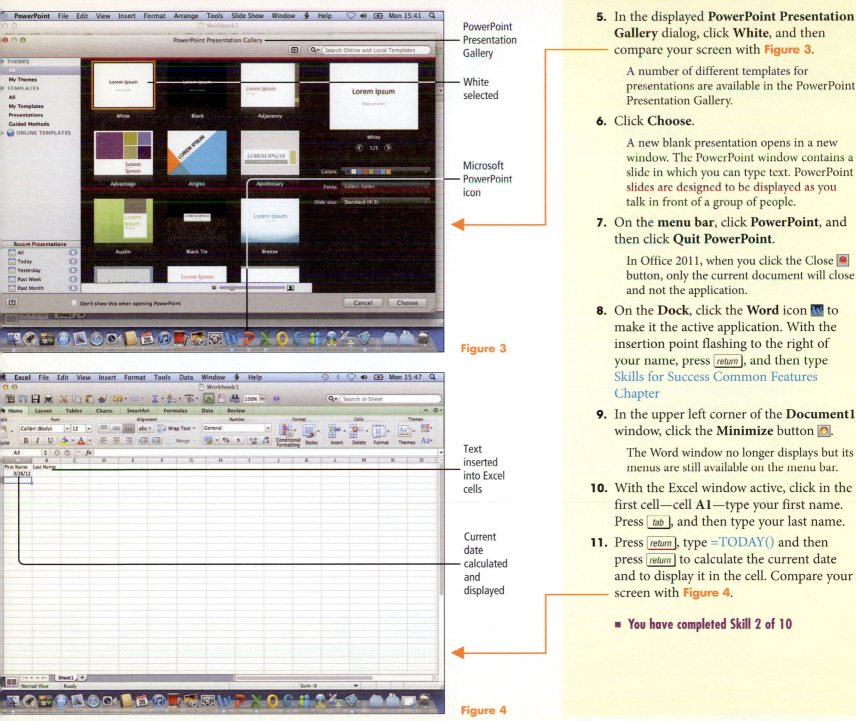

PowerPoint Presentation Gallery

White selected

Microsoft PowerPoint icon

Figure 3

Text inserted into Excel cells

Current date calculated and displayed

Figure 4

5. In the displayed **PowerPoint Presentation Gallery** dialog, click **White**, and then compare your screen with **Figure 3**.

A number of different templates for presentations are available in the PowerPoint Presentation Gallery.

6. Click **Choose**.

A new blank presentation opens in a new window. The PowerPoint window contains a slide in which you can type text. PowerPoint slides are designed to be displayed as you talk in front of a group of people.

7. On the **menu bar**, click **PowerPoint**, and then click **Quit PowerPoint**.

In Office 2011, when you click the Close button, only the current document will close and not the application.

8. On the **Dock**, click the **Word** icon to make it the active application. With the insertion point flashing to the right of your name, press return , and then type Skills for Success Common Features Chapter

9. In the upper left corner of the **Document1** window, click the **Minimize** button.

The Word window no longer displays but its menus are still available on the menu bar.

10. With the Excel window active, click in the first cell—cell **A1**—type your first name. Press tab , and then type your last name.

11. Press return , type =TODAY() and then press return to calculate the current date and to display it in the cell. Compare your screen with **Figure 4**.

■ **You have completed Skill 2 of 10**

► A new document or spreadsheet is stored in the computer's temporary memory (*RAM*) until you save it to a drive.

1. If you are saving your work on a USB flash drive, insert the USB flash drive into the computer now.

2. On the **Dock**, click the **Word** icon 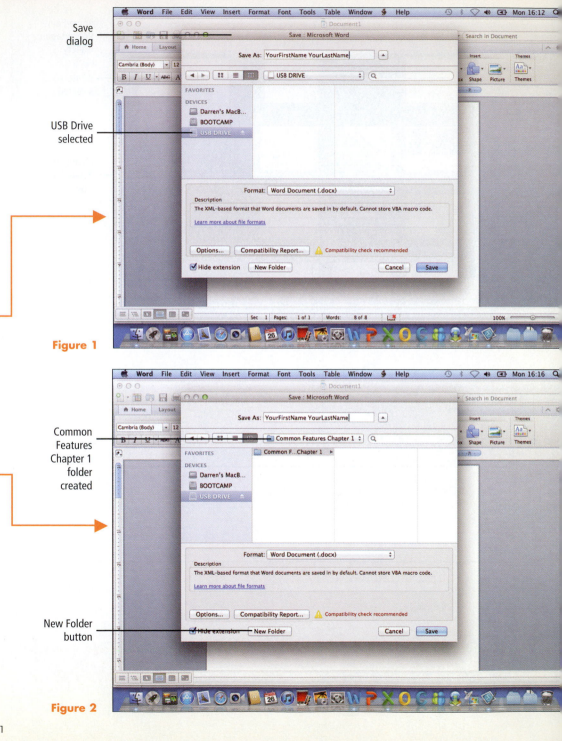 to make it the active application. On the **Standard toolbar**, click the **Save this document** button.

   For new documents, the first time you click the Save this document button, the Save : Microsoft Word dialog opens so that you can name the file.

3. If you are to save your work on a USB drive, under DEVICES scroll down to display the list of drives, and then click your USB flash drive as shown in **Figure 1**. If you are saving your work to another drive, under DEVICES locate and then click that drive.

4. In the **Save: Microsoft Word** dialog, click the **New Folder** button, and then immediately type Common Features Chapter 1

5. Click **Create** to accept the folder name, and then compare your screen to **Figure 2**.

   The new folder is created and then opened in the file list.

   ■ **Continue to the next page to complete the skill**

Save dialog

USB Drive selected

Figure 1

Common Features Chapter 1 folder created

New Folder button

Figure 2

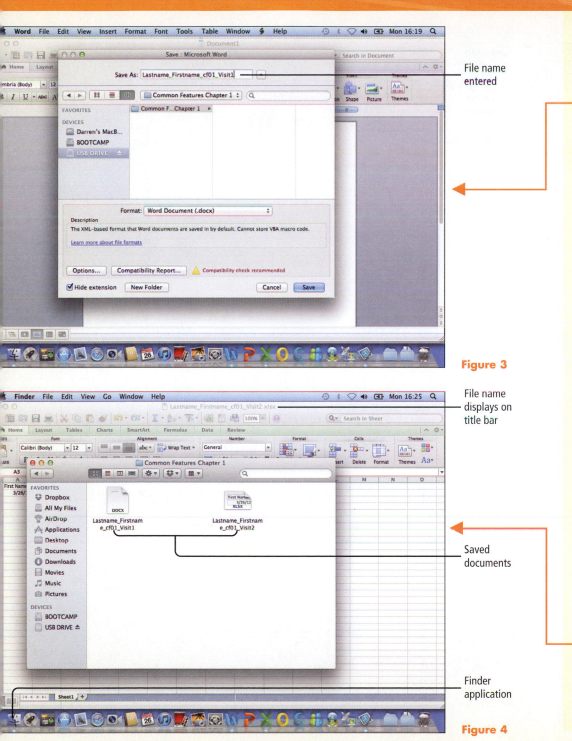

File name entered

Figure 3

File name displays on title bar

Saved documents

Finder application

Figure 4

6. In the **Save As** dialog, in the **File name** box, use your own name to replace the existing text with Lastname_Firstname_ cf01_Visit1

7. Compare your screen with **Figure 3**, and then click **Save**.

   After the document is saved, the name of the file displays on the title bar at the top of the window.

8. On the **Dock**, click the **Finder** icon. Under **DEVICES**, click the drive on which you saved your work, and then double-click the **Common Features Chapter 1** folder. Verify that *Lastname_Firstname_ cf01_Visit1* displays in the file list.

   Finder—an Apple application that enables the user to find and manage files, folders, applications, and attached devices.

9. On the **Dock**, click the **Microsoft Excel** icon to make it the active application. On the **Standard toolbar**, click the **Save this workbook** button.

10. In the displayed dialog, under **DEVICES**, click the drive where you are saving your work, and then click the **Common Features Chapter 1** folder to display its file list.

    If the Devices do not display then try to maximize the dialog or simply scroll down in the sidebar.

11. Click in the **File name** box, replace the existing value with Lastname_Firstname_ cf01_Visit2 and then click the **Save** button.

12. On the **Dock**, click the **Finder** icon and then compare your screen with **Figure 4**.

   ■ **You have completed Skill 3 of 10**

▶ Before printing, it is a good idea to work in *Page Layout view*—a view where you prepare your document or spreadsheet for printing.

1. On the **Dock**, click the **Microsoft Excel** icon 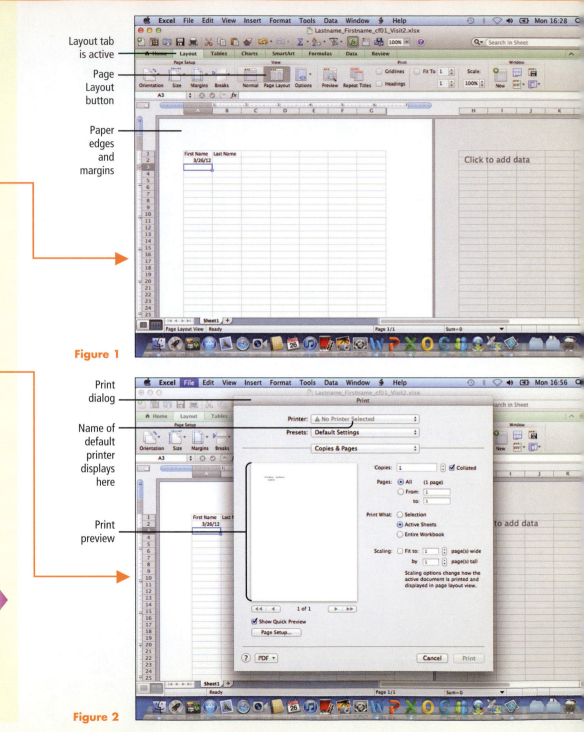.

2. On the Ribbon, click the **Layout tab**, and then in the **View group**, click the **Page Layout** button. Compare your screen with **Figure 1**.

   The worksheet displays the cells, the margins, and the edges of the paper as they will be positioned when you print. The *cell references*—the numbers on the left side and the letters across the top of a spreadsheet that address each cell—will not print.

3. In the **Page Setup group**, click the **Margins** button, and then click **Wide**.

4. On the **menu bar**, click **File**, and then click **Print**. Compare your screen with **Figure 2**.

   The Print dialog has commands and settings that affect your print job and a preview of the printed page. Here, the cell references and *grid lines*—lines between the cells in a table or spreadsheet—do not display because they will not be printed.

5. Next to **Printer**, notice the name of the printer. You will need to retrieve your printout from this printer. If your instructor has directed you to print to a different printer, click the Printer pop-up menu and choose the assigned printer.

   ■ **Continue to the next page to complete the skill**

Layout tab is active

Page Layout button

Paper edges and margins

Figure 1

Print dialog

Name of default printer displays here

Print preview

Figure 2

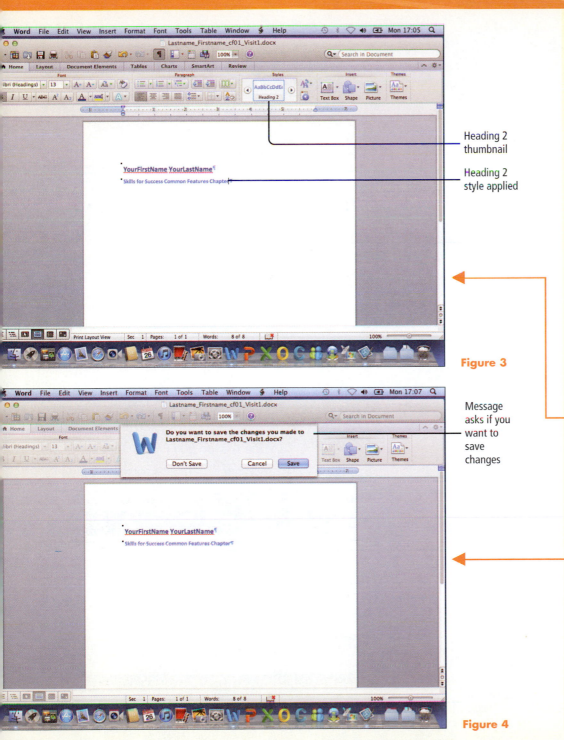

Heading 2
thumbnail

Heading 2
style applied

Figure 3

Message
asks if you
want to
save
changes

Figure 4

6. Check your *Course Assignment Sheet* or *Course Syllabus,* or consult with your instructor to determine whether you are to print your work for this chapter. If you are to print your work, select the Printer, and then click the Print button. If you printed the spreadsheet, retrieve the printout from the printer. If you do not want to print at this time, click the Cancel button.

7. On the **menu bar**, click **File**, and then click **Save**.

    Because you have already named the file, the Save As dialog does not display.

8. On the **menu bar**, click **Excel**, and then click **Quit Excel** to close the spreadsheet and quit Excel.

9. In the Word document, verify that the insertion point is in the second line of text.

10. On the **Home tab**, in the **Styles group**, click the **Heading 2** thumbnail. Compare your screen with **Figure 3**.

11. Click **File**, and then click **Print** to display the Print dialog. If you are printing your work for this chapter, click the Print button, and then retrieve your printout from the printer. Otherwise, click Cancel.

12. On the **menu bar**, click **Word**, click **Quit Word**, and then compare your screen with **Figure 4**.

    When you close a window with changes that have not yet been saved, a message will remind you to save your work.

13. Read the displayed message, and then click **Save**.

■ **You have completed Skill 4 of 10**

▶ This book often instructs you to open a student data file so that you do not need to start the project with a blank document.

▶ The student data files and instructions for downloading them are located at www.pearsonhighered.com/skills. Your instructor may have provided an alternate location to obtain these files.

1. On the **Dock**, click **Safari** 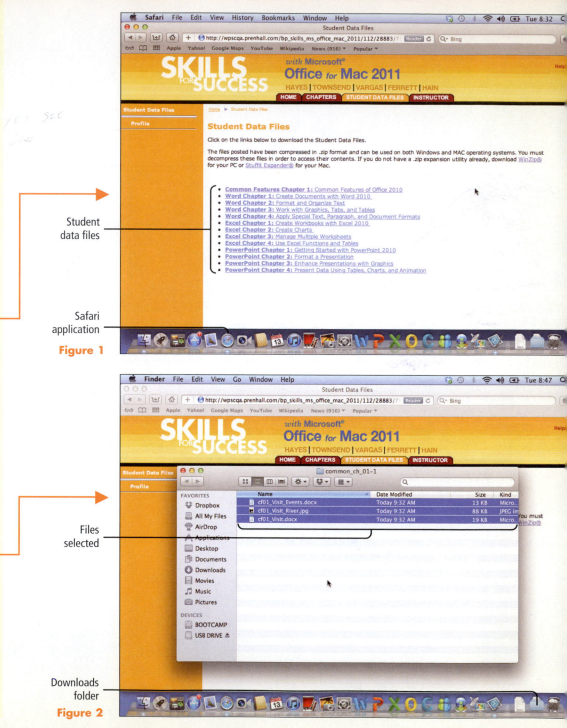, navigate to www.pearsonhighered.com/skills, and then click the hyperlink for the edition of the book that you are using.

   Safari —the default Web browser that comes preinstalled on an Apple Macintosh computer.

2. On the Web page, click **Student Data Files**—or similar—hyperlink, and then compare your screen with **Figure 1**.

3. Click the **Common Features Chapter 1: Common Features of Office 2011** hyperlink.

   Wait for the documents to download.

4. On the **Dock**, click the **Downloads** folder, and then from the displayed list of downloads click the **common_ch_1_01** folder.

5. In the **Finder** window, click the **cf01_Visit_Events.docx** file. Press and hold the ⇧ shift key and then click the **cf01_Visit.docx** file. Compare your screen with **Figure 2**.

   All three files are now selected.

   ▪ **Continue to the next page to complete the skill** ➡

Student data files

Safari application

Figure 1

Files selected

Downloads folder

Figure 2

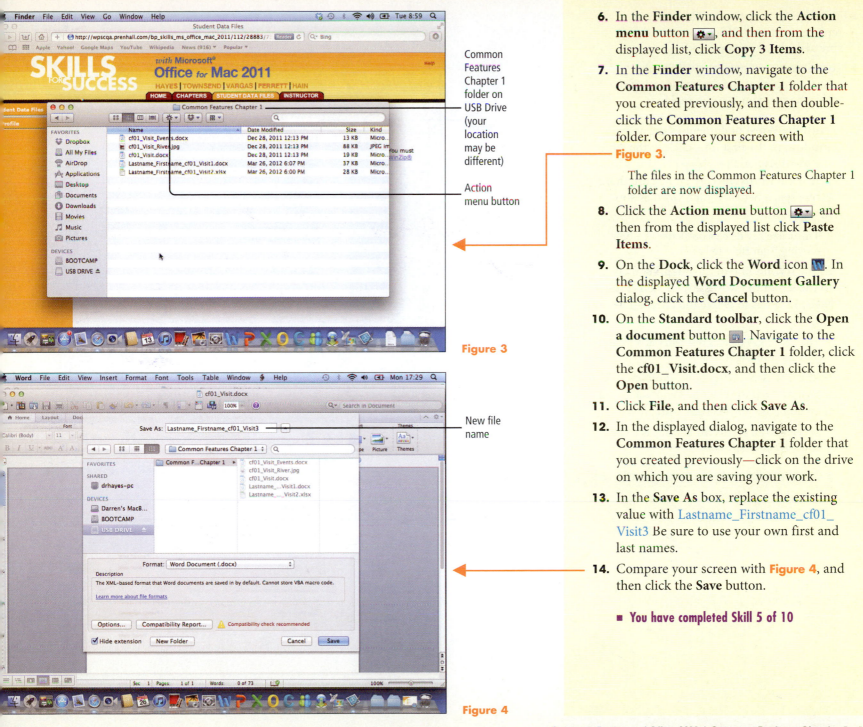

Common Features Chapter 1 folder on USB Drive (your location may be different)

Action menu button

Figure 3

New file name

Figure 4

6. In the **Finder** window, click the **Action menu** button, and then from the displayed list, click **Copy 3 Items**.

7. In the **Finder** window, navigate to the **Common Features Chapter 1** folder that you created previously, and then double-click the **Common Features Chapter 1** folder. Compare your screen with **Figure 3**.

> The files in the Common Features Chapter 1 folder are now displayed.

8. Click the **Action menu** button, and then from the displayed list click **Paste Items**.

9. On the **Dock**, click the **Word** icon. In the displayed **Word Document Gallery** dialog, click the **Cancel** button.

10. On the **Standard toolbar**, click the **Open a document** button. Navigate to the **Common Features Chapter 1** folder, click the **cf01_Visit.docx**, and then click the **Open** button.

11. Click **File**, and then click **Save As**.

12. In the displayed dialog, navigate to the **Common Features Chapter 1** folder that you created previously—click on the drive on which you are saving your work.

13. In the **Save As** box, replace the existing value with Lastname_Firstname_cf01_Visit3 Be sure to use your own first and last names.

14. Compare your screen with **Figure 4**, and then click the **Save** button.

■ **You have completed Skill 5 of 10**

▶ To *edit* is to insert text, delete text, or replace text in an Office document, spreadsheet, or presentation.

▶ To edit text, you need to position the insertion point at the desired location or select the text you want to replace.

1. With the **Word** document as the active window, in the first line, click to the left of the word *Aspen*. Press `delete` 12 times to delete the words *the City of*. Be sure there is one space between each word as shown in **Figure 1**.

   The delete key deletes one letter at a time moving from right to left.

2. In the second line of the document, click to the left of the words *Aspen Falls*. Press `delete` 12 times to delete the phrase *The City of*.

   The delete key deletes one letter at a time moving from right to left.

3. In the line *Area Attractions,* double-click the word *Area* to select it. Type Local and then compare your screen with **Figure 2**.

   When a word is selected, it is replaced by whatever you type next.

■ **Continue to the next page to complete the skill** ▶

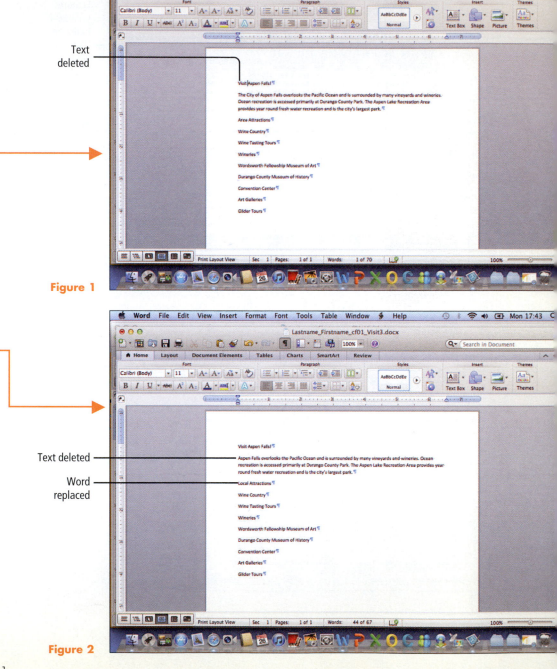

Text deleted

Figure 1

Text deleted

Word replaced

Figure 2

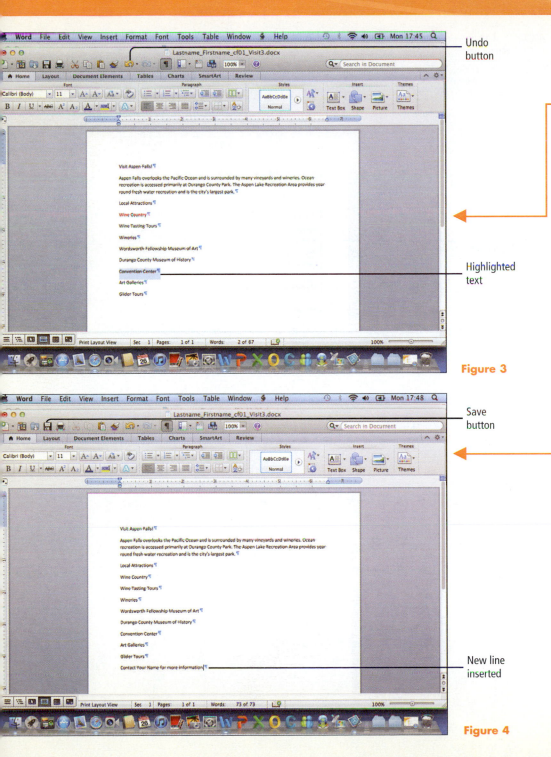

Undo button

Highlighted text

Figure 3

Save button

New line inserted

Figure 4

4. Place the pointer approximately 1 inch to the left of the line *Convention Center*. When the ◢ pointer displays, click one time, and then compare your screen with **Figure 3**.

   Placing the pointer in the Selection bar and then clicking is a way to select an entire line with a single click.

5. With the entire line still selected, press `delete` to delete the line.

6. On the **Standard toolbar**, click the **Undo** button ◙ one time. Notice the *Convention Center* line displays again.

   When you perform an incorrect action, clicking the Undo button often returns your document to its previous state.

7. At the end of the last line—*Glider Tours*—click between the last word and the paragraph formatting mark (¶). Press `return` to insert a new line.

8. With the insertion point in the new line, type Contact Your Name for more information. Be sure to use your first and last names in place of *Your Name*. Compare your screen with **Figure 4**.

9. On the **Standard toolbar**, click **Save this document** 🖫.

   When a document has already been saved with the desired name, click the Save button—the Save As dialog is not needed.

   ■ **You have completed Skill 6 of 10**

► The *copy* command places a copy of the selected text or object in the *Clipboard*—a temporary storage area that holds text or an object that has been cut or copied.

► You can move text by moving it to and from the Clipboard or by dragging the text.

1. Click **File**, and then click **Open**. In the **Open : Microsoft Word** dialog, if necessary, navigate to the student files and display the contents of the **Common Features Chapter 1** folder. Click **cf01_ Visit_Events**, and then click **Open**.

2. On the **menu bar**, click **Edit**, and then click **Select All**. Compare your screen with **Figure 1**.

3. With all of the document text selected, on the **Standard toolbar**, click the **Copy** button .

4. In the upper left corner of the Word document window, click **Close** . You do not need to save changes—you will not turn in this student data file.

5. In **Lastname_Firstname_cf01_Visit3**, click to place the insertion point to the left of the line that starts *Contact Your Name*.

6. On the **menu bar**, click **Edit**, point to— but do not click—the Paste menu item. Compare your screen with **Figure 2**.

    There are a number of different paste options.

■ **Continue to the next page to complete the skill**

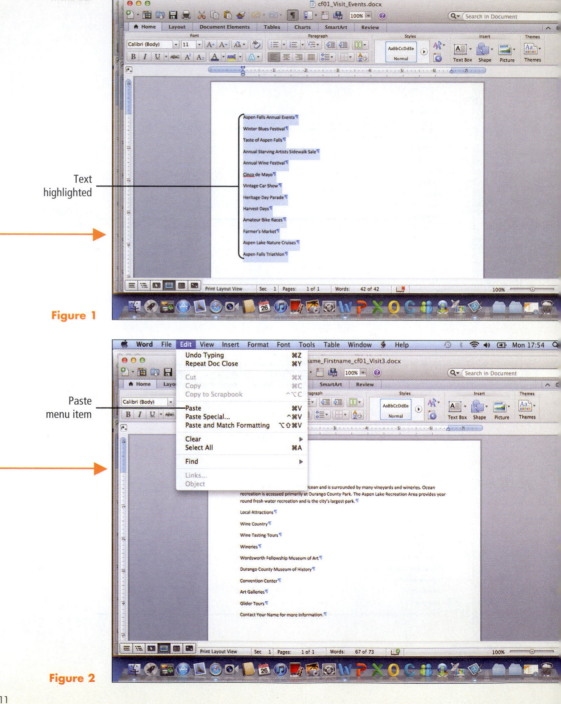

Edit on menu bar

Text highlighted

Figure 1

Paste menu item

Figure 2

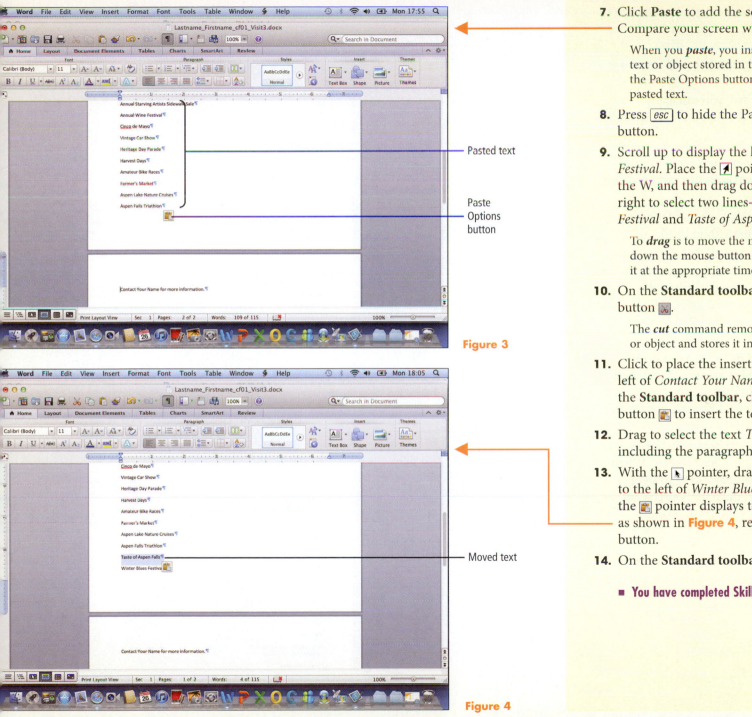

Pasted text

Paste
Options
button

Figure 3

Moved text

Figure 4

7. Click **Paste** to add the selected text. Compare your screen with **Figure 3**.

   When you *paste*, you insert a copy of the text or object stored in the Clipboard and the Paste Options button displays near the pasted text.

8. Press esc to hide the Paste Options button.

9. Scroll up to display the line *Winter Blues Festival*. Place the ↗ pointer to the left of the W, and then drag down and to the right to select two lines—*Winter Blues Festival* and *Taste of Aspen Falls*.

   To *drag* is to move the mouse while holding down the mouse button and then to release it at the appropriate time.

10. On the **Standard toolbar**, click the **Cut** button ✂.

    The *cut* command removes the selected text or object and stores it in the Clipboard.

11. Click to place the insertion point to the left of *Contact Your Name,* and then on the **Standard toolbar**, click the **Paste** button 📋 to insert the text.

12. Drag to select the text *Taste of Aspen Falls,* including the paragraph mark.

13. With the ↖ pointer, drag the selected text to the left of *Winter Blues Festival.* When the 📋 pointer displays to the left of *Winter* as shown in **Figure 4**, release the mouse button.

14. On the **Standard toolbar**, click **Save** 💾.

   ■ **You have completed Skill 7 of 10**

► To *format* is to change the appearance of the text—for example, changing the text color to red.

► Before formatting text, you first need to select the text that will be formatted.

► Once text is selected, you can apply formatting using the Ribbon or the Mini toolbar.

1. Scroll to the top of the document, and then click anywhere in the first line, *Visit Aspen Falls!*

2. On the **Home tab**, in the **Styles group**, click the **Heading 1** thumbnail.

3. Click in the paragraph, *Local Attractions,* and then in the **Styles group**, click the **Heading 2** thumbnail. Click in the paragraph, *Aspen Falls Annual Events,* and then apply the **Heading 2** style. Compare your screen with **Figure 1**.

4. On the **Home tab**, in the **Font group**, click the **Font Size arrow** A⌄, and then from the list, click **28** to increase the size of the selected text. Compare your screen with **Figure 2**.

5. Place the pointer approximately 1 inch to the left of the line *Wine Country*. When the ⬈ pointer displays, drag straight down. When all the lines between and including *Wine Country* and *Glider Tours* are selected, release the left mouse button.

■ **Continue to the next page to complete the skill** ➤

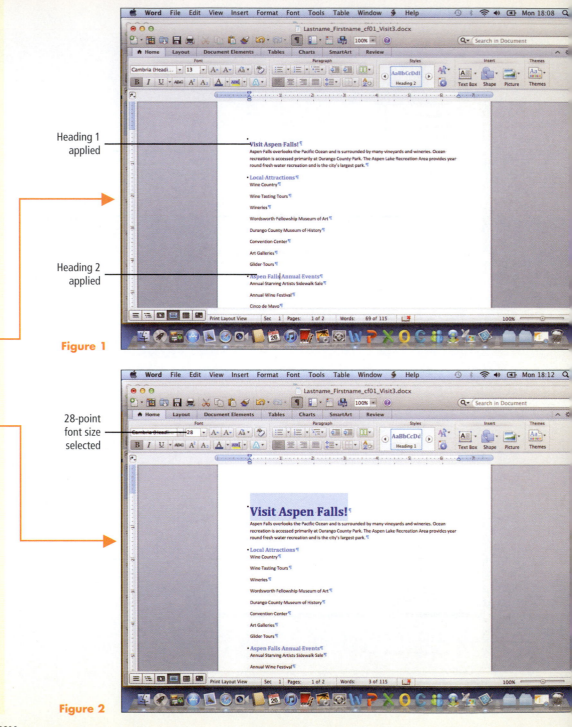

Heading 1 applied

Heading 2 applied

Figure 1

28-point font size selected

Figure 2

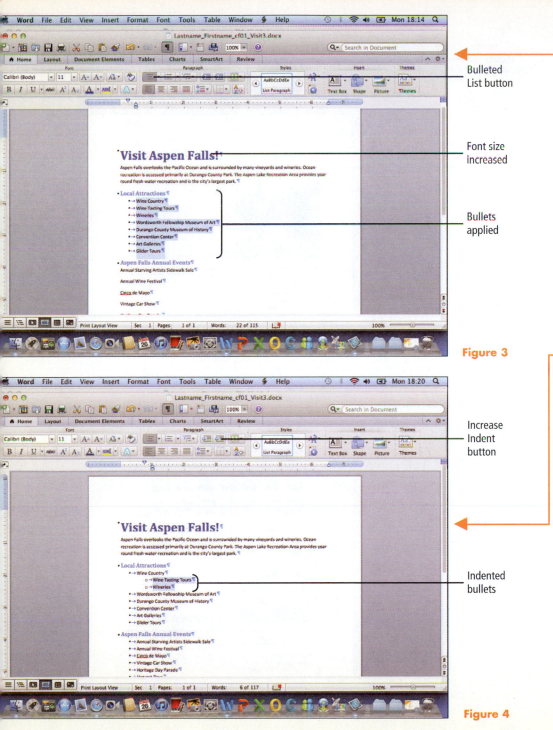

Bulleted
List button

Font size
increased

Bullets
applied

Figure 3

Increase
Indent
button

Indented
bullets

Figure 4

6. On the Ribbon, in the **Paragraph group**, click the **Bulleted List** button ⊟▾, and then compare your screen with **Figure 3**.

   A **Bulleted List** is used to create a list of items with a symbol denoting each item.

7. Click to the left of *Annual Starving Artists Sidewalk Sale*. Scroll down to display the bottom of the page. Press and hold ⎵shift⎵ while clicking to the right of *Winter Blues Festival* to select all of the text between and including *Annual Starving Artists Sidewalk Sale* and *Winter Blues Festival*.

8. In the **Paragraph group**, click the **Bulleted List** button ⊟▾.

9. Scroll to the top of the document. Use either technique just practiced to select *Wine Tasting Tours* and *Wineries*.

10. In the **Paragraph group**, click the **Increase Indent** button 🔳 one time. Compare your screen with **Figure 4**.

11. On the **Standard toolbar**, click **Save** 🖫.

   ■ **You have completed Skill 8 of 10**

► Each Ribbon tab contains commands organized into groups. Some tabs display only when a certain type of object is selected—a graphic, for example.

1. On the first line, click to place the insertion point at the beginning of the document.

2. On the **Home tab**, in the **Insert group**, click the **Picture** button, and then from the displayed list, click **Picture from File**.

3. In the **Choose a Picture** dialog, navigate as needed to display the contents of the student files in the **Common Features Chapter 1** folder. Click **cf01_Visit_River. jpg**, and then click the **Insert** button. Compare your screen with **Figure 1**.

> When a picture is selected, the Format Picture tab displays. On the Format Picture tab, in the Picture Styles group, a *gallery*—a visual display of choices from which you can choose—displays thumbnails. The entire gallery can be seen by clicking the More button to the right and below the first row of thumbnails. The More button displays when you move the mouse over the gallery.

4. On the **Format tab**, in the **Picture Styles group**, click the **More** button ▼ to display the **Picture Styles** gallery. In the gallery, point to the fourth thumbnail in the first row—**Drop Shadow Rectangle**—to display the ScreenTip. Compare your screen with **Figure 2**.

> A *ScreenTip* is informational text that displays when you point to a command or a thumbnail on the Ribbon.

5. Click the **Drop Shadow Rectangle** thumbnail to apply the picture style.

■ **Continue to the next page to complete the skill** ➤

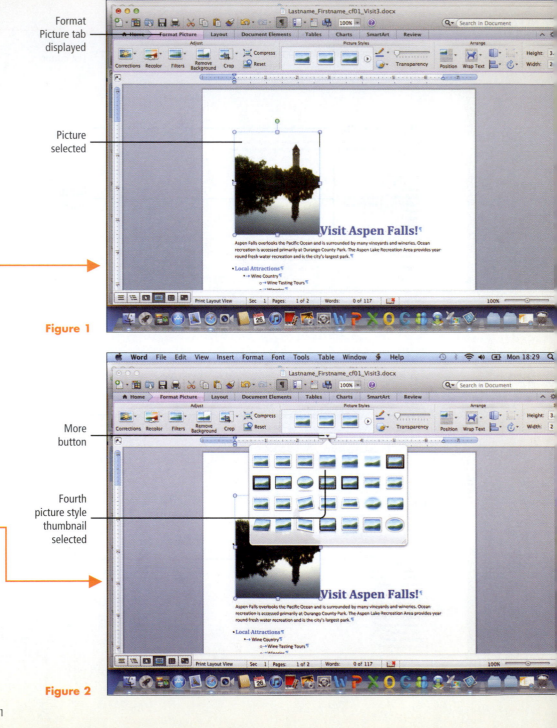

Format Picture tab displayed

Picture selected

Figure 1

More button

Fourth picture style thumbnail selected

Figure 2

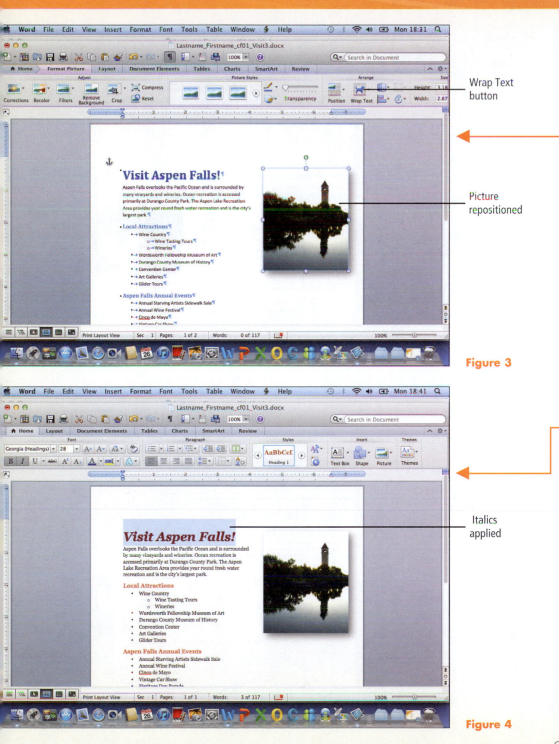

Wrap Text
button

Picture
repositioned

Figure 3

Italics
applied

Figure 4

6. On the **Format Picture tab**, in the **Arrange group**, click the **Wrap Text** button, and then from the list of choices, click **Square**.

7. Point to the picture, and then with the pointer, drag the picture to the right side of the page as shown in **Figure 3**.

8. Click a blank area of the page, and then notice the Picture Tools Format tab no longer displays.

9. On the **Home tab**, in the **Themes group**, click the **Themes** button.

10. In the **Themes** gallery, click the **Civic** thumbnail.

11. On the **menu bar**, click **View**, and then from the displayed list, click **Full Screen**.

12. Move the pointer to the top of the screen until a menu displays, and then click the **Exit** button.

13. Select the text *Visit Aspen Falls!* on the **Home tab**, in the **Font group**, and then click the **Italic** button I. Compare your screen with **Figure 4**.

14. **Save** the document.

■ **You have completed Skill 9 of 10**

► Commands can be accessed in *dialogs*—boxes where you can select multiple settings.

► You can also access commands by pressing the `control` key and then clicking objects in a document.

1. In the paragraph that starts *Aspen Falls overlooks the Pacific Ocean,* **triple-click**—click three times fairly quickly without moving the mouse—to highlight the entire paragraph.

2. Press and hold the `control` key, and then with the pointer ⬐ over the highlighted text, click the mouse button once. Compare your screen with **Figure 1**.

   A shortcut menu displays.

3. Click **Font** to open the **Font** dialog.

4. In the **Font** dialog, click the **Advanced** button. Click the **Spacing arrow**, and then click **Expanded**.

5. To the right of the **Spacing** box, click the **By spin box up arrow** three times to display *1.3 pt*. Compare your screen with **Figure 2**, and then click **OK** to close the dialog and apply the changes.

   ■ **Continue to the next page to complete the skill** ➤

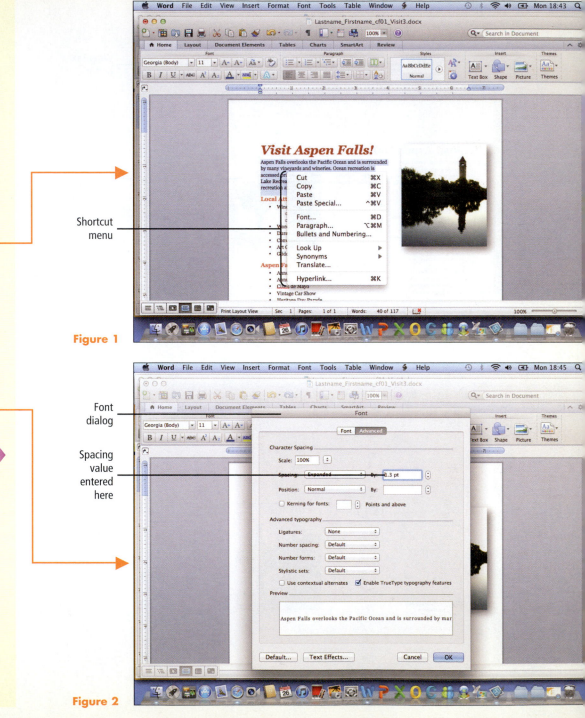

Shortcut menu

Figure 1

Font dialog

Spacing value entered here

Figure 2

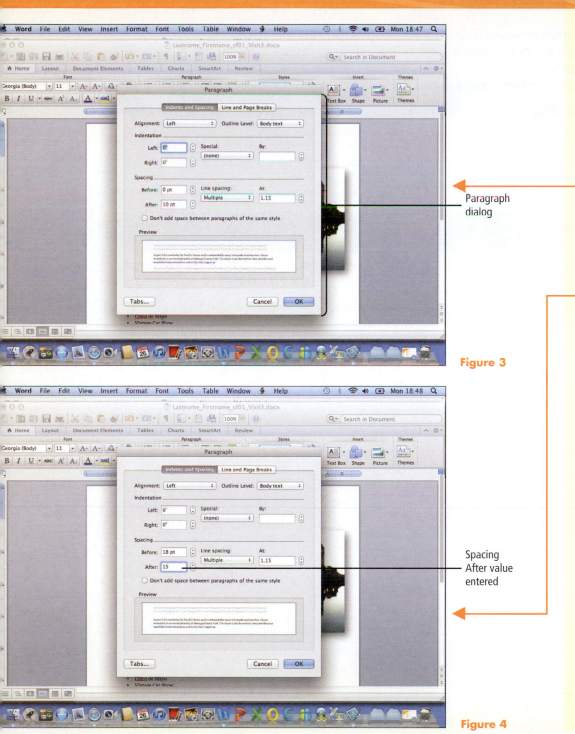

Paragraph dialog

Figure 3

Spacing After value entered

Figure 4

6. With the paragraph still selected, press and hold the control key, and then with the pointer over the highlighted text, click the mouse button once.

   A shortcut menu displays. A *shortcut menu* displays a list of commands related to the type of object that you reference.

7. From the displayed shortcut menu, click the **Paragraph** command, and then compare your screen with **Figure 3**.

8. In the **Paragraph** dialog, under **Spacing**, click the **Before spin up arrow** three times to display *18 pt*.

9. In the **After** box, highlight the existing value, and then type 15 Compare your screen with **Figure 4**, and then click **OK**.

10. If your instructor asks you to print your work, click the File tab, click Print, and then click the Print button.

11. Click **Save this document** 🖫.

12. On the **menu bar**, click **Word**, and then click **Quit Word**. Close the **Finder** application.

   Done! You have completed Skill 10 of 10, and your document is complete!

The following More Skills are located at **www.pearsonhighered.com/skills.** Please note that only More Skills that can be performed on a Macintosh computer are included in this section; therefore, the numbering is not always sequential.

More Skills 12 Use Microsoft Office Help

Microsoft Office 2011 has a Help system in which you can search for articles that show you how to accomplish tasks.

In More Skills 12, you will use the Office 2011 Help system to view an article on how to customize the Help window.

To begin, open your web browser, navigate to www.pearsonhighered.com/skills, locate the name of your textbook, and then follow the instructions on the website.

More Skills 13 Organize Files

Over time, you may create hundreds of files using Microsoft Office. To find your files when you need them, they need to be well-organized. You can organize your computer files by carefully naming them and by placing them into folders.

In More Skills 13, you will create, delete, and rename folders. You will then copy, delete, and move files into the folders that you created.

To begin, open your web browser, navigate to www.pearsonhighered.com/skills, locate the name of your textbook, and then follow the instructions on the website.

Key Terms

Bulleted List 19

Cell 6

Cell reference 10

Clipboard 16

Copy 16

Cut 17

Dialog 22

Drag 17

Edit 14

Finder 9

Format 18

Gallery 20

Grid line 10

Insertion point 5

Page Layout view 10

Paste 17

RAM 8

Safari 12

ScreenTip 20

Shortcut menu 23

Toggle button 5

Triple-click 22

Online Help Skills

1. **Start** Safari or another web browser. In the **address bar**, type microsoft.com/mac/how-to and then press ⟨return⟩ to display the Office for Mac 2011 Website.

   This website provides you with helpful links to get started, reviews of what is new, and tutorials about Office 2011.

2. Scroll down, and then click **Office for Mac 2011 training**.

3. Under **Video Series**, click **Word Basics**.

4. Click **Start**, and then compare your screen with **Figure 1**.

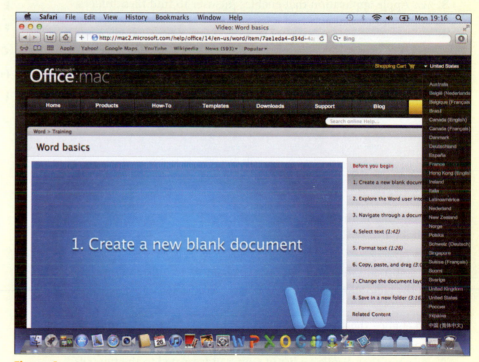

Figure 1

5. Turn on your speakers or put on headphones, and then watch the video to see if you can answer the following questions: How can you change the line spacing in a Word document to 2.0? How can you change the default Margins to Narrow? How can you change the Orientation of your Word document to Landscape?

Matching

Match each term in the second column with its correct definition in the first column by writing the letter of the term on the blank line in front of the correct definition.

____ **1.** A vertical line that indicates where text will be inserted when you start typing.

____ **2.** A line between the cells in a table or spreadsheet.

____ **3.** An Apple application that enables the user to find files, folders, applications, and attached devices.

____ **4.** A view where you prepare your document or spreadsheet for printing.

____ **5.** Quickly click the left mouse button two times without moving the mouse.

____ **6.** To insert text, delete text, or replace text in an Office document, spreadsheet, or presentation.

____ **7.** A command that moves a copy of the selected text or object to the Clipboard.

____ **8.** A command that removes the selected text or object and stores it in the Clipboard.

____ **9.** To change the appearance of the text.

____ **10.** A menu that displays a list of commands related to the type of object that you referenced by clicking.

A Copy

B Cut

C Double-click

D Edit

E Format

F Grid line

G Insertion point

H Page Layout

I Safari

J Shortcut

Multiple Choice

Choose the correct answer.

1. The flashing vertical line that indicates where text will be inserted when you start typing.
   A. Cell reference
   B. Insertion point
   C. KeyTip

2. A button used to turn a feature both on and off.
   A. Contextual button
   B. On/Off button
   C. Toggle button

3. The box formed by the intersection of a row and column.
   A. Cell
   B. Cell reference
   C. Insertion point

4. Until you save a document, it is stored only here.
   A. Clipboard
   B. Live Preview
   C. RAM

5. The combination of a number on the left side and a letter on the top of a spreadsheet that addresses a cell.
   A. Coordinates
   B. Cell reference
   C. Insertion point

6. A temporary storage area that holds text or an object that has been cut or copied.
   A. Clipboard
   B. Dialog
   C. Live Preview

7. To move the mouse while holding down the mouse button and then to release it at the appropriate time.
   A. Copy
   B. Paste
   C. Drag

8. Informational text that displays when you point to commands or thumbnails on the Ribbon.
   A. Live Preview
   B. ScreenTip
   C. Shortcut menu

9. A visual display of choices from which you can choose.
   A. Gallery
   B. Options menu
   C. Shortcut menu

10. Displays a list of commands related to the type of object that you reference.
    A. Shortcut menu
    B. ScreenTip
    C. ToolTip

Topics for Discussion

1. You have briefly worked with three Microsoft Office programs: Word, Excel, and PowerPoint. Based on your experience, describe the overall purpose of each of these programs.

2. Many believe that computers enable offices to go paperless—that is, to share files electronically instead of printing and then distributing them. What are the advantages of sharing files electronically, and in what situations would it be best to print documents?

Create Documents with Word 2011

- Microsoft Office Word is one of the most common productivity programs that individuals use on a computer.

- Word is used to create simple documents, such as memos, reports, letters, or mailing labels, and to create sophisticated documents that include tables and graphics.

- Entering text, formatting text, and navigating within a Word document are the first basic skills you need to work efficiently with Word.

- You can change the font and font size and add emphasis to text, but use caution not to apply too many different formats to your text. This can be distracting to the reader.

- It is easy to insert a picture into a Word document, and doing so increases the visual appeal and the reader's interest. Pictures should be clearly associated with the surrounding text and should not be inserted just to have a picture in the document.

- It is never acceptable to have errors in spelling, grammar, or word usage in your documents; you can use Word features to prevent this from happening.

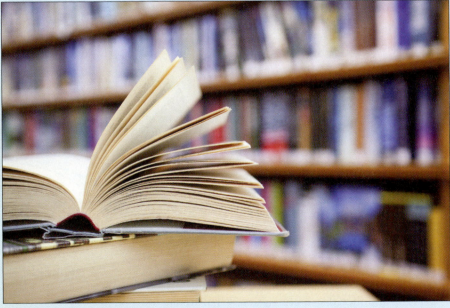

© Slickpics | Dreamtime.com

Aspen Falls City Hall

In this chapter, you will assist Douglas Hopkins, Library Director, to create a letter to Janis Imlay of Aspen Falls Community College requesting her students to update the logo for the Aspen Falls Publi Library.

In this project, you will create a one-page business letter, and the create a second page detailing the programs and activities available at the library. You will insert a clip art image, and then set the text to wrap around the image. Finally, you will check the spelling and gram mar in the document and add the file name to the document footer.

**Time to complete all
10 skills – 60 to 75 minutes**

Student data files needed for this chapter:

New blank Word document
w01_Library_Activities
w01_Library_Logo

You will save your documents as:

Lastname_Firstname_w01_Library
Lastname_Firstname_w01_Library_2004

Outcome

Using the skills in this chapter, you will be able to work with Word documents like this:

SKILLS

Skills 1-10 Training

At the end of this chapter you will be able to:

Skill 1   Create New Documents and Enter Text
Skill 2   Edit Text and Use Keyboard Shortcuts
Skill 3   Select Text
Skill 4   Insert Text from Other Documents
Skill 5   Change Fonts, Font Sizes, and Font Styles
Skill 6   Insert and Work with Graphics
Skill 7   Check Spelling and Grammar
Skill 8   Use the Thesaurus and Set Proofing Options
Skill 9   Create Document Footers
Skill 10   Work with the Print Page Function and Save Documents in Other Formats

MORE SKILLS

Skill 11   Split and Arrange Windows
Skill 12   Insert Symbols

ASPEN FALLS PUBLIC LIBRARY
255 Elm Street
Aspen Falls, CA 93463

May 5, 2013

Dr. Janis Imlay
Aspen Falls Community College
1 College Drive
Aspen Falls, CA 93463
Dear Dr. Imlay:
Subject: New Logo for Library
Thank you so much for your letter offering the services of your graphic design students for library-related projects. We currently have a project in mind that might benefit both the library and your students.
We want to update our logo to more accurately reflect the wide variety of services ordered in a modern library. A logo contest would be a great idea. Call me at (805) 555-1011 to discuss this further.
I have attached a list of library activities to give the students an idea of some of the things we do.
Sincerely,

Douglas Hopkins, Director

Lastname_Firstname_w01_Library_RevLibrary Document   1

► When you start Microsoft Office Word 2011, you can either select a blank document or choose from a template.

1. On the **Dock,** click the **Microsoft Word 2011** 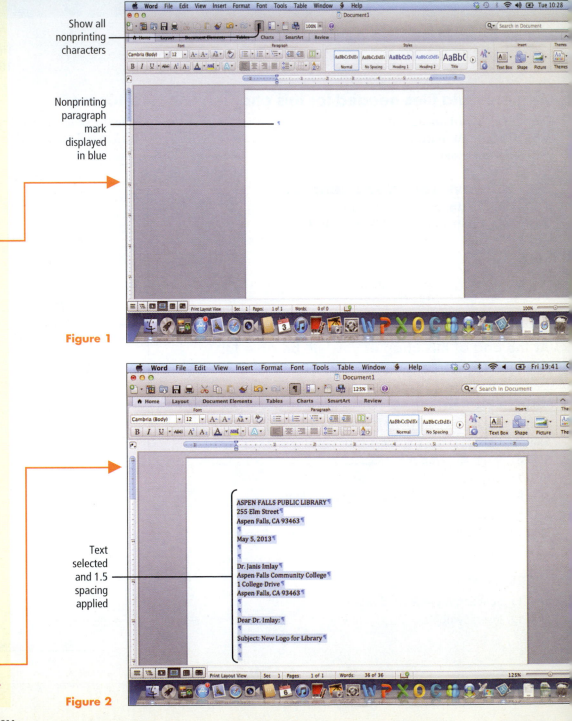 icon. If a previous Word document displays, Close 🔴 the document, then, on the menu bar, click File, and then click New.

2. In the displayed **Word Document Gallery** dialog, make sure that **Blank** is selected, and then click the **Choose** button.

3. On the **Standard toolbar,** click the **Show all nonprinting characters** button ¶ until it displays in blue indicating that it is active, as shown in **Figure 1**.

   When you press ⌐return⌐, ⌐spacebar⌐, or ⌐tab⌐ on your keyboard, characters display in your document to represent these keystrokes. These characters do not print and are referred to as *formatting marks* or *nonprinting characters*.

4. In all uppercase letters, type ASPEN FALLS PUBLIC LIBRARY and press ⌐return⌐. Type 255 Elm Street and press ⌐return⌐. Type Aspen Falls, CA 93463 and press ⌐return⌐ two times.

5. Type May 5, 2013 and press ⌐return⌐ three times; type Dr. Janis Imlay and press ⌐return⌐; type Aspen Falls Community College and press ⌐return⌐; type 1 College Drive and press ⌐return⌐; and type Aspen Falls, CA 93463 and press ⌐return⌐ two times.

6. Type Dear Dr. Imlay: and press ⌐return⌐ two times. Type Subject: New Logo for Library and press ⌐return⌐ two times.

7. Hold down the ⌐command ⌘⌐ key and then press ⌐A⌐. All of the text in the document is selected. On the **Home tab,** in the **Paragraph group,** click the **Line Spacing** button ⌐, and then click **1.15**. Compare your screen with **Figure 2**.

■ **Continue to the next page to complete the skill**

Show all nonprinting characters

Nonprinting paragraph mark displayed in blue

Figure 1

Text selected and 1.5 spacing applied

Figure 2

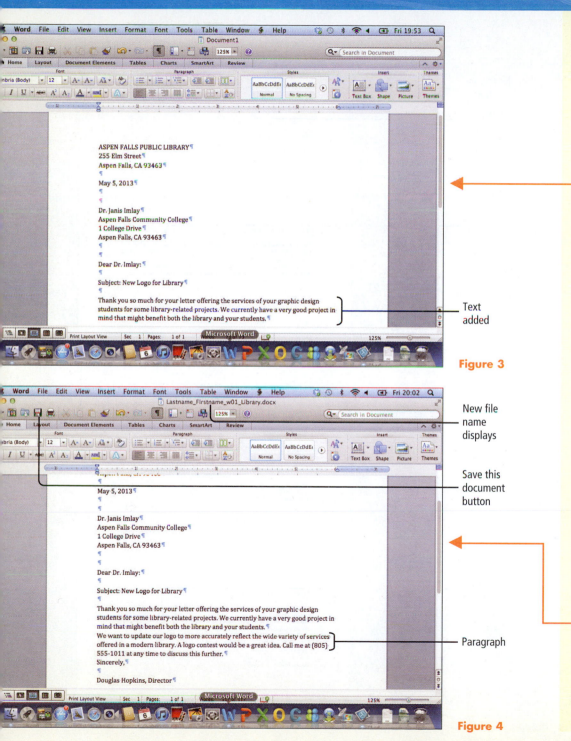

Text
added

Figure 3

New file
name
displays

Save this
document
button

Paragraph

Figure 4

8. Click at the end of the document, and then type the following, inserting only one space after the period at the end of a sentence: Thank you so much for your letter offering the services of your graphic design students for some library-related projects. We currently have a very good project in mind that might benefit both the library and your students. Compare your screen with **Figure 3**.

As you type, the insertion point moves to the right. At the right margin, Word determines whether the word you are typing will fit within the established margin. If it does not fit, Word moves the entire word to the beginning of the next line. This feature is called *word wrap*. You do not need to press return until you reach the end of a paragraph.

9. Press return , and then type We want to update our logo to more accurately reflect the wide variety of services offered in a modern library. A logo contest would be a great idea. Call me at (805) 555-1011 at any time to discuss this further.

10. Press return and type Sincerely, and then press return two times. Type Douglas Hopkins, Director

11. On the **Standard toolbar,** click the **Save this document** button 🔲. Navigate to the location where you are saving your files, create a folder named Word Chapter 1 and then using your own name, **Save** the document as Lastname_Firstname_w01_ Library

12. Compare your screen with **Figure 4**, and notice that the new file name displays on the title bar.

■ **You have completed Skill 1 of 10**

► You can use a combination of keys on the keyboard to edit a document.

► Pressing delete removes characters to the left of the insertion point, and by default, pressing fn + delete removes characters to the right of the insertion point.

1. On the first line, click to position the insertion point just to the left of the word *ASPEN*.

2. If horizontal and vertical rulers do not display, at the top of the vertical scroll bar, click View, and then click Ruler.

3. Move the pointer to the left of the first line of the document to display the ◢ pointer. Drag down to select the first two lines of the document. On the **Home tab,** in the **Styles group,** click the **No Spacing** button. If necessary, click the More button ▼ to display the No Spacing thumbnail.

   Extra space should be removed between the lines of the letterhead and inside address.

4. Locate the paragraph that begins *Thank you,* and then in the second line, click to position the insertion point just to the right of the word *good*.

5. Press delete five times, and notice that both the word *good* and the extra space between *very* and *good* are removed, as shown in **Figure 1**.

6. In the same paragraph, click to position the insertion point just to the left of the word *very*.

7. Press fn + delete five times, and notice that the word *very* and the extra space are removed, as shown in **Figure 2**.

   This combination of keys—a **keyboard shortcut**—moves the insertion point or carries out a function without accessing a toolbar.

■ **Continue to the next page to complete the skill**

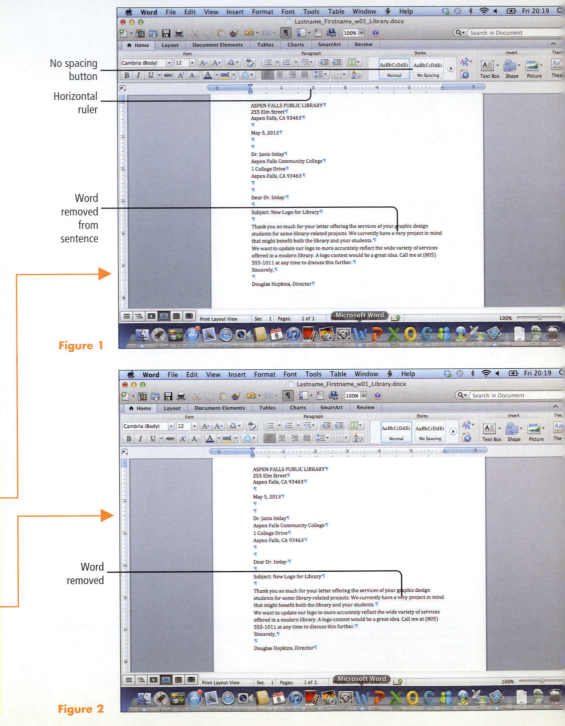

Figure 1

Figure 2

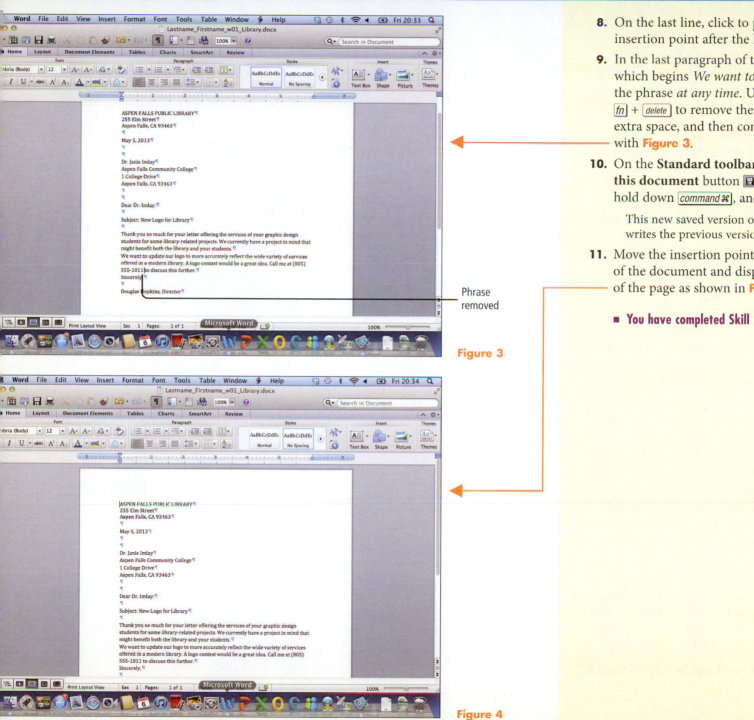

Phrase
removed

Figure 3

Figure 4

8. On the last line, click to position the insertion point after the last word.

9. In the last paragraph of the letter body, which begins *We want to update,* locate the phrase *at any time.* Use either `delete` or `fn` + `delete` to remove the phrase and the extra space, and then compare your screen with **Figure 3**.

10. On the **Standard toolbar,** click the **Save this document** button. Alternately, hold down `command ⌘`, and then press `S`.

   This new saved version of your file overwrites the previous version.

11. Move the insertion point to the beginning of the document and display the top edge of the page as shown in **Figure 4**.

   ■ **You have completed Skill 2 of 10**

► To format text, first select the text, and then make formatting changes. You can also select text and then delete it.

► You can insert text at the insertion point by typing new text. You can also insert text by selecting existing text and then typing new text.

1. In the first line of the document, point just to the left of *ASPEN*. Hold down the mouse button, and then drag to the right to select the entire line, including the paragraph mark. Notice that selected text is highlighted.

2. On the **Home tab,** in the **Paragraph group,** click the **Center Text** button to center the first line of text.

3. Repeat this procedure to center the second and third lines of the library address.

4. In the paragraph that begins *Thank you,* in the first line, point to the word *some,* and then double-click, as shown in **Figure 1.**

5. With the word *some* selected, press delete .

   When you double-click to select and delete a word, the selected word is deleted, along with its following space.

6. In the paragraph *Dr. Janis Imlay,* point to any word and triple-click. Notice that the entire paragraph is selected. On the **Home tab,** in the **Styles group,** click the **No Spacing** button.

7. Repeat this procedure to remove the extra spacing from the two paragraphs below *Dr. Janis Imlay.* Compare your screen with **Figure 2.**

   ■ **Continue to the next page to complete the skill**

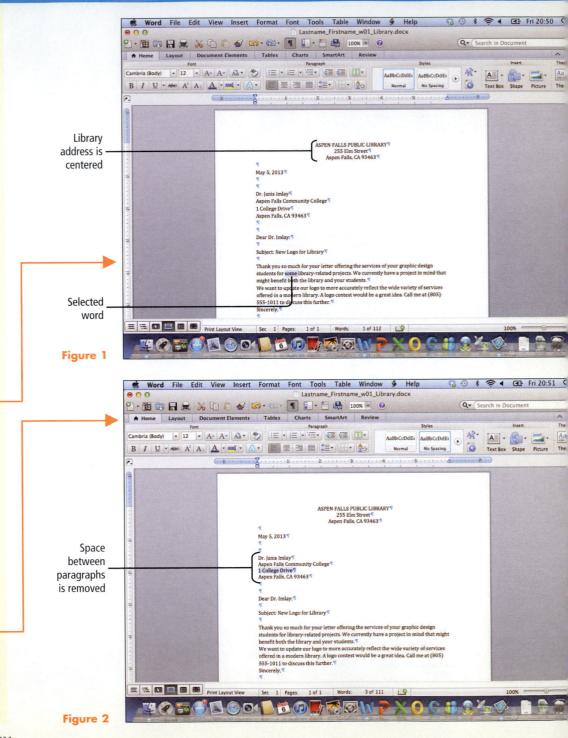

Library address is centered

Selected word

Figure 1

Space between paragraphs is removed

Figure 2

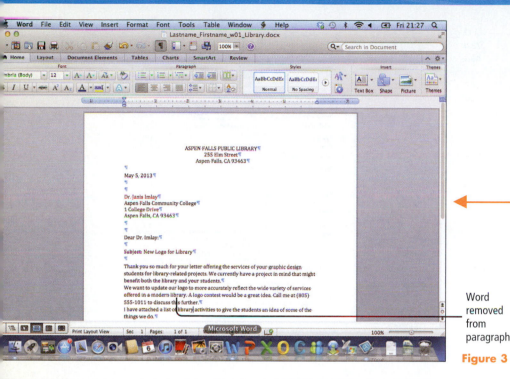

Word removed from paragraph

Figure 3

Selecting Text in a Document

To select	Do this
A portion of text	Hold down the left mouse button and drag from the beginning to the end of the text you want to select.
A word	Double-click the word.
A sentence	Hold down control, and then click anywhere in the sentence.
A paragraph	Triple-click anywhere in the paragraph.
A line	Move the pointer to the left of the line. When the ◤ pointer displays, click one time.
The entire document	Hold down control and press A. Alternately, display the ◤ pointer in the left margin and triple-click.

Figure 4

8. In the paragraph that begins *We want to,* click to position the insertion point at the end of the paragraph—following the period after *further.*

9. Press return one time, and then type I have attached a list of our activities to give the students an idea of some of the things we do.

10. In the same paragraph, double-click the word *our* to select it, type library and then compare your screen with **Figure 3**.

   Recall that when you select a word, phrase, sentence, or paragraph, anything you type will replace all of the selected text.

11. In the paragraph that begins *Thank you,* move the pointer into the left margin area next to the first line of the paragraph. When the ◤ pointer displays, double-click. Notice that the entire paragraph is selected.

12. Click anywhere in the document to deselect the text. Hold down command ⌘, and then press A. Alternately, display the ◤ pointer in the left margin and triple-click to select the entire document.

13. **Save** 🖫 the changes, and then take a moment to examine some ways to select text, described in the table in **Figure 4**.

■ **You have completed Skill 3 of 10**

▶ Objects, such as a text file or a graphic, can be inserted into a document.

▶ Inserted text displays at the insertion point location.

1. Move the insertion point to the end of the document.

2. On the **menu bar,** click **Insert,** then point to **Break,** as shown in **Figure 1**, and then from the displayed list click **Page Break**.

   A *manual page break*—forcing a page to end at a location you specify—is added at the end of Page 1, and a new blank page is created. A manual page break indicator also displays below the text at the bottom of Page 1.

3. Move to the top of the document, and then notice that the active page and the number of pages in the document display on the status bar. Move to the end of the document at the top of Page 2, as shown in **Figure 2**.

4. On the **menu bar,** click **Insert,** and then click **File**.

   The Insert File dialog displays.

■ **Continue to the next page to complete the skill**

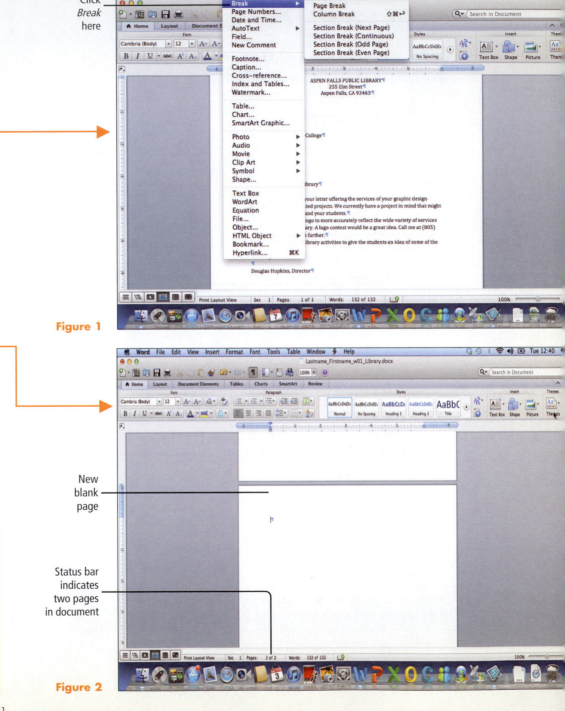

Click *Break* here

Figure 1

New blank page

Status bar indicates two pages in document

Figure 2

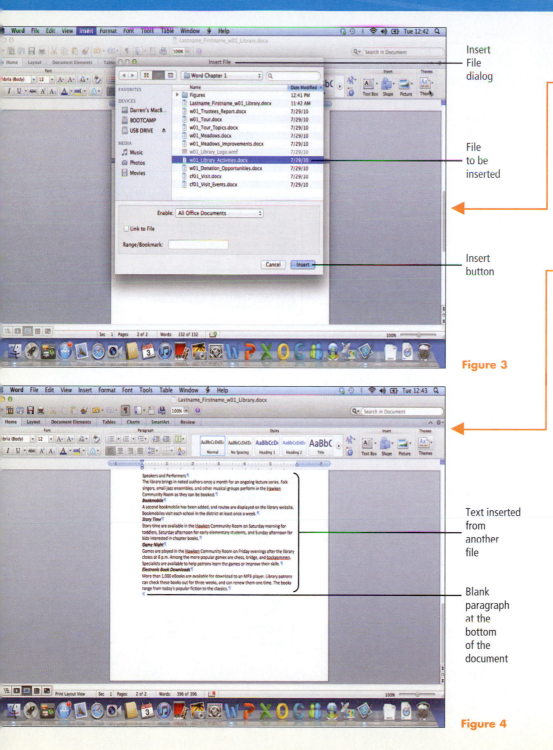

Insert File dialog

File to be inserted

Insert button

Figure 3

Text inserted from another file

Blank paragraph at the bottom of the document

Figure 4

5. Navigate to the location of your student files, and then click the **w01_Library_ Activities** file. Compare your screen with **Figure 3**.

6. In the lower right corner of the **Insert File** dialog, click the **Insert** button.

All of the text from the w01_Library_ Activities file is copied into the current document at the insertion point location. The original file remains unchanged. The spelling and grammar errors in the inserted document will be corrected in Skill 7.

7. Move to the end of the document, and notice that an extra blank paragraph displays, as shown in **Figure 4**.

8. Press delete one time to remove the blank paragraph from the end of the document.

9. Move the insertion point to the beginning of the document, and then **Save** 🖫 the changes.

■ **You have completed Skill 4 of 10**

► A *font* is a set of characters with the same design and shape.

► One way to format text is to change the font or font size.

► You can also add bold, italic, or underline emphasis to make text stand out from surrounding text. Bold, italic, and underline are referred to as *font styles*.

1. Click the **Home tab**. In the **Font group,** notice that Word's default font and size will be the last font style and size that you used.

   Fonts are measured in *points,* with one point equal to 1/72 of an inch.

2. Scroll so that you can view Page 2, click anywhere in the text, and then notice that the font is **Calibri (Headings)** and the font size is **12**.

3. Press command ⌘ + A to select all of the text in the document. In the **Font group,** click the **Font arrow** Calibri (Body) ▾, as shown in **Figure 1**.

4. From the displayed **Font** list, click **Cambria (Body)** to change all of the text in the document to Cambria.

5. With the text still selected, in the **Font group,** click the **Font Size arrow** 11 ▾, and then click **11**.

6. On Page 2, click anywhere in the text to cancel the selection. Notice the change to the font and font size, as shown in **Figure 2**.

■ **Continue to the next page to complete the skill**

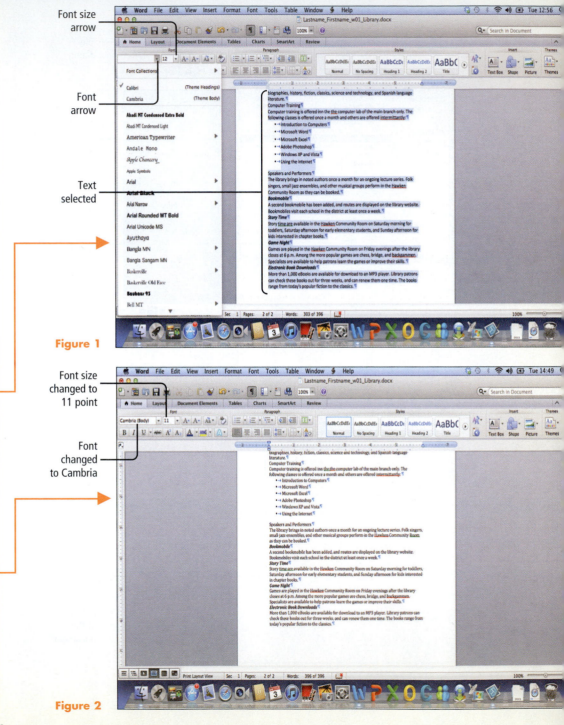

Font size arrow

Font arrow

Text selected

Figure 1

Font size changed to 11 point

Font changed to Cambria

Figure 2

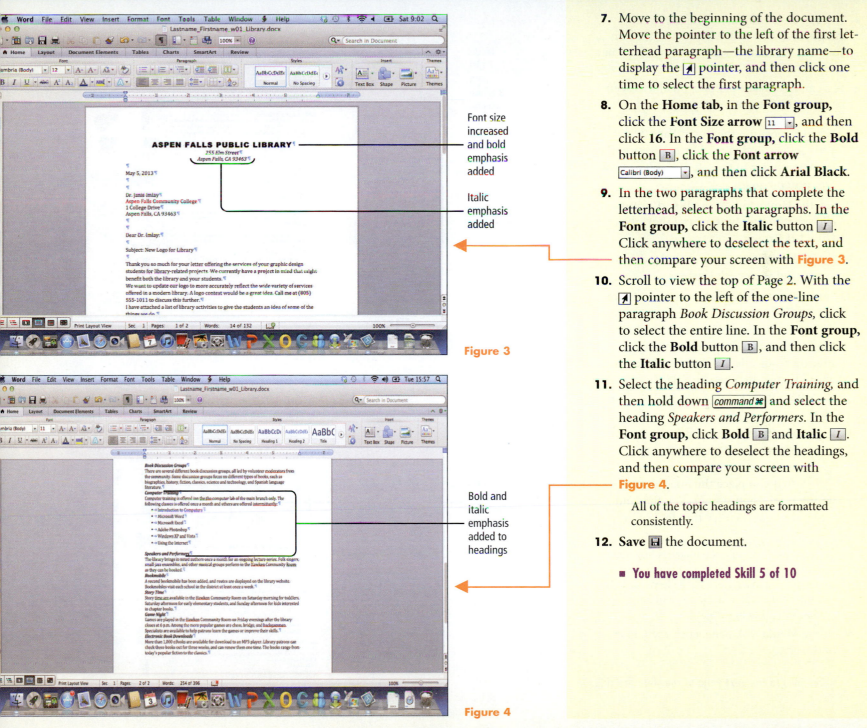

Font size increased and bold emphasis added

Italic emphasis added

Figure 3

Bold and italic emphasis added to headings

Figure 4

7. Move to the beginning of the document. Move the pointer to the left of the first letterhead paragraph—the library name—to display the pointer, and then click one time to select the first paragraph.

8. On the **Home tab,** in the **Font group,** click the **Font Size arrow** 11, and then click **16.** In the **Font group,** click the **Bold** button B, click the **Font arrow** Calibri (Body), and then click **Arial Black.**

9. In the two paragraphs that complete the letterhead, select both paragraphs. In the **Font group,** click the **Italic** button I. Click anywhere to deselect the text, and then compare your screen with **Figure 3.**

10. Scroll to view the top of Page 2. With the pointer to the left of the one-line paragraph *Book Discussion Groups,* click to select the entire line. In the **Font group,** click the **Bold** button B, and then click the **Italic** button I.

11. Select the heading *Computer Training,* and then hold down command ⌘ and select the heading *Speakers and Performers.* In the **Font group,** click **Bold** B and **Italic** I. Click anywhere to deselect the headings, and then compare your screen with **Figure 4.**

  All of the topic headings are formatted consistently.

12. **Save** the document.

  ■ **You have completed Skill 5 of 10**

► You can insert *clip art*—graphics and images included with Microsoft Office or obtained from other sources—anywhere in a document.

► You can also insert pictures that have been saved as files on your computer.

1. Scroll to position the top of Page 2 on your screen, and then click to position the insertion point to the left of the *B* in *Book Discussion Groups*.

2. On the **Home tab,** in the **Insert group,** click the **Picture** button, and then click **Clip Art Browser**.

3. In the **Media** task pane, click the down arrow, and then click **Business**.

4. Scroll down to display the picture shown in **Figure 1**. If you do not see this image, **Close** the **Media** task pane. In the **Insert group,** click **Picture,** and then click **Picture from File**. Navigate to your student files for this chapter. Select and insert the **w01_Library_Logo** file, and skip to **Step 7**.

5. In the **Media** task pane, click the book image indicated in Figure 1. Drag the image to the document as shown in **Figure 2**. If you place the image in the wrong place, then simply click the Undo button 🔄, and then try the step again.

   The image is inserted at the insertion point location. By default, the image is inserted in the text in exactly the same manner that a character is inserted from the keyboard. Some of the text at the bottom of Page 2 may move to a new Page 3.

6. In the **Media** task pane, click the **Close** button 🔴.

   ■ **Continue to the next page to complete the skill** ➤

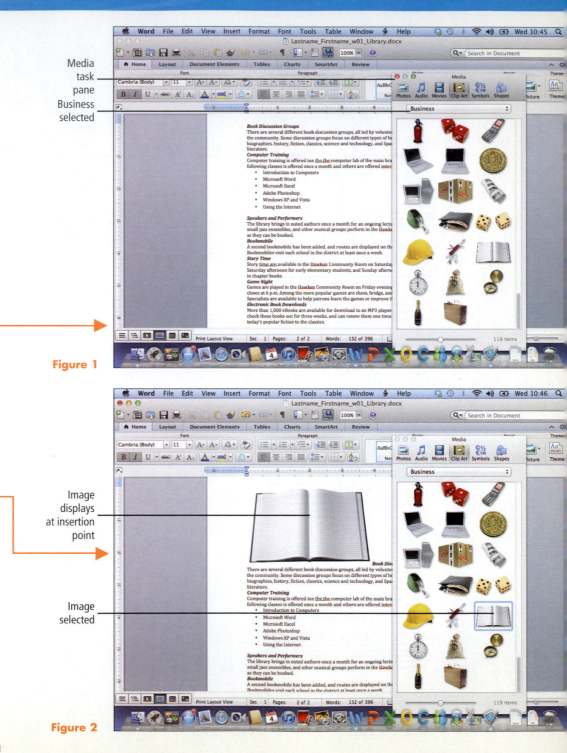

Media task pane

Business selected

Figure 1

Image displays at insertion point

Image selected

Figure 2

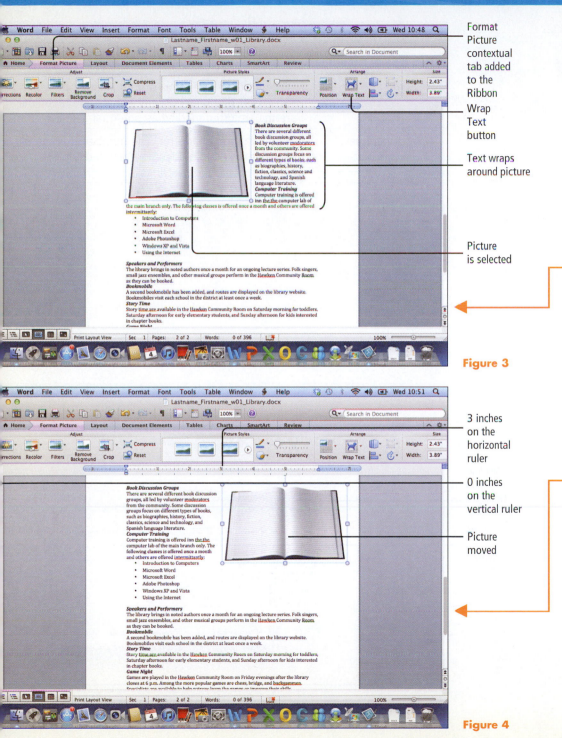

Format
Picture
contextual
tab added
to the
Ribbon

Wrap
Text
button

Text wraps
around picture

Picture
is selected

Figure 3

3 inches
on the
horizontal
ruler

0 inches
on the
vertical ruler

Picture
moved

Figure 4

7. If necessary, click the picture to select it, and then notice that small circles and squares display at the corners and edges of the borders, indicating that the picture is selected. Notice also that a new tab—the **Format Picture** contextual tab—is added to the Ribbon.

8. On the **Format Picture tab,** in the **Arrange group,** click the **Wrap Text** button, and then take a moment to examine the various options for *text wrapping*—the manner in which text displays around an object.

9. From the displayed list, click **Square,** and then compare your screen with **Figure 3**.

10. Be sure the rulers display at the top and left of your document window; if necessary, on the **menu bar,** click **View,** and then click **Ruler.**

11. Point to the selected picture until the ⊹ pointer displays.

12. By using the rulers as a visual guide, drag the picture to the right, positioning the upper left corner of the picture at **3 inches** on the horizontal ruler and at **0 inches** on the vertical ruler. Compare your screen with **Figure 4**. Notice that by wrapping the text around the picture, the number of pages in the document returns to two pages.

13. Adjust the position of the picture as necessary to match the figure, and then **Save** 🖫 the changes.

 ■ **You have completed Skill 6 of 10**

▶ You can respond to potential spelling and grammar errors one at a time, or you can check the entire document.

▶ The number of potential grammar errors displayed by Word depends on your program settings.

1. In the paragraphs near the picture, notice the wavy red and green lines which indicate potential errors in spelling, grammar, and word use as outlined in the table in **Figure 1**.

   One or more of the wavy line colors may be missing, depending on your program settings.

2. Scroll through Page 2 and notice that the name *Hawken* has a wavy red underline in three locations.

   The wavy red underline means the word is not in the Office 2011 main dictionary. Many proper names are not in the main dictionary and are flagged as misspellings.

3. In the middle of Page 2, in the paragraph that begins *The library,* point to *Hawken*.

   Possible corrected spellings display, although this proper name is spelled correctly.

4. On the **menu bar,** click **Tools,** and then click **Spelling and Grammar**.

5. In the displayed **Spelling and Grammar** dialog, click **Ignore All** to remove the underline from all instances of the word *Hawken* in the document. Compare your screen with **Figure 2**.

6. Click **Cancel,** and then scroll to the top of Page 2. Double-click the word *inn* that is flagged with a wavy blue line, which indicates the potentially incorrect use of a word. If your word is not flagged, select the word *inn,* correct the spelling to **in,** and go to **Step 8**.

7. From the shortcut menu, click *in,* to correct the word usage.

   ■ **Continue to the next page to complete the skill** ▶

Proofing Underlines	
This type of underline	**Indicates**
Wavy red line	Potential spelling error; word not found in Microsoft dictionary. Proper names and technical terms are often marked as potential spelling errors.
Wavy green line	Potential grammar error. The number of grammar errors marked in a document depends on the program's proofing settings.

Figure 1

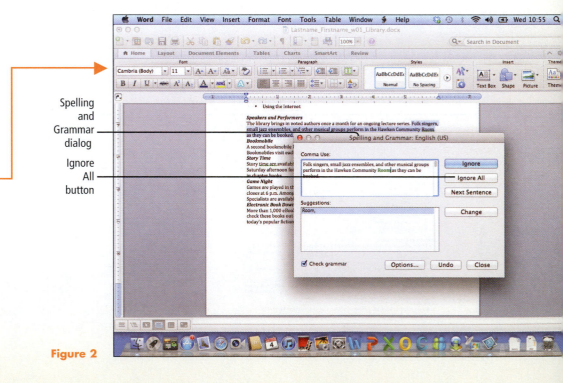

Spelling and Grammar dialog

Ignore All button

Figure 2

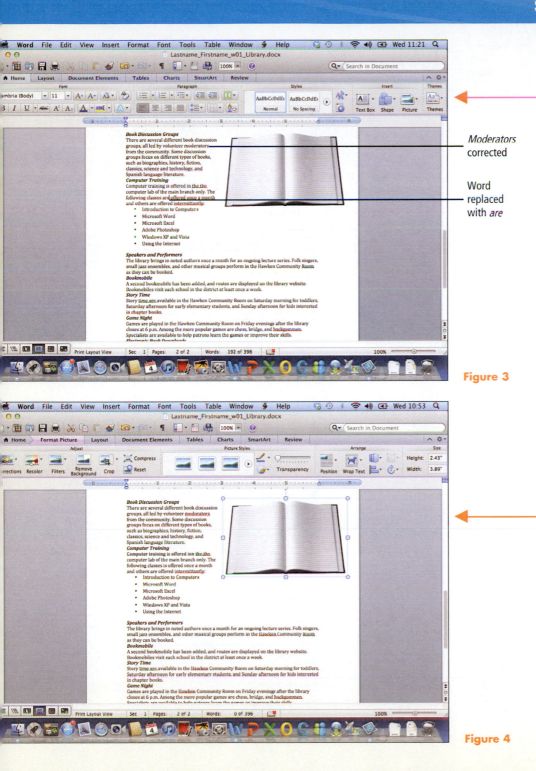

Figure 3

Figure 4

8. Double-click *moderators,* which displays a wavy red line. On the **menu bar,** click **Tools,** and then click **Spelling and Grammar**. Click the correct spelling, *moderators,* and then click **Change**. If a message box displays, then click **No**. Click **Close**.

9. Click to the right of the text *classes is.* Replace the word *is* with *are* Compare your screen with **Figure 3**.

10. Scroll down and notice that there are additional spelling and grammar errors in the document. Move to the beginning of the document. On the **menu bar,** click **Tools,** and then click **Spelling and Grammar**. If a *Verb Confusion* error displays for *ASPEN FALLS,* click **Ignore Once,** and then compare your screen with **Figure 4**.

   The Spelling and Grammar dialog displays a potential error—a repeated word.

11. In the **Spelling and Grammar** dialog, click the **Delete** button to delete the repeated word. Notice for the next selected error, under **Suggestions,** that the correct spelling—*intermittently*—is highlighted. Click the **Change** button to correct the spelling.

12. For the grammatical error *time are,* click **times are,** and then click **Change**.

13. Correct the misspelled word *backgammen* by clicking **Change**.

14. Ignore any other errors, and then when a message indicates that the spelling and grammar check is complete, click **OK**. Save 🖫 your document.

■ **You have completed Skill 7 of 10**

► Proofing tools include Spelling & Grammar checking, a Thesaurus, and Research tools.

► You can set proofing options to provide readability statistics for your document.

1. Scroll to the middle of Page 2 and locate the heading *Speakers and Performers.*

2. Double-click anywhere in *Performers* to select the word. On the **menu bar,** click **Tools,** and then click **Thesaurus.** Notice that a **Reference Tools** task pane displays lists of similar words, as shown in **Figure 1.**

   A *thesaurus* lists words that have the same or similar meaning to the word you are looking up.

3. In the **Reference Tools** task pane, under **Synonyms,** locate and point to *Entertainers,* and then click **Insert.** Notice that *Entertainers* replaces *Performers.* If an extra space displays to the left of *Entertainers,* remove the space.

4. In the second line of the paragraph that begins *Games are played,* locate and click anywhere in the word *Specialists.* Using the technique you just practiced, replace *Specialists* with *Experts.* Compare your screen with **Figure 2.**

5. In the **Reference Tools** task pane, click the **Close** button ⬤. Click anywhere in the document to unselect the text.

6. On the **menu bar,** click **Tools,** and then click the **Word Count** button. Notice that the document statistics display and include the number of pages, words, paragraphs, lines, and characters.

   ■ **Continue to the next page to complete the skill** ▶

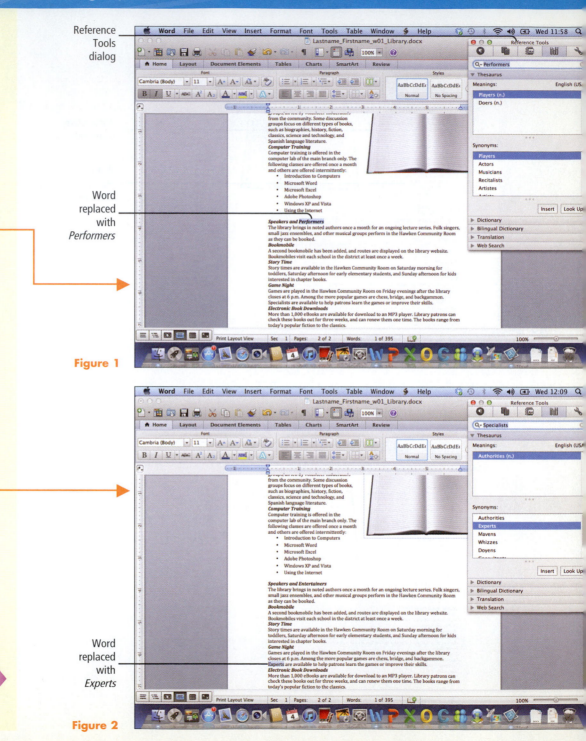

Reference Tools dialog

Word replaced with *Performers*

Figure 1

Word replaced with *Experts*

Figure 2

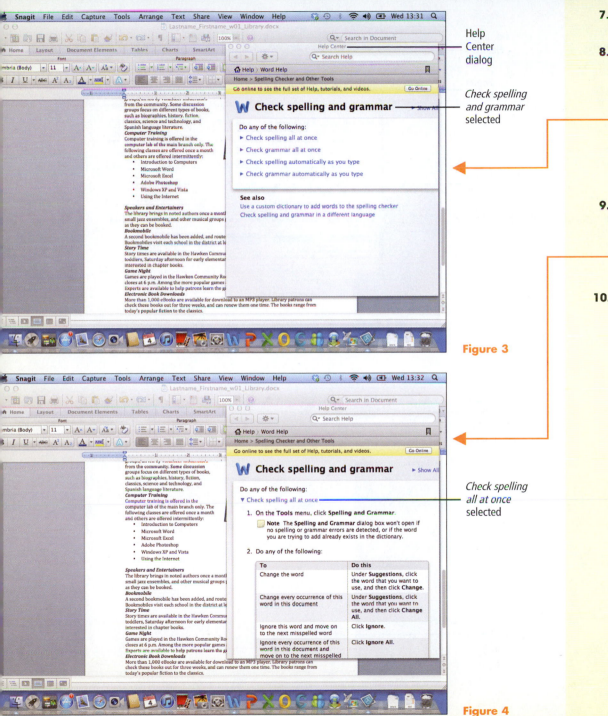

Help Center dialog

Check spelling and grammar selected

Figure 3

Check spelling all at once selected

Figure 4

7. In the **Word Count** dialog, click the **OK** button.

8. On the **menu bar,** click **Help**. In the **Search** box, type proof From the displayed list, click **Check spelling and grammar,** and then compare your screen with **Figure 3**.

   The Proofing options give you control over which potential spelling and grammar errors will be flagged and lets you choose which items or rules to ignore.

9. In the **Help Center** dialog, under **Check spelling and grammar,** click the **Check spelling all at once** link, and then compare your screen with **Figure 4**.

   Read the text provided.

10. **Close** ● the **Help Center** dialog. **Save** 🖫 the document.

   ■ **You have completed Skill 8 of 10**

► A *header* and *footer* are reserved areas for text, graphics, and fields that display at the top (header) or bottom (footer) of each page in a document.

► Throughout this book, you will insert the document file name in the footer of each document.

1. Move to the beginning of the document.

2. Display the **Document Elements tab,** and then in the **Header and Footer group,** click the **Footer** button. Compare your screen with **Figure 1.**

   Word provides several built-in footers. When you want to enter your own text, the Go to Header or Go to Footer command on the Ribbon is used.

3. In the **Footer** gallery, examine the footer formats that are available.

4. From the displayed Footer gallery, click **Bottom Border (Odd Page)**–third choice on the first row. Compare your screen with **Figure 2.**

   Notice that a Header and Footer tab displays.

5. On the **menu bar,** click **Insert,** and then click **Field.**

   A *field* is a category of data—such as a file name, a page number, or the current date—that can be inserted into a document.

■ **Continue to the next page to complete the skill** ➤

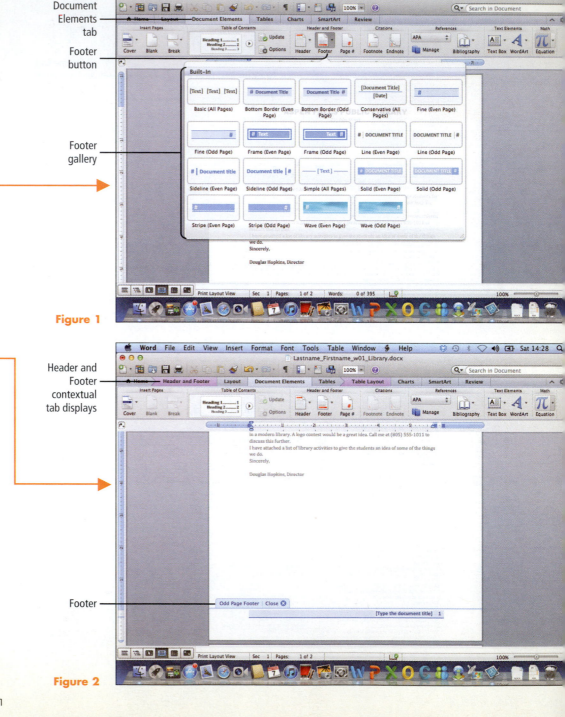

Document Elements tab

Footer button

Footer gallery

Figure 1

Header and Footer contextual tab displays

Footer

Figure 2

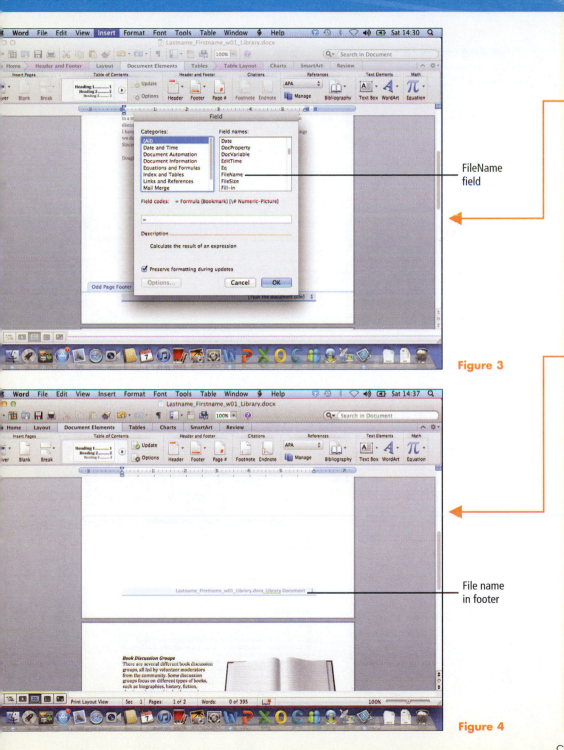

Figure 3

Figure 4

6. In the **Field** dialog, under **Field names**, use the vertical scroll bar to see what types of fields are available, and then locate the **FileName** field. Compare your screen with **Figure 3**.

   When a field name consists of two or more words, the spaces between the words are removed.

7. Under **Field names**, click **FileName**, and then click **OK**.

   The file name is added to the footer.

8. In the **Footer**, click to select [**Type the document title**], press the spacebar once, and then type Library Document

9. Double-click anywhere above the footer to return to the body of the document.

10. Scroll to display the bottom of Page 1 and the top of Page 2, and then compare your screen with **Figure 4**.

    The text in the footer area displays in blue because the footer is inactive; while the document text is active, the footer text cannot be edited.

11. **Save** the document.

   ■ **You have completed Skill 9 of 10**

FileName field

File name in footer

► Before you print a document, it is good practice to preview it on your screen so that you can see any final changes that are necessary.

► You can save documents in different formats so that people who do not have Word can read them.

1. Move to the beginning of the document.

2. Hold down ⌘command ⌘, and then press P, and then compare your screen with **Figure 1**.

    Recall that print settings display on the right side of the Print page, and a preview of the current page of the printed document displays on the left. The Zoom percent displays at the bottom of the preview; yours may vary depending on your screen resolution.

3. Click **Cancel** to close the **Print** dialog.

4. On the **Standard toolbar,** click the [100% ▾] down arrow as shown in **Figure 2**, and then click **125%.**

5. On the **Standard toolbar,** click the [100% ▾] down arrow, and then click **Whole Page**.

    ■ **Continue to the next page to complete the skill**

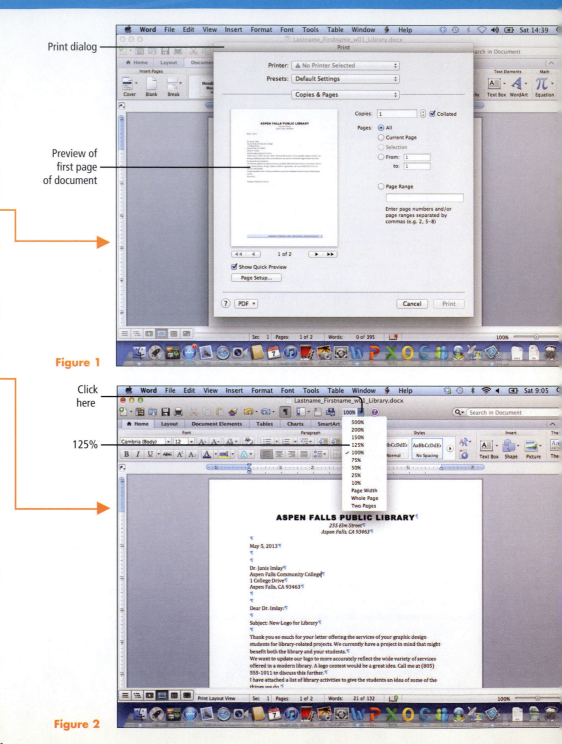

Print dialog

Preview of first page of document

Figure 1

Click here

125%

Figure 2

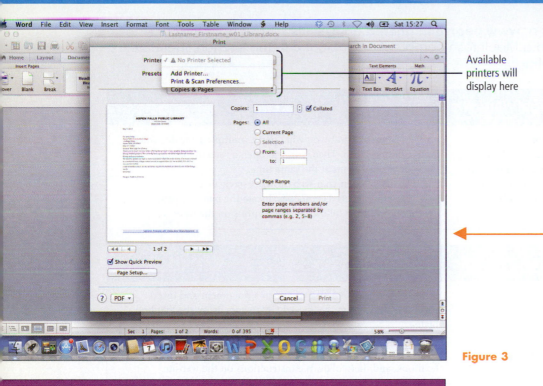

Available printers will display here

Figure 3

Word Save As File Formats

Format	Descriptions
Word Document	Saves the document using the Word 2011 file format.
Word Template	Saves the document so that it can be used over and over, without altering the original document.
Word 97-2004 Document	Saves the file in earlier Word formats so that individuals using earlier versions of the program can open the document.
PDF	Saves the document in the popular Portable Document Format (PDF) display format, which can be opened on most computers.
XPS Document	Saves the document in the Microsoft XPS display format.
Other Formats	Lets you save a document as plain text with no formatting, in a universal file format such as Rich Text Format, or as a web page.

Figure 4

6. Hold down command ⌘, and then press P.

7. In the **Print** dialog, click the **Printer** button, and then compare your screen with **Figure 3**.

   A list of printers that is available to your computer displays, as do other document destinations.

8. From the **Printer** list, select the printer you would like to use.

   You can use the Print page to select a printer, select the number of copies to print, and specify which document pages to print.

9. Be sure that the **Copies** is set to **1**. If you are printing your work for this project, at the bottom of the **Print** page, click the **Print** button—otherwise, click **Cancel**.

10. On the **Standard toolbar,** click **File,** and then click **Save As**. In the **Save As** dialog, click the **Format** box, and then take a moment to examine the most common file formats for Word documents, which are summarized in the table in **Figure 4**.

11. From the list, click **Word 97-2004 Document (.doc)**. Navigate to the **Word Chapter 1** folder, rename the file Lastname_Firstname_w01_Library_2004 and then click **Save**.

    Saving a document in an older format enables people with older software to open the document.

12. On the **menu bar,** click **Word,** and then click **Quit Word**.

13. Submit your printout or files as directed by your instructor.

Done! You have completed Skill 10 of 10, and your document is complete!

The following More Skills are located at **www.pearsonhighered.com/skills**. Please note that only More Skills that can be performed on a Macintosh computer are included in this section; therefore, the numbering is not always sequential.

More Skills ⑪ Split and Arrange Windows

You can split the Word screen, which lets you look at different parts of the same document at the same time. In a multiple-page document, this is convenient for viewing both the first page and the last page at the same time. You can also view two different documents side by side and make comparisons between the two.

In More Skills 11, you will open a multiple-page document and split the screen. Then, you will open a second document and view both documents at the same time.

To begin, open your web browser, navigate to www.pearsonhighered.com/skills, locate the name of your textbook, and then follow the instructions on the website.

More Skills ⑫ Insert Symbols

There are many symbols that are used occasionally, but not often enough to put on a standard computer keyboard. Some examples of commonly inserted symbols include copyright and trademark symbols, mathematical operators, and special dashes that are longer than hyphens. These symbols can be found and inserted from the Symbols group on the Insert tab.

In More Skills 12, you will open a document and insert several symbols from the Special Characters list in the Symbol dialog.

To begin, open your web browser, navigate to www.pearsonhighered.com/skills, locate the name of your textbook, and then follow the instructions on the website.

Key Terms

Clip art 40

Field 46

Font 38

Font style 38

Footer 46

Formatting mark 30

Header 46

Keyboard shortcut 32

Manual page break 36

Nonprinting character 30

Point 38

Text wrapping 41

Thesaurus 44

Word wrap 31

Online Help Skills

1. **Start** Safari  or another web browser. In the **address bar,** type microsoft.com/mac/how-to and then press return to display the home page for Microsoft Office for Mac.

2. Under **Product Help,** click **Word 2011**.

3. In the center of the page under **Word Help,** click the **Preferences and Accessibility** link.

4. Under **Preferences and Accessibility,** click **Word Preferences**.

5. Under **Word Preferences,** click **Automatically save and recover files**.

6. Under **Automatically save and recover files,** click **Change how frequently files are automatically saved,** and then click **Change where to automatically save files**. Compare your screen with **Figure 1**.

Figure 1

7. See if you can answer the following questions: How can you change how often files are automatically saved? How can you change the location of where AutoRecover files are saved to?

Matching

Match each term in the second column with its correct definition in the first column by writing the letter of the term on the blank line in front of the correct definition.

___ **1.** A character that indicates a paragraph, tab, or space on your screen, but that does not print when you print a Word document.

___ **2.** The color of the wavy line that indicates a potential spelling error.

___ **3.** The color of the wavy line that indicates a potential grammar error.

___ **4.** Forces a page to end, and places subsequent text at the top of the next page.

___ **5.** Graphics and images included with Microsoft Office or obtained from other sources.

___ **6.** A reserved area for text, graphics, and fields that displays at the bottom of each page in a document.

___ **7.** A unit of measurement for font sizes.

___ **8.** Automatically moves text from the right edge of a paragraph to the beginning of the next line as necessary to fit within the margins.

___ **9.** A reserved area for text, graphics, and fields that displays at the top of each page in a document.

___ **10.** A category of data—such as a file name, the page number, or the current date—that can be inserted into a document.

A Clip art

B Field

C Formatting mark

D Green

E Header

F Footer

G Manual page break

H Point

I Red

J Word wrap

Multiple Choice

Choose the correct answer.

1. Formatting marks such as paragraph symbols and dots for spaces are also called:
   A. Nonprinting characters
   B. Symbols
   C. Objects

2. When you are typing text and a word will not fit within the established right margin, this Word feature moves the entire word to the next line in the paragraph.
   A. AutoComplete
   B. Word wrap
   C. Alignment

3. With default keyboard settings, to delete the character to the left of the insertion point, press:
   A. control + delete
   B. delete
   C. fn + delete

4. With default keyboard settings, to delete the character to the right of the insertion point, press:
   A. control + delete
   B. delete
   C. fn + delete

5. Pictures can be inserted into a document from here:
   A. Media task pane
   B. Reference Tools task pane
   C. Documents task pane

6. A potential contextual spelling error is indicated by a wavy underline of this color:
   A. Pink
   B. Yellow
   C. Blue

7. To select a sentence, hold down this key, and then click anywhere in the sentence.
   A. control
   B. option
   C. command ⌘

8. A thesaurus may provide the following:
   A. Correct word usage
   B. Words with similar meanings
   C. Reading level of the document

9. To change Proofing tool settings, first display the:
   A. Review tab
   B. Home tab
   C. Spelling and Grammar

10. You can enter the name of the file or page numbers in this area at the bottom of each page of a document:
    A. Footer
    B. Header
    C. Margin

Topics for Discussion

1. What kind of information do you commonly see in the headers and footers of textbooks and magazines? Why do you think publishers include this type of information? In a report, what other type of information might you put in a header or footer?

2. When you check the spelling in a document, one of the options is to add unrecognized words to the dictionary. If you were working for a large company, what types of words do you think you would add to your dictionary?

Skill Check

To complete this document, you will need the following files:

- **New blank Word document**
- **w01_Donation_Opportunities**
- **w01_Donation_Photo**

You will save your document as:

- **Lastname_Firstname_w01_Donation**

1. **Start** Word and open a blank document. On the **Home tab,** click the **Show/Hide** button until it displays in blue. In all uppercase letters, type ASPEN FALLS PUBLIC LIBRARY and press return. Type 255 Elm Street and press return. Type Aspen Falls, CA 93463 and press return two times. Complete the beginning of the letter as follows with the information shown in **Figure 1**.

2. Press return and type Thank you so much for your interest in making a donation to the Aspen Falls Public Library. You asked about potential projects for which we need additional resources, so I have attached a list of possible projects. Press return and type In answer to your question, our library does not have 501c3 status. However, our Friends of the Library group is a 501c3 organization, and all donations to the library through the Friends group are fully tax deductible. Press return two times.

3. Type Sincerely, and press return two times. Type Douglas Hopkins, Director and then move to the line that begins *Aspen Heights.* Select the line. On the **Home tab,** in the **Paragraph group,** click the **Line Spacing** button, and then click **1.5**. Repeat this procedure with the next two lines of the letter.

4. In the paragraph that begins *Thank you,* use delete to erase *so much.* In the same paragraph, double-click *potential,* press delete, and then compare your screen with **Figure 2**.

5. Move to the end of the document. On the **menu bar,** click **Insert,** click **Break,** and then click **Page Break**.

6. On the **menu bar,** click **Insert,** and then click **File**. Locate and insert the file **w01_Donation_Opportunities**. Press delete to remove the blank paragraph at the end of the document.

▪ **Continue to the next page to complete this Skill Check**

May 17, 2013

Mr. Thomas Aldridge

2279 Shoreline Dr.

Aspen Heights, CA 93449

Dear Mr. Aldridge:

Subject: Donation to the Library

Figure 1

Figure 2

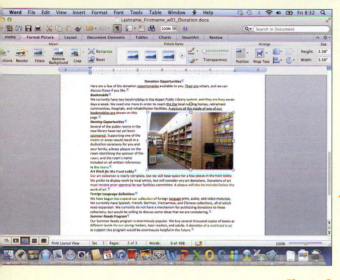

Figure 3

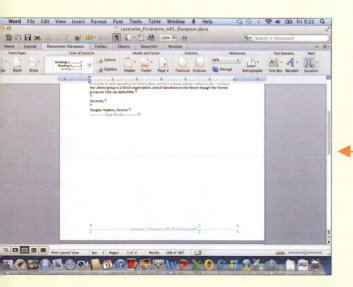

Figure 4

7. Press [command ⌘] + [A]. On the **Home tab,** in the **Font group,** change the **Font Size** to **11** and change the **Font** to **Calibri**. At the top of the document, select the library name. On the **Home tab,** change the **Font** to **Arial Black,** the **Font Size** to **16,** and then click **Bold.**

8. **Save** the document in your **Word Chapter 1** folder as Lastname_Firstname_w01_ Donation Display the top of Page 2. Select the heading *Donation Opportunities,* and then in the **Font group,** click **Bold** and **Center.**

9. Select the heading *Bookmobile,* and then in the **Font group,** click **Bold**. Select the next heading—*Naming Opportunities*—hold down [command ⌘], and then select the rest of the headings displayed in italic. In the **Font group,** click **Bold.**

10. Click to the left of the first *B* in the heading *Bookmobile*. From your student files, insert the picture **w01_Donation_Photo**. With the picture selected, on the **Format Picture tab,** in the **Arrange group,** click the **Wrap Text** button, and then click **Square**. Drag the picture to the right, aligning the right edge at approximately **6.5 inches** on the horizontal ruler and the top edge at approximately **1 inch** on the vertical ruler. Compare your screen with **Figure 3**.

11. Double-click the word, *opportunaties,* that has a wavy red underline, press [control], and then click **opportunities**. In the same paragraph, click the phrase *Their are* that has a wavy green line underline, and then change to **There are**. Move the insertion point to the top of Page 2.

12. On the **menu bar,** click **Tools,** and then click **Spelling & Grammar**. Make the following corrections—your marked errors may differ: For the repeated word *the,* delete the word. In the sentence that begins *A picture,* change to the suggested correction that ends with the word *is*. Correct the misspelling of the word *sponsored,* and change *languge* to *language*. Ignore any other changes except words you might have mistyped on Page 1.

13. On the **Document Elements tab,** in the **Header and Footer group,** click the **Footer** button, and then click **Simple (All Pages)**. Click to select **Type text**. On the **menu bar,** click **Insert,** and then click **Field**. Under **Field names,** scroll down and click **FileName**. Click **OK**. Click **Close**. Compare your document with **Figure 4**.

14. **Save** the document. Click **File,** and then click **Print**. Print or submit the file as directed by your instructor. **Quit** Word.

Done! You have completed the Skill Check

Assess Your Skills 1

To complete this document, you will need the following files:

- w01_Meadows
- w01_Meadows_Improvements
- w01_Meadows_Research

You will save your document as:

- Lastname_Firstname_w01_Meadows

1. **Start** Word and display the formatting marks. Click **File,** and then click **Open**. Navigate to your student files. **Open** the file **w01_Meadows,** save it in your **Word Chapter 1** folder as Lastname_Firstname_w01_Meadows and then add the file name to the footer.

2. In the letterhead, select the first line of text and change the **Font** to **Arial Black** and the **Font Size** to **16**. Select the remaining three lines of the letterhead and add **Bold** emphasis.

3. Move to the end of the document. Type Dear Ms. Jefferson: and press return. Type Subject: Aspen Meadows Branch Improvements and press return. Type the following paragraph: Thank you for your letter of concern about the Aspen Meadows Branch of the Aspen Falls Public Library. This is our smallest branch, and we are working hard to improve the collection and the services offered to our patrons. We have just completed some improvements, which I have detailed on the attached page. We hope these changes will answer some of your concerns. Press return, type Sincerely, and then press return two times. Type Douglas Hopkins, Director and then insert a manual page break.

4. On Page 2, insert the file **w01_Meadows_Improvements**. Select all of the text in the new page and change the **Font** to **Calibri** and the **Font Size** to **11**. Select the report heading that begins *Recent Improvements,* apply **Bold,** change the **Font Size** to **14,** and **Center** the text. Select the three headings on the page—*Collection, Children's Collection,* and *Research Stations*—and apply **Bold** and **Italic** emphasis.

5. Display the **Spelling and Grammar** dialog and on Page 2 fix the following problems: Remove the duplicate *to,* change *a* to *an,* and correct the spelling of *severel* to *several* and *suatable* to *suitable.* Ignore other marked words in the document unless you find typing errors that you made on Page 1.

6. In the last line of the last paragraph that begins *We have added,* double-click to select the word *shown*. Use the **Thesaurus** to change *shown* to **presented**.

7. Move to the blank line at the bottom of Page 2. Press return, and then insert the picture in the file **w01_Meadows_Research**. **Save** the changes, and then compare your document with **Figure 1**. Preview your document, make any necessary changes, and then print or submit the file as directed by your instructor.

Done! You have completed Assess Your Skills 1

Figure 1

Assessment

Assess Your Skills 3 and 4 can be found at **www.pearsonhighered.com/skills**.

MEMORANDUM

TO: Jamie McArthur, Special Services

FROM: Douglas Hopkins, Director

DATE: June 21, 2013

RE: Virtual Tour of the Library

Jamie:

I have been thinking about the suggestion made at the Board of Trustees meeting the other night that we hire an outside company to design a virtual tour of the library. The virtual tour might consist of several modules featuring different topics. I have listed some of the topics on the next page.

Let me know what you think.

Doug

Topics for the Virtual Tour of the New Library

Here is a list I put together of topics I would like to see included if we go ahead with the virtual tour for the Internet:

The Building Exterior

The new building is very striking, and we should have a 360-degree tour of the exterior, including the grounds and the pond. We should also mention the Alvarado architectural firm that we employed to design the building.

The Building Interior

Shots of the interior should include a panorama of our wonderful lobby, and then should move inside to show the collections, the kids' area, the community room, the computer labs, the genealogy room, the office suite, and the board room.

Library Technology

Some of the technology that we show will be physical features, such as computer labs, but some will have to rely on screen shots of technology in action, such as downloading e-books, using the research databases, and some of the adaptive technologies that are available for the disabled. I think it is important that we have a special section that focuses only on technology. This topic will be of special interest to our youngest and oldest patrons.

Friends of the Aspen Falls Public Library Bookshop

The Friends bookshop is a centerpiece of our new library, and needs to have its own module in the virtual tour.

People

I am not sure we should include any of the staff in the virtual tour. Several of them have already indicated that they do not want to be shown in the tours. If we need one or more people for any of the tour modules, we should probably ask for volunteers.

Figure 1

Assess Your Skills 2

To complete this document, you will need the following files:

- w01_Tour
- w01_Tour_Topics

You will save your document as:

- Lastname_Firstname_w01_Tour

1. **Start** Word and display the formatting marks. Open the file **w01_Tour,** save it in your **Word Chapter 1** folder as Lastname_Firstname_w01_Tour and then add the file name to the footer. Select the first line of text and change the **Font** to **Arial** and the **Font Size** to **36,** and then **Center** and **Bold** the title. Add **Bold** emphasis to the four words on the left side of the memo—TO:, FROM:, DATE:, and RE:.

2. Move to the end of the document, type Jamie: and then press return. Type I have been thinking about the suggestion made at the Board of Trustees meeting the other night that we hire an outside company to design a virtual tour of the library. The virtual tour might consist of several different modules featuring different topics. I have listed some of the more interesting things on the next page. Press return, type Let me know what you think. and then press return two times. Type Doug and then add a manual page break.

3. In the text you just typed, use delete to remove the phrase *more interesting*. Double-click the next word—*things*—and type topics to replace it. Locate and double-click the first instance of the word *different*—to the left of *modules*—and then press delete.

4. Position the insertion point at the top of Page 2. Insert the file **w01_Tour_Topics**.

5. On Page 2, select the first line of text, apply **Bold** emphasis, and **Center** the text. Select the five topic titles on the left side of Page 2 and apply **Bold** emphasis. Select all of the text in the document except the title on the first page, and change the **Font Size** to **12**.

6. Move to the top of Page 2. Display the **Spelling and Grammar** dialog. Delete the repeated word *the,* change *interier* to *interior,* change *databasis* to *databases,* and then change *has* to *have.* Correct any mistakes you made on the first page.

7. Position the insertion point at the bottom of the document. Insert and position the clip art image shown in **Figure 1**. Use the **Business** category in the **Media** task pane. (Note: If this image is not available, insert the picture in the student file w01_Library_Logo.) **Close** the **Media** task pane.

8. **Save** the changes and compare your document with **Figure 1**. Preview your document, make any necessary changes, and then print or submit the file as directed by your instructor.

Done! You have completed Assess Your Skills 2

Assess Your Skills Visually

To complete this document, you will need the following file:

- New blank Word document

You will save your document as:

- Lastname_Firstname_w01_Closures

Start Word. Create the document shown in **Figure 1**. **Save** the file as Lastname_Firstname_ w01_Closures in your **Word Chapter 1** folder. To complete this document, use Arial Black sized at 24 points for the title and Cambria sized at 12 points for the rest of the document. After the last paragraph, insert the clip art image shown in **Figure 1** by searching for *holidays*. If you do not see the same image, use any other appropriate clip art. Insert the file name in the footer, and then print or submit the file as directed by your instructor.

Done! You have completed Assess Your Skills Visually

MEMORANDUM

TO: All Library Staff

FROM: Douglas Hopkins, Director

DATE: December 15, 2013

I have listed the days we are going to close the library in 2013. I have listed the holidays, the in-service days, and the days we will close early.

Holidays

We will be closed on New Year's Day, Easter, Memorial Day, the Fourth of July, Labor Day, Thanksgiving, and Christmas.

In-Service Days

We will be closed on April 15th for a session on library security, and on November 7th for a session that will focus on streaming the material handling process.

Close Early

We will close early on New Year's Eve, the day before Easter, the day before Thanksgiving, and Christmas Eve.

Happy Holidays!

Figure 1

Skills in Context

To complete this document, you will need the following files:

- New blank Word document
- w01_Trustees_Report

You will save your document as:

- Lastname_Firstname_w01_Trustees

Using the information provided, compose a letter from Douglas Hopkins, the Director of the Aspen Falls Public Library, to Fran Darcy, the Chair of the Library Board of Trustees. Use the current date and the address used in Skill 1. The letter is regarding the attached report on library operations for the previous year, and it should include the purpose of the letter and provide a very brief summary of the attached document. Save the document as Lastname_Firstname_w01_Trustees On a new page, insert the report **w01_Trustees_Report** and at an appropriate location in the document, insert a representative clip art image. Format the document appropriately. Check the entire document for grammar and spelling, and then insert the file name in the footer. Submit as directed.

Done! You have completed Skills in Context

Skills and You

To complete this document, you will need the following file:

- New blank Word document

You will save your document as:

- Lastname_Firstname_w01_Careers

Using the skills you have practiced in this chapter, compose either a letter or a memo to the director of your college's Career Center inquiring about the skills needed to find a job. Ask if there are upcoming seminars or workshops that you might attend. If you have a picture of yourself, insert it in the memo as a way of introducing yourself. You should include several instances of text formatting somewhere in the document. Save the document as Lastname_Firstname_w01_Careers Check the entire document for grammar and spelling, and insert the file name in the footer. Print or submit the file as directed by your instructor.

Done! You have completed Skills and You

CHAPTER 2

Format and Organize Text

- ▶ Document margins are the spaces that display on the outer edges of a printed page. All four page margins can be adjusted independently.

- ▶ To make paragraphs stand out, add spacing above and below, change the first line indents, and format subheadings. This helps the reader understand the structure of the document, which increases the document's readability.

- ▶ Lists make information easier to understand. Use numbered lists when information is displayed in a sequence and use bulleted lists when information can appear in any order.

- ▶ A footnote or endnote can be inserted when you have supplemental information that does not fit well in the document.

- ▶ When you use quotations or paraphrase information created by someone else, you need to cite your sources.

- ▶ Informal business reports are often formatted using guidelines in *The Gregg Reference Manual* by William A. Sabin. These guidelines specify the way the text is formatted, the way notes display, and the types of citations used.

©Endostock | Dreamstime.com

Aspen Falls City Hall

In this chapter, you will format a report for Cyril Shore, the Director of the Planning Commission. The report will look at the advantages and potential problems of using roof gardens in new or existing construction and will follow the formatting guidelines for an informal business report.

In this project, you will open an existing document and set the margins, line spacing, and paragraph spacing. You will create a bulleted list and a numbered list and format both lists. You will add footnotes and citations, and then create a bibliography for the report.

Time to complete all
10 skills – 60 to 75 minutes

Student data files needed for this chapter:

New blank Word document
w02_Gardens

You will save your document as:

Lastname_Firstname_w02_Gardens

Outcome

Using the skills in this chapter, you will be able to work with Word documents like this:

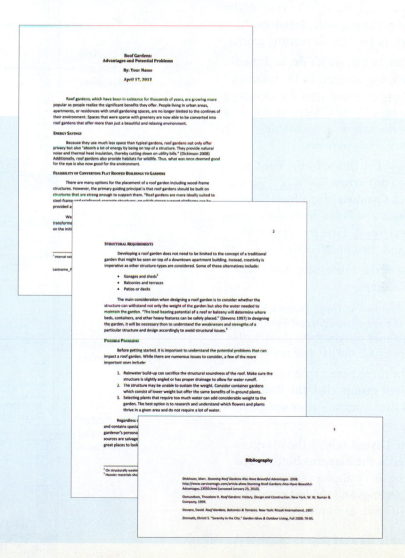

SKILLS

Skills 1-10 Training

At the end of this chapter you will be able to:

Skill 1   Set Document Margins
Skill 2   Align Text and Set Indents
Skill 3   Modify Line and Paragraph Spacing
Skill 4   Format Text Using Format Painter
Skill 5   Find and Replace Text
Skill 6   Create Bulleted and Numbered Lists
Skill 7   Insert and Format Headers and Footers
Skill 8   Insert and Modify Footnotes
Skill 9   Add Citations
Skill 10 Create Bibliographies

MORE SKILLS

Skill 11 Record AutoCorrect Entries
Skill 12 Use AutoFormat to Create Numbered Lists
Skill 13 Format and Customize Lists
Skill 14 Manage Document Properties

► *Margins* are the spaces between the text and the top, bottom, left, and right edges of the paper.

► Each of the margins can be adjusted independently of the other margins.

1. **Start** Word ![W]. If a previous Word document displays, Close ![X] the document, and then, on the menu bar, click File, and then click Open. Navigate to your student files, and then open **w02_Gardens**. If necessary, display the formatting marks.

2. On the menu bar, click **File**, and then click **Save As**. Navigate to the location where you are saving your files, create a folder named Word Chapter 2 and then **Save** the document as Lastname_Firstname_w02_Gardens

3. Press ⟨return⟩ five times. In the **Font group**, click the **Font arrow** Calibri (Body) ▾, and then click **Cambria**. Type Roof Gardens: Advantages and Potential Problems and then press ⟨return⟩. Type By *(Type your name),* and then press ⟨return⟩.

4. Type the current date, and then press ⟨return⟩ two times.

   According to *The Gregg Reference Manual,* the first page of an informal business report uses a 2-inch margin above the title, the author's name, and the date of the report.

5. Select the three paragraphs you just typed. In the **Font group**, click the **Bold** button ![B], and then compare your screen with **Figure 1**.

6. Click the **Layout tab**. In the **Margins group**, click the **Margins** button. The Margins gallery displays several standard margin settings and the last custom setting (if any), as shown in **Figure 2**.

   ■ **Continue to the next page to complete the skill**

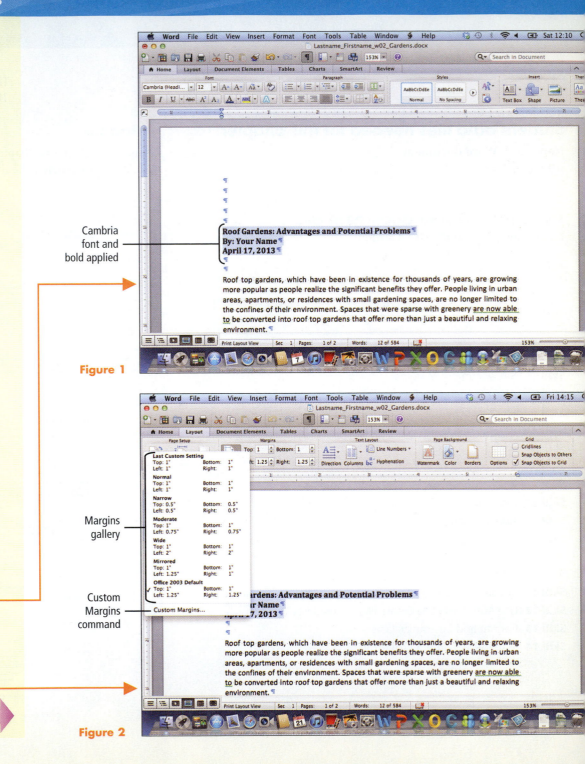

Cambria font and bold applied

Figure 1

Margins gallery

Custom Margins command

Figure 2

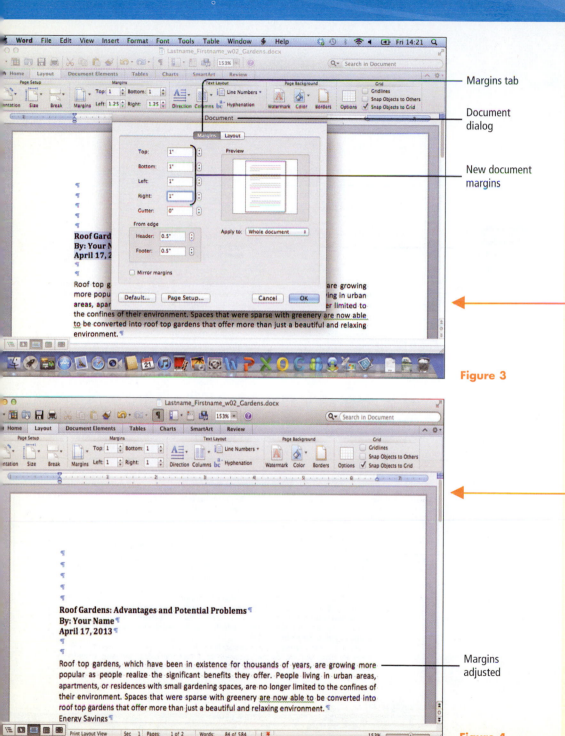

Figure 3

Figure 4

7. At the bottom of the **Margins** gallery, click **Custom Margins**.

   The Page Setup dialog provides you with document formatting options, some of which are not available on the Ribbon.

8. In the **Document** dialog, be sure the **Margins tab** is selected. Press `tab` two times. Under **Margins**, in the **Left** box, with *1.25"* selected, click the **down spin arrow** three times to change the left margin to *1"*. Alternately, with the current margin selected, type the new margin in the margin box.

9. Press `tab`, and then repeat this procedure to change the **Right** margin to *1"*. Compare your screen with **Figure 3**.

10. At the bottom of the **Document** dialog, verify that the **Apply to** box displays *Whole document,* and then click **OK**.

    With *portrait orientation*, the printed page is taller than it is wide; with *landscape orientation*, the printed page width is greater than the page height. Most reports use portrait orientation.

11. Click anywhere in the document to deselect the text. Compare your screen with **Figure 4**, and notice the results of the changes you made to the margins.

12. **Save** 🖫 the document.

    ▪ **You have completed Skill 1 of 10**

Margins tab

Document dialog

New document margins

Margins adjusted

► *Indents* are the position of paragraph lines in relation to the page margins.

► *Horizontal alignment* is the orientation of the left or right edges of the paragraph—for example, flush with the left or right margins.

1. Position the insertion point anywhere in the first paragraph you typed—the title that begins *Roof Gardens*.

   To align a single paragraph, you need only position the insertion point anywhere in the paragraph.

2. On the **Home tab**, in the **Paragraph group**, click the **Align Text Right** button ![icon] to align the title with the right margin.

3. In the **Paragraph group**, click the **Center Text** button ![icon] to center the title between the left and right margins.

4. Select the second and third bold title lines. Click the **Center Text** button ![icon], and then compare your screen with **Figure 1**.

5. In the left margin, point ![icon] to the paragraph that begins *Roof top gardens* and drag down to select that paragraph and the following two paragraphs that begin *Energy Savings* and *Because they use*. Notice that these paragraphs are *justified*—the paragraph text is aligned flush with both the left margin and the right margin.

6. In the **Paragraph group**, click the **Align Text Left** button ![icon]. Compare your screen with **Figure 2**, and then click anywhere to deselect the text.

   These paragraphs are no longer justified.

■ **Continue to the next page to complete the skill**

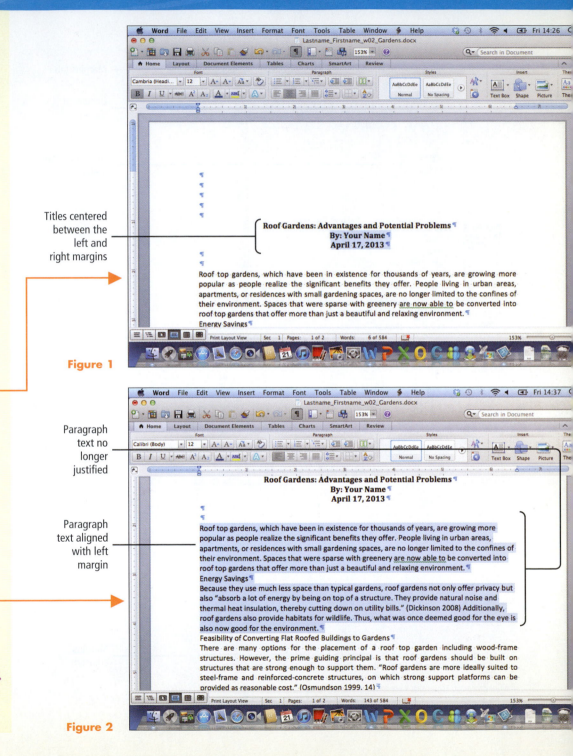

Titles centered between the left and right margins

Figure 1

Paragraph text no longer justified

Paragraph text aligned with left margin

Figure 2

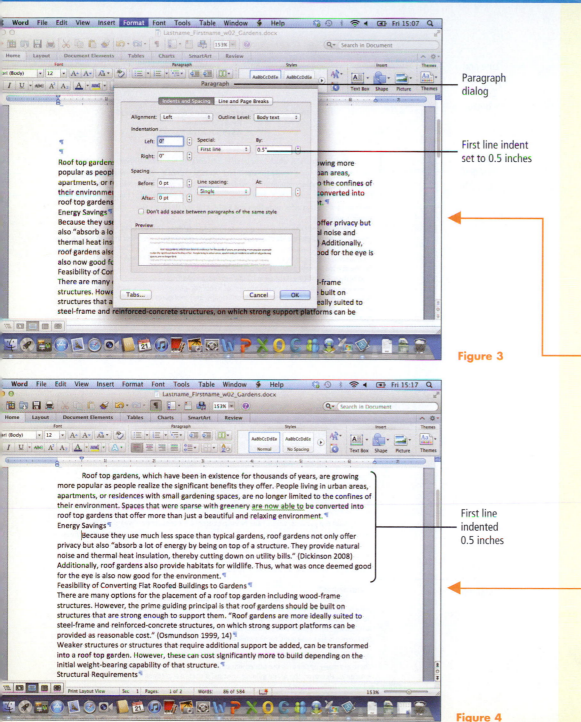

Paragraph
dialog

First line indent
set to 0.5 inches

Figure 3

First line
indented
0.5 inches

Figure 4

7. Below the text that you just aligned, click to the left of the paragraph that begins *Feasibility.* Scroll to the end of the document, hold down $\boxed{shift}$, and then click to the right of the last line in the document. On the **Home tab**, in the **Paragraph group**, click the **Align Text Left** button.

8. Move to the top of the document. Below the centered titles, click to position the insertion point anywhere in the paragraph that begins *Roof top gardens.*

9. On the **menu bar**, click **Format**, and then click **Paragraph**.

   The Paragraph dialog displays, which includes commands that are not available on the Ribbon.

10. Under **Indentation**, click the **Special box arrow**, and then click **First line**. Compare your screen with **Figure 3**.

    The *first line indent* is the location of the beginning of the first line of a paragraph in relationship with the left edge of the remainder of the paragraph. In this case, the *By* box displays *0.5"*, which will indent the first line of the current paragraph one-half inch.

11. Click **OK** to indent the first line of the paragraph.

12. Click anywhere in the paragraph that begins *Because they use,* and repeat the procedure just practiced to indent the first line of the paragraph by 0.5 inches. Compare your screen with **Figure 4**.

13. **Save** the document.

    ■ **You have completed Skill 2 of 10**

► *Line spacing* is the vertical distance between lines of text in a paragraph, and can be adjusted for each paragraph.

► *Paragraph spacing* is the vertical distance above and below each paragraph, and can be adjusted for each paragraph.

1. Below the centered titles, click anywhere in the paragraph that begins *Roof top gardens*.

2. On the **Home tab**, in the **Paragraph group**, click the **Line Spacing** button.

   The current setting is *1.0—single-spacing—* which means that no extra space is added between lines of text. Line spacing of *2.0—double-spacing—*means that the equivalent of a blank line of text displays between each line of text.

3. In the **Line Spacing** list, click **1.15** to change the line spacing, as shown in **Figure 1**.

   Text with a line spacing of 1.15 has been found to be easier to read than single-spaced text.

4. On the **menu bar**, click **Format**, and then click **Paragraph**. In the **Paragraph** dialog, under **Spacing**, click the **After up spin arrow** two times to change the spacing after the paragraph to *12 pt,* and then click **OK**.

5. In the paragraph that begins *Because they use*, repeat the same procedure to set the line spacing to **1.15** and the spacing after to **12 pt**. Notice the change in the spacing between the paragraphs, as shown in **Figure 2**.

   ■ **Continue to the next page to complete the skill**

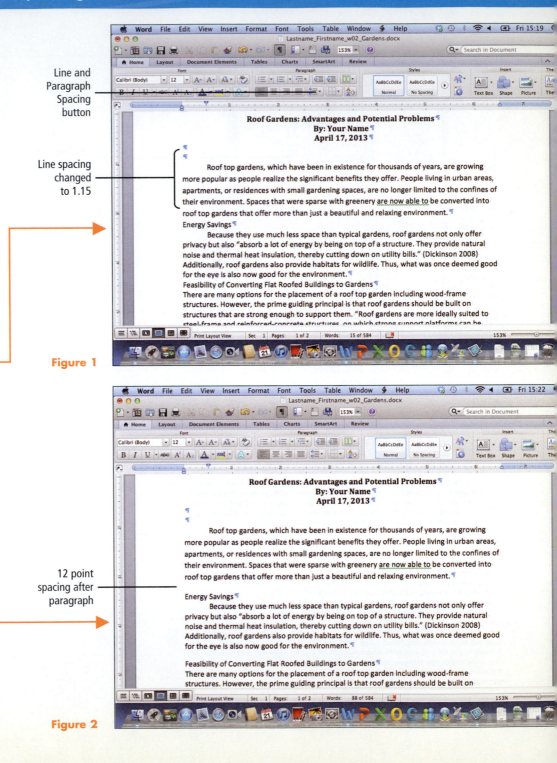

Line and Paragraph Spacing button

Line spacing changed to 1.15

Figure 1

12 point spacing after paragraph

Figure 2

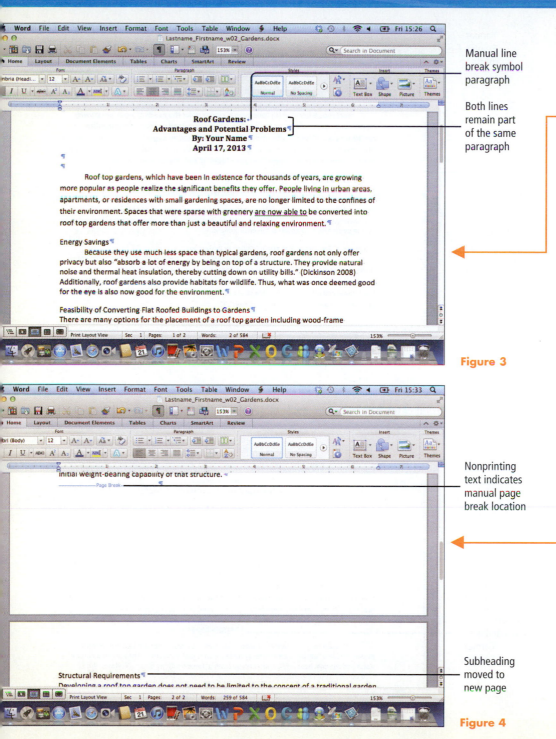

Manual line break symbol paragraph

Both lines remain part of the same paragraph

Figure 3

Nonprinting text indicates manual page break location

Subheading moved to new page

Figure 4

6. At the top of the document, in the first title, position the insertion point to the right of *Roof Gardens:*.

7. Press fn + delete to remove the space, hold down shift, and then press return. Compare your screen with **Figure 3**.

   A *manual line break*—a line break that moves the remainder of the paragraph to a new line while keeping both lines in the same paragraph—is inserted. The manual line break symbol displays when a manual line break is inserted.

8. In the left margin area, point to the left of the first title to display the ↗ pointer, and then drag down to select all of the centered title lines.

9. On the **menu bar**, click **Format**, and then click **Paragraph**. In the **Paragraph** dialog, under **Spacing**, click the **After up spin arrow** two times to add 12 points spacing after each paragraph. Click **OK**.

   No extra spacing was added after the manual line break because both lines are part of the same paragraph.

10. Near the bottom of Page 1, click to position the insertion point to the left of the subheading that begins *Structural Requirements*. On the **menu bar**, click **Insert**, click **Break**, and then click **Page Break**. Compare your screen with **Figure 4**.

    A *manual page break*—a break that moves the text following it to a new page—is inserted. Here, as line spacing and paragraph spacing is changed on Page 1, the text that follows this manual page break will always start on a new page.

11. **Save** 💾 the document.

    ■ **You have completed Skill 3 of 10**

► Use *Format Painter* to copy text formatting quickly from one place to another.

► To use Format Painter on multiple items, double-click the Format Painter button.

1. Near the top of the document, click anywhere in the paragraph that begins *Roof top gardens*.

2. On the **Standard toolbar**, click the **Format Painter** button.

3. Scroll down and point anywhere in the paragraph that begins *There are many*. Notice that the pointer displays.

4. Click anywhere in the paragraph. Notice that the formatting from the original paragraph is applied to the new paragraph, and that the pointer no longer displays. Compare your screen with **Figure 1**.

5. Scroll to the top of the document, click anywhere in the title *By Your Name,* and then on the Standard toolbar click the **Format Painter** button. In the middle of Page 1, move the pointer to the left of the *Energy Savings* subheading until the pointer displays, and then click. Compare your screen with **Figure 2**.

   The font, bold style, centering, and paragraph spacing from the original paragraph are all applied to the new paragraph.

6. With the *Energy Savings* subheading selected, on the **Home tab**, in the **Paragraph group**, click the **Align Text Left** button.

7. On the **menu bar**, click **Format**, and then click **Font**.

■ **Continue to the next page to complete the skill** →

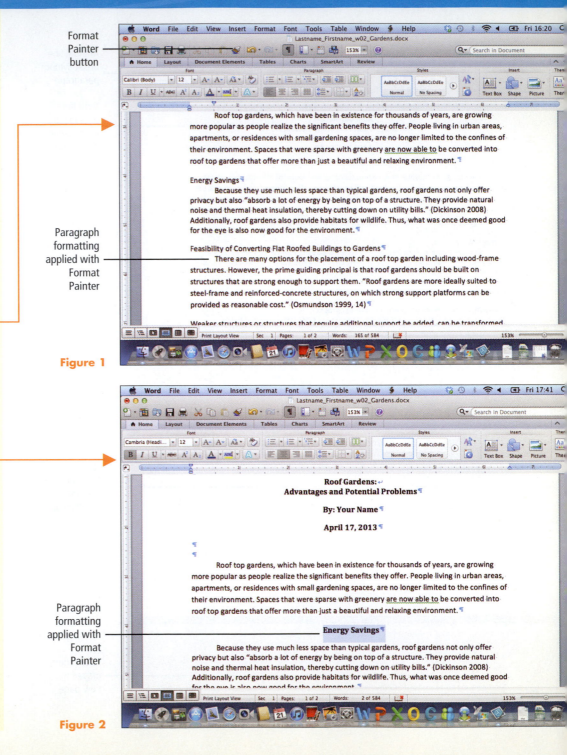

Format Painter button

Paragraph formatting applied with Format Painter

Figure 1

Paragraph formatting applied with Format Painter

Figure 2

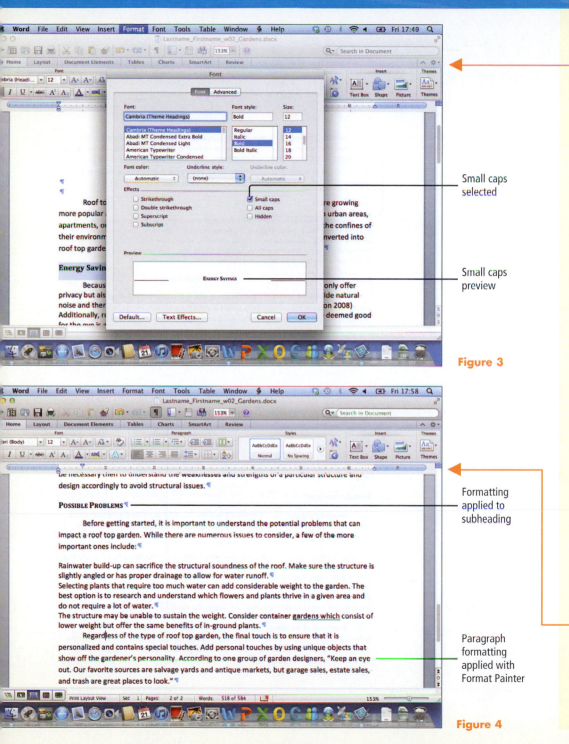

Figure 3

Small caps selected

Small caps preview

Figure 4

Formatting applied to subheading

Paragraph formatting applied with Format Painter

8. In the **Font** dialog, under **Effects**, select the **Small caps** check box. Compare your screen with **Figure 3**.

9. At the bottom of the **Font** dialog, click **OK**.

10. With the text still selected, on the **Standard toolbar**, double-click the **Format Painter** button.

11. Using the pointer, select the remaining three subheadings—*Feasibility of Converting, Structural Requirements,* and *Possible Problems.*

    When you double-click the Format Painter button, it remains on until you turn it off. If you accidentally clicked another paragraph, on the Standard toolbar, click the Undo button and try again.

12. Press esc to turn off Format Painter. Alternately, click the **Format Painter** button.

13. Move to the top of the document, place the insertion point in the paragraph that begins *Roof top gardens,* and then on the **Standard toolbar**, double-click the **Format Painter** button. At the bottom of Page 1, click in the paragraph that begins *Weaker structures.*

14. Move to Page 2, and then click anywhere in the four paragraphs that begin *Developing a roof, The main consideration, Before getting started,* and the final document paragraph *Regardless of the type.*

15. Press esc to turn off Format Painter, and then compare your screen with **Figure 4**.

16. **Save** the document.

    ■ **You have completed Skill 4 of 10**

► The Find command is useful if you know a word or phrase is in a document and you want to locate it quickly.

► Using the Replace command, you can find and then replace words or phrases one at a time, or all at once.

1. Move to the top of the document. On the **menu bar**, click **Edit**, click **Find**, and then click **Find**.

   A Search box displays in the Standard toolbar.

2. In the **Search** box, type space Notice that three instances of the word are highlighted, even though two of them are the plural form of the word—*spaces*. If your screen differs, on the **Standard toolbar**, press command ⌘ + F.

3. In the document, click the third instance of the word, and then compare your screen with **Figure 1**.

4. In the **Search** box, select the existing text, type garden and notice that 24 instances of the word are found.

5. Use the vertical scroll bar to scroll down the list of *garden* instances. Scroll to the bottom of the list.

   The located instances include *garden, gardens, gardening,* and *gardener.*

6. Click to select the last occurrence of the word *garden.*

7. On the **Standard toolbar**, click the **Cut** button ✂ to remove the selected word. Compare your screen with **Figure 2**.

   ■ **Continue to the next page to complete the skill** ➤

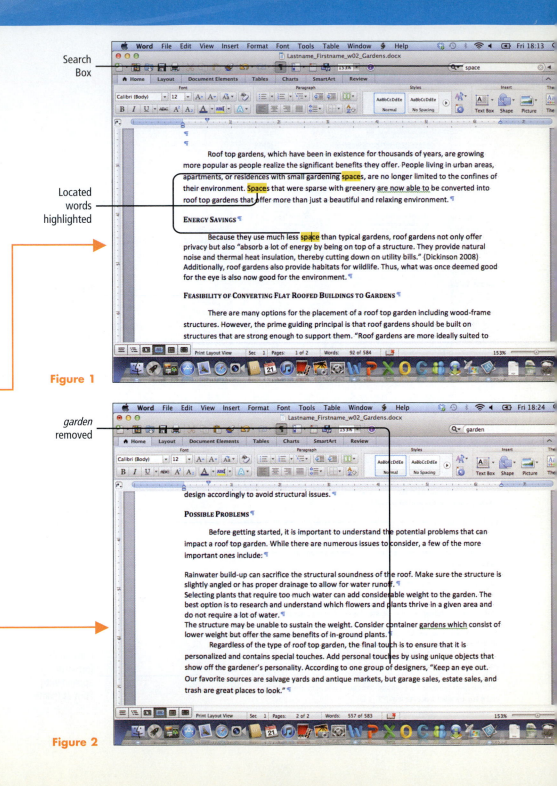

Search Box

Located words highlighted

Figure 1

garden removed

Figure 2

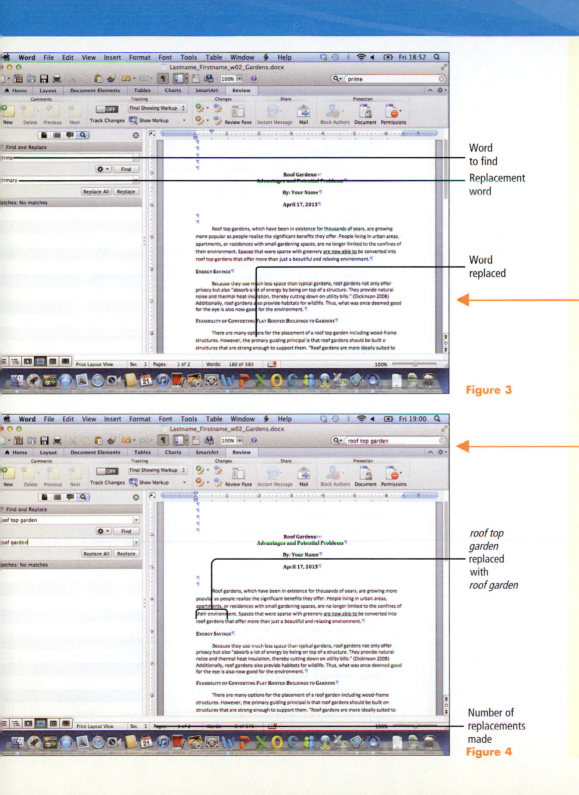

Word to find

Replacement word

Word replaced

Figure 3

roof top garden replaced with roof garden

Number of replacements made

Figure 4

8. Move to the beginning of the document. On the **Review tab**, in the **Changes group**, click the **Review Pane** button. In the Review Pane, click the **Find and Replace** 🔍 button. Notice that the Find and Replace task pane displays and that the previous search term—*garden*—displays in the *Search Document* box.

9. In the **Search Document** box, select the existing text, type prime and press `tab`. In the **Replace With** box, type primary

10. Click the **Find** button to find the first instance of *prime,* and then click the **Replace** button twice. Notice that the word is replaced, as shown in **Figure 3**.

11. Scroll to place the insertion point at the beginning of the document.

12. In the **Find and Replace** task pane, in the **Search Document** box, type roof top garden and in the **Replace With** box, type roof garden

13. Click the **Replace All** button. Compare your screen with **Figure 4**.

> When you do not specify any Find and Replace settings, the replaced text will retain the capitalization used in the original word or phrase.

14. On the **Review tab**, in the **Changes group**, click the **Review Pane** button two times to close the **Review Pane**, and then **Save** 💾 the document.

■ **You have completed Skill 5 of 10**

► A ***bulleted list*** is a list of items with each item introduced by a symbol—such as a small circle or checkmark—in which the list items can be presented in any order.

► A ***numbered list*** is a list of items with each item introduced by a consecutive number or letter to indicate definite steps, a sequence of actions, or chronological order.

1. Near the top of Page 2, in the left margin area, display the ⬈ pointer to the left of the paragraph *Garages and sheds,* and then drag down to select the three paragraphs up to and including the paragraph *Patios or decks.*

2. On the **Home tab**, in the **Paragraph group**, click the **Bulleted List** button ▤▾. Compare your screen with **Figure 1**.

   The symbols used for your bulleted list may vary, depending on the last bullet type used on your computer.

3. With the bulleted list still selected, on the **Home tab**, in the **Paragraph group**, click the **Line Spacing** button ▤▾, and then click **1.15**.

4. In the **Paragraph group**, click the **Increase Indent** button ▤ one time.

   The list moves 0.25 inches to the right.

5. With the bulleted list still selected, on the **menu bar**, click **Format**, and then click **Paragraph**. In the **Paragraph** dialog, under **Spacing**, click the **After up spin arrow** two times to increase the spacing after to *12 pt,* and then click **OK**.

6. Click anywhere in the document and notice that the space was added after the *last item* in the list only, as shown in **Figure 2**.

   ■ **Continue to the next page to complete the skill** ►

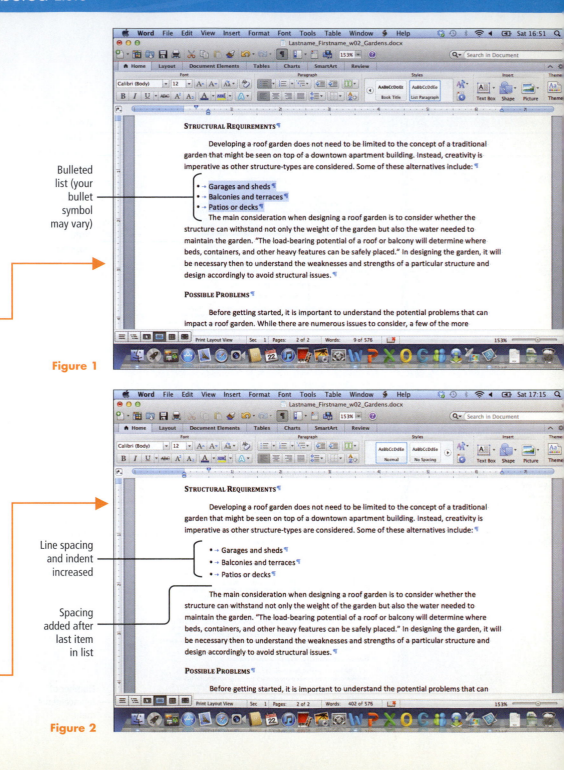

Bulleted list (your bullet symbol may vary)

Figure 1

Line spacing and indent increased

Spacing added after last item in list

Figure 2

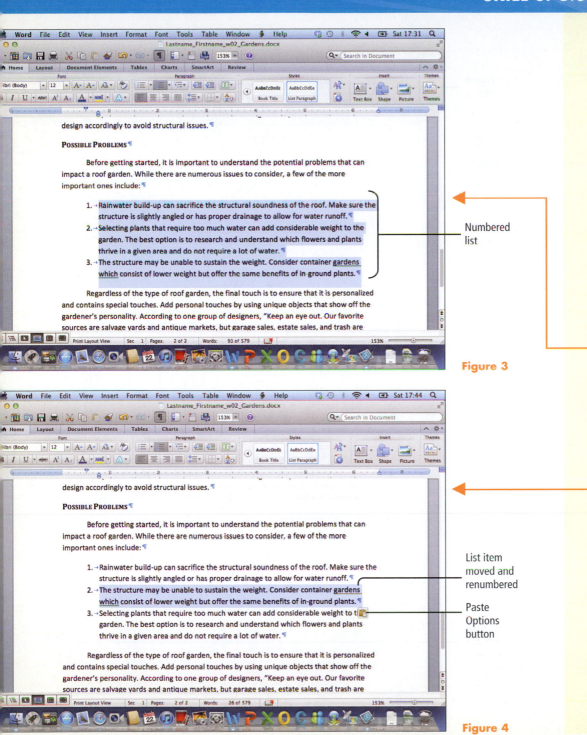

Numbered list

Figure 3

List item moved and renumbered

Paste Options button

Figure 4

7. Scroll to the bottom of Page 2. Select the three paragraphs that begin with *Rainwater build-up* and end with *in-ground plants.*

8. On the **Home tab**, in the **Paragraph group**, click the **Numbered List** button. In the **Paragraph group**, click the **Increase Indent** button one time.

9. With the list still selected, in the **Paragraph group**, click the **Line Spacing** button, and then click **1.15.**

10. On the **menu bar**, click **Format**, and then click **Paragraph**. In the **Paragraph** dialog, under **Spacing**, click the **After up spin arrow** two times to change the spacing after the list to *12 pt*, and then click **OK.** Notice that the space is added only after the last item in the list, as shown in **Figure 3.**

11. In the numbered list, select all of the text in the third item, including the paragraph mark. Do not select the number *3.*

12. Move the pointer over the selected text to display the pointer. Drag the selected text up to the left of *Selecting* in the second item in the list. Compare your screen with **Figure 4.**

> Notice that the step text is moved, the numbering is changed, and the space after the list remains at the bottom of the list. Because dragging text treats the text like it was cut and then pasted, a Paste Options button also displays.

13. **Save** the document.

■ **You have completed Skill 6 of 10**

▶ Headers and footers can include not only text but also graphics and fields—for example, file names and the current date.

▶ You can turn off the headers and footers on the first page of a document.

1. Click at the beginning of the document. On the **menu bar**, click **View**, and then click **Header and Footer**. Notice that the Design contextual tab is added to the Ribbon.

2. Display the **Header and Footer tab**. In the **Insert group**, click the **Page #** button, and then compare your screen with **Figure 1**.

3. Display the **Home tab**, and then in the **Paragraph group**, click the **Align Text Right** button ▤.

4. On the **Header and Footer tab**, in the **Options group**, select the **Different First Page** check box.

   The page number disappears from the header for Page 1 but will display on all other pages of the document.

5. Double-click anywhere in the document to deactivate the header, and then scroll to the top of Page 2. Notice that the page number displays on Page 2, as shown in **Figure 2**.

■ **Continue to the next page to complete the skill**

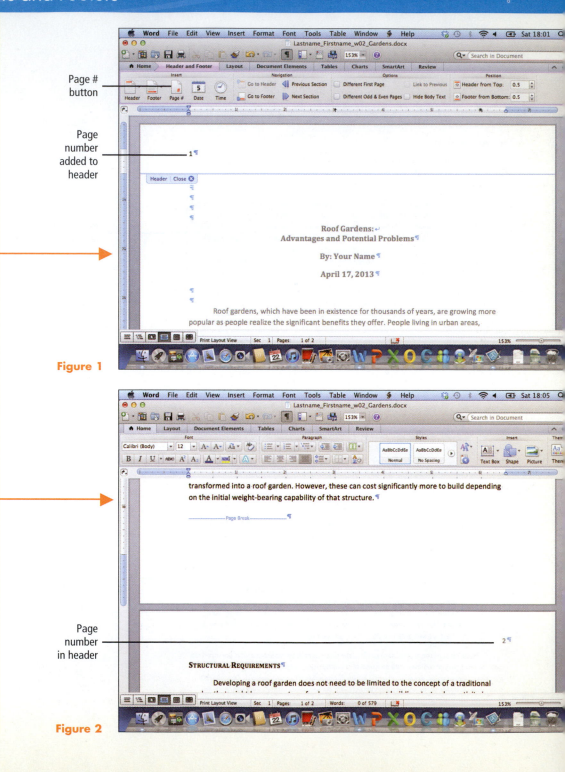

Page # button

Page number added to header

Figure 1

Page number in header

Figure 2

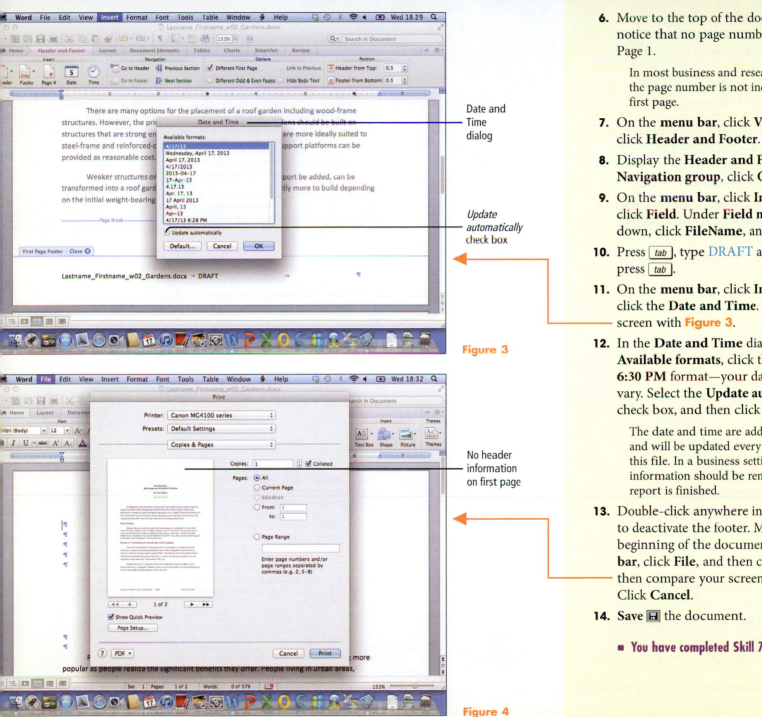

Date and Time dialog

Update automatically check box

Figure 3

No header information on first page

Figure 4

6. Move to the top of the document and notice that no page number displays on Page 1.

   In most business and research reports, the page number is not included on the first page.

7. On the **menu bar**, click **View**, and then click **Header and Footer**.

8. Display the **Header and Footer tab**. In the **Navigation group**, click **Go to Footer**.

9. On the **menu bar**, click **Insert**, and then click **Field**. Under **Field names**, scroll down, click **FileName**, and then click **OK**.

10. Press ⌨ tab ⌨, type DRAFT and then press ⌨ tab ⌨.

11. On the **menu bar**, click **Insert**, and then click the **Date and Time**. Compare your screen with **Figure 3**.

12. In the **Date and Time** dialog, under **Available formats**, click the **4/17/2013 6:30 PM** format—your date and time will vary. Select the **Update automatically** check box, and then click **OK**.

    The date and time are added to the footer and will be updated every time you open this file. In a business setting, the footer information should be removed when the report is finished.

13. Double-click anywhere in the document to deactivate the footer. Move to the beginning of the document. On the **menu bar**, click **File**, and then click **Print**, and then compare your screen with **Figure 4**. Click **Cancel**.

14. Save 💾 the document.

   ▪ **You have completed Skill 7 of 10**

► A *footnote* is a reference placed at the bottom of the page. An *endnote* is a reference placed at the end of a section or a document.

► You can use either numbers or symbols to label footnotes and endnotes.

1. Scroll to the bulleted list near the top of Page 2. At the end of the first bulleted item—*Garages and sheds*—click to position the insertion point.

2. Display the **Document Elements tab**, and then in the **Citations group**, click the **Footnote** button.

> A footnote displays at the bottom of the page with a number *1* before the insertion point. A line is also inserted above the footnote area to separate it from the document text.

3. Type On structurally weaker buildings, potted plants work best. Compare your screen with **Figure 1**.

> Footnotes are used to provide supplemental information that does not fit well in the document.

4. Scroll up to the paragraph below the bulleted list that begins *The main consideration*. Position the insertion point at the end of the paragraph.

5. In the **Citations group**, click the **Footnote** button. Type Heavier materials should be located near load-bearing walls. Compare your screen with **Figure 2**.

> The second footnote displays below the first, and the footnotes are numbered sequentially.

6. On the **menu bar**, click **View**, and then click **Footnotes**.

> You can now edit footnotes here.

■ **Continue to the next page to complete the skill**

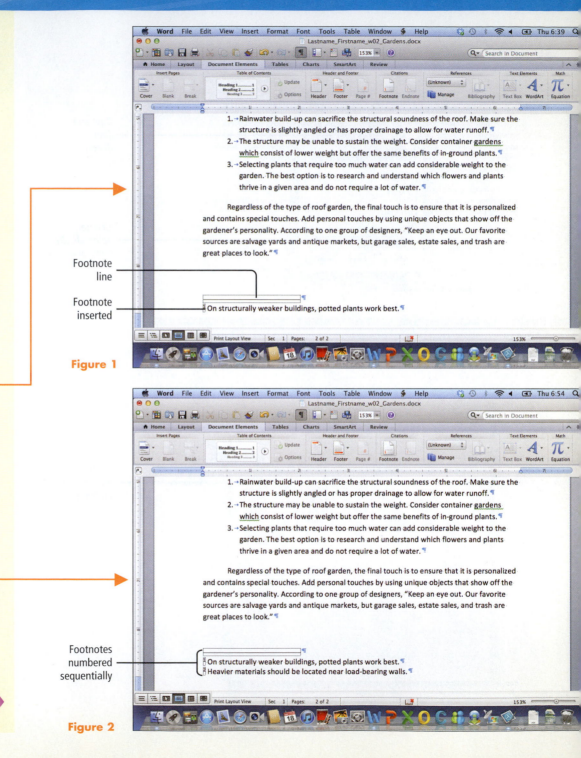

Footnote line

Footnote inserted

Figure 1

Footnotes numbered sequentially

Figure 2

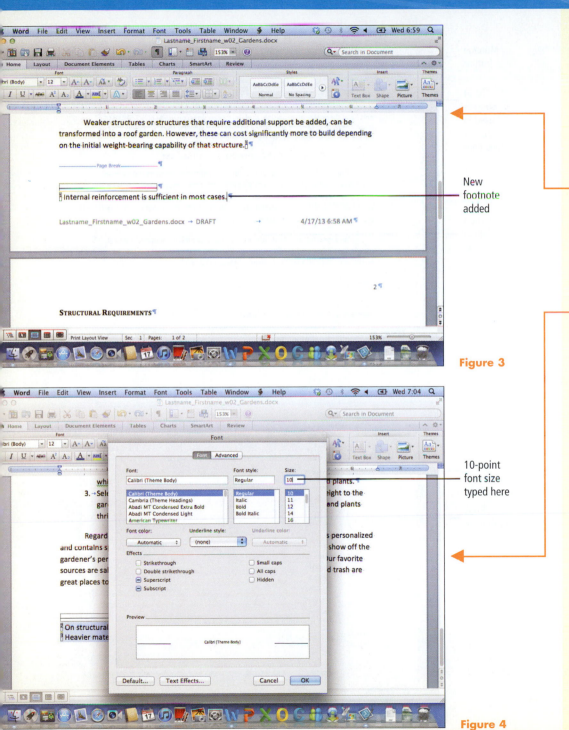

New footnote added

Figure 3

10-point font size typed here

Figure 4

7. Scroll to the last paragraph on Page 1—the one that begins *Weaker structures or structures*. Position the insertion point at the end of that paragraph.

8. On the **menu bar**, click **Insert**, and then click **Footnote**.

9. In the displayed **Footnote and Endnote** dialog, click **Insert**, and then type Internal reinforcement is sufficient in most cases. Compare your screen with **Figure 3**.

   Notice that the new footnote becomes the first footnote.

10. At the bottom of Page 2, select both footnotes. Press command ⌘ + D. In the displayed **Font** dialog, under **Size**, replace the existing value with 10 Compare your screen with **Figure 4**, and then click **OK**.

    Most style manuals call for the footnote text to be the same size as the document text.

11. Scroll to the bottom of Page 1, select the footnote, and change the **Font Size** to **10**.

12. **Save** 🖫 the document.

   ■ **You have completed Skill 8 of 10**

► When you use quotations or detailed information from a reference source, you need to specify the source in the document.

► A *citation* is a note in the document that refers the reader to a source in the bibliography.

1. Display the lower half of Page 1. Notice that two citations are displayed in parentheses.

   Many business reports use an abbreviated citation, which contains the author's last name, the year of publication, and the page number.

2. On the **Document Elements tab**, in the **References group**, click the **Manage** button. Compare your screen with **Figure 1**.

   The sources used in the current document display.

3. **Close** 🔴 the **Citations** task pane. Near the top of Page 2, in the paragraph that begins *The main,* click to the right of the second quotation mark. On the **Document Elements tab**, in the **References group**, click the **Manage** button. On the Citations task pane, click the **Add** button ➕. If a warning box displays, click **Yes**.

4. In the **Create New Source** dialog, if necessary click the **Type of Source arrow**, and then click **Book**. In the **Author** box, type Stevens, David In the **Title** box, type Roof Gardens, Balconies & Terraces

5. For the **Publisher**, type Rizzoli International For the **City** type Milan For the **Year**, type 1997 and then compare your screen with **Figure 2**.

   ■ **Continue to the next page to complete the skill** ➤

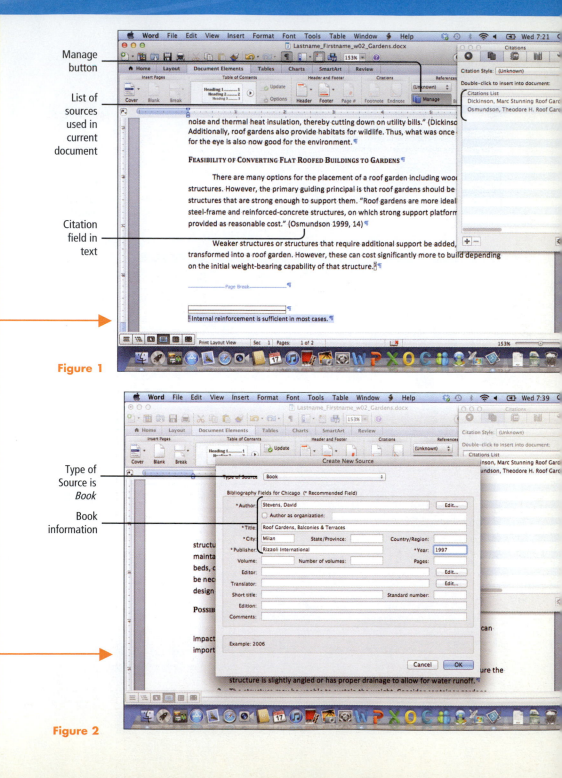

Manage button

List of sources used in current document

Citation field in text

Figure 1

Type of Source is *Book*

Book information

Figure 2

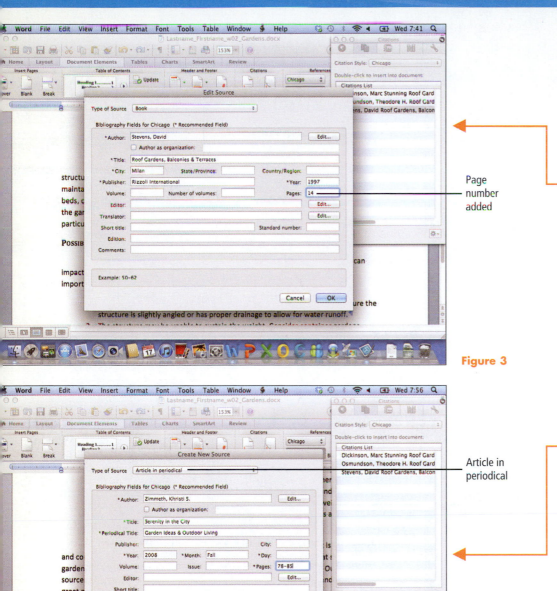

Page number added

Figure 3

Article in periodical

Figure 4

6. In the **Create New Source** dialog, click **OK** to insert an abbreviated citation. Click the new citation one time. On the lower right of the **Citations** task pane, click the **Action menu button** [⚙▾], and then from the menu, click **Edit Source**.

7. In the **Edit Source** dialog, in the **Pages** box, type 14 to add the page number to the citation. Compare your screen with **Figure 3**.

8. In the **Edit Source** dialog, click **OK**. If a message box displays, click **Yes**. Position the insertion point at the end of the document. In the **Citations** task pane, click the **Add** button [+].

9. In the **Create New Source** dialog, click the **Type of Source arrow**, and then click **Article in periodical**. In the **Author** box, type Zimmeth, Khristi S. For the **Title**, type Serenity in the City

10. For the **Periodical Title**, type Garden Ideas & Outdoor Living For the **Year**, type 2008 For the **Month** type Fall For the **Pages**, type 78–85 and then compare your screen with **Figure 4**.

11. In the **Create New Source** dialog, click **OK**. Click the citation in the document, click the **arrow**, and then click **Edit This Citation**.

12. In the **Edit Citation** dialog, in the **Pages** box, type 83 and click **OK**.

    Notice that your new sources are added to the Citations dialog.

13. **Close** [●] the **Citations** task pane.

14. **Save** [💾] the document.

■ **You have completed Skill 9 of 10**

► A *bibliography* is a list of sources referenced in a report, and is listed on a separate page at the end of the report.

► Different styles use different titles for the sources page, including *Works Cited*, *Bibliography*, *References*, or *Sources*.

1. Click to the right of the citation. On the **menu bar**, click **Insert**, click **Break**, and then click **Page Break**. Press return two times.

   The bibliography should begin about two inches from the top of the page.

2. On the **Document Elements tab**, in the **References group**, click the **Bibliography** button to display two built-in bibliographies, as shown in **Figure 1**.

3. From the gallery, click the **Bibliography** thumbnail to insert a bibliography field. If necessary, scroll up to display the inserted bibliography field.

   The bibliography field includes a title and lists the sources cited in the document. The multiple-line references use hanging indents. In a *hanging indent*, the first line extends to the left of the rest of the paragraph.

4. Click in the **Bibliography** title, and then on the **Home tab**, in the **Paragraph group**, click the **Center Text** button to center the title on the page.

5. Click to the right of the title, and then press return to add a blank line between the title and the sources. Compare your screen with **Figure 2**.

6. Display the **Document Elements tab**, and then in the **References group**, click the **Manage** button.

■ Continue to the next page to complete the skill ▶

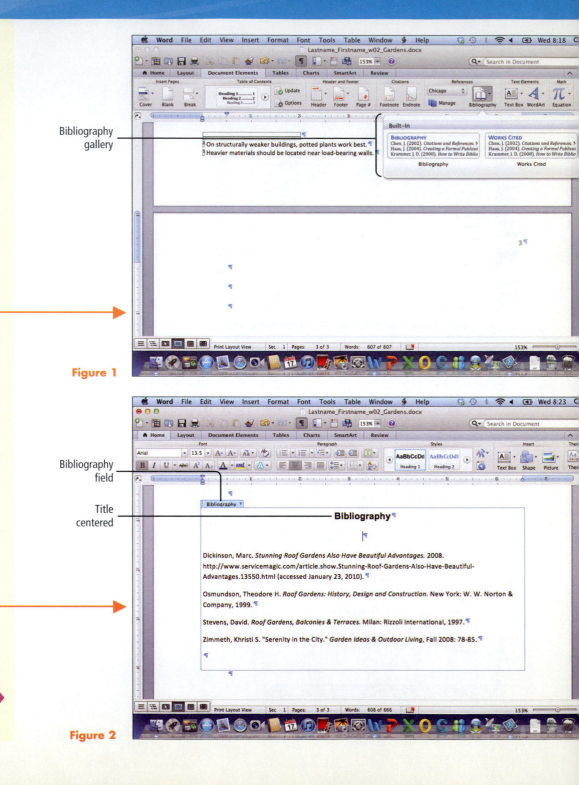

Bibliography gallery

Figure 1

Bibliography field

Title centered

Figure 2

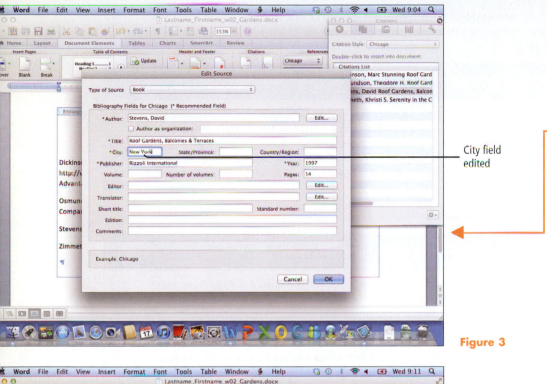

City field edited

Figure 3

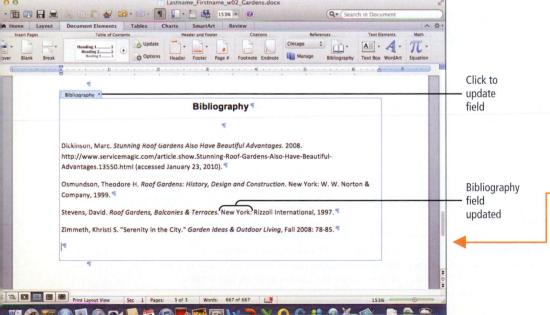

Click to update field

Bibliography field updated

Figure 4

7. In the **Citations** dialog, under **Citations List**, select the *Stevens, David* source. On the lower right of the **Citations** task pane, click the **Action menu button** ⚙▾, and then from the menu, click **Edit Source**.

8. In the **Edit Source** dialog, in the **City** box, select *Milan*. Type New York and then compare your screen with **Figure 3**.

9. Click **OK** to close the dialog, read the displayed message, and then click **Yes**.

   The change will be made to both the current document and the master list.

10. On the lower right of the **Citations** task pane, click the **Action menu button** ⚙▾, and then from the menu, click **Citation Source Manager**. Select the *Stevens, David* source, and then to the right of the Master List, click the **Delete** button. Use the same procedure to remove the *Zimmeth, Khristi S.* source.

    If you are using a computer in a lab or other public area, it is good practice to restore any permanent changes you make to original settings—in this case, remove the sources from the master list.

11. In the **Source Manager** dialog, click **Close. Close** ⬤ the **Citations** task pane. Click in the bibliography. Notice that the change from *Milan* to *New York* has not been made—you must manually update fields when you change them.

12. At the top of the bibliography field, click **Update Citations and Bibliography**. Compare your screen with **Figure 4**.

    The bibliography field is updated to include the change you made in the Source Manager.

13. **Save** 🖫 the document. Submit your printout or files electronically as directed by your instructor. **Quit** Word.

    Done! You have completed Skill 10 of 10, and your document is complete!

More Skills

The following More Skills are located at **www.pearsonhighered.com/skills**. Please note that only More Skills that can be performed on a Macintosh computer are included in this section; therefore, the numbering is not always sequential.

More Skills 11   Record AutoCorrect Entries

If you enable the AutoCorrect feature in Word, when you misspell a word that is contained in the AutoCorrect list, the misspelling is corrected automatically. You can add words that you commonly misspell as you type, or you can open a dialog and add words or phrases that you want to be automatically corrected. This feature can also be used to create shortcuts for phrases that you type regularly.

In More Skills 11, you will open a short document and use two methods to add items to the AutoCorrect Options list.

To begin, open your web browser, navigate to www.pearsonhighered.com/skills, locate the name of your textbook, and then follow the instructions on the website.

More Skills 12   Use AutoFormat to Create Numbered Lists

If you create a lot of numbered lists, Word has an AutoFormat feature that lets you start typing the list, and the program will automatically add numbers and formatting to the list as you type.

In More Skills 12, you will open a document, set the AutoFormat options, and then create a numbered list that is formatted automatically.

To begin, open your web browser, navigate to www.pearsonhighered.com/skills, locate the name of your textbook, and then follow the instructions on the website.

More Skills 13   Format and Customize Lists

In this chapter, you create and format numbered and bulleted lists. There are several other formatting changes you can make to lists. You can change the numbering scheme for numbered lists, and you can change the character used for the bullet symbol. You can also increase or decrease the indent of both types of lists.

In More Skills 13, you will open a document and change the numbering on a numbered list. You will also increase the indent on a bulleted list.

To begin, open your web browser, navigate to www.pearsonhighered.com/skills, locate the name of your textbook, and then follow the instructions on the website.

More Skills 14   Manage Document Properties

Document properties are the detailed information about your document that can help you identify or organize your files, including the name of the author, the title, and keywords. Some document properties are added to the document when you create it. You can add others as necessary.

In More Skills 14, you will open a document, open the Document Properties, and add properties where appropriate.

To begin, open your web browser, navigate to www.pearsonhighered.com/skills, locate the name of your textbook, and then follow the instructions on the website.

Key Terms

Bibliography 80

Bulleted list 72

Citation 78

Double-spacing 66

Endnote 76

First line indent 65

Footnote 76

Format Painter 68

Hanging indent 80

Horizontal alignment 64

Indents 64

Justified 64

Landscape orientation 63

Line spacing 66

Manual line break 67

Manual page break 67

Margins 62

Numbered list 72

Paragraph spacing 66

Portrait orientation 63

Single-spacing 66

Online Help Skills

1. **Start** Safari or another web browser. In the **address bar**, type microsoft.com/mac/how-to and then press return to display the home page for Microsoft Office.

2. Under **Product Help**, click **Word 2011**.

3. Under **Word Help**, click the **Text, Lists, and Bullets** link.

4. Under **Text, Lists, and Bullets**, click **Format a bulleted or numbered list**.

5. Under **Format a bulleted or numbered list**, click **Change the style, color, or font size of bullets**. Compare your screen with **Figure 1**.

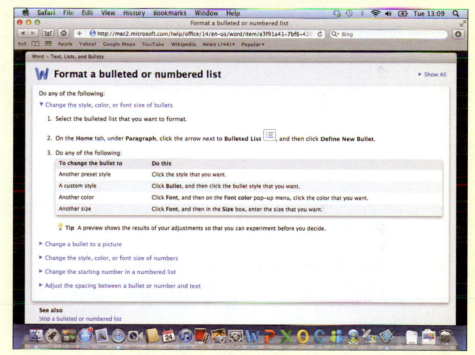

Figure 1

6. See if you can answer the following questions: How do you change the style of bullets in a document? How can you change a bullet to a picture? How can you change the starting number in a numbered list?

Matching

Match each term in the second column with its correct definition in the first column by writing the letter of the term on the blank line in front of the correct definition.

____ **1.** The space between the text and the top, bottom, left, and right edges of the paper when you print the document.

____ **2.** The position of the first line of a paragraph relative to the text in the rest of the paragraph.

____ **3.** The equivalent of a blank line of text displayed between each line of text in a paragraph.

____ **4.** The vertical distance above and below each paragraph in a document.

____ **5.** A command that copies formatting from one place to another.

____ **6.** The command that locates text in a document.

____ **7.** The type of list used for items that are in chronological or sequential order.

____ **8.** A reference added to the end of a section or document.

____ **9.** A list of sources displayed on a separate page at the end of a report.

____ **10.** The command used to display changes made in the Source Manager to a source listed in the bibliography.

A Bibliography

B Double-spacing

C Endnote

D Find

E First line indent

F Format Painter

G Margin

H Numbered

I Paragraph spacing

J Update Field

Multiple Choice

Choose the correct answer.

1. To create your own document margins, use this command at the bottom of the Margins gallery.
   A. Format Paragraph
   B. Document Settings
   C. Custom Margins

2. The placement of paragraph text relative to the left and right document margins is called paragraph:
   A. Alignment
   B. Margins
   C. Orientation

3. The vertical distance between lines in a paragraph is called:
   A. Spacing after
   B. Line spacing
   C. Text wrapping

4. This alignment is used to position paragraph text an equal distance between the left and right margin:
   A. Justify
   B. Center
   C. Middle

5. This type of alignment positions the text so that it is aligned with both the left and right margins.
   A. Justify
   B. Center
   C. Left

6. Hold down `command ⌘` + `D` to display this dialog:
   A. Paragraph
   B. Number
   C. Font

7. Items that can be listed in any order are best presented using which of the following?
   A. Bulleted list
   B. Numbered list
   C. Outline list

8. In a bibliography, this type of indent is used for each reference:
   A. Hanging indent
   B. First line indent
   C. Left alignment

9. To place a note on the same page as the reference source, use which of these?
   A. Footnote
   B. Endnote
   C. Citation

10. This refers to an entry in a bibliography.
    A. Footnote
    B. Citation
    C. Endnote

Topics for Discussion

1. You can build and save a list of master sources you have used in research papers and reports and display them using Manage Sources. What are the advantages of storing sources over time?

2. Paragraph text can be left aligned, centered, right aligned, or justified. Left alignment is the most commonly used. In what situations would you use centered text? Justified text? Can you think of any situations where you might want to use right alignment?

Skill Check

To complete this document, you will need the following file:

- w02_Landscape

You will save your document as:

- Lastname_Firstname_w02_Landscape

1. **Start** Word. Open **w02_Landscape**. **Save** the document in your **Word Chapter 2** folder as Lastname_Firstname_w02_Landscape

2. On the **Layout tab**, in the **Margins group**, click the **Margins** button, and then click **Custom Margins**. Under **Margins**, change the **Left** and **Right** margins to **1**, and then click **OK**. In the second title line, to the right of *By,* type your name.

3. Press command ⌘ + A . On the **Home tab**, in the **Paragraph group**, change the **Line spacing** to **1.15**. On the **menu bar**, click **Format**, and then click **Paragraph**. Change the spacing **After** to **12 pt**, and then click **OK**.

4. Click in the paragraph that begins *Landscaping can be.* On the **Home tab**, in the **Paragraph group**, change the alignment to **Align Text Left**. Display the **Paragraph** dialog, and then under **Indentation**, set the **Special** box to **First line**, and then click **OK**. Compare your screen with **Figure 1**.

5. On the **Standard toolbar**, double-click the **Format Painter** button, and then copy the current paragraph formatting to the paragraphs that begin *When designing, Landscape garden, Time is, Landscape design,* and *In addition;* also the last three paragraphs in the document. Press esc to turn off Format Painter.

6. Near the top of the document, select the subheading *Landscaping as a Weather Barrier.* Press command ⌘ + D to display the **Font** dialog. Apply **Bold** emphasis and **Small caps**, and then click **OK**. Copy the formatting of this subheading to the other two subheadings: *Landscaping That Attracts Butterflies* and *Landscaping to Minimize Water Use.*

7. Click at the beginning of the document. On the **menu bar**, click **Edit**, click **Find**, and then click **Replace** button. In the **Search Document** box, type insure In the **Replace with** box, type ensure and then click **Replace All**. **Save** the document, and then compare your screen with **Figure 2**.

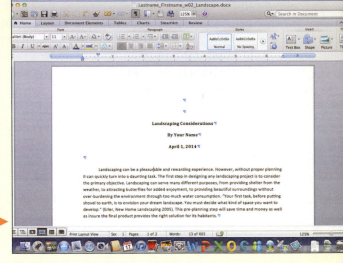

Figure 1

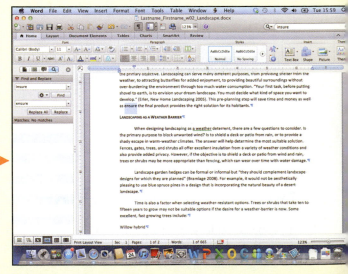

Figure 2

- Continue to the next page to complete this Skill Check ▶

8. Near the bottom of Page 1, locate and select the three tree names, beginning with *Willow hybrid*. In the **Paragraph group**, apply **Bulleted List**, and then click the **Increase Indent** button.

9. Near the top of Page 2, locate and select the four nonindented paragraphs, beginning with *Planting nectar flowers*. In the **Paragraph group**, apply **Numbering**, and then click the **Increase Indent** button.

10. On the **menu bar**, click **View**, and then click **Header and Footer**. On the **Header and Footer tab**, in the **Insert group**, click the **Page #** button. In the **Navigation group**, click **Go to Footer**. On the menu bar, click **Insert**, and then click **Field**. Under **Field names**, click **FileName**, and then click **OK**. In the **Options group**, select the **Different First Page** check box.

11. In the bulleted list, click to the right of *Willow hybrid*. On the **Document Elements tab**, in the **Citations group**, insert the following footnote: The trees grow quickly but do not live very long. On Page 2, at the end of the second item in the numbered list, insert the following footnote: Local nurseries can help you determine which flowers to use. Compare your screen with **Figure 3**.

12. In the **Find and Replace** task pane, in the **Search Document** box, type creating Click **Find** and notice that there is only one instance of the word. In the document, double-click the highlighted word, and then type developing to replace the word.

13. Click at the beginning of the document. In the first paragraph below the title, that begins *Landscaping can be,* locate and click anywhere in the *Erler* citation. Click the citation **arrow**, and then from the menu, click **Edit This Citation**. Click **Yes**. Under **Add**, in the **Pages** box, type 2 Click **OK**. Click the citation **arrow** again, and then click **Edit Source**. In the **Edit Source** dialog, change the title of the book from *New Home Landscaping* to New Complete Home Landscaping and then click **OK**.

14. Click at the end of the document. On the **menu bar**, click **Insert**, click **Break**, and then click **Page Break**. Press `return` two times.

15. On the **Document Elements tab**, in the **References group**, click the **Bibliography**, and then click the **Bibliography** thumbnail. Select the *Bibliography* title, and then on the **Home tab**, in the **Paragraph group**, click the **Center Text** button.

16. **Save** the document, and then submit as directed. Compare your document with **Figure 4**.

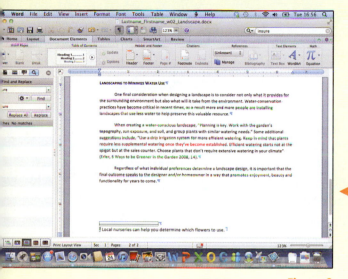

Figure 3

Done! You have completed the Skill Check

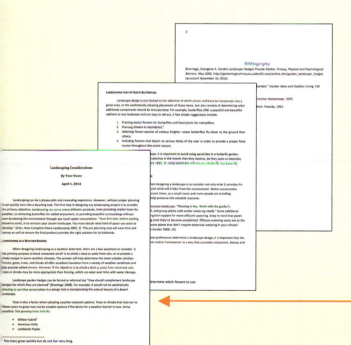

Figure 4

Assess Your Skills 1

To complete this document, you will need the following file:

- w02_Lighting

You will save your document as:

- **Lastname_Firstname_w02_Lighting**

1. **Start** Word. Locate and open **w02_Lighting**, and then **Save** it in your **Word Chapter 2** folder as Lastname_Firstname_w02_Lighting Set the document's **Top** margin to **1"**, and the **Left** and **Right** margins to **1.3"**.

2. Press ⟨return⟩ three times and type Home Lighting For the second title, type By and your name, and then for the third title, type May 25, 2013 Add a blank line following the date.

3. Select *all* of the text in the document. Change the spacing after the paragraphs to *6 pt* and change the **Line Spacing** to **1.15**. Change the paragraph alignment from *Justify* to **Align Text Left**. **Center** all three titles and change their **Font** to **Arial Black**.

4. Near the top of the document, locate the four questions that begin *What is the function*. Change the four questions to a numbered list, and increase the indent one time. Further down the page, select the four lines starting *provide decorative lighting* and ending *substitute for sunlight* and apply a bulleted list with the indent increased one time. At the bottom of the report, repeat this procedure with the three paragraphs (five lines) that begin *Installing* and *Turning lights* and *Understanding*.

5. Near the top of the document, locate the *Interior Lighting* subheading. Add **Bold** emphasis and **Small caps**, and change the

Font to **Arial Black**. Apply the same format to the other two subheadings: *Exterior Lighting* and *Lighting for Energy Efficiency*.

6. For the seven remaining paragraphs that are not titles or lists, indent the first line by *0.5"*.

7. From the **menu bar**, click **Edit**, and then click **Replace**. Search for *lightning*—not *lighting*—and notice how many misuses of the word are found in the document. Change each instance of *lightning* to *lighting*

8. On Page 1, at the end of the last item in the bulleted list, add the following footnote: The color temperature produced by the lighting units needs to be considered.

9. Near the bottom of Page 1, at the end of the paragraph that begins *Consider what the room,* add the following footnote: These can include both permanent and movable light fixtures. Select each footnote and change the **Font Size** to **11** points.

10. On Page 1, insert **Page #** in the header. In the footer, insert the file name. Select the **Different First Page** option.

11. **Save** the document, and then print or submit the file as directed by your instructor. Compare your completed document with **Figure 1**.

Done! You have completed Assess Your Skills 1

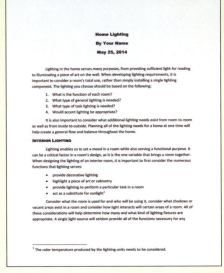

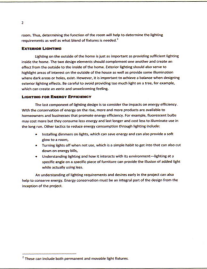

Figure 1

▶ Assess Your Skills 3 and 4 can be found at **www.pearsonhighered.com/skills**.

Assess Your Skills 2

To complete this document, you will need the following file:

- w02_Retrofit

You will save the document as:

- Lastname_Firstname_w02_Retrofit

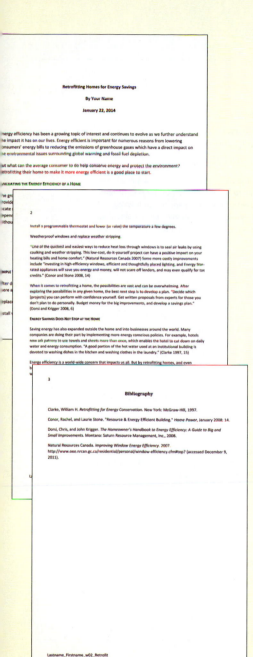

Figure 1

1. **Start** Word. Locate and open **w02_Retrofit**, and then **Save** it in your **Word Chapter 2** folder as Lastname_Firstname_w02_Retrofit Set the document's **Left** and **Right** margins to *1"*.

2. Type your name in the second title line to the right of *By*.

3. Select all of the text in the document. Change the spacing after all paragraphs to *12 pt* and change the **Line Spacing** to **1.15**. Change the paragraph alignment from *Justify* to **Align Text Left**. **Center** the three titles and add **Bold** emphasis.

4. For the three subheadings that begin *Evaluating the Energy* and *Simple Ways* and *Energy Savings Does Not*, apply **Bold** emphasis and the **Small caps** style.

5. On Page 1, select the three paragraphs that begin *Check for drafts*, change them to a numbered list, and then increase the indent one time. Further down the page, select the four paragraphs that begin *Replace light bulbs*, change them to a bulleted list, and then increase the indent one time.

6. At the top of Page 2, click to the right of the quotation mark at the end of the paragraph that ends *credits*. Using the **Chicago** style, insert a new **Article in Periodical** citation. In the **Author** box, type Connor, Rachel; Stone, Laurie The **Title** is Resource & Energy Efficient Building The **Periodical Title** is Home Power The **Year** is 2008 The **Month** is January The **Pages** are 14 (one-page article). Edit the citation field to include the source's page number.

7. Near the bottom of the report, click at the end of the paragraph that begins *Saving energy*. Insert a new **Book** citation. In the **Author** box, type Clark, William H. The **Title** is Retrofitting for Energy Conservation The **Year** is 1997 The **City** is New York The **Publisher** is McGraw-Hill Edit the citation to add 15 as the page number of the quotation.

8. At the end of the document, use a manual page break to create a new page. At the top edge of the last page, insert the built-in **Bibliography**. **Center** the title and add a blank line between the title and the sources. Select the title *Bibliography*, change the **Font Size** to **12** and the **Font Color** to **Black**.

9. On Page 1, insert **Page #** in the header. In the footer, insert the file name, and then select the **Different First Page** option.

10. **Save** the document, and then print or submit the file as directed by your instructor. Compare your completed document with **Figure 1**.

Done! You have completed Assess Your Skills 2

Assess Your Skills Visually

To complete this document, you will need the following file:

- w02_Parks

You will save your document as:

- Lastname_Firstname_w02_Parks

Open the file **w02_Parks**, and then save it in your **Word Chapter 2** folder as Lastname_Firstname_w02_Parks Create the document shown in **Figure 1**.

To complete this document, set the left and right margins to 1.3 inches. All of the text is 12-point Calibri. The list should align with the first line of the indented paragraphs. Because this is a very short document with only one reference—at the end of the second-to-last paragraph—it is placed in a footnote as shown in **Figure 1**. Line spacing should be 1.15, with 6 points of spacing after paragraphs. Below the file name in the footer, add the current date field. Print or submit the file as directed by your instructor.

Done! You have completed Assess Your Skills Visually

Park Designs

By Your Name

May 15, 2014

Parks offer numerous benefits, from providing habitats for local animals and plants to serving as a psychological benefit to its occupants. The benefits of open spaces and fresh air have been well documented. Visiting a park can be relaxing and refreshing, and can even help relieve stress. Parks should be designed to accommodate local needs and conditions. Thus, when designing a park, it is important to consider:

- Who will be using the park?
- What kind of wildlife is indigenous to the area?
- What kind of plant life will live in the park?

ECOLOGICAL IMPACTS

When considering the ecological aspect of a park, it is critical to understand who will be the natural habitants of the park and what structures or plants would foster their well-being? Gaining a thorough understanding and conduction real world observations are recommended in order to understand the local wildlife and how their presence influences the design of the park.

PARK SIZE

The available space can have a huge impact on the design of a park. Small parks "can provide a place away from but close to home, a place that is not too isolated, and a place that avoids some of the problems that can occur in larger parks, crimes, for example."[1]

One additional step in designing a park is to get the opinions and suggestions of the people living in the community. In doing so, it will help to ensure that the final park is something that they have helped to design and will encourage use.

---

[1] Ann Forsyth and Laura Mussacchio, Designing Small Parks: *A Manual for Addressing Social and Ecological Concerns*, Wiley & Sons, New Jersey, 2005, p.14.

Lastname_Firstname_w02_Parks
September 12, 2014

Figure 1

Skills in Context

To complete this document, you will need the following file:

- New blank Word document

You will save your document as:

- Lastname_Firstname_w02_National_Parks

The City of Aspen Falls Planning Department is working with the Travel and Tourism Bureau to explore ways to use the city as the base of operation for tourists who want to visit important sites within a day's drive. Using the skills you practiced in this chapter, create a report on the nearby major nature attractions. These could include Yosemite National Park (250 miles), Death Valley National Park (200 miles), Sequoia National Forest (180 miles), and the Channel Islands National Park (40 miles). Research three of these (or other) national sites, and write the highlights of what a visitor might find at each. Your report should include at least two foot-notes and two citations, one list for each site, and a bibliography. The lists should contain between three and six items each. Format the report in the style practiced in the chapter.

Save the document as Lastname_Firstname_w02_National_Parks Insert the file name and current date in the footer, and check the entire document for grammar and spelling. Print or submit the file as directed by your instructor.

Done! You have completed Skills in Context

Skills and You

To complete this document, you will need the following file:

- New blank Word document

You will save your document as:

- Lastname_Firstname_w02_My_Home

Using the skills you have practiced in this chapter, compose a document about your hometown (or county, region, state, or province). The document should include a top margin of two inches; other margins of one inch each, and a title and subtitle appropriately formatted. You should include three paragraphs of text, with appropriate line spacing and spacing after the paragraphs, with the text left aligned and the first lines indented. You should also include a list of things to see or do in the area, and at least three informational footnotes. If you need to use quotations, include references and a bibliography.

Add the file name and date to the footer. Save the document as Lastname_Firstname_w02_My_Home Check the entire document for grammar and spelling. Print or submit the file as directed by your instructor.

Done! You have completed Skills and You

CHAPTER 3

Work with Graphics, Tabs, and Tables

- ▶ You can enhance the effectiveness of your message and make your document more attractive by adding graphics.

- ▶ Digital images—such as those you have scanned or taken with a digital camera or a cell phone—can be added to a document and formatted using distinctive borders and other interesting and attractive effects.

- ▶ You can organize lists in rows and columns by using tabs.

- ▶ Word tables are used to organize lists and data in columns and rows without needing to create tab settings.

- ▶ You can use tables to summarize and emphasize information in an organized arrangement of rows and columns that make complex information easier to understand at a glance.

- ▶ You can format tables manually or apply a number of different formats quickly using built-in styles.

© Darrinhenry | Dreamstime.com

Aspen Falls City Hall

In this chapter, you will create a flyer for the new Aspen Falls Botanic Gardens for Leah Kim, the Parks and Recreation Director. The flyer w cover hours of operation, upcoming events, and membership rates.

In this project, you will insert, resize, and move pictures, and then apply picture styles and artistic effects. You will set tab stops and us tabs to enter data. You will also create two tables, add rows and columns, format the tables' contents, and modify their layout and desig

Time to complete all
10 skills – 45 to 60 minutes

Student data files needed for this chapter:

w03_Botanical_Gardens   w03_Botanical_Forest
w03_Botanical_Butterfly   w03_Botanical_Events

Outcome

Using the skills in this chapter, you will be able to work with Word documents like this:

You will save your document as:

Lastname_Firstname_w03_Botanical

SKILLS

Skills 1-10 Training

At the end of this chapter you will be able to:

Skill 1   Insert Pictures from Files
Skill 2   Resize and Move Pictures
Skill 3   Format Pictures Using Styles and Artistic Effects
Skill 4   Set Tab Stops
Skill 5   Enter Text with Tab Stops
Skill 6   Apply Table Styles
Skill 7   Create Tables
Skill 8   Add Rows and Columns to Tables
Skill 9   Format Text in Table Cells
Skill 10   Format Tables

MORE SKILLS

Skill 11   Insert Text Boxes
Skill 12   Format with WordArt
Skill 13   Create Tables from Existing Lists
Skill 14   Insert Drop Caps

Aspen Falls Botanical Gardens

The new Aspen Falls Botanical Gardens is located on the western edge of the McMahon Marsh Nature Preserve. There are 22 acres of outdoor gardens, and the Ling Conservatory is filled with tropical plants and flowers. The year-round hours of operation are:

Day	Hours
Monday-Wednesday	10 to 5
Thursday-Friday	10 to 6
Saturday	8 to 5
Sunday	Noon to 5

The Botanical Gardens offers several special events during the year. Among the most popular special events this year include the following:

Event	Month(s)	Description
Butterflies	May and June	Conservatory display of butterflies from around town and around the world
Rainforest	January to April	Wonders of the rain forests are displayed
Photograph Nature	July and August	Nature photography contest for kids, teens, and adults—photos must be from Aspen Falls area
Holiday Decorations	December	Decorations and model trains

Membership rates are as follows:

Memberships		
Group	Ages	Cost
Children	Under 12	Free
Students	Under 18	$ 8.00
Adults	18 to 60	25.00
Seniors	Over 60	12.50

Lastname_Firstname_w03_Botanical_Gardens

► Recall that pictures are inserted at the insertion point location and are positioned in the paragraph in the same manner as a letter or a number.

► You can insert pictures that you have scanned or downloaded from the web, or pictures taken using your digital camera or cell phone.

1. **Start** Word. If a previous Word document displays, Close the document. Then, on the menu bar, click File, and then click Open. Navigate to your student files, and then open **w03_Botanical_Gardens**. If necessary, display the formatting marks.

2. On the **menu bar**, click **File**, and then click **Save As**. Navigate to the location where you are saving your files, create and open a folder named Word Chapter 3 and then **Save** the document as Lastname_Firstname_w03_Botanical

3. Select the document title *Aspen Falls Botanical Gardens*. On the **Home tab**, in the **Font group**, click the **Font arrow** Calibri (Body), locate and then click **Arial Black**. Click the **Font Size arrow** 11, and then click **26**. Click the **Center Text** button, and then compare your screen with **Figure 1**.

4. In the paragraph that begins *The new Aspen Falls,* click to position the insertion point at the beginning of the paragraph.

5. On the **Home tab**, in the **Insert group**, click the **Picture** button, and then click **Picture from File**.

6. In the **Choose a Picture** dialog, navigate to your student files, select **w03_Botanical_Forest**, and then click **Insert**. Compare your screen with **Figure 2**.

■ **Continue to the next page to complete the skill**

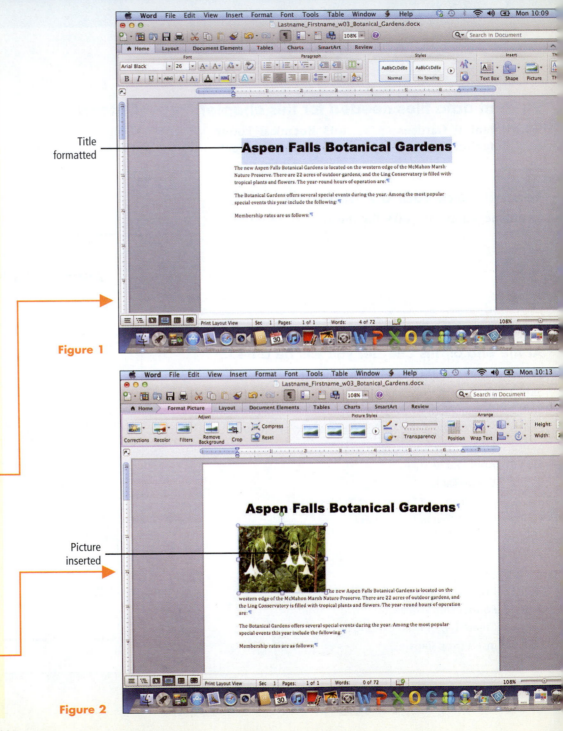

Title formatted

Figure 1

Picture inserted

Figure 2

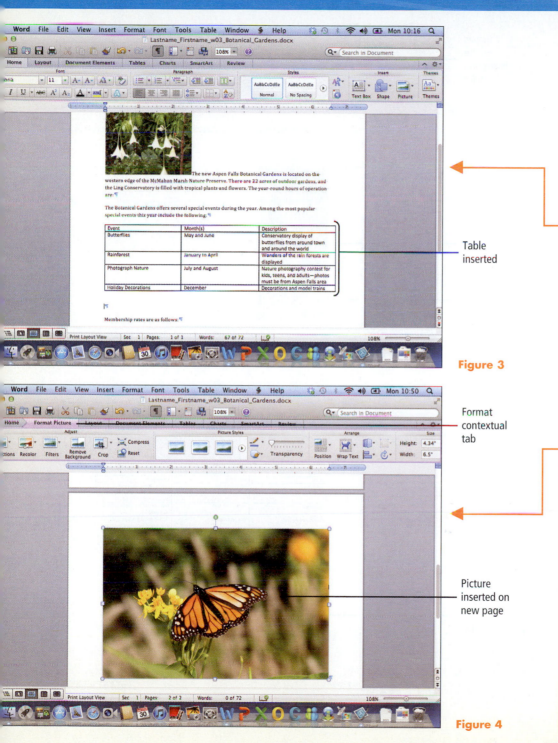

Table inserted

Figure 3

Format contextual tab

Picture inserted on new page

Figure 4

7. At the end of the paragraph that begins *The Botanical Gardens offers,* click to position the insertion point to the right of the colon, and then press return.

8. On the **menu bar**, click **Insert**, and then click **Object**.

9. In the **Object** dialog, click **From File**, navigate to your student files, select **w03_ Botanical_Events**, and then click **Insert** to insert a table. Notice that the insertion point is in the second blank line below the table. Compare your screen with **Figure 3**.

10. With the insertion point still in the second blank paragraph below the inserted table, press the Up Arrow Key ↑ once, and then press delete to remove the first blank paragraph.

11. On the **Home tab**, in the **Insert group**, click the **Picture** button, and then click **Picture from File**. Navigate to your student files, select **w03_Botanical_ Butterfly**, and then click **Insert**. Notice that the Format Picture contextual tab is added to the Ribbon and is the active tab. Compare your screen with **Figure 4**.

    Because the picture is too large to fit in the available space at the bottom of the current page, Word creates a new page.

12. **Save** 🖫 the document.

    ■ **You have completed Skill 1 of 10**

► When you select a picture, *sizing handles*—small squares or circles—display around the picture border, and you can drag these handles to resize the picture.

► You can also resize a picture using the Shape Height and Shape Width buttons on the Format Picture tab.

1. At the top of Page 2, be sure the **w03_Botanical** butterfly picture is selected—sizing handles display around the picture border. Notice that the Format Picture tab displays on the Ribbon.

2. If your rulers do not display, on the menu bar, click View, and then click Ruler.

3. On the right border of the picture, locate the middle—square—sizing handle. Point to the sizing handle to display the pointer, and then drag to the left to **2 inches** on the horizontal ruler, as shown in **Figure 1**.

   The picture does not resize proportionally.

4. On the **Standard toolbar**, click the **Undo** button.

5. Scroll to display the bottom of the picture. Point to the sizing handle in the lower right corner of the picture. When the pointer displays, drag up and to the left until the right border of the picture aligns at approximately **2.5 inches** on the horizontal ruler.

6. If necessary, scroll to view the bottom of the page, and then compare your screen with **Figure 2**.

   The picture is resized proportionally, and the smaller picture fits at the bottom of the first page of the document.

■ **Continue to the next page to complete the skill**

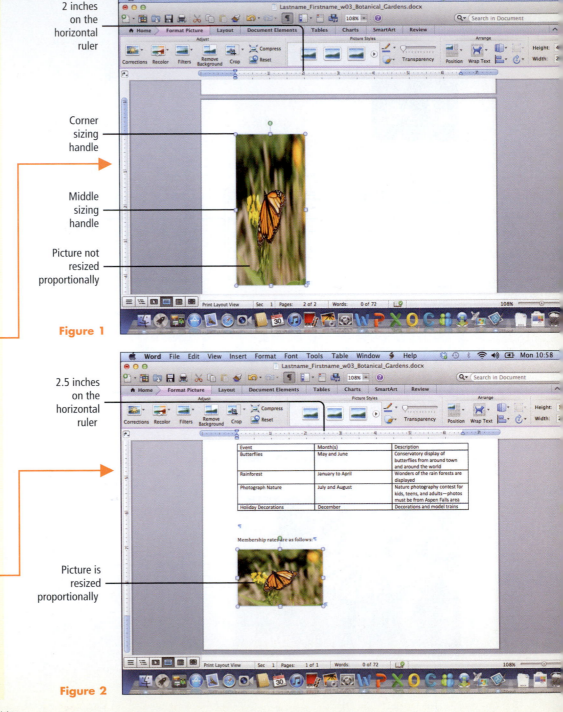

2 inches on the horizontal ruler

Corner sizing handle

Middle sizing handle

Picture not resized proportionally

Figure 1

2.5 inches on the horizontal ruler

Picture is resized proportionally

Figure 2

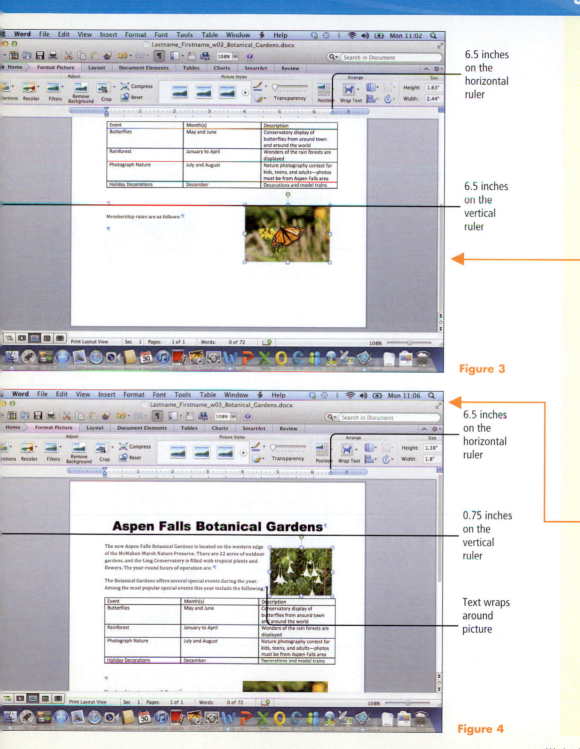

6.5 inches
on the
horizontal
ruler

6.5 inches
on the
vertical
ruler

Figure 3

6.5 inches
on the
horizontal
ruler

0.75 inches
on the
vertical
ruler

Text wraps
around
picture

Figure 4

7. Be sure the picture is still selected. On the **Format Picture tab**, in the **Arrange group**, click the **Wrap Text** button, and then click **Square**.

This setting changes the picture to a *floating object*, which you can move independently of the surrounding text.

8. Point to the picture to display the pointer. Drag the picture to the right so that the right border is aligned approximately at **6.5 inches** on the horizontal ruler and the top border is aligned at approximately **6.5 inches** on the vertical ruler. Compare your screen with **Figure 3**.

9. Move to the top of the document, and then click the picture of the gardens. On the **Format Picture tab**, in the **Size group**, click in the **Width** box, replace the existing value with **1.8** and then press return.

10. On the **Format Picture tab**, in the **Arrange group**, click the **Wrap Text** button, and then click **Square**.

11. Point to the picture to display the pointer. Drag the picture to the right, and align the right border at approximately **6.5 inches** on the horizontal ruler. Align the top border at approximately **0.75 inch** on the vertical ruler. Compare your screen with **Figure 4**, and adjust your picture as necessary.

An *anchor* symbol to the left of the paragraph mark indicates which paragraph the picture is associated with, and the paragraph text wraps around the space filled by the picture.

12. Save the document.

- **You have completed Skill 2 of 10**

► You can add special effects to the texture of a picture to make it look more like a drawing or a painting.

► You can also apply built-in picture styles, such as borders and frames, and then format those borders.

1. Move to the bottom of the document, and then click the picture of the butterfly.

2. In the **Size group**, select the value in the **Width** box `Width: 0.9"`, type 2.75 and then press `return` to change the width of the picture to 2.75 inches. Drag the picture to the left to align the right edge at **6.5 inches** on the horizontal ruler and the top edge at **5.25 inches** on the vertical ruler.

When you need a size that cannot be entered using spin arrows, type the number in the spin box.

3. On the **Format Picture tab**, in the **Picture Styles group**, click the **Picture Effects** button. Point to **Glow**, and then in the first row, click the first effect—**Accent 1, 5 pt glow**. Notice that the edges of the picture have a glow, as shown in **Figure 1**.

A soft edge with a higher number of points will result in a more dramatic fade between the picture and its border.

4. In the **Picture Styles group**, click the **Picture Effects** button, point to **Reflection**, and then in the second row, click the first effect—**Half Reflection, 4 pt offset**.

5. Click anywhere in the text to deselect the picture, and then compare your screen with **Figure 2**.

■ **Continue to the next page to complete the skill**

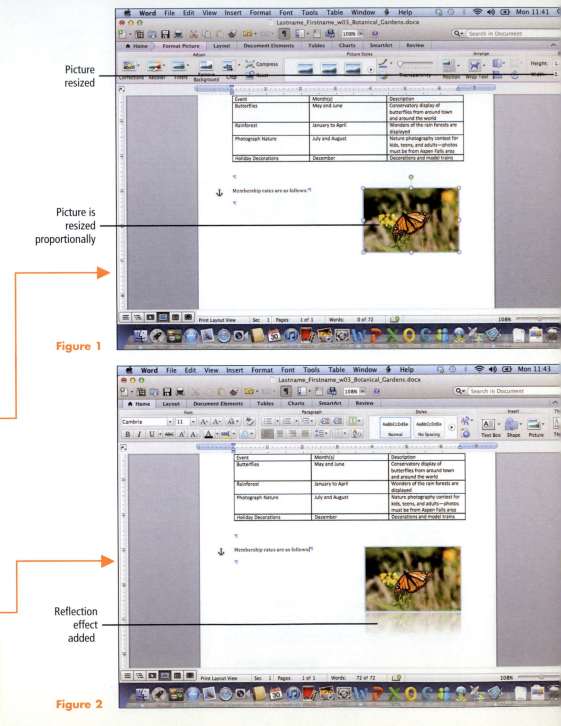

Picture resized

Picture is resized proportionally

Figure 1

Reflection effect added

Figure 2

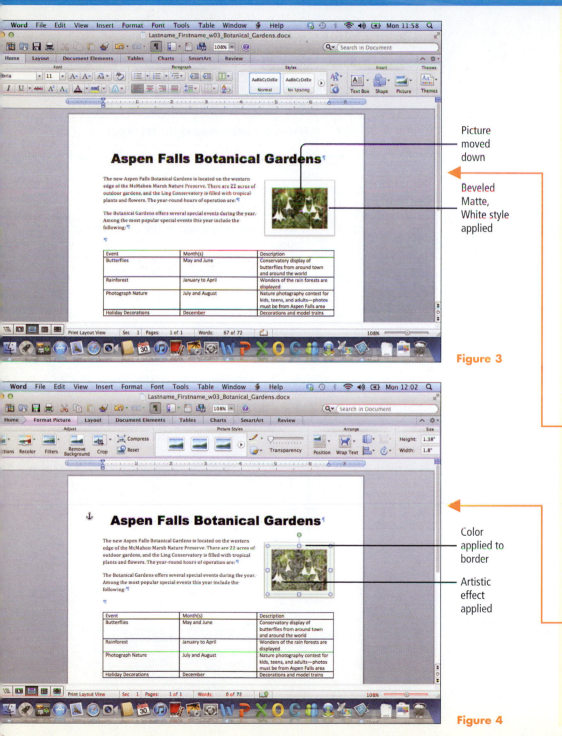

Picture moved down

Beveled Matte, White style applied

Figure 3

Color applied to border

Artistic effect applied

Figure 4

6. Move to the top of the document, and then click the garden picture.

7. With the picture selected, on the **Format Picture tab**, in the **Picture Styles group**, click the **More Down arrow** ▼ to view a gallery of picture styles.

   Some of the styles add height to the picture and can force the document title to the left.

8. In the first row of thumbnails, click the second style—**Beveled Matte, White**.

9. With the picture still selected, press ▼ once so that the document title displays across the screen.

   To move objects in small, precise increments, you can *nudge* them in this manner by selecting the object and then pressing one of the arrow keys. Because the new style increased the size of the picture, the table does not stretch across the screen.

10. At the end of the paragraph that begins *The Botanical Gardens offers*, click to position the insertion point to the right of the colon, and then press return. Compare your screen with **Figure 3**.

11. Click to select the garden picture. On the **Format Picture tab**, in the **Picture Styles group**, click the **Picture Border** button 🖊 down arrow.

12. Under **Theme Colors**, in the second row of colors, click the seventh color— **Accent 3, Lighter 80%**.

13. In the **Adjust group**, click the **Filters** button, and then in the fourth row, click the fifth effect—**Plastic Wrap**. Compare your screen with **Figure 4**.

14. **Save** 🖫 the document.

   ■ **You have completed Skill 3 of 10**

▶ A *tab stop* is a specific location on a line of text marked on the Word ruler to which you can move the insertion point by pressing [tab]. Tabs are used to align and indent text.

▶ Tab stop types are set when you insert the stop; however, you can change the tab stop type using the Tabs dialog.

1. Near the top of the document, click at the end of the paragraph that begins *The new Aspen Falls,* and then press [return].

2. On the left end of the horizontal ruler, notice the **Tab Selector** button [↱]—the icon displayed on your button may vary.

3. Click the button to view the various tab types available. View the information in the table in **Figure 1** to see how each of the tab types is used.

   If you have not added any tab stops to a paragraph, default tab stops are placed every one-half inch on the ruler. These default tab stops are indicated by the small marks at every one-half inch just below the white area of the ruler.

4. With the insertion point still in the blank paragraph, click the **Tab Selector** button [↱] to select the **Left Tab** icon [↱].

5. On the horizontal ruler, point to the mark that indicates **0.5 inch**, and then click one time to insert a left tab stop. Compare your screen with **Figure 2.**

   ■ **Continue to the next page to complete the skill**

Tab Alignment Options

Type	Button	Description
Left	[↱]	The left edge of the text is aligned at the tab stop and extends to the right.
Center	[↥]	Text is centered around the tab stop.
Right	[↰]	The right edge of the text is aligned at the tab stop and extends to the left.
Decimal	[↕]	The decimal point aligns at the tab stop.
Bar	[ǀ]	A vertical bar is inserted in the document at the tab stop.
First Line Indent	[▽]	The first line of a paragraph is indented.
Hanging Indent/ Left Indent	[▤]	The top half of the button indents all lines but the first line in a paragraph. The bottom half moves the left indent of the entire paragraph.

Figure 1

Tab Selector displays Left Tab icon

Left tab stop on horizontal ruler

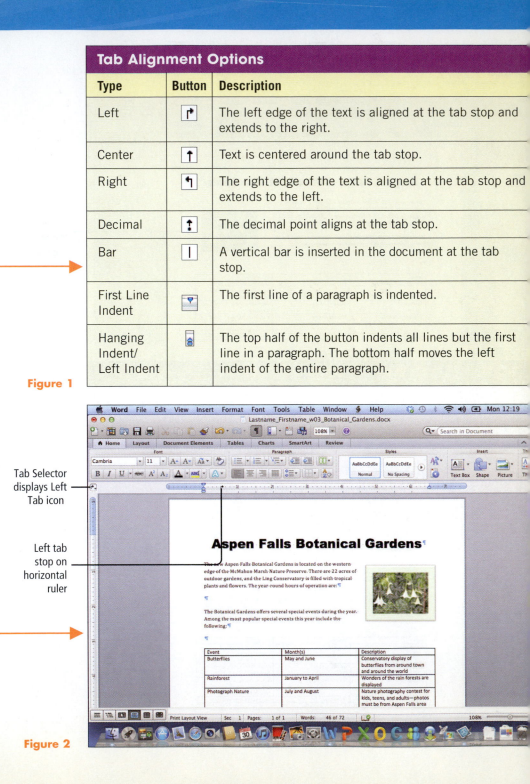

Figure 2

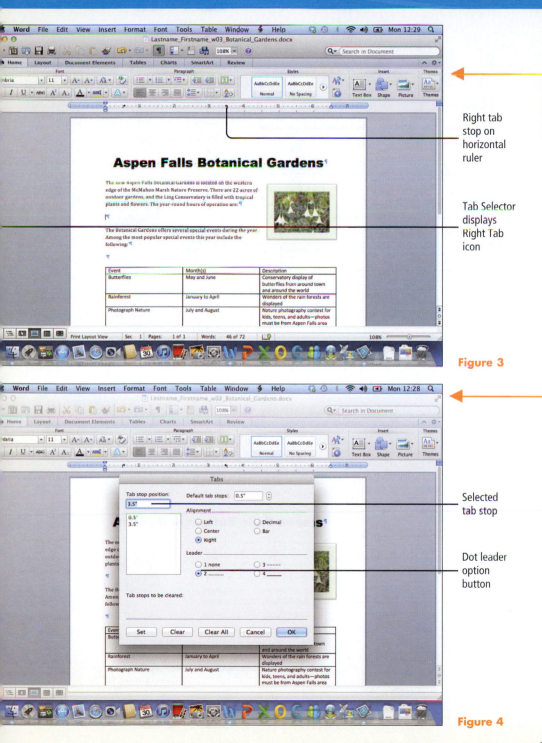

Right tab stop on horizontal ruler

Tab Selector displays Right Tab icon

Figure 3

Selected tab stop

Dot leader option button

Figure 4

6. Click the **Tab Selector** button 📍, and then from the displayed list, click **Right** 📍.

7. On the ruler, point to the mark that indicates **3.5 inches**, and then click the mouse button. Compare your screen with **Figure 3**. Notice that a line indicates the tab location in the document. In this manner, you can determine whether the tab stop is exactly where you want it.

8. On the **menu bar**, click **Format**, and then click **Paragraph**. At the bottom of the displayed **Paragraph** dialog, click the **Tabs** button.

9. In the **Tabs** dialog, in **Tab stop position**, type 3.5. Under **Leader**, select the **2** option button to add a dot leader to the selected tab stop. Near the bottom of the dialog, click the **Set** button, and then compare your screen with **Figure 4**.

A *leader* is a series of characters that form a solid, dashed, or dotted line that fills the space preceding a tab stop; a *leader charac-ter* is the symbol used to fill the space. A *dot leader* is a series of evenly spaced dots that precede a tab stop.

10. In the **Tabs** dialog, click **OK**.

11. Save 💾 the document.

■ **You have completed Skill 4 of 10**

► The Tab key is used to move to the next tab stop in a line of text.

► When you want to relocate a tab stop, you can drag the tab stop marker to a new location on the horizontal ruler.

1. Be sure your insertion point is still in the blank paragraph and the tab stops you entered display on the horizontal ruler.

2. Press [tab] to move the insertion point to the first tab stop you placed on the ruler. Type Day and press [tab] to move to the right tab with the dot leader that you created.

3. Type Hours and press [return]. Compare your screen with **Figure 1**.

    When your insertion point is positioned at a right tab stop and you begin to type, the text moves to the left. When you press [return], the new paragraph displays the same tab stop markers on the ruler as the previous paragraph.

4. Press [tab], type Monday-Wednesday and then press [tab]. Type 10 to 5 and then press [return].

5. Press [tab], type Thursday-Friday and then press [tab]. Type 10 to 6 and then press [return].

6. Press [tab], type Saturday and then press [tab]. Type 8 to 5 and then press [return].

7. Press [tab], type Sunday and then press [tab]. Type Noon to 5 and compare your screen with **Figure 2**.

8. Select the first line of the tabbed list, and then press [command ⌘] + [B].

■ **Continue to the next page to complete the skill**

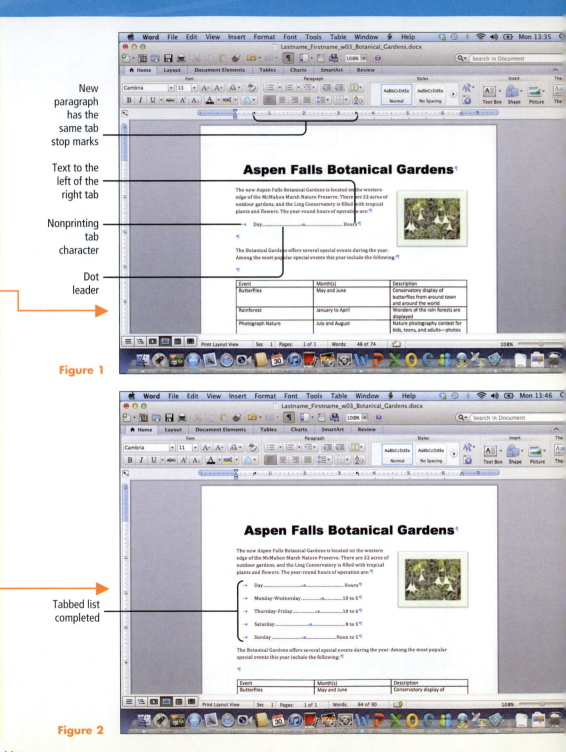

New paragraph has the same tab stop marks

Text to the left of the right tab

Nonprinting tab character

Dot leader

Figure 1

Tabbed list completed

Figure 2

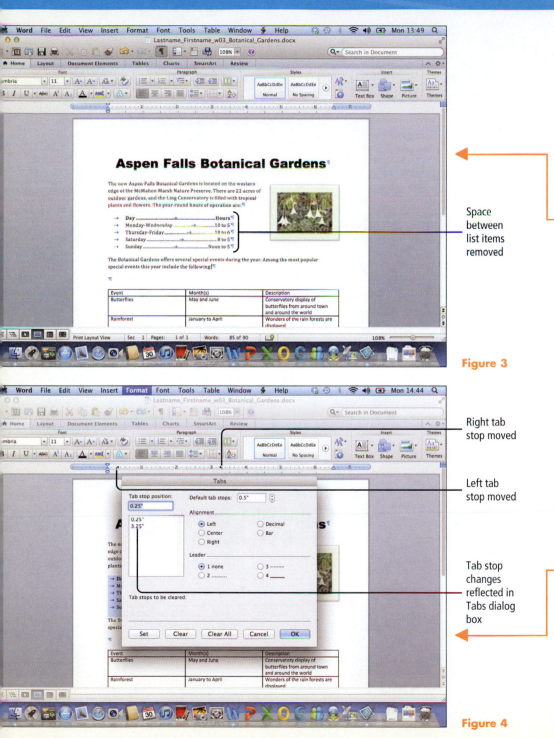

Figure 3

Figure 4

9. Select the first four lines of the tabbed list. Do not select the paragraph that begins *Sunday*.

10. On the **Home tab**, in the **Paragraph group**, click the **Line Spacing** button, and then click **Line Spacing Options**. Under **Spacing**, click the **After down spin arrow** two times to change the space after the selected paragraphs to **0 pt**, and then click **OK**. Click anywhere in the document to deselect the text, and then compare your screen with **Figure 3**.

11. To the left of *Day,* point in the margin area to display the pointer. Then drag down to select all five items in the tabbed list.

12. On the horizontal ruler, point to the left tab mark at **0.5 inch** on the horizontal ruler. When the ScreenTip *Left Tab* displays, drag left to move the tab mark to **0.25 inch** on the horizontal ruler to move each selected line to the new tab location.

13. With the five lines still selected, on the horizontal ruler, point to the right tab mark at **3.5 inches** on the horizontal ruler. When the ScreenTip *Right Tab* displays, drag left to move the tab mark to **3.25 inches** on the horizontal ruler.

14. On the **menu bar**, click **Format**, and then click **Tabs**. Notice that the new tab stop position values display, as shown in **Figure 4**.

15. Click **Cancel** to close the **Tabs** dialog box, and then **Save** the document.

   ▪ **You have completed Skill 5 of 10**

► A *table* consists of rows and columns of text or numbers. Tables summarize data effectively and efficiently.

► You can format each table element individually, or you can apply table styles to the entire table.

1. Scroll as needed to display the table.

    The table contains five rows and three columns. Recall that the intersection of a row and a column in a table is called a *cell*.

2. Double-click the table.

    A new window opens so that the embedded table can be edited.

3. Display the **Tables tab**. In the **Table Styles group**, notice that a number of predesigned styles are available. Using the ScreenTips as your guide, point to the style, **Light Shading – Accent 1**, table— **Light Shading – Accent 1**, as shown in **Figure 1**.

    Because the styles in the first row of the Table Styles gallery display the styles that were used most recently, your first row of thumbnails may vary.

4. In the **Table Styles group**, click the **More Down arrow** ▼.

5. In the **Table Styles** gallery, use the vertical scroll bar to scroll to the bottom of the gallery. Locate the **Medium Grid 3 – Accent 3** style, as shown in **Figure 2**.

6. Click one time to apply the **Medium Grid 3 – Accent 3** style.

    You do not have to select the entire table to apply a built-in style.

■ **Continue to the next page to complete the skill**

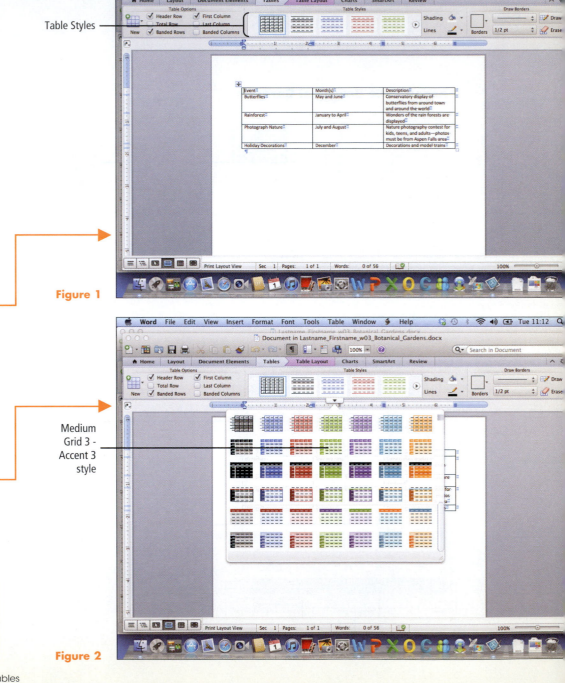

Table Styles

Figure 1

Medium Grid 3 - Accent 3 style

Figure 2

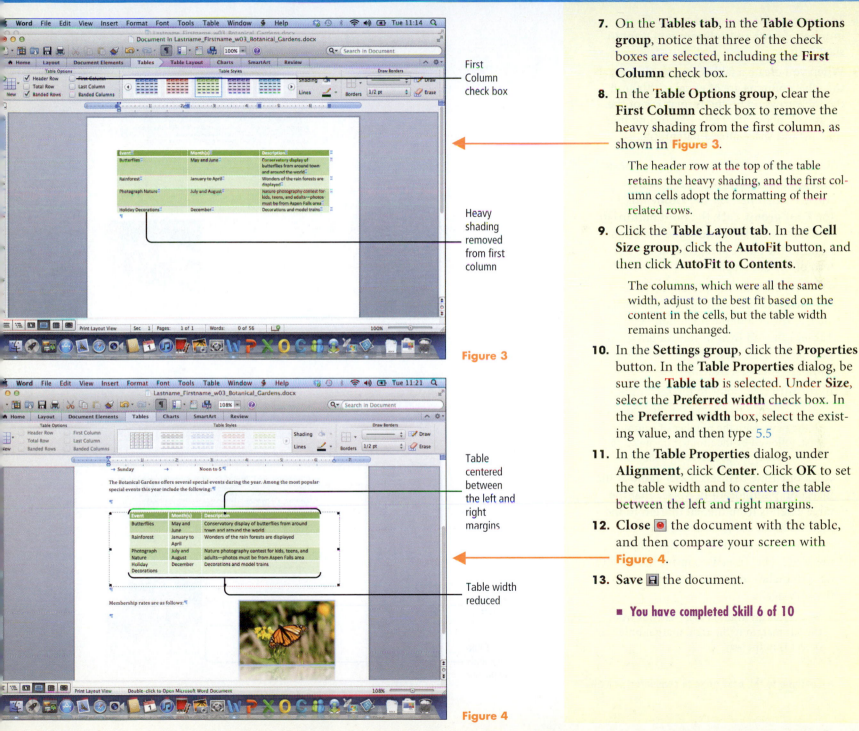

First Column check box

Heavy shading removed from first column

Figure 3

Table centered between the left and right margins

Table width reduced

Figure 4

7. On the **Tables tab**, in the **Table Options group**, notice that three of the check boxes are selected, including the **First Column** check box.

8. In the **Table Options group**, clear the **First Column** check box to remove the heavy shading from the first column, as shown in **Figure 3**.

> The header row at the top of the table retains the heavy shading, and the first column cells adopt the formatting of their related rows.

9. Click the **Table Layout tab**. In the **Cell Size group**, click the **AutoFit** button, and then click **AutoFit to Contents**.

> The columns, which were all the same width, adjust to the best fit based on the content in the cells, but the table width remains unchanged.

10. In the **Settings group**, click the **Properties** button. In the **Table Properties** dialog, be sure the **Table tab** is selected. Under **Size**, select the **Preferred width** check box. In the **Preferred width** box, select the existing value, and then type 5.5

11. In the **Table Properties** dialog, under **Alignment**, click **Center**. Click **OK** to set the table width and to center the table between the left and right margins.

12. Close ⊙ the document with the table, and then compare your screen with **Figure 4**.

13. Save 🖫 the document.

■ **You have completed Skill 6 of 10**

► To create a table, you need to specify the number of rows and columns you want to start with.

► When you create a table using the Insert tab, the table columns are of equal width, and the table rows retain the formatting of the paragraph above the table—including line spacing and space after a paragraph.

1. Near the bottom of the document, locate and select the paragraph that begins *Membership rates*. On the **Home tab**, in the **Font group**, click the **Bold** button B , and then press ▼ to move the insertion point to the blank paragraph at the bottom of the document.

2. **Move** ✥ the butterfly picture up to **6.5 inches** on the vertical ruler, and then click at the end of the document. Click the **Tables tab**, and then in the **Table Options group**, click the **New** button, and then compare your screen with **Figure 1**.

3. In the fifth row, point to the second box.

   The top of the Table gallery displays the size of the table, with the number of columns first, followed by the number of rows—in this instance, you are creating a 2x5 table.

4. Click one time to insert a **2x5 Table** at the insertion point location. Notice that the table extends from the left margin to the picture on the right, as shown in **Figure 2**. If your table extends to the right margin, undo the table insertion, move the picture up to 6 inches on the vertical ruler, and then try again.

   By default, an inserted table extends from the left margin to the right margin unless an object is in the way.

■ **Continue to the next page to complete the skill**

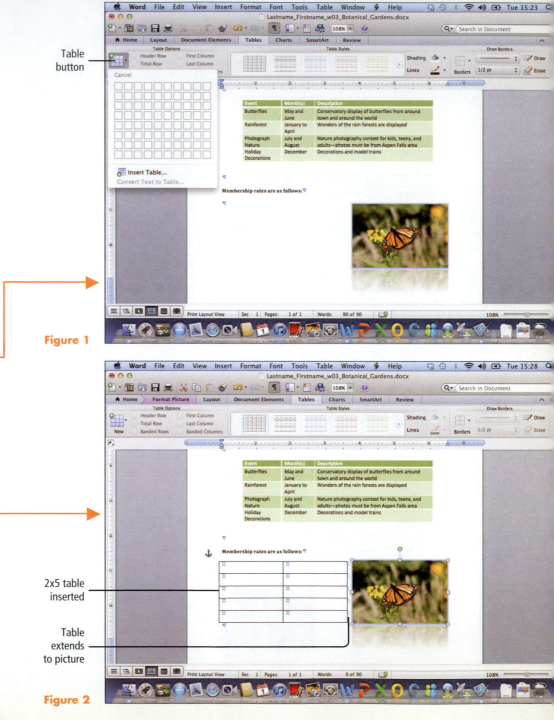

Table button

Figure 1

2x5 table inserted

Table extends to picture

Figure 2

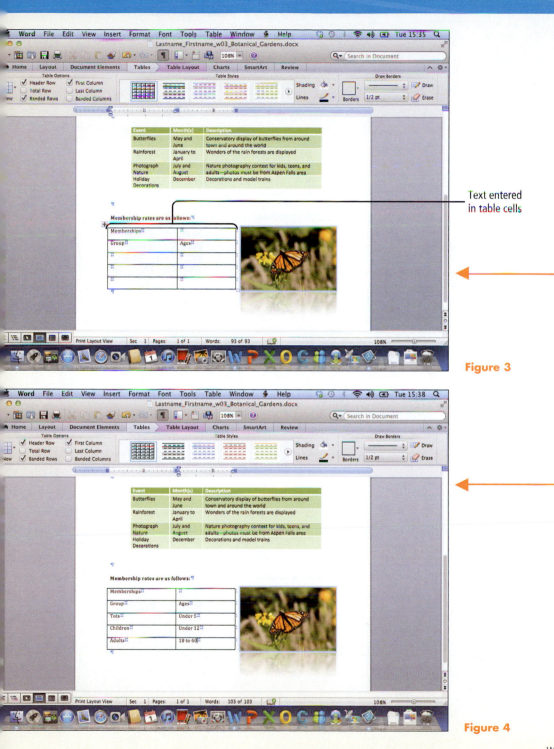

Text entered
in table cells

Figure 3

Figure 4

5. Be sure the insertion point is located in the upper left cell of the new table. Type Memberships and then press `tab`. Notice that the column widths adjust as you type.

> You can use `tab` or the arrow keys to move among cells in a table. When you press `return`, a second line in the same cell is created. If this happens, you can press `delete` or click the **Undo** button to remove the inserted paragraph.

6. Press `tab` again to move to the first cell in the second row.

7. Type Group and then press `tab`. Type Ages and then press `tab`. Compare your screen with **Figure 3**.

8. With the insertion point in the first cell of the third row, type Tots and then press `tab`. Type Under 5 and then press `tab`. Do not be concerned if the widths of the columns continue to change while you are typing.

9. In the first cell of the fourth row, type Children and then press `tab`. Type Under 12 and then press `tab`.

10. In the first cell of the last row, type Adults and then press `tab`. Type 18 to 60 and then compare your screen with **Figure 4**.

11. **Save** the document.

■ **You have completed Skill 7 of 10**

► You can add rows to the beginning, middle, or end of a table, and you can delete one or more rows, if necessary.

► You can add columns to the left or right of the column that contains the insertion point.

1. In the third row of the table, click anywhere in the *Tots* cell.

   To delete a row, you need only position the insertion point anywhere in the row.

2. Click the **Table Layout tab**, and then in the **Rows & Columns group**, click the **Delete** button. From the displayed list, click **Delete Rows**. If you accidentally click Delete Columns, on the Standard toolbar, click the Undo button and try again.

3. Be sure the insertion point is in the *Children* cell. In the **Rows & Columns group**, click the **Below** button. Notice that a blank row is added below the row that contains the insertion point.

4. Type Students and then notice that although the entire row was selected when you started typing, the text was entered into the row's first cell. Press tab, and then type Under 18 Press tab, and then compare your screen with **Figure 1**.

5. In the last row of the table, in the second column, click to the right of *18 to 60*.

6. Press tab to insert a new row at the bottom of the table.

7. Type Seniors and then press tab. Type Over 60 and then compare your screen with **Figure 2**.

■ **Continue to the next page to complete the skill**

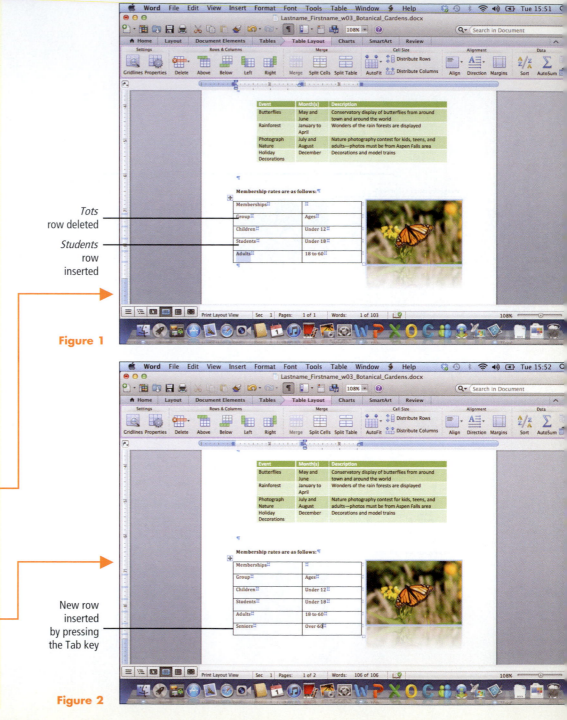

Tots row deleted

Students row inserted

Figure 1

New row inserted by pressing the Tab key

Figure 2

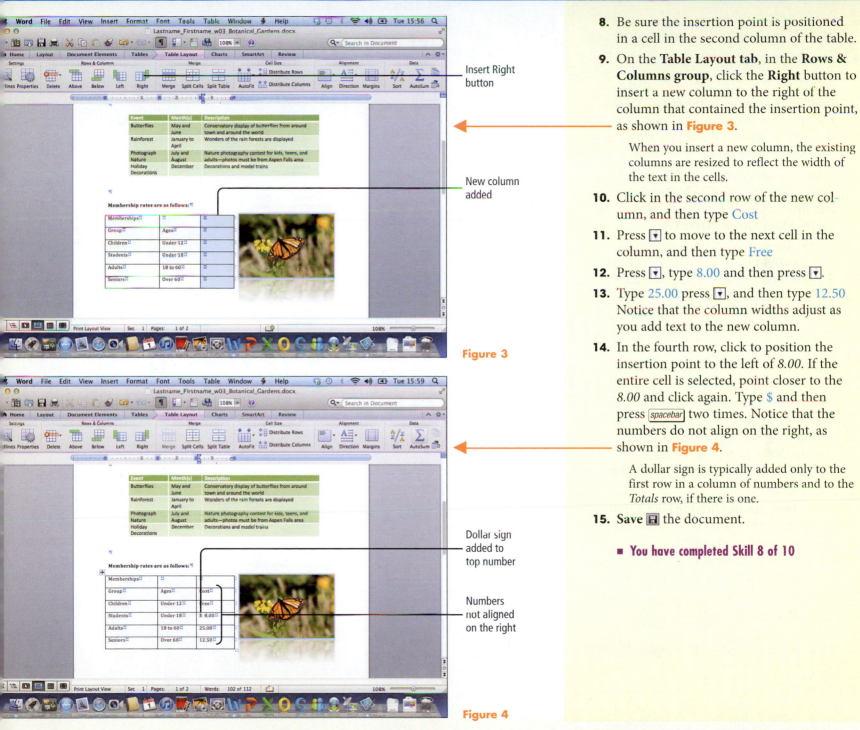

Figure 3

Figure 4

8. Be sure the insertion point is positioned in a cell in the second column of the table.

9. On the **Table Layout tab**, in the **Rows & Columns group**, click the **Right** button to insert a new column to the right of the column that contained the insertion point, as shown in **Figure 3**.

When you insert a new column, the existing columns are resized to reflect the width of the text in the cells.

10. Click in the second row of the new column, and then type Cost

11. Press ▼ to move to the next cell in the column, and then type Free

12. Press ▼, type 8.00 and then press ▼.

13. Type 25.00 press ▼, and then type 12.50 Notice that the column widths adjust as you add text to the new column.

14. In the fourth row, click to position the insertion point to the left of 8.00. If the entire cell is selected, point closer to the 8.00 and click again. Type $ and then press spacebar two times. Notice that the numbers do not align on the right, as shown in **Figure 4**.

A dollar sign is typically added only to the first row in a column of numbers and to the *Totals* row, if there is one.

15. Save ⊟ the document.

■ **You have completed Skill 8 of 10**

► You can format text in tables in the same manner you format text in a document.

► Text and numbers can also be aligned in columns.

1. Position the pointer in the left margin to the left of the first row of the new table to display the ↗ pointer, and then click one time to select the row.

2. Click the **Tables tab**. In the **Table Styles group**, click the **Shading button arrow** 🎨, and then in the first row, click the seventh color—**Olive Green**, **Accent 3**.

3. On the **Home tab**, in the **Font group**, click the **Bold** button **B**. Click the **Font Size arrow**, scroll down, and then click **14**. Click the **Font color arrow**, and then under **Theme Colors**, click the first color in the first row—**Background 1**. Compare your screen with **Figure 1**.

4. Position your pointer in the left margin area next to the second row of the table to display the ↗ pointer, and then click one time to select the row.

5. On the **Home tab**, in the **Font group**, click the **Bold** button **B**. In the **Paragraph group**, click the **Center Text** button ▤.

6. In the **Font group**, click the **Font Color arrow** **A**, and then in the first row, click the seventh color—**Accent 3**. Click anywhere in the document to deselect the row, and then compare your screen with **Figure 2**.

■ **Continue to the next page to complete the skill**

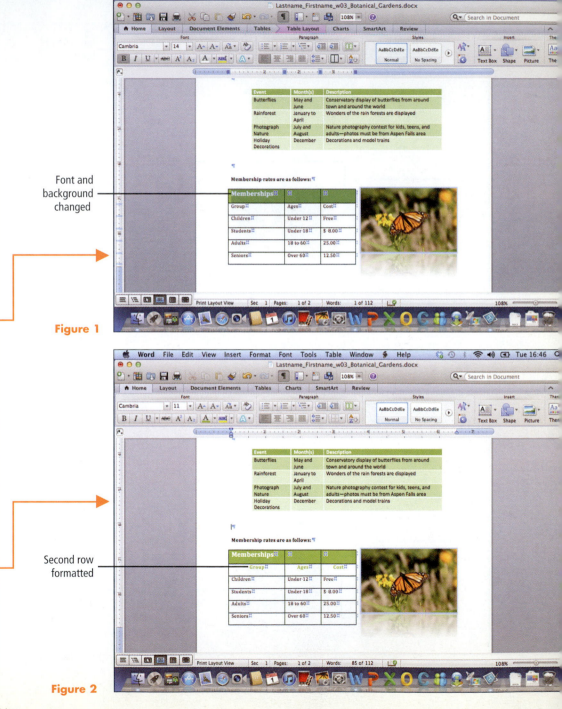

Font and background changed

Figure 1

Second row formatted

Figure 2

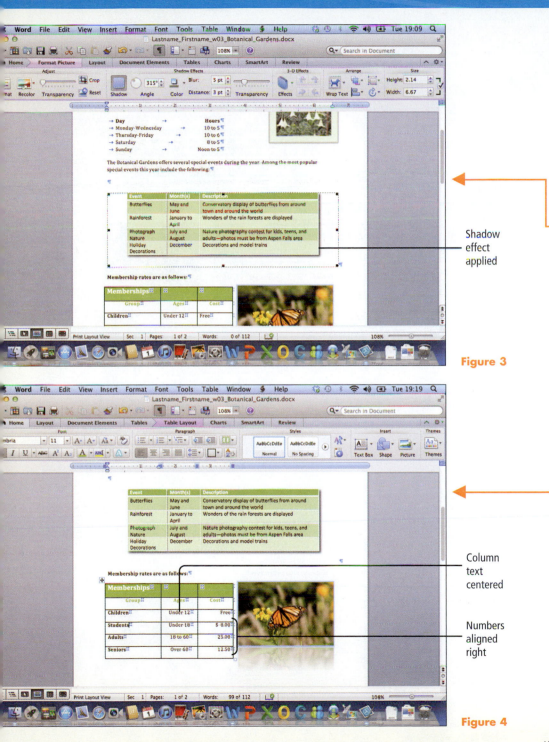

Figure 3

Figure 4

Shadow effect applied

Column text centered

Numbers aligned right

7. In the third row of the table, click anywhere in the cell with the text *Children*. Drag down to select the first cell in rows 3 through 6.

8. In the **Font group**, click the **Bold** button B. Alternately, press command ⌘ + B.

9. Click to select the table above.

   Notice that the table is now a picture and the Format Picture tab displays.

10. On the **Format Picture tab**, in the **Shadow Effects group**, click **Shadow**, and then compare your screen with **Figure 3**.

11. In the lower table, click in the second cell in the third row—*Under 12*. Drag down to select the remaining three cells in the column. In the **Paragraph group**, click the **Center Text** button.

12. In the lower table, click in the third cell in the third row—*Free*. Drag down to select the remaining cells in the column. On the **Home tab**, in the **Paragraph group**, click the **Align Text Right** button.

    Aligning numbers to the right in a column of numbers makes them easier to read.

13. Click anywhere in the document to cancel the selection, and then compare your screen with **Figure 4**.

14. **Save** the document.

    ■ **You have completed Skill 9 of 10**

► You can change the width of table columns by using the AutoFit Contents command or by changing the column widths manually.

► To accommodate a title that spans multiple columns, you can merge cells to create one wide cell.

1. In the lower table, click to position the insertion point anywhere in the first column.

2. Click the **Table Layout tab**. In the **Settings group**, click the **Properties** button. In the **Table Properties** dialog, click the **Column** tab. In the **Preferred width** box, type 1.5

3. In the **Table Properties** dialog, click the **Next Column** —> button. In the **Preferred width** box, type 1.1 Click the **Next Column** —> button, and then in the **Preferred width** box, type 0.8 Click **OK**, and then compare your screen with **Figure 1**.

   When you manually resize table columns, it is good practice to resize the columns from left to right.

4. In the first row of the lower table, click in the first cell and drag to the right to select all of the cells in the row.

5. On the **Table Layout tab**, in the **Merge group**, click the **Merge** button. Click the **Home tab**, and then in the **Paragraph group**, click the **Center Text** button ⊞. Click to deselect the text, and then notice that the text spans all of the columns, as shown in **Figure 2**.

6. Click anywhere in the lower table. Move the pointer ✥, and then click the **Layout Selector** ⊞ to select the entire table.

■ **Continue to the next page to complete the skill** ➤

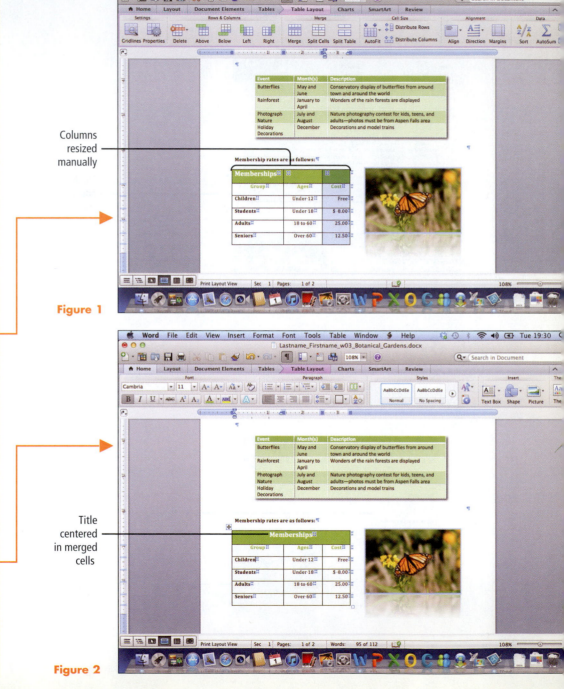

Columns resized manually

Figure 1

Title centered in merged cells

Figure 2

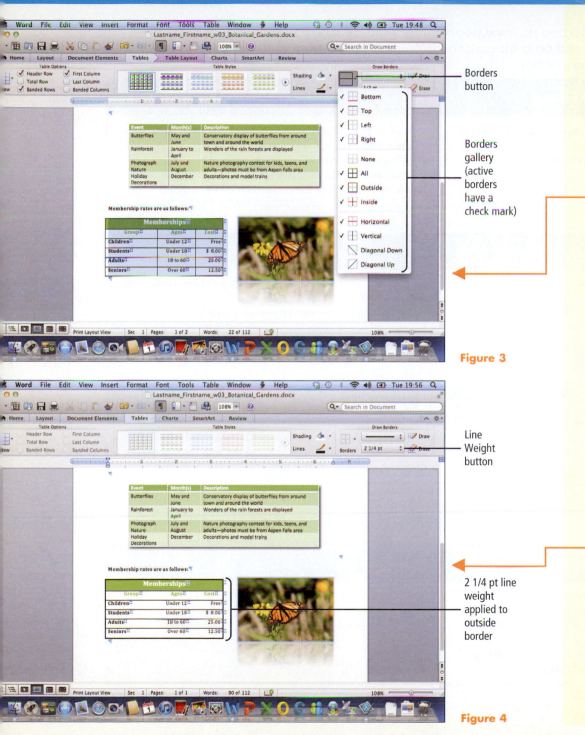

Borders button

Borders gallery (active borders have a check mark)

Figure 3

Line Weight button

2 1/4 pt line weight applied to outside border

Figure 4

7. On the **menu bar**, click **Format**, and then click **Paragraph**. In the **Paragraph** dialog, under **Spacing**, click the **Spacing After down spin arrow** one time to reduce the spacing after to **6 pt**, and then click **OK**.

8. On the **Tables tab**, in the **Draw Borders group**, click the **Borders button arrow**, and then examine the **Borders** gallery. Notice that the borders that are active display with a checkmark, as shown in **Figure 3**.

9. In the **Borders** gallery, click **Left Border**, and notice that the left border is removed from the selected cells.

10. Repeat the same technique to remove the **Right Border** and the **Inside Vertical Border**. Click anywhere in the document to deselect the text.

    Your program may be set to display light, nonprinting grid lines where borders have been removed.

11. In the lower table, move the pointer, and then click the **Layout Selector** to select the entire table.

12. On the **Tables tab**, in the **Draw Borders group**, click the **Line Weight** button, and then click **2 1/4 pt**. Click the **Borders button arrow**, and then click **Outside**. Click anywhere in the document to deselect the table, and then compare your screen with **Figure 4**.

13. Add the file name to the footer. **Save** the document. Print or submit the file as directed by your instructor. **Exit** Word.

    Done! You have completed Skill 10 of 10, and your document is complete!

More Skills

The following More Skills are located at **www.pearsonhighered.com/skills.** Please note that only More Skills that can be performed on a Macintosh computer are included in this section; therefore, the numbering is not always sequential.

More Skills 11 — Insert Text Boxes

Text boxes are floating objects that can be placed anywhere in a document. They are useful when you want to present text in a different orientation from other text. Text boxes function as a document within a document, and they can be resized or moved. Text in a text box wraps in the same manner it wraps in any document.

In More Skills 11, you will open a document and create a text box. You will also resize and format the text box.

To begin, open your web browser, navigate to www.pearsonhighered.com/skills, locate the name of your textbook, and then follow the instructions on the website.

More Skills 12 — Format with WordArt

When you create a flyer or a newsletter, you might want to use a distinctive and decorative title. Word provides a feature called WordArt that you can use to change text into a decorative title.

In More Skills 12, you will open a document and create a title that uses WordArt.

To begin, open your web browser, navigate to www.pearsonhighered.com/skills, locate the name of your textbook, and then follow the instructions on the website.

More Skills 13 — Create Tables from Existing Lists

You can create a new table by using the Table button on the Insert tab. You can also use the Table button to convert a tabbed list into a table.

In More Skills 13, you will open a document and convert a tabbed list into a table. You will also format the table.

To begin, open your web browser, navigate to www.pearsonhighered.com/skills, locate the name of your textbook, and then follow the instructions on the website.

More Skills 14 — Insert Drop Caps

Word provides a number of methods to format text distinctively. To give text the professional look you often see in books and magazines, you can use a large first letter to begin the first paragraph of the document.

In More Skills 14, you will open a document and create a drop cap for the first character of the first paragraph.

To begin, open your web browser, navigate to www.pearsonhighered.com/skills, locate the name of your textbook, and then follow the instructions on the website.

Key Terms

Anchor 97

Dot leader 101

Floating object 97

Leader 101

Leader character 101

Nudge 99

Sizing handle 96

Tab stop 100

Table 104

Online Help Skills

1. **Start** Safari or another web browser. In the **address bar**, type microsoft.com/mac/how-to and then press ⟨return⟩ to display the home page for Microsoft Office 2011.

2. Under **Product Help**, click **Word 2011**.

3. Under Word Help, click Tables.

4. Under Tables, click Convert a table to text or vice versa.

5. Under Convert a table to text or vice versa, click **Convert a table to text**, and then compare your screen with **Figure 1**.

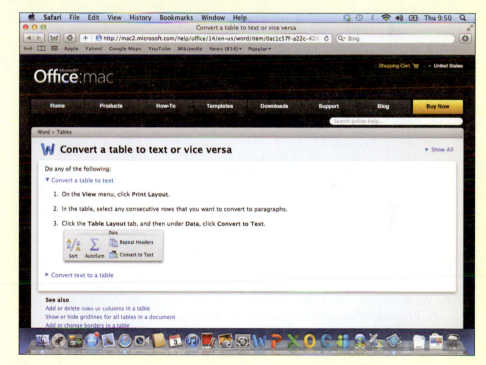

Figure 1

6. Review the content within both links to answer the following questions: How do you convert a table to text? How do you convert text to a table?

Matching

Match each term in the second column with its correct definition in the first column by writing the letter of the term on the blank line in front of the correct definition.

___ **1.** The feature used to change a picture to a floating object so that it can be moved independently of a paragraph.

___ **2.** The type of sizing handle used to resize a picture proportionally.

___ **3.** The formatting feature that makes a picture's edges appear to fade into the picture.

___ **4.** A specific location in the document, marked on the Word ruler, to which you can move using the Tab key.

___ **5.** A series of characters that form a solid, dashed, or dotted line that fills the space preceding a tab stop.

___ **6.** Information presented in rows and columns to summarize and present data effectively and efficiently.

___ **7.** A set of predefined table formats.

___ **8.** When you create a table using the Insert tab, the table columns will all be of this width.

___ **9.** With the insertion point in the last cell in the table, the key used to create a new row at the bottom of the table.

___ **10.** The command used to make the size of the table columns reflect the data in the columns.

A AutoFit Contents

B Corner

C Equal

D Leader

E Soft Edges

F Tab

G Tab Stop

H Table

I Table Styles

J Wrap Text

Multiple Choice

Choose the correct answer.

1. When you select a picture, use these to change the picture height or width.
   - A. Arrow keys
   - B. Sizing handles
   - C. `page up` or `page down`

2. The symbol that indicates which paragraph a picture is associated with.
   - A. Anchor
   - B. Paragraph mark
   - C. Em dash

3. To move a selected picture small distances using an arrow key.
   - A. Drag
   - B. Bump
   - C. Nudge

4. A series of evenly spaced dots that precede a tab.
   - A. Ellipsis
   - B. Tab stop position
   - C. Dot leader

5. When you make a change to a tab stop in the Tabs dialog, click this button to apply the changes.
   - A. Set
   - B. Clear
   - C. Apply

6. The intersection of a row and column in a table.
   - A. Banded row
   - B. Cell
   - C. Banded column

7. The command used to change a picture to make it look more like a drawing or a painting.
   - A. Artistic Effects
   - B. Picture Styles
   - C. Picture Effects

8. Use this key to move from one part of a table to another.
   - A. `option`
   - B. `tab`
   - C. `control`

9. How many columns are in a 3x7 table?
   - A. 3
   - B. 7
   - C. 21

10. Numbers in a table are typically aligned this way.
    - A. Left
    - B. Center
    - C. Right

Topics for Discussion

1. Tables have largely taken the place of tabs in most documents. Can you think of any situations where you might want to use tabs instead of tables? What would you have to do to a table to make it look like a tabbed list?

2. Pictures add interest to your documents when used in moderation. What guidelines would you recommend for using pictures—or any other type of graphics—in a document?

Skill Check

To complete this document, you will need the following files:

- w03_Fitness
- w03_Fitness_Activities
- w03_Fitness_Climber

You will save your document as:

- Lastname_Firstname_w03_Fitness

1. **Start** Word. Click **File**, and then click **Open**. Navigate to your student files and open **w03_Fitness**. Click **File**, click **Save As**, navigate to your **Word Chapter 3** folder, **Save** the document as Lastname_Firstname_w03_Fitness and then add the file name to the footer.

2. In the paragraph that begins *The following,* click to position the insertion point at the beginning of the paragraph. On the **menu bar**, click **Insert**, and then click **Object**. Click the **From File** button. Locate and insert **w03_Fitness_Activities**.

3. Double-click in the first row of the inserted table. On the **Table Layout tab**, in the **Rows & Columns group**, click the **Above** button. In the **Alignment group**, click **Align**, and then click **Center**. In the first cell, type Fitness Area and press ⟨tab⟩. In the second cell, type Reservations and press ⟨tab⟩. In the third cell, type Description and then compare your screen with **Figure 1**. ————

4. Click the **Tables tab**. In the **Table Styles group**, click the **More** button, and then under **Built-In**, in the first row, click the last style—**Light Shading – Accent 6**.

5. On the **Table Layout tab**, in the **Cell Size group**, click the **AutoFit** button, and then click **AutoFit to Contents**.

6. In the **Table Layout group**, click the **Properties** button. In the **Table Properties** dialog, set the **Preferred Width** to 6", and then under **Alignment**, **Center** the table. Click **OK**. Compare with **Figure 2**. **Save** and **Close** the document with the table. —

7. At the end of the paragraph that begins *The following,* position the insertion point after the colon, and then press ⟨return⟩ to create a blank line.

8. Click the **Tables tab**. In the **Tables Options group,** click the **New** button, and then insert a **2x6** table.

- **Continue to the next page to complete this Skill Check** ▶

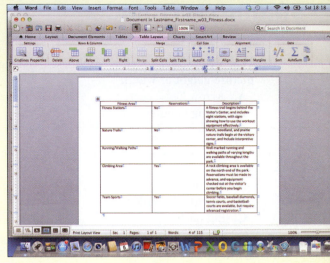

Figure 1

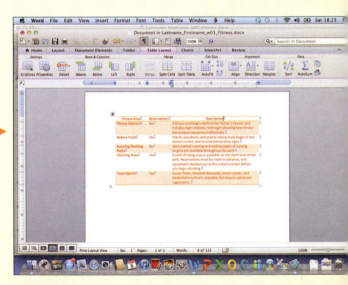

Figure 2

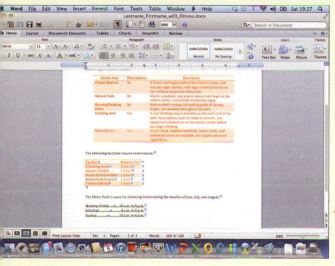

Figure 3

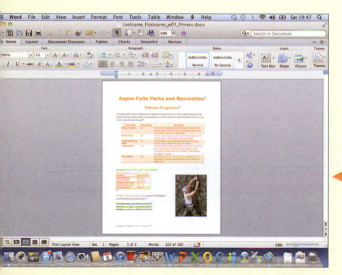

Figure 4

9. Enter the following information in the table:

Facility	Reserve for
Climbing Area	2 hours
Soccer Fields	2 hours
Baseball Diamonds	2 hours
Basketball Courts	1 hour
Tennis Courts	1 hour

10. On the **Tables tab**, apply the same table style you applied to the upper table—**Light Shading – Accent 6**. On the **Table Layout tab**, in the **Cell Size group**, click the **AutoFit** button, and then click **AutoFit to Contents**.

11. Select the five cells that contain numbers. On the **Home tab**, in the **Paragraph group**, click the **Align Text Right** button.

12. Move to the end of the document. On the left side of the horizontal ruler, click the **Tab Selector** button, and then click **Right**. Insert a right tab at **2.5 inches** on the horizontal ruler.

13. Click the **Tab Selector** button, and then click **Tabs**. In the **Tabs** dialog, under **Leader**, select **2**, click **Set**, and then click **OK**. Type the following tabbed list, pressing [tab] before typing the text in the *second* column:

Monday-Friday	10 a.m. to 9 p.m.
Saturday	8 a.m. to 9 p.m.
Sunday	10 a.m. to 6 p.m.

14. Select the first two items in the tabbed list. On the **Home tab**, in the **Paragraph group**, click **Line Spacing**, and then **Line Spacing Options**. Set the **Spacing After** to **0 pt**. Move to the end, and then compare your screen with **Figure 3**.

15. On the **Home tab**, in the **Insert group**, click the **Picture** button, and then locate and **Insert** the **w03_Fitness_Climber** picture. On the **Format Picture tab**, in the **Size group**, select the number in the **Shape Width** box, type **2.5** and then press [return]. In the **Shape Height** box, type **3** and then press [return]. In the **Arrange group**, apply **Square** wrapping.

16. Drag the picture to page 1 so that the upper edge aligns at about **5.75 inches** on the vertical ruler and the right edge aligns at about **6.5 inches** on the horizontal ruler. Adjust the picture position as necessary.

17. On the **Format Picture tab**, in the **Picture Styles group**, click the **Picture Effects** button, point to **Glow**, and then click **Access 1, 5 pt glow**. On the **Standard toolbar**, click the **Zoom** button, and then click **Whole Page**.

18. Click anywhere to deselect the picture, and then compare your document with **Figure 4**. **Save** the document, and submit it as directed. **Exit** Word.

Done! You have completed the Skill Check

Assess Your Skills 1

To complete this document, you will need the following files:

- w03_Run
- w03_Run_Start
- w03_Run_Finish

You will save your document as:

- Lastname_Firstname_w03_Run

1. **Start** Word. Locate and open **w03_Run**, and then save it in your **Word Chapter 3** folder as Lastname_Firstname_w03_Run

2. Add a new third column to the table. In the first cell of the new column, type Start Time and then complete the column with the following:

10:00 a.m.	11:30 a.m.	1:00 p.m.
10:30 a.m.	12:00 p.m.	
11:00 a.m.	12:30 p.m.	

3. Click in the first row of the table and add a new row above the first row. In the first cell of the new row, type Waves for 10K Run

4. Select the table, and then apply the **Light Shading – Accent 6** table style. Apply **AutoFit to Contents** formatting. **Align Text Right** all of the cells in the third column. Apply **Bold** formatting to the titles in row 2.

5. **Merge** the cells in the first row of the table, and then **Center** the text. Select the table, and increase the **Font Size** to **14** points. **Center** the table.

6. Move to the end of the document, and press ⏎ return. Type: There are several requirements for registration in Waves A through E, and these can be found on the attached registration form. Each participant will receive a T-shirt package after the race. Press ⏎ return.

7. Insert a left tab stop at **2 inches** and a right tab stop at **4.5 inches** on the horizontal ruler. Add a dot leader to the right tab stop. Enter the following text to create a tabbed list. *Be sure to press* ⌨ tab *before the first item in each row:*

Category	Cost
Men	$40
Women	40
Children (12 & under)	20
Seniors (62 & older)	25

8. In the first row of the list, **Bold** the titles. For the first four rows in the list, change the **Spacing After** to **0 pt**.

9. Insert the **w03_Run_Start** picture, apply **Square** text wrapping, change the **Width** to **2.8"**, and then position the left edge of the picture at the left margin and the top of the picture at **7 inches** on the vertical ruler. Repeat this procedure with the **w03_Run_Finish** picture, except position the picture at the right margin.

10. Add the file name to the footer. **Save** the document, and then print or submit the file as directed by your instructor. Compare your completed document with **Figure 1**.

Done! You have completed Assess Your Skills 1

Aspen Falls 10K Run
Information

The Aspen Falls Parks and Recreation Department is once again sponsoring the Spring 10K Run. This year, instead of closing down the main streets in town, the entire run will take place in the Aspen Falls Metro Park. The race will start on the boardwalk that separates the lake from the swamp, and will end at the south end of the mid-lake trail. Because of the anticipated increase in runners, we have expanded the number of waves to seven. When you register, be sure to register for the correct wave!

Waves for 10K Run		
Wave	10K Time	Start Time
A	sub 40:00	10:00 a.m.
B	sub 45:00	10:30 a.m.
C	sub 50:00	11:00 a.m.
D	sub 55:00	11:30 a.m.
E	sub 60:00	12:00 p.m.
F	60:00 - 90:00	12:30 p.m.
G	90:00 +	1:00 p.m.

There are several requirements for registration in Waves A through E, and these can be found on the attached registration form. Each participant with receive a T-shirt package after the race.

Category	Cost
Men	$40
Women	40
Children (12 & under)	20
Seniors (62 & older)	25

Lastname_Firstname_w03_Run

Figure 1

Assess Your Skills 2

Assess Your Skills 3 and 4 can be found at **www.pearsonhighered.com/skills**.

To complete this document, you will need the following files:

- w03_Cleanup
- w03_Cleanup_River

You will save your document as:

- Lastname_Firstname_w03_Cleanup

Aspen Falls

Cleanup Day

The annual Spring Cleanup Day is here again, and will take place this year on May 15th. Once again, the Parks and Recreation Department will be coordinating the effort, and we hope to have a turnout even larger than last year. We have identified six areas that need various types of work done. Please call and sign up for one or more of the sessions. Groups are welcome, as always! Here is a list of this year's target areas:

Location	Cleanup Needs
Falls River	The river cleanup will be a little more complicated this year than in past years. Because of low water levels, some old machinery has been uncovered (see the picture below). We need quite a few strong people for this one!
Veterans Park	The park needs mostly trash pickup, but we also need experienced people to trim and prune trees and shrubs.
Metro Park Trails	Get your exercise and help clean up the park! This job will consist mostly of trash pickup, and should be easy work.
Metro Park Woods	We need specialists here. If you have a chainsaw, there are a number of downed trees that need to be removed.
Highways	Cleaning our highways is not the most glamorous of the cleanup opportunities, but it is vital to the perception of our communities by people visiting the city. This is a good project for small groups.
Mt. Joy Cemetery	This old pioneer cemetery needs lots of mowing, trimming, and brush removal. Bring your own equipment.

Lastname_Firstname_w03_Cleanup

Figure 1

---

1. **Start** Word. Locate and open **w03_Cleanup**, and then save it in your **Word Chapter 3** folder as Lastname_Firstname_w03_Cleanup **Center** both document titles, change the **Font** to **Arial Black**, and then change the **Font Color** to the last color under Theme Colors—**Orange**, **Accent 6**, **Darker 50%**. Change the **Font Size** of the first title to **36** points and the **Font Size** of the second title to **24** points. Change the **Spacing After** the first title to **0 pt**.

2. Select the table, and then apply the last table style in the fourth row—**Medium Shading 1 – Accent 6**. Insert a new row at the bottom of the table, and in the new row, type Mt. Joy Cemetery Press ⟨tab⟩, and then type This old pioneer cemetery needs lots of mowing, trimming, and brush removal. Bring your own equipment.

3. Set the **Width** of the first column to **1.5"**. Use the **Table Properties** dialog box to set the **Preferred Width** of the table to **5.5"** and to **Center** the table.

4. In the first row of the table, change the **Font Size** to **14** points, and then **Center** the table titles.

5. At the end of the document, insert the picture **w03_Cleanup_River**. Change the height of the picture to **2"**. Apply **Square** text wrapping, and then drag the picture so that it is centered under the table and the top edge is about 0.25 inch below the table. If you accidentally drag the picture into the table, click the Undo button and try again. If the picture moves to the second page, switch to Two Pages view.

6. With the picture still selected, apply an **Accent 1**, **5 pt glow**, and then apply the fourth picture style in the first row—**Drop Shadow Rectangle**.

7. Add the file name to the footer. **Save** the document, and then print or submit the file as directed by your instructor. Compare your completed document with **Figure 1**.

Done! You have completed Assess Your Skills 2

Assess Your Skills Visually

To complete this document, you will need the following files:

- New blank Word document
- w03_Trails
- w03_Trails_Family
- w03_Trails_Marsh

You will save your document as:

- Lastname_Firstname_w03_Trails

Open a new Word document, and then save it in your **Word Chapter 3** folder as Lastname_Firstname_w03_Trails Create the document shown in **Figure 1**.

To complete this document, add the titles and opening paragraph. The titles are in **Arial Rounded MT Bold 24** points and **16** points, and the space between the titles is **0 pt**. The space after the second title is **6 pt**. Insert the table from the **w03_Trails** file, and format it as shown, with the **Header Row** formatting removed, the width of the first column set at **1.6"**, and the table width **6"**. The font colors are **Automatic**, and the titles are the last color in the last column under Theme Colors—**Orange**, **Accent 6**, **Darker 50%**. Add the **w03_Trails_Family** and **w03_Trails_Marsh** pictures, and then size and position the pictures as shown in **Figure 1**. The **w03_Trails_Family** picture has the **Soft Edge Rectangle** effect applied. Format the **Height** of both pictures to **1.5"**. Add the file name to the footer. **Save** the document, and then print or submit the file as directed by your instructor.

Done! You have completed Assess Your Skills Visually

City of Aspen Falls
Self-Guided Tours

The Aspen Falls Parks and Recreation Department has created several self-guided tours that cover the history of the city and the local environment. Brochures for each of the tours are available at City Hall, all of the park offices, all local schools, and the area libraries.

Historic Houses	Take a walking tour through the historic district of Aspen Falls. Use the self-guided tour guide to learn about the history and architecture of some of our more interesting buildings.
Flower Gardens	Take a tour through the houses in the older part of town, and see some spectacular flower gardens. Because these gardens are on private property, the tours are open only on Sunday afternoons from 1 to 4 p.m.
Bird Watching	Both the nature trails in the Metro Park and the shoreline trails along the ocean offer you plenty of opportunity for birding. The best time of the day is the very early morning.
Marsh Life	A meandering boardwalk trail through the marsh area in the Metro Park gives you the opportunity to see the wide varieties of plant, animal, and insect life in the marsh.
Waterfalls and Rapids	There are actually two trails, along the Falls River and Aspen Creek, that can be walked individually or together, passing a number of small waterfalls and rapids—great for pictures!
Geological Formations	Take a look at the physical evidence of the strike-slip zone between the North American Plate and the Pacific Plate. Interpretive signs are placed at interesting locations along this shoreline trail.

Lastname_Firstname_Trails

Figure 1

Skills in Context

To complete this document, you will need the following files:

- New blank Word document
- w03_Events
- w03_Events_Bird

You will save your document as:

- Lastname_Firstname_w03_Events

Each month, the City of Aspen Falls Parks and Recreation Department hosts events throughout the city. Using the information in the file **w03_Events**, create a flyer that describes and lists the events that will be held during the month of May. Begin with a title and a subtitle, followed by a short descriptive paragraph about the events. Then create the table of events that are going to take place during the specified month. You will need to determine the appropriate number of columns. In the table, include column headings; at the top of the table, include a table title that spans all of the columns. Use an appropriate table style to make the table attractive. Locate and insert a picture or a clip art image that is related to one of the events in some way; you can use the included **w03_Events_Bird** picture if you choose. Format the picture using appropriate picture styles.

Save the document as Lastname_Firstname_w03_Events Insert the file name in the footer, and be sure to check the entire document for grammar and spelling. Print or submit the file as directed by your instructor.

Done! You have completed Skills in Context

Skills and You

To complete this project, you will need the following file:

- New blank Word document

You will save your document as:

- Lastname_Firstname_w03_Resume

Using the skills you have practiced in this chapter, create a resume using a table for the structure. To find information on what to include in a resume, find a book in your library or search for *resume* on the web. To complete your resume, you will need to hide most, if not all, of the table borders. (*Hint*: In this chapter, you merged cells across a row. In the resume, you will probably want to merge cells in a column several times.)

Save the document as Lastname_Firstname_w03_Resume Check the entire document for grammar and spelling. Add the file name to the footer. Print or submit electronically as directed by your instructor.

Done! You have completed Skills and You

CHAPTER 4

Apply Special Text, Paragraph, and Document Formats

▶ Text used in a newsletter is commonly displayed in two or three columns, which is often easier to read than one wide column.

▶ Clip art is included with Microsoft Office, and a clip art graphic is inserted and formatted in much the same way as a picture.

▶ SmartArt graphics display information visually and can add a professional look to a document.

▶ To draw attention to a small amount of text, you can add a border and shading to the paragraph.

▶ You can use the mail merge feature in Word to create mailing labels to distribute flyers or brochures.

▶ In a mail merge, you can take an existing list of names and addresses fro[m] other Office applications and insert them into a mailing labels documen[t].

©Lipik | Dreamstime.com

Aspen Falls City Hall

In this chapter, you will assist Todd Austin, the Aspen Falls Tourism Director, in creating a newsletter about winter activities. You will als[o] create mailing labels so that the newsletter can be mailed to potenti[al] visitors to the city.

In this project, you will create a one-page flyer with an artistic title and a two-column format. You will add text effects to article headings, and then add page and paragraph borders and border shading. You will insert a clip art graphic and create a SmartArt graphic. Finall[y] you will create mailing labels by merging data from one file to a labe[l] template.

Time to complete all
10 skills – 60 to 90 minutes

60-90 min.

Student data files needed for this chapter:

New blank Word Document
w04_Festival
w04_Festival_Addresses

You will save your documents as:

Lastname_Firstname_w04_Festival
Lastname_Firstname_w04_Festival_Addresses
Lastname_Firstname_w04_Festival_Labels

SKILLS

Skills 1-10 Training

At the end of this chapter you will be able to:

Skill 1 Create Multiple-Column Text
Skill 2 Insert a Column Break
Skill 3 Apply and Format Text Effects
Skill 4 Use Quick Styles
Skill 5 Add Borders and Shading to Paragraphs and Pages
Skill 6 Insert and Format Clip Art Graphics
Skill 7 Insert SmartArt Graphics
Skill 8 Format SmartArt Graphics
Skill 9 Create Labels Using Mail Merge
Skill 10 Preview and Print Mail Merge Documents

MORE SKILLS

Skill 11 Create Resumes from Templates

Outcome

Using the skills in this chapter, you will be able to create a Word document like this:

Aspen Falls Winter News

ASPEN FALLS SPONSORS WINTER JAZZ & BLUES FESTIVAL

Aspen Falls is proud to announce that the city will be this year's sponsor of the Winter Jazz & Blues Festival. Founded in 1980, the festival takes place at the Aspen Falls Lakefront Park just southwest of the city. To go along with the music, the festival also features an array of food and beverages from restaurants in the area. Micro beers and wine from the Aspen Falls winery region will also be available. A variety of retail stores will also be selling CDs, books, shirts, hats, and other paraphernalia.

For further information, contact Mary Lou Pietela at (805) 555-5454.

Jazz & Blues Festival Wins Greener Festival Award

Aspen Falls Winter Jazz & Blues Festival has been awarded the Environmentally Responsible Festival Award. Ten festivals were presented the awards this year for their efforts in promoting and sponsoring environmentally responsible festivals.

The award is based on scoring in several areas such as event management, waste management recycling and water management. Points are awarded for festivals that can show an active plan to reduce on-site waste, recycle and compost wherever possible, reuse water and use sustainable power.

Some of the Jazz & Blues Festival efforts include the promotion of Refuse, Reuse, Reduce, Recycle, only allow recyclable materials within the festival site, observing the 'leave no trace' program and using parking income to help protect the nearby wetlands.

Refuse
↓
Reuse
↓
Reduce
↓
Recycle

► In a brochure or flyer, using multiple columns makes text easier to read.

► Two or three columns are typically used on a standard 8 1/2″ × 11″ page.

1. **Start** Word. If a previous Word document displays, then Close the document, and then, on the menu bar, click File, and then click **Open**. Open **w04_Festival**, create a folder named Word Chapter 4 and then **Save** the document as Lastname_Firstname_ w04_Festival Add the file name to the footer. If necessary, display formatting marks.

2. Locate the paragraph that begins *Aspen Falls Sponsors,* and then position the pointer to the left of the first word in the paragraph. Drag down to the end of the document—including the paragraph mark in the last paragraph.

3. On the **Home tab**, in the **Paragraph group**, click the **Columns** button, and then click **Two**. If necessary, scroll up, and notice that the text is formatted in two uneven columns, as shown in **Figure 1**.

   A section break displays above the two-column text. A *section* is a portion of a document that can be formatted differently from the rest of the document. A *section break* marks the end of one section and the beginning of another section.

4. With the text still selected, on the **menu bar**, click **Format,** and then click **Paragraph**. In the **Paragraph** dialog, click the **After down spin arrow** one time to change the space after the paragraphs to **6 pt**, and then click **OK**.

5. On the **Home tab**, in the **Font group**, click the **Font arrow** Calibri (Body), and then scroll down and select **Comic Sans MS**. Click the **Font Size arrow** 11, and then click **11**. Compare your screen with **Figure 2**.

   ■ **Continue to the next page to complete the skill**

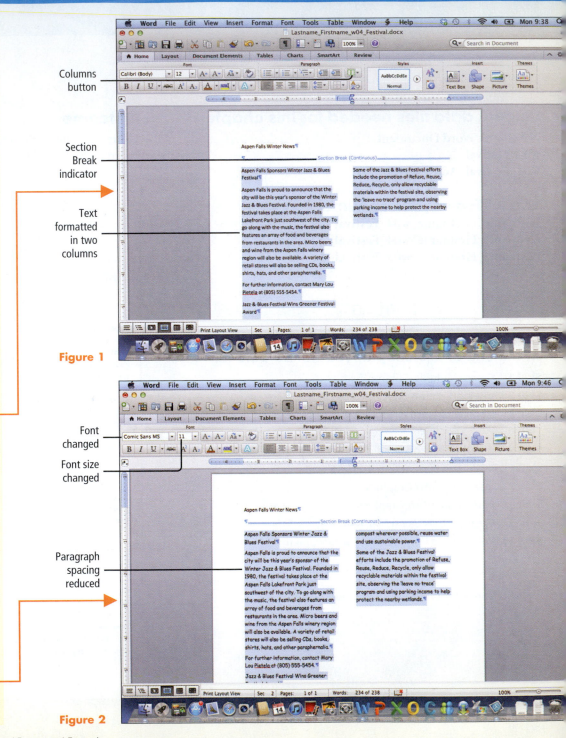

Columns button

Section Break indicator

Text formatted in two columns

Figure 1

Font changed

Font size changed

Paragraph spacing reduced

Figure 2

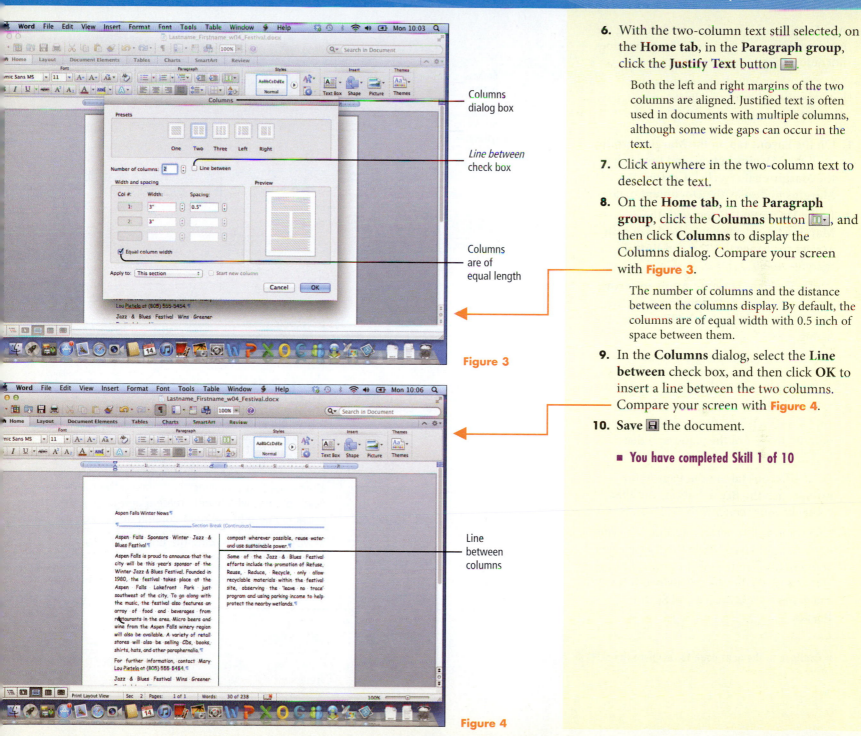

Columns dialog box

Line between check box

Columns are of equal length

Figure 3

Line between columns

Figure 4

6. With the two-column text still selected, on the **Home tab**, in the **Paragraph group**, click the **Justify Text** button.

   Both the left and right margins of the two columns are aligned. Justified text is often used in documents with multiple columns, although some wide gaps can occur in the text.

7. Click anywhere in the two-column text to deselect the text.

8. On the **Home tab**, in the **Paragraph group**, click the **Columns** button, and then click **Columns** to display the Columns dialog. Compare your screen with **Figure 3**.

   The number of columns and the distance between the columns display. By default, the columns are of equal width with 0.5 inch of space between them.

9. In the **Columns** dialog, select the **Line between** check box, and then click **OK** to insert a line between the two columns. Compare your screen with **Figure 4**.

10. **Save** the document.

   ■ **You have completed Skill 1 of 10**

▶ A *column break* forces the text following the break to the top of the next column but does not automatically create a new page.

▶ You can increase or decrease the space between the columns to adjust the document layout.

1. On the **Layout tab**, in the **Margins group**, click the **Margins** button, and then below the **Margins** gallery, click **Custom Margins** to display the **Document** dialog.

2. In the **Document** dialog, with the **Margins tab** selected, use the **down spin arrows** to change the **Top** and **Bottom** margins to **0.8"**.

3. Under **Preview**, click the **Apply to arrow**, and then click **Whole document**. At the bottom of the dialog, click **OK** to close the dialog.

   If the document has multiple sections, by default the settings from the Document dialog apply only to the current section.

4. Near the bottom of the document, in the left column, click to position the insertion point to the left of the paragraph that begins *The award is based*.

5. On the **Layout tab**, in the **Page Setup group**, click the **Break** button, and then compare your screen with **Figure 1**.

6. Take a moment to examine common types of breaks displayed in the Breaks gallery and described in the table in **Figure 2**. Notice that the breaks are divided into two categories—Page Breaks and Section Breaks.

■ **Continue to the next page to complete the skill**

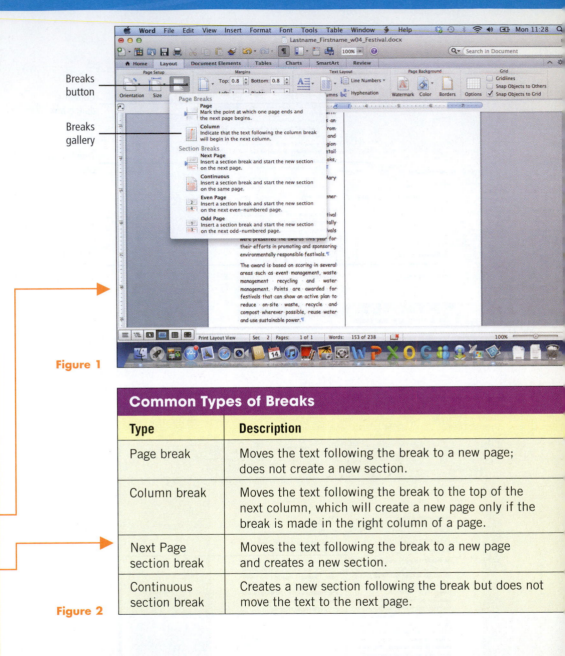

Breaks button

Breaks gallery

Figure 1

Figure 2

Common Types of Breaks

Type	Description
Page break	Moves the text following the break to a new page; does not create a new section.
Column break	Moves the text following the break to the top of the next column, which will create a new page only if the break is made in the right column of a page.
Next Page section break	Moves the text following the break to a new page and creates a new section.
Continuous section break	Creates a new section following the break but does not move the text to the next page.

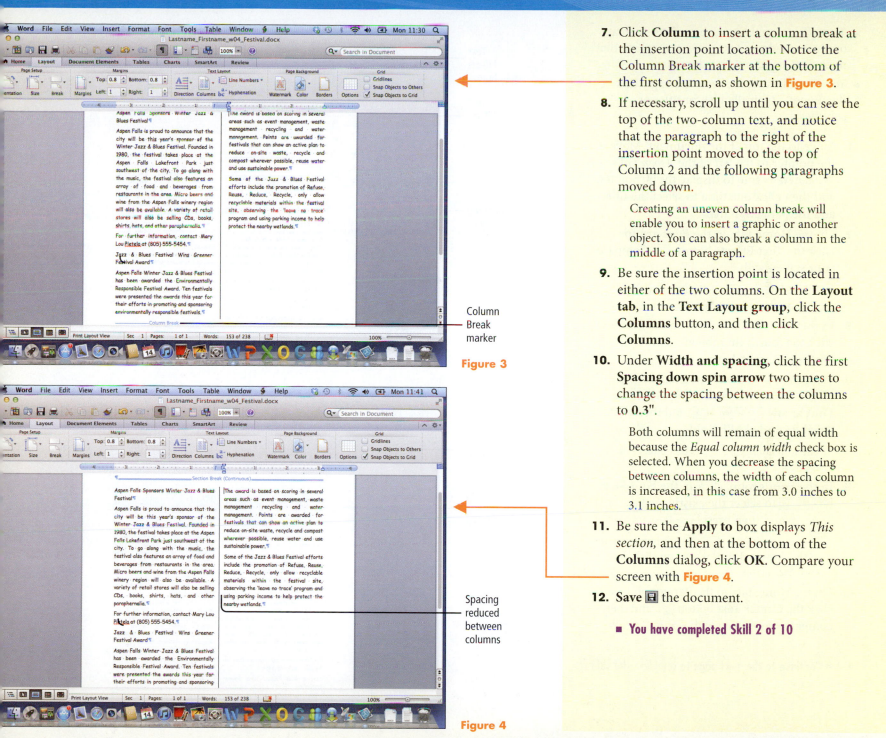

Column Break marker

Figure 3

Spacing reduced between columns

Figure 4

7. Click **Column** to insert a column break at the insertion point location. Notice the Column Break marker at the bottom of the first column, as shown in **Figure 3**.

8. If necessary, scroll up until you can see the top of the two-column text, and notice that the paragraph to the right of the insertion point moved to the top of Column 2 and the following paragraphs moved down.

    Creating an uneven column break will enable you to insert a graphic or another object. You can also break a column in the middle of a paragraph.

9. Be sure the insertion point is located in either of the two columns. On the **Layout tab**, in the **Text Layout group**, click the **Columns** button, and then click **Columns**.

10. Under **Width and spacing**, click the first **Spacing down spin arrow** two times to change the spacing between the columns to 0.3".

    Both columns will remain of equal width because the *Equal column width* check box is selected. When you decrease the spacing between columns, the width of each column is increased, in this case from 3.0 inches to 3.1 inches.

11. Be sure the **Apply to** box displays *This section,* and then at the bottom of the **Columns** dialog, click **OK**. Compare your screen with **Figure 4**.

12. **Save** the document.

    ■ **You have completed Skill 2 of 10**

▶ *Text effects* are decorative formats, such as outlines, shadows, text glow, and colors, that make text stand out in a document.

▶ You should use text effects sparingly in a document—typically just for titles or subtitles.

1. Move to the top of the document. Move the pointer to the left of the *Aspen Falls Winter News* title to display the pointer, and then click one time to select the title and the paragraph mark.

2. On the **Home tab**, in the **Font group**, click the **Text Effects** button. Compare your screen with **Figure 1**.

   A Text Effects gallery displays as well as several other text formatting options.

3. In the **Text Effects** gallery, in the first row, click the fourth thumbnail—**Fill–White, Outline–Accent 1**.

4. With the title text still selected, on the **Home tab**, in the **Font group**, click the **Font arrow** Calibri (Body), and then click **Arial Rounded MT Bold**.

   The font changes, but the text effect is still applied.

5. In the **Font group**, click in the **Font Size** box 11 to select the existing value. Type 38 and then press return.

   By typing the font size, you are not restricted to the displayed sizes when you click the Font Size arrow.

6. On the **Home tab**, in the **Paragraph group**, click the **Center Text** button, and then compare your screen with **Figure 2**.

■ **Continue to the next page to complete the skill**

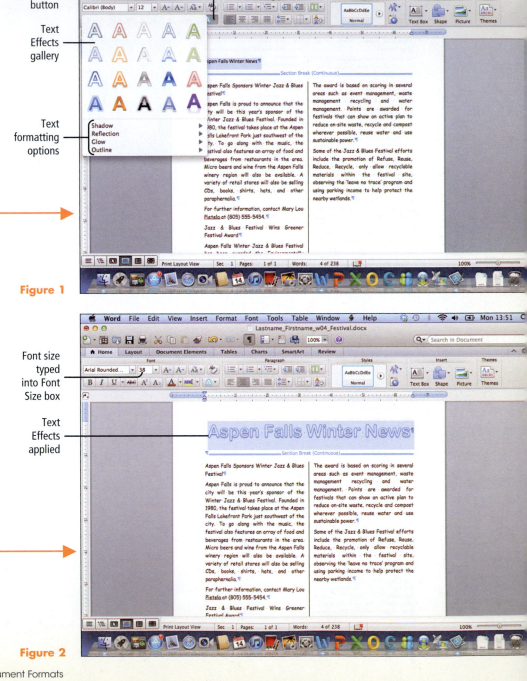

Text Effects button

Text Effects gallery

Text formatting options

Figure 1

Font size typed into Font Size box

Text Effects applied

Figure 2

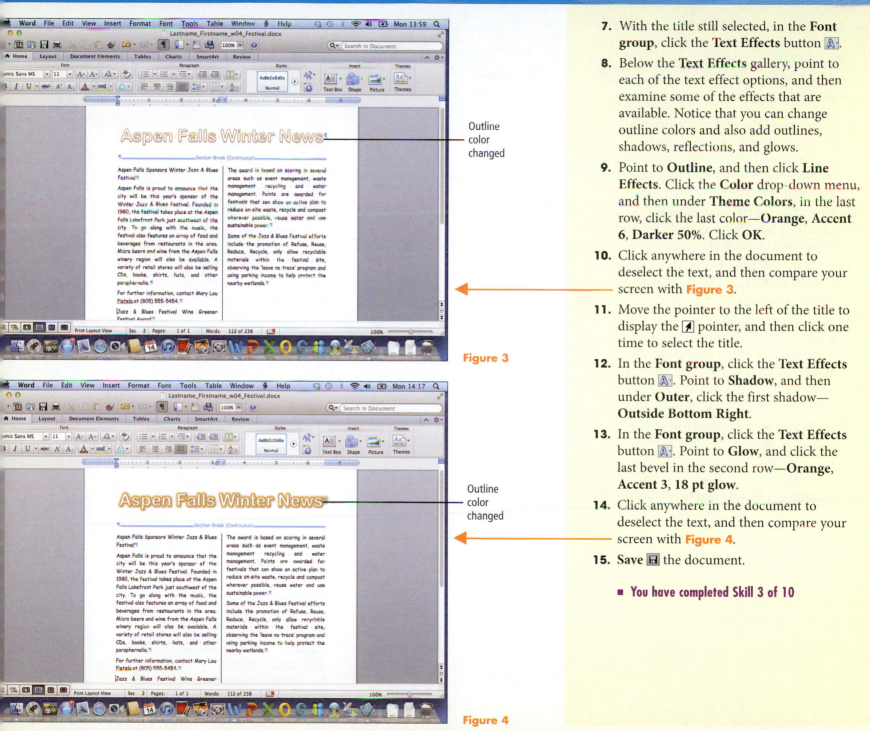

Figure 3

Outline color changed

Outline color changed

Figure 4

7. With the title still selected, in the **Font group**, click the **Text Effects** button.

8. Below the **Text Effects** gallery, point to each of the text effect options, and then examine some of the effects that are available. Notice that you can change outline colors and also add outlines, shadows, reflections, and glows.

9. Point to **Outline**, and then click **Line Effects**. Click the **Color** drop-down menu, and then under **Theme Colors**, in the last row, click the last color—**Orange, Accent 6, Darker 50%**. Click **OK**.

10. Click anywhere in the document to deselect the text, and then compare your screen with **Figure 3**.

11. Move the pointer to the left of the title to display the pointer, and then click one time to select the title.

12. In the **Font group**, click the **Text Effects** button. Point to **Shadow**, and then under **Outer**, click the first shadow— **Outside Bottom Right**.

13. In the **Font group**, click the **Text Effects** button. Point to **Glow**, and click the last bevel in the second row—**Orange, Accent 3, 18 pt glow**.

14. Click anywhere in the document to deselect the text, and then compare your screen with **Figure 4**.

15. **Save** the document.

■ **You have completed Skill 3 of 10**

▶ A *style* is a predefined set of formats that can be applied to text, a paragraph, a table cell, or a list.

▶ A *Quick Style* is a style that can be accessed from a Ribbon gallery of thumbnails.

1. At the top of the left column, move the pointer to the left of the subtitle that begins *Aspen Falls Sponsors* to display the ◢ pointer, and then drag down to select both lines of text.

2. On the **Home tab**, in the **Styles group**, click the **More Down arrow** [▼] to display the **Quick Styles** gallery.

3. From the displayed **Quick Styles** gallery click **Heading 2**, and then compare your screen with **Figure 1**.

4. With the text still selected, in the **Font group**, click the **Font Size arrow** [11 ▼], and then click **16**. In the **Paragraph group**, click the **Center Text** button [≡]. Click anywhere to deselect the title, and then compare your screen with **Figure 2**.

   The black square to the left of the subtitle indicates that it will always stay with the next paragraph.

■ **Continue to the next page to complete the skill** ➤

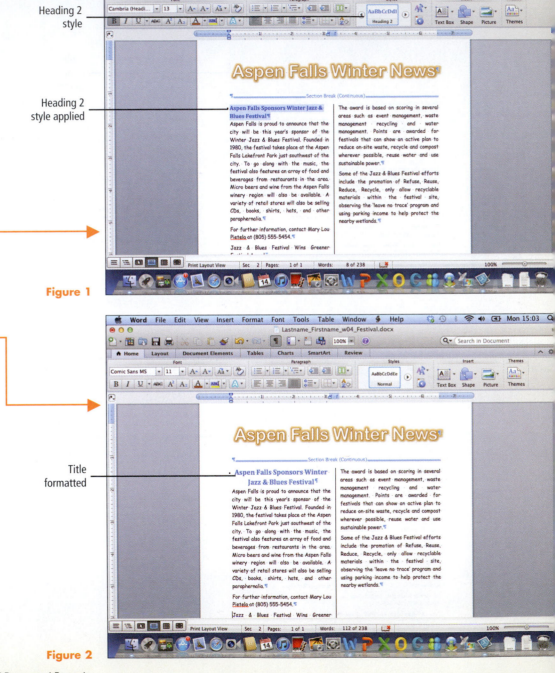

Heading 2 style

Heading 2 style applied

Figure 1

Title formatted

Figure 2

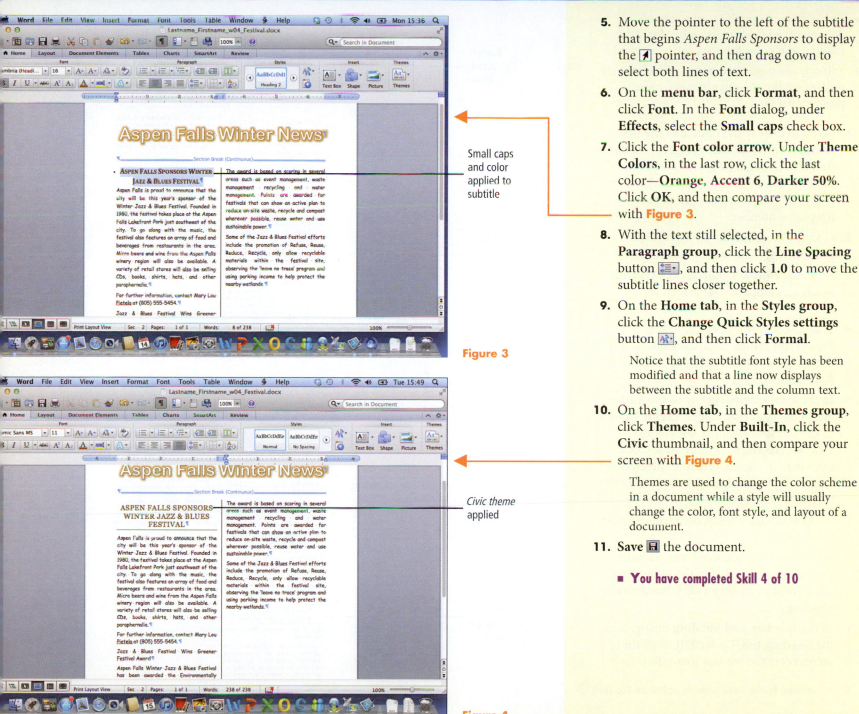

Small caps and color applied to subtitle

Figure 3

Civic theme applied

Figure 4

5. Move the pointer to the left of the subtitle that begins *Aspen Falls Sponsors* to display the ⬈ pointer, and then drag down to select both lines of text.

6. On the **menu bar**, click **Format**, and then click **Font**. In the **Font** dialog, under **Effects**, select the **Small caps** check box.

7. Click the **Font color arrow**. Under **Theme Colors**, in the last row, click the last color—**Orange**, **Accent 6**, **Darker 50%**. Click **OK**, and then compare your screen with **Figure 3**.

8. With the text still selected, in the **Paragraph group**, click the **Line Spacing** button 🔲▾, and then click **1.0** to move the subtitle lines closer together.

9. On the **Home tab**, in the **Styles group**, click the **Change Quick Styles settings** button 🔲▾, and then click **Formal**.

   Notice that the subtitle font style has been modified and that a line now displays between the subtitle and the column text.

10. On the **Home tab**, in the **Themes group**, click **Themes**. Under **Built-In**, click the **Civic** thumbnail, and then compare your screen with **Figure 4**.

    Themes are used to change the color scheme in a document while a style will usually change the color, font style, and layout of a document.

11. **Save** 🔲 the document.

■ **You have completed Skill 4 of 10**

▶ To make a paragraph stand out in a document, add a paragraph border. Add shading and color for even more impact.

▶ You can use page borders to frame flyers or posters, giving the documents a more professional look.

1. Scroll to display the middle of the first column. Select the last paragraph in the first article, beginning with *For further information*. Be sure to include the paragraph mark to the right of the telephone number.

2. On the **Home tab**, in the **Paragraph group**, click the **Borders button** .

3. From the **Borders** gallery, click **Outside**, and then compare your screen with **Figure 1**.

4. With the text still selected, in the **Paragraph group**, click the **Center Text** button . In the **Font group**, click the **Bold** button B.

5. In the **Font group**, click the **Font Color arrow** , and then under **Theme Colors**, in the last row, click the last color— **Orange**, **Accent 6**, **Darker 50%**. Click anywhere in the document to deselect the text, and then compare your screen with **Figure 2**.

   The font color matches the document title and subtitles.

6. Select all of the bordered text, including the paragraph mark. On the **menu bar**, click **Format**, and then click **Borders and Shading**.

7. In the **Borders and Shading** dialog, click the **Shading tab**. Under **Fill**, click the second color in the last row—**Tan**.

■ **Continue to the next page to complete the skill** ➤

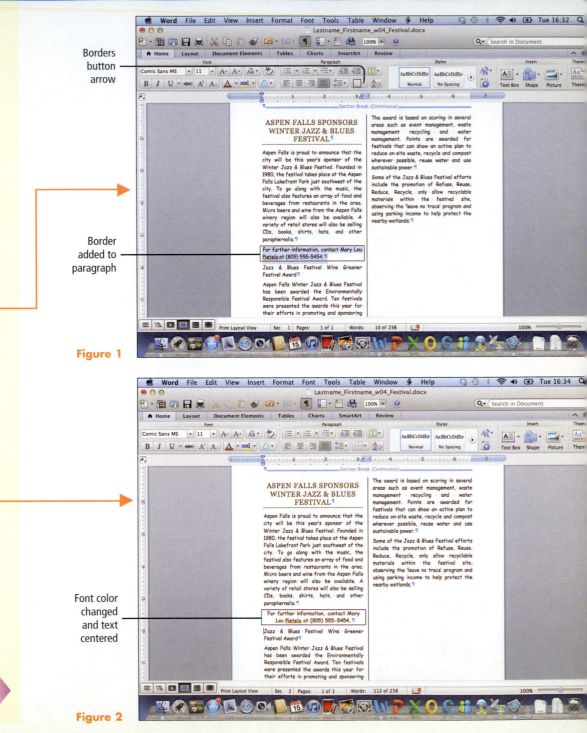

Borders button arrow

Border added to paragraph

Figure 1

Font color changed and text centered

Figure 2

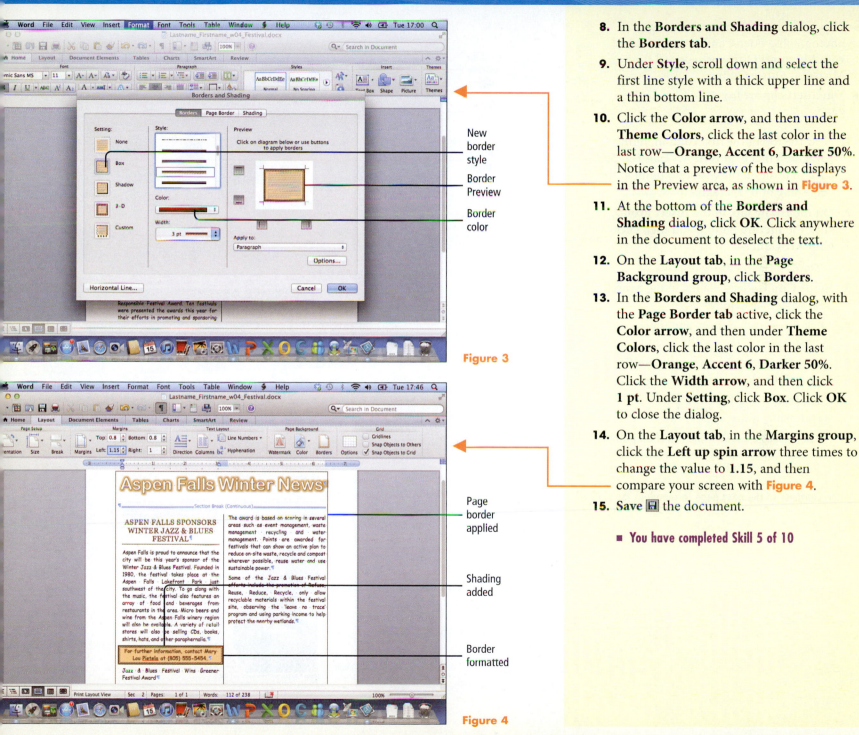

Figure 3

Figure 4

New border style

Border Preview

Border color

Page border applied

Shading added

Border formatted

8. In the **Borders and Shading** dialog, click the **Borders tab**.

9. Under **Style**, scroll down and select the first line style with a thick upper line and a thin bottom line.

10. Click the **Color arrow**, and then under **Theme Colors**, click the last color in the last row—**Orange, Accent 6, Darker 50%**. Notice that a preview of the box displays in the Preview area, as shown in **Figure 3**.

11. At the bottom of the **Borders and Shading** dialog, click **OK**. Click anywhere in the document to deselect the text.

12. On the **Layout tab**, in the **Page Background group**, click **Borders**.

13. In the **Borders and Shading** dialog, with the **Page Border tab** active, click the **Color arrow**, and then under **Theme Colors**, click the last color in the last row—**Orange, Accent 6, Darker 50%**. Click the **Width arrow**, and then click **1 pt**. Under **Setting**, click **Box**. Click **OK** to close the dialog.

14. On the **Layout tab**, in the **Margins group**, click the **Left up spin arrow** three times to change the value to **1.15**, and then compare your screen with **Figure 4**.

15. **Save** 💾 the document.

■ **You have completed Skill 5 of 10**

► *Clip art* is a set of images, drawings, photographs, videos, and sound included with Microsoft Office or accessed from Microsoft Office Online.

► You insert clip art from the Clip Art task pane.

1. Near the top of the first column, in the paragraph that begins *Aspen Falls is proud,* click to position the insertion point at the beginning of the paragraph.

2. On the **Home tab**, in the **Insert group**, click the **Picture** button, and then click **Clip Art Gallery**.

   The Clip Gallery dialog displays.

3. In the **Clip Gallery** dialog, in the **Search** box, type microphone

4. Click the **Search** button, and then compare your screen with **Figure 1**.

5. Locate the *microphone* image identified in **Figure 1**. Click to select the image.

6. Click **Insert**, and then compare your screen with **Figure 2**.

   The image is placed at the insertion point as an *inline* image—as if it were a character from the keyboard.

■ **Continue to the next page to complete the skill**

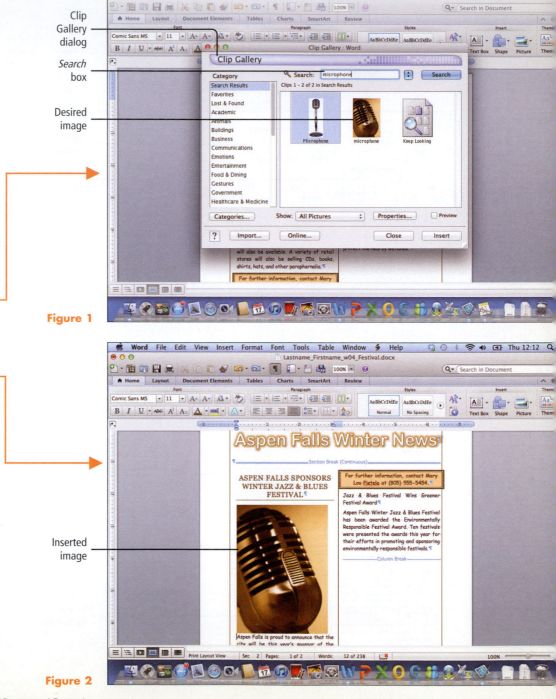

Clip Gallery dialog

Search box

Desired image

Figure 1

Inserted image

Figure 2

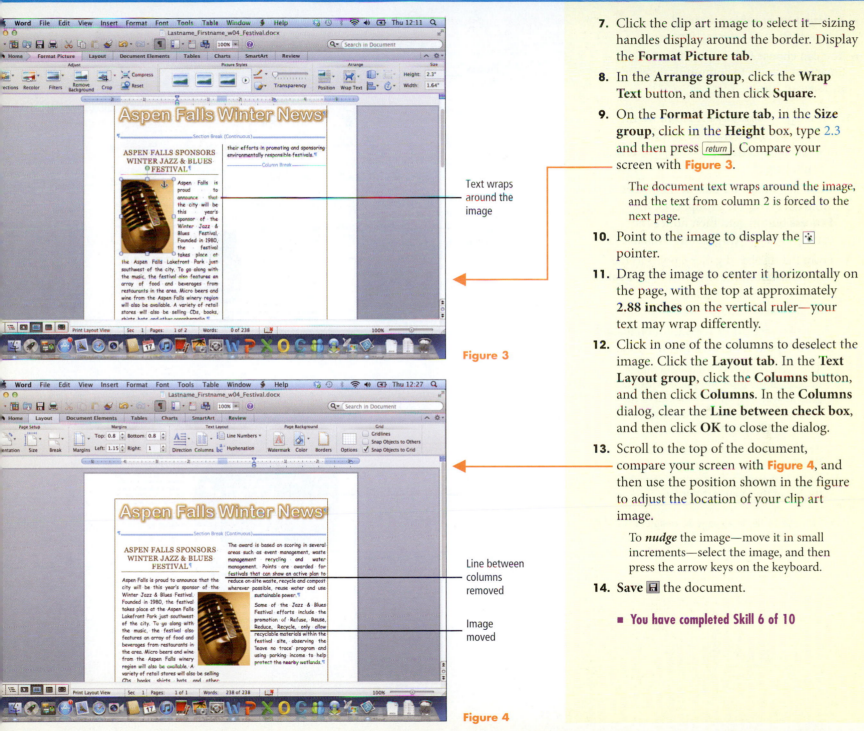

Figure 3

Figure 4

7. Click the clip art image to select it—sizing handles display around the border. Display the **Format Picture tab**.

8. In the **Arrange group**, click the **Wrap Text** button, and then click **Square**.

9. On the **Format Picture tab**, in the **Size group**, click in the **Height** box, type 2.3 and then press return. Compare your screen with **Figure 3**.

   The document text wraps around the image, and the text from column 2 is forced to the next page.

10. Point to the image to display the ⊕ pointer.

11. Drag the image to center it horizontally on the page, with the top at approximately **2.88 inches** on the vertical ruler—your text may wrap differently.

12. Click in one of the columns to deselect the image. Click the **Layout tab**. In the **Text Layout group**, click the **Columns** button, and then click **Columns**. In the **Columns** dialog, clear the **Line between check box**, and then click **OK** to close the dialog.

13. Scroll to the top of the document, compare your screen with **Figure 4**, and then use the position shown in the figure to adjust the location of your clip art image.

   To *nudge* the image—move it in small increments—select the image, and then press the arrow keys on the keyboard.

14. **Save** 🖫 the document.

   ■ **You have completed Skill 6 of 10**

► A **SmartArt graphic** is a visual representation of information.

► You can choose from many different SmartArt layouts to communicate your message or ideas.

1. Press [fn] + [command ⌘] + [←] to move the insertion point to the end of the document, and then press [return] to create a blank line.

2. Click the **SmartArt tab**. In the **Insert SmartArt Graphic group**, click the **Process** button, and then notice the variety of SmartArt graphics available.

3. From the displayed gallery, point to the second layout in the fifth row—**Vertical Process** (the exact location of this SmartArt may vary), as shown in **Figure 1**.

4. Click the **Vertical Process** thumbnail, and then compare your screen with **Figure 2**.

   The Vertical Process SmartArt graphic displays at the insertion point, with the graphic width equal to the width of the column. A contextual tab is added to the Ribbon—a Format tab.

   The SmartArt outline displays sizing handles, which consist of a series of dots, and a Text Pane button, which displays on the left of the SmartArt border.

■ **Continue to the next page to complete the skill**

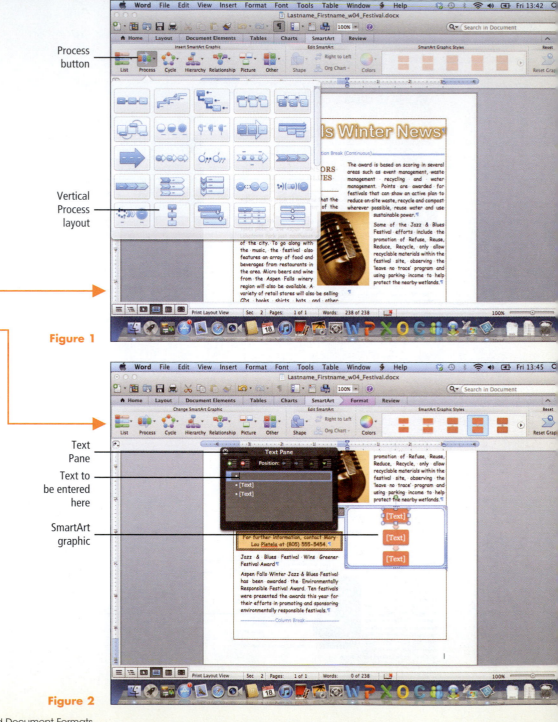

Process button

Vertical Process layout

Figure 1

Text Pane

Text to be entered here

SmartArt graphic

Figure 2

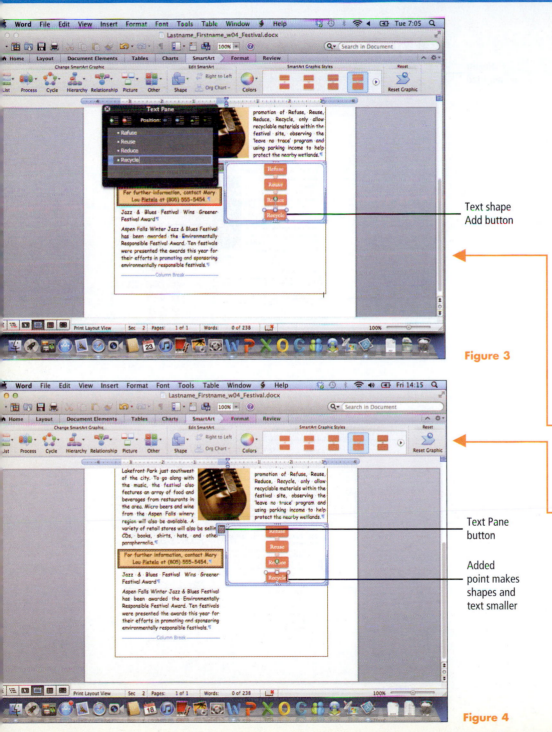

Text shape
Add button

Figure 3

Text Pane
button

Added
point makes
shapes and
text smaller

Figure 4

5. Click in the top [**Text**] shape, type Refuse and then notice that the shape resizes as you type. The font size also adjusts automatically.

   [Text] is *placeholder text*—reserved space in shapes into which you enter your own text. If no text is entered, the placeholder text will not print.

6. In the second shape, click the [**Text**] placeholder, and then type Reuse

   To move to the next [Text] shape, you must click in the shape—you cannot use [tab] to move from one shape to the next.

7. In the **Text Pane**, click in the third [**Text**] placeholder, and then type Reduce Notice that while you type in the bulleted list, the text also displays in the third SmartArt shape.

   To move to the next [Text] shape in the Text pane, you can also press [▲] or [▼].

8. In the **Text Pane**, click the **Text Shape Add** button ▦ to display another bullet point. Type Recycle and then compare your screen with **Figure 3**. Notice that the shapes and the text in the shapes became smaller when you added an item to the list.

9. **Close** ⊗ the **Text Pane**, and then compare your screen with **Figure 4**.

10. **Save** 🖫 the document.

   ■ **You have completed Skill 7 of 10**

► When you change the height or width of a SmartArt graphic, the shapes and the text will automatically adjust to fit the available space.

► In a SmartArt graphic, you can also format the text, the backgrounds, and the borders of the shapes.

1. Click the border of the SmartArt graphic to select it—be sure you select the outer border, not the border of one of the blue shapes. Click the **Format tab**.

2. In the **Size group**, click the **Height box up spin arrow** as necessary to increase the height of the graphic to **3 inches**. Compare your screen with **Figure 1**.

   When you change the height or width of a SmartArt graphic, the graphic width is not resized proportionally; however, the text font size increases to fit the new shape size.

3. Click anywhere on the border of the top shape—*Refuse*. Hold down shift then click the other three shapes to select all four shapes in the SmartArt graphic.

4. With all four shapes selected, in the **Size group**. Click the **Width box up spin arrow** as necessary to increase the width of the graphic to **2.5 inches**.

5. In the **Shape Styles group**, click the **Fill button arrow**. Under **Theme Colors**, click the last color in the last row—**Orange, Accent 6, Darker 50%**.

6. In the **Text Styles group**, click the **Text Fill button arrow** 🅰. Under **Theme Colors**, click the last color in the third row—**Orange, Accent 6, Lighter 60%**. Compare your screen with **Figure 2**.

■ **Continue to the next page to complete the skill** ➡

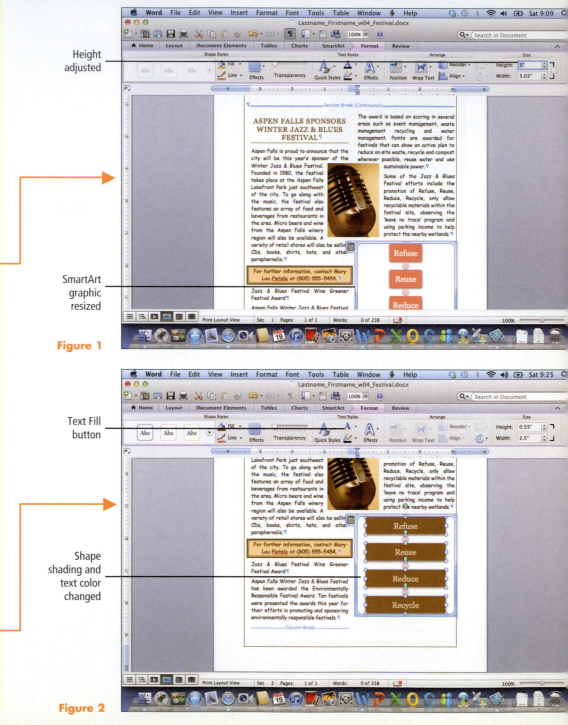

Height adjusted

SmartArt graphic resized

Figure 1

Text Fill button

Shape shading and text color changed

Figure 2

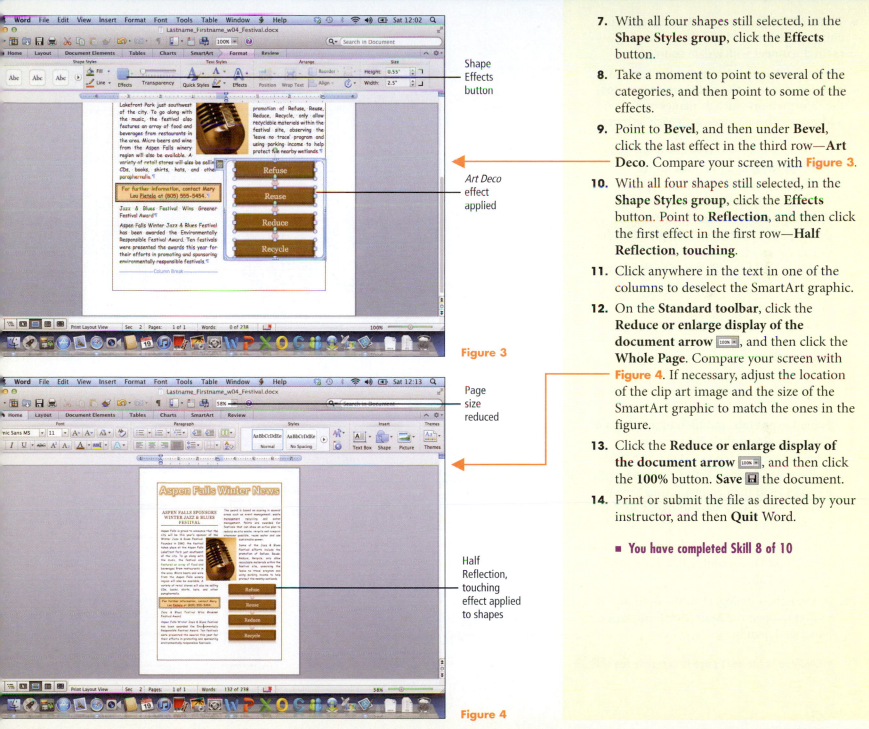

Shape
Effects
button

Art Deco
effect
applied

Figure 3

Page
size
reduced

Half
Reflection,
touching
effect applied
to shapes

Figure 4

7. With all four shapes still selected, in the **Shape Styles group**, click the **Effects** button.

8. Take a moment to point to several of the categories, and then point to some of the effects.

9. Point to **Bevel**, and then under **Bevel**, click the last effect in the third row—**Art Deco**. Compare your screen with **Figure 3**.

10. With all four shapes still selected, in the **Shape Styles group**, click the **Effects** button. Point to **Reflection**, and then click the first effect in the first row—**Half Reflection, touching**.

11. Click anywhere in the text in one of the columns to deselect the SmartArt graphic.

12. On the **Standard toolbar**, click the **Reduce or enlarge display of the document arrow** ⌷100%⌷, and then click the **Whole Page**. Compare your screen with **Figure 4**. If necessary, adjust the location of the clip art image and the size of the SmartArt graphic to match the ones in the figure.

13. Click the **Reduce or enlarge display of the document arrow** ⌷100%⌷, and then click the **100%** button. **Save** ⊟ the document.

14. Print or submit the file as directed by your instructor, and then **Quit** Word.

■ **You have completed Skill 8 of 10**

▶ The ***mail merge*** feature in Word is used to customize letters or labels by combining a main document with a data source.

▶ The ***main document*** contains the text that remains constant; the ***data source*** contains the information—such as names and addresses—that changes with each letter or label.

1. **Start** Word 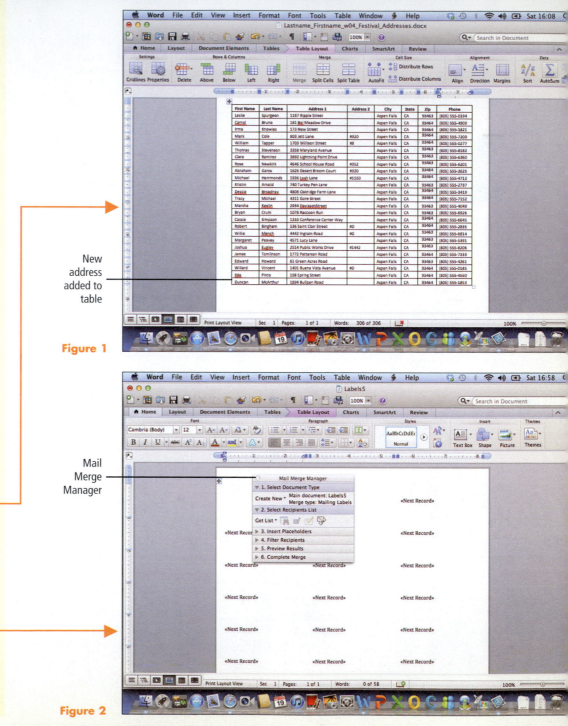. If a previous Word document displays, then Close ⬤ the document. **Open** the document **w04_ Festival_Addresses**, and then **Save** the document in your **Word Chapter 4** folder as Lastname_Firstname_w04_Festival_ Addresses Add the file name to the footer.

2. Take a moment to examine the table of names and addresses.

   This table will be the data source for the mailing labels you will create to use with the festival flyer you created earlier in this chapter.

3. Scroll to the bottom of the table. Click in the bottom row of the table. Click the **Table Layout tab**, and then in the **Rows & Columns group** click **Below**. Enter the information for Duncan McArthur 1894 Bullpen Road Aspen Falls CA 93464 (805) 555-1853 and then compare your screen with **Figure 1**. **Save** 💾, and then **Close** ⬤ the document.

4. On the **menu bar**, click **File** and then click **New Blank Document**. Click **Tools**, and then click **Labels**.

5. In the **Labels** dialog, click the **Mail Merge** button to open the **Mail Merge Manager** pane, as shown in **Figure 2**.

   ■ **Continue to the next page to complete the skill** ▶

New address added to table

Figure 1

Mail Merge Manager

Figure 2

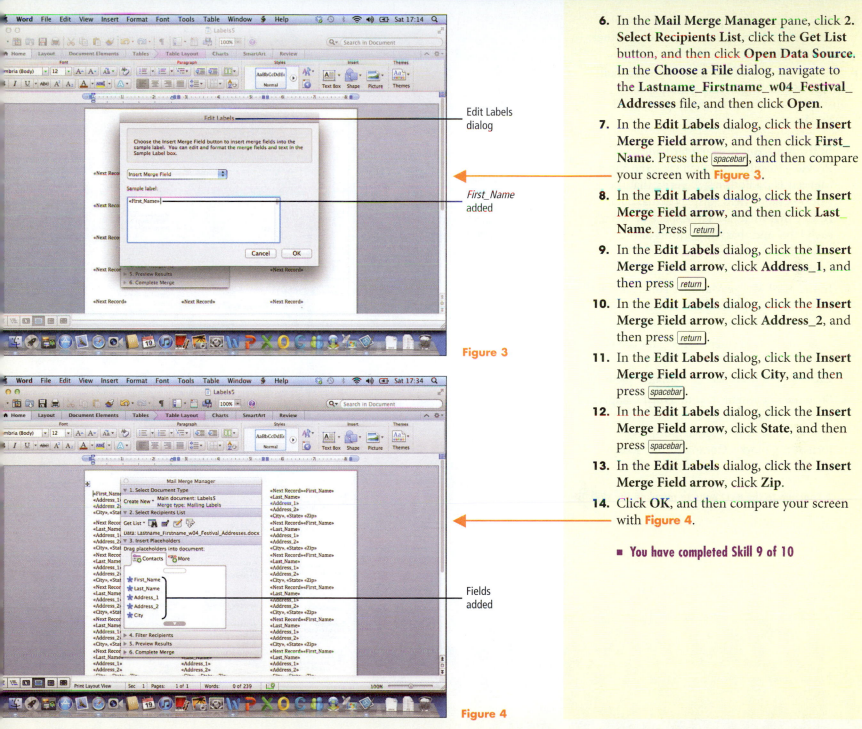

Edit Labels dialog

First_Name added

Figure 3

Fields added

Figure 4

6. In the **Mail Merge Manager** pane, click **2. Select Recipients List**, click the **Get List** button, and then click **Open Data Source**. In the **Choose a File** dialog, navigate to the **Lastname_Firstname_w04_Festival_ Addresses** file, and then click **Open**.

7. In the **Edit Labels** dialog, click the **Insert Merge Field arrow**, and then click **First_ Name**. Press the [spacebar], and then compare your screen with **Figure 3**.

8. In the **Edit Labels** dialog, click the **Insert Merge Field arrow**, and then click **Last_ Name**. Press [return].

9. In the **Edit Labels** dialog, click the **Insert Merge Field arrow**, click **Address_1**, and then press [return].

10. In the **Edit Labels** dialog, click the **Insert Merge Field arrow**, click **Address_2**, and then press [return].

11. In the **Edit Labels** dialog, click the **Insert Merge Field arrow**, click **City**, and then press [spacebar].

12. In the **Edit Labels** dialog, click the **Insert Merge Field arrow**, click **State**, and then press [spacebar].

13. In the **Edit Labels** dialog, click the **Insert Merge Field arrow**, click **Zip**.

14. Click **OK**, and then compare your screen with **Figure 4**.

■ **You have completed Skill 9 of 10**

► It is good practice to preview your labels before printing them so you can see whether formatting changes are necessary.

► You can check the final results of your mail merge by printing first to plain paper instead of the more expensive preprinted label sheets.

1. In the **Mail Merge Manager** pane, click **5. Preview Results**, and then click the **View Merged Data** button. Verify that the Address Block fields display actual data. Notice that there is a large space between each label and that the bottoms of the labels that have two address lines, as shown in **Figure 1**.

2. In the **Mail Merge Manager** pane, click **6. Complete Merge**, and then verify that **All** is selected in the pull-down menu.

   Step 6 allows the user to select only certain fields to merge.

3. **Close** the **Mail Merge Manager** pane.

4. **Save** the document in your **Word Chapter 4** folder as Lastname_Firstname_w04_Festival_Labels If necessary, display formatting marks. Compare your screen with **Figure 2**.

■ **Continue to the next page to complete the skill**

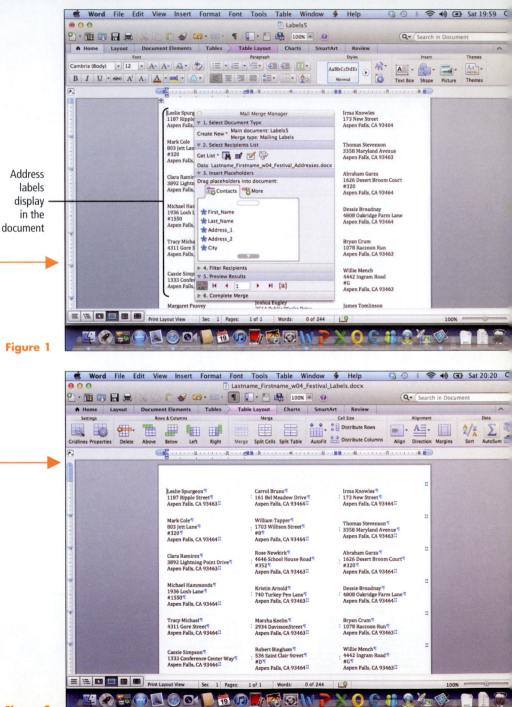

Address labels display in the document

Figure 1

Figure 2

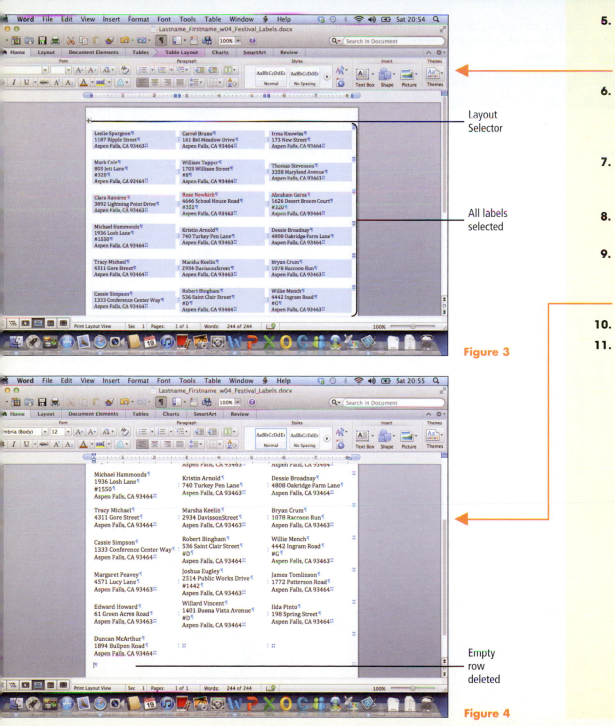

Layout Selector

All labels selected

Figure 3

Empty row deleted

Figure 4

5. Move the mouse up to the top left of the page until the ☒ pointer displays. Click the **Layout Selector** ⊞, and then compare your screen with **Figure 3**.

6. On the **Home tab**, in the **Font group**, click the **Font down arrow** [Calibri (Body) ▾], and then from the displayed list click **Cambria**.

7. On the **Home tab**, in the **Font group**, click the **Font Size down arrow** [11 ▾], and then from the displayed list click **14**.

8. Scroll to the bottom of the document and click anywhere in the bottom row.

9. Display the **Table Layout tab**, in the **Rows & Columns group**, click the **Delete** button, and then click **Delete Rows**. Compare your screen with **Figure 4**.

10. **Save** 🖫 the document.

11. Print or submit the files as directed by your instructor. **Quit** Word.

Done! You have completed Skill 10 of 10, and your document is complete!

More Skills

The following More Skills are located at **www.pearsonhighered.com/skills**. Please note that only More Skills that can be performed on a Macintosh computer are included in this section; therefore, the numbering is not always sequential.

More Skills 11 Create Resumes from Templates

Templates are predesigned document structures that enable you to create a new document quickly. Word templates are available for many document types, including memos, letters, business cards, and fax cover sheets. Several different resumes templates are also available.

In More Skills 11, you will open a resumes template, and then complete the resume.

To begin, open your web browser, navigate to www.pearsonhighered.com/skills, locate the name of your textbook, and then follow the instructions on the website.

Key Terms

Clip art 136

Column break 128

Data source 142

Mail merge 142

Main document 142

Nudge 137

Placeholder text 139

Quick Style 132

Section 126

Section break 126

SmartArt graphic 138

Style 132

Text effect 130

Online Help Skills

1. **Start** Safari 🧭 or another web browser. In the **address bar**, type microsoft.com/ mac/how-to and then press ⟨return⟩ to display the home page for Microsoft Office.

2. Under **Product Help**, click **Word 2011**.

3. Under **Word Help**, click **Mass Mailings**.

4. Under **Mass Mailings**, click **Create a data source for a mail merge**.

5. Under **Create a data source for a mail merge**, click **Create a data source in Word**, and then compare your screen with **Figure 1**.

6. Review the content within both links to answer the following question: How do you create a Word document data source for a mail merge?

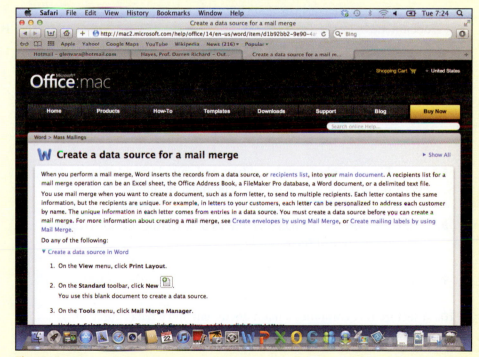

Figure 1

Matching

Match each term in the second column with its correct definition in the first column by writing the letter of the term on the blank line in front of the correct definition.

____ **1.** In mail merge, the command used to modify all labels based on changes made to the original label.

____ **2.** In the Columns gallery, the command that displays the Columns dialog.

____ **3.** A style displayed on the Ribbon.

____ **4.** A set of decorative formats that make text stand out in a document.

____ **5.** A portion of a document that can be formatted differently from the rest of the document.

____ **6.** A format that makes a paragraph stand out from the rest of the text.

____ **7.** A set of images, photographs, videos, and sound provided by Microsoft that is available on your computer or online.

____ **8.** To move an object in small increments by selecting the object, and then pressing one of the arrow keys.

____ **9.** Text that reserves space in a SmartArt shape but does not print.

____ **10.** A feature that combines a main document and a data source to create customized letters or tables.

A Border

B Clip art

C Mail merge

D Columns

E Nudge

F Placeholder

G Quick Style

H Section

I Text effects

J Update Labels

Multiple Choice

Choose the correct answer.

1. The default width assigned to columns.
   A. Proportional
   B. Equal
   C. Unbalanced

2. A predefined set of text formats that can be applied from the Ribbon.
   A. Quick Style
   B. SmartArt
   C. Clip art

3. A picture is inserted into a document using this format.
   A. Centered
   B. Text wrapped
   C. Inline

4. Moves the text to the right of the insertion point to the top of the next column.
   A. Page break
   B. Column break
   C. Continuous break

5. A type of break that is used to create a new section that can be formatted differently from the rest of the document.
   A. Page
   B. Column
   C. Continuous

6. To change the color of the background in a paragraph, add this to the text background.
   A. Shading
   B. A border
   C. Text emphasis

7. Reserved spaces in shapes into which you enter your own text.
   A. Text effects
   B. Placeholder text
   C. Data sources

8. A graphic visual representation of information.
   A. Text effects
   B. Clip art
   C. SmartArt

9. Used by a mail merge document, this file contains information such as names and addresses.
   A. Data source
   B. Main document
   C. Merge document

10. In a mail merge document, this document contains the text that remains constant.
    A. Data source
    B. Main document
    C. Merge document

Topics for Discussion

1. In this chapter, you practiced inserting a clip art image in a document. When do you think clip art images are most appropriate, and in what kind of documents might clip art images be inappropriate? If you had to create a set of rules for using clip art in a document, what would the top three rules be?

2. In this chapter, you used the mail merge feature in Word to create mailing labels. With mail merge, you can also insert one field at a time—and the fields do not have to be just names and addresses. Can you think of any situations where you might want to insert fields in a letter or another document?

Skill Check

To complete this document, you will need the following files:

- w04_Cars
- w04_Cars_Judges

You will save your documents as:

- Lastname_Firstname_w04_Cars
- Lastname_Firstname_w04_Cars_Labels

1. **Start** Word, and open **w04_Cars**. **Save** the document in your **Word Chapter 4** folder as Lastname_Firstname_w04_Cars Add the file name to the footer.

2. Locate the paragraph *This Year's Show,* and then select the document text from that point to the end of the document. On the **Home tab**, in the **Paragraph group,** click **Justify Text**. On the **Layout tab**, in the **Text Layout group**, click the **Columns** button, and then click **Two**.

3. Position the insertion point at the beginning of the paragraph *Featured Cars*. On the **Layout tab**, in the **Page Setup group**, click the **Break** button, and then click **Column**. Compare your screen with **Figure 1**.

4. Select the document title. On the **Home tab**, in the **Styles group**, click the **More** button, and then click **Title**.

5. In the **Font group**, click the **Text Effects** button, and then in the fourth row of the gallery, click the first thumbnail—**Gradient Fill Blue**, **Accent 1**, **Outline–White**, **Glow–Accent 2**. **Center** the title, and then change the **Font Size** to 42 pt.

6. Select the subtitle *This Year's Show*. On the **menu bar**, click **Format**, and then click **Font**. Under **Font style**, click **Bold**. Under **Size**, click **16**. Click the **Font Color arrow**, and then under **Theme Colors**, click the sixth color in the first row—**Red**, **Accent 2**. Under **Effects**, select the **Small caps** check box, and then click **OK**. In the **Paragraph group**, click the **Center Text** button.

7. Click the **Format Painter** button one time, and then select the second subtitle—*Featured Cars*. Compare your screen with **Figure 2**.

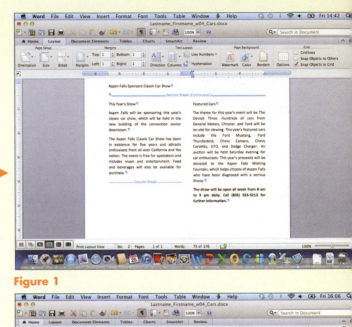

Figure 1

Figure 2

- Continue to the next page to complete this Skill Check

8. Click anywhere in the document. On the **Home tab**, in the **Insert group**, click the **Picture** button, and then click **Clip Art Gallery**.

9. In the **Clip Gallery** dialog, in the **Search for** box, type road and then click **Search**. Click the image shown in **Figure 3** (or a similar image if this one is not available). Click **Insert**. Select the image. On the **Format Picture tab**, in the **Arrange group**, click the **Wrap Text** button, and then click **Tight**. On the **Format Picture tab**, in the **Size group**, change the **Width** to 2.5". Move the image to the position shown in **Figure 3**.

10. Select the last paragraph in the document. On the **menu bar**, click **Format**, and then click **Borders and Shading**. Under **Setting**, click **Box**. Click the **Shading tab**. Under **Fill**, click the second color in the last row—**Tan**. Click **OK**.

11. Click anywhere in the document. On the **SmartArt tab**, in the **Insert SmartArt Graphics group**, click **Relationship**, click the **Funnel** layout—the third layout in the first row.

12. For the four bullets, type Chevy and Chrysler and Ford and Classic Cars and then **Close** the Text Pane. Click the border of the SmartArt image. On the **Format tab**, in the **Arrange group**, click the **Arrange** button. Click the **Position** button, and then under **With Text Wrapping**, in the third row, click the second button. Click the **Size** button, and decrease the **Height** to 1.6".

13. On the **Format tab**, in the **Shape Styles group**, click the **Effects** button, point to **Shadow**, and then click the first style under **Outer—Outside Bottom Right**. Deselect the SmartArt graphic, and then compare your document with **Figure 3**. **Save** and **Exit** Word.

14. **Start** Word with a blank document. On the **menu bar**, click **Tools**, and then click **Labels**. In the **Labels** dialog, under **Label**, make sure that **Avery standard**, **5160** is selected. Click **Mail Merge**. Click **Get List**, and then click **Open Data Source**. Locate and open **w04_Cars_Judges**.

15. In the **Edit Labels** dialog, click the **Insert Merge Field arrow**, and then add all name and address fields. Click **OK**.

16. Click **5. Preview Results**, click the **View Merged Data** button 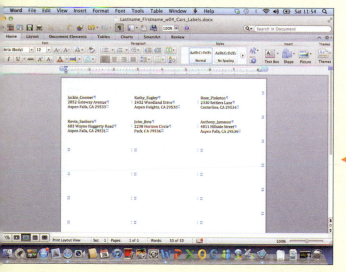, and then **Close** the **Mail Merge Manager**. Delete the last row in the table. **Save** the document in your **Word Chapter 4** folder as Lastname_Firstname_w04_Cars_Labels and add the file name to the footer. Compare your document with **Figure 4**.

17. **Save** and then submit your documents as directed. **Quit** Word but do not save changes to any other documents.

Done! You have completed the Skill Check

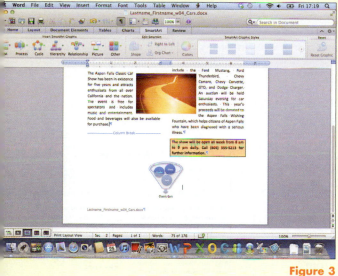

Figure 3

Figure 4

Assess Your Skills 1

To complete this document, you will need the following file:

- w04_Cruises

You will save your document as:

- Lastname_Firstname_w04_Cruises

1. **Start** Word. Locate and open **w04_Cruises**, save it in your **Word Chapter 4** folder as Lastname_Firstname_w04_Cruises and then add the file name to the footer. Select the title *Aspen Lake Cruises*—including the paragraph mark—and then on the **Home tab**, apply the **Intense Quote** Quick Style.

2. With the title still selected, change the title font size to **36** points. Apply the **Gradient Fill – Blue**, **Accent 1** text effect—the fourth effect in the third row. Then apply an **Outside Bottom Left** text effect shadow—under **Outer**, the third effect in the first row.

3. Starting with the *Aspen Lake Nature Cruise* subtitle, select all of the text to the end of the document, and then change it to a two-column format. **Justify** the two-column text. Display the **Columns** dialog, and then change the **Spacing** between the columns to **0.3"**. At the left side of the *Valentine's Day Cruise!* subtitle, insert a column break.

4. Select the *Aspen Lake Nature Cruise* subtitle, and then apply **Bold**, **Italic**, and **Center** alignment. Change the font size to **16** points, the font color to **Blue**, **Accent 1**, and then apply the **Small caps** effect.

5. Using the **Format Painter** tool, copy the formatting for the subtitle you just formatted and apply the formatting to the *Valentine's Day Cruise!* subtitle.

6. Position the insertion point at the beginning of the last paragraph, which begins *Book online or call*. Use the **Clip Gallery** dialog to search the Clip Art media type for skyscape and then insert the image shown in **Figure 1**. If that clip art image is not available, find a similar image.

7. Change the width of the clip art image to **3"**. Change the **Wrap Text** to **Top and Bottom**, and then center the image horizontally in the column, as shown in **Figure 1**.

8. At the bottom of the first column, select the last paragraph, including the paragraph mark. Add an **Outside Border** to the paragraph. Display the **Borders and Shading** dialog. Change the border width to **1.5 pt**, the border color to **Dark Blue**, **Text 2**, and the shading fill to **Pale Blue**—the sixth color in the last row.

9. Add a **Box** style page border that is **0.5 pt** wide, with a **Color** of **Dark Blue**, **Text 2**.

10. Compare your document with **Figure 1**. **Save** your document, and then submit it as directed.

Done! You have completed Assess Your Skills 1

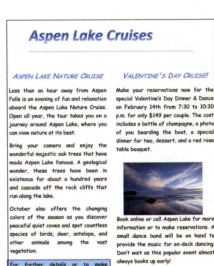

Figure 1

Assess Your Skills 3 and 4 can be found at **www.pearsonhighered.com/skills**.

Assess Your Skills 2

To complete this document, you will need the following files:

- w04_Competition
- w04_Competition_Addresses

You will save your documents as:

- Lastname_Firstname_w04_Competition
- Lastname_Firstname_w04_Competition_Labels

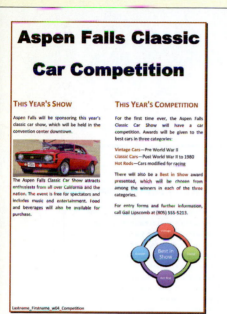

Lastname_Firstname_w04_Competition

Lastname_Firstname_w04_Competition_Labels

Figure 1

1. **Start** Word. Locate and open **w04_Competition**, save it in your **Word Chapter 4** folder as Lastname_Firstname_w04_Competition and then add the file name to the footer.

2. Select the document title. Change the title text to **Arial Black**, **42** points, and **Center** the text. Change the *title* **Line Spacing** to **1.0**, and the **Spacing After** to **0 pt**. With the title still selected, apply the **Outside Bottom Right** text effect—the first effect in the first row, in **Shadow**, under **Outer**. Apply an **Orange, Accent 2, 8 pt Glow** text effect—the last Glow effect in the first row.

3. Move to the end of the document. Insert a **Cycle** SmartArt graphic using the **Radial Cycle** layout—the fourth style in the second row. In the center circle, type Best in Show

4. In the **Text Pane**, fill in the empty bullet points with the following text:

   Vintage
   Classic
   Hot Rod
   Custom

5. **Close** the Text pane. Change the SmartArt **Height** to **2.3"** and the **Width** to **3.5"**. On the **Format tab**, apply the **Perspective Above** SmartArt Style—the first style in the second row under Perspective, in 3-D Rotation.

6. With the SmartArt graphic still selected, **Change Colors** to **Colorful–Accent Colors**—the first style under Colorful.

7. Insert a **Shadow** page border with the **Orange**, **Accent 6**, **Darker 50%** color and a width of **3 pt**. **Save** your document, and then **Exit** Word.

8. Create a new blank document. Start the mail merge process to create **Labels** using **Avery US Letter**, **Product number 5160**. Use the **w04_Competition_Addresses** document as the data source. Add an **Address Block**, and accept all address block defaults, and then **Update Labels** and preview the results. Merge all the labels into a single document. Delete the two bottom rows of the table.

9. **Save** the mail merge document in your **Word Chapter 4** folder as Lastname_Firstname_w04_Competition_Labels and then add the file name to the footer. Compare your completed documents with **Figure 1**. **Quit** Word—do not save the original mail merge document. Print or submit your documents as directed.

Done! You have completed Assess Your Skills 2

Assess Your Skills Visually

To complete this document, you will need the following file:

- w04_Heritage_Days

You will save your document as:

- Lastname_Firstname_w04_Heritage_Days

Start Word, and open **w04_Heritage_Days**. Create a flyer as shown in **Figure 1**. **Save** the file as Lastname_Firstname_w04_Heritage_Days in your **Word Chapter 4** folder.

To complete this document, apply the **Title** Quick Style, with a font size of **26 pt**. Break the column as indicated. In the bordered text, apply the **Dark Blue, Text 2** text effect and border colors and **Pale Blue** shading. Use the same border color for the page border. Set all border widths to **3 pt**. Insert the **Clip Art** image shown in **Figure 1** using windmills as the search term, and change its **Width** to **2"**—use a substitute if this image is not available.

For the subtitles, use an **18**-point font size, **Small caps,** and **Center** the titles. Use the same color you used for the borders. For the SmartArt graphic, in the **Relationship** category, apply the **Converging Radial** layout. Adjust the graphic to **6.5"** wide and **3"** high, and then apply the **Shadow, Outer, Outside Bottom Right** effect. Insert the file name in the footer, and then print or submit it electronically as directed.

Done! You have completed Assess Your Skills Visually

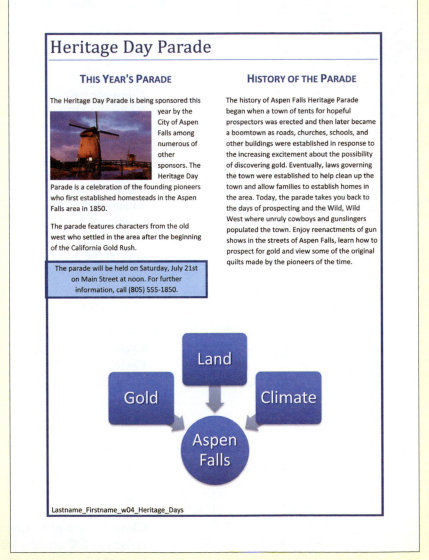

Figure 1

Skills in Context

To complete this document, you will need the following file:

- New blank Word document

You will save your document as:

- Lastname_Firstname_w04_Attractions

Create a flyer about the attractions around Aspen Falls. Use the web to research northern California for ideas—you could research attractions such as sailing, nature trails, bird watching, waterfalls, wineries, and so on. The flyer should have a formatted title and a subtitle, and then two-column text describing the area's attractions. Your completed document should include a page border, a paragraph or paragraphs with a paragraph border and shading, a clip art image, and a SmartArt graphic of your choice. You can include a picture if you would like to do so.

Save the document as Lastname_Firstname_w04_Attractions Insert the file name in the footer, and be sure to check the entire document for grammar and spelling. Print or submit the file electronically as directed.

Done! You have completed Skills in Context

Skills and You

To complete this document, you will need the following file:

- New blank Word document

You will save your document as:

- Lastname_Firstname_w04_Family

Using the skills you have practiced in this chapter, create a flyer to send to family members about family events coming up during the next year. The flyer should have a formatted title and a subtitle, and then two-column text describing the various events. Your completed document should include a page border, a paragraph with a paragraph border and shading, a clip art image, and a SmartArt graphic of your choice.

Save the document as Lastname_Firstname_w04_Family Check the entire document for grammar and spelling. Print or submit the file electronically as directed.

Done! You have completed Skills and You

CHAPTER 1

Create Workbooks with Excel 2011

▶ Microsoft Office Excel 2011 is used worldwide to create workbooks and to analyze data that is organized into columns and rows.

▶ After data is entered into Excel, you can perform calculations on the numerical data and analyze the data to make informed decisions.

▶ When you make changes to one or more number values, you can immediately see the effect of those changes in totals and charts that rely on those values.

▶ An Excel workbook can contain a large amount of data—up to 16,384 columns and 1,048,576 rows.

▶ The basic skills you need to work efficiently with Excel include entering and formatting data and navigating within Excel.

▶ When planning your worksheet, think about what information will form the rows and what information will form the columns. Generally, rows are used to list the items and columns to group or describe the items in the list.

© Conchala | Dreamstime.com

Aspen Falls City Hall

In this chapter, you will assist Amado Pettinelli, Outdoor Recreation Supervisor, to create an Excel workbook that will display the bike rentals at the various locations in the Aspen Lake Recreation Area. In this project, you will create a new Excel workbook and enter data that shows how many bikes are rented by children and adults at different locations in city parks. You will format the data, construct formulas, and insert functions. You will calculate the percentage of bikes rented by adults at each of the locations. To complete the workbook, you will check the spelling in the workbook and create a footer.

Time to complete all
10 skills – 60 to 90 minutes

Student data file needed for this chapter:

New blank Excel workbook

You will save your spreadsheet as:

Lastname_Firstname_e01_Bikes

Outcome

Using the skills in this chapter, you will be able to work with Excel spreadsheets like this:

SKILLS

Skills 1-10 Training

At the end of this chapter you will be able to:

Skill 1 Create and Save New Workbooks

Skill 2 Enter Worksheet Data and Merge and Center Titles

Skill 3 Construct Addition and Subtraction Formulas

Skill 4 Construct Multiplication and Division Formulas

Skill 5 Adjust Column Widths and Apply Cell Styles

Skill 6 Use the SUM Function

Skill 7 Copy Formulas and Functions Using the Fill Handle

Skill 8 Format, Edit, and Check the Spelling of Data

Skill 9 Create Footers and Change Page Settings

Skill 10 Display and Print Formulas and Scale Worksheets for Printing

MORE SKILLS

Skill 11 Create New Workbooks from Templates

Skill 12 Use Range Names in Formulas

Skill 13 Change Themes

Skill 14 Manage Document Properties

	A	B	C	D	E	F	G	H
1			Aspen Falls Parks and Recreation					
2			Bike Rentals at Aspen Lake Recreation Area					
3	Location	Children	Adult	Total	Difference	Rental Fee	Total Fees	
4	North	139	51	190	88	$ 6	$ 1,140	
5	South	108	60	168	48	7	1,176	
6	Central	153	93	246	60	7	1,722	
7	East	175	82	257	93	10	2,570	
8	West	246	170	416	76	7	2,912	
9	Total	821	456	1277			$ 9,520	
10								
11								
12	Percent of Adult Bikes Rented							
13	North	26.8%						
14	South	35.7%						
15	Central	37.8%						
16	East	31.9%						
17	West	40.9%						
18								
19								
20								

Bike Rentals

Normal View   Ready

► In Excel you can begin with a template or a new blank *workbook*—a file that you can use to organize various kinds of related information. A workbook contains *worksheets*, also called *spreadsheets*—the primary documents that you use in Excel to store and work with data.

► The worksheet forms a grid of vertical columns and horizontal rows. The small box where one column and one row meet is a cell.

1. On the **Dock,** click the **Microsoft Excel** icon 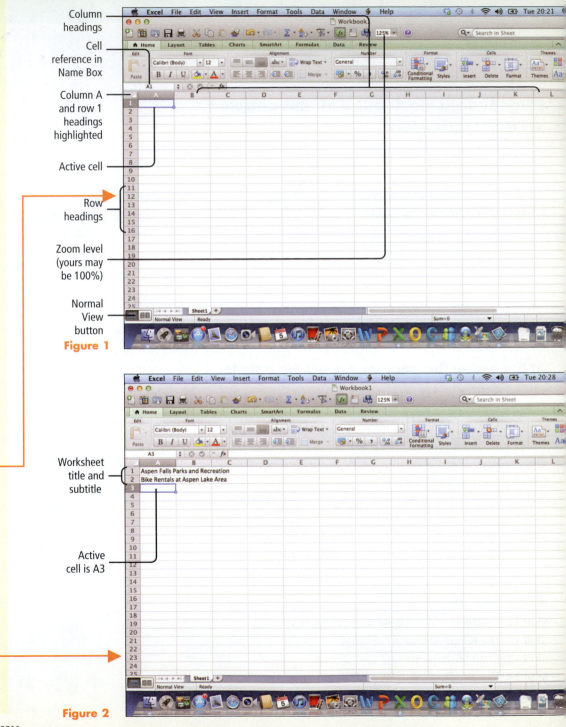. In the displayed **Excel Workbook Gallery** dialog, make sure that Excel Workbook is selected, and then click **Choose**. In the lower left, if necessary, click the **Normal View** button. On the **Standard toolbar,** notice the zoom—the magnification level.

   Your zoom level should be 100%, but most figures in this chapter are zoomed to 125%.

2. Verify the cell in the upper left corner is the *active cell*—the cell outlined in blue in which data is entered when you begin typing. Notice that columns have alphabetical headings across the top, and rows have numerical headings down the left side, as shown in **Figure 1**.

   When a cell is active, the headings for the column and row in which the cell is located are highlighted. The column letter and row number that identify a cell is the *cell address*, also called the *cell reference*.

3. In cell **A1,** type Aspen Falls Parks and Recreation and then press [return] to store the entry.

4. In cell **A2,** type Bike Rentals at Aspen Lake Area and then press [return]. Compare your screen with **Figure 2**.

■ **Continue to the next page to complete the skill**

Column headings

Cell reference in Name Box

Column A and row 1 headings highlighted

Active cell

Row headings

Zoom level (yours may be 100%)

Normal View button

Figure 1

Worksheet title and subtitle

Active cell is A3

Figure 2

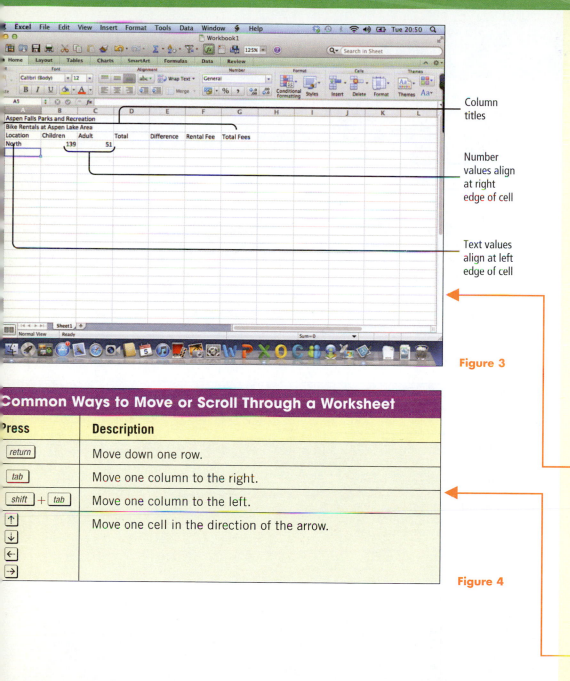

Column titles

Number values align at right edge of cell

Text values align at left edge of cell

Figure 3

Common Ways to Move or Scroll Through a Worksheet

Press	Description
return	Move down one row.
tab	Move one column to the right.
shift + tab	Move one column to the left.
↑ ↓ ← →	Move one cell in the direction of the arrow.

Figure 4

5. Type Location and press tab to make the cell to the right—**B3**—active.

6. With cell **B3** the active cell, type the following titles, pressing tab between each title:

   Children
   Adult
   Total
   Difference
   Rental Fee
   Total Fees

   Titles above columns help readers understand the data.

   To correct typing errors, click a cell and retype the data—the new typing will replace the existing data.

7. Click cell **A4,** type North and then press tab. Type 139 and press tab. Type 51 and then press return.

   Data in a cell is called a *value*. You can have a *text value* (*North*) or a *number value* (*139*). A text value is also referred to as a *label*.

8. Notice that the text values align at the left cell edge, and number values align at the right cell edge, as shown in **Figure 3**.

9. On the **Standard toolbar,** click **Save** 🖫. In the **Save As** dialog, navigate to the location where you are saving your files. Click **New Folder,** type Excel Chapter 1 and then click **Create**. In the **Save As** box, using your own name, name the workbook Lastname_Firstname_e01_Bikes and then press return.

   Common methods to move between cells in an Excel worksheet are summarized in the table in **Figure 4**.

- **You have completed Skill 1 of 10**

► Multiple cells can be selected by dragging so that the selection can be edited, formatted, copied, or moved.

1. In cell **A5,** type Soutth and press `tab`. (You will correct the spelling in Skill 8.)

2. In cell **B5,** type 108 and press `tab`. In cell **C5,** type 60 and press `return`.

3. In row 6 and row 7, enter the following data:

   | Easst | 75 | 32 |
   | West | 246 | 170 |

4. In cell **A8,** type Total and press `return`. Compare your screen with **Figure 1**.

5. Click cell **B1,** type Worksheet and press `return`. Notice that the text in cell A1 is **truncated**—cut off.

   When text is too long to fit in a cell and the cell to the right of it contains data, the text will be truncated.

6. Click cell **A1,** and then above column D, locate the **formula bar**—a bar below the Ribbon that displays the value contained in the active cell and is used to enter or edit values or formulas. Compare your screen with **Figure 2**.

   Data displayed in a cell is the **displayed value**. Data displayed in the formula bar is the **underlying value**. Displayed values often do not match their underlying values.

7. On the **Standard toolbar,** click the **Undo** button to remove the text in cell B1. Notice that the text in cell A1 now overlaps the cells to the right because those cells are empty.

   ■ **Continue to the next page to complete the skill**

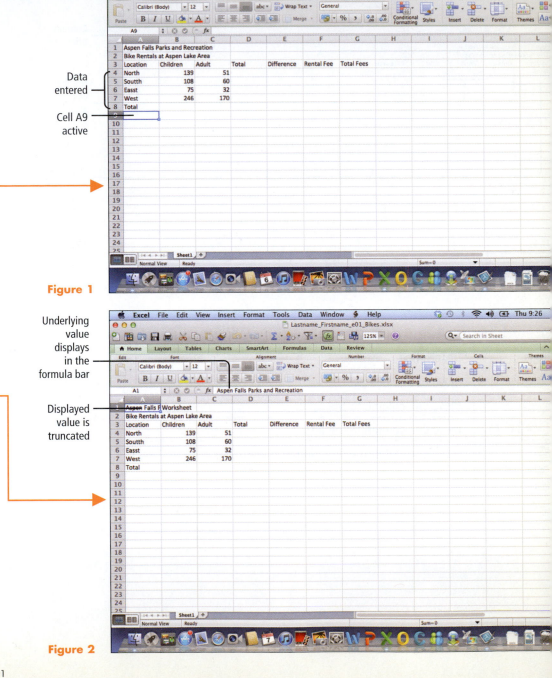

Data entered

Cell A9 active

Figure 1

Underlying value displays in the formula bar

Displayed value is truncated

Figure 2

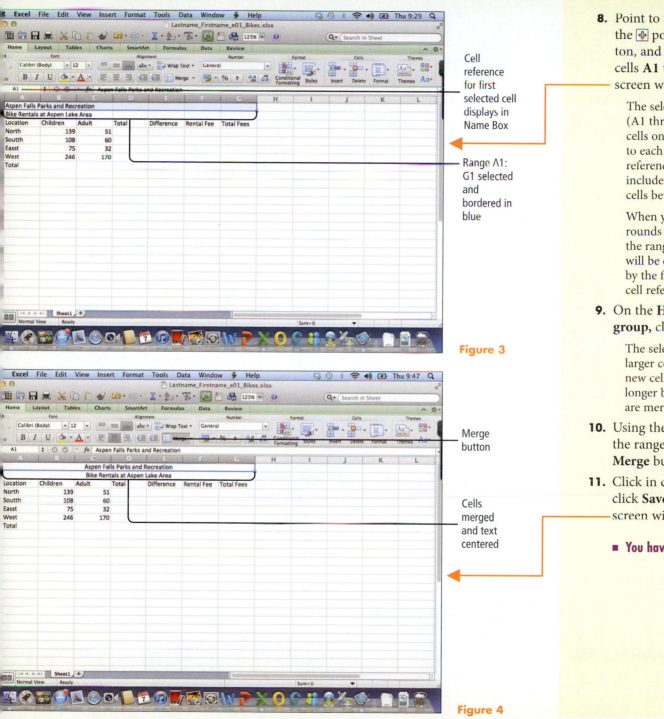

Figure 3

Cell reference for first selected cell displays in Name Box

Range A1: G1 selected and bordered in blue

Merge button

Cells merged and text centered

Figure 4

8. Point to the middle of cell **A1** to display the ⊞ pointer. Hold down the mouse button, and then drag to the right to select cells **A1** through **G1**. Compare your screen with **Figure 3**.

   The selected range is referred to as *A1:G1* (A1 through G1). A **range** is two or more cells on a worksheet that are adjacent (next to each other). A colon (:) between two cell references indicates a range of cells that includes the two cell references and all the cells between them.

   When you select a range, a thick line surrounds the range and all but the first cell in the range are shaded. The first cell reference will be displayed in the *Name Box*—an area by the formula bar that displays the active cell reference.

9. On the **Home tab,** in the **Alignment group,** click the **Merge** button.

   The selected range, A1:G1, merges into one larger cell, and the data is centered in the new cell. The cells in B1 through G1 can no longer be individually selected because they are merged into cell A1.

10. Using the technique just practiced, select the range **A2:G2,** and then click the **Merge** button.

11. Click in cell A1. On the **Standard toolbar,** click **Save** 🖫, and then compare your screen with **Figure 4**.

   ▪ **You have completed Skill 2 of 10**

► A cell's underlying value can be a text value, a number value, or a formula. A *formula* is an equation that performs mathematical calculations on number values in the worksheet.

► Formulas begin with an equal sign and often include an *arithmetic operator*—a symbol that specifies a mathematical operation such as addition or subtraction.

1. Study the symbols that Excel uses to perform mathematical operations, as summarized in the table in **Figure 1**.

2. In cell **D4,** type =B4+C4 and then press return .

> The total number of bikes rented for the North location equals the sum of the values in cells B4 and C4, which is *190*, the sum of 139 and 51.
>
> When you type a formula, you might see a brief display of function names that match the first letter you type. This Excel feature, called *Formula AutoComplete*, assists in inserting formulas.

3. In cell **D5,** type the formula to add cells B5 and C5, =B5+C5 and then press return .

4. In cell **D6,** type = and then click cell **B6.** Notice that *B6* is inserted into the formula, and cell **B6** is surrounded by a moving border indicating that it is part of an active formula as shown in **Figure 2**.

5. Type + Click cell **C6,** and then press return to display the result *107*.

> You can either type formulas or construct them by pointing and clicking in this manner.

■ **Continue to the next page to complete the skill**

Symbols Used in Excel for Arithmetic Operators	
Operator Symbol	**Operation**
+ (plus sign)	Addition
- (minus sign)	Subtraction (also negation)
* (asterisk)	Multiplication
/ (forward slash)	Division
% (percent sign)	Percent
^ (caret)	Exponentiation

Figure 1

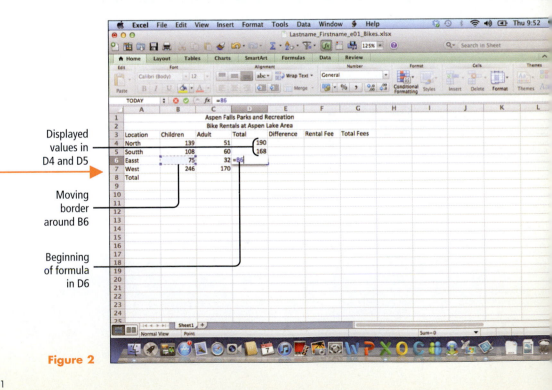

Displayed values in D4 and D5

Moving border around B6

Beginning of formula in D6

Figure 2

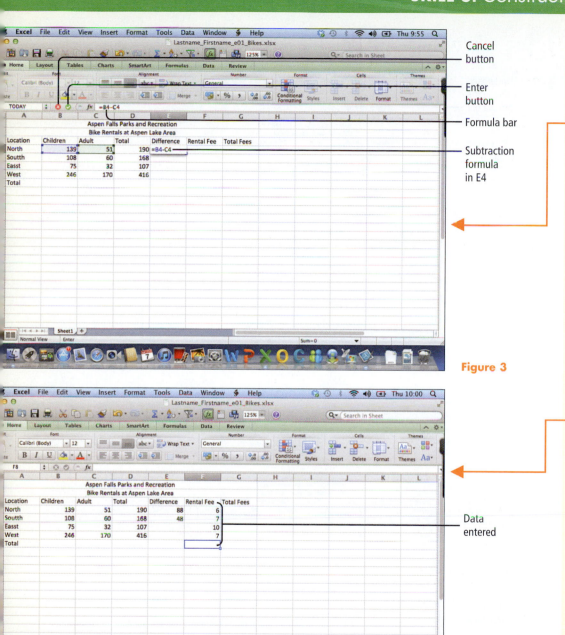

Cancel button

Enter button

Formula bar

Subtraction formula in E4

Figure 3

Data entered

Figure 4

6. In cell **D7**, use point and click to construct a formula that adds cells **B7** and **C7**.

7. In cell **E4**, type =B4-C4 On the **formula bar,** notice that the **Cancel** and **Enter** buttons display to the left of the formula as shown in **Figure 3**.

   If you make an error entering a formula, you can click the Cancel button and then start over. Alternately, you can press the esc key.

8. On the **formula bar,** click the **Enter** button to confirm the entry while keeping cell **E4** the active cell. Notice that the underlying value for cell **E4** displays as a formula in the **formula bar** and the display value *88* displays in the cell as a result of the formula.

9. In cell **E5**, use point and click to enter the formula =B5-C5 to display the difference for the South location. (You will complete the column E formulas in Skill 7.)

10. Type the following data using the ▼ to move to the next row, and then compare your screen with **Figure 4**.

Cell	Value
F4	6
F5	7
F6	10
F7	7

11. **Save** the workbook.

   ■ **You have completed Skill 3 of 10**

► The four most common operators for addition (+), subtraction (-), multiplication (*), and division (/) can be found on any standard keyboard.

1. In cell **G4,** type =D4*F4—the formula that multiplies the total North bikes rented by its rental fee. On the **formula bar,** click the **Enter** button ⬮, and then compare your screen with **Figure 1**. ───────

   The *underlying formula*—the formula as displayed in the formula bar—multiplies the value in cell D4 (*190*) by the value in cell F4 (*6*) and displays the result in cell G4 (*1140*).

2. In the range **G5:G7,** enter the following formulas:

Cell	Formula
G5	=D5*F5
G6	=D6*F6
G7	=D7*F7

3. In cell **A11,** type Percent of Adult Bikes Rented and then press ⌐return⌐.

4. Select cells **A11:B11**. On the **Home tab,** in the **Alignment group,** click the **Merge button arrow,** and then on the displayed list, click **Merge Across**. Compare your screen with **Figure 2**. ───────

   Merge Across will merge the selected cells without centering. (You will widen the columns in Skill 5.)

■ **Continue to the next page to complete the skill**

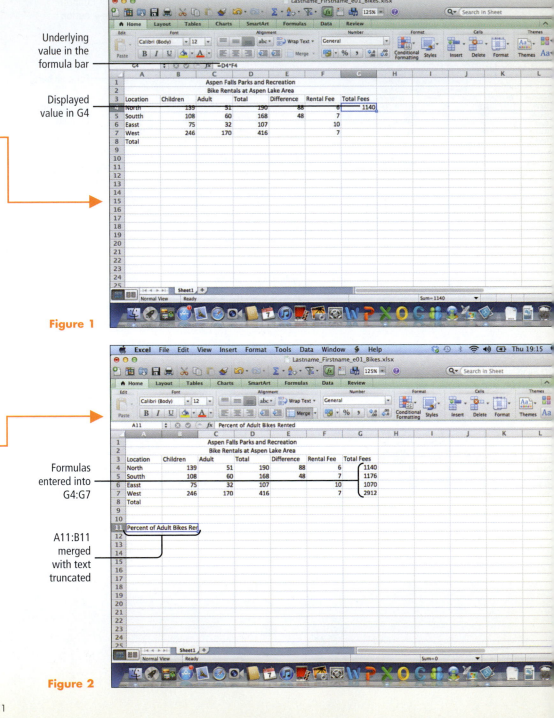

Underlying value in the formula bar ──

Displayed value in G4 ──

Figure 1

Formulas entered into G4:G7 ──

A11:B11 merged with text truncated ──

Figure 2

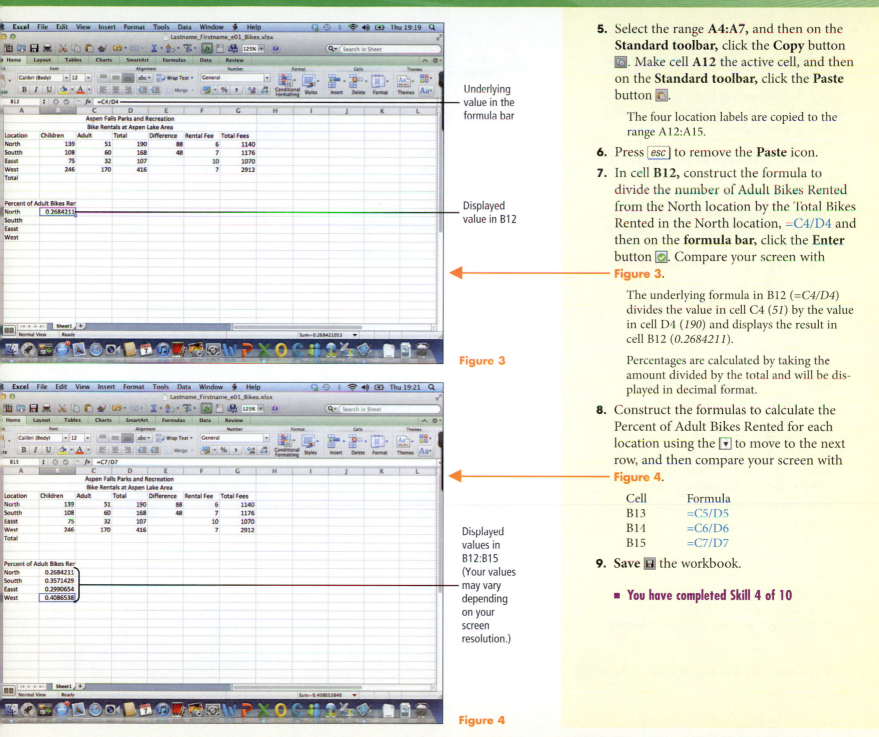

Underlying value in the formula bar

Displayed value in B12

Figure 3

Displayed values in B12:B15 (Your values may vary depending on your screen resolution.)

Figure 4

5. Select the range **A4:A7,** and then on the **Standard toolbar,** click the **Copy** button . Make cell **A12** the active cell, and then on the **Standard toolbar,** click the **Paste** button .

   The four location labels are copied to the range A12:A15.

6. Press esc to remove the **Paste** icon.

7. In cell **B12,** construct the formula to divide the number of Adult Bikes Rented from the North location by the Total Bikes Rented in the North location, =C4/D4 and then on the **formula bar,** click the **Enter** button . Compare your screen with **Figure 3**.

   The underlying formula in B12 (=C4/D4) divides the value in cell C4 (51) by the value in cell D4 (190) and displays the result in cell B12 (0.2684211).

   Percentages are calculated by taking the amount divided by the total and will be displayed in decimal format.

8. Construct the formulas to calculate the Percent of Adult Bikes Rented for each location using the to move to the next row, and then compare your screen with **Figure 4**.

Cell	Formula
B13	=C5/D5
B14	=C6/D6
B15	=C7/D7

9. **Save** the workbook.

   ▪ **You have completed Skill 4 of 10**

▶ The letter that displays at the top of a column is the *column heading*. The number that displays at the left of a row is the *row heading*.

▶ Recall that formatting is the process of specifying the appearance of cells or the overall layout of a worksheet.

1. At the top of column **A,** point to the right border of the column **A** heading to display the ⊞ pointer.

2. Drag to the right until the ScreenTip indicates *Width: 13.00 (1.15 inches).* Release the mouse button, and then compare your screen with **Figure 1.**

   The default column width will display 10.00 (0.90 inches) when formatted in the standard font. Here, the width has been increased to display more characters.

3. In the column **B** heading, point anywhere to display the ⬇ pointer, and then drag right to select columns **B** through **G.**

4. With columns **B:G** selected, point to the right boundary of any selected column heading to display the ⊞ pointer, and then drag to the right until the width in the ScreenTip indicates *Width: 12.00 (1.07 inches).* Release the mouse button, and then compare your screen with **Figure 2.**

5. Point to the row **1** heading, and then with the ➡ pointer, click to select the entire row. Point to the bottom boundary of the row heading to display the ⊞ pointer, and then drag down until the height in the ScreenTip indicates *Height 22.00 (0.31 inches).* Release the mouse button.

■ **Continue to the next page to complete the skill** ▶

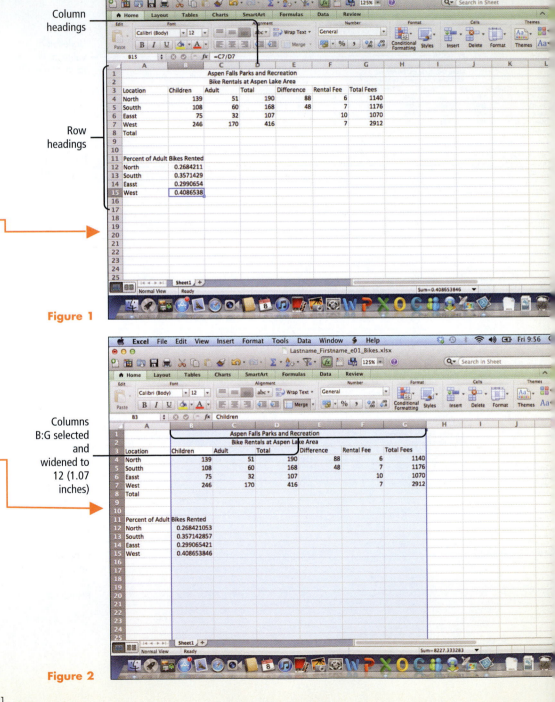

Column headings

Row headings

Figure 1

Columns B:G selected and widened to 12 (1.07 inches)

Figure 2

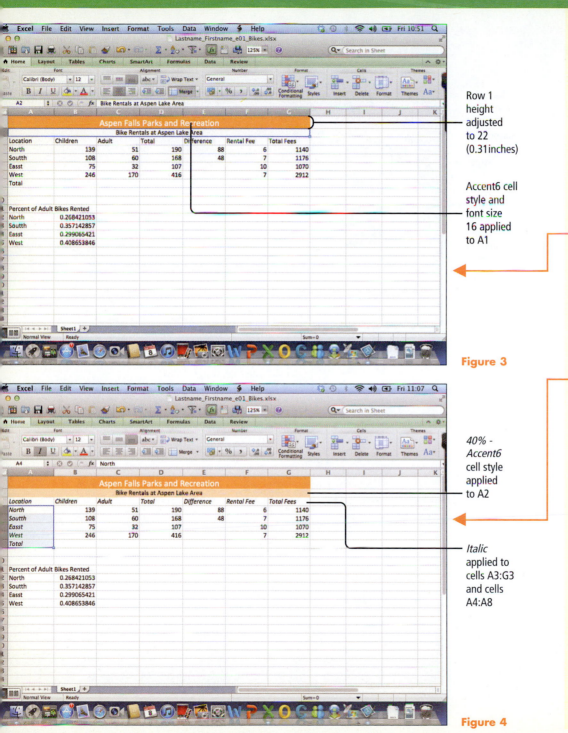

Row 1 height adjusted to 22 (0.31 inches)

Accent6 cell style and font size 16 applied to A1

Figure 3

40% - Accent6 cell style applied to A2

Italic applied to cells A3:G3 and cells A4:A8

Figure 4

6. Click cell **A1,** which is a merged and centered cell. In the **Format group,** click the **Styles** button. In the **Cell Styles** gallery, review the list of styles available.

   A *cell style* is a prebuilt set of formatting characteristics, such as font, font size, font color, cell borders, and cell shading.

7. Under **Themed Cell Styles,** scroll down, and then click the **Accent6** style. In the **Font group,** click the **Font Size arrow** 12 ▼, and then click **16.** Click cell **A2,** and then compare your screen with **Figure 3**.

8. In cell **A2,** using the technique you just practiced, from the **Cell Styles** gallery, apply the **40%–Accent6** cell style.

9. Select the range **A3:G3.** In the **Font group**, click the **Italic** button *I* to apply italic to the text within each of the selected cells.

10. Select the range **A4:A8,** press command ⌘ + I . Compare your screen with **Figure 4**.

11. **Save** 🖫 the workbook.

   ■ **You have completed Skill 5 of 10**

▶ You can create your own formulas, or you can use a *function*—a prewritten Excel formula that takes a value or values, performs an operation, and returns a value or values.

▶ The Sum button is used to insert common functions into a worksheet.

▶ When cell references are used in a formula or function, editing the values in those cells results in the formula or function automatically recalculating a new result.

1. Click cell **B8**. On the **Standard toolbar,** click the **Sum** button ∑. Notice that the range **B4:B7** is surrounded by a moving border, and *=SUM(B4:B7)* displays in cell **B8** and in the **formula bar** as shown in **Figure 1**.

   SUM is an Excel function that adds all the numbers in a range of cells. The range in parentheses, *(B4:B7),* indicates the range of cells on which the SUM function will be performed.

   When the Sum button is used, Excel first looks *above* the selected cell for a suitable range of cells to sum. When no suitable data is detected, Excel then looks to the *left* and proposes a range of cells to sum.

2. Press [return] to display the function result—*568*.

3. Select the range **C8:D8**. On the **Standard toolbar,** click the **Sum** button ∑, and then compare your screen with **Figure 2**.

■ **Continue to the next page to complete the skill**

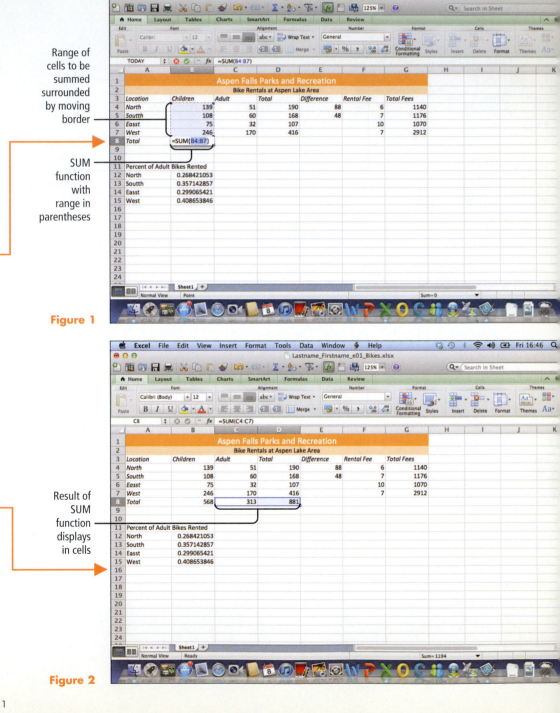

Range of cells to be summed surrounded by moving border

SUM function with range in parentheses

Figure 1

Result of SUM function displays in cells

Figure 2

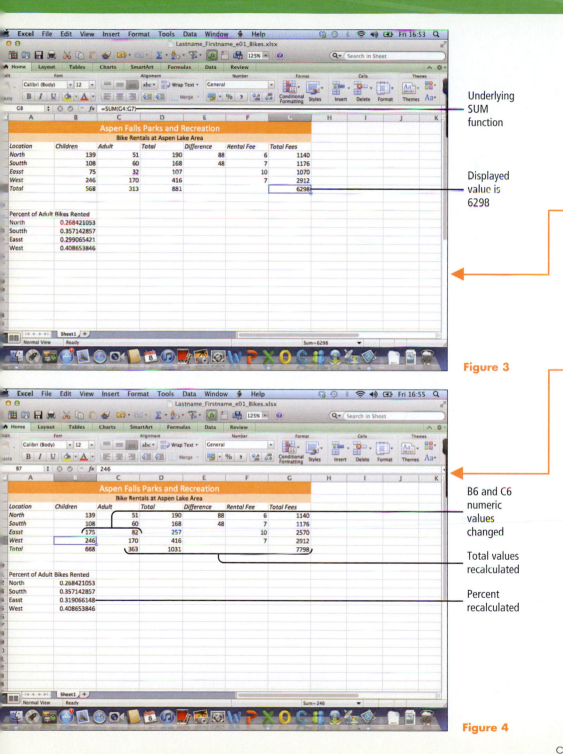

Underlying SUM function

Displayed value is 6298

Figure 3

B6 and C6 numeric values changed

Total values recalculated

Percent recalculated

Figure 4

4. Click cell **C8,** and then in the **formula bar,** verify that the SUM function adds the values in the range *C4:C7.*

5. Click cell **D8,** and verify that the SUM function adds the values in the range *D4:D7.*

6. Using the technique just practiced, in cell **G8,** insert the SUM function to add the values in the range **G4:G7.** Select cell **G8,** and then compare your screen with **Figure 3.**

7. In cell **B6,** type 175 Watch the total in cell **B8** update as you press [tab].

   In cell B8, the displayed value changed to 668, but the underlying formula remained the same.

8. In cell **C6,** type 82 and then press [return] to update the values in cells that contain formulas referring to cell C6 as shown in **Figure 4.**

9. **Save** 🖫 the workbook.

   ■ **You have completed Skill 6 of 10**

► Text, numbers, formulas, and functions can be copied down rows and also across columns to insert formulas and functions quickly.

► When a formula is copied to another cell, Excel adjusts the cell references relative to the new location of the formula.

1. Click cell **E5**.

   To use the fill handle, first select the cell that contains the content you want to copy—here the formula =B5-C5.

2. With cell **E5** selected, point to the ***fill handle***—the small blue square in the lower right corner of the selection—until the ⊞ pointer displays as shown in **Figure 1**.

3. Drag the ⊞ pointer down to cell **E7**, and then release the mouse button.

4. Click cell **E6**, and verify the formula copied from E5 is =B6-C6. Click cell **E7**, and verify the copied formula is =B7-C7 as shown in **Figure 2**.

   In each row, Excel copied the formula but adjusted the cell references *relative to* the row number—B5 changed to B6 and then to B7. This adjustment is called a ***relative cell reference*** because it refers to cells based on their position *in relation to* (relative to) the cell that contains the formula.

■ **Continue to the next page to complete the skill**

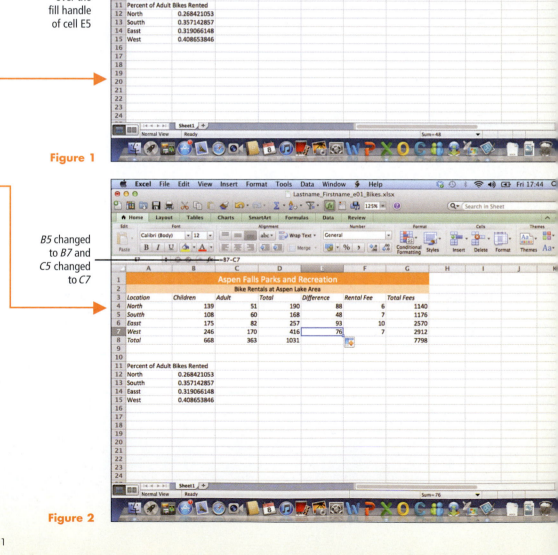

⊞

pointer displays over the fill handle of cell E5

Figure 1

B5 changed to *B7* and *C5* changed to *C7*

Figure 2

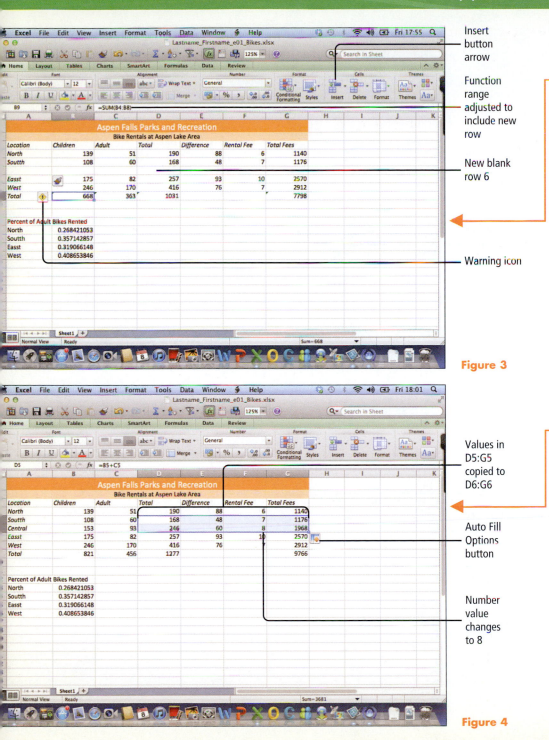

Figure 3

Figure 4

5. Click cell **A6**. In the **Cells group**, click the **Insert button arrow,** and then click **Insert Rows**. Click cell **B9**, and then compare your screen with **Figure 3**.

> The function in cell B9 automatically updates to include the new row.
>
> When you insert a new row or column, the cell references and the ranges in formulas or in functions adjust to include the new row or column.

6. In cell **A6**, type Central and then press tab . Notice that the formatting (italic) from cell A7 was applied to the inserted row.

7. In cell **B6,** type 153 and then press tab to enter the value and update the column total in cell **B9** to *821*.

8. In cell **C6,** type 93 and press tab .

9. Select cells **D5:G5**. Point to the fill handle so that the ⊞ pointer displays, and then drag the ⊞ pointer down one row. Release the mouse button, and notice the **Auto Fill Options** button 🔲 displays as shown in **Figure 4**.

> When you copy number values using the fill handle, the numbers automatically increment for each row or column. Here, the number value in cell F5 increased by one when it was copied to cell F6.

10. Click the **Auto Fill Options** button 🔲, and then click **Copy Cells**.

> With the Copy Cells option, number values are literally copied and do not increment. Here, the number value in cell F6 changes to 7.

11. Save 🖫 the workbook.

■ **You have completed Skill 7 of 10**

▶ Always check spelling after you have finished formatting and editing your worksheet data.

1. Click cell **A15,** and repeat the technique used previously to insert a new row.

2. In cell **A15,** type Central and then press `return`. Click cell **B14,** and then use the fill handle to copy the formula down to cell **B15**. Compare your screen with **Figure 1**.

3. Click cell **A2**. Click in the **formula bar,** and then use the arrow keys to move to the left of the word *Area*. Type Recreation Add a space as needed, and then press `return`.

4. Click cell **F4,** and then with the ⊞ pointer, drag right from cells **F4** to **G4**. Hold down `command ⌘`, and then click cell **G9**.

> You can select nonadjacent ranges by holding down `command ⌘`.

5. In the **Format group,** click the **Styles** button, scroll down, and then under **Number Format,** click **Currency [0]**.

6. Select the range **B13:B17**. In the **Number group,** click the **Percent Style** button **%**, and then click the **Increase Decimal** button one time.

> The Increase Decimal and Decrease Decimal buttons do not actually add or remove decimals, but they change how the underlying decimal values *display* in the cells.

7. Select the range **B9:D9**. Hold down `command ⌘`, and then click cell **G9**. In the **Format group,** click the **Styles** button. Under **Titles and Headings,** click the **Total** style. Click cell **A10,** and then compare your screen with **Figure 2**.

■ **Continue to the next page to complete the skill** ➤

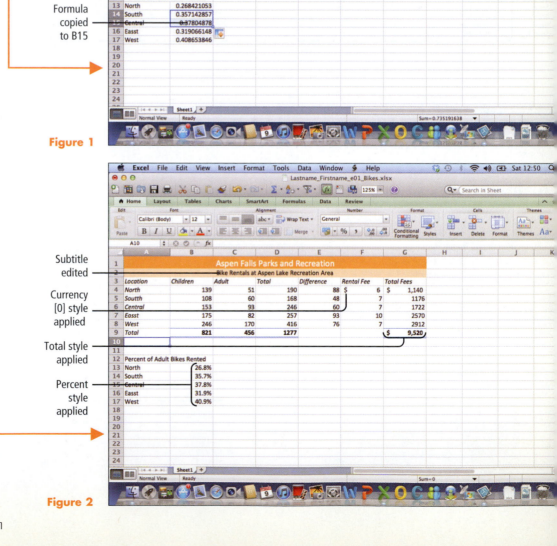

Central entered in new row

Formula copied to B15

Figure 1

Subtitle edited

Currency [0] style applied

Total style applied

Percent style applied

Figure 2

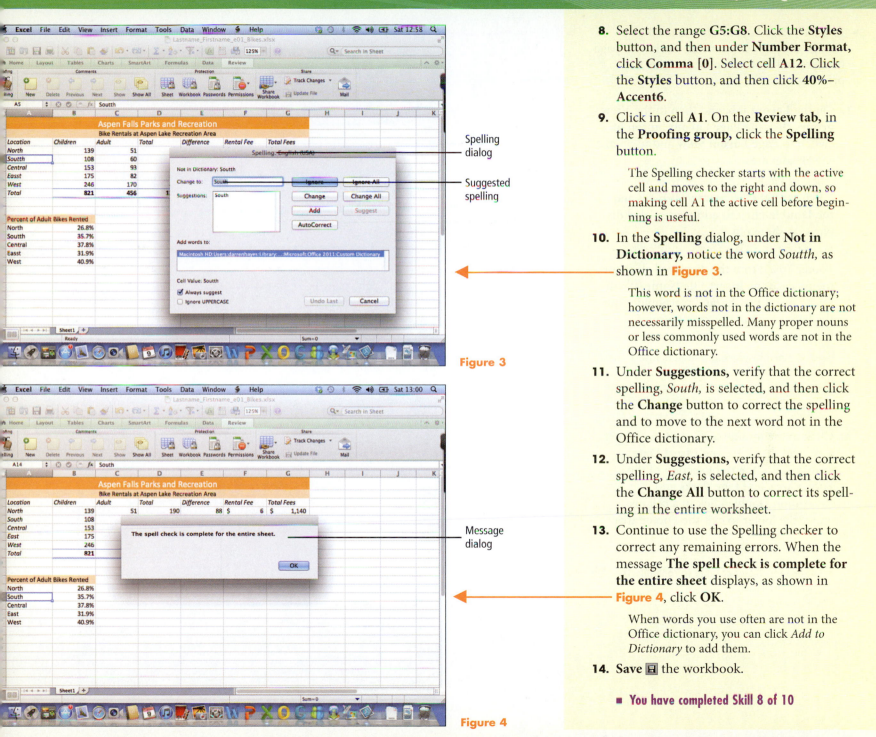

Spelling dialog

Suggested spelling

Figure 3

Message dialog

Figure 4

8. Select the range **G5:G8**. Click the **Styles** button, and then under **Number Format,** click **Comma [0]**. Select cell **A12**. Click the **Styles** button, and then click **40%– Accent6**.

9. Click in cell **A1**. On the **Review tab,** in the **Proofing group,** click the **Spelling** button.

> The Spelling checker starts with the active cell and moves to the right and down, so making cell A1 the active cell before beginning is useful.

10. In the **Spelling** dialog, under **Not in Dictionary,** notice the word *Southh,* as shown in **Figure 3**.

> This word is not in the Office dictionary; however, words not in the dictionary are not necessarily misspelled. Many proper nouns or less commonly used words are not in the Office dictionary.

11. Under **Suggestions,** verify that the correct spelling, *South,* is selected, and then click the **Change** button to correct the spelling and to move to the next word not in the Office dictionary.

12. Under **Suggestions,** verify that the correct spelling, *East,* is selected, and then click the **Change All** button to correct its spelling in the entire worksheet.

13. Continue to use the Spelling checker to correct any remaining errors. When the message **The spell check is complete for the entire sheet** displays, as shown in **Figure 4**, click **OK**.

> When words you use often are not in the Office dictionary, you can click *Add to Dictionary* to add them.

14. Save ⊞ the workbook.

■ **You have completed Skill 8 of 10**

▶ In Excel, *Page Layout view* is used to change the page orientation, work with page headers and footers, or set margins for printing.

1. On the **Layout tab,** and then in the **View group,** click the **Page Layout** button to switch to **Page Layout view** and to open the Header area.

2. Click in **Page 1.** Use the ▼ to scroll down until the 🖳 pointer displays and the **Double-click to add footer** label displays, as shown in **Figure 1.**

3. Double-click in the left section of the Footer area. From the displayed shortcut menu, click the **Insert File Name** 🔳 button to insert the *& [File]* placeholder into the left section of the Footer area. Compare your screen with **Figure 2.**

   Predefined headers and footers insert placeholders with instructions for printing. Here, the *& [File]* placeholder instructs Excel to insert the file name when the worksheet is printed.

4. Click in the middle section of the Footer area, and then click the **Insert Date** 🔳 button. Click the right section of the Footer area, and type Parks and Recreation Double-click in a cell just above the footer to exit the Footer area.

■ **Continue to the next page to complete the skill**

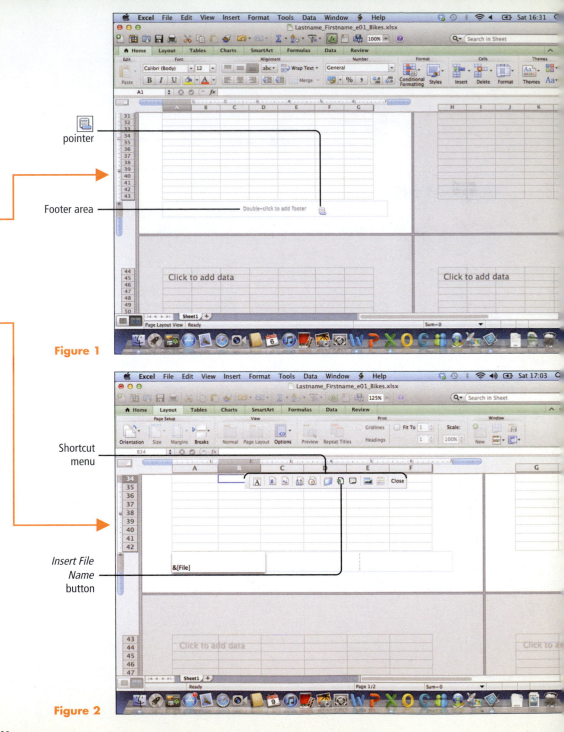

pointer

Footer area

Figure 1

Shortcut menu

Insert File Name button

Figure 2

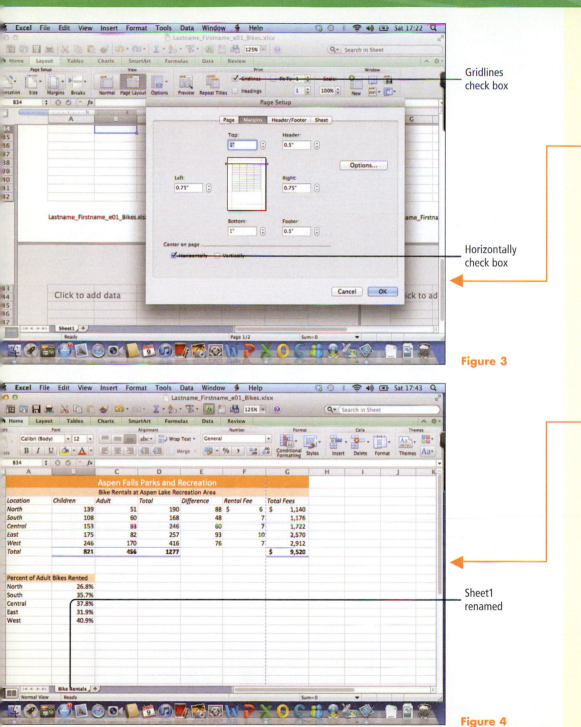

Gridlines
check box

Horizontally
check box

Figure 3

Sheet1
renamed

Figure 4

5. On the **Layout tab,** in the **Print group,** select the **Gridlines** check box. In the **Page Setup group,** click the **Margins** button, and then click **Custom Margins.** In the **Page Setup** dialog, under **Center on page,** select the **Horizontally** check box, and then compare your screen with **Figure 3.** Click **OK.**

   The gridlines on the worksheet are shifted to the right.

6. Click the **Home tab.** On the lower left side of the status bar, click the **Normal View** button ⊞ to return to Normal view, and then scroll to the top of the worksheet.

   Normal view maximizes the number of cells visible on the screen. The page break—the dotted line between columns F and G—indicates where one page ends and a new page begins.

7. At the bottom of your worksheet, press and hold [control], and then click the **Sheet1** sheet tab. From the shortcut menu, click **Rename.** Type Bike Rentals and then press [return]. Compare your screen with **Figure 4.**

8. **Save** ⊞ the workbook. On the **menu bar,** click **File,** and then click **Print.** If you are directed by your instructor to print, select a printer, and then click **Print.**

   ■ **You have completed Skill 9 of 10**

► Underlying formulas and functions can be displayed and printed.

► When formulas are displayed in cells, the orientation and worksheet scale might need to be changed so that the worksheet prints on a single page.

1. Click the **Formulas tab,** and then in the **Function group,** click the **Show** button, and then click **Show Formulas** button to display the underlying formulas in the cells as shown in **Figure 1**.

   Columns become wider when formulas are displayed. Here, the printed worksheet extends to a second page.

2. Display the **Layout tab**. In the **Print group,** click the **Preview** button.

   A preview of the worksheet displays as a PDF. To the right of the file name, notice that *(page 1 of 3)* displays, which indicates that the worksheet will print on three pages.

3. On the **menu bar,** click **Go,** and then click **Next Item** to view the second page. Repeat this step to move to the third page. Compare your screen with **Figure 2**.

4. On the **menu bar,** click **Preview,** and then click **Quit Preview**.

5. On the **Layout tab,** in the **Page Setup group,** click the **Orientation** button, and then click **Landscape** so that the orientation will be wider than it is tall.

   ■ **Continue to the next page to complete the skill**

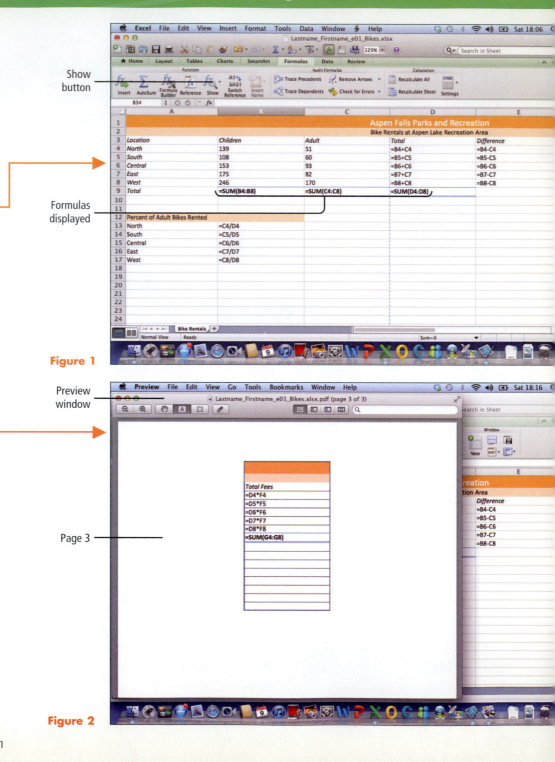

Show button

Formulas displayed

Figure 1

Preview window

Page 3

Figure 2

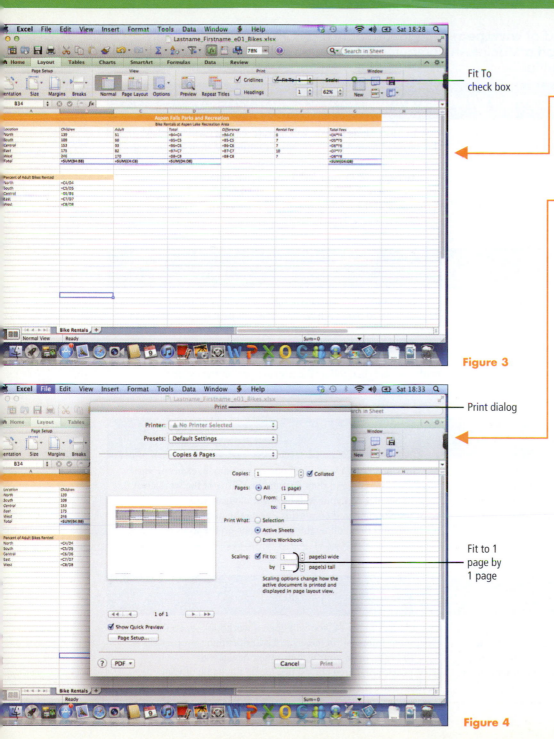

Fit To check box

Figure 3

Print dialog

Fit to 1 page by 1 page

Figure 4

6. On the **Layout tab,** in the **Print group,** select the **Fit To** check box. Make sure that *1* displays in each of the *Fit To* boxes. The scaling is one page wide by one page tall as shown in **Figure 3**.

   Scaling adjusts the size of the printed worksheet to fit on the number of pages that you specify. Notice that the Scale has changed.

7. On the **menu bar,** click **File,** and then click **Print**. Compare your screen with **Figure 4**.

   1 of 1 displays at the bottom middle of the Print page to notify you that the worksheet will now print on one page.

8. If you are directed by your instructor to submit a printout of your formulas, click the **Print** button.

9. Click the **Formulas** tab. In the **Function group,** click **Show,** and then click **Show Formulas**.

   The values are displayed.

10. **Save** 🖫 the workbook, and then **Quit** Excel.

11. Submit your printouts or file as directed by your instructor.

   Done! You have completed Skill 10 of 10, and your document is complete!

More Skills

The following More Skills are located at **www.pearsonhighered.com/skills**. Please note that only More Skills that can be performed on a Macintosh computer are included in this section; therefore, the numbering is not always sequential.

More Skills Create New Workbooks from Templates

Templates are used to build workbooks without having to start from scratch. You can save one of your own workbooks as a template to use again, or you can download one of many predefined templates from Microsoft Office Online.

In More Skills 11, you will modify a Time Card template downloaded from Microsoft Office Online and then use the template to create a new weekly time card.

To begin, open your web browser, navigate to www.pearsonhighered.com/skills, locate the name of your textbook, and then follow the instructions on the website.

More Skills Use Range Names in Formulas

Instead of using cell references in formulas and functions, you can assign names that refer to the same cell or range. Range names can be easier to remember than cell references, and they can add meaning to formulas, making them easier for you and others to understand.

In More Skills 12, you will open a workbook and practice various ways to name cell ranges. You will then use the names in formulas.

To begin, open your web browser, navigate to www.pearsonhighered.com/skills, locate the name of your textbook, and then follow the instructions on the website.

More Skills Change Themes

Office themes are used to apply a coordinated set of colors, fonts, and graphic effects with a single click. You can use the Office themes, which were developed by graphics professionals, to provide a consistent and polished look and feel for all of your worksheets.

In More Skills 13, you will open a workbook, examine various Office themes, and then change the theme of the worksheet.

To begin, open your web browser, navigate to www.pearsonhighered.com/skills, locate the name of your textbook, and then follow the instructions on the website.

More Skills 14 Manage Document Properties

Document properties are the detailed information about your workbook that can help you identify or organize your files, including the name of the author, the title, and keywords. Some workbook properties are added to the workbook when you create it. You can add others as necessary.

In More Skills 14, you will open a workbook, open the Document Information Panel, and add document properties.

To begin, open your web browser, navigate to www.pearsonhighered.com/skills, locate the name of your textbook, and then follow the instructions on the website.

Key Terms

Active cell 158

Arithmetic operator 162

Cell address 158

Cell reference 158

Cell style 167

Column heading 166

Displayed value 160

Fill handle 170

Formula 162

Formula AutoComplete 162

Formula bar 160

Function 168

Label 159

Name Box 161

Normal view 175

Number value 159

Page Layout view 174

Range 161

Relative cell reference 170

Row heading 166

Spreadsheet 158

SUM 168

Text value 159

Truncated 160

Underlying formula 164

Underlying value 160

Value 159

Workbook 158

Worksheet 158

Online Help Skills

1. **Start** Safari or another web browser. In the **address bar,** type microsoft.com/mac/how-to and then press $\boxed{return}$ to display the home page for Microsoft Office.

   This website provides you with helpful links to get started, find out what is new and tutorials about Office 2011.

2. Under **Product Help,** click **Excel 2011**.

3. Under **Excel Help**, click **Training**.

4. Under **Training**, click **Video: Excel basics**.

5. Click **Start** two times, and then compare your screen with **Figure 1**.

Figure 1

6. Turn on your speakers or put on headphones, and then click **Start** to watch the video to see if you can answer the following questions: How can you format numbers in cells with different currency symbols? How can you insert a column into a spreadsheet? How can you save a workbook in a different file format?

Matching

Match each term in the second column with its correct definition in the first column by writing the letter of the term on the blank line in front of the correct definition.

____ **1.** An Excel file that contains one or more worksheets.

____ **2.** The primary document that you use in Excel to store and work with data, and which is formatted as a pattern of uniformly spaced horizontal and vertical lines.

____ **3.** Another name for a worksheet.

____ **4.** The cell, surrounded by a blue border, ready to receive data or be affected by the next Excel command.

____ **5.** The identification of a specific cell by its intersecting column letter and row number.

____ **6.** Data in a cell—text or numbers.

____ **7.** Data in a cell made up of text only.

____ **8.** Data in a cell made up of numbers only.

____ **9.** Another name for a text value.

____ **10.** An Excel window area that displays the address of a selected cell.

A Active cell

B Cell reference

C Label

D Name Box

E Number value

F Spreadsheet

G Text value

H Value

I Workbook

J Worksheet

Multiple Choice

Choose the correct answer.

1. The data displayed in a cell.
   - A. Viewed value
   - B. Inspected value
   - C. Displayed value

2. In Excel, this performs mathematical calculations on number values.
   - A. Method
   - B. Formula
   - C. System

3. A view that maximizes the number of cells visible on the screen.
   - A. Page Layout view
   - B. Standard view
   - C. Normal view

4. The column letter and row number that identify a cell.
   - A. Cell window
   - B. Cell address
   - C. Cell file name

5. An Excel window area that displays the value contained in the active cell.
   - A. Formula bar
   - B. Workbook
   - C. Name Box

6. Symbols that specify mathematical operations such as addition or subtraction.
   - A. Hyperlinks
   - B. Bookmarks
   - C. Arithmetic operators

7. The number that displays at the left of a row.
   - A. Row heading
   - B. Row name
   - C. Row border

8. A prewritten Excel formula.
   - A. A formula
   - B. A function
   - C. An exponent

9. The small blue square in the lower right corner of the active cell.
   - A. Border
   - B. Fill handle
   - C. Edge

10. Page headers and footers can be changed in this view.
    - A. Print preview
    - B. Page Layout view
    - C. Normal view

Topics for Discussion

1. What is the advantage of using cell references instead of actual number values in formulas and functions?

2. What are some things you can do to make your worksheet easier for others to read and understand?

According to the Introduction to this chapter, how do you decide which information to put in columns and which to put in rows?

Skill Check

To complete this project, you will need the following file:

- **New blank Excel document**

You will save your spreadsheet as:

- **Lastname_Firstname_e01_Sales**

1. **Start** Excel. In cell **A1,** type Aspen Falls Parks and Recreation and then in cell **A2,** type Concession Sales at Durango County Park In cell **A3,** type Location and then pressing ⌨tab after each title, type Food, Drinks, Total Sales, and Difference

2. In rows **4** through **8,** enter the following data starting in cell **A4:**

Carol's Ice Cream	5794	3448	Joe's Candy	5821	4721
Jerry's Fudge	3950	2520	Alice's Fresh Fruit	9515	8661
Ray's Tacos	7488	7015			

3. In cell **D4,** type =B4+C4 and then in cell **E4,** type =B4-C4 Select the range **D4:E4.** Point to the fill handle, and then drag down through row **8.** Compare your screen with **Figure 1.**

4. **Save** the workbook in your **Excel Chapter 1** folder with the name Lastname_Firstname_e01_Sales

5. On the **Layout tab,** in the **View group,** click the **Page Layout** button. Click in **Page 1,** scroll down, and then double-click in the center of the footer. Click the **Insert File Name** button. Double-click in a cell just above the footer, and then in the **View group** click **Normal.** Move to the top of the worksheet.

6. In cell **A9,** type Totals and then select the range **B9:D9.** On the **Standard toolbar,** click the **Sum** button.

7. Select cell **A7.** On the **Home tab,** in the **Cells group,** click the **Insert button arrow,** and then click **Insert Rows.** In the new row **7,** type the data David's Biscotti, 7183, and 5492

8. Select the range **D6:E6,** and then use the fill handle to copy the formulas down one row.

9. In cell **A13,** type Drinks as a Percent of Total Sales

10. Select the range **A4:A9,** and then on the **Standard toolbar,** click the **Copy** button. Click cell **A14,** and then on the **Standard toolbar,** click the **Paste** button. Press ⌨esc, and then compare your screen with **Figure 2.**

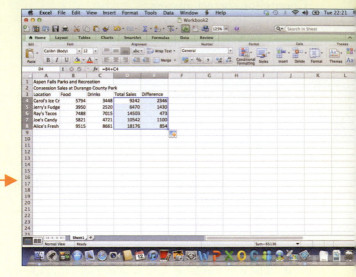

Figure 1

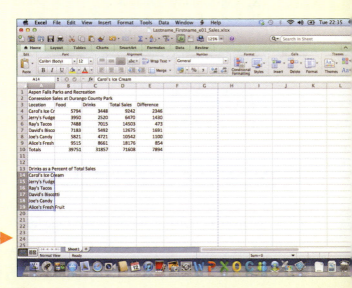

Figure 2

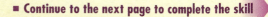

- **Continue to the next page to complete the skill**

11. In cell **B14,** type =C4/D4 and then on the **formula bar,** click the **Enter** button. In cell **B14,** use the fill handle to copy the formula down through row **19.** Compare your screen with **Figure 3.**

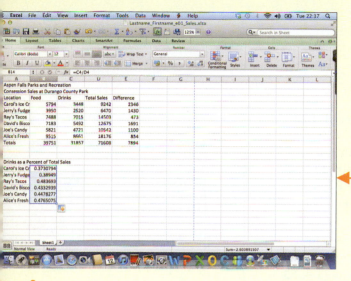

12. Select the range **A1:E1,** and then on the **Home tab,** in the **Alignment group,** click the **Merge** button. In the **Format group,** click the **Styles** button, and then click **Accent4.** In the **Font group,** click the **Font Size arrow,** and then click **16.** Select the range **A2:E2,** and then in the **Alignment group,** click the **Merge** button. Click the **Styles** button, and then click **60%–Accent4.**

13. Select columns **A:E,** point to the right boundary of any selected column heading, drag to a column width of *16.00 (1.40 inches),* and then release the mouse button.

14. Select the range **A3:E3.** Hold down command ⌘, and then select the range **A4:A10.** In the **Font group,** click the **Italic** button.

15. Select range **B4:E4.** Hold down command ⌘, and then select the range **B10:D10.** In the **Format group,** click the **Styles** button, and then click **Currency [0].** Select the range **B10:D10.** Click the **Styles** button, and then click the **Total** style. Select the range **B5:E9,** click the **Styles** button, and then click **Comma [0].**

16. Select the range **A13:B13.** In the **Alignment group,** click the **Merge button arrow,** and then click **Merge Across.** Click the **Styles** button, and then click **40%–Accent4.**

17. Select the range **B14:B19.** In the **Number group,** click the **Percent Style** button, and then click the **Increase Decimal** button one time.

18. Click in cell **A1.** On the **Review tab,** in the **Proofing group,** click the **Spelling** button, and then correct any spelling errors.

19. Move the cursor over the **Sheet1 sheet tab,** press control, click the mouse, and from the shortcut menu, click **Rename.** Type Concessions and then press return.

20. On the **Layout tab,** in the **Page Setup group,** click **Orientation,** and then click **Landscape.**

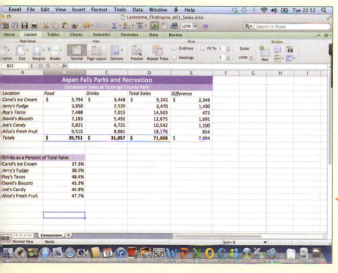

21. **Save,** and then compare your screen with **Figure 4.** If asked by your instructor, print the worksheet. If asked by your instructor, display and format the worksheet formulas as described in Skill 10, and then print the worksheet.

22. **Quit** Excel. Submit the printouts or file as directed by your instructor.

Done! You have completed the Skill Check

Figure 3

Figure 4

Assess Your Skills 1

To complete this project, you will need the following file:

- e01_Fees

You will save your spreadsheet as:

- **Lastname_Firstname_e01_Fees**

1. **Start** Excel. From your student data files, open **e01_Fees**. Save the workbook in your **Excel Chapter 1** folder as Lastname_Firstname_e01_Fees Add the file name to the worksheet's left footer, add the current date to the center footer, and then type Tax Rates in the right footer. Return to **Normal** view.
2. For the range **A1:E1,** merge and center and apply the **Accent5** cell style. Increase the font size to **18** points. For the range **A2:E2,** merge and center and apply the **40%–Accent5** cell style. Widen column **A** to *20.00 (1.74 inches)*. For all column and row titles, apply **Italic**.
3. For the range **E5:E13,** insert the **SUM** function to add the three fees for each row. In the range **B14:E14,** insert the **SUM** function to provide totals for each column.
4. Select the nonadjacent ranges **B5:E5** and **B14:E14**. Apply the **Currency [0]** cell style.
5. Select the range **B6:E13,** and then apply the **Comma** [0] cell style. Select the range **B14:E14,** and then apply the **Total** cell style.
6. Insert a new row above row 7. In cell **A7,** type Silkworth Hiking Area and as the fees for the new location, type 14257 and 9625 and 10925 Use the fill handle to copy the formula in cell **E6** to cell **E7**.
7. **Copy** the location names from the range **A5:A14** to the range **A20:A29**.
8. In cell **B19,** type New Tax Rate In cells **B20** and **B21,** type .03 In cells **B22** and **B23,** type .05 and in cell **B24,** type .06 Use the fill handle to copy the value in cell **B24** down through cell **B29**. Select the range **B20:B29,** and then apply the **Percent Style** number format.
9. In cell **C19,** type New Tax Collections In cell **C20,** enter a formula that calculates the new tax charged by the city by multiplying cell **E5** by cell **B20**. In cell **C20,** use the fill handle to copy the formula down through cell **C29**.
10. Rename the **Sheet1** sheet tab as City Fees and then delete **Sheet2** and **Sheet3**.
11. Use **Page Setup** to center the worksheet **Horizontally**. Set the **Gridlines** to print.
12. Check and correct any spelling errors, ignoring the proper names.
13. Print or submit the workbook electronically as directed by your instructor. If you are instructed to do so, display the worksheet formulas, scale the worksheet to print on one page, and then print.
14. Compare your completed worksheet with **Figure 1**. **Save** the workbook, and then **Quit** Excel.

Done! You have completed Assess Your Skills 1.

Aspen Falls				
Annual Collection of City Fees				
Location	*Entrance Fees*	*Overnight Fees*	*Parking Fees*	*Total Fees*
Aspen Lakes	$ 16,593.00	$ 9,385.00	$ 13,618.00	$ 39,596.00
Behrendt Park	14,093	6,965	10,885	31,943
Silkworth Hiking Area	14,257	9,625	10,925	34,807
Hansen Hills	15,182	7,775	13,446	36,403
Terry Park	14,621	5,695	12,437	32,753
Cornish Forest	17,178	7,645	13,971	38,794
Schroder Picnic Area	16,418	-	16,927	33,345
Hamilton Hills Park	13,668	9,253	19,344	42,265
Rodman Biking Path	13,136	-	20,367	33,503
Haack Scuba Center	14,622	-	17,560	32,182
Total	$ 149,768.00	$ 56,343.00	$ 149,480.00	$ 355,591.00
	New Tax Rate	New Tax Collections		
Aspen Lakes	3%	$ 1,187.88		
Behrendt Park	3%	$ 958.29		
Silkworth Hiking Area	5%	$ 1,740.35		
Hansen Hills	5%	$ 1,820.15		
Terry Park	6%	$ 1,965.18		
Cornish Forest	6%	$ 2,327.64		
Schroder Picnic Area	6%	$ 2,000.70		
Hamilton Hills Park	6%	$ 2,535.90		
Rodman Biking Path	6%	$ 2,010.18		
Haack Scuba Center	6%	$ 1,930.92		

Lastname_Firstname_e01_Fees 6/13/2012 Tax Rates

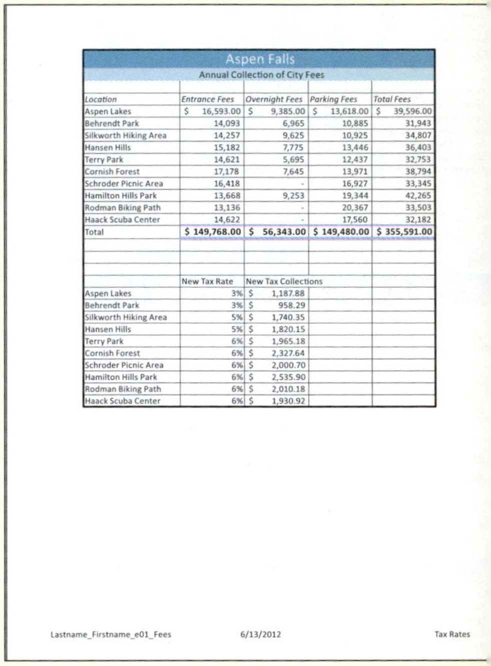

Figure 1

Assess Your Skills 2

Assess Your Skills 3 and 4 can be found at www.pearsonhighered.com/skills.

To complete this project, you will need the following file:

- e01_Visitors

You will save your spreadsheet as:

- Lastname_Firstname_e01_Visitors

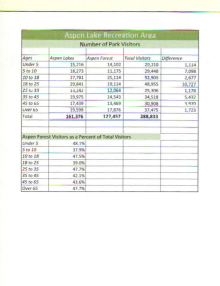

Aspen Lake Recreation Area
Number of Park Visitors

Ages	Aspen Lakes	Aspen Forest	Total Visitors	Difference
Under 5	15,216	14,102	29,318	1,114
5 to 10	18,273	11,175	29,448	7,098
10 to 18	27,791	25,114	52,905	2,677
18 to 25	29,841	19,114	48,955	10,727
25 to 35	14,242	12,064	25,306	1,178
35 to 45	19,975	14,543	34,518	5,432
45 to 65	17,439	13,469	30,908	3,970
Over 65	19,599	17,876	37,475	1,723
Total	161,376	127,457	288,833	

Aspen Forest Visitors as a Percent of Total Visitors

Under 5	48.1%
5 to 10	37.9%
10 to 18	47.5%
18 to 25	39.0%
25 to 35	47.7%
35 to 45	42.1%
45 to 65	43.6%
Over 65	47.7%

Lastname_Firstname_e01_Visitors   6/13/2012

Figure 1

1. **Start** Excel. From the student data files, open **e01_Visitors.** Save the workbook in your **Excel Chapter 1** folder as Lastname_Firstname_e01_Visitors Add the file name to the worksheet's left footer, and then add the current date to the right footer. Return to **Normal** view.

2. In cell **D5,** construct a formula to add cells **B5** and **C5.** In cell **E5,** construct a formula to subtract cell **C5** from **B5.** Use the fill handle to copy the formulas in **D5:E5** down through row **11.**

3. In cell **A12,** type Total and then in row **12,** insert the SUM function to total columns **B:D.**

4. Insert a new row above row **7,** and then in the new cell, **A7,** type 10 to 18 In cell **B7,** type 27791 and in cell **C7** type 25114

5. Use the fill handle to copy the formulas in the range **D6:E6** down one row.

6. Merge and center the range **A1:E1,** and then apply the **Accent3** cell style. Increase the font size to **18.** Merge and center the range **A2:E2,** and then apply the **40%–Accent3** cell style. Increase the font size to **14.**

7. Widen column **A** to *10.00 (0.90 inches),* and then widen columns **B:E** to *14.00 (1.24 inches).*

8. For the column and row titles, apply **Italic.** In the range **B5:E13,** apply the **Comma [0]** cell style, and then in range **B13:D13,** apply the **Total** cell style.

9. In cell **A16,** type Aspen Forest Visitors as a Percent of Total Visitors For the range **A16:D16,** apply the **Merge Across** alignment and the **40%–Accent3** cell style.

10. **Copy** the age groups from the range **A5:A12,** and **Paste** them to the range **A17:A24.**

11. In cell **B17,** construct a formula to divide *Aspen Forest Visitors*—cell **C5**—by *Total Visitors*—cell **D5.** In cell **B17,** apply the **Percent** number style and display one decimal. Use the fill handle to copy the formula down through row **24.**

12. Rename the sheet tab Park Visitors and then delete **Sheet2** and **Sheet3.**

13. Check for and correct any spelling errors.

14. Use Page Setup to center the page **Horizontally.** Set the **Gridlines** to print, and then **Save** the workbook.

15. Print or submit the workbook electronically as directed by your instructor. If you are instructed to do so, display the worksheet formulas, scale the worksheet to print on one page, and then print.

16. Compare your completed worksheet with **Figure 1.** **Save** and then **Quit** Excel.

Done! You have completed Assess Your Skills 2

Assess Your Skills Visually

To complete this project, you will need the following file:

- New blank Excel workbook

You will save your spreadsheet as:

- Lastname_Firstname_e01_Boats

Open a new blank workbook, and then **Save** the workbook as Lastname_Firstname_e01_Boats Create the worksheet shown in **Figure 1**. The width of column A is 14.00 (1.24 inches) and the width of columns B:F is 11.00 (0.99 inches). Construct formulas that display the results shown in columns D and F, row 11, and the range B15:B21. The title uses the **Accent6** cell style, and the font size is **14**. The subtitle uses the **40%–Accent6** cell style, and the font size is **12**. The title and subtitle should be merged and centered. Using **Figure 1** as your guide, apply the **Currency [0]** cell style, the **Comma [0]** cell style, the **Total** cell style, the **Percent** number style, and the **Italic** format. On the range **A14:C14,** use **Merge Across** and apply the **40%–Accent6** cell style. Rename the Sheet1 sheet tab as Boat Rentals and delete any unused worksheets. Check and correct any spelling errors. Add the file name to the left footer. **Save** the workbook, and then print or submit the file as directed by your instructor.

Done! You have completed Assess Your Skills Visually

Aspen Falls Parks and Recreation					
Hourly Boat Rentals at Aspen Lake Recreation Area					
Location	Canoes	Kayaks	Total Hours	Hourly Fee	Total Fees
North	178	175	353	$ 50.00	$ 17,650.00
South	251	158	409	60	24,540
Central	112	148	260	75	19,500
Main Entrance	401	370	771	80	61,680
Kid's Corner	491	296	787	40	31,480
East	292	189	481	50	24,050
West	143	193	336	50	16,800
Total	1,868	1,529	3,397		$ 195,700

Canoe Hours as a Percent of Total Hours	
North	50.4%
South	61.4%
Central	43.1%
Main Entrance	52.0%
Kid's Corner	62.4%
East	60.7%
West	42.6%

Lastname_Firstname_e01_Boats

Figure 1

Skills in Context

To complete this project, you will need the following file:

- e01_Employees

You will save your spreadsheet as:

- Lastname_Firstname_e01_Employees

Open the workbook **e01_Employees,** and then save the workbook as Lastname_Firstname_e01_Employees The city of Aspen Falls wants to total and compare the number of employees at its recreation areas. Using the skills you practiced in this chapter, insert formulas that calculate the total workers for each park, the total workers in each job category, and the Aspen Lakes employees as a percentage of the total employees. Format the worksheet as appropriate, and adjust column widths as necessary to display all data. Insert the file name in the footer, and check for spelling errors. Save the workbook, and then print or submit the file as directed by your instructor.

Done! You have completed Skills in Context.

Skills and You

To complete this project, you will need the following file:

- New blank Excel workbook

You will save your spreadsheet as:

- Lastname_Firstname_e01_My_College

Select six popular courses at your college, for example, *Algebra, Introduction to Computers, Biology, American History,* and so on. Consult your college's course schedule, and note the number of sections for each course that are offered in the Fall term and in the Spring term. Using the skills you have practiced in this chapter, create a worksheet to calculate the total number of sections for each course. SUM the total number of courses for the Fall term and for the Spring term. Below this data, calculate the Fall sections of each course as a percentage of the total courses offered by your school. Add appropriate titles and formatting. Save the workbook as Lastname_Firstname_e01_My_College and then add the file name to the left footer. Delete unused worksheets, check the worksheet for spelling, and then save the workbook. Print or submit the file as directed by your instructor.

Done! You have completed Skills and You.

CHAPTER 2

Create Charts

- ▶ After data is entered into Excel, you can create a visual representation of the data in the form of charts.

- ▶ Excel provides various types of charts that can make your data easier to understand.

- ▶ Column charts show data changes over a period of time or illustrate comparisons among items.

- ▶ Pie charts illustrate how each part relates to the whole. Pie charts display the relative sizes of items in a single data series.

- ▶ Charts can be enhanced with effects such as 3-D and soft shadows to create compelling graphical summaries.

- ▶ Excel helps you find errors by displaying error values, such as #### when a column is not wide enough to display the contents, or #DIV/0! when a formula's divisor is 0 or refers to an empty cell.

- ▶ A workbook can be formatted quickly by changing its overall theme or by changing its theme colors, fonts, or effects.

© Yanc | Dreamstime.com

Aspen Falls City Hall

In this chapter, you will assist Thelma Perkins, a Risk Management Specialist in the Finance Department, to complete an Excel workbook on the projected first quarter revenue for Aspen Falls. The workbook will display graphical representations of the data in charts. In this project, you will open an existing workbook, construct formulas containing absolute cell references, and copy the formulas to other cells. You will create and format column charts and pie charts and change chart effects. You will insert text boxes and WordArt. To complete the workbook, you will modify the chart sheets to meet printing requirements.

Time to complete all
10 skills – 60 to 90 minutes

Student data file needed for this chapter:

e02_Revenue

Outcome

Using the skills in this chapter, you will be able to work with Excel spreadsheets like this:

You will save your spreadsheet as:

Lastname_Firstname_e02_Revenue

SKILLS

Skills 1-10 Training

At the end of this chapter you will be able to:

Skill 1 Open Existing Workbooks and Align Text

Skill 2 Construct and Copy Formulas Containing Absolute Cell References

Skill 3 Format Numbers

Skill 4 Create Column Charts

Skill 5 Format Column Charts

Skill 6 Create Pie Charts and Chart Sheets

Skill 7 Apply 3-D Effects and Rotate Pie Chart Slices

Skill 8 Explode and Color Pie Slices and Insert Text Boxes

Skill 9 Update Charts and Insert WordArt

Skill 10 Prepare Chart Sheets for Printing

MORE SKILLS

Skill 11 Insert and Edit Comments

Skill 12 Change Chart Types

Skill 13 Copy Excel Data to Word Documents

Skill 14 Fill Series Data into Worksheet Cells

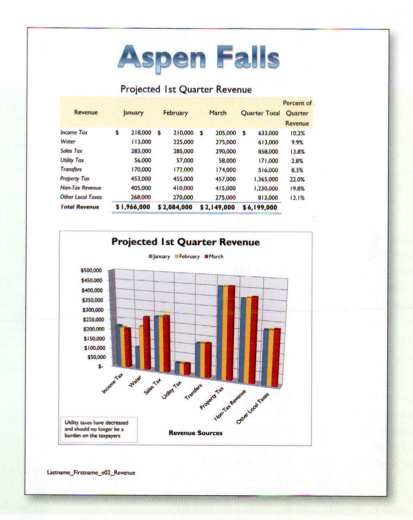

► The *Text wrap* format displays text on multiple lines within a cell.

► A *document theme*—a set of design elements providing a unified look for colors, fonts, and graphics—can be applied.

1. On the **Dock,** click the **Microsoft Excel** icon. In the displayed **Excel Workbook Gallery** dialog, make sure that **Excel Workbook** is selected, and then click **Choose**. On the **menu bar,** click **File,** and then click **Open**. In the **Open** dialog, navigate to your student data files. Select **e02_Revenue,** and then click the **Open** button. Compare your screen with **Figure 1**.

2. Click **File,** and then click **Save As**. Navigate to the location where you are saving your files, create a folder named Excel Chapter 2 and then **Save** the workbook as Lastname_Firstname_e02_Revenue

3. Display the **Layout tab,** and then in the **View group,** click the **Page Layout** button. On **Page 1,** use the ▼ to scroll down until the 🖺 pointer displays and the **Double-click to add footer** label displays. Double-click in the left section of the Footer area. Click the **Insert File Name** 🗐 button to insert the *&[File]* placeholder into the left section of the Footer area.

4. Double-click in a cell above the footer. In the **View group,** click the **Normal** button 🖾, then scroll to the top of the worksheet.

5. In the column heading area, point to the right boundary of column **A** to display the ➕ pointer displayed. Double-click to **AutoFit** or automatically change the column width. Compare your screen with **Figure 2**.

   ■ **Continue to the next page to complete the skill**

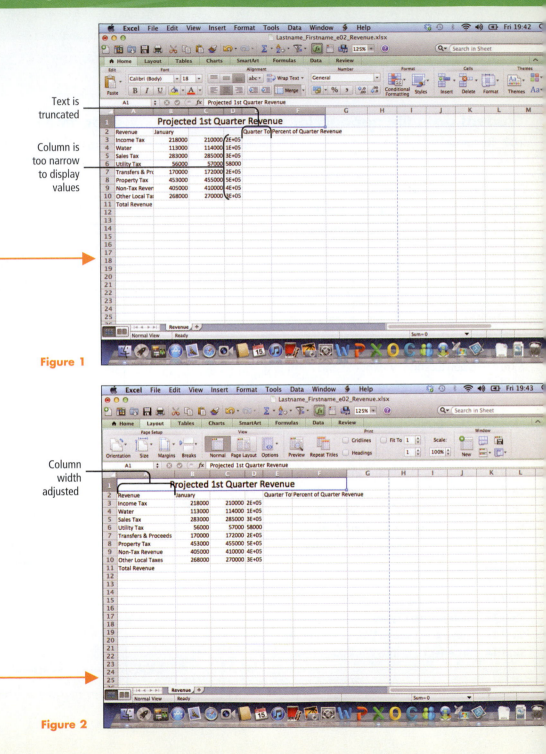

Text is truncated

Column is too narrow to display values

Figure 1

Column width adjusted

Figure 2

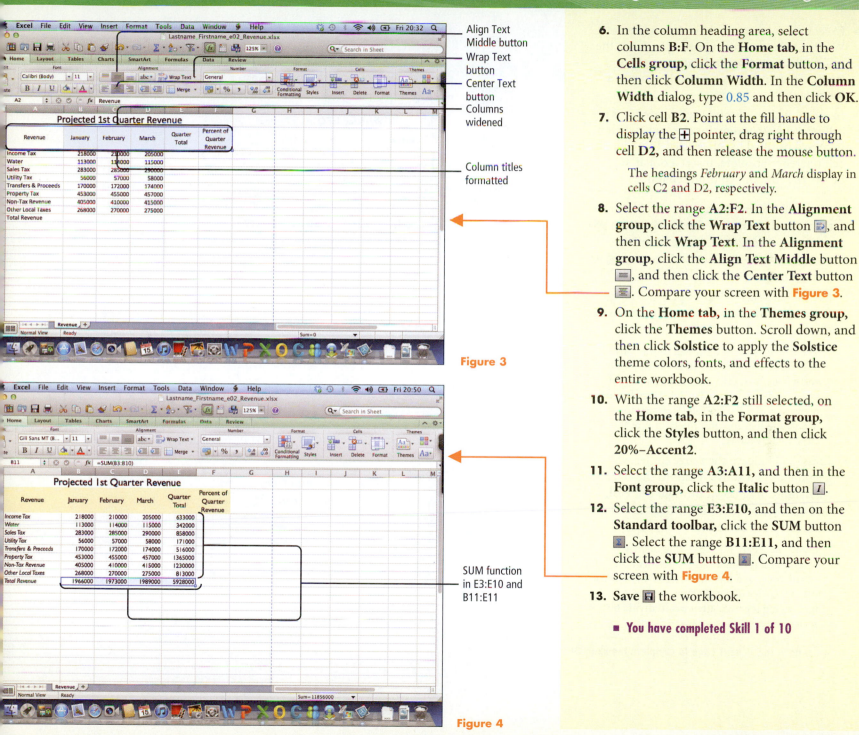

Align Text
Middle button

Wrap Text
button

Center Text
button

Columns
widened

Column titles
formatted

Figure 3

SUM function
in E3:E10 and
B11:E11

Figure 4

6. In the column heading area, select columns **B:F.** On the **Home tab,** in the **Cells group,** click the **Format** button, and then click **Column Width.** In the **Column Width** dialog, type 0.85 and then click **OK.**

7. Click cell **B2.** Point at the fill handle to display the ⊞ pointer, drag right through cell **D2,** and then release the mouse button.

   The headings *February* and *March* display in cells C2 and D2, respectively.

8. Select the range **A2:F2.** In the **Alignment group,** click the **Wrap Text** button, and then click **Wrap Text.** In the **Alignment group,** click the **Align Text Middle** button, and then click the **Center Text** button. Compare your screen with **Figure 3.**

9. On the **Home tab,** in the **Themes group,** click the **Themes** button. Scroll down, and then click **Solstice** to apply the **Solstice** theme colors, fonts, and effects to the entire workbook.

10. With the range **A2:F2** still selected, on the **Home tab,** in the **Format group,** click the **Styles** button, and then click **20%–Accent2.**

11. Select the range **A3:A11,** and then in the **Font group,** click the **Italic** button *I*.

12. Select the range **E3:E10,** and then on the **Standard toolbar,** click the **SUM** button. Select the range **B11:E11,** and then click the **SUM** button. Compare your screen with **Figure 4.**

13. **Save** 🖫 the workbook.

   ■ **You have completed Skill 1 of 10**

▶ Excel uses rules to check for formula errors. When a formula breaks one of the rules, the cell displays an *error indicator*—a green triangle that indicates a possible error in a formula.

▶ In a formula, an ***absolute cell reference*** is a cell reference that remains the same when it is copied or filled to other cells. To make a cell reference absolute, insert a dollar sign before the row and column reference.

1. Click cell **F3,** and then type =E3/E11 On the **formula bar,** click the **Enter** button to display *0.10678138*. In the **Number group,** click the **Percent Style** button to display *11%*.

2. Double-click cell **F3** to display the range finder, and then compare your screen with **Figure 1**.

    The *range finder* outlines all of the cells referenced in a formula. It is useful for verifying which cells are used in a formula and for editing formulas. Here, *Income Tax* revenue is divided by *Total Revenue* to determine that Income Tax is 11% of the city's total revenue.

3. Press [esc] to leave the range finder while keeping cell **F3** active. Point to the cell **F3** fill handle, drag down through cell **F10,** and then release the mouse button. Compare your screen with **Figure 2**.

    Error values are messages that display whenever a formula cannot perform the calculations in a formula. The *#DIV/0!* error value displays in a cell whenever the underlying formula attempts to divide by zero.

    ■ **Continue to the next page to complete the skill**

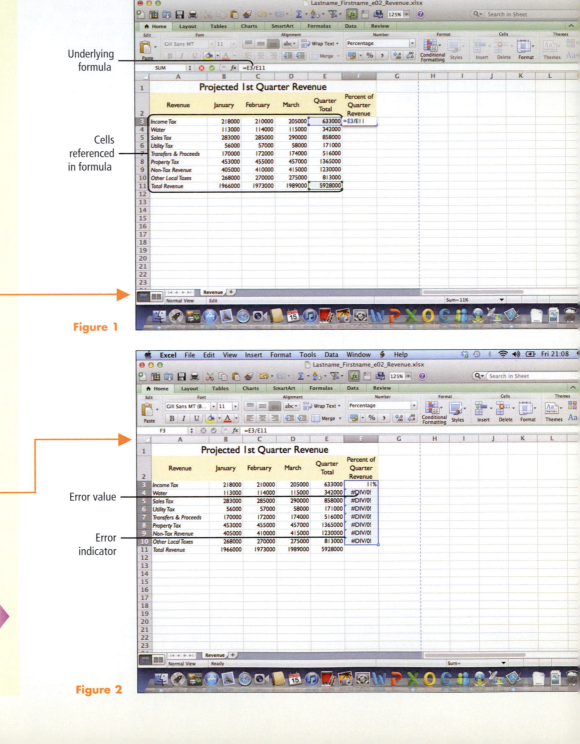

Underlying formula

Cells referenced in formula

Figure 1

Error value

Error indicator

Figure 2

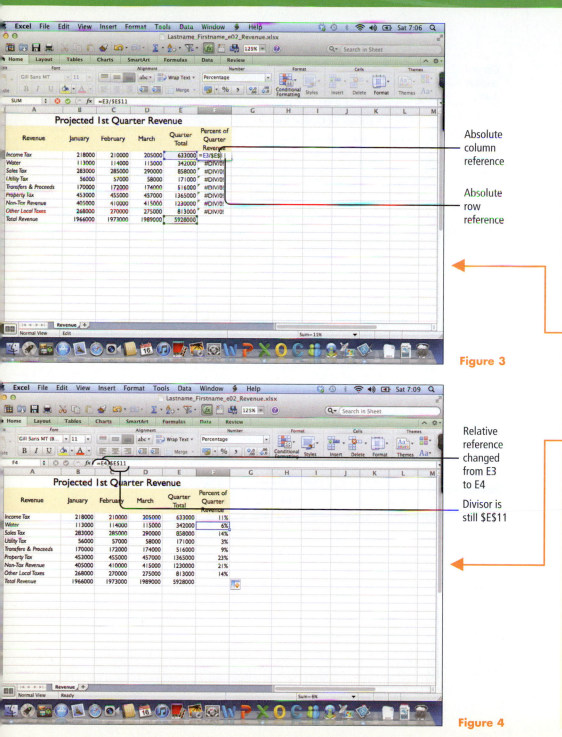

Figure 3

Absolute column reference

Absolute row reference

Relative reference changed from E3 to E4

Divisor is still E11

Figure 4

4. Click cell **F4**. To the left of the cell, point to the displayed **Error Checking** button to display the ScreenTip—*The formula or function used is dividing by zero or empty cells.*

5. Double-click cell **F4** to display the range finder.

   The formula was copied with a relative cell reference. In the copied formula, the cell reference to cell E4 is correct, but the formula is dividing by the value in cell E12, an empty cell. In this calculation, the divisor must always be cell E11.

6. Press [esc], and then double-click cell **F3**. Move the insertion point to the middle of the formula—to the left of *E11*—and then type $ Click to the left of 11, and then type $ to make the cell reference absolute, as shown in **Figure 3**.

7. On the **formula bar,** click the **Enter** button. In cell **F3**, point to the fill handle, and then drag the fill handle to copy the formula down through cell **F10**.

8. Click cell **F4**. Notice that the divisor refers to cell **E11**, as shown in **Figure 4**.

   The cell reference for the *Water Quarter Total* changed relative to its row; however, the value used as the divisor—*Total Revenue* in cell E11—remained absolute.

9. Press the ▼ repeatedly, and notice that the divisor remains constant—E11—while the quotient changes relative to the row.

10. **Save** the workbook.

   ■ **You have completed Skill 2 of 10**

► A *number format* is a specific way that Excel displays numbers. By default, Excel displays the *General format*—a number format that does not display commas or trailing zeros to the right of a decimal point.

► The *Accounting number format* applies comma separators where appropriate, inserts a fixed dollar sign aligned at the left edge of the cell, applies two decimal places, and leaves a small amount of space at both the right and left edges of the cell to accommodate parentheses for negative numbers.

► The *Comma cell style* adds commas where appropriate and applies the same formatting as the Accounting number format but without a dollar sign.

1. Click cell **B3,** and then on the **Home tab,** in the **Number group,** notice that *General* displays, as shown in **Figure 1**.

2. Select the range **B3:E3,** hold down command ⌘, and then select the range **B11:E11.**

3. With the two nonadjacent ranges selected, on the **Home tab,** in the **Number group,** click the **Currency** button 🢒, and then click the **Decrease Decimal** button 🢒 two times to remove the decimal places. Compare your screen with **Figure 2**.

   Financial worksheets typically display dollar signs only in the first row and in the total row.

   ■ **Continue to the next page to complete the skill**

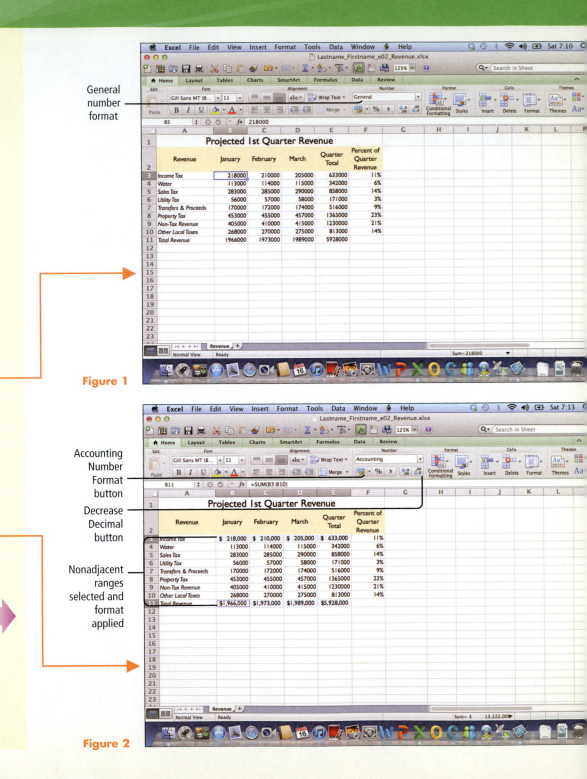

General number format

Figure 1

Accounting Number Format button

Decrease Decimal button

Nonadjacent ranges selected and format applied

Figure 2

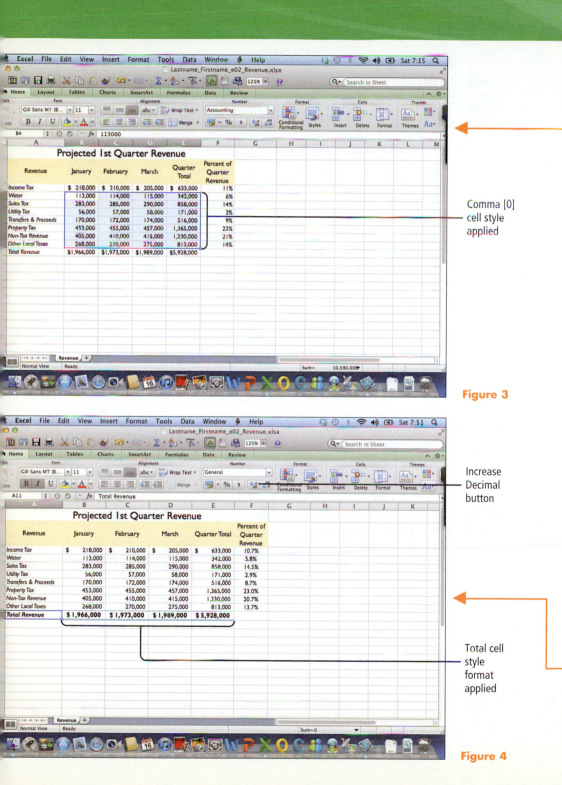

Figure 3

Comma [0] cell style applied

Increase Decimal button

Total cell style format applied

Figure 4

4. Select the range **B4:E10**. In the **Format group,** click the **Styles** button, scroll down, and then under **Number Format,** click **Comma [0]**. Compare your screen with **Figure 3**.

   The Comma [0] cell style inserts commas and rounds the values so that no decimals display.

5. Select the range **F3:F10**. In the **Number group,** click the **Increase Decimal** button one time to add one decimal to the applied **Percent** style. In the **Alignment group,** click the **Center Text** button.

6. Select the range **B11:E11**. In the **Format group,** click the **Styles** button, and then under **Titles and Headings,** click **Total.**

   The *Total cell style* applies a single top border, which indicates that calculations were performed on the numbers above, and a double bottom border, which indicates that the calculations are complete. Notice that the values for *Total Revenue* do not display properly—##### displays for the value. This means that the column is not wide enough to display the entire contents and the displayed value is truncated.

7. In the column heading area, select columns **B:E**. With columns **B:E** selected, point to the right boundary of any selected column heading to display the pointer, and then drag to the right until the width in the ScreenTip indicates *Width: 12.00 (1.07 inches)*. Release the mouse button.

8. Click in cell **A11**. On the **Home tab,** in the **Font group,** click the **Bold** button. Compare your screen with **Figure 4**.

9. **Save** the workbook.

   ■ **You have completed Skill 3 of 10**

▶ A **chart** is a graphic representation of data used to show comparisons, patterns, and trends.

▶ A **column chart** is useful for illustrating comparisons among related numbers.

1. Select the range **A2:D10**—do *not* include the *Quarter Total* column or the *Total Revenue* row in your selection. On the **Charts tab,** in the **Insert Chart group,** click the **Column** button to display the **Chart** gallery, as shown in **Figure 1**.

2. In the **Chart** gallery, under **2-D Column,** click the first chart—**Clustered Column.** On the Ribbon, notice that the **Chart Layout** and **Format** contextual tabs display, as shown in **Figure 2**.

   When you insert a chart, borders surround the chart data and an embedded chart is inserted. An **embedded chart** is a chart that is placed on the worksheet containing the data. Embedded charts are beneficial when you want to view or print a chart with its source data.

3. Along the bottom of the chart, locate the names of the revenue categories.

   An **axis** is a line bordering the chart plot area used as a frame of reference for measurement. The **category axis** is the axis that displays the category labels. A **category label** is nonnumeric text that identifies the categories of data. Here, the worksheet's row titles are used for the category labels. For column charts, the category axis is the **x-axis**—the horizontal axis of a chart.

   ■ **Continue to the next page to complete the skill** ➤

Clustered Column chart

Chart gallery

Figure 1

Chart Tools contextual tabs display

Borders around chart data

Embedded column chart

Category axis

Figure 2

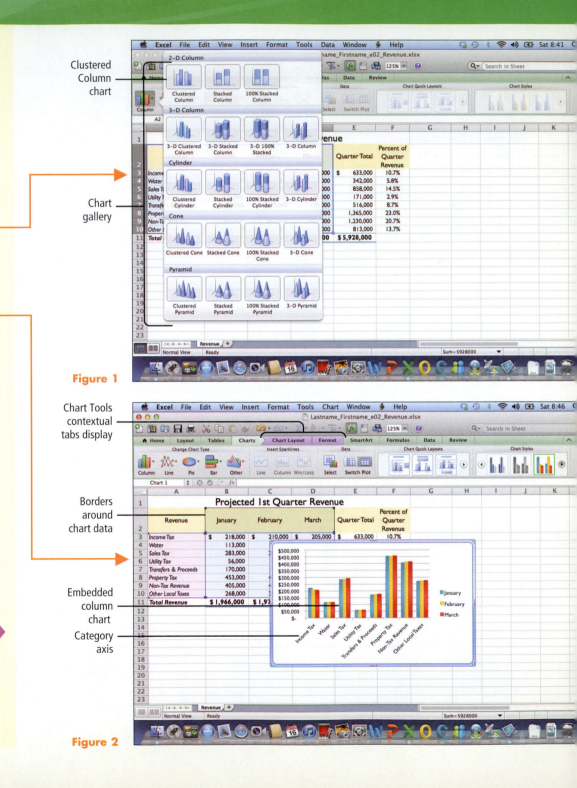

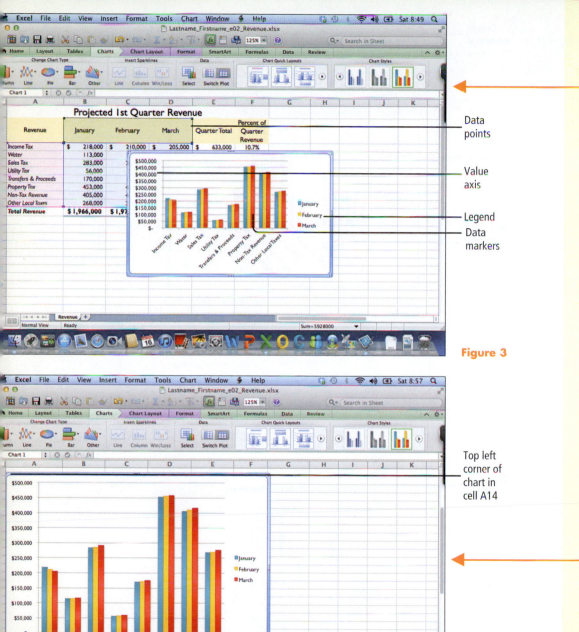

Figure 3

Figure 4

4. On the left side of the chart, locate the numerical scale, and then on the right side, locate the months displayed in the legend. Compare your screen with **Figure 3**.

In the worksheet, each cell bordered in blue is referred to as a *data point*—a chart value that originates in a worksheet cell. Each data point is represented in a chart by a *data marker*—a column, a bar, an area, a dot, a pie slice, or another symbol that represents a single data point.

The *value axis* is the axis that displays the worksheet's numeric data. In a column chart, the value axis is the *y-axis*—the vertical axis of a chart.

Data points that are related to one another form a *data series*, and each data series has a unique color or pattern represented in the chart *legend*—a box that identifies the patterns or colors that are assigned to the data series or categories in the chart. Here, each month is a different data series, and the legend shows the color assigned to each month.

5. Point to the upper border of the chart to display the ⊕ pointer, and then move the chart to position its upper left corner in cell **A14**.

6. Scroll to display row **29,** and then point to the lower right corner of the chart. With the ⬉ pointer, drag to position the lower right corner in the middle of cell **F36,** as shown in **Figure 4**.

7. **Save** 🖫 the workbook.

■ **You have completed Skill 4 of 10**

▶ You can customize individual chart elements by using the buttons on the Chart Tools contextual tabs.

▶ You can modify the look of a chart by applying a *chart layout*—a prebuilt set of chart elements that can include a title, a legend, or labels—or by applying a *chart style*—a prebuilt chart format that applies an overall visual look to a chart by modifying its graphic effects, colors, and backgrounds.

1. If necessary, click the border of the chart to select the chart. On the **Charts tab,** in the **Change Chart Type group,** click the **Column** button. In the displayed gallery, under **3-D Column,** click **3-D Clustered Column**.

    The chart is changed from a two-dimensional chart to a three-dimensional chart. *3-D,* which is short for *three-dimensional*, refers to an image that appears to have all three spatial dimensions—length, width, and depth.

2. In the **Chart Quick Layouts group,** click the **More** button ⏷, and then click **Layout 9**–third thumbnail on the third row—to add the chart title and the axes titles, as shown in **Figure 1.**

3. At the top of the chart, click the text *Chart Title,* and type Projected 1st Quarter Revenue Verify that your text replaced any existing text.

4. In the **Chart Styles group,** click the **More** button ⏷, and then click the second thumbnail on the fifth row. Compare your screen with **Figure 2.**

    ▪ **Continue to the next page to complete the skill**

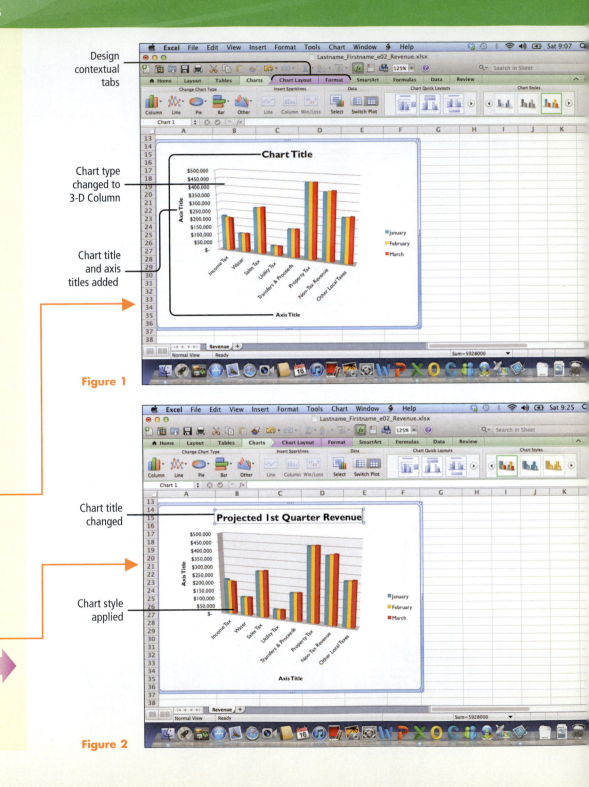

Design contextual tabs

Chart type changed to 3-D Column

Chart title and axis titles added

Figure 1

Chart title changed

Chart style applied

Figure 2

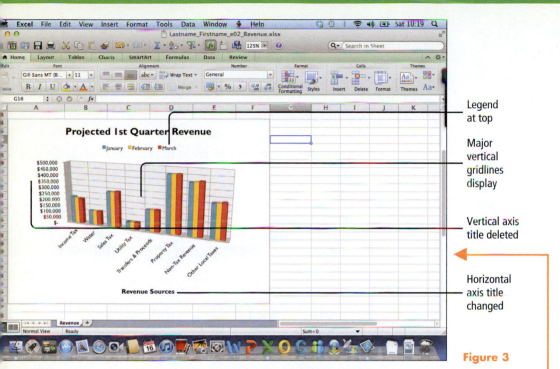

Legend at top

Major vertical gridlines display

Vertical axis title deleted

Horizontal axis title changed

Figure 3

Chart Types Commonly Used in Excel

Chart type	Use to
Column	Illustrate data changes over a period of time or illustrate comparisons among items.
Line	Illustrate trends over time, with time displayed along the horizontal axis and the data point values connected by a line.
Pie	Illustrate the relationship of parts to a whole.
Bar	Illustrate comparisons among individual items.
Area	Emphasize the magnitude of change over time.

Figure 4

5. Below the horizontal axis, click the text *Axis Title*. Type Revenue Sources Verify that your text replaced any existing text.

6. In the chart, highlight the *Revenue Sources* axis title. With the 🔲 pointer over the title, press and hold control, and then click the mouse. From the displayed shortcut menu, click **Format Text**. In the **Format Text** dialog, in the **Font size** box replace the existing value with 12 Click **OK**.

7. To the left of the vertical axis, click the text *Axis Title*. Press delete to delete the vertical axis title.

   The vertical axis title is deleted, and the chart automatically resizes to use the additional space.

8. On the **Chart Layout tab,** in the **Labels group,** click the **Legend** button. From the displayed list, click **Legend at Top** to move the legend to the top of the chart.

   When you move chart elements such as the legend, the chart automatically resizes.

9. In the **Axes group,** click the **Gridlines** button. Point to **Vertical Gridlines,** and then click **Major Gridlines** to display vertical grid lines between each category.

10. Click cell **G16** to deselect the chart. **Save** 🔲 the workbook, and then compare your screen with **Figure 3**.

11. Take a moment to examine the various types of charts available in Excel, as summarized in **Figure 4**.

   ■ **You have completed Skill 5 of 10**

▶ A *pie chart* displays the relationship of parts to a whole.

▶ A *chart sheet* is a workbook sheet that contains only a chart and is useful when you want to view a chart separately from the worksheet data.

1. Select the range **A3:A10**. Hold down command ⌘, and then select the range **E3:E10** to select the nonadjacent quarter totals.

2. On the **Charts tab,** in the **Insert Chart group,** click the **Pie** button. Under **3-D Pie,** click the first chart—**3-D Pie.**

   The row labels in the range A3:A10 identify the slices of the pie chart. The quarter totals in the range E3:E10 are the data series that determine the size of each pie slice.

3. On the **menu bar,** click **Chart,** and then click **Move Chart.** In the **Move Chart** dialog, select the **New sheet** option button. In the **New sheet** box, replace the highlighted text *Chart1* by typing Revenue Chart as shown in **Figure 1.**

4. In the **Move Chart** dialog, click **OK** to move the pie chart to a chart sheet.

5. On the **Charts tab,** in the **Chart Quick Layouts group,** click the **More** button ⊡, and then click **Layout 5**—second thumbnail on the second row. Compare your screen with **Figure 2.**

   With Chart Layout 5, the chart title displays at the top of the chart, the legend is deleted, and the category names display in each pie slice.

6. Use the technique practiced earlier to change the **Chart Title** to Aspen Falls Projected 1st Quarter Revenue

   ■ **Continue to the next page to complete the skill** ▶

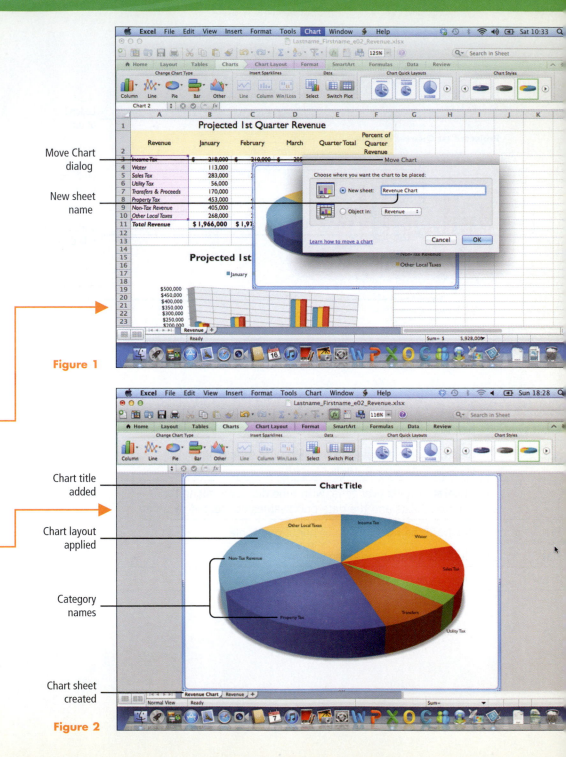

Move Chart dialog

New sheet name

Figure 1

Chart title added

Chart layout applied

Category names

Chart sheet created

Figure 2

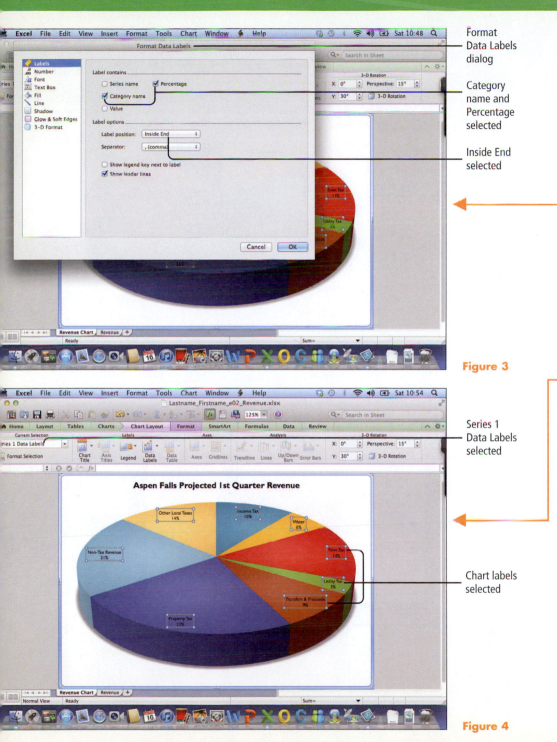

Format Data Labels dialog

Category name and Percentage selected

Inside End selected

Figure 3

Series 1 Data Labels selected

Chart labels selected

Figure 4

7. On the **Chart Layout tab,** in the **Labels group,** click the **Data Labels** button, and then click **Data Label Options**.

8. In the **Format Data Labels** dialog, on the left, click **Labels**. Under **Label contains,** verify that the **Category name** check box is selected, and then select the **Percentage** check box. Clear any other check boxes in this group. Under **Label position,** select the **Inside End** option button, and then compare your screen with **Figure 3**.

9. In the left side of the **Format Data Labels** dialog, click **Number**. Clear the **Linked to source** check box. Under **Category,** click **Percentage**. In the **Decimal places** box, replace the value with 1 Click to select the **Linked to source** check box, and then click **OK**.

10. In the **Current Selection group,** verify that *Series 1 Data Labels* displays, as shown in **Figure 4**. If necessary, click the Chart Elements arrow, and then click Series 1 Data Labels.

    You can use the Chart Elements list to select any chart element.

11. With all of the data labels selected, on the **Home tab,** in the **Font group,** click the **Bold** button ⧉, and then change the **Font Size** to 12.

12. On the **menu bar,** click **View,** and then click **Header and Footer**. In the **Page Setup** dialog, click the **Customize Footer** button. Verify that the insertion point is in the **Left section** box, and then click the **Insert File Name** button ⧉. Click **OK** two times to insert a footer that will display when the chart sheet is printed.

13. **Save** ⧉ the workbook.

    ■ **You have completed Skill 6 of 10**

▶ You can modify chart elements by changing the fill color or texture, or by adding an effect such as a shadow, glow, reflection, or bevel.

▶ You can rotate pie chart slices to present a different visual perspective of the chart.

1. Click the edge of any pie slice to deselect the data labels and to select all of the pie slices—*Series 1*. Compare your screen with **Figure 1**.

2. On the **Format tab,** in the **Chart Element Styles group,** click the **Effects** button. Point to **Bevel,** and then at the bottom of the **Bevel** gallery, click **Bevel Options**.

3. In the **Format Data Series** dialog, under **Bevel,** click the **Top button arrow.** In the gallery, click the **Circle** thumbnail. Click the **Bottom button arrow,** and then click the **Circle** thumbnail.

4. Under **Bevel,** in the four **Width** and **Height** spin boxes, replace the existing value with 512 pt and then compare your screen with **Figure 2**.

5. In the **Format Data Series** dialog, click the **Depth & Surface** tab. Under **Surface,** click the **Material button arrow,** and then click the third thumbnail—**Plastic**. In the lower right corner of the dialog, click the **OK** button.

6. On the **Format tab,** in the **Chart Element Styles group,** click the **Effects** button, and then point to **Shadow**. At the bottom of the **Shadow** gallery, under **Perspective,** click the third thumbnail—**Perspective Bottom**.

   ■ **Continue to the next page to complete the skill** ▶

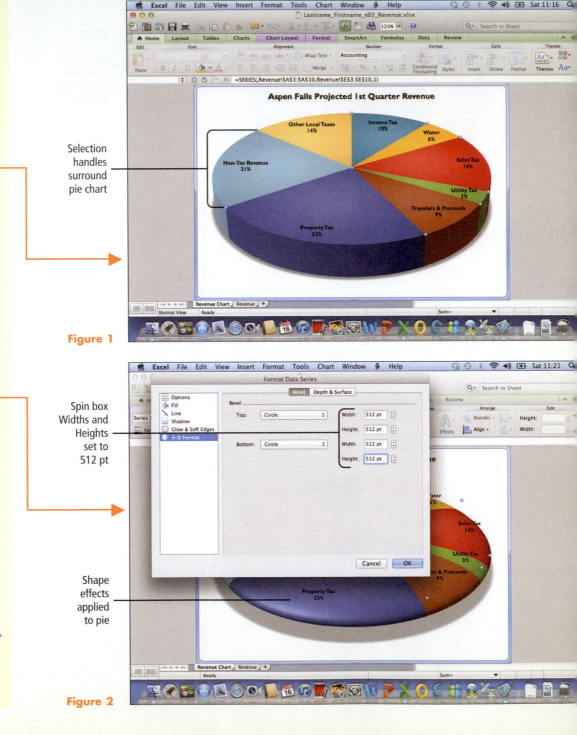

Selection handles surround pie chart

Figure 1

Spin box Widths and Heights set to 512 pt

Shape effects applied to pie

Figure 2

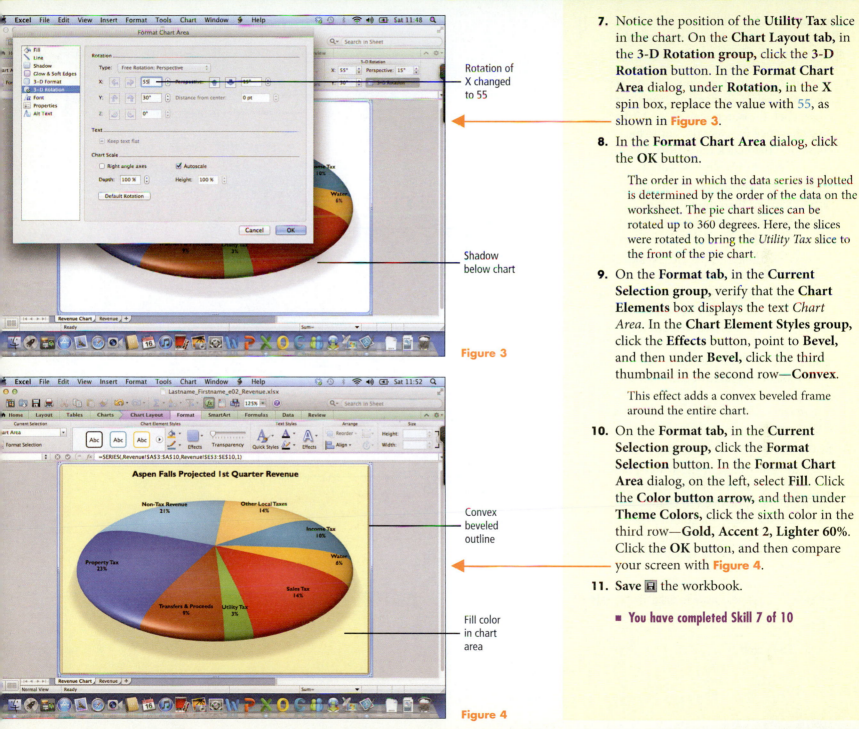

Rotation of
X changed
to 55

Shadow
below chart

Figure 3

Convex
beveled
outline

Fill color
in chart
area

Figure 4

7. Notice the position of the **Utility Tax** slice in the chart. On the **Chart Layout tab,** in the **3-D Rotation group,** click the **3-D Rotation** button. In the **Format Chart Area** dialog, under **Rotation,** in the **X** spin box, replace the value with **55,** as shown in **Figure 3**.

8. In the **Format Chart Area** dialog, click the **OK** button.

   The order in which the data series is plotted is determined by the order of the data on the worksheet. The pie chart slices can be rotated up to 360 degrees. Here, the slices were rotated to bring the *Utility Tax* slice to the front of the pie chart.

9. On the **Format tab,** in the **Current Selection group,** verify that the **Chart Elements** box displays the text *Chart Area.* In the **Chart Element Styles group,** click the **Effects** button, point to **Bevel,** and then under **Bevel,** click the third thumbnail in the second row—**Convex**.

   This effect adds a convex beveled frame around the entire chart.

10. On the **Format tab,** in the **Current Selection group,** click the **Format Selection** button. In the **Format Chart Area** dialog, on the left, select **Fill**. Click the **Color button arrow,** and then under **Theme Colors,** click the sixth color in the third row—**Gold, Accent 2, Lighter 60%**. Click the **OK** button, and then compare your screen with **Figure 4**.

11. **Save** 🖫 the workbook.

   ■ **You have completed Skill 7 of 10**

► You can *explode*—pull out one or more slices—of a 3-D pie chart to emphasize a specific slice or slices in a pie chart.

1. Click in the shaded area outside the pie chart to deselect all elements. On the pie chart, click the outer edge of the **Utility Tax** slice once to select the entire pie chart, and then click the **Utility Tax** slice again to select only the one pie slice.

2. Point to the **Utility Tax** slice to display the ❖ pointer, and then drag the slice away from the center of the pie, as shown in **Figure 1**.

   Notice the Utility Tax pie slice exploded—pulled away from the pie.

3. With the **Utility Tax** slice still selected, on the **Format tab,** in the **Current Selection group,** click the **Format Selection** button. In the left side of the **Format Data Point** dialog, click **Fill**. On the **Solid tab,** click the **Color button arrow,** and then under **Theme Colors,** click the ninth color in the fourth row—**Brown, Accent 5, Lighter 40%**. Compare your screen with **Figure 2**.

4. In the dialog, click the **OK** button.

5. Click the inner edge of the **Water** pie slice to select only that pie slice. Use the technique just practiced to change the *Water* pie slice solid fill color to the last color in the fourth row—**Indigo, Accent 6, Lighter 40%**. Click the **OK** button.

   ■ **Continue to the next page to complete the skill** ➤

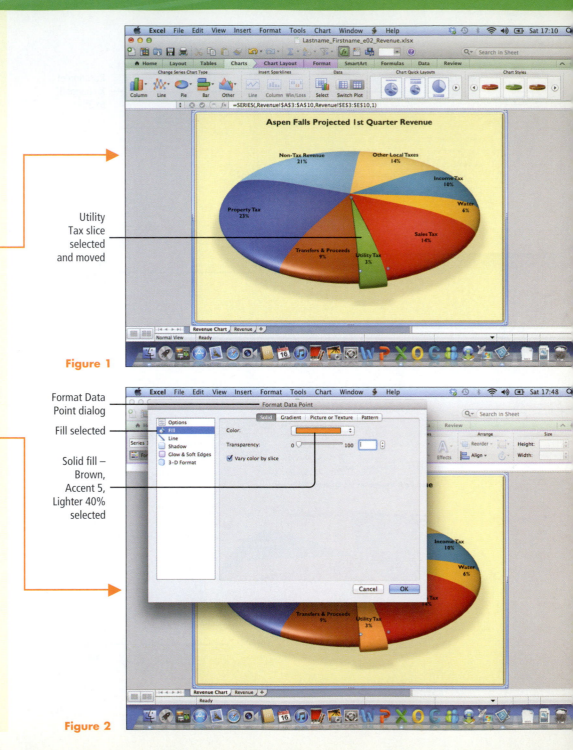

Utility Tax slice selected and moved

Figure 1

Format Data Point dialog

Fill selected

Solid fill – Brown, Accent 5, Lighter 40% selected

Figure 2

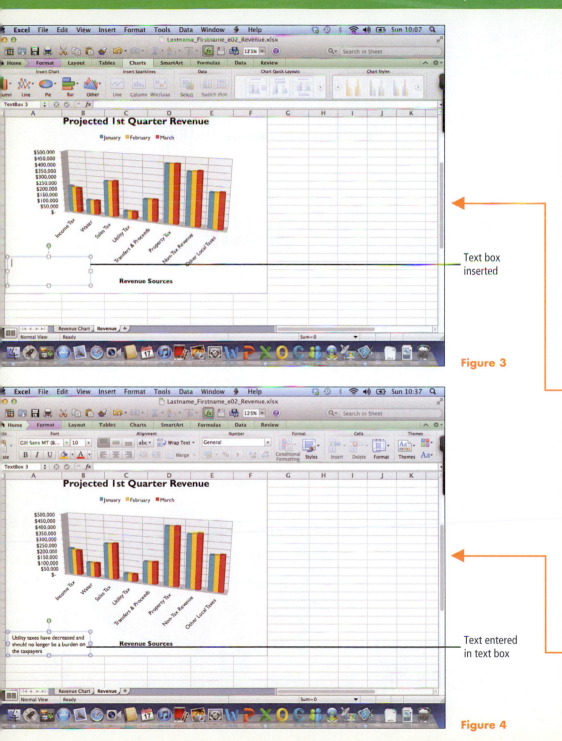

Figure 3

Text box inserted

Figure 4

Text entered in text box

6. On the chart, click the **Utility Tax** category label once to select all data labels, and then click the **Utility Tax** data label again to select only that one data label. Point to the *Utility Tax* data label's bottom border, and then with the ⊕ pointer, drag the *Utility Tax* data label to the edge of the exploded slice. Adjust the size and position of the data label or text box as needed.

7. In the sheet tab area at the bottom of the workbook, click the **Revenue** sheet tab to display the worksheet. If necessary, scroll down, and then click in an empty cell below the chart. On the **menu bar,** click **Insert,** and then click **Text Box.**

8. Position the displayed A pointer just to the left of the **Revenue Sources** title on the Horizontal Axis. Hold down the left mouse button, and then drag down and to the right to draw the text box approximately, as shown in **Figure 3**.

9. Release the mouse button to insert the text box. With the insertion point blinking inside the text box, type Utility taxes have decreased and should no longer be a burden on the taxpayers

10. Select all the text in the text box. On the **Home tab,** in the **Font group,** click the **Font Size arrow** 12 ▾, and then click **10.** If necessary, resize the text box to display all the text.

11. Point to the top border of the text box so that the ⊕ pointer displays and then with the ⊕ pointer, drag to position the text box to the bottom of the plot area, as shown in **Figure 4**.

12. **Save** 🖫 the workbook.

■ **You have completed Skill 8 of 10**

▶ Recall that a chart's data series and category labels are linked to the source data in the worksheet. When worksheet values are changed, the chart is automatically updated.

▶ *Sheet tabs* are the labels along the lower border of the workbook window that identify each worksheet or chart sheet.

1. Click cell **C4,** type 225000 and then press return to accept the new value. If necessary, scroll down to view the chart. Notice the *Water* value for the month of *February* is updated, as shown in **Figure 1**.

   The data marker—the column—representing this data point is updated on the column chart.

2. Click cell **D4,** type 275000 and then press return. In cell **F4,** notice the Water revenue now represents 9.9% of the projected 1st Quarter Revenue.

3. Click the **Revenue Chart** sheet tab to display the pie chart and then move the *Utility Tax* data label to the edge of the slice. Verify that in the pie chart, the slice for *Water* displays *10%*, as shown in **Figure 2**.

   When underlying data is changed, the pie chart percentages and pie slices are automatically recalculated and resized.

4. Click the **Revenue** sheet tab, and then in cell **A7,** change *Transfers & Proceeds* to Transfers Press return), and then scroll down to verify that the column chart category label also changed.

   ■ **Continue to the next page to complete the skill** ➡

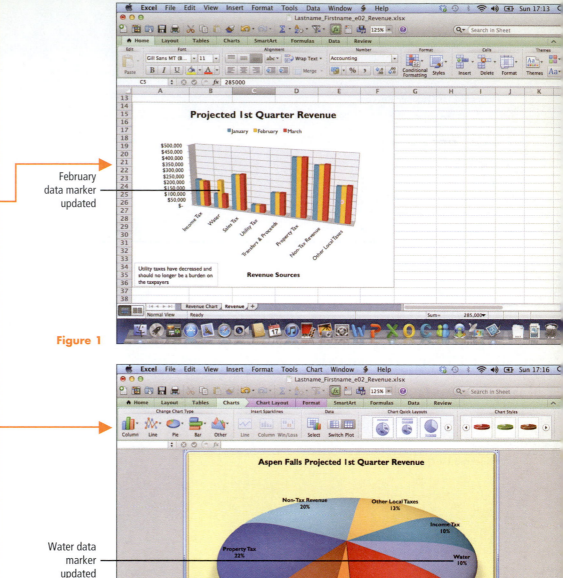

February data marker updated

Figure 1

Water data marker updated

Figure 2

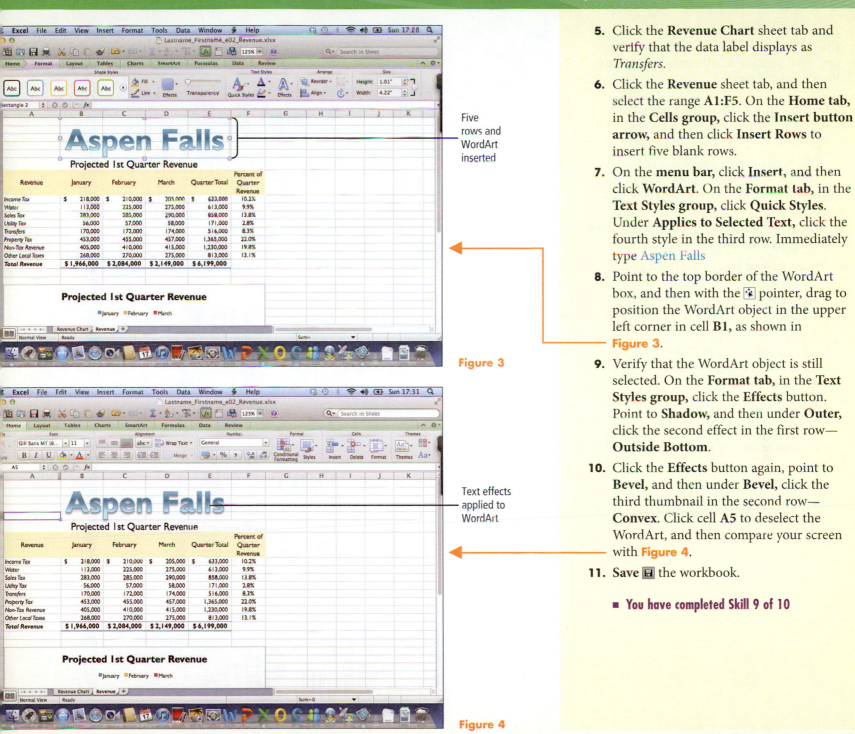

Five rows and WordArt inserted

Figure 3

Text effects applied to WordArt

Figure 4

5. Click the **Revenue Chart** sheet tab and verify that the data label displays as *Transfers*.

6. Click the **Revenue** sheet tab, and then select the range **A1:F5**. On the **Home tab,** in the **Cells group,** click the **Insert button arrow,** and then click **Insert Rows** to insert five blank rows.

7. On the **menu bar,** click **Insert,** and then click **WordArt**. On the **Format tab,** in the **Text Styles group,** click **Quick Styles.** Under **Applies to Selected Text,** click the fourth style in the third row. Immediately type Aspen Falls

8. Point to the top border of the WordArt box, and then with the ✛ pointer, drag to position the WordArt object in the upper left corner in cell **B1,** as shown in **Figure 3**.

9. Verify that the WordArt object is still selected. On the **Format tab,** in the **Text Styles group,** click the **Effects** button. Point to **Shadow,** and then under **Outer,** click the second effect in the first row—**Outside Bottom**.

10. Click the **Effects** button again, point to **Bevel,** and then under **Bevel,** click the third thumbnail in the second row—**Convex**. Click cell **A5** to deselect the WordArt, and then compare your screen with **Figure 4**.

11. **Save** 🖫 the workbook.

■ **You have completed Skill 9 of 10**

► Before you print an Excel worksheet, you should preview the printed document. If you need to make adjustments, you can use Page Layout view.

1. On the **Layout tab,** in the **View group,** click **Preview.** Compare your screen with **Figure 1.**

   The Preview application opens and indicates that the worksheet will print on two pages. If you scroll down, you will notice that Page 2 is blank.

2. On the **menu bar,** click **Preview,** and then click **Quit Preview.**

3. On the **Layout tab,** in the **Print group,** click the **Fit To** check box. In the **View group,** click **Preview.** Compare your screen with **Figure 2.**

   Notice *1 of 1* displays at the top of the screen, indicating that the WordArt, the data, and the column chart will all print on one page.

4. On the **menu bar,** click **Preview,** and then click **Quit Preview.**

   ■ **Continue to the next page to complete the skill**

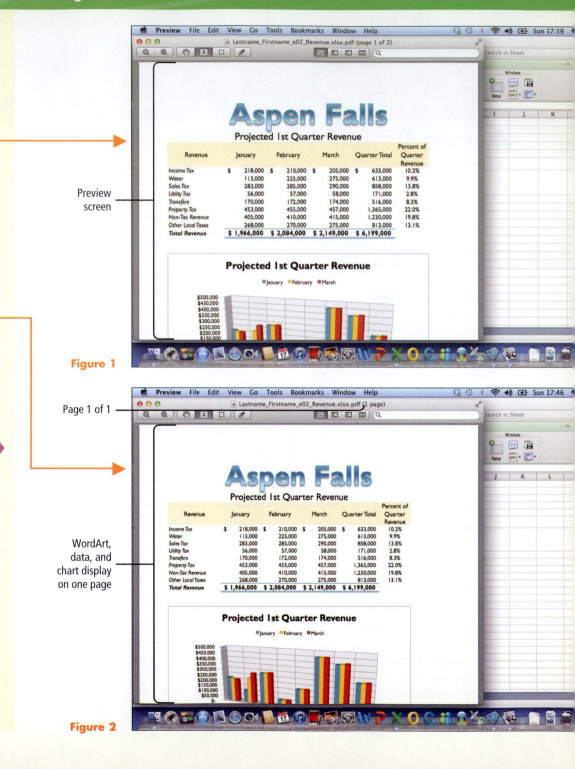

Preview screen

Figure 1

Page 1 of 1

WordArt, data, and chart display on one page

Figure 2

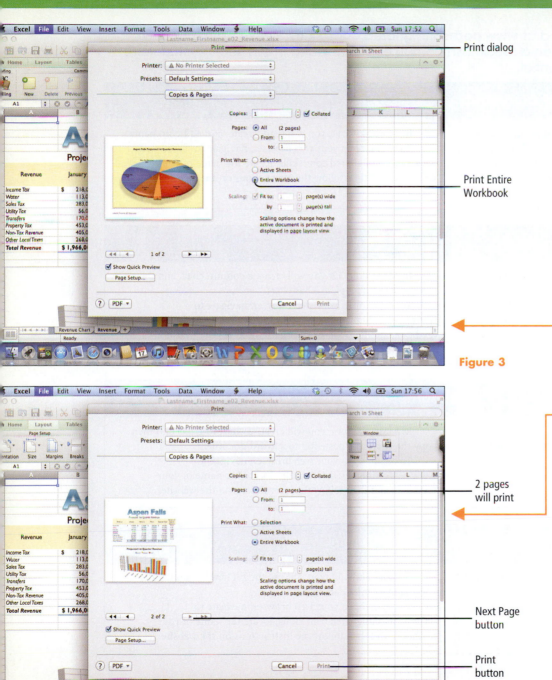

Print dialog

Print Entire
Workbook

Figure 3

2 pages
will print

Next Page
button

Print
button

Figure 4

5. In the **Page Setup group,** click the **Margins** button, and then click **Custom Margins**. In the **Page Setup** dialog, under **Center on page,** select the **Horizontally** check box, and then click **OK**.

6. Click in cell **A1**. On the **Review tab,** in the **Proofing group,** click the **Spelling** button, and then check the spelling of the worksheet. When the message *The spell check is complete for the entire sheet* displays, click **OK**.

7. **Save** 🔲 the workbook.

8. On the **menu bar,** click **File,** and then click **Print**. Under **Print What,** click the **Entire Workbook** option button. Notice at the bottom of the screen, *1 of 2* displays, and the chart sheet with the pie chart is the first page, as shown in **Figure 3**.

9. At the bottom of the screen, click the **Next Page** button ▶ to preview the worksheet containing your WordArt, the data, and the column chart. Compare your screen with **Figure 4**, and then print the workbook, or submit the file as directed by your instructor. If you are instructed to do so, display and format the worksheet formulas, and then print the formulas.

10. **Close** 🔴 the workbook, and then **Quit** Excel.

Done! You have completed Skill 10 of 10, and your document is complete!

The following More Skills are located at **www.pearsonhighered.com/skills**. Please note that only More Skills that can be performed on a Macintosh computer are included in this section; therefore, the numbering is not always sequential.

More Skills Insert and Edit Comments

You can add comments to cells in a worksheet to provide reminders, to display clarifying information about data within the cells, or to document your work. When you point to a cell that contains a comment, the comment and the name of the person who created the comment display.

In More Skills 11, you will read, create, and edit comments. To begin, open your web browser, navigate to www.pearsonhighered.com/skills, locate the name of your textbook, and then follow the instructions on the website.

More Skills Change Chart Types

After you create a chart, a different chart type might be easier for the readers of your chart to understand. For example, you can change a column chart to a bar chart. Both a column chart and a bar chart are good choices to illustrate comparisons among items; however, a bar chart might be a better choice when the axis labels are lengthy.

In More Skills 12, you will create a column chart and then change the chart type to a bar chart. To begin, open your web browser, navigate to www.pearsonhighered.com/skills, locate the name of your textbook, and then follow the instructions on the website.

More Skills Copy Excel Data to Word Documents

You can copy the data and objects created in one application to another application, saving time and providing accuracy because data is entered only one time.

In More Skills 13, you will create a chart in Excel and then copy the chart and paste it into a Word document. To begin, open your web browser, navigate to www.pearsonhighered.com/skills, locate the name of your textbook, and then follow the instructions on the website.

More Skills Fill Series Data into Worksheet Cells

Instead of entering data manually, you can use the fill handle or the fill command to enter data that follow a pattern or series—for example, hours, days of the week, or numeric sequences such as even numbers.

In More Skills 14, you will use the fill handle and the fill command to enter data in cells. To begin, open your web browser, navigate to www.pearsonhighered.com/skills, locate the name of your textbook, and then follow the instructions on the website.

Key Terms

3-D 198

Absolute cell reference 192

Accounting number format . . 194

Area chart 199

AutoFit 190

Axis 196

Bar chart 199

Category axis 196

Category label 196

Chart 196

Chart layout 198

Chart sheet 200

Chart style 198

Column chart 196

Comma cell style 194

Data marker 197

Data point 197

Data series 197

Document theme 190

Embedded chart 196

Error indicator 192

Error value 192

Explode 204

General format 194

Legend 197

Line chart 199

Number format 194

Pie chart 200

Range finder 192

Sheet tab 206

Text wrap 190

Three-dimensional 198

Total cell style 195

Value axis 197

X-axis 196

Y-axis 197

Online Help Skills

1. **Start** Safari or another web browser. In the **address bar,** type microsoft.com/mac/ how-to and then press `return` to display the home page for Microsoft Office.

   This website provides you with helpful links to get started, find out what is new, and tutorials about Office 2011.

2. Under **Product Help,** click **Excel 2011.**

3. Under **Excel Help,** click **Charts and Graphics.**

4. Under **Charts and Graphics,** click **Charts.**

5. Under **Charts,** click **Video: Get started with charts.**

6. Click **Start,** and then click **Start** on the next screen to begin the video. Compare your screen with **Figure 1.**

Figure 1

7. Turn on your speakers or put on headphones, and then watch the video to see if you can answer the following questions: What is a combination chart? How can you reuse a chart?

Matching

Match each term in the second column with its correct definition in the first column by writing the letter of the term on the blank line in front of the correct definition.

___ **1.** A command with which you can display text on multiple lines within a cell.

___ **2.** A cell reference that refers to a cell by its fixed position in a worksheet and that does not change when the formula is copied.

___ **3.** A specific way that Excel displays numbers.

___ **4.** The default format that Excel applies to numbers—whatever you type in the cell will display, with the exception that trailing zeros to the right of a decimal point will not display.

___ **5.** The Excel number format that applies a comma separator where appropriate, inserts a fixed dollar sign aligned at the left edge of the cell, applies two decimal places, and leaves a small amount of space at both the right and left edges of the cell to accommodate parentheses for negative numbers.

___ **6.** A graphic representation of data in a worksheet that shows comparisons, patterns, and trends.

___ **7.** The chart axis that is usually the horizontal axis and contains categories.

___ **8.** The chart axis that is usually the vertical axis and contains data.

___ **9.** To pull out one or more slices of a 3-D pie chart to emphasize a specific slice or slices.

___ **10.** A set of design elements that provides a unified look for colors, fonts, and graphics.

A Absolute cell reference

B Accounting number format

C Category axis

D Chart

E Explode

F General format

G Number format

H Theme

I Text wrap

J Value axis

Multiple Choice

Choose the correct answer.

1. Automatically changing the column width to accommodate the longest column entry is called:
   A. Drag and drop
   B. AutoFit
   C. Auto adjust

2. A green triangle that indicates a possible error in a formula is called:
   A. An error indicator
   B. A message
   C. A dialog launcher

3. The Excel feature that outlines all of the cells referenced in a formula is the:
   A. Formula finder
   B. Cell finder
   C. Range finder

4. A chart type useful for illustrating comparisons among related numbers is called:
   A. A pie chart
   B. An area chart
   C. A column chart

5. A chart placed on a worksheet with the source data is:
   A. A chart sheet
   B. A column chart
   C. An embedded chart

6. The chart data points related to one another are known as a:
   A. Column
   B. Data series
   C. Chart point

7. The box that identifies the patterns or colors assigned to the data series in a chart is called a:
   A. Legend
   B. Dialog
   C. Message box

8. A predesigned combination of chart elements is referred to as a:
   A. 3-D chart
   B. Chart layout
   C. Chart

9. The chart type that displays the relationship of parts to a whole is:
   A. A pie chart
   B. An area chart
   C. A column chart

10. A worksheet that contains only a chart is referred to as a:
    A. Worksheet
    B. Chart area
    C. Chart sheet

Topics for Discussion

1. Search some current newspapers and magazines for examples of charts. Which charts catch your eye and why? Do the charts appeal to you because of their color or format? Is something intriguing revealed to you in the chart that you have never considered before? What are some formatting changes that you think make a chart interesting and valuable to a reader?

2. Why is it important to present accounting and financial information in a manner that is attractive and easy to read? What are some of the ways that Excel can help you do so?

Skill Check

To complete this project, you will need the following file:

- e02_Expenses

You will save your spreadsheet as:

- Lastname_Firstname_e02_Expenses

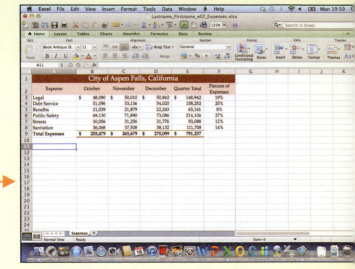

1. **Start** Excel, and open the file **e02_Expenses**. **Save** the file in your **Excel Chapter 2** folder as Lastname_Firstname_e02_Expenses Insert the file name in the left footer and then return to **Normal** view.

2. On the **Home tab,** in the **Themes group,** click the **Themes** button, and then click **Hardcover**.

3. Click cell **B2,** and then use the fill handle to fill the months into the range **C2:D2**. Select the range **A2:F2**. On the **Home tab,** in the **Alignment group,** click the **Wrap Text, Align Text Middle,** and **Center Text** buttons.

4. Select **E3:E8,** and then on the **Standard toolbar,** click the **SUM** button. In the range **B9:E9,** use the **SUM** function to calculate the *Total Expenses*.

5. In cell **F3,** type =E3/E9 and then on the formula bar, click the **Enter** button. Use the fill handle to fill the formula down through cell **F8**. With the range **F3:F8** still selected, in the **Number group,** click the **Percent Style** button. In the **Alignment group,** click the **Center Text** button.

Figure 1

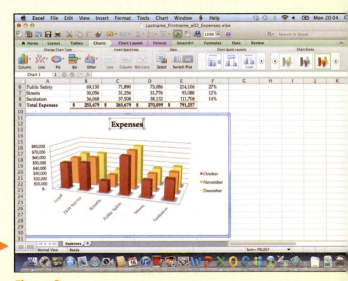

6. Select the range **B3:E3,** hold down command ⌘, and then select the range **B9:E9**. In the **Number group,** click the **Accounting** button, and then click the **Decrease Decimal** button two times. Select the range **B4:E8**. In the **Format group,** click the **Styles** button, and then click **Comma [0]**. Select the range **B9:E9,** click the **Styles** button, and then click **Total**. Click cell **A11,** and then compare your screen with **Figure 1**.

7. Select the range **A2:D8**. On the **Charts tab,** in the **Insert Chart group,** click the **Column** button, and then click **3-D Column**. Move the chart below the data, and then resize the chart to display in approximately the range **A11:F30**. On the **Charts tab,** in the **Chart Quick Layouts group,** click **Layout 1**. Click the **Chart Title,** type Expenses and then compare your screen with **Figure 2**.

Figure 2

■ Continue to the next page to complete this Skill Check ▶

8. Select the nonadjacent ranges **A3:A8** and **E3:E8**. On the **Charts tab,** in the **Insert Chart group,** click the **Pie** button, and then click **3-D Pie**.

9. On the **menu bar,** click **Chart,** and then click **Move Chart**. In the **Move Chart** dialog, select the **New sheet** option button, type the sheet name Expenses Chart and then click **OK**.

10. For the pie chart, apply the **Layout 1** chart layout, and then change the **Chart Title** to 4th Quarter Expenses Select the title, and then change the **Font Size** to **28**.

11. Select the data labels, and then change the **Font Size** to **14** and apply the **Bold** format.

12. Click the **Chart Area**. On the **Chart Layout tab,** in the **Current Selection group,** click the **Format Selection** button. In the **Format Chart Area** dialog, click **Fill**. Click the **Color button arrow,** and then click **Accent 3, Lighter 80%**. Click **OK**.

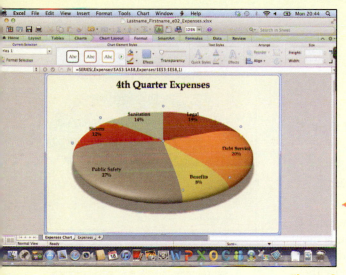

13. Click the edge of a pie slice to select all of the slices. On the **Format tab,** in the **Chart Element Styles group,** click the **Effects** button, point to **Bevel,** and then click **Bevel Options**. Click the **Top button arrow,** and then click the **Circle** thumbnail. Click the **Bottom button arrow,** and then click the **Circle** thumbnail. Set the four Bevel **Width** and **Height** spin boxes to 250 pt and then click **OK**. Compare your screen with **Figure 3**.

Figure 3

14. On the **menu bar,** click **View,** and then click **Header and Footer**. In the **Page Setup** dialog, click the **Customize Footer** button. Verify that the insertion point is in the Left section, click the **Insert File Name** button, and then click **OK** two times.

15. Click the **Expenses** sheet tab. Select the range **A1:F6**. On the **Home tab,** in the **Cells group,** click the **Insert button arrow,** and then click **Insert Rows**. On the **menu bar,** click **Insert,** and then click **WordArt**. Immediately type City Expenses and then move the WordArt to the top of the worksheet. On the **Format** tab, in the **Text Styles group,** click **Quick Styles,** and then in the third row, click the fourth thumbnail—**Dark Red**. Click anywhere outside the WordArt.

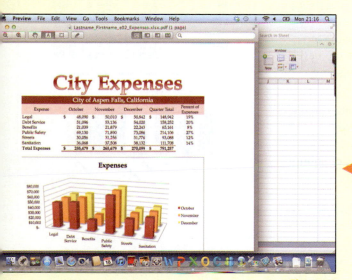

16. Click the **Layout tab**. In the **Print group,** select the **Fit To** check box. In the **Page Setup group,** click the **Margins** button, and then click **Custom Margins**. In the **Page Setup** dialog, select the **Horizontally** check box, and then click **OK**. In the **Print group,** click the **Preview** button.

Figure 4

17. Compare your screen with **Figure 4**. **Save** the workbook, and then print or submit the file as directed by your instructor.

Done! You have completed the Skill Check

Assess Your Skills 1

To complete this project, you will need the following file:

- e02_Assets

You will save your spreadsheet as:

- Lastname_Firstname_e02_Assets

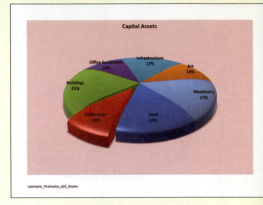

1. **Start** Excel, and open the file **e02_Assets**. **Save** the workbook in your **Excel Chapter 2** folder as Lastname_Firstname_e02_Assets Add the file name in the worksheet's left footer, and then return to **Normal** view.

2. In the ranges **D4:D10** and **B11:D11**, use the SUM function to total the rows and the columns. Select the ranges **B4:D4** and **B11:D11**, apply the **Accounting** number format, and format the range so that no decimals display. For the range **B5:D10**, apply the **Comma [0]** cell style. In the range **B11:D11**, apply the **Total** cell style.

3. Insert a **3-D Clustered Column** chart based on the range **A3:C10**. Move the chart below the data, and then resize the chart to approximately the range **A13:D30**. Change the chart layout to show the legend at the top of the chart. Change the legend font size to **12**. Delete the chart title.

4. Insert a **3-D Pie** chart based on the nonadjacent ranges **A4:A10** and **D4:D10**. Move the pie chart to a chart sheet named Capital Assets Chart and then apply **Layout 1**. Change the chart title to Capital Assets

5. For the data labels, apply **Bold,** and then change the **Font Size** to **14**.

6. Format the **Chart Area** with **Solid fill,** and then change the **Color** to **Red, Accent 2, Lighter 60%**.

7. For all the slices—in Series 1, change the **3-D Rotation** of **X** to **140,** and then explode the **Collections** pie slice. Verify that all data labels display on a pie slice. If necessary, move the **Collections** pie slice back toward the center of the pie to display the labels on the slices. Display the **3-D Format** settings in the **Format Data Series** dialog. Change the top bevel to **Circle** and then change the top bevel **Width** and **Height** to **1000 pt** Change the **Material** setting to **Metal**.

8. For the chart sheet, add a footer with the file name in the left section. Compare your **worksheet** and **chart sheet** with **Figure 1**. **Save** the workbook, and then print or submit the file as directed by your instructor.

Done! You have completed Assess Your Skills 1

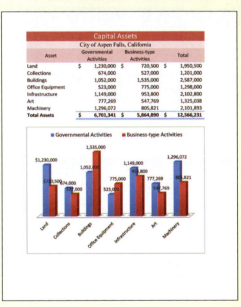

Figure 1

Assess Your Skills 2

To complete this project, you will need the following file:

- e02_Debt

You will save your spreadsheet as:

- Lastname_Firstname_e02_Debt

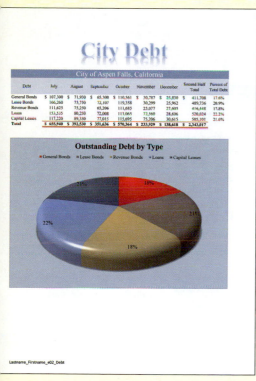

Figure 1

1. **Start** Excel, and open the file **e02_Debt**. **Save** the workbook in your **Excel Chapter 2** folder as Lastname_Firstname_e02_Debt Add the file name in the worksheet's left footer, and then return to **Normal** view.

2. Apply the **Newsprint** theme. In cell **B2**, type July and then **Auto Fill** the months through cell **G2**.

3. In cell **I3**, calculate the *Percent of Total Debt*. In the formula, use an absolute cell reference when referring to cell **H8**. Copy the formula down through cell **I7**, and then format the results as percentages with one decimal place. Center the results in the cell.

4. Select the ranges **B3:H3** and **B8:H8**, and then apply the **Accounting** number format and display zero decimal places. In the range **B4:H7**, apply the **Comma [0]** cell style, and in the range **B8:H8**, apply the **Total** cell style.

5. Insert a **3-D Pie** chart based on the nonadjacent ranges **A3:A7** and **H3:H7**. Move the pie chart below the data, and then resize the chart so that it displays approximately in the range **A11:I38**. Apply **Layout 2**.

6. Change the **Chart Title** to Outstanding Debt by Type and then change the chart title **Font Size** to **20**. Select the data labels, and then change the **Font Size** to **14**. Select the legend, and then change the **Font Size** to **12**. Display the legend at the bottom of the chart.

7. Format the **Chart Area** to display a **Solid fill** using the ninth color in the third row—**Blue-Gray, Accent 5, Lighter 60%**.

8. Display the **Format Data Series** dialog. Set a **Top Divot 3-D Bevel**, set the top **Width** and **Height** to 50 pt and change the **Material** setting to **Soft Edge**.

9. Insert seven rows at the top of the worksheet. Insert **WordArt**, using a **Blue-Gray** style, and **Half-Reflection touching**. Change the WordArt text to City Debt and then move the WordArt to the top of the worksheet, centering it in the seven blank rows.

10. View the worksheet in **Print Layout** view. Verify that the WordArt, data, and pie chart all print on one page. If necessary, adjust the **Fit To** so that all objects are on one page.

11. **Save** the workbook, and then print or submit the file as directed by your instructor. Compare your completed workbook with **Figure 1**.

Done! You have completed Assess Your Skills 2

Assess Your Skills Visually

To complete this project, you will need the following file:

- e02_Net_Assets

You will save your spreadsheet as:

- Lastname_Firstname_e02_Net_Assets

Start Excel, and open the file **e02_Net_Assets**. **Save** the workbook in your **Excel Chapter 2** folder as Lastname_Firstname_e02_Net_Assets Create the worksheet and chart sheet, as shown in **Figure 1**. Apply the **Solstice** theme. **Auto Fill** the months in row **4**. Insert totals using the **SUM** function. Calculate the *Percent of Total Net Assets* using an absolute cell reference, and then format the values as shown. Create the 3-D pie chart and move the chart to a chart sheet, as shown in the figure. Apply the **Layout 1** chart layout, and then format the chart title and data labels as shown. Format the 3-D pie chart with the **Circle** bevel 3-D shape effect on both the top and bottom, with all the widths and heights set to 512 pt Use the **Metal** surface and add a shadow and chart area fill. **Explode** the *Power* pie slice and rotate the pie chart as shown. Insert the file name in the left footer of both sheets. Check the spelling of the worksheet. **Save** the file, and then print or submit it as directed by your instructor.

Done! You have completed Assess Your Skills Visually

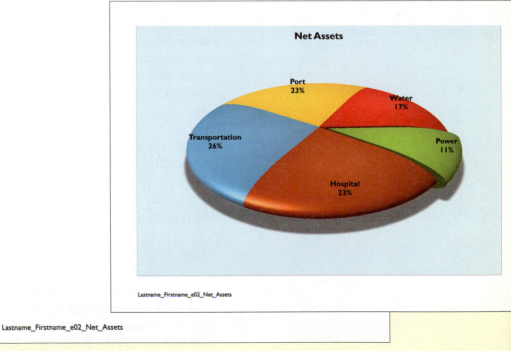

Aspen Falls					
Net Assets					
Business-type Activities					
Activity	July	August	September	Total	Percent of Total Net Assets
Transportation	$ 268,755	$ 275,082	$ 282,086	$ 825,923	25.9%
Port	242,886	245,688	247,253	735,827	23.1%
Water	175,885	180,256	193,008	549,149	17.2%
Power	117,006	108,832	115,038	340,876	10.7%
Hospital	213,468	250,865	275,066	739,399	23.2%
Total Net Assets:	$ 1,018,000	$ 1,060,723	$ 1,112,451	$ 3,191,174	

Lastname_Firstname_e02_Net_Assets

Lastname_Firstname_e02_Net_Assets

Figure 1

Skills in Context

To complete this project, you will need the following file:

- e02_Budget

You will save your spreadsheet as:

- Lastname_Firstname_02_Budget

During the fourth quarter of this year, the Accounting Department developed a summary of the proposed Aspen Falls budget. Open the file **e02_Budget,** and then save the workbook in your **Excel Chapter 2** folder as Lastname_Firstname_e02_Budget Apply a theme of your choice. Compute the totals and the percentage by which each budget item makes up the total budget. Use an absolute cell reference when computing the percentages. Format the values appropriately. Create an embedded column chart that effectively compares the budget data for the three

months. Create an attractive pie chart on a separate chart sheet that describes the quarter percentages. Insert blank rows at the top of the worksheet, and then insert a WordArt with the text Proposed Budget Format the WordArt appropriately. Insert the file name in the left footer of both sheets. Save the workbook, and then print or submit the workbook file as directed by your instructor.

Done! You have completed Skills in Context

Skills and You

To complete this project, you will need the following file:

- New blank Excel workbook

You will save your spreadsheet as:

- Lastname_Firstname_e02_Personal_Budget

What items in your monthly budget might you be able to reduce? A pie chart can point out items on which you might be over-spending without realizing it. Create a worksheet for a month's worth of your expenses. Total the expenses, and then create a pie chart to show the percentage by which each item makes up your monthly budget. Format the pie chart appropriately. Insert the

filename in the left footer of the worksheet, and then return to **Normal** view. Save the workbook as Lastname_Firstname_e02_Personal_Budget and print or submit the workbook electronically as directed by your instructor.

Done! You have completed Skills and You

CHAPTER 3

Manage Multiple Worksheets

▶ Organizations typically create workbooks that contain multiple worksheets. In such a workbook, the first worksheet often summarizes the detailed information in the other worksheets.

▶ In an Excel workbook, you can insert, delete, and reorder worksheets.

▶ By grouping worksheets, you can edit and format the data in multiple worksheets at the same time. Data that you edit on the active sheet is reflected in all of the selected sheets.

▶ When you have a large amount of data to organize in a workbook, dividing the data into logical elements, such as locations or time periods, and then placing each element in a separate worksheet makes sense. In other words, design a system of worksheets instead of trying to fit all of the information on a single worksheet.

▶ You can copy information from one worksheet, and then paste it in a different worksheet.

▶ You can manage multiple worksheets by color coding each sheet tab so that you can quickly locate the detailed information.

▶ Multiple math operators can be used in one formula, and a formula can refer to a cell in another worksheet.

©Arne9001 | Dreamstime.com

Aspen Falls City Hall

In this chapter, you will work with Excel workbooks for Leah Kim, the Parks and Recreations Director in Aspen Falls. She is interested in how many local visitors, families, and international tourists have visited the city parks. In this project, you will work with grouped worksheets to display the formatting used on one worksheet on all selected worksheets. You will create formulas that use multiple math operators. You will construct formulas that refer to cells in other Excel workbooks, and you will create a clustered bar chart.

Time to complete all
10 skills – 60 to 90 minutes

Student data file needed for this chapter:

e03_Visitors

You will save your file as:

Lastname_Firstname_e03_Visitors

Outcome

Using the skills in this chapter, you will be able to work with Excel spreadsheets like this:

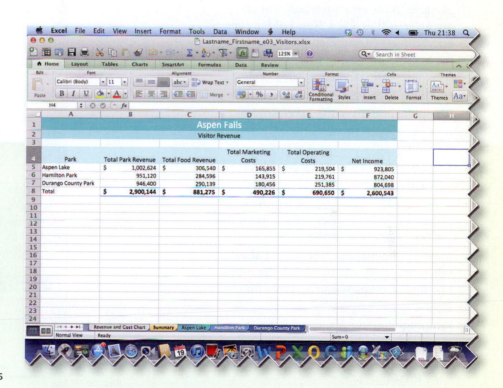

SKILLS

Skills 1–10 Training

At the end of this chapter you will be able to:

Skill 1 Work with Sheet Tabs

Skill 2 Enter and Format Dates

Skill 3 Clear Cell Contents and Formats

Skill 4 Move, Copy, Paste, and Paste Options

Skill 5 Work with Grouped Worksheets

Skill 6 Use Multiple Math Operators in a Formula

Skill 7 Format Grouped Worksheets

Skill 8 Insert and Move Worksheets

Skill 9 Construct Formulas That Refer to Cells in Other Worksheets

Skill 10 Create Clustered Bar Charts

MORE SKILLS

Skill 11 Create Organization Charts

Skill 12 Create Line Charts

Skill 13 Set and Clear Print Areas

Skill 14 Insert Hyperlinks

► When a workbook contains more than one worksheet, you can navigate (move) among worksheets by clicking the sheet tabs.

► To view sheet tabs, use the four *tab scrolling buttons*—the buttons to the left of the sheet tabs used to display Excel sheet tabs that are not in view.

1. **Start** Excel 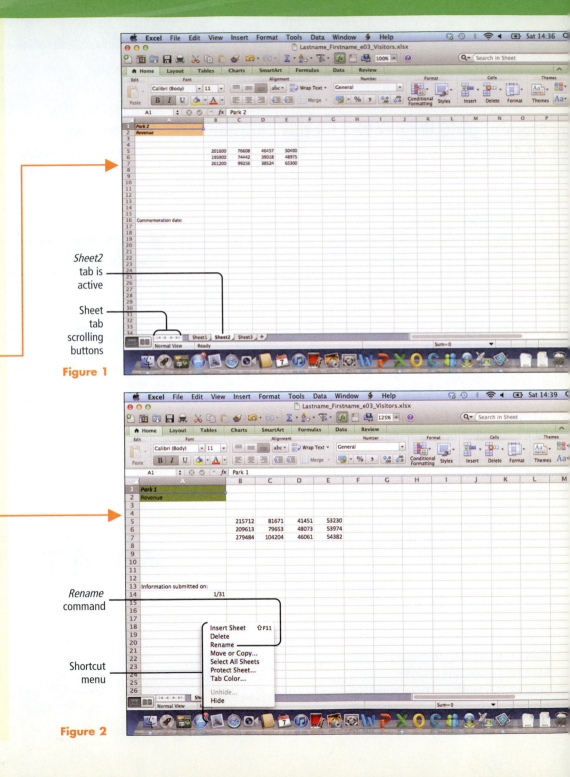, and then open **e03_ Visitors**. On the **menu bar,** click **File,** and then click **Save As**. In the **Save As** dialog, navigate to the location where you are saving your files. Click **New Folder,** type Excel Chapter 3 and then press return . In the **Save As** box, using your own name, type Lastname_Firstname_e03_Visitors and then press return .

2. Along the bottom of the Excel window, click the **Sheet2 sheet tab,** and then compare your screen with **Figure 1**.

3. Click the **Sheet1 sheet tab**. In cell **A1,** notice the text *Park 1*.

   The first worksheet becomes the active sheet, and cell A1, which is formatted with a green background, displays *Park 1*.

4. Move the pointer over the **Sheet1 sheet tab,** press control , and then click the mouse one time. Compare your screen with **Figure 2**.

5. From the shortcut menu, click **Rename**. On the **Sheet1 sheet tab,** verify the tab name is selected, and then type Aspen Lake Press return .

   You can use up to 31 characters in a sheet tab name. Strive for a short but meaningful name.

■ **Continue to the next page to complete the skill** ▶

Sheet2 tab is active

Sheet tab scrolling buttons

Figure 1

Rename command

Shortcut menu

Figure 2

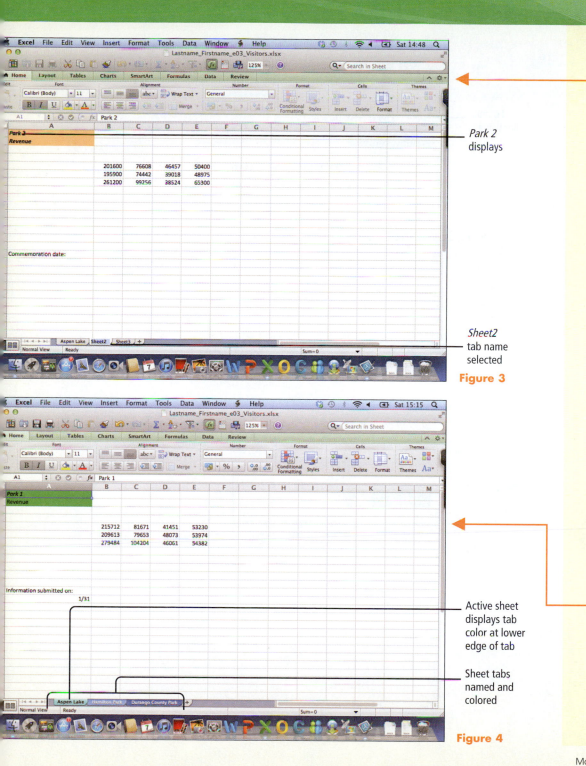

Park 2 displays

Sheet2 tab name selected

Figure 3

Active sheet displays tab color at lower edge of tab

Sheet tabs named and colored

Figure 4

6. Double-click the **Sheet2 sheet tab** to make it the active sheet and to select the sheet name, as shown in **Figure 3**.

7. With the *Sheet2* sheet tab name selected, type Hamilton Park and then press return.

8. Using either of the two methods just practiced, rename the **Sheet3 sheet tab** as Durango County Park and then press return.

9. Verify that the *Durango County Park* sheet is the active worksheet. On the **Home tab,** in the **Themes group,** click the **Colors** button Colors ▾. Scroll down, and then click **Waveform** to change the theme colors for this workbook.

10. On the **menu bar,** click **Format,** point to **Sheet,** and then click **Tab Color** to display the colors associated with the *Waveform* theme colors. On the **Tab Color** pane, click the fourth color in the first row—**Text 2**. **Close** the **Tab Color** pane. Alternately, press control, click the mouse one time, and then click Tab Color.

    When a worksheet is active, the sheet tab font will be bold.

11. Use the technique just practiced to change the sheet tab color of the **Hamilton Park tab** to the sixth color in the first row—**Accent 2**.

12. Change the sheet tab color of the **Aspen Lake sheet tab** to the last color in the first row—**Accent 6**. Close the Tab Color pane. Compare your screen with **Figure 4**.

13. **Save** the workbook.

    ■ **You have completed Skill 1 of 10**

► When you enter a date, it is assigned a *serial number*—a sequential number.

► Dates are stored as sequential serial numbers so they can be used in calculations.

► When you type any of the following values into cells, Excel interprets them as dates: *7/4/10, 4-Jul, 4-Jul-10, Jul-10*. When typing in these date formats, the [-] (hyphen) key and the [/] (forward slash) key function identically.

► You can enter months using the entire name or the first three characters. Years can be entered as two digits or four digits. When you leave the year off, the current year will be inserted.

1. On the **Aspen Lake sheet,** click cell **A14,** and then notice that in the cell the date displays as *1/31*. In the **formula bar,** notice that the underlying value displays as *1/31/2012,* as shown in **Figure 1.**

2. On the **Home tab,** in the **Number group,** click the **Number Format arrow,** as shown in **Figure 2.**

> Here you can select popular date, time, and number formats, or click *More Number Formats* at the bottom of the list to display additional built-in number formats.

■ **Continue to the next page to complete the skill**

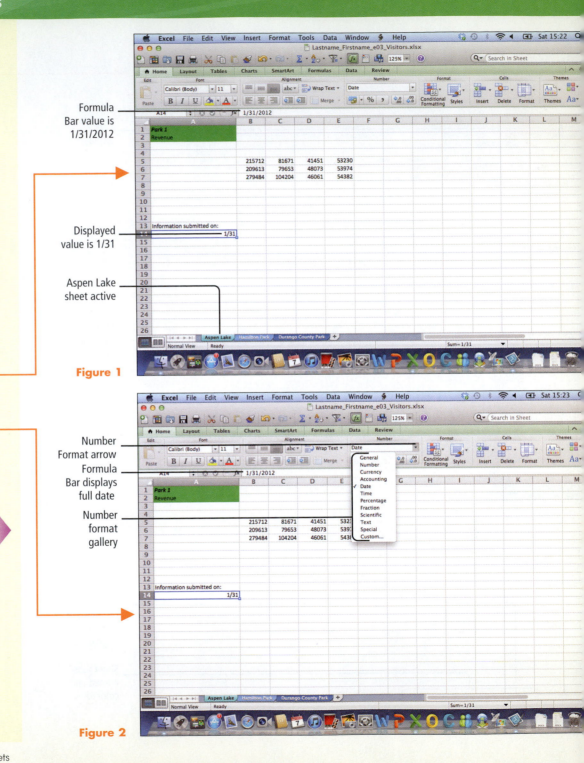

Formula Bar value is 1/31/2012

Displayed value is 1/31

Aspen Lake sheet active

Figure 1

Number Format arrow

Formula Bar displays full date

Number format gallery

Figure 2

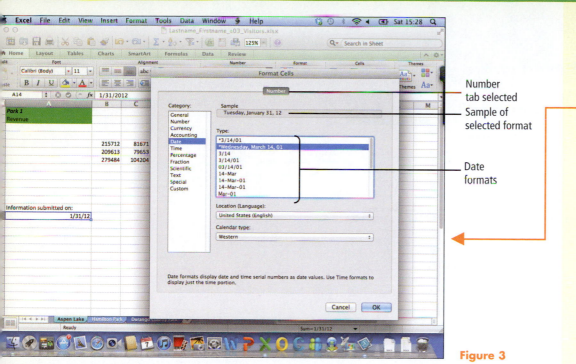

Number tab selected

Sample of selected format

Date formats

Figure 3

Date Format AutoComplete

Date Typed As	Completed by Excel As
7/4/11	7/4/2011
7-4-98	7/4/1998
7/4 or 7-4	4-Jul (current year assumed)
July 4 or Jul 4	4-Jul (current year assumed)
Jul/4 or Jul-4	4-Jul (current year assumed)
July 4, 1998	4-Jul-98
July 2012	Jul-12
July 1998	Jul-98

Figure 4

3. At the bottom of the **Number Format** list, click **Custom**. In the displayed **Format Cells** dialog, under **Category,** click **Date**. Under **Type,** click *Wednesday, March **14, 01** to show a sample of the selected date format, as shown in **Figure 3**.

> The date *Wednesday, March 14, 2001* will not display in your worksheet. This is a sample of a format that can be applied to your current date.

4. Under **Type,** scroll down, click **March 14, 2001,** and then click **OK**.

> The date January 31, 2012 displays in cell A14.

5. Click the **Hamilton Park sheet tab** to make it the active worksheet, and then click cell **A17**. Type 8/11/98 and then on the **formula bar,** click the **Enter** button.

> In cell A17, the year changed from *98* to *1998*. When a two-digit year between 30 and 99 is entered, a 20th-century date is assumed.

6. Click the **Durango County Park sheet tab,** and then click cell **A17**. Hold down control and press ; —the semicolon key. Press return to confirm the entry.

> The control + ; shortcut enters the current date, obtained from your computer, into the selected cell using the default date format. The table in **Figure 4** summarizes how Excel interprets various date formats.

7. **Save** the workbook.

> ▪ **You have completed Skill 2 of 10**

▶ Cells can contain formatting, comments, and *contents*—underlying formulas and data.

▶ You can clear the contents of a cell, the formatting of a cell, or both.

1. Click the **Aspen Lake sheet tab** to make it the active worksheet, and then click cell **A1**. On the **menu bar**, click **Edit**, point to **Clear**, and then click **Contents**.

    Alternately, you can press delete to clear the contents of a cell.

2. Look at cell **A1**, and verify that text has been cleared but that the fill color applied to the cell still displays, as shown in **Figure 1**.

    Deleting the contents of a cell does *not* delete the formatting of the cell.

3. In cell **A1**, type Aspen Lake and then on the **formula bar**, click the **Enter** button.

4. With cell **A1** still selected, on the **menu bar**, click **Edit**, point to **Clear**, and then click **Formats**. Compare your screen with **Figure 2**.

    Clear *Formats* deletes the formatting from the cell but does not delete the cell contents.

■ **Continue to the next page to complete the skill** ➜

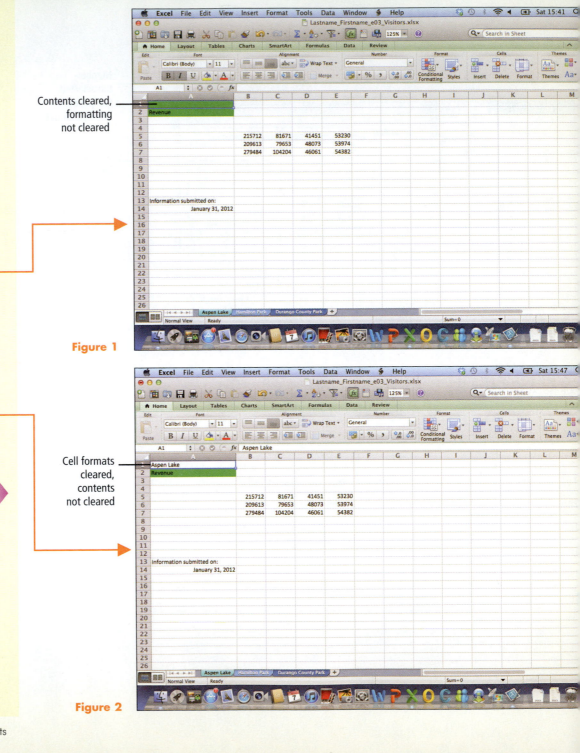

Contents cleared, formatting not cleared

Figure 1

Cell formats cleared, contents not cleared

Figure 2

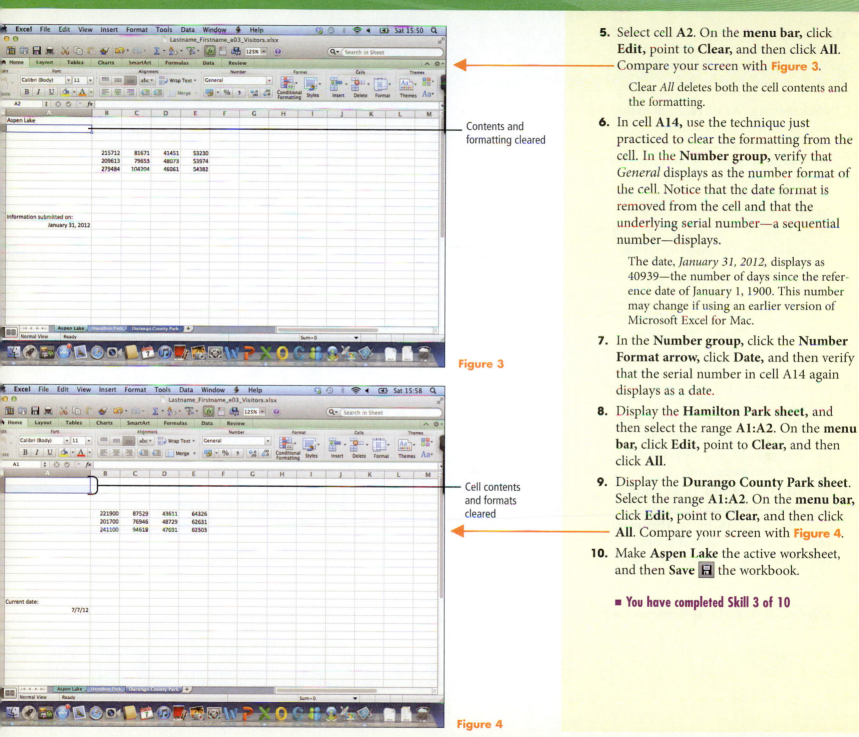

Contents and formatting cleared

Figure 3

Cell contents and formats cleared

Figure 4

5. Select cell **A2**. On the **menu bar,** click **Edit,** point to **Clear,** and then click **All.** Compare your screen with **Figure 3.**

   Clear *All* deletes both the cell contents and the formatting.

6. In cell **A14,** use the technique just practiced to clear the formatting from the cell. In the **Number group,** verify that *General* displays as the number format of the cell. Notice that the date format is removed from the cell and that the underlying serial number—a sequential number—displays.

   The date, *January 31, 2012,* displays as 40939—the number of days since the reference date of January 1, 1900. This number may change if using an earlier version of Microsoft Excel for Mac.

7. In the **Number group,** click the **Number Format arrow,** click **Date,** and then verify that the serial number in cell A14 again displays as a date.

8. Display the **Hamilton Park sheet,** and then select the range **A1:A2.** On the **menu bar,** click **Edit,** point to **Clear,** and then click **All.**

9. Display the **Durango County Park sheet**. Select the range **A1:A2.** On the **menu bar,** click **Edit,** point to **Clear,** and then click **All.** Compare your screen with **Figure 4.**

10. Make **Aspen Lake** the active worksheet, and then **Save** the workbook.

■ **You have completed Skill 3 of 10**

▶ Data from cells and ranges can be copied and then pasted to other cells in the same worksheet, to other worksheets, or to worksheets in another workbook.

1. Select the range **A13:A14**. Point to the lower edge of the black border surrounding the selected range until the 🖑 pointer displays. Drag downward until the ScreenTip displays *A16:A17,* and then release the mouse button to complete the move. Compare your screen with **Figure 1**.

   Drag and drop is a method of moving objects in which you point to the selection and then drag it to a new location.

2. Click cell **A4,** type Visitor Type and then press ⎆tab . Type the following titles in row **4,** pressing ⎆tab after each title: Park Revenue, Food Revenue, Marketing Costs, Operating Costs, Net Income

3. Select columns **B:F**. In the **Cells group,** click the **Format** button, and then click **Column Width**. In the **Column Width** dialog, with the displayed number selected, type 1.25 and then click **OK**. Compare your screen with **Figure 2**.

4. Select the range **A4:F4**. In the **Format group,** click the **Styles** button, and then click **20% - Accent6**. In the **Alignment group,** click the **Wrap Text** button, click **Wrap Text,** and the **Center Text** button 📄.

   ■ **Continue to the next page to complete the skill** ➡

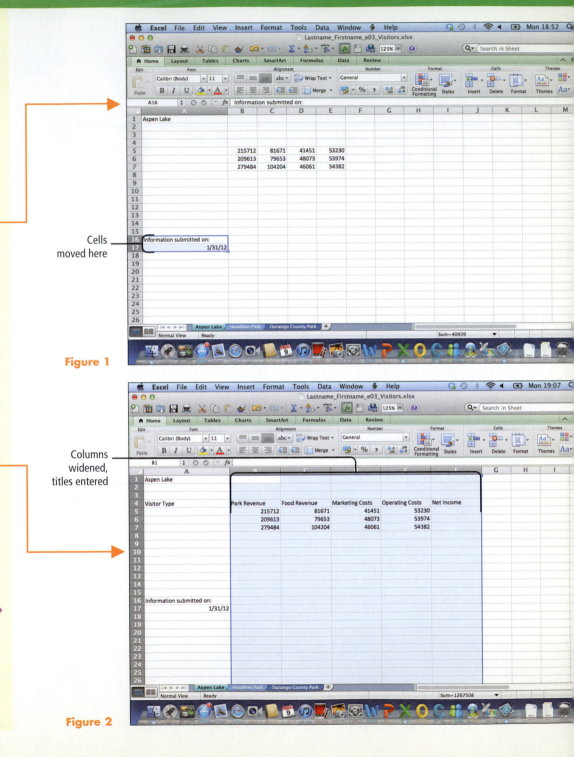

Cells moved here

Figure 1

Columns widened, titles entered

Figure 2

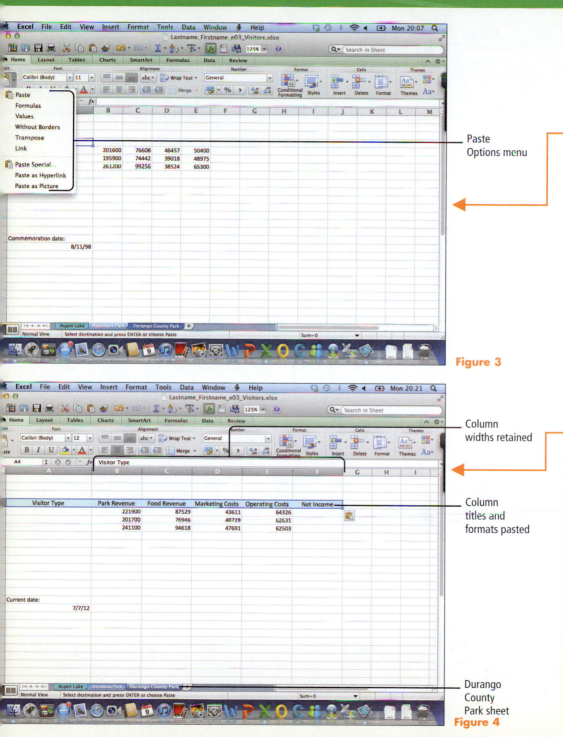

Paste Options menu

Figure 3

Column widths retained

Column titles and formats pasted

Durango County Park sheet

Figure 4

5. With the range **A4:F4** still selected, on the **Standard toolbar,** click the **Copy** button.

6. Display the **Hamilton Park sheet,** and then click cell **A4.** In the **Edit group,** click the **Paste** button arrow to display the **Paste** menu, as shown in **Figure 3.**

7. Click **Paste Special,** and then under **Paste** click to select the **Column widths** option. Click **OK.**

   The column widths from the source worksheet are retained.

8. On the **Standard toolbar,** click the **Paste** button.

   When pasting a range of cells, you need to select only the cell in the upper left corner of the *paste area*—the target destination for data that has been cut or copied.

9. Display the **Durango County Park** worksheet, and then click cell **A4.** Using the technique just practiced, paste the column titles using the Paste option **Column widths.** Compare your screen with **Figure 4.**

10. Display the **Aspen Lake sheet,** and then **Save** workbook.

   ■ **You have completed Skill 4 of 10**

▶ You can group any number of worksheets in a workbook. After the worksheets are grouped, you can edit data or format cells in all of the grouped worksheets at the same time.

▶ Grouping worksheets is useful when you are creating or modifying a set of worksheets that are similar in purpose and structure.

1. Move the pointer over the **Aspen Lake sheet tab,** press control, and then click the mouse one time. From the shortcut menu, click **Select All Sheets**.

2. At the top of the window, on the title bar, verify that *[Group]* displays, as shown in **Figure 1**.

   All the worksheets are selected, as indicated by *[Group]* on the title bar.

3. Click cell **A5,** type Local and then press return. In cell **A6,** type Domestic and then press return. In cell **A7,** type International and then press return.

4. Select the range **A5:A7**. In the **Format group,** click the **Styles** button, scroll down, and then click **40% - Accent6**.

5. Display the **Hamilton Park sheet** and verify that the row labels and formats you entered on the **Aspen Lake sheet** display. Compare your screen with **Figure 2**.

   Data and formats are entered on all grouped worksheets.

   ■ **Continue to the next page to complete the skill** ➔

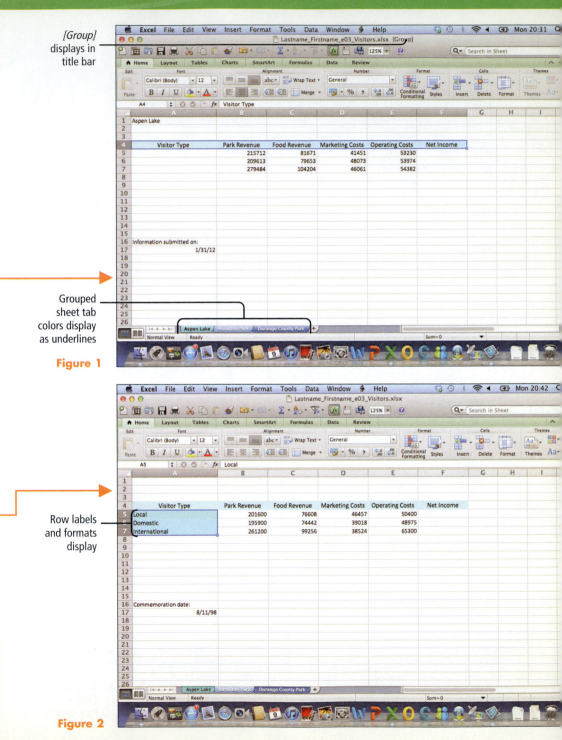

[Group] displays in title bar

Grouped sheet tab colors display as underlines

Figure 1

Row labels and formats display

Figure 2

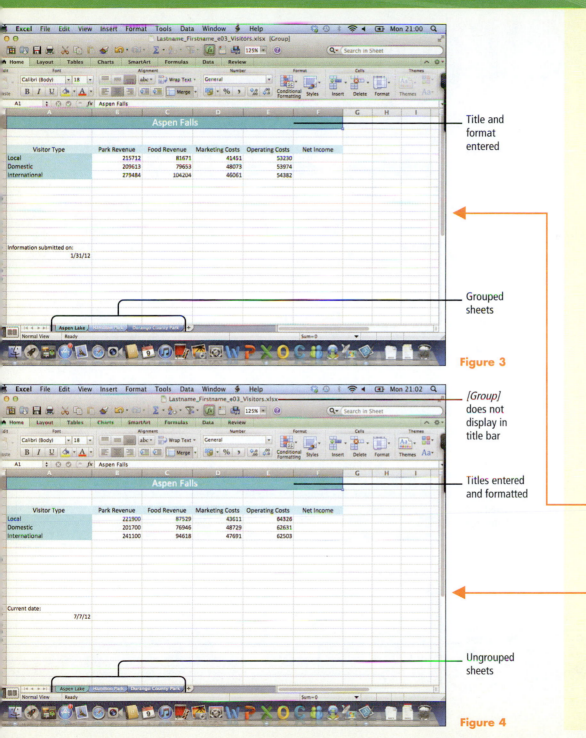

Title and format entered

[Group] does not display in title bar

Grouped sheets

Titles entered and formatted

Ungrouped sheets

Figure 3

Figure 4

6. Display the **Durango County Park sheet** to verify that the labels and formats have been entered. In the sheet tab area, verify that both the *Aspen Lake* sheet tab and the *Hamilton Park* sheet tab display a solid color, indicating that they are no longer active in the group. Also verify that at the top of your window *[Group]* no longer displays on the title bar.

Selecting a single sheet cancels a grouping. Because the worksheets were grouped, the text and formatting was entered into all of the selected sheets. In this manner, you can make the same changes to all selected worksheets in a workbook at the same time.

7. Move the pointer over the **Aspen Lake sheet tab,** press control, and then click the mouse one time. From the shortcut menu, click **Select All Sheets**.

[Group] displays on the title bar.

8. In cell **A1**, press delete, type Aspen Falls and then press return. Select the range **A1:F1**. In the **Alignment group,** click the **Merge** button. In the **Format group,** click the **Styles** button, scroll down, and then click **Accent6**. In the **Font group,** click the **Font Size** button arrow 12, and then click **18**. Compare your screen with **Figure 3**.

9. Display the **Durango County Park sheet,** and verify that the same changes have been made to this worksheet. **Save** the workbook, and then compare your screen with **Figure 4**.

■ **You have completed Skill 5 of 10**

► When you combine several math operators in a single formula, Excel follows a set of mathematical rules for performing calculations within a formula, called *operator precedence*. First, expressions within parentheses are calculated. Second, multiplication and division are performed before addition and subtraction.

► When a formula contains operators with the same precedence level, Excel evaluates the operators from left to right. Multiplication and division are considered to be on the same level of precedence. Addition and subtraction also are considered to be on the same level of precedence.

1. Display the **Aspen Lake sheet**. Click cell **A2,** type Aspen Lake and then press ⏎. Display the **Hamilton Park sheet**. Click cell **A2,** type Hamilton Park and then press ⏎. Display the **Durango County Park sheet**. Click cell **A2,** type Durango County Park and then press ⏎. Compare your screen with **Figure 1**.

2. Move the pointer over the **Durango County Park sheet tab,** press control, and then click the mouse one time. From the shortcut menu, click **Select All Sheets**.

3. Select the range **A2:F2,** and then in the **Alignment group,** click the **Merge** button. In the **Format group,** click the **Styles** button, and then click **40% - Accent6**.

4. Click cell **A13,** type Submitted by: and then press ⏎. In cell **A14,** using your first and last names, type Your Name and then press ⏎. Compare your screen with **Figure 2**.

■ **Continue to the next page to complete the skill**

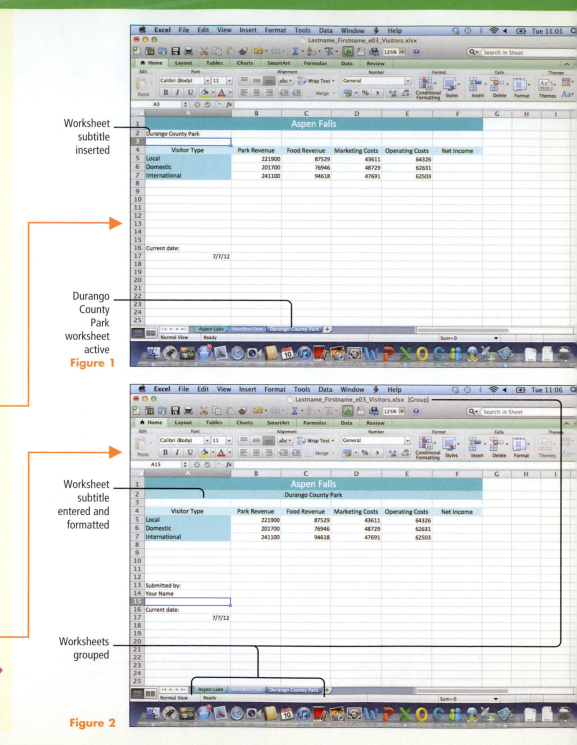

Worksheet subtitle inserted

Durango County Park worksheet active
Figure 1

Worksheet subtitle entered and formatted

Worksheets grouped

Figure 2

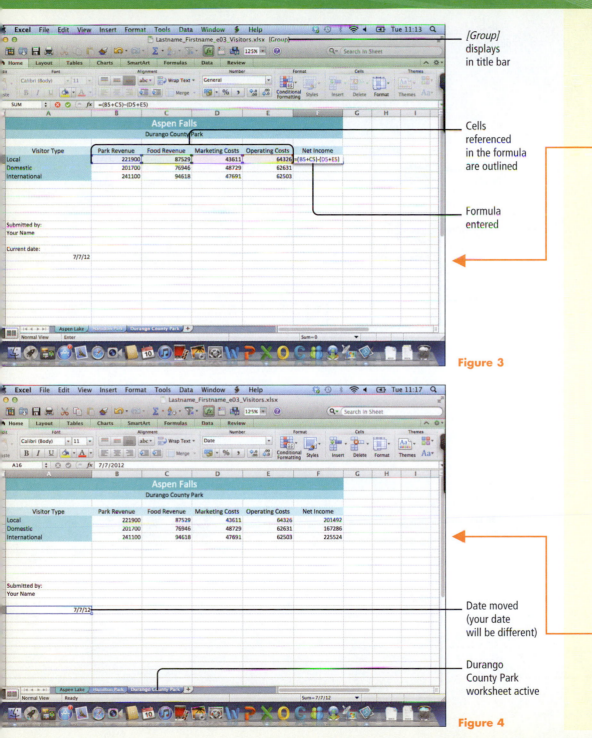

Figure 3

Figure 4

5. Verify that *[Group]* still displays on the title bar. If necessary, move the pointer over one of the sheet tabs, press `control`, and then click the mouse one time. From the shortcut menu, click **Select All Sheets**. Click cell **F5**, enter the formula =(B5+C5)-(D5+E5) and then compare your screen with **Figure 3**.

> The formula *Net Income = Total Revenue – Total Cost* is represented by *(Park Revenue + Food Revenue) – (Marketing Costs + Operating Costs)*. By placing parentheses in the formula, the revenue is first added, the costs are added next, and then the total costs are subtracted from the total revenues. Without the parentheses, the formula would give an incorrect result.

6. On the **formula bar,** click the **Enter** button. Use the **fill handle** to copy the formula down through cell **F7**.

> Recall that because the worksheets are grouped, the formulas have been entered on all three worksheets.

7. Verify that the formula results display in the **Hamilton Park** and **Aspen Lake** sheets.

8. Click the **Durango County Park sheet tab** to make it the active worksheet, and verify that the worksheets are no longer grouped. Click cell **A17,** and then point to the upper edge of the black border surrounding the cell until the pointer displays. Drag up to move the cell contents up to cell **A16**. In the message box *Do you want to replace the contents of the selected cells?* click **OK**. Compare your screen with **Figure 4**.

9. **Save** the workbook.

■ **You have completed Skill 6 of 10**

▶ When worksheets are grouped, any changes made to a single worksheet are made to each worksheet in the group. For example, if you change the width of a column or add a row, all the worksheets in the group are changed in the same manner.

1. Move the pointer over the **Hamilton Park sheet tab,** press control, and then click the mouse one time. From the shortcut menu, click **Select All Sheets**.

2. In the row heading area, point to row 7 to display the ➡ pointer. Click to select the row.

3. On the **Home tab,** in the **Cells group,** click the **Insert** button to insert a new blank row above the *International* row. In cell **A7,** type Families press tab, and then compare your screen with **Figure 1**.

4. Click the **Aspen Lake sheet tab** to make it the active worksheet and to cancel the grouping of the worksheets. Beginning in cell **B7,** enter the following *Families* data for Aspen Lake:

   297815   41012   30270   57918

5. Click the **Hamilton Park sheet tab,** and then beginning in cell **B7,** enter the following *Families* data for Hamilton Park:

   292420   34290   19916   55086

6. Click the **Durango County Park sheet tab,** and then beginning in cell **B7,** enter the following *Families* data for Durango County Park:

   281700   31046   40425   61925

7. Click each of the sheet tabs, and then verify that you entered the values correctly. Click the **Durango County Park sheet tab,** and then compare your screen with **Figure 2**.

▪ **Continue to the next page to complete the skill** ➡

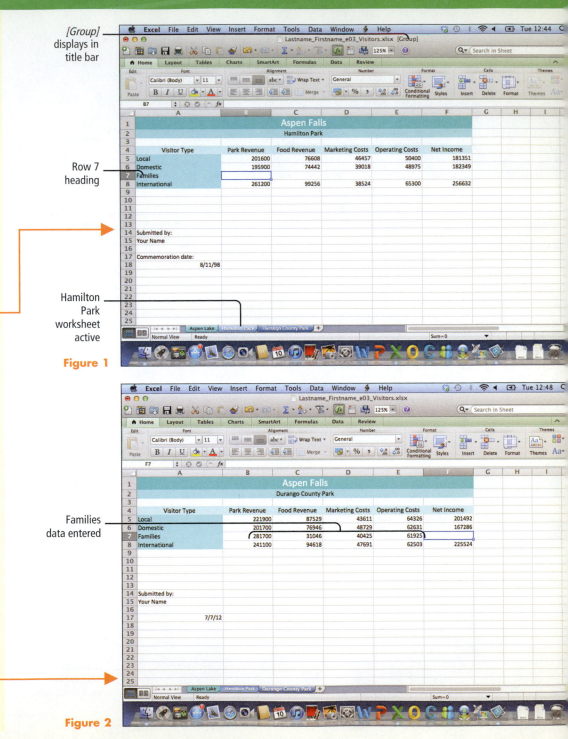

[Group] displays in title bar

Row 7 heading

Hamilton Park worksheet active

Figure 1

Families data entered

Figure 2

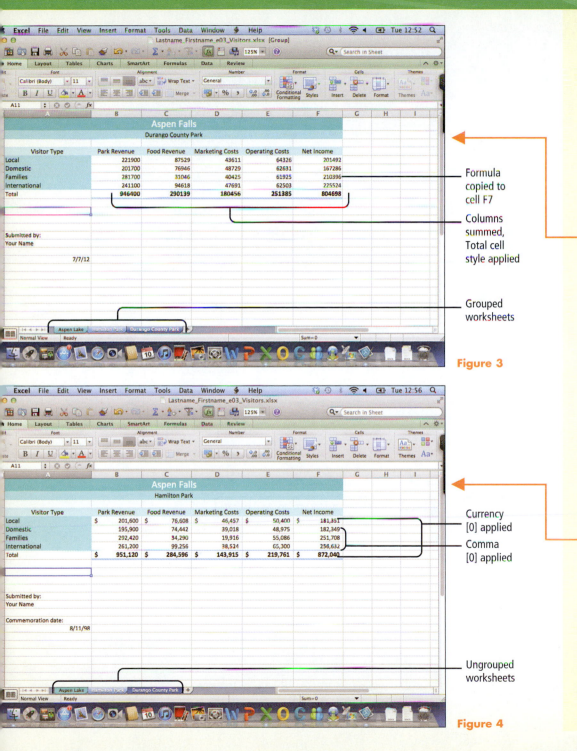

Figure 3

Figure 4

Formula copied to cell F7

Columns summed, Total cell style applied

Grouped worksheets

Currency [0] applied

Comma [0] applied

Ungrouped worksheets

8. Move the pointer over the **Durango County Park sheet tab,** press `control`, and then click the mouse one time. From the shortcut menu, click **Select All Sheets.** Click cell **F6,** and then use the **fill handle** to copy the formula down to cell **F7.**

9. In cell **A9,** type Total and then press `return`. Select the range **B9:F9.** On the **Standard toolbar,** click the **Sum** button. With the range still selected, in the **Format group,** click the **Styles** button, and then click **Total.** Click cell **A11,** and then compare your screen with **Figure 3.**

10. Select the range **B5:F5,** hold down `command ⌘`, and then select the range **B9:F9.** In the **Format group,** click the **Styles** button, scroll down, and then click **Currency [0].**

11. Select the range **B6:F8,** click the **Styles** button, and then click **Comma [0].**

12. Display the **Aspen Lake sheet,** and then verify that the same formulas were entered and the same formatting was applied.

    On the Aspen Lake worksheet, the formula in cell F9 displays as the value *$923,805.*

13. Click the **Hamilton Park sheet tab** to make it the active worksheet, and verify that the formulas and formatting changes were made. Click cell **A11,** and then compare your screen with **Figure 4.**

    On the Hamilton Park worksheet, the formula in cell F9 displays as the value *$872,040.*

14. Click the **Durango County Park sheet tab,** and verify that the formula in cell **F9** displays as the value *$804,698.*

15. **Save** the workbook.

- **You have completed Skill 7 of 10**

► To organize a workbook, you can move sheet tabs into any order you desire.

► You can add new worksheets to accommodate new information.

1. To the right of the **Durango County Park sheet tab,** click the **Insert Sheet** button.

   A new blank worksheet is inserted with a unique name such as *Sheet1* or *Sheet2*.

2. Double-click the **sheet tab** just inserted, type Summary and then press return. Compare your screen with **Figure 1**.

3. In cell **A4,** type Park and then press tab. In cell **B4,** type Total Park Revenue and then press tab. In cell **C4,** type Total Food Revenue and then press tab. In cell **D4,** type Total Marketing Costs and then press tab. In cell **E4,** type Total Operating Costs and then press tab. In cell **F4,** type Net Income and then press return. Compare your screen with **Figure 2**.

4. Select cell **A1,** and then in the **Cells group,** click the **Format** button, and then click **Column Width**. In the **Column Width** dialog, type 1.5 and then click **OK**. Select columns **B:F,** and then using the same technique, widen the columns to *1.5*.

5. Display the **Aspen Lake sheet,** and click cell **A4**. Click the **Copy** button. Display the **Summary sheet,** and then select the range **A4:F4**. Click the **Paste button arrow** and then from the displayed menu click **Paste Special**. In the **Paste Special** dialog, under **Paste,** click to select the **Formats** option, and then click **OK**.

   The formatting is applied to the range A4:F4.

■ **Continue to the next page to complete the skill** ➤

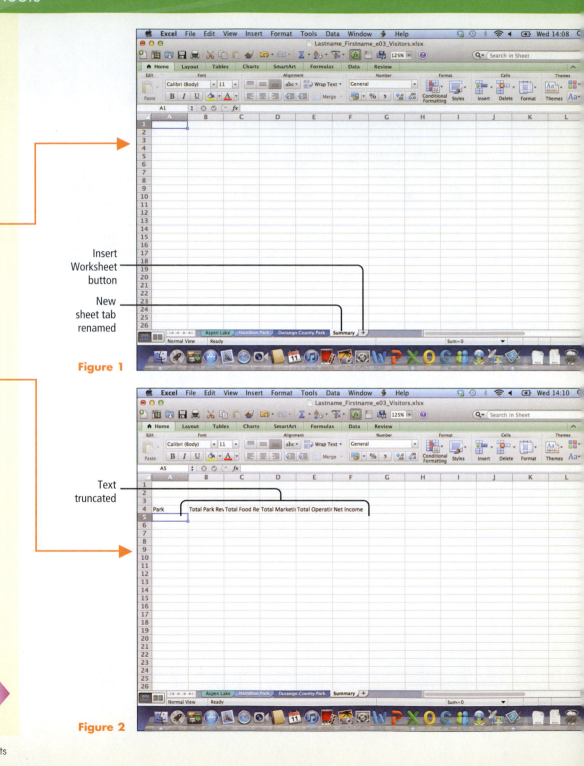

Insert Worksheet button

New sheet tab renamed

Figure 1

Text truncated

Figure 2

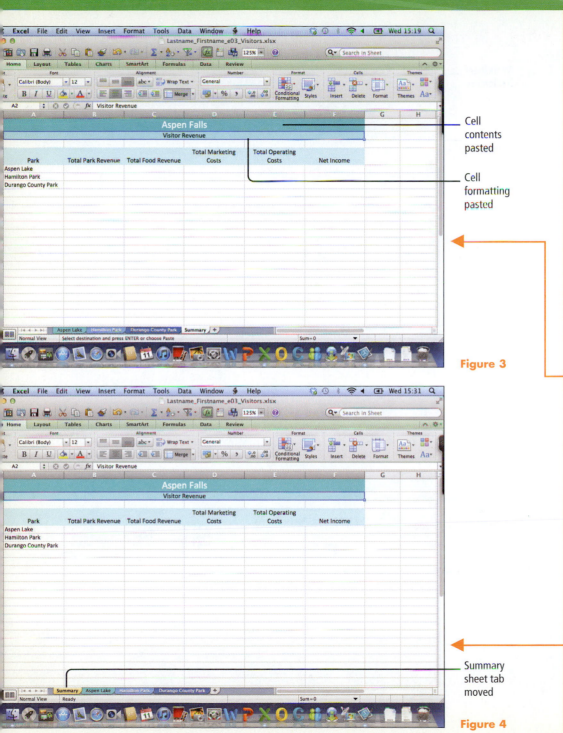

Cell contents pasted

Cell formatting pasted

Figure 3

Summary sheet tab moved

Figure 4

6. In cell **A5**, type Aspen Lake and then press `return`. In cell **A6**, type Hamilton Park and then in cell **A7**, type Durango County Park.

7. Display the **Aspen Lake sheet,** and click cell **A1**. On the **Standard toolbar,** click the **Copy** button. Display the **Summary sheet,** and click cell **A1**. Press `command ⌘` + `V`.

    The cell contents, including both the text *Aspen Falls* and the formatting, are pasted.

8. On the **Summary sheet,** in cell **A2**, type Visitor Revenue and press `return`. Display the **Aspen Lake sheet,** and click cell **A2**. Click the **Copy** button. Display the **Summary sheet,** and click cell **A2**. On the **Home tab,** in the **Edit group,** click the **Paste button arrow** and then from the displayed menu click **Paste Special.** In the **Paste Special** dialog, under **Paste,** click to select the **Formats** option, and then click **OK.** Compare your screen with **Figure 3**.

    Only the cell formatting is pasted.

9. With the **Summary sheet tab** selected, on the **menu bar,** click **Format,** point to **Sheet,** and then click **Tab Color.** Click the ninth color in the first row—**Gold, Accent 5. Close** the **Tab Color** pane.

10. Point to the **Summary sheet tab,** hold down the mouse button to display a small black triangle—a caret—and then notice that a small paper icon attaches to the mouse pointer.

11. Drag to the left until the caret and mouse pointer are to the left of the **Aspen Lake tab**. Release the mouse button to complete the worksheet move, as shown in **Figure 4**.

12. **Save** the workbook.

■ **You have completed Skill 8 of 10**

► A *summary sheet* is a worksheet that displays and summarizes totals from other worksheets. A *detail sheet* is a worksheet with cells referred to by summary sheet formulas.

► Changes made to the detail sheets that affect their totals will automatically recalculate and display on the summary sheet.

1. On the **Summary sheet,** click cell **B5.** Type = and then click the **Aspen Lake sheet tab**. On the **Aspen Lake sheet,** click cell **B9,** and then press return.

   The Summary worksheet displays the value from cell B9 in the Aspen Lake worksheet.

2. Click cell **B5.** In the **formula bar,** notice that the cell reference in the underlying formula includes both a worksheet reference and a cell reference, as shown in **Figure 1**.

   By using a formula of this type, changes made to cell B9 of the *Aspen Lake* worksheet will be automatically updated in this *Summary* worksheet.

3. Click cell **B6,** type = and then click the **Hamilton Park sheet tab**. On the **Hamilton Park sheet,** click cell **B9,** and then press return.

4. On the **Summary sheet,** repeat the technique just practiced to place the value in cell **B9** from the **Durango County Park sheet** in cell **B7** of the **Summary sheet**.

5. On the **Summary sheet,** select the range **B5:B7.** Point to the **fill handle,** and then drag to the right to fill the formulas through column **F.** Click cell **F7,** and compare your screen with **Figure 2**.

■ **Continue to the next page to complete the skill**

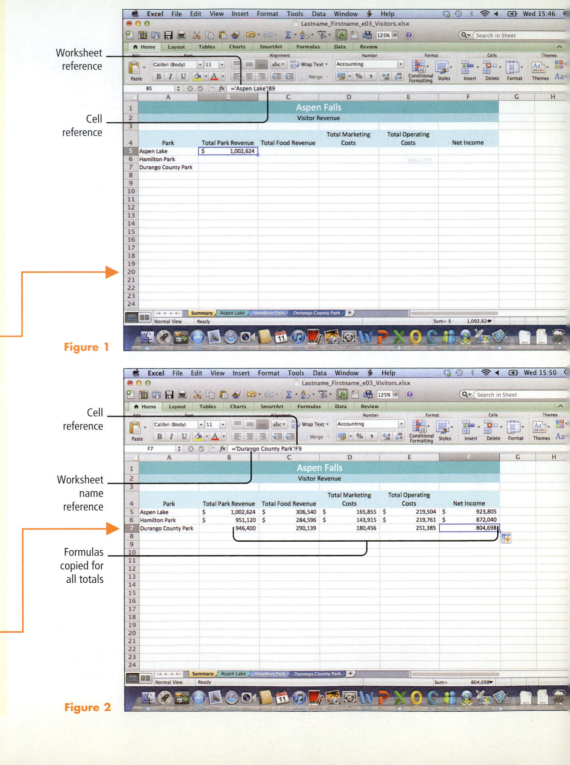

Figure 1

Figure 2

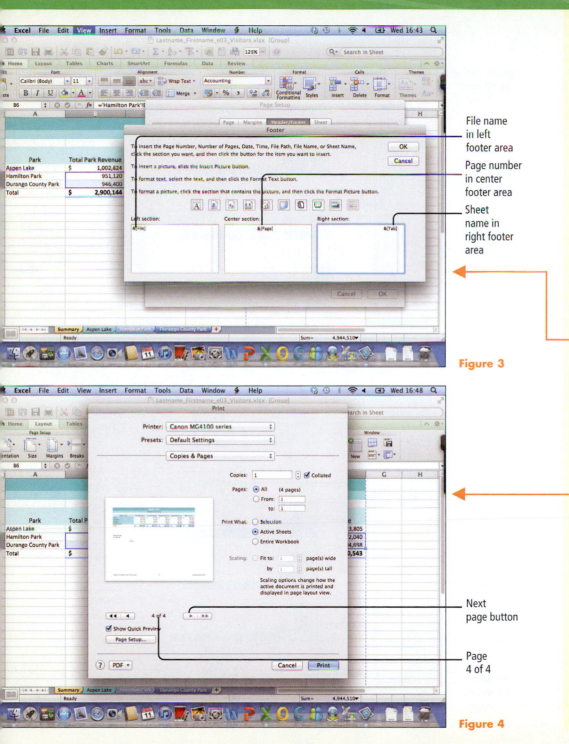

File name in left footer area

Page number in center footer area

Sheet name in right footer area

Figure 3

Next page button

Page 4 of 4

Figure 4

6. On the **Summary sheet,** in cell **A8,** type Total and then select the range **B8:F8.** On the **Standard toolbar,** click the **Sum** button , and then apply the **Total** cell style. Select the range **B6:F7,** and then apply the **Comma [0]** cell style.

7. Move the pointer over the **Summary sheet tab,** press control, and then click the mouse one time. From the shortcut menu, click **Select All Sheets.** On the **menu bar,** click **View,** and then click **Header and Footer.** Click the **Customize Footer** button. With the insertion point in the **Left section,** click **Insert File Name** .

8. Click in the **Center section** of the footer, and then click the **Insert Page Number** button . Click in the **Right section,** and then click the **Insert Sheet Name** button . Compare your screen with **Figure 3,** and then click **OK** two times.

9. On the **Layout tab,** in the **Page Setup group,** click **Orientation,** and then click **Landscape.** On the **menu bar,** click **File,** and then click **Print.** At the bottom of the screen, click the **Next Page** button three times to view each of the four worksheets, and then compare your screen with **Figure 4.**

    Because the worksheets are grouped, all four worksheets will be previewed and the footer will display in each worksheet.

10. Click **Cancel.** Move the pointer over the **Summary sheet tab,** press control, and then click **Ungroup Sheets.**

11. **Save** the workbook.

   ■ **You have completed Skill 9 of 10**

► A *clustered bar chart* is a chart type that is useful when you want to compare values across categories. Bar charts organize categories along the vertical axis and values along the horizontal axis.

1. On the **Summary sheet,** select the range **A4:E7.** On the **Charts tab,** in the **Insert Chart group,** click the **Bar** button, and then under **2-D Bar,** click **Clustered Bar.**

2. On the **menu bar,** click **Chart,** and then click **Move Chart.** In the **Move Chart** dialog, select the **New sheet** option button, if necessary, type Revenue and Cost Chart and then click **OK.**

   The chart is moved to a chart sheet.

3. On the **Charts tab,** in the **Data group,** click the **Switch Plot by column** button. Compare your screen with **Figure 1.**

   Because you want to look at revenue and costs by location, displaying the locations on the vertical axis is useful.

4. In the **Chart Quick Layouts group,** click the **More** button ⮟, and then click **Layout 8.** In the **Chart Styles group,** click the **More** button ⮟, and then click **Style 26**—second thumbnail in the fourth row.

5. On the **Chart Layout tab,** in the **Axes group,** click the **Axes** button. Point to **Horizontal Axis,** and then click **Axis Options.** On the left side of the **Format Axis** dialog, click **Text Box,** and then on the right, in the **Custom angle box,** type -40 Click **OK,** and then compare your screen with **Figure 2.**

   ■ **Continue to the next page to complete the skill** ➤

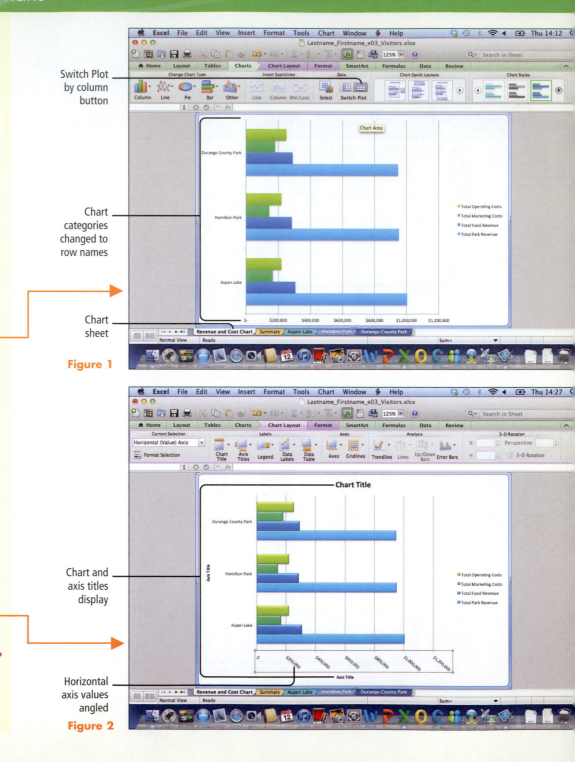

Switch Plot by column button

Chart categories changed to row names

Chart sheet

Figure 1

Chart and axis titles display

Horizontal axis values angled

Figure 2

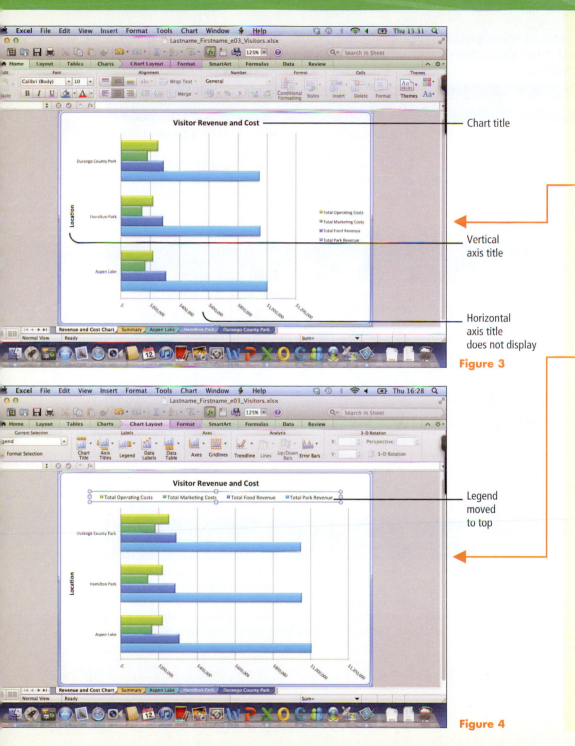

Chart title

Vertical axis title

Horizontal axis title does not display

Figure 3

Legend moved to top

Figure 4

6. Click the **Chart Title**. Type Visitor Revenue and Cost

7. On the left side of the chart, click the vertical **Axis Title**. Type Location Select the *Location* title, and then on the **Home tab,** in the **Font group,** change the **Font Size** to **14.** At the bottom of the chart, click the horizontal **Axis Title,** press delete, and then compare your screen with **Figure 3.**

8. On the **Chart Layout tab,** in the **Labels group,** click the **Legend** button, and then click **Legend Options.** In the **Format Legend** dialog, select the **Top** option button. On the left, click **Line,** and then on the right, click the **Color button arrow,** and then click **Accent 2.** Click **OK.** On the **Home tab,** in the **Font group,** change the **Font Size** to **12.** Compare your screen with **Figure 4.**

9. On the **menu bar,** click **View,** and then click **Header and Footer.** In the **Page Setup** dialog, click the **Customize Footer** button. Click the **Insert File Name** button, and then click **OK** two times.

10. **Save** the workbook. Print or submit your file as directed by your instructor. To print, on the **menu bar,** click **File,** and then click **Print.** Under **Settings,** click **Print Active Sheets,** and then click **Print Entire Workbook.** Click the **Print** button. **Quit** Excel.

Done! You have completed Skill 10 of 10, and your document is complete!

More Skills

The following More Skills are located at **www.pearsonhighered.com/skills**. Please note that only More Skills that can be performed on a Macintosh computer are included in this section; therefore, the numbering is not always sequential.

More Skills 11 Create Organization Charts

You can add SmartArt graphics to a worksheet to create timelines, illustrate processes, or show relationships. When you click the SmartArt button on the Ribbon, you can select from among a broad array of graphics, including an organization chart. An organization chart graphically represents the relationships between individuals and groups in an organization.

In More Skills 11, you will insert and modify a SmartArt graphic organization chart.

To begin, open your web browser, navigate to www.pearsonhighered.com/skills, locate the name of your textbook, and then follow the instructions on the website.

More Skills 12 Create Line Charts

Use a line chart when you want to compare more than one set of values over time. Time is displayed along the bottom axis and the data point values are connected with a line. The curves and directions of the lines make trends obvious to the reader.

In More Skills 12, you will create a line chart comparing three sets of values.

To begin, open your web browser, navigate to www.pearsonhighered.com/skills, locate the name of your textbook, and then follow the instructions on the website.

More Skills 13 Set and Clear Print Areas

If you are likely to print the same portion of a particular worksheet over and over again, you can save time by setting a print area.

In More Skills 13, you will set print areas in a worksheet.

To begin, open your web browser, navigate to www.pearsonhighered.com/skills, locate the name of your textbook, and then follow the instructions on the website.

More Skills 14 Insert Hyperlinks

You can insert a hyperlink in a worksheet that can link to a file, a location in a file, a web page on the World Wide Web, or a web page on an organization's intranet. Creating a hyperlink in a workbook is a convenient way to provide quick access to related information.

In More Skills 14, you will insert hyperlinks to related information on the web and to other worksheets in the workbook.

To begin, open your web browser, navigate to www.pearsonhighered.com/skills, locate the name of your textbook, and then follow the instructions on the website.

Key Terms

Clustered bar chart 240

Contents 226

Detail sheet 238

Drag and drop 228

Operator precedence 232

Paste area 229

Serial number 224

Summary sheet 238

Tab scrolling button 222

Online Help Skills

1. **Start** Safari or another web browser. In the **address bar,** type microsoft.com/mac/how-to and then press ⎇return⎇ to display the home page for Microsoft Office.

   This website provides you with helpful links to get started, find out what is new and tutorials about Office 2011.

2. Under **Product Help,** click **Excel 2011**.

3. Under **Excel Help,** click **Charts and Graphics**.

4. Under **Charts and Graphics,** click **Fills, Shadows, and Effects**.

5. Click **Add effects to text,** and then compare your screen with **Figure 1**.

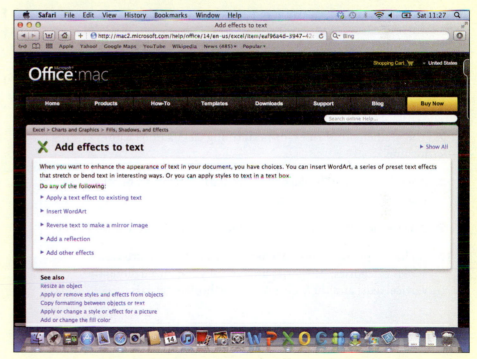

Figure 1

6. Click through each of the links on the page and then answer the following questions. What types of effects can be applied to text in a chart? How do you remove an effect from an object? How can you make a picture look 3-D?

Matching

Match each term in the second column with its correct definition in the first column by writing the letter of the term on the blank line in front of the correct definition.

____ **1.** The labels along the lower border of the workbook window that identify each worksheet.

____ **2.** Buttons to the left of the sheet tabs used to display Excel sheet tabs that are not in view.

____ **3.** A sequential number assigned to a date.

____ **4.** The underlying formulas and data in a cell.

____ **5.** A method of moving or copying the content of selected cells in which you point to the selection and then drag it to a new location.

____ **6.** The target destination for data that has been cut or copied.

____ **7.** The mathematical rules for performing calculations within a formula.

____ **8.** A worksheet that displays and summarizes totals from other worksheets in a workbook.

____ **9.** A worksheet that contains the detailed information in a workbook.

____ **10.** A chart type that is useful when you want to compare values across categories; categories are typically organized along the vertical axis, and the values along the horizontal axis.

A Contents

B Clustered bar chart

C Detail sheet

D Drag and drop

E Operator precedence

F Paste area

G Serial number

H Sheet tabs

I Summary sheet

J Tab scrolling buttons

Multiple Choice

Choose the correct answer.

1. In an Excel workbook, you can do this.
   A. Insert only one worksheet
   B. Move worksheets
   C. Move only one worksheet

2. Grouped worksheets can be edited and formatted in this way.
   A. All at the same time
   B. Only one worksheet at a time
   C. Only once

3. Deleting the contents of a cell also deletes this.
   A. Only the contents
   B. Only the format
   C. Both contents and format

4. When pasting a range of cells, this cell needs to be selected in the paste area.
   A. Bottom right cell
   B. Center cell
   C. Top left cell

5. When grouping worksheets in a workbook, you can group this number of worksheets.
   A. Only two
   B. Only three
   C. Any number

6. If a workbook contains grouped worksheets, this word will display on the title bar.
   A. [*Collection*]
   B. [*Set*]
   C. [*Group*]

7. When a formula contains operators with the same precedence level, the operators are evaluated in this order.
   A. Left to right
   B. Right to left
   C. From the center out

8. Addition and this mathematical operator are considered to be on the same precedence level.
   A. Multiplication
   B. Division
   C. Subtraction

9. Changes made in a detail worksheet will automatically recalculate and display on this sheet.
   A. Summary
   B. Final
   C. Outline

10. In a chart, the legend can be located here.
    A. The detail sheet
    B. The top of the chart
    C. The summary sheet

Topics for Discussion

1. Think of the various departments and discipline areas at your college. Provide an example of workbooks containing data that could be organized into identically detailed worksheets and then summarized in a summary sheet. Can you think of any examples specifically for your college athletic department?

2. Illustrate some examples of how a formula's results will be incorrect if parentheses are not used to group calculations in the order they should be performed. Think of averaging three test scores and how you would write the formula to get a correct result.

Skill Check

To complete this project, you will need the following file:

- e03_Payroll

You will save your workbook as:

- Lastname_Firstname_e03_Payroll

1. **Start** Excel, and open the file **e03_Payroll**. **Save** the workbook in your **Excel Chapter 3** folder as Lastname_Firstname_e03_Payroll

2. Double-click the **Sheet1 sheet tab,** type Courthouse and then press ⌐return⌐. Press ⌐control⌐, click the mouse button over the **Courthouse sheet tab,** click **Tab Color,** and then click **Blue, Accent 2**. Use the same technique to rename **Sheet2** as City Center and then apply the tab color **Gold, Accent 4**. Rename **Sheet3** as Community Center and then apply the tab color **Red, Accent 3**. Close the **Tab Color** pane.

3. Press ⌐control⌐, click the mouse button over a **sheet tab,** and then click **Select All Sheets**. Add the file name in the worksheets left footer, and then add the sheet name in the right footer.

4. In cell **A4,** type Job Title and then press ⌐tab⌐. In cell **B4,** type Total Gross Pay In cell **C4,** type Income Tax In cell **D4,** type Social Security (FICA) Tax In cell **E4,** type Health Insurance In cell **F4,** type Net Pay

5. Select the range **A4:F4,** and then apply the cell style **40% - Accent3**. In the **Alignment group,** click the **Wrap Text** and the **Center Text** buttons. Click cell **A10,** and then compare your screen with **Figure 1**.

6. Verify that the worksheets are still grouped. In cell **F5,** type =B5-(C5+D5+E5) and then press ⌐return⌐ to construct the formula to compute the Net Pay as *Total Gross Pay – (Income Tax + Social Security (FICA) Tax + Health Insurance)*. In cell **F5,** use the **fill handle** to copy the formula down through cell **F8**.

7. Select the range **B9:F9**. On the **Standard toolbar,** click the **Sum** button, and then apply the **Total** cell style. Select the nonadjacent ranges **B5:F5** and **B9:F9,** and then apply the **Currency [0]** cell style. In the range **B6:F8,** apply the **Comma [0]** cell style. Double-click a **sheet tab** to ungroup the worksheets. Click cell **A10,** and then compare your screen with **Figure 2**.

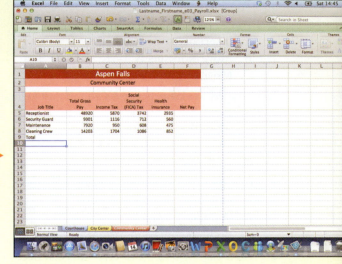

Figure 1

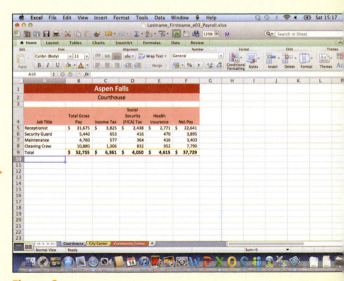

Figure 2

 ■ **Continue to the next page to complete this Skill Check**

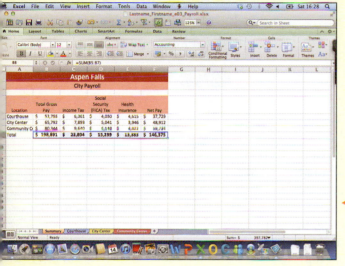

Figure 3

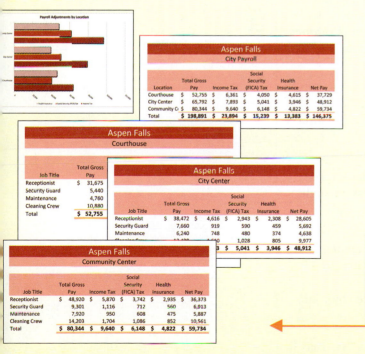

Figure 4

8. Insert a new worksheet. Rename the new sheet tab Summary and then change the **Tab Color** to **Orange, Accent 1**. Move the **Summary sheet** to the first position in the workbook.

9. Display the **Courthouse sheet,** select the range **A1:F4,** and then click **Copy**. Display the **Summary sheet** and then click cell **A1**. Click the **Paste button arrow** and then click **Paste**. In cell **A2**, type City Payroll and then in cell **A4**, type Location In cell **A5**, type Courthouse In cell **A6**, type City Center In cell **A7**, type Community Center and then in cell **A8**, type Total

10. Click **B5,** type = and then click the **Courthouse sheet tab**. On the **Courthouse sheet,** click cell **B9,** and then press ⏎ return . Use the same technique in cells **B6** and **B7** to place the *Total Gross Pay* amounts from the *City Center* and the *Community Center* worksheets on the *Summary* worksheet.

11. On the **Summary sheet,** select the range **B5:B7,** and then use the **fill handle** to copy the formulas to the right through column **F**. Select the range **B8:F8**. On the **Standard toolbar,** click the **SUM** button, and then apply the **Total** cell style. Compare your screen with **Figure 3**.

12. On the **Summary sheet,** select the nonadjacent ranges **A4:A7** and **C4:E7**. On the **Charts tab,** in the **Insert Chart group,** click the **Bar** button, and then click **Clustered Bar**. On the **menu bar,** click **Chart,** and then click **Move Chart**. Rename the chart sheet Payroll Chart

13. On the **Charts tab,** in the **Data group,** click the **Plot** button. In the **Chart Styles group,** click the **More** button, and then click **Style 13**. In the **Chart Quick Layouts group,** click **Layout 3**. Click the **Chart Title,** type Payroll Adjustments by Location On the **Chart Layout tab,** in the **Axes group,** click the **Axes** button, point to **Horizontal Axis,** and then click **Axis Options**. On the left, click **Text Box**. In the **Custom angle** box, type -40 and then click **OK**.

14. On the **menu bar,** click **View,** and then click **Header and Footer**. In the **Page Setup** dialog, click the **Customize Footer** button, and then in the **Left section,** click the **Insert File Name** button. Click **OK** two times.

15. **Save** the workbook. Group the worksheets. On the **menu bar,** click **File,** and then click **Print**. Click the **Next Page** button to view the five sheets. Compare your workbook with **Figure 4**. Print or submit the file as directed by your instructor.

Done! You have completed the Skill Check

Assess Your Skills 1

To complete this workbook, you will need the following file:

- e03_Water

You will save your workbook as:

- Lastname_Firstname_e03_Water

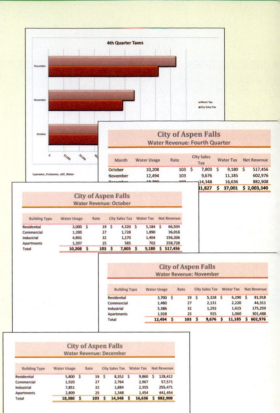

Figure 1

1. **Start** Excel, and open the file **e03_Water**. **Save** the workbook in your **Excel Chapter 3** folder as Lastname_Firstname_e03_Water Rename **Sheet1** as October and then apply the sheet tab color **Dark Red, Accent 2**.

2. Group the sheets. In cell **F5**, construct a formula to compute *Net Revenue = (Water Usage * Rate) + (City Sales Tax + Water Tax)*. Copy the formula down. In row **9**, sum the columns. In the range **B9:F9**, apply the **Total** cell style.

3. In the nonadjacent ranges **C5:F5** and **C9:F9**, apply the **Currency [0]** cell style, and then in the ranges **B5:B9** and **C6:F8**, apply the **Comma [0]** cell style.

4. Insert a new worksheet. Rename the new sheet tab Summary and apply the sheet tab color **Orange, Accent1**. Move the new sheet tab to make it the first worksheet in the workbook. Delete any extra, unused worksheets.

5. Group the sheets. Add the file name in the left footer and the sheet name in the right footer. Return to **Normal View,** and then ungroup the sheets.

6. Copy the range **A1:F4** from any of the other worksheets, and then on the **Summary sheet,** click cell **A1**. On the **Standard toolbar,** click the **Paste** button. Change the title of cell **A2** to Water Revenue: 4th Quarter and then change the title in cell **A4** to Month In cell **A5,** type October and then use the fill

handle to fill cells **A6** and **A7** with *November* and *December*. In cell **A8**, type Total

7. In the *Summary* worksheet, enter a formula in cell **B5** setting the cell equal to cell **B9** in the *October* worksheet. Enter the *Water Usage* total from the *November* and the *December* worksheets in cells **B6** and **B7**. In the *Summary* worksheet, select the range **B5:B7,** and then use the **fill handle** to copy the formulas to the right through column **F**.

8. In row **8,** sum column **B** and the columns **D:F,** and then apply the **Total** cell style to the cells. In the range **D6:F7,** apply the **Comma [0]** cell style. In the ranges **D5:F5** and **D8:F8,** apply the **Currency [0]** cell style.

9. Insert a **Clustered Bar chart** using the nonadjacent ranges **A4:A7** and **D4:E7** as the source data. Move the chart to a chart sheet with the sheet name Tax Chart

10. Apply the **Style 28** chart style, and then apply the **Layout 1** chart quick layout. For the **Horizontal Axis,** set the **Custom angle** to -40°. Change the **Chart Title** to 4th Quarter Taxes

11. On the **chart sheet,** add the file name in the left footer. **Save** the workbook. Compare your completed workbook with **Figure 1**. Print or submit the file as directed by your instructor.

Done! **You have completed Assess Your Skills 1**

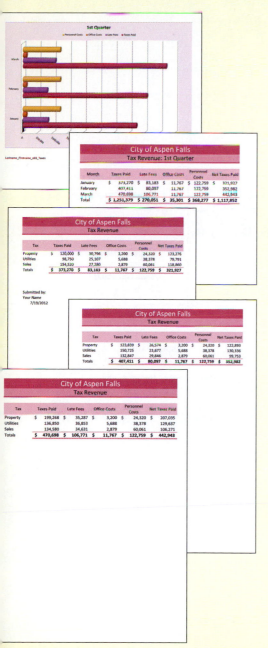

Assess Your Skills 3 and 4 can be found at **www.pearsonhighered.com/skills.**

Assess Your Skills 2

To complete this workbook, you will need the following file:

- e03_Taxes

You will save your workbook as:

- **Lastname_Firstname_e03_Taxes**

1. **Start** Excel, and open the file **e03_Taxes**. **Save** the workbook in your **Excel Chapter 3** folder as Lastname_Firstname_e03_Taxes

2. Rename the **Sheet1** sheet tab as January and then apply the sheet tab color **Pink, Text 2**. In cell **A13,** using your first and last names, type Your Name and then in cell **A14** enter the current date.

3. Group the sheets. In cell **F5**, construct a formula to compute *Net Taxes = (Taxes Paid + Late Fees) – (Office Costs + Personnel Costs)*. Copy the formula down, and then in row **8,** sum the columns.

4. In the ranges **B5:F5** and **B8:F8,** apply the **Currency [0]** cell style; in the range **B8:F8,** apply the **Total** cell style; and then in the range **B6:F7,** apply the **Comma [0]** cell style.

5. Insert a new sheet, rename the sheet tab Summary and then change the sheet tab color to **Black, Text 1**. Move the sheet to the first position in the workbook. Copy the range **A1:F4** from another sheet, and then paste the range into the *Summary* sheet using the **Paste** button. Delete any extra unused worksheets.

6. Group the sheets. Add the file name in the left footer and the sheet name in the right footer. Return to **Normal** view, and then ungroup the sheets.

7. On the **Summary sheet,** change the title in cell **A2** to Tax Revenue: 1st Quarter and then change the title in cell **A4** to Month In the

range **A5:A7,** enter the months January, February, and March and in cell **A8,** type Total

8. In cell **B5,** enter a formula setting the cell equal to cell **B8** in the *January* worksheet. Enter the total *Taxes Paid* from the *February* and the *March* worksheets in cells **B6** and **B7** of the **Summary sheet**. In the *Summary* worksheet, copy the range **B5:B7** to the right through column **F**.

9. In the range **B8:F8,** sum the columns, and then apply the **Total** cell style. In the range **B6:F7,** apply the **Comma [0]** cell style.

10. Select the range **A4:E7,** and then from the **Bar Chart** gallery, insert a **Clustered Cylinder** chart. Move the chart to a chart sheet with the sheet tab name Tax Chart In the **Data group,** click the **Plot** button. Apply the **Layout 1** chart quick layout and the **Style 26** chart style. Change the chart title to 1st Quarter

11. Show the **Legend** at the top of the chart. For the **Horizontal Axis,** set the **Text Box** to **Custom angle** of -40°. Click in the **Chart Area**. On the **Chart Layout tab,** in **Current Selection,** click **Format Selection,** and then select the color **Light PinkBackground 2**. Add the file name in the left footer of the chart sheet.

12. **Save** the workbook. Print or submit the file as directed by your instructor. Compare your completed workbook with **Figure 1**.

Done! **You have completed Assess Your Skills 2**

Figure 1

Assess Your Skills Visually

To complete this workbook, you will need the following file:

- e03_Parking

You will save your workbook as:

- Lastname_Firstname_e03_Parking

Open the file **e03_Parking,** and save the workbook in your **Excel Chapter 3** folder as Lastname_Firstname_e03_Parking Complete the three detail sheets, as shown in **Figure 1**. To compute the *Net Income,* group the worksheets, and then use the formula *Net Income = (Parking Meters + Parking Tickets) – (Maintenance Cost + Personnel Costs).* Sum the columns, and then apply appropriate number formats. Create the summary sheet for the 2nd Quarter with the totals from each month and the titles, as shown in the figure. Insert a **Clustered Bar** chart, and then move the chart to a chart sheet with the sheet tab name Parking Chart Apply the **Style 27** chart style and the **Layout 1** quick chart layout. For the chart title, type Parking Revenue and Cost and show the legend at the top. Angle the horizontal axis at **-40°**. On all worksheets, add a footer with the file name in the left section and the sheet name in the right section. Delete any unused blank worksheets. **Save** the workbook, and then print or submit the workbook electronically as directed by your instructor.

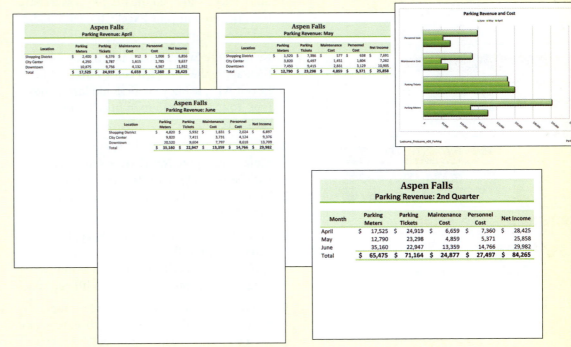

Figure 1

Done! You have completed Assess Your Skills Visually

Skills in Context

To complete this workbook, you will need the following file:

- e03_Center

You will save your workbook as:

- Lastname_Firstname_e03_Center

During each quarter, the city tracked the rental revenue at the City Center. Open the file **c03_Center,** and then save the workbook in your **Excel Chapter 3** folder as Lastname_Firstname_e03_Center For each quarter, compute the net income using the formula *Net Income = Income – (Indirect Costs + Direct Costs).* Total the columns, and format the numbers appropriately. Create a worksheet named Summary containing the totals for each quarter. Use the same column titles that are on the detail worksheets in the range B4:E4, and change the row titles in the range A4:A7. Total and format the numbers on the *Summary* worksheet. Insert a clustered bar chart, and move the chart to a chart sheet. Format the chart appropriately. On all sheets, insert the file name in the left footer and the sheet name in the right footer. Delete any unused blank worksheets. Save the workbook, and then print or submit the workbook electronically as directed by your instructor.

Done! You have completed Skills in Context

Skills and You

To complete this workbook, you will need the following file:

- New blank Excel workbook

You will save your workbook as:

- Lastname_Firstname_e03_Repairs

How much does it cost your family to own, operate, and maintain more than one vehicle? Recording the cost of owning each vehicle and then comparing the costs might reveal that one or more of your vehicles are costing more in repairs or gasoline than you want to spend. Create a worksheet for each vehicle your family uses. Use months as the row names, and use *Payment, Insurance, Gasoline,* and *Maintenance and Repairs* as the column names. Record three months of data, and then format the data appropriately. Create a summary sheet for the vehicles. Create a clustered bar chart, and move the chart to a chart sheet. Switch the rows and columns as necessary so that the vehicles form the vertical axis. You might find that one or more vehicles is using much more gasoline or costing more in repairs and maintenance than you realized. Save the workbook in your **Excel Chapter 3** folder as Lastname_Firstname_e03_Repairs and submit the workbook as directed by your instructor.

Done! You have completed Skills and You

CHAPTER 4

Use Excel Functions and Tables

▶ Functions are prewritten formulas that have two parts—the name of the function and the arguments that specify the values or cells to be used by the function.

▶ The Excel Function Library contains hundreds of special functions that perform complex calculations quickly. Some of the categories in the Function Library are statistical, financial, logical, date and time, and math and trigonometry.

▶ Conditional formatting helps you see important trends and highlight exceptions in your data by applying various formats such as colored gradients, data bars, or icons.

▶ You can convert data organized in rows and columns into an Excel table.

▶ An Excel table helps you manage information by providing ways to sort and filter the data and to analyze the data using summary rows and calculated columns. You can generate charts from the data in an Excel table.

©Wellfordt | Dreamstime.com

Aspen Falls City Hall

In this chapter, you will create Excel worksheets for Rachel Brewer, the Aspen Falls Fire Marshal. She is looking at the firefighting equipment inventory and wants to know if equipment needs to be reordered and if new suppliers should be contacted for quotes when replacing equipment. In this project, you will use the Excel functions SUM, AVERAGE, MIN, MAX, and IF to generate useful information for the fire marshal. You will apply conditional formatting to highlight outlying data and create sparklines to display trends. To modify data, you will use the Find and Replace tool. Finally, you will create and format Excel tables, and then search the tables for data.

**Time to complete all
10 skills – 60 to 90 minutes**

**60-90
min.**

Student data file needed for this chapter:

e04_Fire_Equipment

Outcome

Using the skills in this chapter, you will be able to work with Office documents like this:

You will save your workbook as:

Lastname_Firstname_e04_Fire_Equipment

SKILLS

Skills 1-10 Training

At the end of this chapter you will be able to:

Skill 1   Use the SUM and AVERAGE Functions

Skill 2   Use the MIN and MAX Functions

Skill 3   Move Ranges with Functions, Add Borders, and Rotate Text

Skill 4   Use the IF Function

Skill 5   Apply Conditional Formatting with Custom Formats, Data Bars, and Sparklines

Skill 6   Use Find and Replace and Insert the NOW Function

Skill 7   Freeze and Unfreeze Panes

Skill 8   Create and Sort Excel Tables

Skill 9   Use the Search Filter in Excel Tables

Skill 10   Convert Tables to Ranges, Hide Rows and Columns, and Format Large Worksheets

MORE SKILLS

Skill 11   Apply Conditional Color Scales with Top and Bottom Rules

Skill 12   Use the Payment (PMT) Function

Skill 13   Create PivotTable Reports

Skill 14   Use Goal Seek

► A *function* is a prewritten formula that takes input, performs an operation, and returns a value. Functions are used to simplify and shorten formulas.

► *Statistical functions* are predefined formulas that describe a collection of data—for example, totals, counts, and averages.

► The *AVERAGE function* adds a group of values and then divides the result by the number of values in the group.

1. **Start** Excel ✕, and then open **e04_Fire_ Equipment**. On the **menu bar,** click **File,** and then click **Save As**. In the **Save As** dialog, navigate to the location where you are saving your files. Click **New Folder,** type Excel Chapter 4 and then press return . In the **Save As** box, type Lastname_ Firstname_e04_Fire_Equipment and then press return .

2. Click cell **C4**. On the **Standard toolbar,** click the **SUM** button Σ, and then compare your screen with **Figure 1**.

3. With the insertion point in the function parentheses, click cell **A12,** and then press command ⌘ + shift + ▼ to select the range **A12:A70**. On the formula bar, click the **Enter** button to display the result *1745,* as shown in **Figure 2**.

   The range in parentheses is the function *argument*—the values that a function uses to perform operations or calculations. The arguments each function uses are specific to that function. Common arguments include numbers, text, cell references, and range names.

   ■ **Continue to the next page to complete the skill** ➤

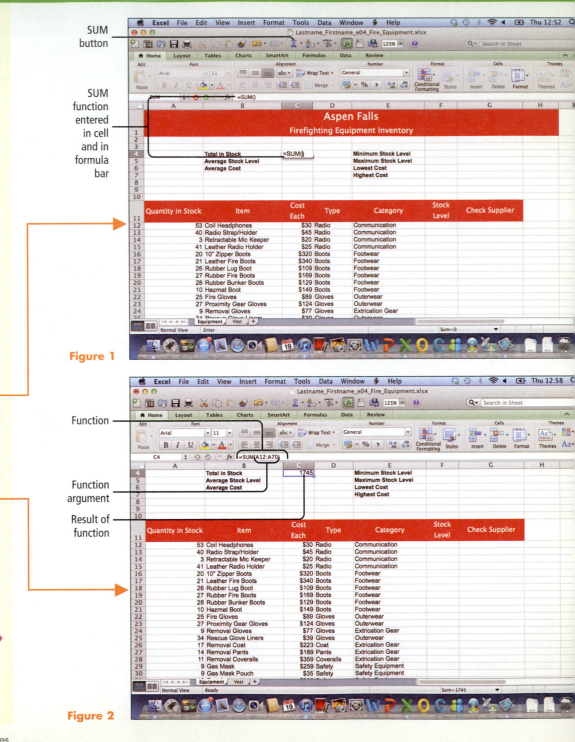

Figure 1

Figure 2

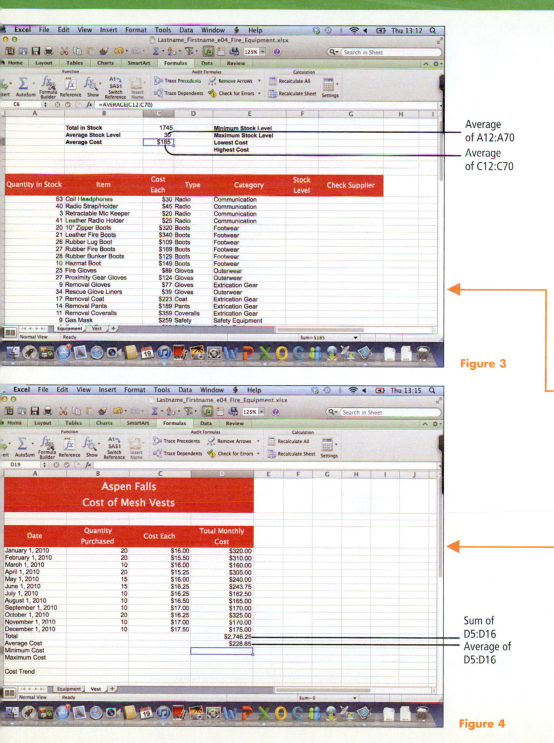

Average of A12:A70

Average of C12:C70

Figure 3

Sum of D5:D16

Average of D5:D16

Figure 4

4. Click cell **C5**. On the **Formulas tab,** in the **Function group,** click the **AutoSum button arrow** ∑, and then in the list of functions, click **Average**. In the formula bar and in the cell, notice that Excel proposes to average the value in cell *C4*.

   When data is above or to the left of a selected cell, a function will suggest a range. Often, you will need to edit a suggested range.

5. With cell **C4** highlighted in the function argument, select the range **A12:A70,** and then on the formula bar, click the **Enter** button to display the result *29.5763*. On the **Home tab,** in the **Format group,** click the **Styles** button, and then click **Comma [0]**.

6. Click cell **C6**. On the **Formulas tab,** in the **Function group,** click the **AutoSum button arrow** ∑, and then in the list, click **Average**. Select the range **C12:C70,** and then click the **Enter** button. If necessary, scroll up to display the result *$185,* as shown in **Figure 3**.

7. Click the **Vest sheet tab,** and then click cell **D17**. Using the techniques just practiced, enter the **SUM** function using the argument range **D5:D16,** and then press return . In cell **D18,** enter the **AVERAGE** function using the argument range **D5:D16,** and then click the **Enter** button. Verify that cell **D17** is not included in the Average range. Compare your sheet to **Figure 4**.

8. Move the pointer over the **Vest sheet tab,** press control , and then click the mouse. From the displayed menu, click **Select All Sheets**. Display the worksheet footers, insert the **File Name** in the left footer and the **Sheet Name** in the right footer. Return to **Normal** view and then scroll to the top of the worksheet.

9. **Save** 💾 the workbook.

▪ **You have completed Skill 1 of 10**

▶ The *MIN function* returns the smallest value in a range of cells.

▶ The *MAX function* returns the largest value in a range of cells.

1. Make the **Equipment** sheet the active sheet. Click cell **F4**. In the **Function group,** click the **AutoSum button arrow** Σ, and then in the list, click **Min**. With the insertion point in the function, select the range **A12:A70,** and then on the formula bar, click the **Enter** button ☑ to display the result *3*.

   The MIN function evaluates all of the values in the range A12:A70 and then returns *3*, the lowest value found in the range.

2. Click cell **F5**. In the **Function group,** click the **AutoSum button arrow** Σ, and then in the list, click **Max**.

   The MAX function automatically suggests the argument F4 because the cell above contains a value.

3. With cell **F4** selected in the function argument, select the range **A12:A70,** and then on the formula bar, click the **Enter** button ☑ to display the result *90*, as shown in **Figure 1**.

   The MAX function evaluates all of the values in the range A12:A70 and then returns the highest value found.

4. Click cell **A12,** type 146 and then press return . In cell **A13,** type 2 and then press return . Verify that the MIN and MAX functions in cells **F4** and **F5** now display the lowest and highest values in the range **A12:A70**. Verify that the SUM and AVERAGE functions also automatically recalculated, as shown in **Figure 2**.

   ■ Continue to the next page to complete the skill ➤

Result of MAX function

Figure 1

Function results recalculated

Value changed to 146

Figure 2

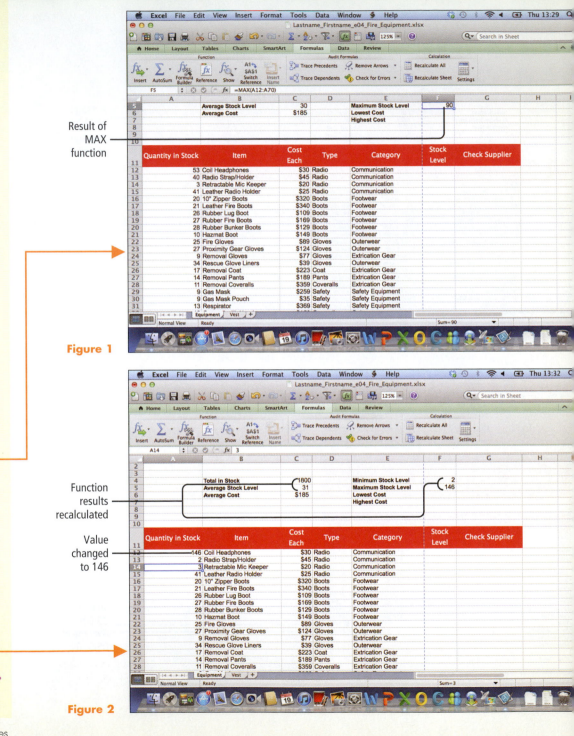

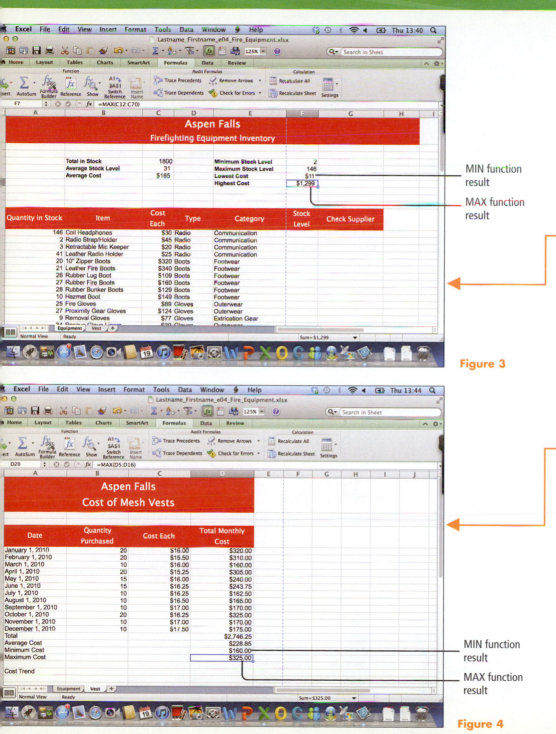

MIN function result

MAX function result

Figure 3

MIN function result

MAX function result

Figure 4

5. In cell **F6**, repeat the technique just practiced to insert the **MIN** function using the range **C12:C70** as the argument in the parentheses. Verify that the result is *$11*.

6. In cell **F7**, insert the **MAX** function to return the highest cost in the range **C12:C70**. Verify that the result is *$1,299*. Scroll down to view the worksheet, and verify that the lowest and highest values in column **C** were selected from each of the ranges for the MIN and MAX functions. Compare your screen with **Figure 3**.

7. Make the **Vest** worksheet the active sheet.

8. In cell **D19**, insert the MIN function to evaluate the lowest monthly cost in the range **D5:D16** as the argument in the parentheses. Do not include the *Total* or *Average Cost* values in the range. Verify that the result is *$160.00*.

9. In cell **D20**, insert the MAX function to evaluate the highest monthly cost in the range **D5:D16** as the argument. Verify that the result is *$325.00*, as shown in **Figure 4**.

10. **Save** 🖫 the workbook.

■ **You have completed Skill 2 of 10**

▶ You can move a range of cells containing formulas or functions without changing the cell references in those formulas or functions.

▶ Borders and shading emphasize a cell or a range of cells, and rotated or angled text draws attention to text on a worksheet.

1. Make the **Equipment** worksheet the active sheet. Select the range **E4:F7**. Point to the top edge of the selected range to display the 👆 pointer. Drag the selected range up until the ScreenTip displays the range *E3:F6,* and then release the mouse button to complete the move. Compare your screen with **Figure 1**.

2. Select the range **B4:C6,** and then using the technique you just practiced, move the range to **E7:F9.**

3. On the **Formulas tab,** in the **Function group,** click the **Show** button, and then click **Show Formulas** to display the functions in the cells. Scroll to the right, and then click cell **F2**. Notice that the cell references in the functions did not change, as shown in **Figure 2**.

4. In the **Function group,** click the **Show** button, and then click **Show Formulas** to display the function results in the cells.

5. Select the range **F3:F4**. Hold down command ⌘, and then select the range **F7:F8**. With the nonadjacent cells selected, on the **Home tab,** in the **Format group,** click the **Styles** button, and then click **Comma [0].**

6. Select the range **A11:G11**. On the **menu bar,** click **Format,** and then click **Cells**. In the **Format Cells** dialog, click the **Border button**. On the right, under **Style,** click the sixth line style in the second column, and then under **Border** click **Bottom Border**. Click **OK.**

■ **Continue to the next page to complete the skill**

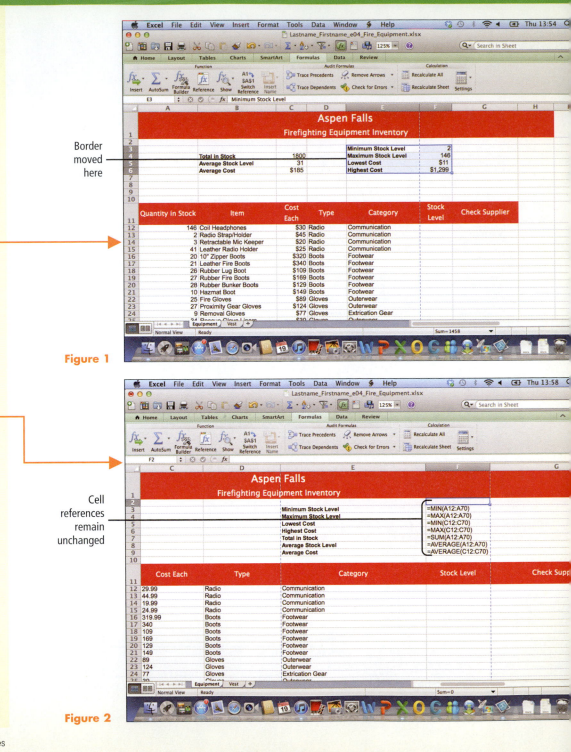

Border moved here

Figure 1

Cell references remain unchanged

Figure 2

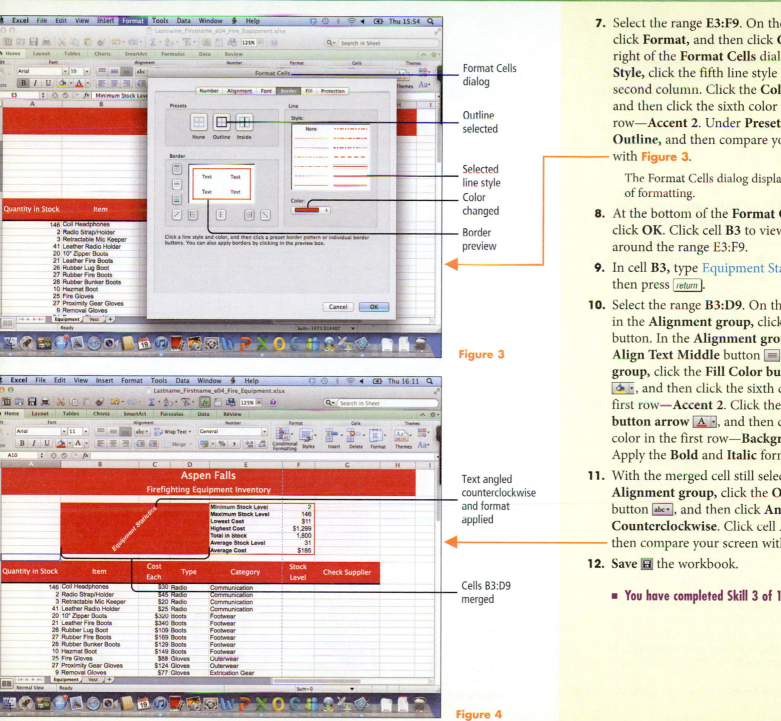

Format Cells
dialog

Outline
selected

Selected
line style

Color
changed

Border
preview

Figure 3

Text angled
counterclockwise
and format
applied

Cells B3:D9
merged

Figure 4

7. Select the range **E3:F9**. On the **menu bar,** click **Format,** and then click **Cells.** In the right of the **Format Cells** dialog, under **Style,** click the fifth line style in the second column. Click the **Color arrow,** and then click the sixth color in the first row—**Accent 2.** Under **Presets,** click **Outline,** and then compare your screen with **Figure 3.**

   The Format Cells dialog displays a preview of formatting.

8. At the bottom of the **Format Cells** dialog, click **OK.** Click cell **B3** to view the border around the range **E3:F9.**

9. In cell **B3,** type Equipment Statistics and then press return .

10. Select the range **B3:D9.** On the **Home tab,** in the **Alignment group,** click the **Merge** button. In the **Alignment group,** click the **Align Text Middle** button ☰. In the **Font group,** click the **Fill Color button arrow** ◇▾, and then click the sixth color in the first row—**Accent 2.** Click the **Font Color button arrow** A▾, and then click the first color in the first row—**Background 1.** Apply the **Bold** and **Italic** format.

11. With the merged cell still selected, in the **Alignment group,** click the **Orientation** button abc▾, and then click **Angle Counterclockwise.** Click cell **A10,** and then compare your screen with **Figure 4.**

12. **Save** ⊞ the workbook.

   ■ **You have completed Skill 3 of 10**

▶ A *logical test* is any value or expression that can be evaluated as TRUE or FALSE.

▶ A *logical function* applies a logical test to determine whether a specific condition is met. *Criteria* are the conditions specified in the logical test.

▶ The *IF function* checks whether criteria are met and then returns one value when the condition is TRUE and another value when the condition is FALSE.

1. Click cell **F12.** On the **menu bar,** click **Insert,** and then click **Function**.

2. On the **Formula Builder** task pane, click in the **Search for a function** box, and then type if In the displayed results, under **Logical,** double-click **IF**.

   An *Arguments* section displays in the Formula Builder.

3. With the insertion point in the **value1** box, type A12<10

   The logical test *A12<10* will look at the value in cell A12 and determine whether the value is less than 10. The expression *<10* includes the < comparison operator, which means *less than*. A *comparison operator* compares two values and returns either TRUE or FALSE. The table in **Figure 1** lists commonly used comparison operators.

4. Press [tab] to move the insertion point to the **then** box, and then type Order

5. Press [tab] to move the insertion point to the **else** box, type Level OK and then compare your screen with **Figure 2**.

   Quotation marks display around *Order* and will automatically be inserted around *Level OK* after you press [return]. In function arguments, text values are surrounded by quotation marks.

■ **Continue to the next page to complete the skill** ➤

Comparison Operators	
Comparison Operator Symbol	**Definition**
=	Equal to (A1=B1)
>	Greater than (A1>B1)
<	Less than (A1<B1)
>=	Greater than or equal to (A1>=B1)
<=	Less than or equal to (A1<=B1)
<>	Not equal to (A1<>B1)

Figure 1

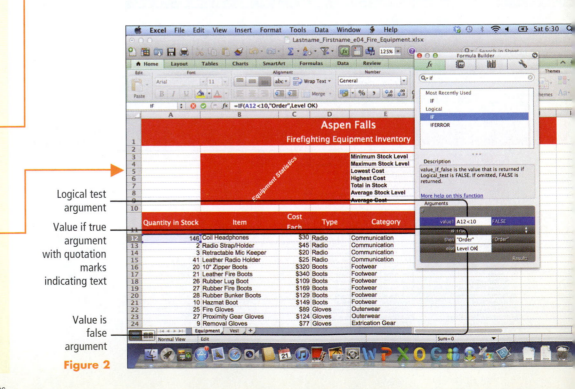

Logical test argument

Value if true argument with quotation marks indicating text

Value is false argument

Figure 2

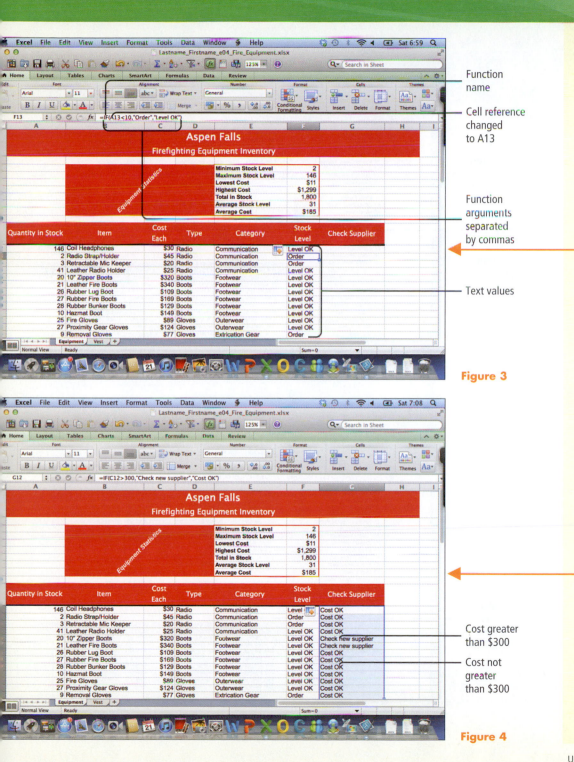

Figure 3

Figure 4

6. Press ⌐return⌐, and then **Close** ◉ the **Formula Builder** task pane to display the result *Level OK* in cell **F12**.

The IF function tests whether cell A12 is less than 10. If this condition were TRUE, *Order* would display. Because cell A12 contains the value *146*, the condition is FALSE, and *Level OK* displays in cell F12.

7. In cell **F12**, point to the fill handle to display the ⊞ pointer, and then double-click to copy the function down through cell **F70**. Click cell **F13**, and then compare your screen with **Figure 3**.

When a function has multiple arguments, each argument is separated by a comma.

When the function was copied down to cell F13, the cell reference changed from A12 to A13.

8. Click cell **G12**. On the **menu bar,** click **Insert,** and then click **Function**. On the **Formula Builder** task pane, under **Most Recently Used,** double-click **IF**. In the **value1** box, type C12>300 and then press ⌐tab⌐. In the **then** box, type Check new supplier and then press ⌐tab⌐. In the **else** box, type Cost OK Press ⌐return⌐, and then **Close** ◉ the **Formula Builder** task pane. In cell **G12**, point to the fill handle to display the ⊞ pointer, and then double-click to copy the function down through cell **G70**. Compare your screen with **Figure 4**.

In each row, the function evaluates the value in column C. When the value in column C is greater than $300, the text *Check new supplier* displays. Otherwise, the text *Cost OK* displays.

9. **Save** 🖫 the workbook.

■ **You have completed Skill 4 of 10**

► *Conditional formatting* is a format, such as cell shading or font color, that is applied to cells when a specified condition is true.

► Conditional formatting makes analyzing data easier by emphasizing cell values.

1. Click cell **F12**. Press $\boxed{\text{command} \ \mathcal{H}}$ + $\boxed{\text{shift}}$ + $\boxed{\blacktriangledown}$ to select the range **F12:F70**.

2. On the **Home tab,** in the **Format group,** click the **Conditional Formatting** button. On the list, point to **Highlight Cells Rules,** and then click **Text that Contains**. In the **New Formatting Rule** dialog, with the insertion point in the text box, type Order as shown in **Figure 1**.

3. In the **New Formatting Rule** dialog, click **OK**.

    Within the range F12:F70, cells that contain the text *Order* display with light red fill and dark red text formatting.

4. Using the technique just practiced, select the range **G12:G70**. Click the **Conditional Formatting** button, point to **Highlight Cells Rules,** and then click **Text That Contains**. In the text box, type Check new supplier Click the **Format with box arrow,** and on the list, click **yellow fill with dark yellow text**. Compare your screen with **Figure 2**.

    The Text That Contains dialog is used to specify the formatting to apply when the condition is true—here, if the cell contains the text *Check new supplier*. Within the selected range, if a cell contains the text *Check new supplier,* the conditional format is applied.

■ **Continue to the next page to complete the skill** ➡️

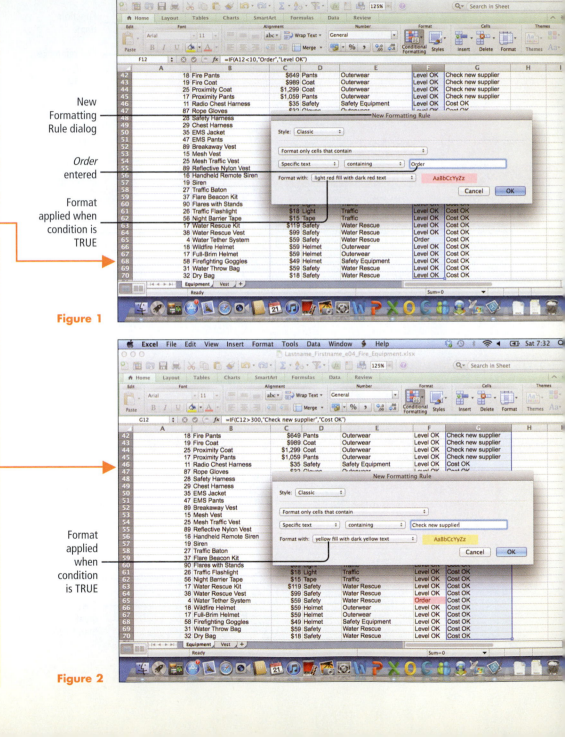

New Formatting Rule dialog

Order entered

Format applied when condition is TRUE

Figure 1

Format applied when condition is TRUE

Figure 2

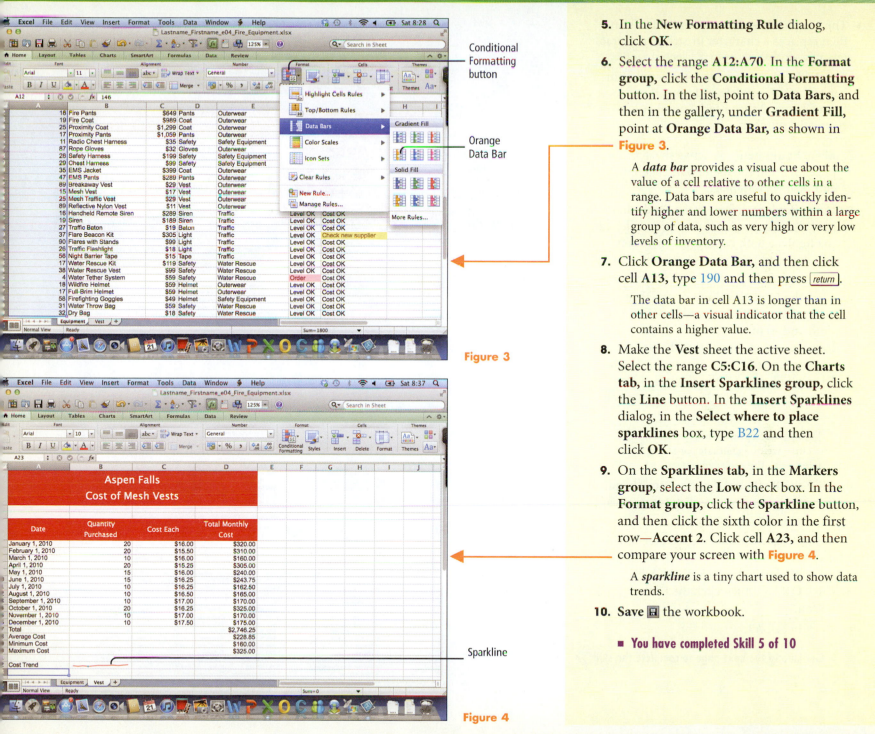

Conditional Formatting button

Orange Data Bar

Figure 3

Sparkline

Figure 4

5. In the **New Formatting Rule** dialog, click **OK**.

6. Select the range **A12:A70**. In the **Format group,** click the **Conditional Formatting** button. In the list, point to **Data Bars,** and then in the gallery, under **Gradient Fill,** point at **Orange Data Bar,** as shown in **Figure 3.**

A *data bar* provides a visual cue about the value of a cell relative to other cells in a range. Data bars are useful to quickly identify higher and lower numbers within a large group of data, such as very high or very low levels of inventory.

7. Click **Orange Data Bar,** and then click cell **A13,** type 190 and then press [return].

The data bar in cell A13 is longer than in other cells—a visual indicator that the cell contains a higher value.

8. Make the **Vest** sheet the active sheet. Select the range **C5:C16**. On the **Charts tab,** in the **Insert Sparklines group,** click the **Line** button. In the **Insert Sparklines** dialog, in the **Select where to place sparklines** box, type B22 and then click **OK.**

9. On the **Sparklines tab,** in the **Markers group,** select the **Low** check box. In the **Format group,** click the **Sparkline** button, and then click the sixth color in the first row—**Accent 2**. Click cell **A23,** and then compare your screen with **Figure 4.**

A *sparkline* is a tiny chart used to show data trends.

10. **Save** 🖫 the workbook.

■ **You have completed Skill 5 of 10**

▶ The *Find and Replace* command finds and then replaces a character or string of characters in a worksheet or in a selected range.

▶ The *NOW function* returns the serial number of the current date and time. Recall from Chapter 3 that a serial number is a sequential number.

1. Make **Equipment** the active sheet. Click in cell **A1**. On the **menu bar,** click **Edit,** and then click **Replace**.

2. In the **Replace** dialog, in the **Find what** box, type Removal and then press `tab`. In the **Replace with** box, type Extrication and then compare your screen with **Figure 1**.

3. Click the **Find Next** button, and then verify that cell **B24** is highlighted. In the **Find and Replace** dialog, click the **Replace** button. Verify that the first occurrence of *Removal* was replaced with *Extrication* and that the second occurrence—in cell **B26**—is automatically located.

   The Replace option will replace a single occurrence of a character or string of characters with the replacement value.

4. Click the **Replace All** button, and then in the message box, notice that **3 instances** were replaced, as shown in **Figure 2**.

   The Replace All option replaces all matches of an occurrence of a character or string of characters with the replacement value.

5. Click **OK,** and then click the **Close** button.

6. Click in cell **A1**.

   ■ **Continue to the next page to complete the skill**

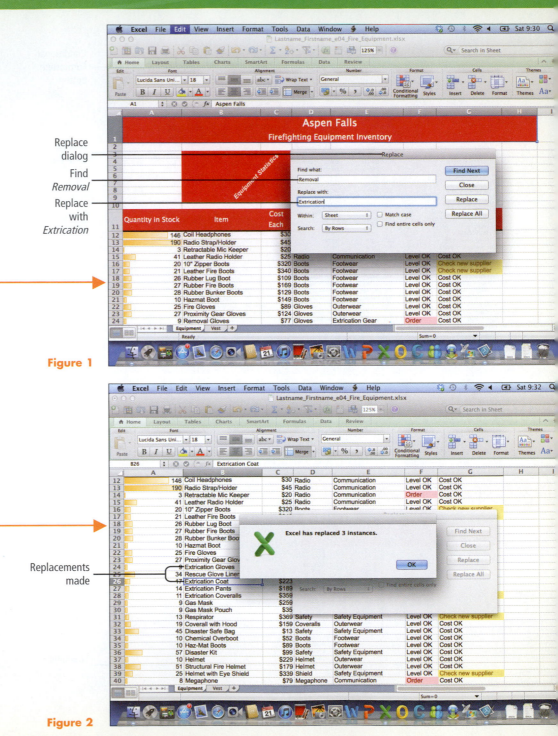

Figure 1

Figure 2

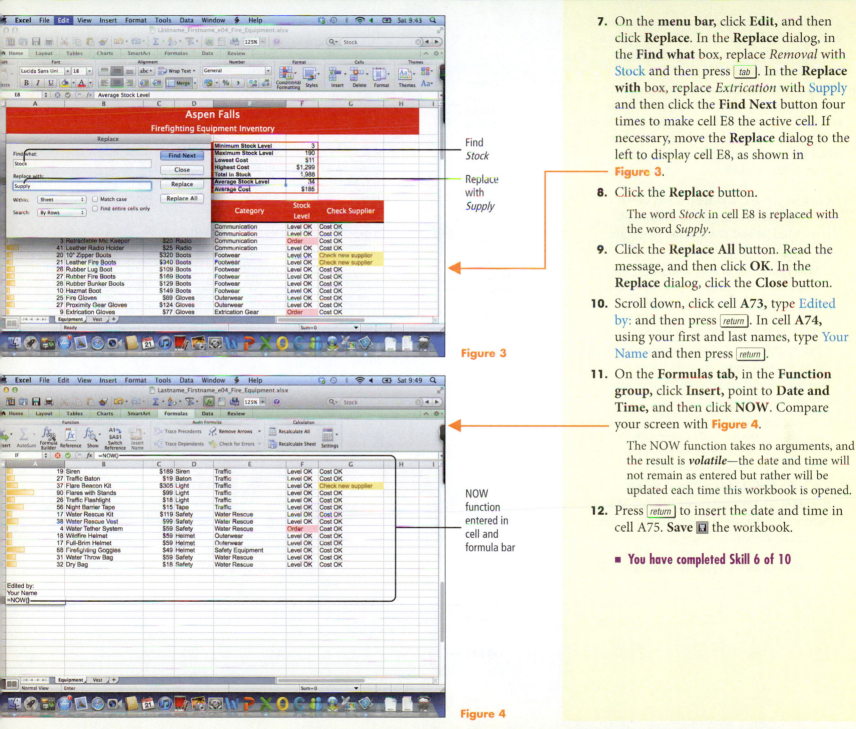

Figure 3

Figure 4

7. On the **menu bar,** click **Edit,** and then click **Replace.** In the **Replace** dialog, in the **Find what** box, replace *Removal* with Stock and then press tab . In the **Replace with** box, replace *Extrication* with Supply and then click the **Find Next** button four times to make cell E8 the active cell. If necessary, move the **Replace** dialog to the left to display cell E8, as shown in **Figure 3.**

8. Click the **Replace** button.

   The word *Stock* in cell E8 is replaced with the word *Supply*.

9. Click the **Replace All** button. Read the message, and then click **OK.** In the **Replace** dialog, click the **Close** button.

10. Scroll down, click cell **A73,** type Edited by: and then press return . In cell **A74,** using your first and last names, type Your Name and then press return .

11. On the **Formulas tab,** in the **Function group,** click **Insert,** point to **Date and Time,** and then click **NOW.** Compare your screen with **Figure 4.**

   The NOW function takes no arguments, and the result is *volatile*—the date and time will not remain as entered but rather will be updated each time this workbook is opened.

12. Press return to insert the date and time in cell A75. **Save** 💾 the workbook.

   ■ **You have completed Skill 6 of 10**

► The *Freeze Panes* command keeps rows or columns visible when you are scrolling in a worksheet. The frozen rows and columns become separate panes.

► When you freeze panes, you determine the specific rows or columns that you want to remain visible when scrolling. You will likely find it easier to work with large worksheets when you can always view the identifying row or column labels.

1. Click in cell **A1,** and then scroll down until row **50** displays at the bottom of your window and the column labels are out of view, as shown in **Figure 1**.

   When you scroll in large worksheets, the column and row labels may not be visible, which can make identifying the purpose of each row or column difficult. You may see different rows depending on the zoom level.

2. Click in cell **C15**. On the **Layout tab,** in the **Window group,** click the **Freeze Panes** button, and then click **Freeze Panes**.

   By selecting cell C15, the rows above and the columns to the left of C15 are frozen. A line displays along the upper border of row 15 and on the left border of column C.

3. Click the **Scroll Down** and **Scroll Right** arrows, and then click cell **M80**. Notice that the top and left panes remain frozen, as shown in **Figure 2**.

   ■ **Continue to the next page to complete the skill** ➜

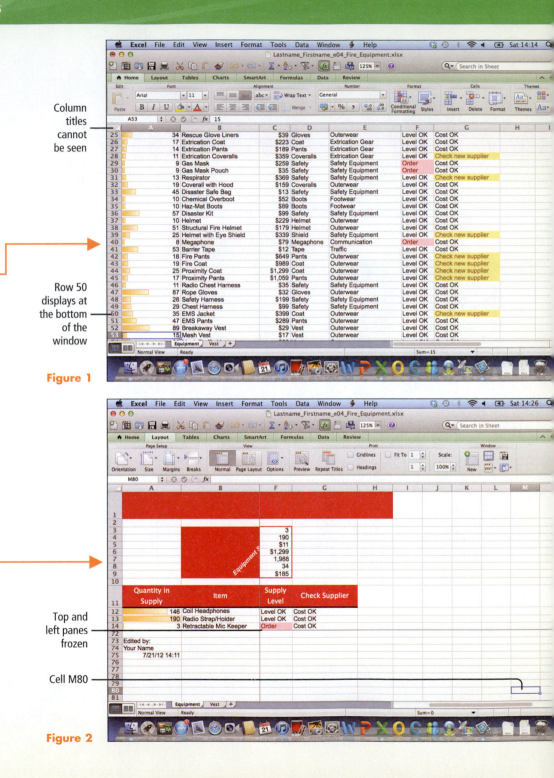

Column titles cannot be seen

Row 50 displays at the bottom of the window

Figure 1

Top and left panes frozen

Cell M80

Figure 2

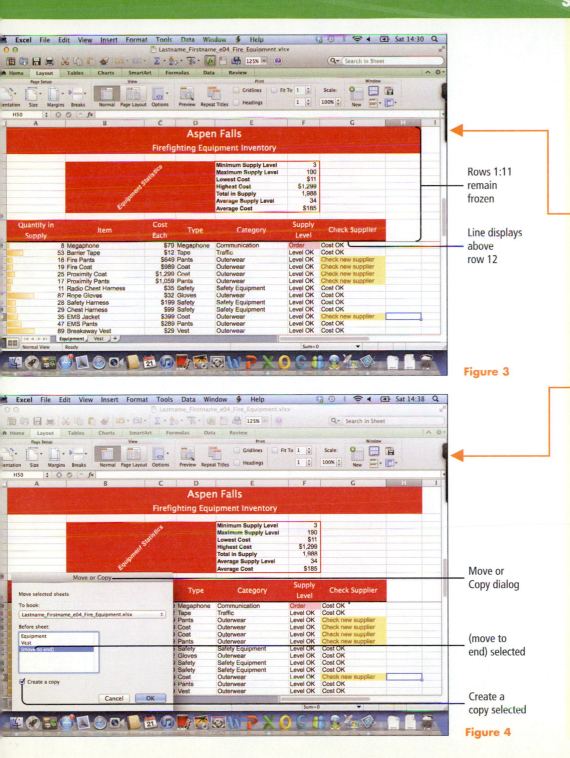

Rows 1:11 remain frozen

Line displays above row 12

Figure 3

Move or Copy dialog

(move to end) selected

Create a copy selected

Figure 4

4. In the **Window group,** click the **Freeze Panes** button, and then click **Unfreeze.**

   The rows and columns are no longer frozen, and the border no longer displays on row 15 and on column C.

5. Click cell **A12.** In the **Window group,** click the **Freeze Panes** button, and then click **Freeze Panes.**

6. Watch the row numbers below row **11** as you scroll down to row **50.** Compare your screen with **Figure 3.**

   The titles in row 1 through row 11 stay frozen while the remaining rows of data continue to scroll.

7. Move the pointer over the **Equipment** sheet tab, press control and then click the mouse button. From the list, click **Move or Copy.** In the **Move or Copy** dialog, click (**move to end**), and then select the **Create a copy** check box. Compare your screen with **Figure 4.**

8. In the **Move or Copy** dialog, click **OK.**

   A copy of the *Equipment* worksheet is created, and the new sheet tab is named *Equipment (2).*

9. Move the pointer over the **Equipment (2)** sheet tab, press control and then click the mouse button. Click **Rename,** type Sort by Cost and then press return. In the **Window group,** click the **Freeze Panes** button, and then click **Unfreeze.** Click the **Equipment** sheet tab, and verify that on this worksheet, the panes are still frozen.

10. **Save** 🖫 the workbook.

■ **You have completed Skill 7 of 10**

► To analyze a group of related data, you can convert a range into an *Excel table*—a series of rows and columns that contain related data. Data in an Excel table are managed independently from the data in other rows and columns in the worksheet.

► Data in Excel tables can be sorted in a variety of ways—for example, in ascending order or by color.

1. Click the **Sort by Cost** sheet tab, and then click cell **A11**. On the **Tables tab,** in the **Table Options group,** click the **New** button, and then compare your screen with **Figure 1**. —————

   The range A11:G70 is automatically selected because there are no blank rows or columns in the range. In the Excel table, formatting is applied and the header row displays filter arrows in each column.

2. On the **Tables tab,** in the **Table Styles group,** click the **More** button ☑, and then under **Light,** click **Table Style Light 10**.

3. Click cell **H11,** type Total Cost and then press ⏎ to automatically include the column in the Excel table.

4. In **H12,** type =A12*C12 and then press ⏎ to create a *calculated column*—a column in an Excel table that uses a single formula that adjusts for each row—as shown in **Figure 2**. —————

   ■ **Continue to the next page to complete the skill** ➤

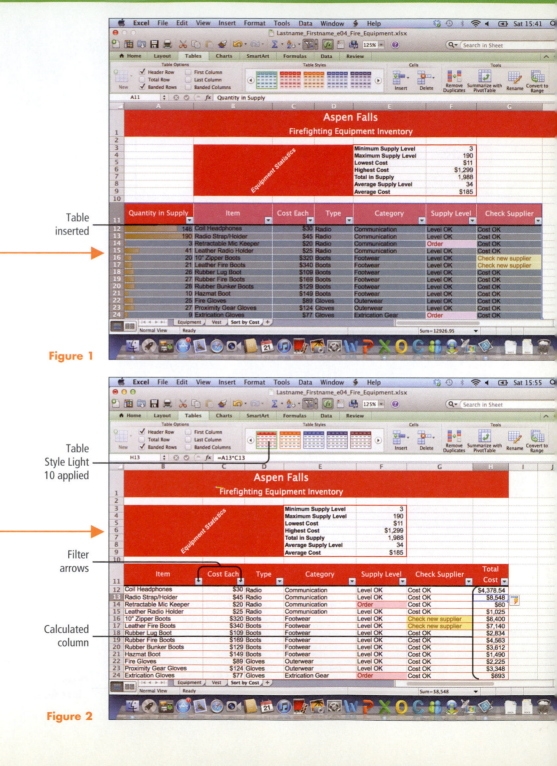

Table inserted

Figure 1

Table Style Light 10 applied

Filter arrows

Calculated column

Figure 2

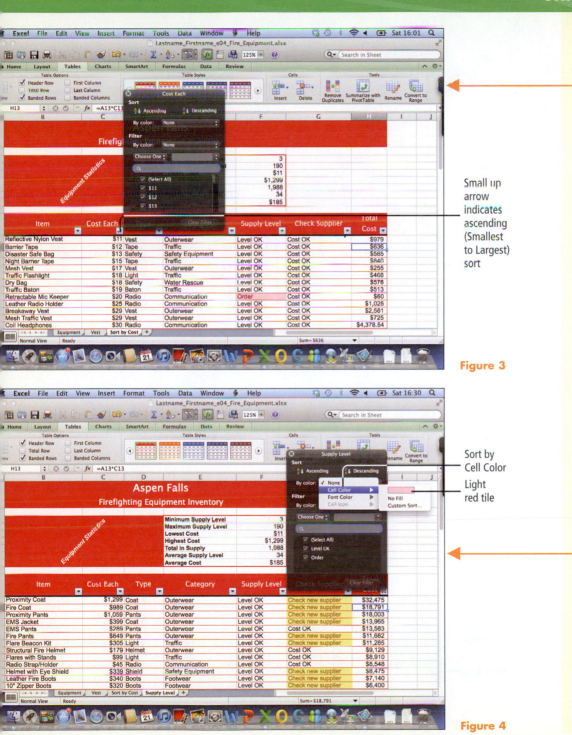

Figure 3

Figure 4

5. In the header row of the Excel table, click the **Cost Each filter arrow,** and then click the **Ascending** button. Compare your screen with **Figure 3**.

> The rows in the table are sorted by the *Cost Each* values, from the lowest to the highest, as indicated by the up arrow on the column's filter button.

6. Close ⬛ the task pane. In the header row, click the **Total Cost filter arrow,** and then click the **Descending** button. **Close** ⬛ the task pane.

> The rows in the table are now sorted from the highest to lowest *Total Cost* value, and the small arrow in the Total Cost filter arrow points down, indicating a descending sort. The previous sort on the *Cost Each* column no longer displays.

7. Move the pointer over the **Sort by Cost** sheet tab, press control and then click the mouse button. Click **Move or Copy**. In the **Move or Copy** dialog, click (**move to end**), select the **Create a copy** check box, and then click **OK**.

8. Move the pointer over the **Sort by Cost (2)** sheet tab, press control and then click the mouse button. Click **Rename,** type Supply Level and then press return.

9. In the **Supply Level** worksheet, click the **Supply Level filter arrow**. Click the **By color arrow,** and then point to **Cell Color,** as shown in **Figure 4**.

> If you have applied manual or conditional formatting to a range of cells, you can sort by these colors.

10. In the **Sort by Color** list, under **Cell Color,** click the **light red tile** to display the six items that need to be ordered first in the Excel table. **Close** ⬛ the task pane.

11. Save 🖫 the workbook.

▪ **You have completed Skill 8 of 10**

The following callouts appear in the figures:

Small up arrow indicates ascending (Smallest to Largest) sort

Sort by Cell Color

Light red tile

► You can *filter* data to display only the rows of a table that meet specified criteria. Filtering temporarily hides rows that do not meet the criteria.

1. On the **Supply Level** worksheet, click the **Category filter arrow**. From the menu, clear the **(Select All)** check box to clear all the check boxes. Select the **Safety Equipment** check box, and then click **Close**. Compare your screen with **Figure 1**.

   In the *Category* column, only the rows containing *Safety Equipment* display. The rows not meeting this criteria are hidden from view.

2. Click anywhere in the table. On the **Tables tab,** in the **Table Options group,** select the **Total Row** check box.

   The ***total row*** option displays as the last row in an Excel table and provides functions in drop-down lists for each column. Here, *Total* displays in cell A71. In cell H71, the number *$33,816* indicates the SUM of the Total Cost column for the filtered rows.

3. In the Total row, click cell **C71,** and then click the arrow that displays to the right of the selected cell. In the list, click **Average**. Compare your screen with **Figure 2**.

   Excel averages only the visible rows in column C—here, *$150* is the average cost.

4. In the header row, click the **Type filter arrow**. From the menu, clear the **Helmet** and the **Shield** check boxes, and then click **Close**.

   Filters can be applied to more than one column. Here, both the Type and Category columns are filtered.

   ■ **Continue to the next page to complete the skill** →

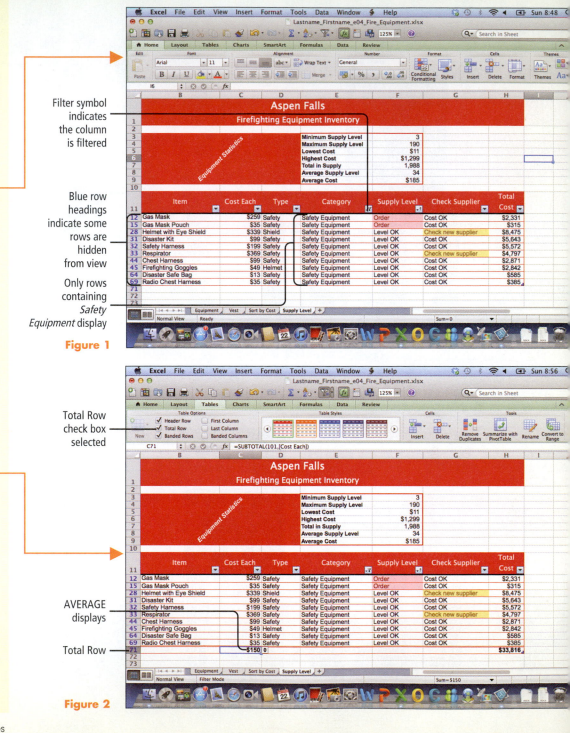

Filter symbol indicates the column is filtered

Blue row headings indicate some rows are hidden from view

Only rows containing *Safety Equipment* display

Figure 1

Total Row check box selected

AVERAGE displays

Total Row

Figure 2

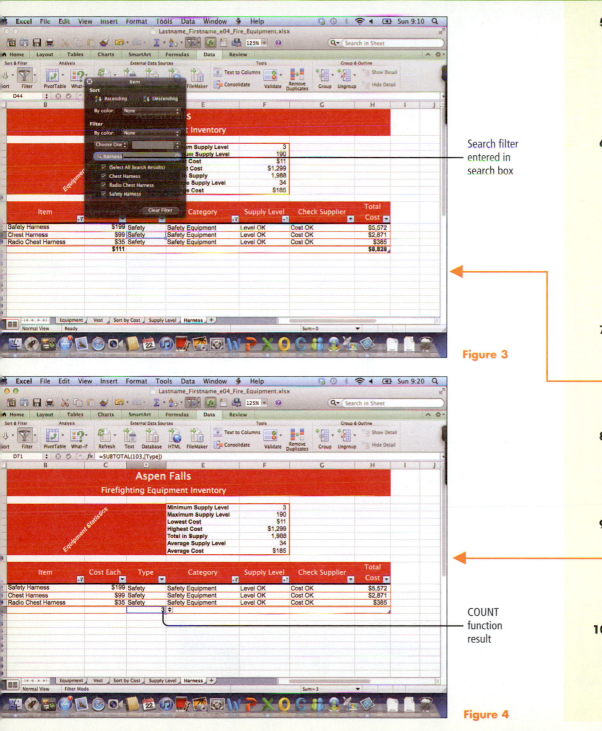

Search filter entered in search box

Figure 3

COUNT function result

Figure 4

5. Move the pointer over the **Supply Level** sheet tab, press ⌃control⌃ and then click the mouse button. Using the techniques you just practiced, create a copy of the worksheet and move the sheet to the end. Rename the **Supply Level (2)** sheet tab as Harness

6. With the **Harness** worksheet active, click any cell in the filtered column to make the Excel table active. On the **Data tab,** in the **Sort & Filter group,** click the **Filter button arrow,** and then click **Clear Filter** to clear all the filters and to display all the rows in the Excel table.

   In the Harness worksheet, all the filters are cleared and all the rows in the Excel table redisplay. On the Supply Level worksheet, the filters are still applied.

7. In the header row, click the **Item filter arrow.** From the menu, in the **Search** box, type harness and then compare your screen with **Figure 3.**

   The three rows containing the text *harness* display.

8. Click **Close** ◉. In the Total row, click cell **C71.** Click the displayed arrow, and then on the list, click **None.** In cell **H71,** repeat the same technique to remove the total from the Total Cost column.

9. Click cell **D71,** click the displayed arrow, and then click **Count.** Compare your screen with **Figure 4.**

   Only the filtered rows are counted. In this manner, you can determine how many items meet a filter criteria.

10. **Save** 🖬 the workbook.

■ **You have completed Skill 9 of 10**

► After sorting, filtering, and totaling an Excel table, you can convert the Excel table into a range.

► When a large worksheet is too wide or too long to print on a single page, row and column headings can be printed on each page or the worksheet can be formatted to print on a single page.

1. Move the pointer over the **Harness** sheet tab, press control and then click the mouse button. Create a copy of the sheet at the end of the workbook, and rename the new sheet Inventory

2. Click cell **A11**. On the **menu bar,** click **Data,** point to **Table Tools,** and then click **Convert to Range.** Read the message box, click **Yes,** and then compare your screen with **Figure 1**.

   When converting an Excel table into a range, all filters are removed and the heading row no longer displays filter buttons. Any existing sorts and formatting remain.

3. On the **Layout tab,** in the **View group,** click the **Page Layout** button, and then notice that the content displays across two pages. In the **Print group,** click to select the **Fit To** check box. Click the **Tall spin button** one time to select **2**.

4. Click the **Equipment** sheet tab. In the **Print group,** click to select the **Fit To** check box. Click the **Tall spin button** one time to select **2**.

5. In the **View group,** click the **Repeat Titles** button, and then in the **Page Setup** dialog, under **Print titles,** click in the **Rows to repeat at top** box, if necessary. Compare your screen with **Figure 2**.

   ■ **Continue to the next page to complete the skill**

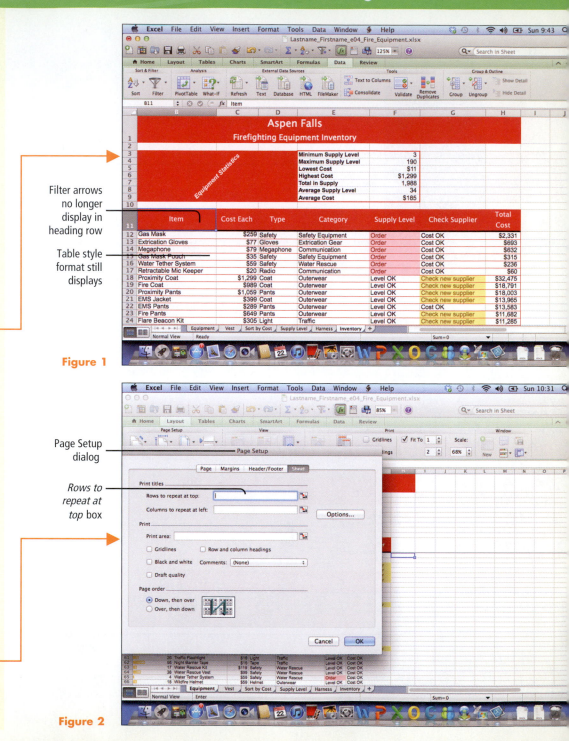

Filter arrows no longer display in heading row

Table style format still displays

Figure 1

Page Setup dialog

Rows to repeat at top box

Figure 2

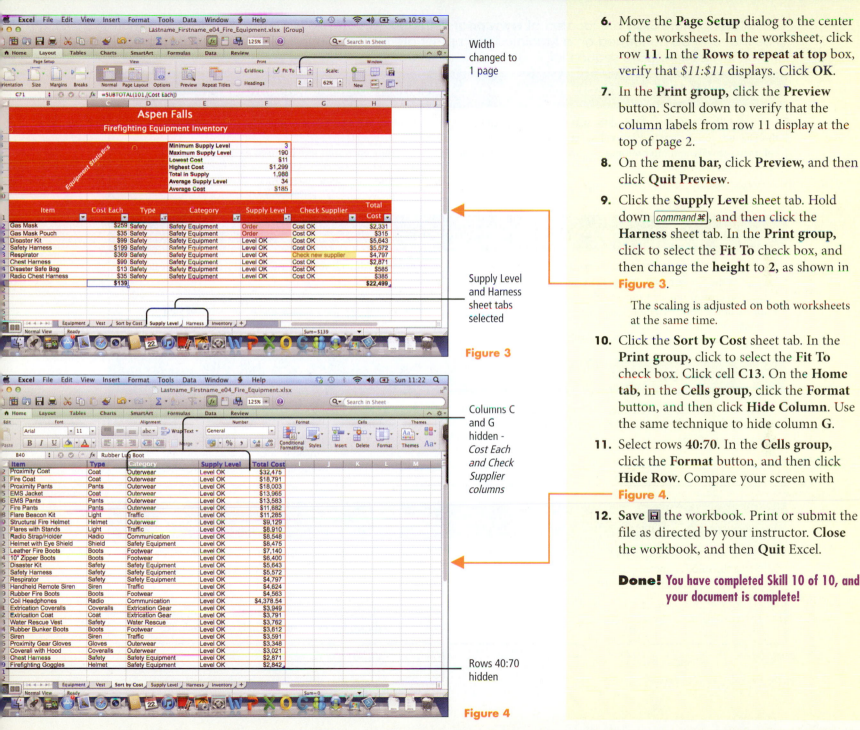

Width changed to 1 page

Supply Level and Harness sheet tabs selected

Figure 3

Columns C and G hidden - *Cost Each and Check Supplier columns*

Rows 40:70 hidden

Figure 4

6. Move the **Page Setup** dialog to the center of the worksheets. In the worksheet, click row **11**. In the **Rows to repeat at top** box, verify that *$11:$11* displays. Click **OK**.

7. In the **Print group,** click the **Preview** button. Scroll down to verify that the column labels from row 11 display at the top of page 2.

8. On the **menu bar,** click **Preview,** and then click **Quit Preview**.

9. Click the **Supply Level** sheet tab. Hold down command ⌘, and then click the **Harness** sheet tab. In the **Print group,** click to select the **Fit To** check box, and then change the **height** to **2,** as shown in **Figure 3**.

   The scaling is adjusted on both worksheets at the same time.

10. Click the **Sort by Cost** sheet tab. In the **Print group,** click to select the **Fit To** check box. Click cell **C13**. On the **Home tab,** in the **Cells group,** click the **Format** button, and then click **Hide Column**. Use the same technique to hide column **G**.

11. Select rows **40:70**. In the **Cells group,** click the **Format** button, and then click **Hide Row**. Compare your screen with **Figure 4**.

12. **Save** 💾 the workbook. Print or submit the file as directed by your instructor. **Close** the workbook, and then **Quit** Excel.

   Done! You have completed Skill 10 of 10, and your document is complete!

More Skills

The following More Skills are located at **www.pearsonhighered.com/skills**. Please note that only More Skills that can be performed on a Macintosh computer are included in this section; therefore, the numbering is not always sequential.

More Skills Apply Conditional Color Scales with Top and Bottom Rules

In addition to the conditional formats you have applied in this chapter, you can apply color scales, which apply different colors to the cells, and top/bottom rules, which format the highest or lowest values.

In More Skills 11, you will apply the additional types of conditional formats.

To begin, open your web browser, navigate to www.pearsonhighered.com/skills, locate the name of your textbook, and then follow the instructions on the website.

More Skills Use the Payment (PMT) Function

The PMT function calculates the periodic payment for any loan given the loan amount, interest rate, and length of the loan. When you borrow money from a bank, the amount charged for your use of the borrowed money is called interest, and the interest amount is included in the PMT function.

In More Skills 12, you will use the PMT function to calculate various loan payments.

To begin, open your web browser, navigate to www.pearsonhighered.com/skills, locate the name of your textbook, and then follow the instructions on the website.

More Skills Create PivotTable Reports

A PivotTable report is an interactive way to summarize large amounts of data quickly, to analyze numerical data in depth, and to answer unanticipated questions about your data.

In More Skills 13, you will create a PivotTable report, pivot the data, and then filter the data.

To begin, open your web browser, navigate to www.pearsonhighered.com/skills, locate the name of your textbook, and then follow the instructions on the website.

More Skills Use Goal Seek

Goal Seek is a method to find a specific value for a cell by adjusting the value of another cell. With Goal Seek, you work backward from the desired outcome to find the necessary input to achieve your goal.

In More Skills 14, you will use Goal Seek to determine how much money can be borrowed to achieve a specific monthly payment.

To begin, open your web browser, navigate to www.pearsonhighered.com/skills, locate the name of your textbook, and then follow the instructions on the website.

Key Terms

Argument 254

AVERAGE function 254

Calculated column 268

Comparison operator 260

Conditional formatting 262

Criteria 260

Data bar 263

Excel table 268

Filter 270

Find and Replace 264

Freeze Panes 266

Function 254

IF function 260

Logical function 260

Logical test 260

MAX function 256

MIN function 256

NOW function 264

Sparkline 263

Statistical function 254

Total row 270

Volatile 265

Online Help Skills

1. **Start** Safari or another web browser. In the **address bar,** type microsoft.com/mac/how-to and then press ⎡return⎤ to display the home page for Microsoft Office.

   This website provides you with helpful links to get started, find out what is new, and tutorials about Office 2011.

2. Under **Product Help,** click **Excel 2011**.

3. Under **Excel Help,** click **Formulas**.

4. Under **Formulas,** click **Creating Formulas**.

5. Click **Switch between relative and absolute references,** and then compare your screen with **Figure 1**.

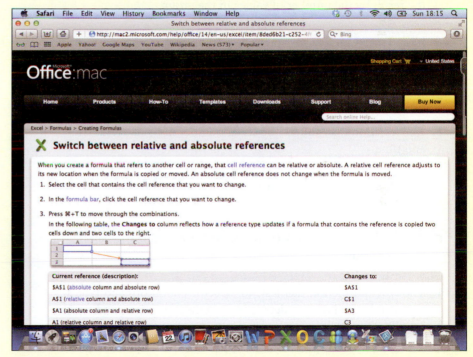

Figure 1

6. Read through the page and then answer the following questions. What is an absolute reference? How do you make an absolute row in a formula? How do you make an absolute column in a formula?

Matching

Match each term in the second column with its correct definition in the first column by writing the letter of the term on the blank line in front of the correct definition.

____ **1.** A prewritten formula that performs calculations by using specific values in a particular order or structure.

____ **2.** A column in an Excel table that uses a single formula that adjusts for each row.

____ **3.** The Excel function that adds a group of values and then divides the result by the number of values in the group.

____ **4.** In an Excel function, the values in parentheses used to perform calculations or operations.

____ **5.** A type of function that summarizes a group of measurements.

____ **6.** The function that returns the serial number of the current date and time.

____ **7.** An Excel function that determines the smallest value in a selected range of values.

____ **8.** An Excel function that determines the largest value in a selected range of values.

____ **9.** The type of function that tests for specific conditions and typically uses conditional tests to determine whether specified conditions are TRUE or FALSE.

____ **10.** Conditions that you specify.

A Arguments

B AVERAGE

C Calculated column

D Criteria

E Function

F Logical functions

G MAX

H MIN

I NOW

J Statistical functions

Multiple Choice

Choose the correct answer.

1. This type of test has an outcome of TRUE or FALSE.
   A. Logical
   B. Rational
   C. Normal

2. This function checks whether criteria are met and returns one value if TRUE and another value if FALSE.
   A. BRANCH
   B. TRUE
   C. IF

3. After sorting, filtering, and totaling an Excel table, an Excel table can be converted into this.
   A. Link
   B. Pane
   C. Range

4. This word describes a format, such as cell shading, that is applied to cells when a specified condition is true.
   A. Filtered
   B. Conditional
   C. Calculated

5. This word describes a function that is updated each time the workbook is opened.
   A. Volatile
   B. Changeable
   C. Unstable

6. This command ensures that header rows and columns remain visible when a worksheet is scrolled.
   A. Total Panes
   B. Excel Panes
   C. Freeze Panes

7. This term refers to related data organized in rows and columns that is managed independently from other data in the worksheet.
   A. Pane
   B. Excel table
   C. Window

8. This command displays only the rows of a table that meet specified criteria.
   A. Filter
   B. Standard
   C. Chart

9. This row displays as the last row in an Excel table and provides summary statistics.
   A. Total
   B. Sorted
   C. Changeable

10. These symbols are inserted into logical functions to determine whether a condition is true or false—(<) and (=), for example.
    A. Comparison operators
    B. Mathematical operators
    C. Logical symbols

Topics for Discussion

1. Think about current news stories, including sports stories, and identify one or more in which statistical functions such as AVERAGE, MIN, or MAX play an important part. For example, when reporting about home prices, the average home price is frequently quoted.

2. Sorting and filtering are two of the most valuable ways to analyze data. If you were presented with an Excel table containing names and addresses, what are some of the ways you might sort or filter the data? If you were presented with an Excel table of a day's cash transactions at your college's cafeteria, what are some ways you could sort, filter, and total?

Skill Check

To complete this project, you will need the following file:

- e04_Surplus

You will save your workbook as:

- Lastname_Firstname_e04_Surplus

1. **Start** Excel, and then open the file **e04_Surplus**. Save the workbook in your **Excel Chapter 4** folder, using your own name, as Lastname_Firstname_e04_Surplus Insert the file name in the worksheet's left footer and the sheet name in the right footer. Return to **Normal** view.

2. Click cell **B4,** and then on the **Standard toolbar,** click the **SUM** button. With the insertion point in the function parentheses, select the range **F9:F48,** and then press [return]. With cell **B5** active, on the **Standard toolbar,** click the **SUM button arrow,** and then click **Average.** Select the range **F9:F48,** and then press [return]. Using the same range, in cell **B6,** enter the **MAX** function. Compare your screen with **Figure 1.**

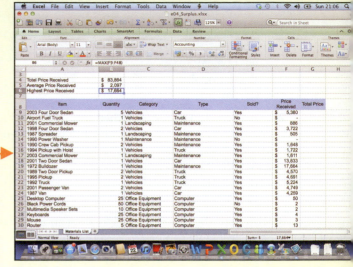

Figure 1

3. Select the range **A4:B6.** Point to the right edge of the selected range, and then drag the cells to **D4:E6.** With the range still selected, on the **menu bar,** click **Format,** and then click **Cells.** If necessary click **Border,** click **Outline,** and then click **OK.**

4. In cell **B4,** type Surplus and press [return], and then merge and center the title in the range **B4:C6.** In the **Alignment group,** click the **Align Text Middle** button. Click the **Orientation** button, and then click **Angle Counterclockwise.** Click the **Fill Color button arrow,** and then click the color in the fourth row and sixth column— **Blue, Accent 2, Lighter 40%.**

5. Click cell **G9.** On the **menu bar,** click **Insert,** and then click **Function.** In the **Search** box, type if and then double-click **IF** under **Most Recently Used** or **Logical.** In the **value1** box, type E9="Yes" In the **then** box, type B9*F9 In the **else** box, type 0 press [return], and then click **Close.** Copy the function down through cell **G48,** and then on the **Home tab,** in the **Format group,** click the **Styles** button and apply **Currency [0]** to the range. Compare your screen with **Figure 2.**

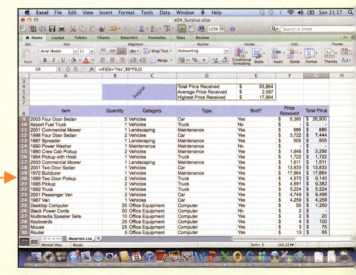

Figure 2

■ **Continue to the next page to complete this Skill Check**

6. Select cell **A1.** On the **menu bar,** click **Edit,** and then click **Replace.** In the **Find what** box, type Sedan In the **Replace with** box, type Car and then click **Replace All.** Click **OK,** and then **Close** the dialog.

7. Click cell **A9.** On the **Layout tab,** in the **Window group,** click the **Freeze Panes** button, and then click **Freeze Panes.**

8. Move the pointer over the **Materials List** sheet tab, press `control` and then click the mouse button. Click **Move or Copy.** In the **Move or Copy** dialog, click (**move to end),** select the **Create a copy** check box, and then click **OK.** Rename the new sheet tab as Price by Car

9. With the *Price by Car* worksheet active, in the **Window group,** click the **Freeze Panes** button, and then click **Unfreeze.** On the **Tables tab,** in the **Table Options group,** click the **New** button. In the **Table Styles group,** click the **More** button, and then under **Light,** click **Table Style Light 17.**

10. Click the **Type filter arrow,** and then clear the **(Select All)** check box. Select the **Car** check box, and then click **Close.** Click the **Total Price filter arrow,** click **Descending,** and then click **Close.** On the **Tables tab,** in the **Table Options group,** select the **Total Row** check box. Click cell **B49,** click the arrow that displays, and from the list, click **Sum.**

11. Select the range **F9:F48.** On the **Home tab,** in the **Format group,** click the **Conditional Formatting** button, point to **Data Bars,** and then click the first choice in the second row—**Orange Data Bar.** Click cell **A9,** and then compare your screen with **Figure 3.**

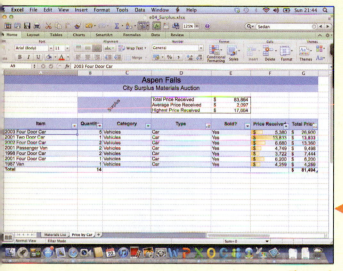

Figure 3

12. Create a copy of the *Price by Car* worksheet, and then rename the new sheet tab Pickups Click the **Type filter arrow,** and then select the **Select All** check box. Click **Close.** Click the **Item filter arrow.** In the **Search** box, type Pickup and then click **Close.**

13. Move the pointer over the sheet tab, press `control` and then click the mouse button. Click **Select All Sheets.** On the **Layout tab,** in the **Page Setup group,** click the **Orientation** button, and then click **Landscape.** In the **Print group,** select the **Fit To** check box.

14. Click the **Materials List** sheet tab, and then in the **Print group,** click the **Repeat Titles** button. In the **Page Setup** dialog, click in the **Rows to repeat at top** box, click row **8,** and then press `return`.

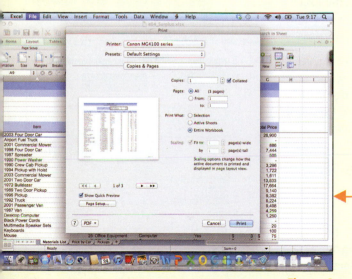

Figure 4

15. **Save** the workbook. Click **File,** and then click **Print.** Under **Print What,** click **Entire Workbook.** Compare your workbook with **Figure 4.** Print or submit the file as directed by your instructor. **Close** the workbook, and then **Quit** Excel.

Done! You have completed the Skill Check

Assess Your Skills 1

To complete this project, you will need the following file:

- e04_Water

You will save your workbook as:

- Lastname_Firstname_e04_Water

1. **Start** Excel, and open the file **e04_Water**. Save the workbook in your **Excel Chapter 4** folder, using your own name, as Lastname_Firstname_e04_Water Insert the file name in the worksheet's left footer and the sheet name in the right footer. Return to **Normal** view.

2. Click cell **F4**. From the **Standard toolbar,** insert the **AVERAGE** function using the range **F12:F41** as the argument. For each cell in the range **F5:F7**, insert the appropriate **Statistical** functions using the values in column **G** as the function arguments.

3. In cell **H12,** insert the **IF** function with the following logical arguments. For the logical test, check whether the **Farm Water** result is greater than the **MCL, TT, or MRDL** value in the same row. If the logical test is true, Yes should display. If the logical test is false, No should display. **Center** the result in the cell, and then copy the function down through cell **H41.**

4. Verify that the range **H12:H41** is selected, and then apply a **Highlight** conditional format that will display any cells that indicate *Yes* formatted with **Light Red Fill with Dark Red Text**.

5. Convert the range **A11:H41** to an Excel table, and then apply the **Table Style Light 16** table style.

6. Create a copy of the *Water* worksheet, and then rename the new sheet tab Chlorine On the *Chlorine* worksheet, filter the table to display only the contaminant Chlorine For the Excel table, display the **Total Row**. In cell **E42,** display the **AVERAGE,** and then in cell **H42,** select **None**. In cell **A42,** change the title to Average

7. Create a copy of the *Chlorine* worksheet, and then rename the new sheet tab Farm Water In the *Farm Water* worksheet, convert the Excel table to a range, and then hide columns **C** and **G**. In cell **A12,** freeze the panes.

8. Click the **Water** sheet tab. In the Excel table, click the **Contaminants filter arrow,** and then click **Ascending**. Select the range **D4:F7,** and then apply a **Thick Box Border**. Click cell **A43,** type High Test Trend and then in cell **A44,** insert the **NOW** function.

9. Select the range **G12:G41**. Using the selected range, insert a **Line Sparkline** in cell **B43,** and then display its **High Point**.

10. Select all the worksheets. Scale both the **Width** and **Height** to **1 page**. **Save** your workbook. Click **File,** click **Print,** and then compare your workbook with **Figure 1**. Print or submit the file as directed by your instructor. **Close** the workbook, and then **Quit** Excel.

Done! You have completed Assess Your Skills 1

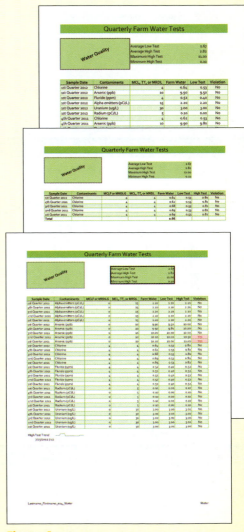

Figure 1

Assess Your Skills 2

Assess Your Skills 3 and 4 can be found at **www.pearsonhighered.com/skills.**

To complete this project, you will need the following file:

- e04_Roof

You will save your workbook as:

- Lastname_Firstname_e04_Roof

Lastname_Firstname_e04_Roof

Garden Inventory

Figure 1

1. **Start** Excel, and open the file **e04_Roof**. Save the workbook in your **Excel Chapter 4** folder, using your own name, as Lastname_Firstname_e04_Roof Insert the file name in the worksheet's left footer and the sheet name in the right footer. Return to **Normal** view.

2. In the range **B4:B7**, insert the appropriate statistical functions using the appropriate ranges. Move the range **A4:B7** to **D4:E7**.

3. In cell **A4**, type Top Growth and then merge and center the cell across the range **A4:A7**. In the merged cell, apply **Align Text Middle**, a **Thick Box Border**, the **Fill Color Dark Green, Accent 4, Lighter 60%**, and then change the orientation to **Angle Counterclockwise**.

4. In cell **F10**, insert the **IF** function with the following logical arguments. For the logical test, check whether the **Quantity in Stock** is greater than **20**. If the logical test is true, No should display. If the logical test is false, Reorder should display. **Center** the result in the cell.

5. Copy the function in cell **F10** down through cell **F68**. In the range **F10:F68**, apply a **Highlight** conditional format that will display any cells that indicate *Reorder* formatted with **Light Red Fill**.

6. Find and replace all occurrences of Ground Cover with Herb

7. Convert the range **A9:F68** to an Excel table, and then apply the **Table Style Medium 12** table style. In cell **G9**, type Total Cost and then in cell **G10**, enter the formula to calculate the *Cost Each* multiplied by the *Quantity in Stock*. In columns **A:G**, AutoFit the column width.

8. Scale the page **Width** to **1 page** and the page **Height** to **2 pages**, and then set the titles in row **9** to repeat on each printed page.

9. Create a copy of the worksheet, and then rename the new sheet tab Plants On the *Plants* worksheet, filter the Excel table to display the categories **Bush, Flower,** and **Vegetation**. Sort the table in alphabetical order by **Item**.

10. Display the **Total Row,** and then in **E69,** display the column's **SUM**.

11. **Save** the workbook. Compare your workbook with **Figure 1**. Print or submit the file as directed by your instructor. **Close** the workbook, and then **Quit Excel**.

Done! You have completed Assess Your Skills 2

Assess Your Skills Visually

To complete this project, you will need the following file:

- e04_Art

You will save your workbook as:

- **Lastname_Firstname_e04_Art**

Start Excel, and open the file **e04_Art.** Save the workbook in your **Excel Chapter 4** folder, using your own name, as Lastname_Firstname_e04_Art Add the file name in the worksheet's left footer and the sheet name in the right footer. In the range **E4:E7,** apply appropriate functions to calculate the results shown. In column **F,** use the **IF** logical function indicating *Insure* for art with a value greater than $50,000. Apply conditional formatting to the **Insurance** column, as shown in **Figure 1**. Create a copy of the worksheet, and rename the new sheet tab Paintings Convert the data to an Excel table, and format with the **Table Style Light 14.** Filter the table to show only the **Painting** category, and sort the table by **Location.** Insert the **Total Row** as shown in **Figure 1. Save** the workbook. Print or submit the file as directed by your instructor. **Close** the workbook, and then **Quit** Excel.

Done! You have completed Assess Your Skills Visually

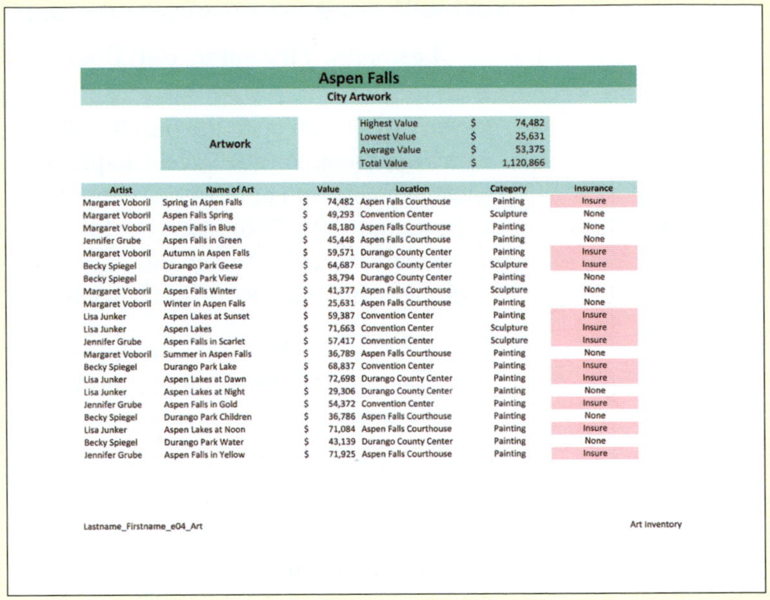

Aspen Falls

City Artwork

Artwork

Highest Value	$	74,482
Lowest Value	$	25,631
Average Value	$	53,375
Total Value	$	1,120,866

Artist	Name of Art	Value	Location	Category	Insurance
Margaret Voboril	Spring in Aspen Falls	$ 74,482	Aspen Falls Courthouse	Painting	Insure
Margaret Voboril	Aspen Falls Spring	$ 49,293	Convention Center	Sculpture	None
Margaret Voboril	Aspen Falls in Blue	$ 48,180	Aspen Falls Courthouse	Painting	None
Jennifer Grube	Aspen Falls in Green	$ 45,448	Aspen Falls Courthouse	Painting	None
Margaret Voboril	Autumn in Aspen Falls	$ 59,571	Durango County Center	Painting	Insure
Becky Spiegel	Durango Park Geese	$ 64,687	Durango County Center	Sculpture	Insure
Becky Spiegel	Durango Park View	$ 38,794	Durango County Center	Painting	None
Margaret Voboril	Aspen Falls Winter	$ 41,377	Aspen Falls Courthouse	Sculpture	None
Margaret Voboril	Winter in Aspen Falls	$ 25,631	Aspen Falls Courthouse	Painting	None
Lisa Junker	Aspen Lakes at Sunset	$ 59,387	Convention Center	Painting	Insure
Lisa Junker	Aspen Lakes	$ 71,663	Convention Center	Sculpture	Insure
Jennifer Grube	Aspen Falls in Scarlet	$ 57,417	Convention Center	Sculpture	Insure
Margaret Voboril	Summer in Aspen Falls	$ 36,789	Aspen Falls Courthouse	Painting	None
Becky Spiegel	Durango Park Lake	$ 68,837	Convention Center	Painting	Insure
Lisa Junker	Aspen Lakes at Dawn	$ 72,698	Durango County Center	Painting	Insure
Lisa Junker	Aspen Lakes at Night	$ 29,306	Durango County Center	Painting	None
Jennifer Grube	Aspen Falls in Gold	$ 54,372	Convention Center	Painting	Insure
Becky Spiegel	Durango Park Children	$ 36,786	Aspen Falls Courthouse	Painting	None
Lisa Junker	Aspen Lakes at Noon	$ 71,084	Aspen Falls Courthouse	Painting	Insure
Becky Spiegel	Durango Park Water	$ 43,139	Durango County Center	Painting	None
Jennifer Grube	Aspen Falls in Yellow	$ 71,925	Aspen Falls Courthouse	Painting	Insure

Lastname_Firstname_e04_Art   Art Inventory

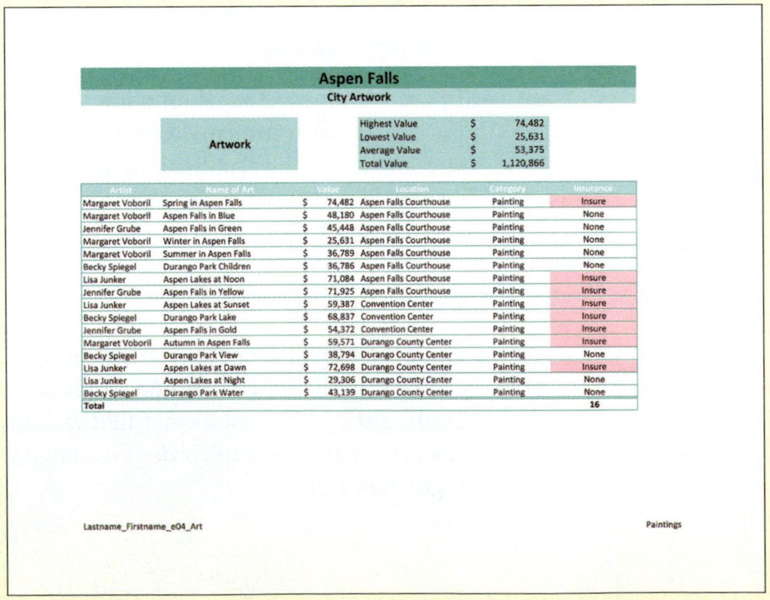

Aspen Falls

City Artwork

Artwork

Highest Value	$	74,482
Lowest Value	$	25,631
Average Value	$	53,375
Total Value	$	1,120,866

Artist	Name of Art	Value	Location	Category	Insurance
Margaret Voboril	Spring in Aspen Falls	$ 74,482	Aspen Falls Courthouse	Painting	Insure
Margaret Voboril	Aspen Falls in Blue	$ 48,180	Aspen Falls Courthouse	Painting	None
Jennifer Grube	Aspen Falls in Green	$ 45,448	Aspen Falls Courthouse	Painting	None
Margaret Voboril	Winter in Aspen Falls	$ 25,631	Aspen Falls Courthouse	Painting	None
Margaret Voboril	Summer in Aspen Falls	$ 36,789	Aspen Falls Courthouse	Painting	None
Becky Spiegel	Durango Park Children	$ 36,786	Aspen Falls Courthouse	Painting	None
Lisa Junker	Aspen Lakes at Noon	$ 71,084	Aspen Falls Courthouse	Painting	Insure
Jennifer Grube	Aspen Falls in Yellow	$ 71,925	Aspen Falls Courthouse	Painting	Insure
Lisa Junker	Aspen Lakes at Sunset	$ 59,387	Convention Center	Painting	Insure
Becky Spiegel	Durango Park Lake	$ 68,837	Convention Center	Painting	Insure
Jennifer Grube	Aspen Falls in Gold	$ 54,372	Convention Center	Painting	Insure
Margaret Voboril	Autumn in Aspen Falls	$ 59,571	Durango County Center	Painting	Insure
Becky Spiegel	Durango Park View	$ 38,794	Durango County Center	Painting	None
Lisa Junker	Aspen Lakes at Dawn	$ 72,698	Durango County Center	Painting	Insure
Lisa Junker	Aspen Lakes at Night	$ 29,306	Durango County Center	Painting	None
Becky Spiegel	Durango Park Water	$ 43,139	Durango County Center	Painting	None
Total					16

Lastname_Firstname_e04_Art   Paintings

Figure 1

Skills in Context

To complete this project, you will need the following file:

- e04_Schools

You will save your workbook as:

- Lastname_Firstname_e04_Schools

Start Excel, and open the file **e04_Schools.** Save the workbook in your **Excel Chapter 4** folder, using your own name, as Lastname_Firstname_e04_Schools Add the file name in the worksheet's left footer. View the worksheet, and decide how best to summarize the data effectively. Add titles and statistical functions similar to those you used in this chapter. In column D, use a logical function to calculate whether a class needs a Teacher Aide—a class needs a Teacher Aide if the class size is greater than 30. Format the data as an Excel table, add a **Total Row,** and sort the Excel table from largest to smallest class size. Set the titles in row 12 to repeat on each page. Copy the worksheet, and then in the new worksheet, apply a filter to display the classes that need a teacher aide. Rename the new sheet tab with a worksheet name that describes the filter. **Save** the workbook. Print or submit the file as directed by your instructor. **Close** the workbook, and then **Quit** Excel.

Done! You have completed Skills in Context

Skills and You

To complete this project, you will need the following file:

- New blank Excel workbook

You will save your workbook as:

- Lastname_Firstname_e04_Budget

Do you ever try to figure out where your money goes? Make a list of major spending categories, such as Housing, Transportation, Food, Clothing, Entertainment, Gifts, Personal Care, and so on. Within each category, make a list of Types. For example, within Clothing, you might have Work Clothes, Leisure Clothes, or Special Occasion Clothes. Next, for a one-week or a one-month period, keep an exact record of every financial transaction you make. In an Excel worksheet, use a new row for every transaction.

Record the amount and a description of the transaction and assign a type and a category. Use Excel's table feature to sort and filter your information to see how much you are spending for specific types of expenses. Save your workbook as Lastname_Firstname_e04_Budget and submit the workbook as directed by your instructor.

Done! You have completed Skills and You

CHAPTER 1

Getting Started with PowerPoint 2011

- ► Microsoft PowerPoint is a presentation graphics software program that you can use to present information effectively to your audience by creating electronic slide presentations and handouts.

- ► There are four views in PowerPoint—Normal, Slide Sorter, Slide Show, and Reading.

- ► Normal view is used to edit and format your presentation.

- ► Slide Sorter view is used to organize your presentation. In Slide Sorter view, you can see an overall view of your presentation and easily move and delete slides.

- ► In Slide Show view, your presentation displays as an electronic slide show.

- ► Reading view is optimized for viewing a presentation on a computer screen—for example, during an online conference.

©Goldenkb | Dreamstime.com

Aspen Falls City Hall

In this chapter, you will create documents for the Aspen Falls City Hall, which provides essential services for the citizens and visitors of Aspen Falls, California. In this project, you will assist Evelyn Stone, Director of Human Resources, in developing a presentation that she will use for an orientation for new interns at City Hall.

You will create a presentation with eight slides, by editing and formatting text, modifying slide layouts, and inserting and formatting a picture. You will also add speaker notes to the presentation and print handouts and notes pages.

Time to complete all
10 skills – 60 to 75 minutes

Student data files needed for this chapter:

p01_Interns
p01_Interns_Logo
p01_Interns_City_Hall

You will save your presentation as:

Lastname_Firstname_p01_Interns

Outcome

Using the skills in this chapter, you will be able to work with PowerPoint presentations like this:

Skills 1-10 Training

SKILLS

At the end of this chapter you will be able to:

Skill 1 Open, View, and Save Presentations
Skill 2 Edit and Replace Text in Normal View
Skill 3 Format Slide Text
Skill 4 Check Spelling and Use the Thesaurus
Skill 5 Insert Slides and Modify Slide Layouts
Skill 6 Insert and Format Pictures
Skill 7 Organize Slides Using Slide Sorter View
Skill 8 Apply Slide Transitions and View Slide Shows
Skill 9 Insert Headers and Footers and Print Presentation Handouts
Skill 10 Add Notes Pages and Print Notes

MORE SKILLS

Skill 11 Type Text in the Outline Tab
Skill 12 Use Keyboard Shortcuts
Skill 13 Move and Delete Slides in Normal View
Skill 14 Design Presentations for Audience and Location

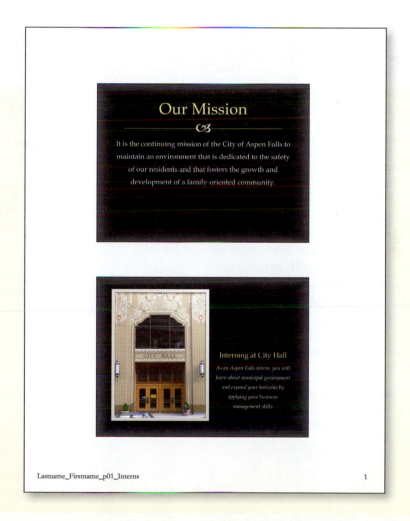

► When you start PowerPoint 2011, a new blank presentation displays.

► Save your changes frequently so that you do not lose any of your editing or formatting changes.

1. On the **Dock**, click the **Microsoft PowerPoint** icon 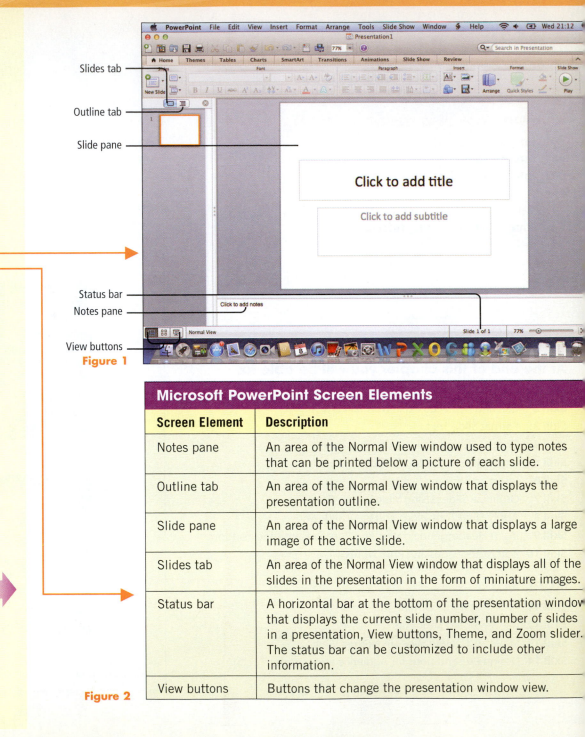.

2. In the displayed **PowerPoint Presentation Gallery**, with the **White** template selected, click **Choose**.

3. Take a moment to identify the main parts of the PowerPoint window as shown in **Figure 1** and described in the table in **Figure 2**.

   The PowerPoint window is divided into three parts—the Slide pane, the left pane containing the Slides and Outline tabs, and the Notes pane. The status bar displays the View and Zoom buttons and indicates the presentation design, the displayed slide number, and the number of slides in the presentation.

4. On the **menu bar**, click **File**, and then click **Open**. In the **Open : Microsoft PowerPoint** dialog, navigate to your student data files. Select **p01_Interns** and then click the **Open** button—or press ⌐return⌐—to display **Slide 1** in the Slide pane.

   A *slide* is an individual page in a presentation and can contain text, pictures, tables, charts, and other multimedia or graphic objects.

   ■ **Continue to the next page to complete the skill**

Figure 1

Figure 2

Microsoft PowerPoint Screen Elements

Screen Element	Description
Notes pane	An area of the Normal View window used to type notes that can be printed below a picture of each slide.
Outline tab	An area of the Normal View window that displays the presentation outline.
Slide pane	An area of the Normal View window that displays a large image of the active slide.
Slides tab	An area of the Normal View window that displays all of the slides in the presentation in the form of miniature images.
Status bar	A horizontal bar at the bottom of the presentation window that displays the current slide number, number of slides in a presentation, View buttons, Theme, and Zoom slider. The status bar can be customized to include other information.
View buttons	Buttons that change the presentation window view.

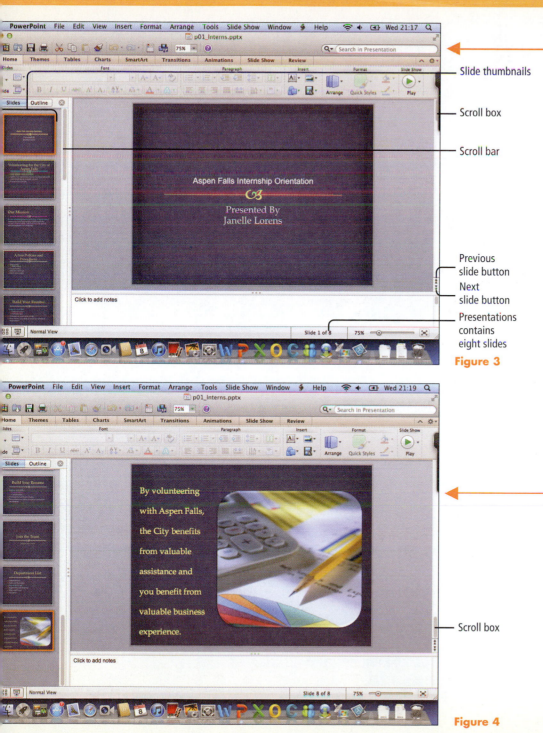

Slide thumbnails

Scroll box

Scroll bar

Previous slide button

Next slide button

Presentations contains eight slides

Figure 3

Scroll box

Figure 4

5. Click **Maximize** , and then compare your screen with **Figure 3**.

At the left side of the PowerPoint window, on the Slides tab, the slide *thumbnails*—miniature images of presentation slides—and slide numbers display. A scroll bar to the right of the slide thumbnails is used to view additional slides. You can click a slide thumbnail to display it in the Slide pane. At the right side of the window, another scroll bar displays a scroll box and the Next Slide and Previous Slide buttons used to navigate in your presentation.

6. At the left of the PowerPoint window, on the **Slides tab**, click **Slide 2** to display it in the Slide pane. Click the slide thumbnails for **Slides 3** through **5** to view each slide. As you view each slide, notice that the vertical scroll bar at the right side of the PowerPoint window moves, indicating the relative location in the presentation of the slide that you are viewing.

7. At the right side of the PowerPoint window, point to the vertical scroll box, and then hold down the mouse button. A ScreenTip displays the slide number and slide title. Drag down to display **Slide 8**, and then compare your screen with **Figure 4**.

8. Drag the scroll box up to display **Slide 1**.

9. On the **menu bar**, click **File**, and then click **Save As**. Navigate to the location where you are saving your files, create a folder named PowerPoint Chapter 1 and then using your own name, save the presentation as Lastname_Firstname_p01_Interns

■ **You have completed Skill 1 of 10**

► In *Normal view*, the PowerPoint window is divided into three areas—the Slide pane, the left pane containing the Slides and Outline tabs, and the Notes pane.

► Individual lines of bulleted text on a slide are referred to as *bullet points*.

► Bullet points are organized in list levels similar to an outline. A *list level* is identified by the indentation, size of text, and bullet assigned to that level.

► You can use the Replace command to change multiple occurrences of the same text in a presentation.

1. Display **Slide 3**, which contains two *placeholders*—boxes with rectangular borders that are part of most slide layouts and that hold text or objects such as charts, tables, and pictures.

2. Near the end of the paragraph, click to the left of the letter *c* in the word *community* so that the insertion point displays before the word *community*, as shown in **Figure 1**.

3. Type family-oriented and then press spacebar to insert the text to the left of the word *community*.

4. Display **Slide 2**, click at the end of the last bullet point—*Expand your network*—and then press return .

5. Press tab to create a second-level, indented bullet point. Type Professional contacts and then press return . Type Mentors and friends and then compare your slide with **Figure 2**.

   Pressing return at the end of a bullet point results in a new bullet point at the same list level.

■ **Continue to the next page to complete the skill**

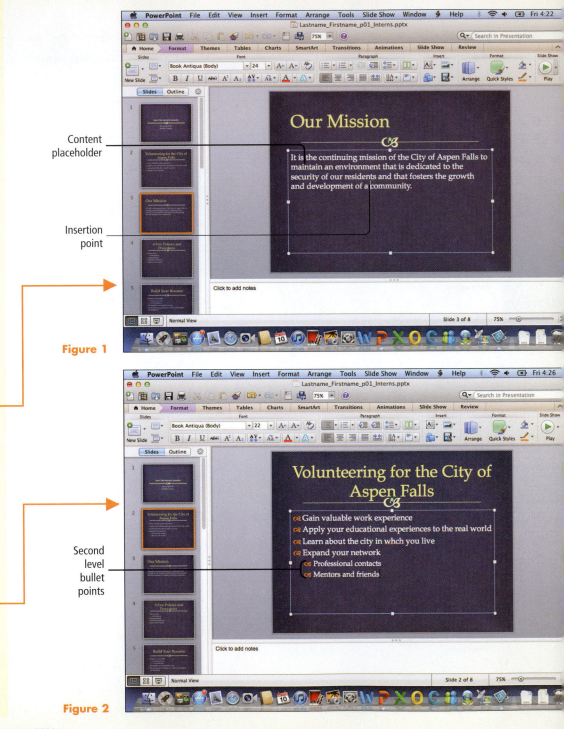

Content placeholder

Insertion point

Figure 1

Second level bullet points

Figure 2

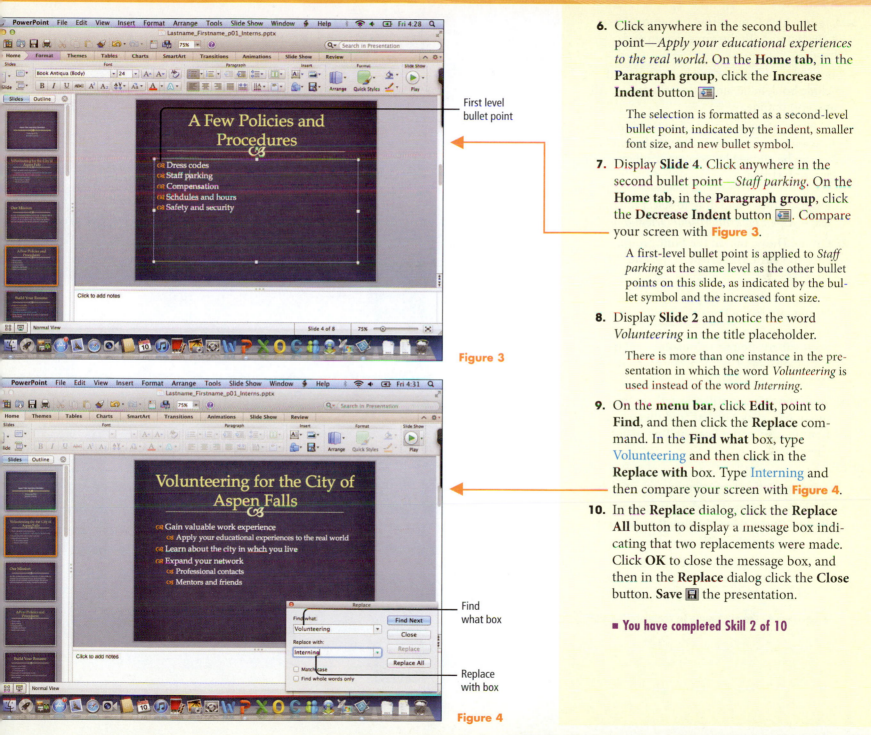

Figure 3

Find what box

Replace with box

Figure 4

6. Click anywhere in the second bullet point—*Apply your educational experiences to the real world*. On the **Home tab**, in the **Paragraph group**, click the **Increase Indent** button.

The selection is formatted as a second-level bullet point, indicated by the indent, smaller font size, and new bullet symbol.

7. Display **Slide 4**. Click anywhere in the second bullet point—*Staff parking*. On the **Home tab**, in the **Paragraph group**, click the **Decrease Indent** button. Compare your screen with **Figure 3**.

A first-level bullet point is applied to *Staff parking* at the same level as the other bullet points on this slide, as indicated by the bullet symbol and the increased font size.

8. Display **Slide 2** and notice the word *Volunteering* in the title placeholder.

There is more than one instance in the presentation in which the word *Volunteering* is used instead of the word *Interning*.

9. On the **menu bar**, click **Edit**, point to **Find**, and then click the **Replace** command. In the **Find what** box, type Volunteering and then click in the **Replace with** box. Type Interning and then compare your screen with **Figure 4**.

10. In the **Replace** dialog, click the **Replace All** button to display a message box indicating that two replacements were made. Click **OK** to close the message box, and then in the **Replace** dialog click the **Close** button. **Save** the presentation.

■ **You have completed Skill 2 of 10**

► A *font*, which is measured in *points*, is a set of characters with the same design and shape.

► Font styles and effects emphasize text and include bold, italic, underline, shadow, small caps, and outline.

► The horizontal placement of text within a placeholder is referred to as *text alignment*. Text can be aligned left, centered, aligned right, or justified.

1. Display **Slide 1** and drag to select the title text—*Aspen Falls Internship Orientation*

2. On the **Home tab**, in the **Font group**, click the **Font Size** arrow `18`, and then click **32**.

3. With the title text still selected, on the **Home tab**, in the **Font group**, click the **Font** arrow `Calibri (Body)`. Scroll the **Font** gallery, point to **Consolas**, and then click **Consolas**. Compare your screen with **Figure 1**.

4. With the title text still selected, on the **menu bar**, click **Format**, and then click **Font** to display the **Format Text** dialog, as shown in **Figure 2**.

   The Font dialog provides additional font style and effect formatting options.

5. With **Font** selected on the left, under **Basic Effects**, select the **Small caps** check box, and then click **OK**.

   With small caps, lowercase characters are capitalized but are smaller than characters that were typed as capital letters.

   ■ **Continue to the next page to complete the skill**

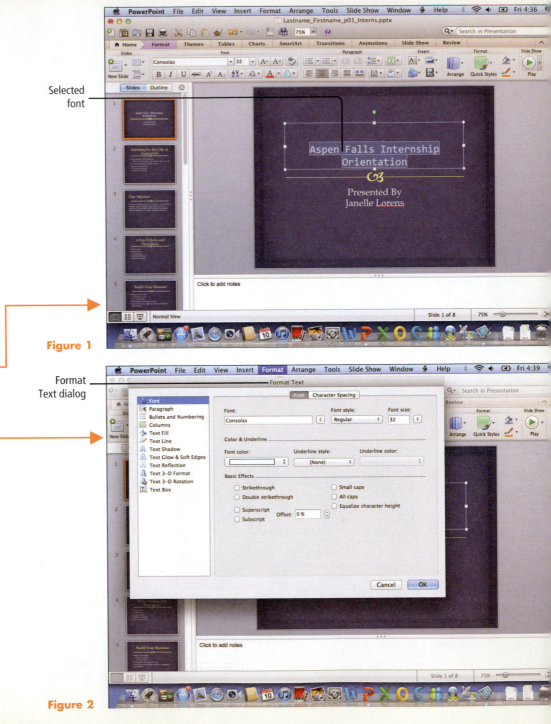

Selected font

Figure 1

Format Text dialog

Figure 2

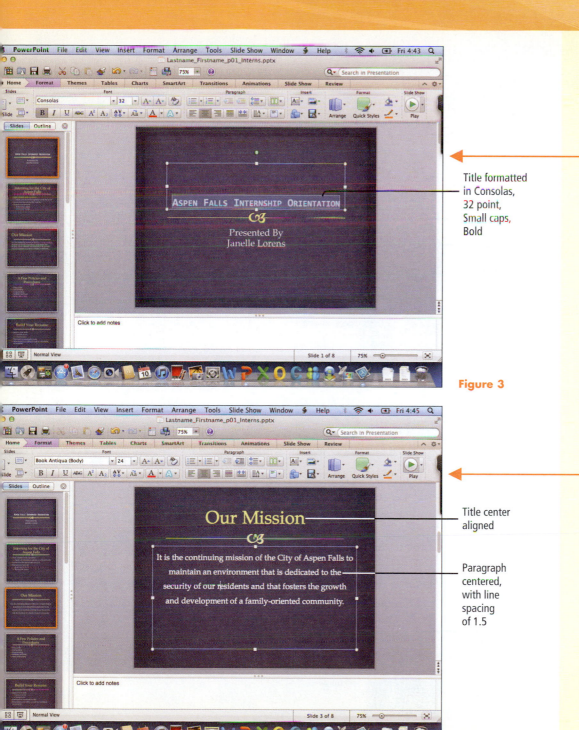

Title formatted in Consolas, 32 point, Small caps, Bold

Figure 3

Title center aligned

Paragraph centered, with line spacing of 1.5

Figure 4

6. With the title still selected, in the **Font group**, click the **Bold** button B, and then click the **Italic** button I.

7. If necessary, select the title. On the **Home tab**, in the **Font group**, click the **Italic** button I to turn off the italic formatting. Compare your slide with **Figure 3**.

  You can use the Mini toolbar, the Ribbon, or the Font dialog to apply font styles and effects.

8. Display **Slide 3** and click the title text to select the title placeholder.

9. On the **Home tab**, in the **Paragraph group**, click the **Center Text** button to center align the title text.

10. Click anywhere in the content placeholder that contains the paragraph. In the **Paragraph group**, click the **Center Text** button to center align the paragraph within the content placeholder.

11. In the **Paragraph group**, click the **Line Spacing** button. In the displayed list, click **1.5** to increase the space between lines in the paragraph. Compare your slide with **Figure 4**.

12. **Save** the presentation.

■ **You have completed Skill 3 of 10**

▶ PowerPoint compares slide text with the words in the Office 2011 main dictionary. Words that are not in the main dictionary are marked with a red wavy underline.

▶ You can correct spelling errors using the shortcut menu or the spell check feature.

▶ The *thesaurus* is a research tool that provides a list of *synonyms*—words with the same meaning—for text that you select.

1. Display **Slide 5**. Notice that the word *ability* is flagged with a red wavy underline, indicating that it is misspelled.

2. Click in the word *ability,* press control, and then click the mouse button to display the shortcut menu with suggested solutions for correcting the misspelled word, as shown in **Figure 1**.

3. From the shortcut menu, click **ability** to correct the spelling of the word.

4. Display **Slide 1**. In the subtitle, notice that the name *Lorens* is flagged as misspelled, although it is a proper name and is spelled correctly.

    Proper names are sometimes flagged as misspelled even though they are correctly spelled.

5. Click in the word *Lorens,* press control, click the mouse button, and from the shortcut menu, click **Ignore All**. Compare your slide with **Figure 2**.

    The Ignore All option instructs PowerPoint to ignore all occurrences of a word that is not in the main dictionary but that is spelled correctly. Thus, the red wavy underline is removed.

■ **Continue to the next page to complete the skill** ➜

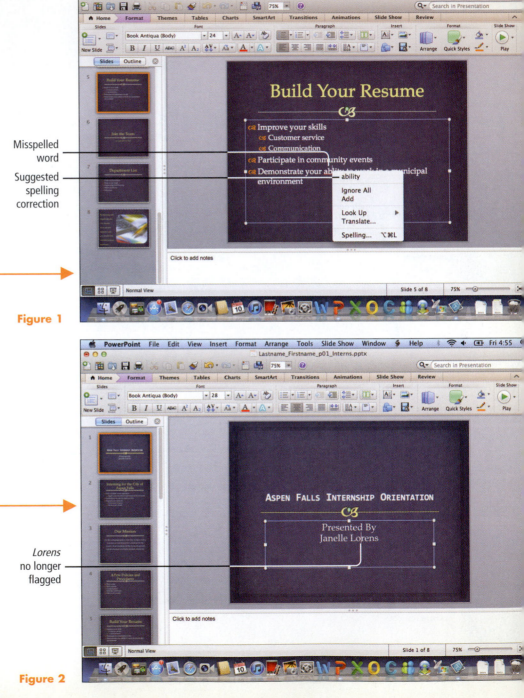

Misspelled word

Suggested spelling correction

Figure 1

Lorens no longer flagged

Figure 2

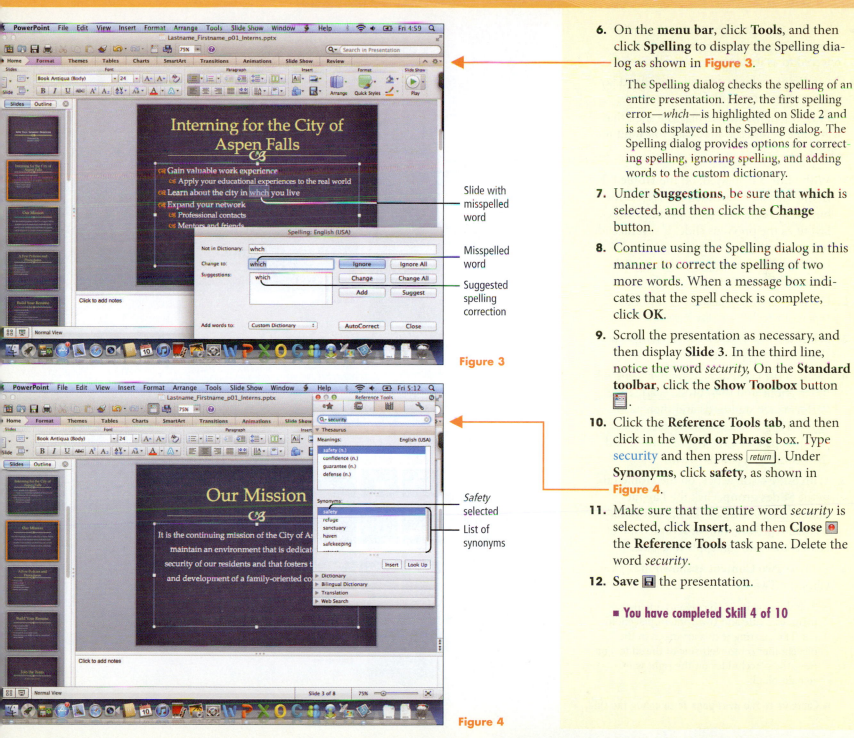

Slide with misspelled word

Misspelled word

Suggested spelling correction

Figure 3

Safety selected

List of synonyms

Figure 4

6. On the **menu bar**, click **Tools**, and then click **Spelling** to display the Spelling dialog as shown in **Figure 3**.

   The Spelling dialog checks the spelling of an entire presentation. Here, the first spelling error—*whch*—is highlighted on Slide 2 and is also displayed in the Spelling dialog. The Spelling dialog provides options for correcting spelling, ignoring spelling, and adding words to the custom dictionary.

7. Under **Suggestions**, be sure that **which** is selected, and then click the **Change** button.

8. Continue using the Spelling dialog in this manner to correct the spelling of two more words. When a message box indicates that the spell check is complete, click **OK**.

9. Scroll the presentation as necessary, and then display **Slide 3**. In the third line, notice the word *security,* On the **Standard toolbar**, click the **Show Toolbox** button ▣.

10. Click the **Reference Tools tab**, and then click in the **Word or Phrase** box. Type security and then press return. Under **Synonyms**, click **safety**, as shown in **Figure 4**.

11. Make sure that the entire word *security* is selected, click **Insert**, and then **Close** ⊗ the **Reference Tools** task pane. Delete the word *security.*

12. **Save** ▣ the presentation.

   ▪ **You have completed Skill 4 of 10**

▶ The arrangement of the text and graphic elements or placeholders on a slide is referred to as its *layout*.

▶ PowerPoint includes several predefined layouts used to arrange slide elements.

▶ To insert a new slide, display the slide that will come before the slide that you want to insert.

1. With **Slide 3** displayed, on the **Home tab**, in the **Slides group**, click the **New Slide** button to add a new slide with the same layout as the previous slide. If several slide layouts display, in the Slides group click the Layout button, and then click Title and Content.

2. Click in the title placeholder, and then type Your Role as a City Intern

3. Select the title text, and then change the **Font Size** 18 ▾ to **48**.

4. Click in the content placeholder. Type Job descriptions and then press return. Type Performance standards and then press return. Type Evaluations and then press return. Type Full-time opportunities and then compare your slide with **Figure 1**.

5. With **Slide 4** still active, on the **Home tab**, in the **Slides group**, click the **Layout** button to display the *Layout gallery*— a visual representation of several content layouts that you can apply to a slide.

6. Point to **Two Content** as shown in **Figure 2**. Click the **Two Content** thumbnail.

   The slide layout is changed to one that includes a title and two content placeholders. The existing text is arranged in the placeholder on the left side of the slide. For now, the placeholder on the right will remain blank.

▪ **Continue to the next page to complete the skill**

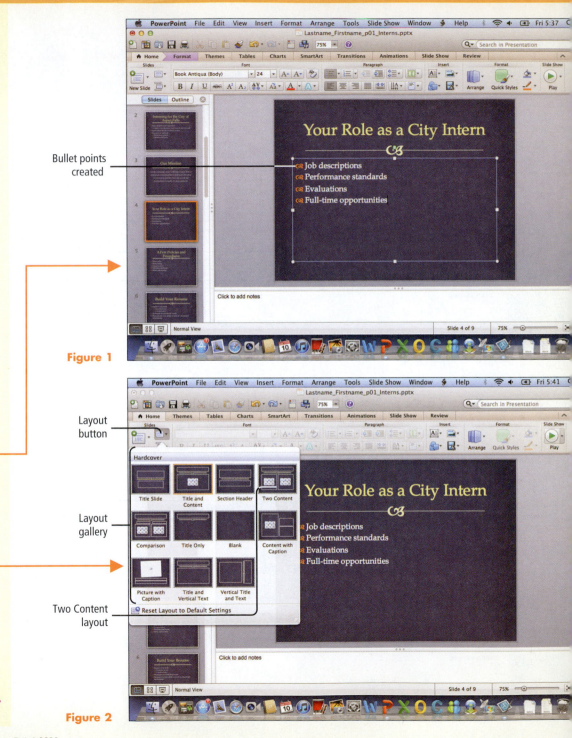

Bullet points created

Figure 1

Layout button

Layout gallery

Two Content layout

Figure 2

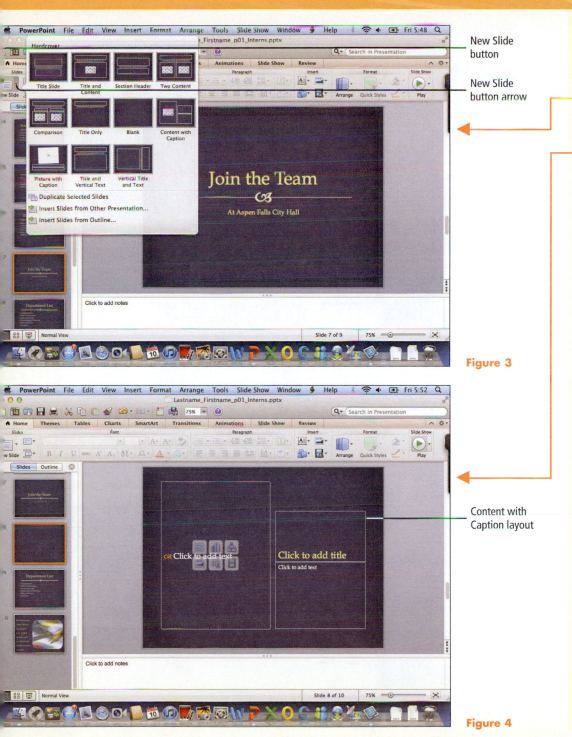

New Slide button

New Slide button arrow

Figure 3

Content with Caption layout

Figure 4

7. If necessary, use the scroll box to display **Slide 7**. On the **Home tab**, in the **Slides group**, click the **New Slide button arrow** and notice that no slide layout is selected as shown in **Figure 3**.

8. In the displayed **Layout** gallery, click **Content with Caption** as shown in **Figure 4**. If you inserted a new slide without displaying the gallery, on the Home tab, in the Slides group, click Layout, and then click Content with Caption.

9. Click in the title placeholder, and then type Interning at City Hall

10. Select the title, and then change the **Font Size** 18 to **24** and **Center** the text.

11. Click in the placeholder below the title. Type As an Aspen Falls intern, you will learn about municipal government and expand your horizons by applying your business management skills

12. Select the sentence that you typed, and then **Center** the text, change the **Font Size** 18 to **18**, and apply **Italic** _I_. In the **Paragraph group**, click the **Line Spacing** button , and then click **1.5**.

13. Save the presentation.

■ **You have completed Skill 5 of 10**

► In PowerPoint, *clip art* refers to images included with Microsoft Office or from Microsoft Office Online.

► *Pictures* are images created with a scanner, digital camera, or graphics software saved with a graphic file extension such as .jpg, .tif, or .png.

1. Display **Slide 4**. In the content placeholder on the right, click the **Insert Picture from File** button as shown in **Figure 1**.

2. In the **Choose a Picture** dialog, navigate to your student files for this chapter, click **p01_Interns_Logo**, and then click **Insert**.

   The inserted picture is selected, as indicated by the *sizing handles*—circles or squares surrounding a selected object that are used to adjust its size. When you point to a circular sizing handle, a diagonal resize pointer— or —displays, indicating that you can resize the image proportionally, both vertically and horizontally. When you point to a square sizing handle, a vertical resize pointer or horizontal resize pointer displays, indicating the direction in which you can size the image.

3. Notice the **Format Picture** contextual tool displays as shown in **Figure 2**.

   Contextual tools enable you to perform commands related to the selected object, and they display one or more contextual tabs that contain related groups of commands used for working with the selected object. The Format Picture contextual tab contains four groups.

   ■ **Continue to the next page to complete the skill**

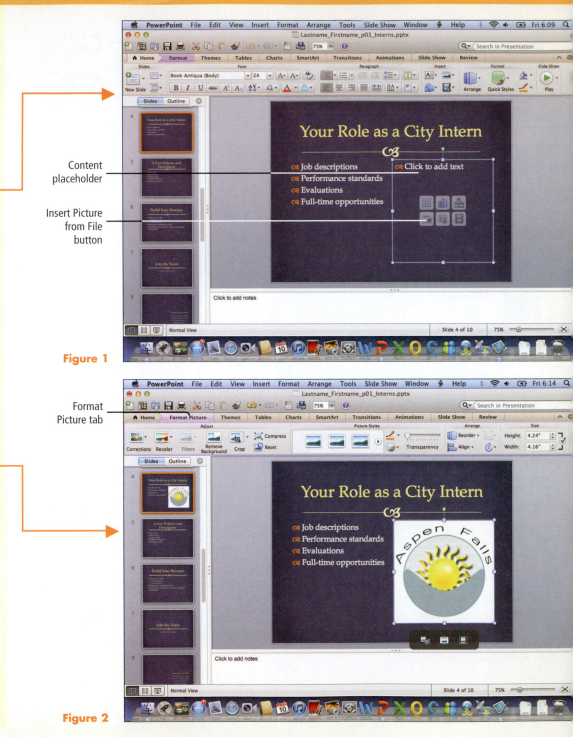

Content placeholder

Insert Picture from File button

Figure 1

Format Picture tab

Figure 2

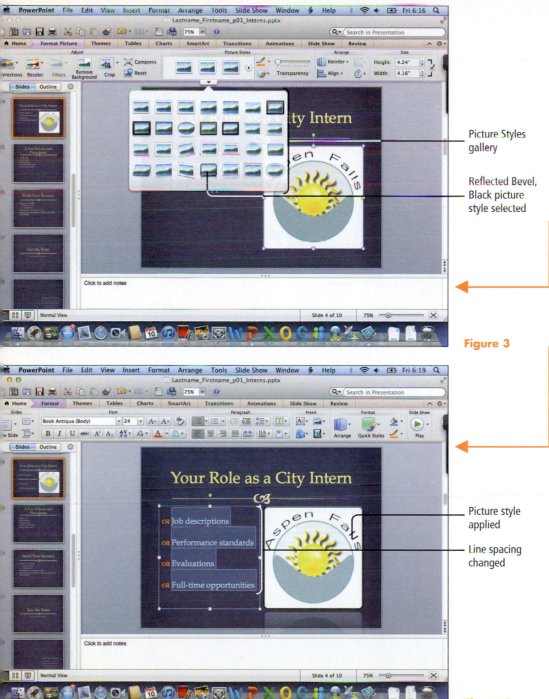

Figure 3

Figure 4

Picture Styles gallery

Reflected Bevel, Black picture style selected

Picture style applied

Line spacing changed

4. On the **Format Picture tab**, in the **Picture Styles group**, click the **More** button ▾ to display the **Picture Styles** gallery.

> A *picture style* is a prebuilt set of formatting borders, effects, and layouts applied to a picture.

5. In the **Picture Styles** gallery, move your pointer over several of the picture styles to display the ScreenTip identifying the style.

6. Using the ScreenTip to verify your selection, point to the picture style on the bottom row—**Reflected Bevel**, **Black**—as shown in **Figure 3**.

7. Click **Reflected Bevel**, **Black** to apply the style to the picture.

8. In the left placeholder, select the four bullet points. On the **Home tab**, in the **Paragraph group**, click the **Line Spacing** button ⬛▾, and then click **2.0**. Compare your slide with **Figure 4**.

> The additional line spacing balances the text with the picture.

9. Display **Slide 8**. In the content placeholder on the left, click the **Insert Picture from File** button ⬛▾. In the **Choose a Picture** dialog, navigate to your student files for this chapter, click **p01_Interns_City_Hall**, and then click **Insert**.

10. On the **Format Picture tab**, in the **Picture Styles group**, click the third style—**Metal Frame**.

11. **Save** ⬛ the presentation.

> ■ **You have completed Skill 6 of 10**

▶ *Slide Sorter view* displays all of the slides in your presentation as thumbnails.

▶ Slide Sorter view is used to rearrange and delete slides, to apply formatting to multiple slides, and to get an overall impression of your presentation.

▶ In Slide Sorter view, you can select multiple slides by holding down [*shift*] or [*command ⌘*].

1. In the lower left corner of the PowerPoint window, locate the **View** buttons as shown in **Figure 1**, and then click the **Slide Sorter view** button [⊞] to display all of the slide thumbnails.

2. If necessary, scroll the presentation so that Slides 7 through 10 are visible. Click **Slide 7** and notice that a thick outline surrounds the slide, indicating that it is selected. Hold down [*shift*] and click **Slide 10** so that Slides 7 through 10 are selected.

    Using [*shift*] enables you to select a group of sequential slides.

3. With the four slides selected, hold down [*command ⌘*] and then click **Slides 7** and **8**. Notice that only Slides 9 and 10 are now selected, as shown in **Figure 2**.

    Using [*command ⌘*] enables you to select or deselect non-adjacent slides.

    ■ **Continue to the next page to complete the skill**

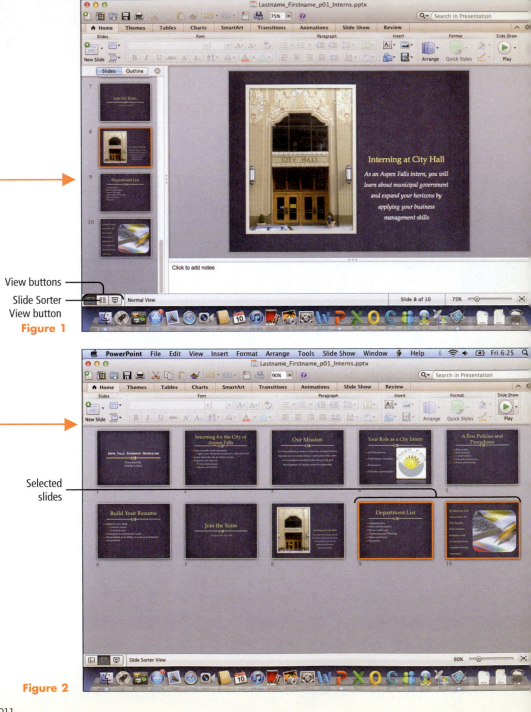

View buttons

Slide Sorter View button

Figure 1

Selected slides

Figure 2

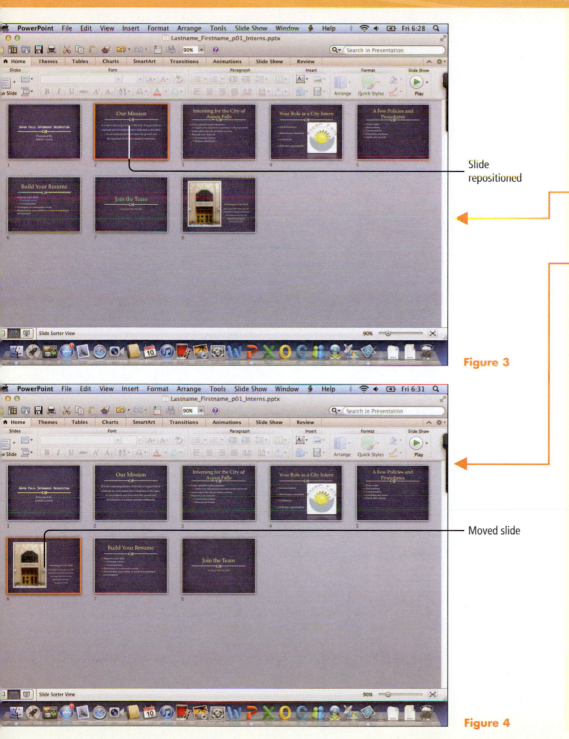

Slide repositioned

Figure 3

Moved slide

Figure 4

4. Press `delete` to delete Slides 9 and 10 and notice that your presentation contains eight slides.

5. If necessary, use the scroll bar so that **Slide 3** is visible. Click **Slide 3** to select it.

6. Point to **Slide 3**, hold down the mouse button, and then drag the slide to the left of **Slide 2**. Release the mouse button to move the slide, and then compare your screen with **Figure 3**.

7. Point to **Slide 8**, and then drag to the right of **Slide 5**. Release the mouse button to move the slide, and then compare your screen with **Figure 4**.

8. Double-click **Slide 1** to return the presentation to Normal view with Slide 1 displayed.

9. Save 🖫 the presentation.

■ **You have completed Skill 7 of 10**

► When a presentation is viewed as an electronic slide show, the entire slide fills the computer screen, and when your computer is connected to a projection system, an audience can view your presentation on a large screen.

► *Slide transitions* are motion effects that occur in Slide Show view when you move from one slide to the next during a presentation.

► You can choose from a variety of transitions, and you can control the speed and method with which the slides advance during a presentation.

1. With **Slide 1** displayed, click the **Transitions tab**. In the **Transition to This Slide group**, click the **More** button ⬇ to display the **Transitions** gallery as shown in **Figure 1**.

   The slide transitions are organized in three groups—Subtle, Exciting, and Dynamic Content.

2. View the displayed transition effects, using the **More** button ⬇ as necessary to display the gallery.

3. In the **Transition to This Slide group**, click the **More** button ⬇, and then under **Exciting**, click **Zoom**.

4. In the **Transition to This Slide group**, click the **Effect Options** button, and then compare your screen with **Figure 2**.

   The Effect Options menu lists the directions from which a slide transition displays.

5. Click **Out** to change the direction from which the slide transitions.

   ■ **Continue to the next page to complete the skill**

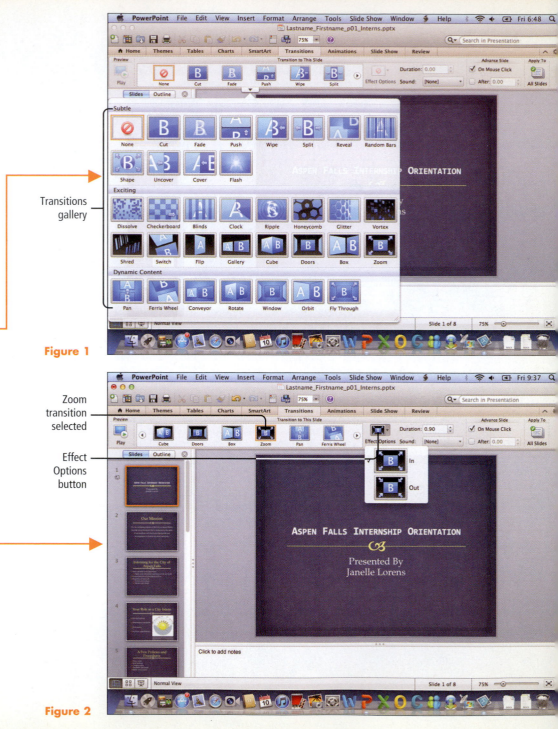

Transitions gallery

Figure 1

Zoom transition selected

Effect Options button

Figure 2

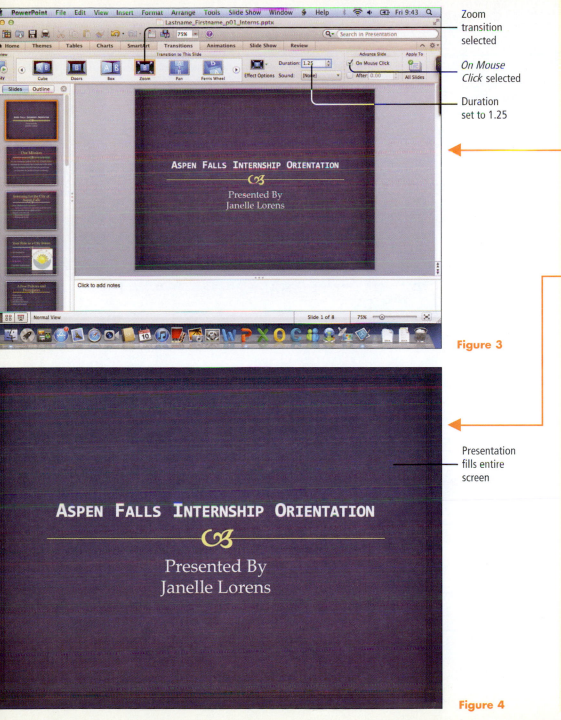

Zoom transition selected

On Mouse Click selected

Duration set to 1.25

Figure 3

Presentation fills entire screen

Figure 4

6. In the **Transition to This Slide group**, click in the **Duration** box, type 1.25 thus slowing down the transition to 1.25 seconds.

7. Verify that under **Advance Slide**, the **On Mouse Click** check box is selected so that the slides advance only when the mouse button is clicked or the [spacebar] is pressed, as shown in **Figure 3**.

8. In the **Apply To group**, click the **All Slides** button to apply the transition setting to all of the slides in the presentation.

9. Click the **Slide Show tab**. In the **Play Slide Show group**, click **From Start**. The slide show begins, and the first slide fills the entire screen as shown in **Figure 4**.

10. Click the mouse button to advance to the second slide, noticing the transition as Slide 1 moves off the screen and Slide 2 displays. Continue to click through the presentation and view each slide. After the last slide displays, click to return to Slide 1 in Normal view.

11. Save the presentation.

■ **You have completed Skill 8 of 10**

▶ A *header* is text that prints at the top of each sheet of slide handouts. A *footer* is text that displays at the bottom of every slide or that prints at the bottom of a sheet of slide handouts.

▶ *Slide handouts* are printed images of a single slide or multiple slides on a sheet of paper.

1. On the **menu bar**, click **View**, and then click **Header and Footer** to display the Header and Footer dialog.

   In the Header and Footer dialog, the Slide tab is used to insert a footer on each individual slide. For most projects in this textbook, you will insert headers and footers on the Notes and Handouts tab.

2. In the **Header and Footer** dialog, click the **Notes and Handouts tab**, and then compare your screen with **Figure 1**.

3. Under **Include on page**, if necessary, clear the Date and time check box and the Header check box so that these items are omitted. Select the **Page number** check box so that the page number prints on the slide handouts.

4. Select the **Footer** check box, and then notice that the insertion point displays in the Footer box. Using your own first and last name, type Lastname_Firstname_p01_Interns and then compare your screen with **Figure 2**.

   ■ **Continue to the next page to complete the skill** ▶

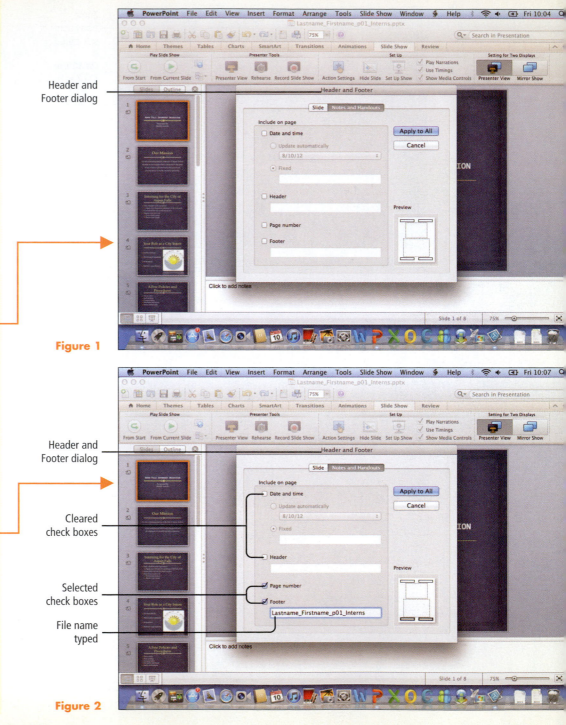

Header and Footer dialog

Figure 1

Header and Footer dialog

Cleared check boxes

Selected check boxes

File name typed

Figure 2

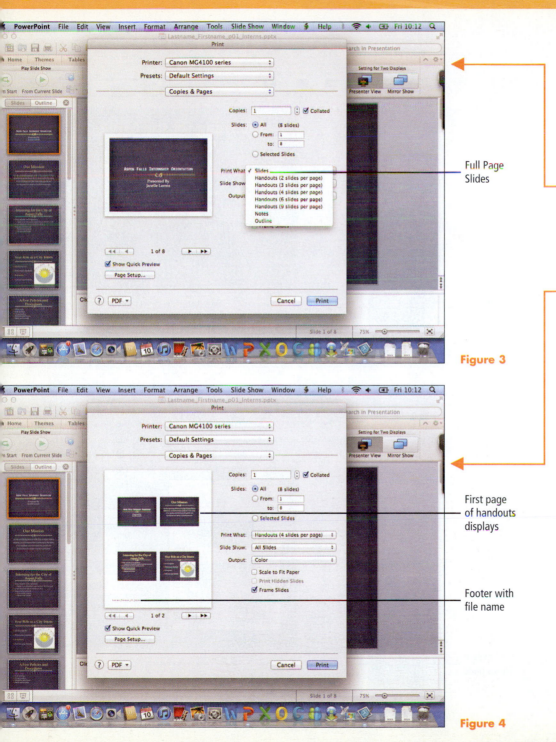

Full Page
Slides

Figure 3

First page
of handouts
displays

Footer with
file name

Figure 4

5. In the **Header and Footer** dialog, click the **Apply to All** button.

6. On the **menu bar**, click **File**, and then click **Print**.

   The Print page has tools you can use to select your desired print settings and displays a preview of your presentation exactly as it will print.

7. In the **Print** dialog, click the **Print What** button arrow, as shown in **Figure 3**.

   Depending upon the type of printer connected to your computer, your slides may display in color, grayscale, or black and white.

8. Click **Handouts (4 slides per page)**, and then compare your screen with **Figure 4**.

   Your presentation includes eight slides, and the first handout displays the first four slides. The footer displays on the handouts, not on the slides.

9. At the lower left of the window, click the Next Page button ▶ to display the second page of slide handouts, containing Slides 5 though 8.

10. If you are instructed to print your work for this project, click the Print button. Otherwise, click Cancel.

11. **Save** 🖫 the presentation.

   ■ **You have completed Skill 9 of 10**

▶ The ***Notes pane*** is an area of the Normal view window used to type notes that can be printed below a picture of each slide.

▶ ***Notes Pages*** are printouts that contain the slide image in the top half of the page and speaker notes typed in the Notes pane in the lower half of the page.

▶ During a presentation, refer to your notes to review important points that you want to make while running a slide show.

1. Display **Slide 3**. Below the slide, click in the **Notes pane** and type There are numerous advantages to completing an internship with the Aspen Falls City Hall. Browse the city website to view comments made by interns from previous years. Compare your screen with **Figure 1**.

2. Select the text that you typed in the **Notes pane**, click the **Home tab**, and then change the **Font Size** to **18**.

   In the Notes pane, the size of the text does not change. When you print the notes, the increased font size displays so that you can easily view the printed notes during the presentation.

3. Display **Slide 6**. Click in the **Notes pane** and type Ask your advisor for additional information on opportunities in other city departments. Compare your screen with **Figure 2**.

4. On **Slide 6**, select the text that you typed in the **Notes pane**, and then change the **Font Size** to **18**.

   ■ **Continue to the next page to complete the skill**

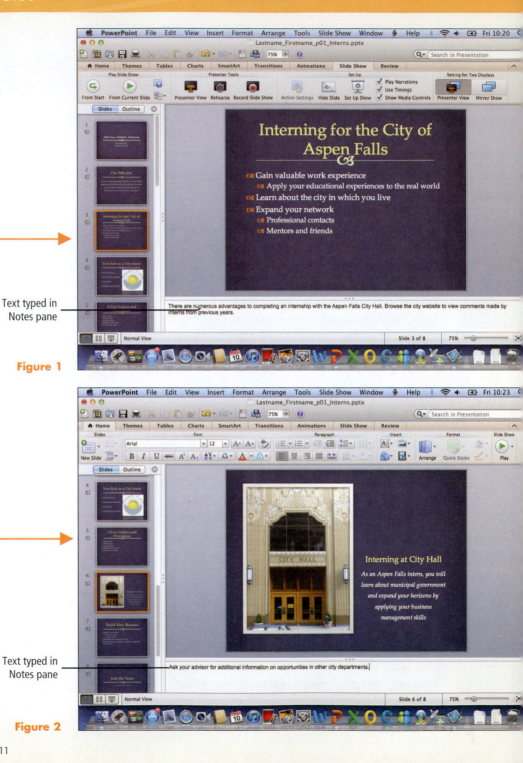

Text typed in Notes pane

Figure 1

Text typed in Notes pane

Figure 2

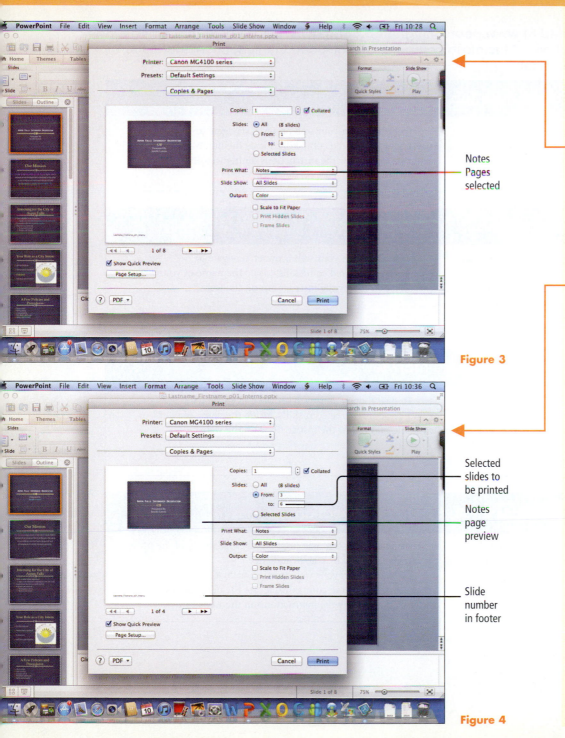

Notes Pages selected

Figure 3

Selected slides to be printed

Notes page preview

Slide number in footer

Figure 4

5. Display **Slide 1**. On the **menu bar**, click **File**, and then click **Print** and notice that under **Settings** the previous print selection—*Handouts (4 slides per page)*—displays.

6. Click the **Print What button arrow**, and then click **Notes**. Compare your screen with **Figure 3**.

> Because notes were not typed for Slide 1, the slide displays at the top of the Notes Page, and the lower portion of the Notes Page is blank.

7. Under **Slides**, click the **From** option button. In the **From** box, type 3 and press tab, type 6 and then compare your screen with **Figure 4**.

> When selected slides are printed, page numbers in the headers or footers display the slide number. Here, the upper part of the Notes Page displays Slide 3, and the lower part displays the notes in 18-point font size. Below the Notes Page, a page counter indicates that two pages will print.

8. If your instructor asks you to print this project, click the **Print** button.

9. **Save** 🖫 the presentation, and then **Quit** PowerPoint. Submit the printout or file as directed by your instructor.

Done! You have completed Skill 10 of 10, and your presentation is complete!

The following More Skills are located at **www.pearsonhighered.com/skills.** Please note that only More Skills that can be performed on a Macintosh computer are included in this section; therefore, the numbering is not always sequential.

More Skills Type Text in the Outline Tab

The Outline tab is used when you want to create several slides that are composed primarily of text.

In More Skills 11, you will open a presentation and then type text in the Outline tab for two slides.

To begin, open your web browser, navigate to www.pearsonhighered.com/skills, locate the name of your textbook, and follow the instructions on the website.

More Skills Use Keyboard Shortcuts

You can use keyboard shortcuts to apply commands instead of clicking buttons on the Ribbon or shortcut menu.

In More Skills 12, you will open a presentation and use keyboard shortcuts to apply font styles, change text alignment, and save a presentation.

To begin, open your web browser, navigate to www.pearsonhighered.com/skills, locate the name of your textbook, and follow the instructions on the website.

More Skills Move and Delete Slides in Normal View

Slides can be moved in Normal view using the Slides tab. You can select multiple slides using `command ⌘` and `shift`, and then delete or drag the selected slides to a new location in the presentation.

In More Skills 13, you will open a presentation, select and delete one slide, and then select and move a slide.

To begin, open your web browser, navigate to www.pearsonhighered.com/skills, locate the name of your textbook, and follow the instructions on the website.

More Skills Design Presentations for Audience and Location

When you design a presentation, you should consider the size of the room in which the presentation will be viewed and the number of people who will be present.

In More Skills 14, you will review design tips for presenting in a large room, and then you will open a presentation and review

formatting changes that will improve the readability of the presentation when viewed by a large audience.

To begin, open your web browser, navigate to www.pearsonhighered.com/skills, locate the name of your textbook, and follow the instructions on the website.

Key Terms

Bullet point 288

Clip art. 296

Contextual tools 296

Font 290

Footer. 302

Header 302

Layout 294

Layout gallery 294

List level. 288

Normal view 288

Notes Page. 304

Notes pane. 304

Picture 296

Picture style. 297

Placeholder 288

Point. 290

Sizing handle 296

Slide 286

Slide handout 302

Slide Sorter view. 298

Slide transition 300

Synonym 292

Text alignment 290

Thesaurus 292

Thumbnail. 287

Online Help Skills

1. **Start** Safari or another web browser. In the **address bar**, type microsoft.com/mac/how-to and then press `return` to display the home page for Microsoft Office.

   This website provides you with helpful links to get started, find out what is new, and tutorials about Office 2011.

2. Under **Get Started**, click **PowerPoint 2011**.

3. Click the **PowerPoint Basics tutorial** link.

4. Under **PowerPoint basics**, click **Add content to slides**, and then compare your screen with **Figure 1**.

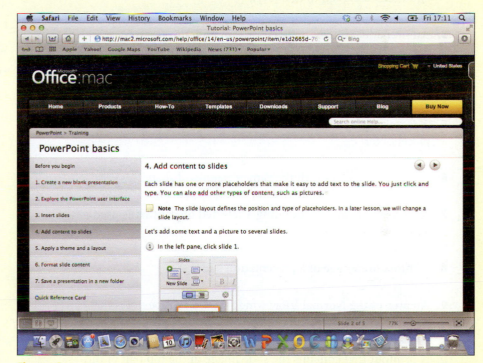

Figure 1

5. Read through the page, click to view the next page and then answer the following questions. How do you insert a clip art image? How do you add a theme to a slide? How can you change the layout of a slide?

Matching

Match each term in the second column with its correct definition in the first column. Write the letter of the term on the blank line in front of the correct definition.

____ **1.** The PowerPoint view in which the window is divided into three panes—the Slide pane, the pane containing the Slides and Outline tabs, and the Notes pane.

____ **2.** Levels of text on a slide identified by the indentation, size of text, and bullet assigned to that level.

____ **3.** An individual line of bulleted text on a slide.

____ **4.** A box with rectangular borders that are part of most slide layouts and that hold text or objects such as charts, tables, and pictures.

____ **5.** A feature that changes the horizontal placement of text within a placeholder.

____ **6.** A set of characters with the same design and shape.

____ **7.** A circle or square surrounding a selected object that is used to adjust its size.

____ **8.** A miniature image of a presentation slide.

____ **9.** An area of the Normal View window used to type notes that can be printed below a picture of each slide.

____ **10.** A printout that contains the slide image in the top half of the page and speaker notes typed in the Notes pane in the lower half of the page.

A Bullet point

B Font

C List level

D Normal

E Notes page

F Notes pane

G Placeholder

H Sizing handle

I Text alignment

J Thumbnail

Multiple Choice

Choose the correct answer.

1. A research tool that provides a list of synonyms.
   A. Reviewer
   B. Spell check
   C. Thesaurus

2. Words with the same meaning.
   A. Synonyms
   B. Antonyms
   C. Prepositions

3. The arrangement of the text and graphic elements or placeholders on a slide.
   A. Layout
   B. Gallery
   C. Design

4. Images included with Microsoft Office or from Microsoft Office Online.
   A. Pictures
   B. Vector graphics
   C. Clip art

5. Tools used to perform specific commands related to a selected object.
   A. Contextual tools
   B. ScreenTips
   C. Tool galleries

6. A prebuilt set of formatting borders, effects, and layouts applied to a picture.
   A. Artistic effects
   B. Picture styles
   C. Picture designs

7. A motion effect that occurs in Slide Show view when you move from one slide to the next during a presentation.
   A. Animation
   B. Slide transition
   C. Custom effect

8. Text that prints at the top of a sheet of slide handouts or notes pages.
   A. Page numbers
   B. Header
   C. Footer

9. Text that displays at the bottom of every slide or that prints at the bottom of a sheet of slide handouts.
   A. Page numbers
   B. Header
   C. Footer

10. Printed images of a single slide or multiple slides on a sheet of paper.
    A. Notes
    B. Slide handout
    C. Footer

Topics for Discussion

1. PowerPoint 2011 provides a number of slide transitions that you can apply to your presentation. Do you think that it is important to apply one consistent transition to the entire presentation instead of applying a different transition to each slide? Why or why not?

2. When you applied the transition to the slides in the project in this chapter, you verified that the slides should advance when the mouse is clicked instead of advancing automatically after a few seconds. Why do you think that presentation slides should be advanced when the speaker clicks the mouse button instead of automatically?

Skill Check

- **p01_Park**
- **p01_Park_River**

You will save your presentation as:

- **Lastname_Firstname_p01_Park**

1. **Start** PowerPoint. From your student files, open **p01_Park**. Save the file in your **PowerPoint Chapter 1** folder, using your own name, as Lastname_Firstname_ p01_Park

2. On **Slide 1**, select the title text—*Community Park Proposal*. In the **Font group**, click the **Font** arrow, and then click **Garamond**. Click the **Font Size** arrow, and then click **48**. On the **menu bar**, click **Format**, and then click **Font**. In the **Format Text** dialog, select **Small caps**, and then click **OK**.

3. In the subtitle, click to the right of the word *Aspen,* and then, adding spaces as necessary, type Falls

4. On the **menu bar**, click **Edit**, point to **Find**, and then click **Replace**. In the **Find what** box, type north and then in the **Replace with** box, type south Click **Replace All**. Click **OK**, and then **Close** the **Replace** dialog.

5. Display **Slide 2**. Click in the title, and then in the **Paragraph group**, click **Center Text**. Select all of the bullet points. In the **Paragraph group**, click the **Line Spacing** button, and then click **1.5**.

6. Click anywhere in the third bullet point. In the **Paragraph group**, click the **Decrease Indent** button. Click in the last bullet point. In the **Paragraph group**, click the **Increase Indent** button, and then compare your slide with **Figure 1**.

7. Display **Slide 3**. On the **Home tab**, in the **Slides group**, click the down arrow on the **New Slide** button. In the gallery, click **Title Slide**. In the title placeholder, type What will we do with the land at the current park location?

8. In the subtitle placeholder, type Develop or Remodel and then change the subtitle text **Font Size** to **36**. Compare your slide with **Figure 2**.

9. On the **menu bar**, click **Tools**, and then click **Spelling**. Click **Change** to accept the spelling for *Municipal,* and then ignore the spelling for *Ramsburg*. **Close** the message box.

- ▶ **Continue to the next page to complete this Skill Check** ➤

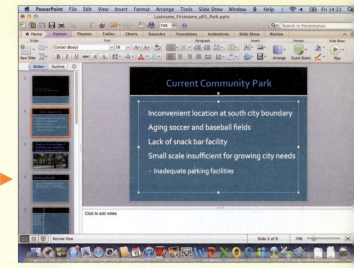

Figure 1

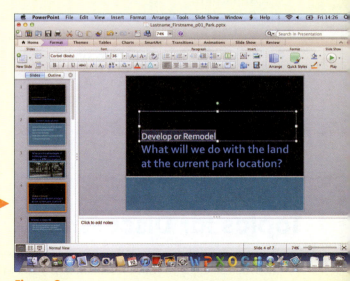

Figure 2

10. Display **Slide 6**. Double-click the word *entrance*. On the **Standard toolbar**, click **Toolbox**, type entrance and press ⏎ return, click **entry**, click **Insert**, and then click **Close**.

11. On the right side of **Slide 6**, click the **Insert Picture from File** button. From your student files, insert **p01_Park_River**. On the left side of the slide, select the text in the content placeholder. On the **Home tab**, in the **Paragraph group**, click the **Line Spacing** button, and then click **1.5**. Compare your slide with **Figure 3**.

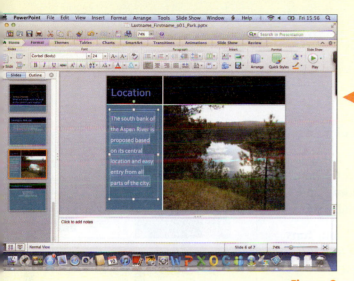

12. Display **Slide 3**, and then select the picture. On the **Format Picture tab**, in the **Picture Styles group**, click the **More** button, and then click the eleventh thumbnail—**Compound Frame, Black**.

13. Display **Slide 5**. On the **Home tab**, in the **Slides group**, click the **Layout** button, and then click **Two Content**. In the placeholder on the right, type Remodeling the park will increase the number of recreational facilities and then press ⏎ return. Type Less expensive to remodel than develop

14. In the lower left corner of the PowerPoint window, click the **Slide Sorter** button. Select **Slide 7**, and then press ⏎ delete. Point to **Slide 6**, and then drag to position before **Slide 4** to move the slide. On the status bar, locate the View buttons, and then click the **Normal view** button.

15. On the **Transitions tab**, in the **Transition to This Slide group**, click the **More** button, and then under **Subtle**, click **Wipe**. In the **Timing group**, click in the **Duration** box and type 1.25 Click **All Slides**.

16. On the **Slide Show tab**, in the **Play Slide Show group**, click **From Start**, and then press the mouse button to advance through the slide show until you return to Normal view or press ⏎ esc.

17. Display **Slide 2**. In the **Notes pane**, type The growing population in Aspen Falls warrants additional recreation facilities. Select the text and then change the **Font Size** to **18**.

18. On the **menu bar**, click **View**, and then click the **Header and Footer**. Click the **Notes and Handouts tab**. Select the **Page number** check box, and then select the **Footer** check box. In the **Footer** box, type Lastname_Firstname_p01_Park and then click **Apply to All**.

Figure 3

19. **Save** the presentation, and then compare your completed presentation with **Figure 4**.

20. Print the presentation or submit the file as directed by your instructor, and then **Quit** PowerPoint.

Figure 4

Done! You have completed the Skill Check

Assess Your Skills 1

To complete this project, you will need the following files:

- p01_Commission
- p01_Commission_Members

You will save your presentation as:

- Lastname_Firstname_p01_Commission

1. **Start** PowerPoint. From the student files that accompany this textbook, open **p01_Commission**. **Save** the presentation in your **PowerPoint Chapter 1** folder, using your own name, as Lastname_Firstname_p01_Commission

2. On **Slide 1**, center the subtitle, change the font to **Arial** and the font size to **32**, and then apply **Small caps**.

3. Display **Slide 2**, and then change the layout to **Two Content**. In the placeholder on the right, from your student files, insert the picture **p01_Commission_Members**, and then apply the **Compound Frame**, **Black** picture style.

4. With **Slide 2** still active, insert a new slide with the **Title and Content** layout. In the slide title, type Commission Responsibilities and then in the content placeholder, type the following four bullet points:

   Review new expansion plans
   Residential and commercial
   Recommend amendments to Planning Codes
   Design and development standards

5. Increase the list indent of the second and fourth bullet points, and then select all of the bullet points and change the line spacing to **1.5**.

6. Use the thesaurus to change the word *expansion* to *development*.

7. Display **Slide 5**, and then change the layout to **Section Header**.

8. Display the presentation in **Slide Sorter** view, and then move **Slide 5** between **Slides 3** and **4**. Return the presentation to **Normal view**.

9. Apply the **Push** transition with the **From Top** effect option. Change the **Duration** to 1.50 Apply the transition to all slides, and then view the slide show from the beginning.

10. Display **Slide 5**, and then in the **Notes pane**, type The Planning Commission is actively developing a plan for new construction in the city based on demographic projections through the year 2015 Change the speaker notes font size to **18**.

11. Correct all spelling errors in the presentation.

12. In the **Notes and Handouts** footer, insert the page number and the file name Lastname_Firstname_p01_Commission

13. Display the **Print** page, and then display **Handouts (6 slides per page)**. Compare your completed presentation with **Figure 1**. **Save** the presentation, and then print or submit the file as directed by your instructor.

Done! You have completed Assess Your Skills 1

Figure 1

Assess Your Skills 3 and 4 can be found at **www.pearsonhighered.com/skills.**

Assess Your Skills 2

To complete this presentation, you will need the following files:

- p01_Convention
- p01_Convention_Catering

You will save your presentation as:

- Lastname_Firstname_p01_Convention

1. **Start** PowerPoint. From your student files, open **p01_Convention**. **Save** the presentation in your **PowerPoint Chapter 1** folder, using your own name, as Lastname_Firstname_p01_Convention

2. Display **Slide 3**. In the first bullet point, after the word *Professional,* type meeting and adjust spacing as necessary. Decrease the list indent for the fourth bullet point, and then increase the list indent for the fifth bullet point. Replace all instances of Hall with Center and then correct the spelling throughout the presentation.

3. Display **Slide 1**. Change the title font to **Arial Black** and the font size to **36**. Change the title alignment to **Align Text Right**. Select the sub-title, apply **Italic** and **Small caps**, and then **Align Text Right**.

4. Display **Slide 4**, and then apply the same formatting to the title and subtitle as you did to the title and subtitle on Slide 1.

5. Display **Slide 2**. Select all four bullet points, and then change the line spacing to **1.5**. Apply the **Double Frame**, **Black** picture style to the picture.

6. With **Slide 2** still selected, insert a new slide with the **Picture with Caption** layout. In the title placeholder, type Outstanding Culinary Selections

7. In the caption placeholder, located below the title, type Professional catering staff Change the caption font size to **18**. In the picture placeholder, from your student files, insert the picture **p01_Convention_Catering**.

8. Display the presentation in **Slide Sorter** view. Delete **Slide 6**, and then move **Slide 4** between **Slides 1** and **2**. For all slides, apply the **Split** transition with the **Vertical In** effect option. View the slide show from the beginning.

9. Display **Slide 2** in **Normal** view, and then in the **Notes pane**, type The convention center is conveniently located in central Aspen Falls. Change the speaker notes font size to **18**.

10. In the **Notes and Handouts** footer, insert the page number and the file name Lastname_Firstname_p01_Convention

11. Compare your completed presentation with **Figure 1**. **Save** your presentation, and then print or submit the file as directed by your instructor. **Quit** PowerPoint.

Done! You have completed Assess Your Skills 2

Figure 1

Assess Your Skills Visually

To complete this presentation, you will need the following files:

- p01_Daycare
- p01_Daycare_Playground

You will save your presentation as:

- Lastname_Firstname_p01_Daycare

Open the file **p01_Daycare**. Save the file in your **PowerPoint Chapter 1** folder, using your own name, as Lastname_Firstname_p01_Daycare and then format the single slide presentation as a flyer as shown in **Figure 1**. To complete this presentation flyer, change the title font to **Corbel** font size **36**. Change the font size for all other text to **18**. In the placeholder on the right, insert the picture **p01_Daycare_Playground** and apply the **Soft Edge Rectangle** picture style. In the Notes and Handouts footer, insert the page number and the file name Lastname_Firstname_p01_Daycare and then print or submit the file as directed by your instructor. **Quit** PowerPoint.

Done! You have completed Assess Your Skills Visually

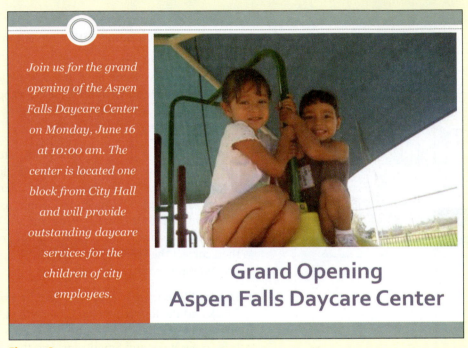

Figure 1

Skills in Context

To complete this presentation, you will need the following files:

- p01_Opening
- p01_Opening_Outdoor
- p01_Opening_Children

You will save your presentation as:

- Lastname_Firstname_p01_Opening

From your student files, open the **p01_Opening** presentation. Change the layout of Slide 2 to **Picture with Caption** and insert the **p01_Opening_Outdoor** picture in the picture placeholder. Apply an appropriate picture style. In the caption placeholder, change the font, font size, font effects, and line spacing so that the slide is formatted attractively. Insert a new Slide 3 using a layout of your choice. In the title placeholder, type Grand Opening Events and then for the slide content, provide a list of events that will take place at the grand opening ceremony, such as continental breakfast, arts and crafts, children's events, and teacher introductions.

At the end of the presentation, insert a slide using either the Content with Caption or the Picture with Caption layout. Use this slide to remind people of the date and time of the grand opening. Insert the picture **p01_Opening_Children** on this slide and apply an appropriate picture style. Apply slide transitions to all of the slides in the presentation and correct the spelling. Insert the file name and page number in the Notes and Handouts footer. Save your presentation, using your own name, as Lastname_Firstname_p01_Opening and then print or submit the file as directed by your instructor. **Quit** PowerPoint.

Done! You have completed Skills in Context

Skills and You

To complete this presentation, you will need the following file:

- p01_PowerPoint

You will save your presentation as:

- Lastname_Firstname_p01_PowerPoint

From your student files, open **p01_PowerPoint**, and then on the first slide, add your name to the subtitle placeholder. Add a slide that describes your reasons for wanting to learn PowerPoint. Add a slide with the Content with Caption layout and on it describe how you plan to use PowerPoint personally or professionally. If you have a picture of yourself, add it to this slide, and then change font size and line spacing as necessary. If you do not have a picture of yourself, use a picture that depicts how you plan to use PowerPoint.

Insert a final slide with the Section Header layout and enter text that briefly summarizes in two lines—the title line and the subtitle line—your presentation. Add a footer to the presentation with the file name and page number, and then check spelling in the presentation. Save the presentation, using your own name, as Lastname_Firstname_p01_PowerPoint and then print or submit the file as directed by your instructor. **Quit** PowerPoint.

Done! You have completed Skills and You

CHAPTER 2

Format a Presentation

- ▶ Formatting is the process of changing the appearance of the text, layout, or design of a slide.

- ▶ Apply formatting to text and images to enhance your slides in a manner that conveys your message to your audience.

- ▶ Apply PowerPoint themes to your presentation to create dynamic and professional slides.

- ▶ Customize your presentation design by changing font colors, bullet symbols, and slide backgrounds.

©Stephano Lunaradi | Dreamstime.com

Aspen Falls City Hall

In this chapter, you will create documents for the Aspen Falls City Hall, which provides essential services for the citizens and visitors of Aspen Falls, California. In this project, you will create a new presentation that the Human Resources Department will use for professional development classes for the Utilities Department Customer Care Representatives.

You will start with a blank presentation, apply a design, and create six slides. You will format slide backgrounds with styles, pictures, and textures; format text with WordArt; and modify bulleted and numbered lists.

Time to complete all
10 skills – 60 to 75 minutes

Student data files needed for this chapter:

p02_CS_Building   p02_CS_Representative
p02_CS_Headset   p02_CS_Telephone

Outcome

Using the skills in this chapter, you will be able to work
with PowerPoint presentations like this:

You will save your presentation as:

Lastname_Firstname_p02_CS

SKILLS

Skills 1-10 Training

At the end of this chapter you will be able to:

Skill 1 Create New Presentations
Skill 2 Change Presentation Themes
Skill 3 Apply Font and Color Themes
Skill 4 Format Slide Backgrounds with Styles
Skill 5 Format Slide Backgrounds with Pictures and Textures
Skill 6 Format Text with WordArt
Skill 7 Change Character Spacing and Font Color
Skill 8 Modify Bulleted and Numbered Lists
Skill 9 Move and Copy Text and Objects
Skill 10 Use Format Painter and Clear All Formatting

MORE SKILLS

Skill 11 Edit Slide Masters
Skill 12 Save and Apply Presentation Templates
Skill 14 Design Presentations with Contrast

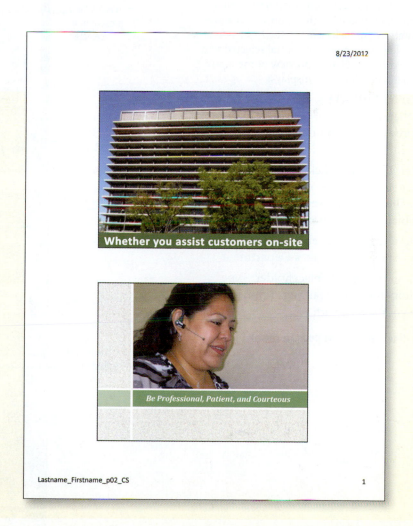

► When you start PowerPoint, the PowerPoint Presentation Gallery displays.

► In a new, blank presentation, black or grey text displays on a white background.

1. On the **Dock**, click the **Microsoft PowerPoint** icon 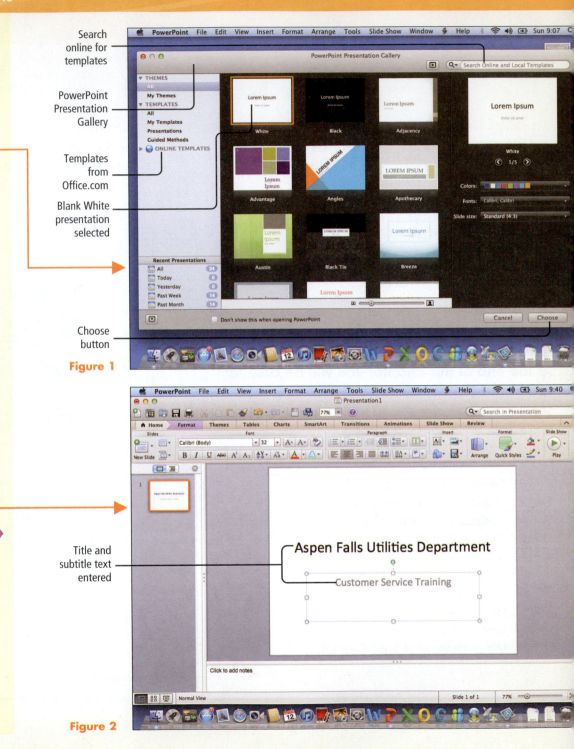. Compare your screen with **Figure 1**.

   The PowerPoint Presentation Gallery displays available templates, themes, and templates that you can download from Office. com. A *template* is a file upon which a presentation can be based. On the right side of the New page, a preview of the selected template displays. Here, a preview of the Blank presentation template displays.

2. Under **TEMPLATES**, click **Presentations**, and then click several templates to display the preview of each on the right side of the window.

3. Under **THEMES**, click **All**, and then click **White**. On the lower-right side of the window, click the **Choose** button to display a new blank presentation.

4. Click in the title placeholder, and then type Aspen Falls Utilities Department

5. Click in the subtitle placeholder. Type Customer Service Training and then compare your screen with **Figure 2**.

   ■ **Continue to the next page to complete the skill**

Search online for templates

PowerPoint Presentation Gallery

Templates from Office.com

Blank White presentation selected

Choose button

Figure 1

Title and subtitle text entered

Figure 2

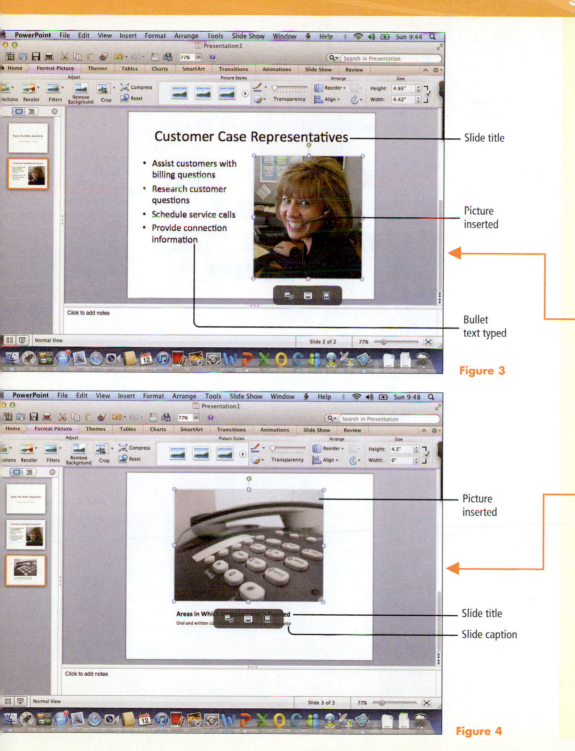

Figure 3

Figure 4

6. On the **Home tab**, in the **Slides group**, click the **New Slide button arrow**. In the gallery, click the **Two Content** thumbnail to insert a slide with the **Two Content** layout. In the title placeholder, type Customer Care Representatives

7. Click in the placeholder on the left, and then type the following four bullet points:

   Assist customers with billing questions
   Research customer questions
   Schedule service calls
   Provide connection information

8. In the placeholder on the right, click the **Insert Picture from File** button 🖼▾, and then from your student files, insert the picture **p02_CS_Representative**. Compare your slide with **Figure 3**.

9. On the **Home tab**, in the **Slides group**, click the **New Slide button arrow**. In the gallery, click **Picture with Caption**. In the title placeholder, type Areas in Which Improvement Is Needed In the text placeholder, type Oral and written communications and telephone etiquette

10. In the picture placeholder, from your student files, insert **p02_CS_Telephone**, and then compare your slide with **Figure 4**.

11. On the **Standard toolbar**, click **Save**. Navigate to the location where you are saving your files, create a folder named PowerPoint Chapter 2 and then using your own name, save the document as Lastname_Firstname_p02_CS

   ■ **You have completed Skill 1 of 10**

▶ The presentation *theme* is a set of unified design elements—colors, fonts, and graphics—that provides a unique look for your presentation.

▶ The Office theme is the default theme applied to new presentations.

▶ To give the presentation a consistent design, choose one theme for all of the slides in the presentation.

1. Display **Slide 1**. On the **Themes tab**, in the **Themes group**, click the **More** button ⊡ to display the **Themes** gallery.

2. Under **Built-In**, point to the third theme—*Adjacency*—and then compare your screen with **Figure 1**. ━━━━

   Under Built-In, the default themes—White and Black—display first. After the White and Black default themes, the themes are arranged alphabetically and are identified by their ScreenTips.

3. Under **Built-In**, locate and click **Median** to apply the theme to all of the slides in the presentation. Compare your screen with **Figure 2**. ━━━━

4. Display **Slide 3**, and then select the title *Areas in Which Improvement Is Needed*. On the **Home tab**, in the **Paragraph group**, click the **Center Text** button ☰.

   ■ **Continue to the next page to complete the skill**

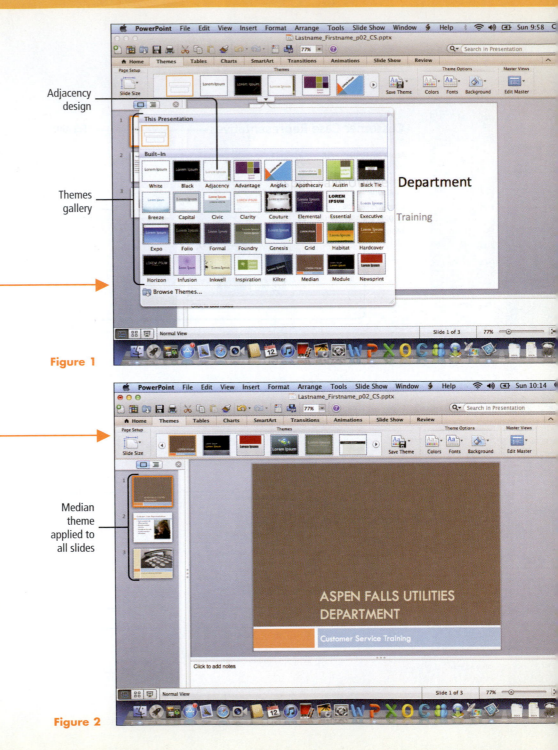

Adjacency design

Themes gallery

Figure 1

Median theme applied to all slides

Figure 2

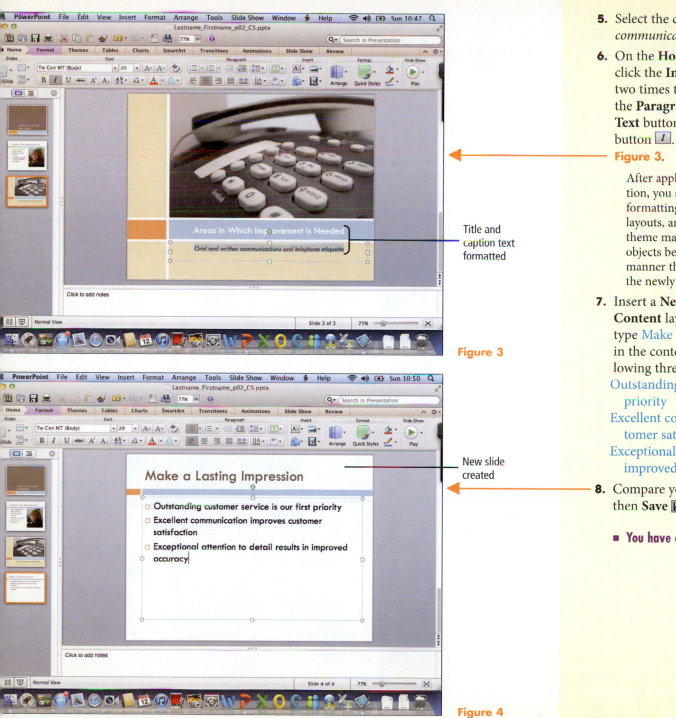

Title and
caption text
formatted

Figure 3

New slide
created

Figure 4

5. Select the caption text *Oral and written communications and telephone etiquette.*

6. On the **Home tab**, in the **Font group**, click the **Increase Font Size** button two times to change the font size to **20**. In the **Paragraph group**, click the **Center Text** button, and then click the **Italic** button. Compare your slide with **Figure 3**.

   After applying a new theme to a presentation, you should review each slide and make formatting changes as necessary. The fonts, layouts, and spacing associated with one theme may require that existing text and objects be resized or moved to display in a manner that is consistent and attractive in the newly applied theme.

7. Insert a **New Slide** with the **Title and Content** layout. In the title placeholder, type Make a Lasting Impression and then in the content placeholder, type the following three bullet points:

   Outstanding customer service is our first priority

   Excellent communication improves customer satisfaction

   Exceptional attention to detail results in improved accuracy

8. Compare your slide with **Figure 4**, and then **Save** the presentation.

   ■ **You have completed Skill 2 of 10**

▶ Customize the presentation theme by changing the colors, fonts, effects, and background styles applied to a presentation.

▶ When you are using several pictures in a presentation, choose theme colors that complement the pictures you select.

1. Display **Slide 1**. On the **Themes tab**, in the **Theme Options group**, click the **Fonts** button and **Background** button in the group to view the available slide design options, as shown in **Figure 1**.

2. On the **Themes tab**, in the **Theme Options group**, click the **Colors** button to display a list of color themes.

   Theme colors are composed of a set of coordinated colors that are applied to the backgrounds, objects, and text in a presentation. The Median theme color is selected because the Median theme is applied to the presentation.

3. Click **Foundry** to change the theme colors of the presentation, and then compare your screen with **Figure 2**.

   You can apply a design theme to the presentation—in this case Median—and then change the colors by applying a different theme color. Although the presentation colors change, the overall design of the presentation and the slide layouts continue to be formatted using the Median theme.

   ■ **Continue to the next page to complete the skill**

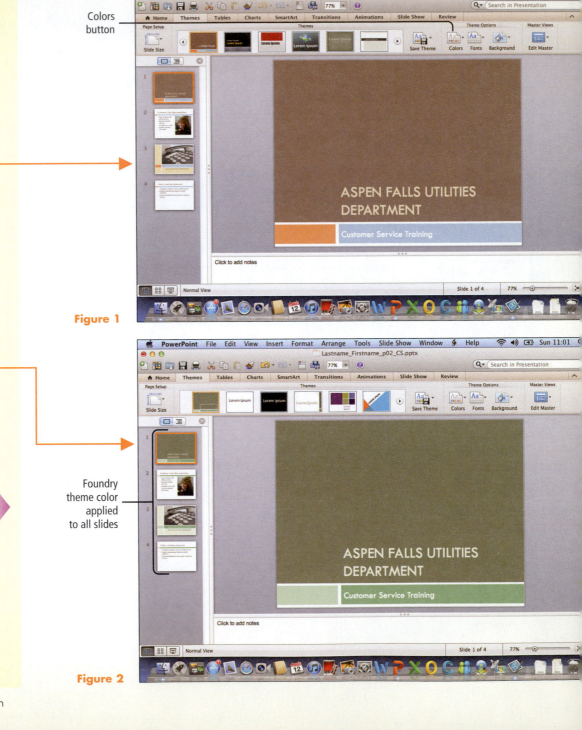

Colors button

Figure 1

Foundry theme color applied to all slides

Figure 2

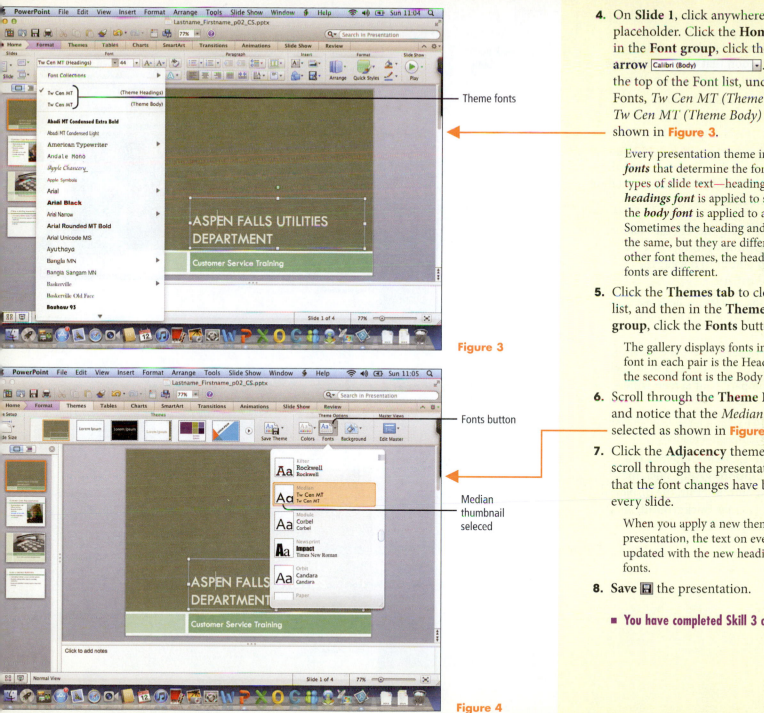

Figure 3

Figure 4

4. On **Slide 1**, click anywhere in the title placeholder. Click the **Home tab**, and then in the **Font group**, click the **Font button arrow** Calibri (Body). Notice that at the top of the Font list, under Theme Fonts, *Tw Cen MT (Theme Headings)* and *Tw Cen MT (Theme Body)* display, as shown in **Figure 3**.

> Every presentation theme includes *theme fonts* that determine the font applied to two types of slide text—headings and body. The *headings font* is applied to slide titles, and the *body font* is applied to all other text. Sometimes the heading and body fonts are the same, but they are different sizes. In other font themes, the heading and body fonts are different.

5. Click the **Themes tab** to close the Font list, and then in the **Theme Options group**, click the **Fonts** button.

> The gallery displays fonts in pairs. The first font in each pair is the Headings font, and the second font is the Body font.

6. Scroll through the **Theme Fonts** gallery, and notice that the *Median* theme font is selected as shown in **Figure 4**.

7. Click the **Adjacency** theme, and then scroll through the presentation. Notice that the font changes have been applied to every slide.

> When you apply a new theme font to the presentation, the text on every slide is updated with the new heading and body fonts.

8. **Save** 🖫 the presentation.

■ **You have completed Skill 3 of 10**

▶ You can customize the presentation design by applying a background style to your slides. A *background style* is a slide background fill variation that combines theme colors in different intensities or patterns.

▶ Background styles can be applied to a single slide or to all of the slides in the presentation.

▶ After you apply a background style, you can reset the background so that the original background associated with the presentation is applied to the slide.

1. Display **Slide 2**. On the **Themes tab**, in the **Theme Options group**, click the **Background** button to display the **Background** gallery.

   The styles that display are designed to coordinate with the theme color applied to the presentation.

2. Point to each background and view the style applied to the slide, and then click **Style 10**. Compare your screen with **Figure 1**.

   The Style 10 background style is applied to every slide in the presentation.

3. Display **Slide 1**. On the **Themes tab**, in the **Theme Options group**, click the **Background** button. From the displayed menu, click **Format Background**, and then compare your screen with **Figure 2**.

   ■ **Continue to the next page to complete the skill**

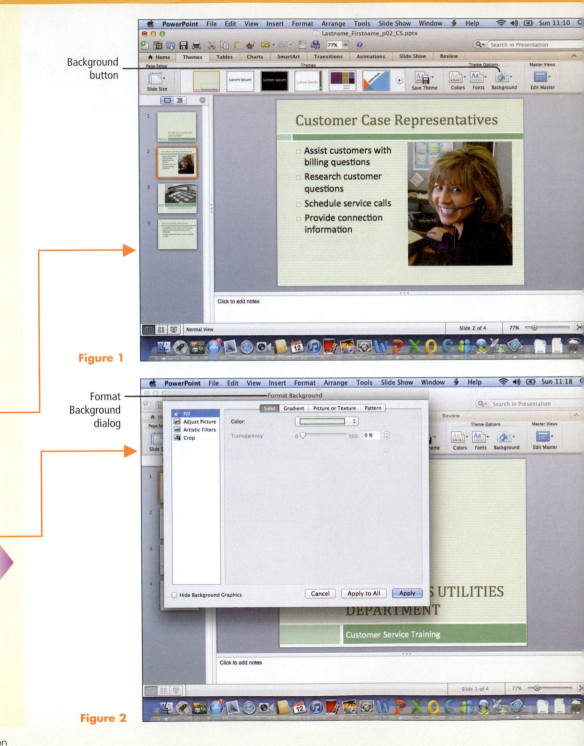

Background button

Figure 1

Format Background dialog

Figure 2

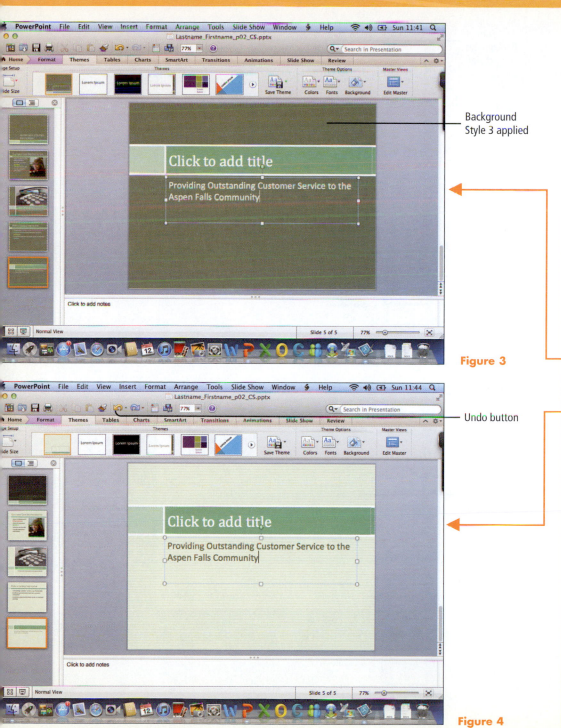

Background Style 3 applied

Figure 3

Undo button

Figure 4

4. In the **Format Background** dialog, click the **Color button arrow**. From the displayed list, under **Theme Colors**, click **Black**, **Text 1**, **Lighter 15%**—second color on the fifth row. Click the **Apply** button.

   The background style is applied only to Slide 1. To apply a background style to multiple slides, click the Apply to All button.

5. Display **Slide 4**, and then insert a **New Slide** with the **Section Header** layout. Notice that the new slide has the same background as Slides 2 through 4.

6. Leave the title placeholder blank. In the text placeholder, type Providing Outstanding Customer Service to the Aspen Falls Community

7. With **Slide 5** selected, on the **Themes tab**, in the **Theme Options group**, click the **Background** button. Click **Style 3**. Compare your slide with **Figure 3**.

8. With **Slide 5** displayed, on the **Standard toolbar**, click the **Undo** button ⟲. Compare your screen with **Figure 4**.

   The slide background is changed back to the previous design formatting.

9. **Save** 🖫 the presentation.

   ■ **You have completed Skill 4 of 10**

▶ A slide can be formatted by inserting a picture or a texture on the slide background.

1. Display **Slide 4**, and then insert a **New Slide** with the **Title Only** layout.

2. On the **Themes tab**, in the **Theme Options group**, click the **Background** button, and then click **Format Background**. Compare your screen with **Figure 1**.

3. In the **Format Background** dialog, click the **Picture or Texture** tab, and then click the **Choose Picture** button.

4. In the **Choose a Picture** dialog, navigate to your student files for this chapter, and then click **p02_CS_Building**. Click **Insert** to insert the picture on the slide background.

5. In the **Format Background** dialog, click in the **Transparency** box, select the entry, and then type 25

6. Click the **Apply** button.

   Notice that the picture is tiled.

7. In the **Theme Options group**, click the **Background** button, and then click **Format Background**. Click the **Picture or Texture** tab button, and then click the **Tile** check box to unselect the Tile effect. Compare your screen with **Figure 2**.

8. In the **Format Background** dialog, click the **Apply** button.

   ■ **Continue to the next page to complete the skill**

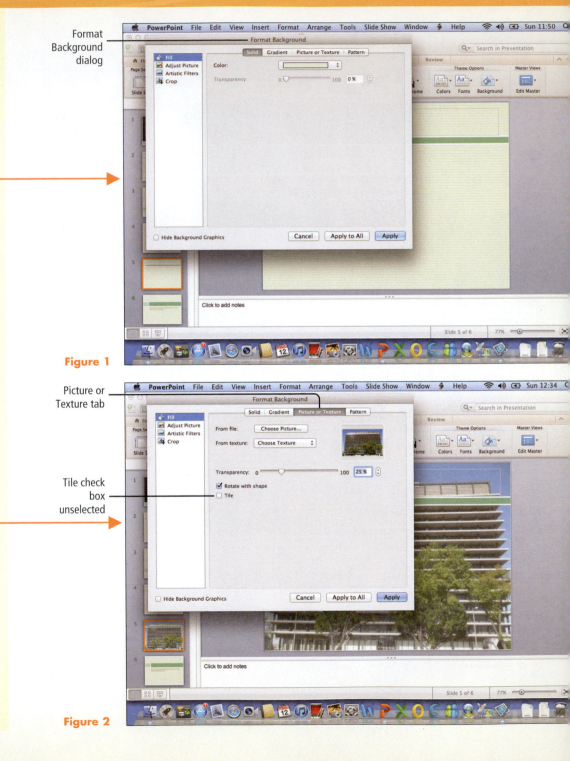

Format Background dialog

Figure 1

Picture or Texture tab

Tile check box unselected

Figure 2

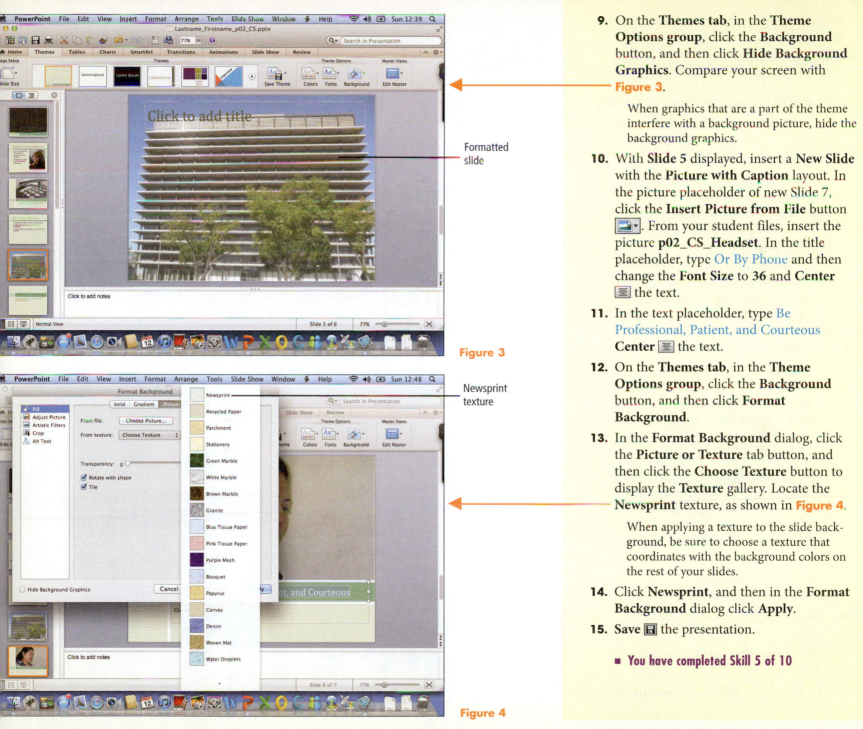

Figure 3

Formatted slide

Newsprint texture

Figure 4

9. On the **Themes tab**, in the **Theme Options group**, click the **Background** button, and then click **Hide Background Graphics**. Compare your screen with **Figure 3**.

> When graphics that are a part of the theme interfere with a background picture, hide the background graphics.

10. With **Slide 5** displayed, insert a **New Slide** with the **Picture with Caption** layout. In the picture placeholder of new Slide 7, click the **Insert Picture from File** button. From your student files, insert the picture **p02_CS_Headset**. In the title placeholder, type Or By Phone and then change the **Font Size** to **36** and **Center** the text.

11. In the text placeholder, type Be Professional, Patient, and Courteous Center the text.

12. On the **Themes tab**, in the **Theme Options group**, click the **Background** button, and then click **Format Background**.

13. In the **Format Background** dialog, click the **Picture or Texture** tab button, and then click the **Choose Texture** button to display the **Texture** gallery. Locate the **Newsprint** texture, as shown in **Figure 4**.

> When applying a texture to the slide background, be sure to choose a texture that coordinates with the background colors on the rest of your slides.

14. Click **Newsprint**, and then in the **Format Background** dialog click **Apply**.

15. Save the presentation.

- **You have completed Skill 5 of 10**

► *WordArt* is a text style used to create decorative effects in your presentation.

► You can insert new WordArt or you can convert existing text to WordArt.

1. Display **Slide 1**, and then select the title text.

2. On the **Format tab**, in the **Text Styles group**, click the **Quick Styles** button to view the WordArt gallery.

3. Under **Applies to Selected Text**, in the first row, point to the fourth WordArt style—**Fill - White**, **Outline – Accent 1**—as shown in **Figure 1**. Click the thumbnail and **Center** ≣ the title text.

4. Select the subtitle text. On the **Format tab**, in the **Text Styles group**, click the **Quick Styles** button. In the **WordArt** gallery, under **Applies to All Text in the Shape**, click the second WordArt style—**Fill - Black**, **Background 1**, **Metal Bevel**—and then **Center** ≣ the text.

5. Display **Slide 5**. On the **Home tab**, in the **Slides group**, click the **Layout** button, and then click the **Blank** thumbnail to change the slide layout.

6. On the **Home tab**, in the **Insert group**, click the **Text** button ⬚, and then click **WordArt**. With the *Your Text Here* placeholder text selected, in the **Text Styles group**, click **Quick Styles**, and then click the third WordArt style—**Fill - White**, **Drop Shadow**. Compare your screen with **Figure 2**.

   On the slide, a WordArt placeholder displays *Your Text Here*.

7. With the WordArt text selected, type Whether you assist customers on-site

   The placeholder expands to accommodate the text.

   ■ **Continue to the next page to complete the skill** ►

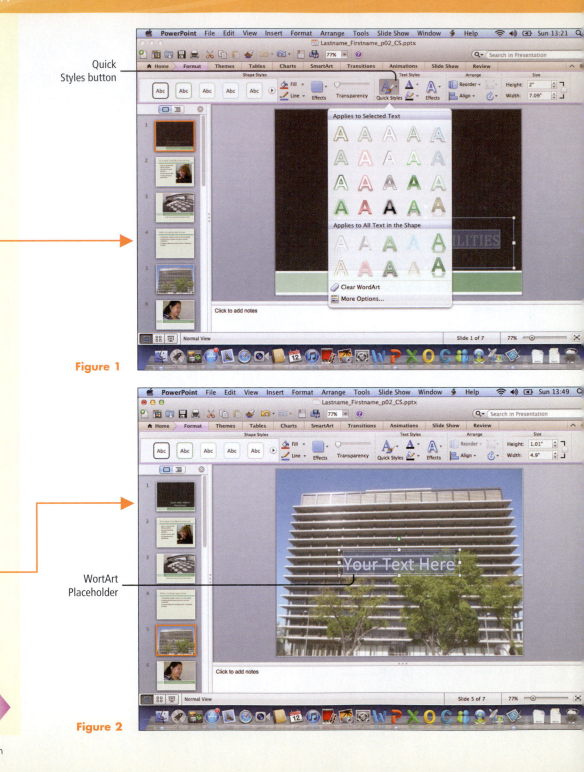

Quick Styles button

Figure 1

WortArt Placeholder

Figure 2

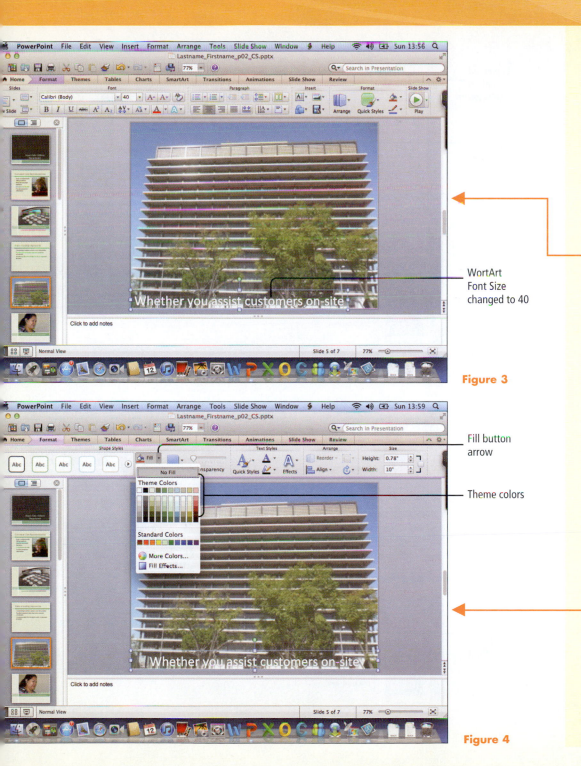

WortArt
Font Size
changed to 40

Figure 3

Fill button
arrow

Theme colors

Figure 4

8. Select the **WordArt** text. On the **Home tab**, in the **Font group**, click the **Font Size arrow** 18 , and then click **40** to resize the WordArt.

9. Point to the outer edge of the WordArt placeholder to display the move pointer.

10. While holding down the mouse button, drag down and to the left so that the lower-left corner of the WordArt placeholder aligns with the lower-left corner of the slide, and then release the mouse button to move the WordArt, as shown in **Figure 3**.

11. Select the WordArt text, point to its square, center-right sizing handle to display the pointer. Drag to the right so that the right edge of the WordArt placeholder aligns with the right edge of the slide.

12. On the **Format tab**, in the **Shape Styles group**, click the **Fill button arrow** to display the **Fill** gallery.

   The colors in the top row of the Fill gallery are the Foundry theme colors. The colors in the rows below the first row are light and dark variations of the theme colors and coordinate with the color theme. These colors can be used to change the *fill color*—the inside color of text or an object—so that the WordArt text displays prominently against the picture on the background.

13. Under **Theme Colors**, in the last row, click the sixth color—**Light Green**, **Accent 2**, **Darker 50%**—as shown in **Figure 4**.

   The WordArt text contrasts with the green fill color and the title is clearly visible on the slide.

14. Save the presentation.

   ■ **You have completed Skill 6 of 10**

▶ When a selected font displays text that appears crowded in a placeholder, expand the horizontal spacing between characters.

▶ When a selected font displays text with excessive horizontal spacing, condense the spacing between characters.

▶ You can change font colors to create contrast and emphasis on a slide.

1. If necessary, display **Slide 5**, and then select the WordArt text at the bottom of the slide. On the **Home tab**, in the **Font group**, click the **Bold** button **B**.

   The bold text contrasts well with the dark background of the placeholder, but the characters are spaced tightly together.

2. With the text still selected, on the **Home tab**, in the **Font group**, click the **Character Spacing** button, and then in the list click **Character Spacing Options**. In the **Format Text** dialog, click the **Spacing arrow**, and then click **Expanded**. In the **By** box, select the entry, and then type 1.6 to expand the spacing between characters by 1.6 points. Compare your dialog with **Figure 1**, and then click **OK** to apply the character spacing.

3. Display **Slide 3**, and then select the title. In the **Font group**, click the **Character Spacing** button, and then click **Tight** to reduce the amount of space between each character. Compare your slide with **Figure 2**.

   ■ **Continue to the next page to complete the skill**

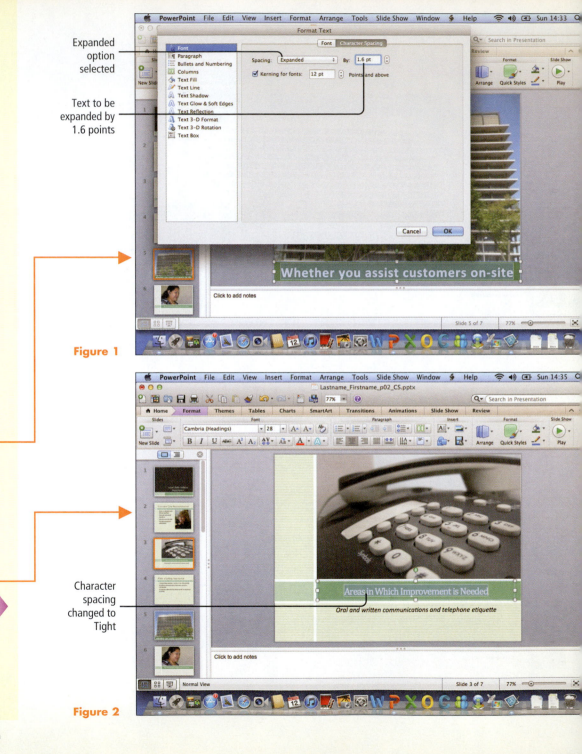

Expanded option selected

Text to be expanded by 1.6 points

Figure 1

Character spacing changed to Tight

Figure 2

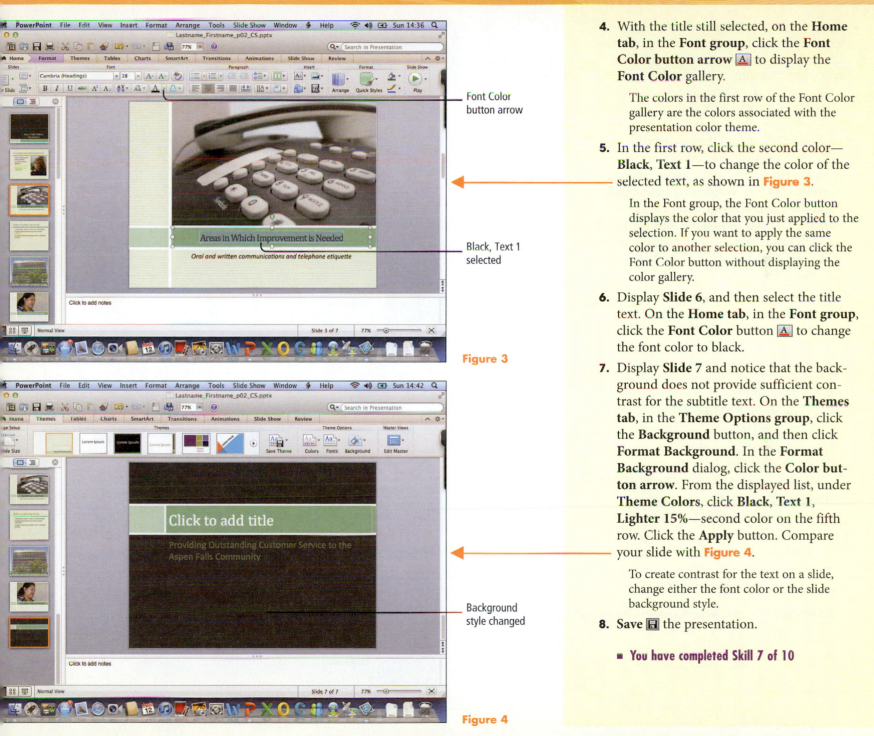

Font Color
button arrow

Black, Text 1
selected

Figure 3

Background
style changed

Figure 4

4. With the title still selected, on the **Home tab**, in the **Font group**, click the **Font Color button arrow** to display the **Font Color** gallery.

The colors in the first row of the Font Color gallery are the colors associated with the presentation color theme.

5. In the first row, click the second color—**Black, Text 1**—to change the color of the selected text, as shown in **Figure 3**.

In the Font group, the Font Color button displays the color that you just applied to the selection. If you want to apply the same color to another selection, you can click the Font Color button without displaying the color gallery.

6. Display **Slide 6**, and then select the title text. On the **Home tab**, in the **Font group**, click the **Font Color** button to change the font color to black.

7. Display **Slide 7** and notice that the background does not provide sufficient contrast for the subtitle text. On the **Themes tab**, in the **Theme Options group**, click the **Background** button, and then click **Format Background**. In the **Format Background** dialog, click the **Color button arrow**. From the displayed list, under **Theme Colors**, click **Black, Text 1, Lighter 15%**—second color on the fifth row. Click the **Apply** button. Compare your slide with **Figure 4**.

To create contrast for the text on a slide, change either the font color or the slide background style.

8. **Save** the presentation.

▪ **You have completed Skill 7 of 10**

▶ The presentation theme includes default bullet styles for the bullet points in content placeholders. You can customize a bullet symbol by changing its style, color, and size.

▶ A numbered list can be applied to bullet points in place of bullet symbols.

1. Display **Slide 4**, and then in the content placeholder, select the three bullet points. On the **Home tab**, in the **Paragraph group**, click the **Numbering** button ⬚▾, and then compare your screen with **Figure 1**. If you clicked the Numbering button arrow and a gallery displays, in the first row, click the second Numbering option—1, 2, 3.

   The bullet symbols are replaced by numbers. The default color for the numbers—light green—is based on the Foundry color theme.

2. With the three numbered list items selected, click the **Numbering button arrow** ⬚▾, and then below the gallery, click **Numbering Options**.

3. In the **Format Text** dialog, on the **Numbering tab**, click the **Color** button. Under **Theme Colors**, in the last row, point to the seventh color—**Sky Blue**, **Accent 3**, **Darker 50%**—as shown in **Figure 2**. Click to apply the new color.

4. In the **Size** box, replace the number with 100 so that the numbers will be the same size as the text. Click **OK** to apply the changes to the numbers in the list.

   ▪ **Continue to the next page to complete the skill** ▶

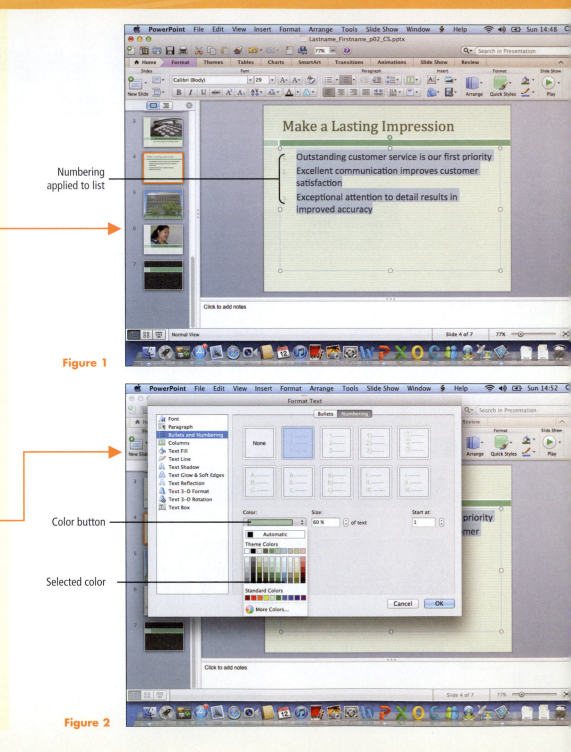

Numbering applied to list

Figure 1

Color button

Selected color

Figure 2

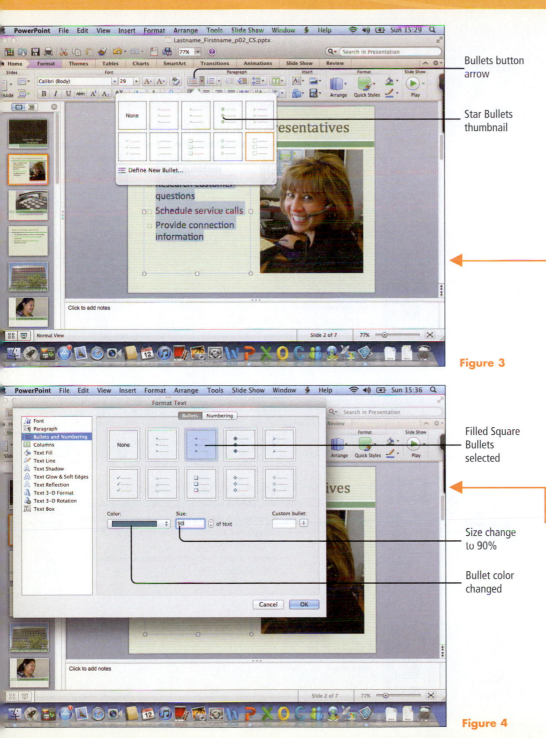

Bullets button arrow

Star Bullets thumbnail

Figure 3

Filled Square Bullets selected

Size change to 90%

Bullet color changed

Figure 4

5. Display **Slide 2**. In the content place-holder, select the four bullet points.

6. With the four bullet points selected, on the **Home tab**, in the **Paragraph group**, click the **Bullets button arrow** to display the **Bullets** gallery. If your bullets disappeared, click the Bullets button again, and then repeat Step 6, making sure to click the Bullets *button arrow* instead of the Bullets *button*.

   The gallery displays several bullet characters that you can apply to the selection.

7. Point to the **Star Bullets** thumbnail as shown in **Figure 3**, and then click the thumbnail to change the bullet style for the selection.

8. With the four bullet points selected, click the **Bullets button arrow**, and then below the gallery, click **Define New Bullet**.

9. In the **Format Text** dialog, on the **Bullets tab**, in the first row of the bullet gallery, click **Filled Square Bullets**. Click the **Color** button. Under **Theme Colors**, in the last row, click the seventh color—**Sky Blue**, **Accent 3**, **Darker 50%**.

10. In the **Size** box, replace the number with 90 and then compare your dialog with **Figure 4**.

11. Click **OK** to apply the bullet style, color, and size, and then **Save** the presentation.

   ■ **You have completed Skill 8 of 10**

► The Cut command removes selected text or graphics from your presentation and places the selection in the Office Clipboard.

► The Clipboard is a temporary storage area maintained by your operating system.

► The Copy command duplicates a selection and places it in the Office Clipboard.

1. Display **Slide 4**. In the content place-holder, position the pointer over the number 3, and notice the ⊕ pointer that displays.

2. With the pointer positioned over the number 3, click the mouse button, and notice that the number and the related text are selected.

   Clicking a list number or bullet symbol is an efficient way to select the entire point.

3. On the **Standard toolbar**, click the **Cut** button ✂ to remove the item from the slide and send it to the Clipboard. Compare your screen with **Figure 1**.

4. In the second numbered list item, click in front of the *E* in the word *Excellent*. On the **Standard toolbar**, click the **Paste** button 📋 to paste the selection to the new location. Notice that below the pasted text, the Paste Options button displays as shown in **Figure 2**, providing options for formatting pasted text. Also notice that the points are automatically renumbered when the order is changed.

   ■ **Continue to the next page to complete the skill**

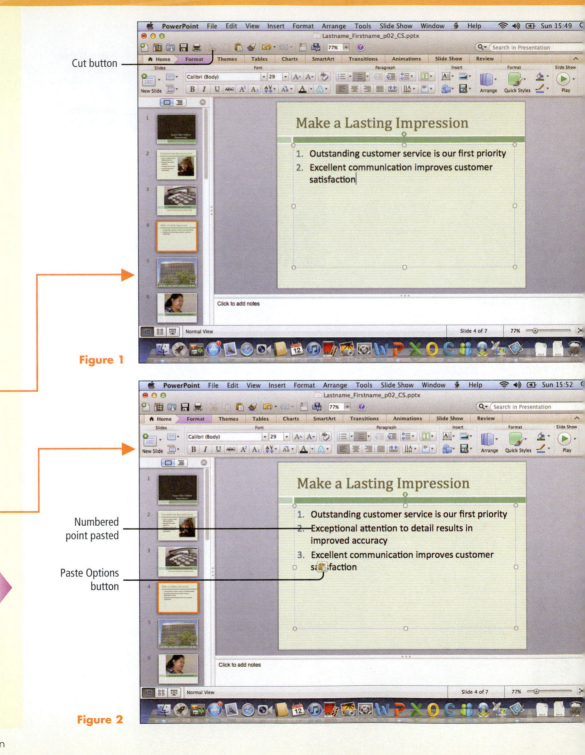

Cut button

Figure 1

Numbered point pasted

Paste Options button

Figure 2

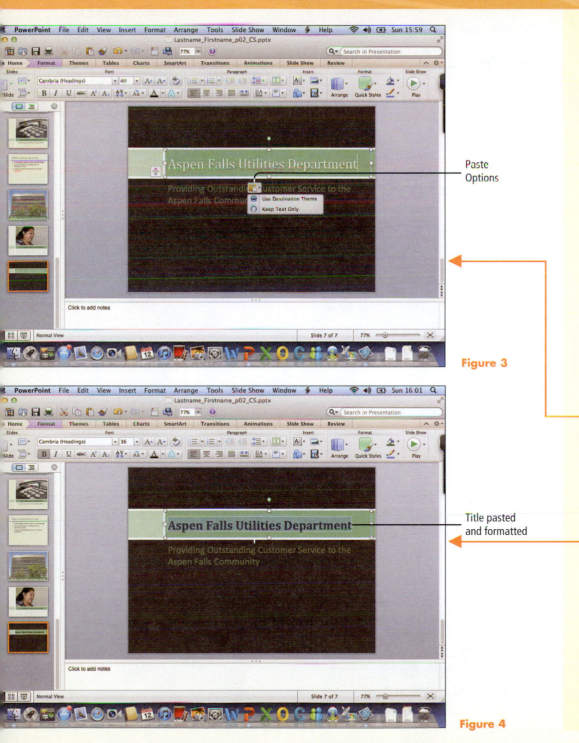

Paste
Options

Figure 3

Title pasted
and formatted

Figure 4

5. Click the **Paste Options** button to view the options.

   Use Destination Theme applies the formatting of the slide to which the text is pasted. *Keep Text Only* removes all formatting from the selection. The Paste Options button remains on the screen until you perform another action.

6. Display **Slide 1**, and then select the title text. Point to the selection, press control, click the mouse button, and then from the shortcut menu, click **Copy**.

   There are multiple methods you can use to cut, copy, and paste text, including the shortcut menu and the buttons in the Clipboard group. You can also use the keyboard shortcuts—command ⌘ + X to cut, command ⌘ + C to copy, and command ⌘ + V to paste.

7. Display **Slide 7**. With the pointer over the title placeholder, press control, click the mouse button, and then from the shortcut menu click **Paste**. Click the **Paste Options** button to display the shortcut menu as shown in **Figure 3**, and then notice the two paste options.

8. On the shortcut menu, click the last button—**Keep Text Only**.

9. Select the title text. Apply **Bold** B, change the **Font Color** A to **Black, Text 1**, and then change the **Font Size** to **36**. Compare your slide with **Figure 4**.

10. **Save** the presentation.

   ■ **You have completed Skill 9 of 10**

▶ *Format Painter* copies *formatting* from one selection of text to another, thus ensuring formatting consistency in your presentation.

▶ You can use the Clear All Formatting button to revert to the font formatting associated with the original slide layout.

1. Display **Slide 3**, and then select the word *Oral*. On the **Standard toolbar**, click the **Format Painter** button 🖌, and then position the 🖌 pointer anywhere in the Slide pane. Compare your screen with **Figure 1**.

   The pointer displays with a small paintbrush attached to it, indicating that Format Painter is active.

2. Display **Slide 6**. Drag the pointer over the caption text—*Be Professional, Patient, and Courteous*.

   The selected text is now formatted in italic 20-point characters as was the text on Slide 3. Notice that only the formatting was applied; the text was not copied. The 🖌 pointer is no longer active.

3. If necessary, select the caption text—*Be Professional, Patient, and Courteous*. On the **Home tab**, in the **Font group**, click the **Clear Formatting** button 🔲 to revert to the default font formatting for this slide layout.

   Use the Clear Formatting button to revert to the original formatting on a slide.

4. With the caption text still selected, apply **Bold** B and **Italic** I. Compare your slide with **Figure 2**.

   ■ **Continue to the next page to complete the skill** ➤

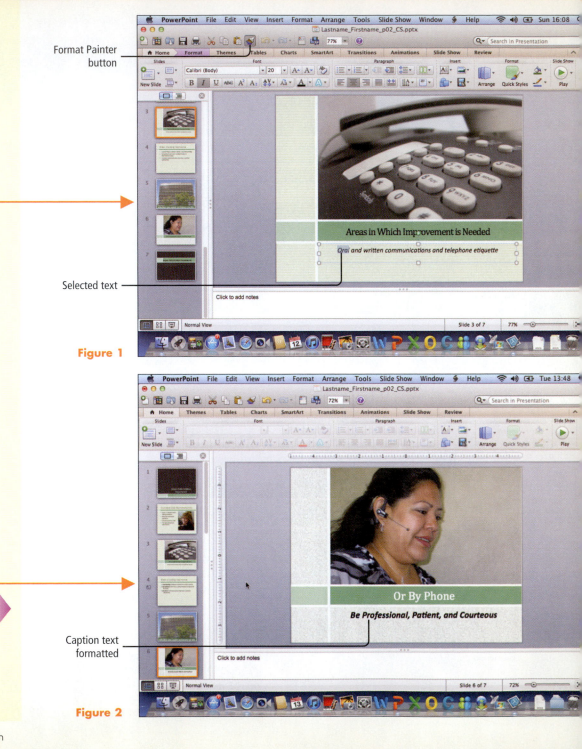

Format Painter button

Selected text

Figure 1

Caption text formatted

Figure 2

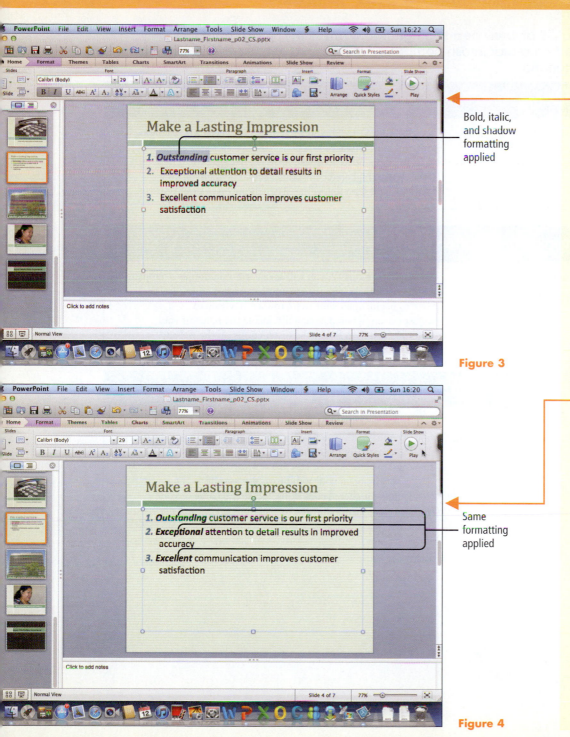

Bold, italic, and shadow formatting applied

Figure 3

Same formatting applied

Figure 4

5. Display **Slide 4**. In the first item, select the text *Outstanding*. On the **Home tab**, in the **Font group**, click the **Bold** button **B** and the **Italic** button *I*. Compare your slide with **Figure 3**.

6. With the text *Outstanding* still selected, on the **Standard toolbar**, *double-click* the **Format Painter** button.

   To apply formatting to multiple selections, double-click the Format Painter button.

7. In the second numbered item, click the word *Exceptional* to apply the selected formatting to the text. Notice that the pointer is still active.

8. In the third numbered item, click the word *Excellent*. If you were unable to apply the formatting to the word *Excellent*, repeat Step 6, and then try again.

9. To turn off Format Painter, on the **Standard toolbar**, click the **Format Painter** button. Alternately, press `esc`. Compare your slide with **Figure 4**.

10. Apply the **Wipe** transition with the **Effect Options** changed to **From Top** to all of the slides, and then view the slide show from the beginning.

11. Insert a **Header and Footer** on the **Notes and Handouts** that includes the **Date and time** updated automatically, a **Page number**, and the **Footer** Lastname_Firstname_p02_CS

12. **Save** the presentation. Print your presentation or submit electronically, as directed by your instructor. **Quit** PowerPoint.

Done! You have completed Skill 10 of 10, and your presentation is complete!

The following More Skills are located at **www.pearsonhighered.com/skills.** Please note that only More Skills that can be performed on a Macintosh computer are included in this section; therefore, the numbering is not always sequential.

More Skills Edit Slide Masters

When you are formatting a presentation and want to change the format for every slide in the presentation, modify the slide master. The slide master holds information about the colors, fonts, and other objects that display on your slides.

In More Skills 11, you will edit a slide master by changing its font and bullet styles.

To begin, open your web browser, navigate to www.pearsonhighered.com/skills, locate the name of your textbook, and then follow the instructions on the website.

More Skills Save and Apply Presentation Templates

You can design your own custom presentation and save it as a template so that you can easily apply the template to another presentation.

In More Skills 12, you will save a presentation as a template and then apply the template to another presentation.

To begin, open your web browser, navigate to www.pearsonhighered.com/skills, locate the name of your textbook, and then follow the instructions on the website.

More Skills Design Presentations with Contrast

Contrast is an important element of slide design because it enables the audience to clearly view presentation text, images, and objects.

In More Skills 14, you will review design principles that will assist you in creating contrast on your slides. You will view two slides and compare the difference in contrast created by using color and images.

To begin, open your web browser, navigate to www.pearsonhighered.com/skills, locate the name of your textbook, and then follow the instructions on the website.

Key Terms

Background style 324

Body font 323

Fill color 329

Format Painter 336

Headings font 323

Template 318

Theme 320

Theme color 322

Theme font 323

WordArt 328

Online Help Skills

1. **Start** Safari or another web browser. In the **address bar**, type microsoft.com/ mac/how-to and then press ⌷return⌷ to display the home page for Microsoft Office.

   This website provides you with helpful links to get started, find out what is new, and tutorials about Office 2011.

2. Under **Product Help**, click **PowerPoint 2011**.

3. Click the **Themes** link.

4. Click **Create and apply your own theme**, and then compare your screen with **Figure 1**.

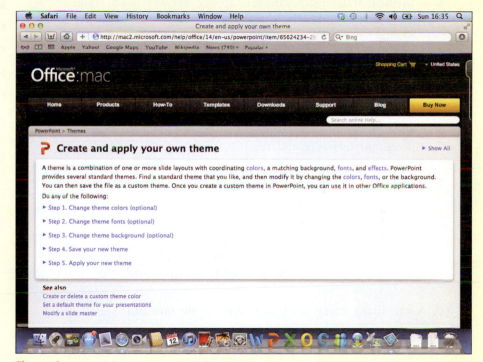

Figure 1

5. On the right of your screen, click **Show All**, read the displayed content and then answer the following questions. How do you change a theme's font? How can you create your own theme in PowerPoint? How can you apply a theme that you created to slides?

Matching

Match each term in the second column with its correct definition in the first column by writing the letter of the term on the blank line in front of the correct definition.

____ **1.** A file upon which a presentation can be based.

____ **2.** A set of unified design elements that provides a look for your presentation, using colors, fonts, and graphics.

____ **3.** A theme that determines the font applied to two types of slide text—headings and body.

____ **4.** A font applied to slide titles.

____ **5.** A font applied to all slide text except titles.

____ **6.** A slide background fill variation that combines theme colors in different intensities or patterns.

____ **7.** A text style used to create decorative effects in a presentation.

____ **8.** The inside color of text or an object.

____ **9.** A command that removes selected text or graphics from a presentation, and then moves the selection to the Clipboard.

____ **10.** A temporary storage area maintained by the operating system.

A Background style

B Body font

C Clipboard

D Cut

E Fill color

F Headings font

G Template

H Theme

I Theme font

J WordArt

Multiple Choice

Choose the correct answer.

1. The process of changing the appearance of the text, layout, or design of a slide.
   A. Editing
   B. Designing
   C. Formatting

2. The area of the PowerPoint window in which the user view displays: Normal, Slide Sorter, or Slide Show.
   A. Status bar
   B. Task pane
   C. Slide pane

3. The default theme in PowerPoint.
   A. Apex
   B. Office
   C. Urban

4. The coordinating set of colors applied to presentation backgrounds, objects, and text.
   A. Theme color
   B. Color palette
   C. Color gallery

5. A set of unified design elements that provides a unique look for your presentation using colors, fonts, and graphics.
   A. Sepia
   B. Gradient fill
   C. Theme

6. A format that you can change to create contrast and emphasis on a slide.
   A. Alignment
   B. Font color
   C. Layout

7. The command used to duplicate a selection.
   A. Format Painter
   B. Cut
   C. Copy

8. The command used to copy formatting from one selection to another.
   A. Format Painter
   B. Cut
   C. Copy

9. A command used to revert to font formatting associated with the original slide layout.
   A. Clear All Formatting
   B. Reset Format
   C. Reset Slide Layout

10. The mouse action necessary when Format Painter is used on multiple selections.
    A. Single-click
    B. Double-click
    C. Triple-click

Topics for Discussion

1. PowerPoint 2011 includes several themes that you can apply to your presentations. What should you consider when choosing a design theme for the presentations that you create?

2. Format Painter is an important tool used to maintain consistent formatting in a presentation. Why is consistency important when you format the slides in your presentations?

Skill Check

To complete this presentation, you will need the following files:

- New blank presentation
- p02_Plaza_Fountain

You will save your presentation as:

- Lastname_Firstname_p02_Plaza

1. **Start** PowerPoint and open a blank presentation. Type the slide title The Plaza at Aspen Falls and the subtitle Opening Ceremony **Save** the file in your **PowerPoint Chapter 2** folder, using your own name, as Lastname_Firstname_p02_Plaza

2. Insert a **New Slide** with the **Title and Content** layout. In the title placeholder, type Event Activities In the text placeholder, type four bullet points:

   Ribbon cutting and Welcome address and Continental breakfast and Grand prize raffle

3. On the **Themes tab,** in the **Themes group**, click the **More** button. Under **Built-In,** click **Urban Pop**. In the **Themes Options group**, click the **Fonts** button, and then click **Advantage**. Click the **Colors** button, and then click **Breeze**. In the **Themes Options group**, click the **Background** button, and then click **Style 3**. Compare your screen with **Figure 1**.

4. Insert a **New Slide** with the **Blank** layout. On the **Themes tab**, in the **Themes Options group**, click the **Background** button, and then click **Format Background**. In the **Format Background** dialog, select **Picture or Texture**, then click the **Choose Picture** button. From your student files, insert **p02_Plaza_Fountain**. Click **Apply**.

5. Insert a **New Slide** with the **Content with Caption** layout. Type the slide title Join the Celebration! In the left placeholder, type four bullet points:

   July 25 at 10 a.m. and Free events and Retail locations and park will be open and Raffle at 6 p.m.

6. Select the bullet points and change the **Line Spacing** to **1.5**. In the **Paragraph group,** click the **Bullets button arrow,** and then click **Define New Bullet**. Click **Arrow Bullets,** and then click the **Color** button. In the third row, click the sixth color—**Sky Blue, Accent 2, Lighter 60%**. In the **Size** box, type 80 and then click **OK**. Compare your screen with **Figure 2**.

- Continue to the next page to complete this Skill Check

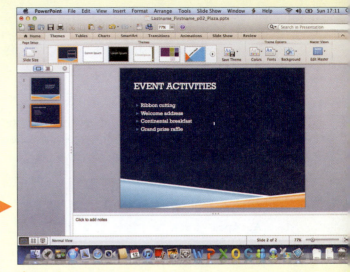

Figure 1

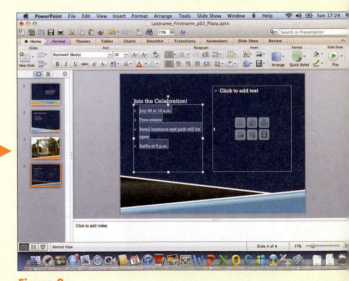

Figure 2

7. On the **Themes tab**, in the **Theme Options group**, click the **Background** button, and then click **Format Background**. Select **Picture or Texture**, and then click the **Choose Texture** button. Click **Purple Mesh**, and then click **Apply**.

8. Display **Slide 2**, and then select the four bullet points. On the **Home tab**, in the **Paragraph group**, click the **Numbering** button.

9. Display **Slide 3**. On the **Themes tab**, in the **Theme Options group**, click the **Background** button, and then click **Hide Background Graphics**. On the **menu bar**, click **Insert**, and then click **WordArt**. Click the third WordArt style—**Fill - White**, **Drop Shadow**—and then replace the WordArt text with Ribbon cutting to take place at the fountain

10. Change the **Font Size** to **36**, and then point to the outer edge of the WordArt place-holder. Drag to align the placeholder with the lower-left corner of the slide. Size the WordArt so that it extends from the left to the right edge of the slide.

11. On the **Format tab**, in the **Shape Styles group**, click the **Fill button arrow**. Under **Theme Colors**, in the last row, click the tenth color—**Dark Red**, **Accent 6**, **Darker 50%**. Compare your screen with **Figure 3**.

Figure 3

12. Display **Slide 1**. On the **Themes tab**, in the **Theme Options group**, click the **Background** button, and then click **Format Background**. Click the **Color** button, and then under **Theme Colors**, click **Blue**, **Accent 1**—fifth color on the first row. Click **Apply**. Select the title. On the **Format tab**, in the **Text Styles group**, click the **Quick Styles** button, and then under **Applies to Selected Text**, click the last style—**Gradient Fill - Brown**, **Accent 4**, **Reflection**.

13. On the **Standard toolbar**, click the **Copy** button. Display **Slide 4**, and then click in the text placeholder on the right. On the **Standard toolbar**, click the **Paste** button. Click the **Bulleted List** button to remove the bullet. Change the **Font Size** to **40**, and then **Center** the text.

14. Display **Slide 1**. Select the subtitle. Apply **Bold** and **Italic**, and then on the **Standard toolbar**, click the **Format Painter** button.

15. Display **Slide 4**, and then drag the **Format Painter** pointer over the title—*Join the Celebration!* **Center** the title and change the **Font Color** to **Orange**, **Accent 1**.

16. Insert a **Header and Footer** on the **Notes and Handouts** with the **Date and time**, the **Page number**, and the **Footer** Lastname_Firstname_p02_Plaza

Figure 4

17. **Save** the presentation, and then compare your presentation with **Figure 4**. Print or submit the file as directed by your instructor.

Done! You have completed the Skill Check

Assess Your Skills 1

To complete this presentation, you will need the following files:

- New blank presentation
- p02_AFD_Engines
- p02_AFD_Fireman

You will save your presentation as:

- Lastname_Firstname_p02_Station

1. **Start** PowerPoint and display a blank presentation. Apply the **Foundry** theme. Change the theme font to **Orbit**. **Save** the file in your **PowerPoint Chapter 2** folder, using your own name, as Lastname_Firstname_p02_Station

2. In the title placeholder, type Aspen Falls Fire District and then in the subtitle placeholder, type New Station Proposal Change the subtitle **Font Size** to **36**, and the **Font Color** to **Beige**, **Accent 5**, **Lighter 80%**.

3. Insert a **New Slide** with the **Title and Content** layout. In the content placeholder, type the following bullet points:

   Add 3 engines and 15 firefighters and Locate in southern area of city and Fund by municipal bonds

4. Display **Slide 1**. **Copy** the subtitle and **Paste** the selection to the title placeholder on **Slide 2**. Delete any extra blank lines.

5. Insert a **New Slide** with the **White** layout. On the slide background, from your student files, insert the picture **p02_AFD_Engines**. Deselect the **Tile** check box. Hide background graphics.

6. Insert the third WordArt style—**Fill - White**, **Drop Shadow**—with the text Proposed Engine Additions Drag the WordArt to the upper-left corner of the slide. Size the

WordArt so that it extends from the left to the right edge of the slide. Change the shape fill color to **Black**, **Background 1**.

7. Insert a **New Slide** with the **Title and Content** layout. In the title placeholder, type Rationale In the text placeholder, type four bullet points:

   Reduced emergency response time and Increased population growth and Expanded city boundaries and Increased commercial density

8. To the **Slide 4** title, apply the fourth WordArt style—**Fill - White**, **Outline - Accent 1**. Use **Format Painter** to apply the same style to the **Slide 1** subtitle. Change the subtitle text **Font Size** to **36**. If necessary, Align Right the subtitle.

9. Display **Slide 4**, and then insert a **New Slide** with the **Picture with Caption** layout. Display **Slide 1**, and then **Copy** the title and **Paste** it in the **Slide 5** title. In the text placeholder, type Dedicated to serving our community Change the **Font Size** to **32**. In the picture placeholder, from your student files, insert **p02_AFD_Fireman**. Apply the **Soft Edge Rectangle** picture style.

10. Insert a **Header and Footer** on the **Notes and Handouts**. Include the date, page number, and the footer Lastname_Firstname_p02_Station

Figure 1

11. Compare your presentation with **Figure 1**. **Save** your presentation, and then print or submit the file as directed by your instructor.

Done! You have completed Assess Your Skills 1

Assess Your Skills 3 and 4 can be found at **www.pearsonhighered.com/skills**.

Assess Your Skills 2

To complete this presentation, you will need the following file:

- p02_Loans

You will save your presentation as:

- Lastname_Firstname_p02_Loans

Lastname_Firstname_p02_Loans   1

Figure 1

1. **Start** PowerPoint. From your student files, open **p02_Loans**. Change the theme color to **Horizon**, and change the theme font to **Venture**. Apply background **Style 12** to the entire presentation, and then **Save** the file in your **PowerPoint Chapter 2** folder, using your own name, as Lastname_Firstname_p02_Loans

2. Display **Slide 4**, and then move the picture above the slide text.

3. Display **Slide 1**, select the title, and then apply the last WordArt style—**Fill - Orange**, **Accent 1**, **Metal Bevel**, **Reflection**. Change the font size to **40**. Use **Format Painter** to apply the same formatting to the title on **Slide 4**.

4. Display **Slide 1**, and then select the subtitle. Apply **Bold**, and then expand the character spacing by **1** point. Increase the **Font Size** to **24**. Use **Format Painter** to apply the same formatting to the subtitle on **Slide 4**.

5. Display **Slide 2**. Change the bullet style to **Star Bullets**, and then change the **Size** to 90% of text. Move the last bullet point so that it is the first bullet point. Apply the **Rotated**, **White** picture style to the picture.

6. Display **Slide 3**, and then in the first bullet point, select the first word—*Apply*. Change

the **Font Color** to the fourth color in the first row—**Orange, Text 2**. Apply **Bold** and **Italic**, and then use **Format Painter** to apply the same formatting to the first word of each of the remaining bullet points. Convert the bullets to a numbered list, and change the **Color** of the numbers to **White, Text 1**.

7. Display **Slide 1**, and then format the slide background by applying the **Green Marble** texture. Apply the same background style to **Slide 4**.

8. With **Slide 4** displayed, apply the **Double Frame, Black** picture style to the picture.

9. Apply the **Wipe** transition to all of the slides in the presentation. View the slide show from the beginning.

10. Insert a **Header and Footer** on the **Notes and Handouts** that includes the page number and a footer with the text Lastname_Firstname_p02_Loans

11. Compare your completed presentation with **Figure 1**. **Save** your presentation, and then print or submit the file as directed by your instructor.

Done! You have completed Assess Your Skills 2

Assess Your Skills Visually

To complete this presentation, you will need the following files:

- New blank presentation
- p02_Natural_History_Museum

You will save your presentation as:

- Lastname_Firstname_p02_Museum

1. **Start** a new, blank presentation, and create the first two slides of a presentation, as shown in **Figure 1**. To complete these two slides, apply the **Pushpin** theme. On **Slide 1**, change the title font size to **54**, and change the subtitle font size to **32**. On **Slide 2,** format the slide background by using the picture found in your student files—**p02_Natural_History_Museum**. Insert the appropriate WordArt style, type the text, and change the WordArt font size to **48**. Move and format the shape **Fill** color as indicated in the figure. **Save** your presentation as Lastname_Firstname_p02_Museum and then insert the date, file name, and page number in the **Notes and Handouts** footer. **Save** the presentation, and then print or submit the file as directed by your instructor.

   Done! You have completed Assess Your Skills Visually

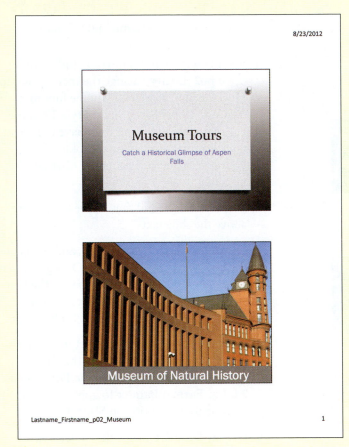

Figure 1

Skills in Context

To complete this presentation, you will need the following file:

- New blank presentation

You will save your presentation as:

- Lastname_Firstname_p02_Celebration

Each year the City of Aspen Falls hosts a Fourth of July celebration at the Aspen Falls Community Park. Using the skills you practiced in this chapter, create a presentation with five slides that describes the city's Fourth of July events, which include a parade, barbecue, games, arts and crafts fair, and fireworks. Create an appropriate title slide, and then on the second and third slides, provide a description of the event location and the celebration schedule. On the fourth slide, format the background with a picture that depicts the event and include WordArt text that briefly describes the picture. On the fifth slide, provide a summary using the Section Header layout.

Apply an appropriate theme and change fonts and colors as necessary. Save the presentation as Lastname_Firstname_p02_Celebration and then Insert the file name and page number in the Notes and Handouts footer. Save the presentation, and then print or submit the file as directed by your instructor.

Done! You have completed Skills in Context

Skills and You

To complete this presentation, you will need the following file:

- New blank presentation

You will save your presentation as:

- Lastname_Firstname_p02_City

Using the skills you have practiced in this chapter, create a presentation with six slides describing a city that you would like to visit. Apply an appropriate theme and change the fonts and colors themes. On at least one slide, format the slide background with a picture that depicts the city that you choose. On the first slide, format the slide title by using a WordArt style. Include in your presentation a numbered list that indicates at least four things that you would like to do or see in the city that you choose. The remaining slides may include information about the people, culture, and activities of the city.

Format the last slide with the Section Header layout, and enter text that briefly summarizes your presentation. Insert the file name and page number in the Notes and Handouts footer, and then check spelling in the presentation. Save the presentation, using your own name, as **Lastname_Firstname_p02_City** and then print or submit the file as directed by your instructor.

Done! You have completed Skills and You

CHAPTER 3

Enhance Presentations with Graphics

▶ Appropriate presentation graphics visually communicate your message and help your audience understand the points you want to convey.

▶ Review the graphics that you use, the text on your slides, and your spoken words to ensure that your presentation is coherent, precise, and accurate.

▶ Review the procedures in your organization so that you are familiar with how presentations are shared using slide libraries and other file sharing procedures.

▶ When effective and illustrative diagrams are needed, you can use SmartArt graphics to list information and show processes and relationships.

▶ When your slides contain many bullet points, consider replacing the bullet points with SmartArt graphics to add interest and variety.

©Cheryl Casey | Dreamstime.com

Aspen Falls City Hall

In this chapter, you will create documents for the Aspen Falls City Hall, which provides essential services for the citizens and visitors of Aspen Falls, California. In this project, you will work with Eugene Garner, Benefits Specialist, to create a presentation describing the benefits that are extended to the members of the Aspen Falls Employee Alliance.

You will start with a blank presentation, apply a design, and create six slides. You will insert, size, move, and align clip art and shapes, and you will add text and apply styles to shapes. You will also insert and format a video and a SmartArt graphic.

Time to complete all
10 skills – 60 to 75 minutes

Student data files needed for this chapter:

New blank PowerPoint
   presentation
p03_Alliance_Orientation
p03_Alliance_Director

p03_Alliance_Park
p03_Alliance_Canyon
p03_Alliance_Boat

You will save your presentation as:

Lastname_Firstname_p03_Alliance

Outcome

Using the skills in this chapter, you will be able to work
with PowerPoint presentations like this:

SKILLS

Skills 1-10 Training

At the end of this chapter you will be able to:

Skill 1   Insert Slides from Other Presentations
Skill 2   Insert, Size, and Move Clip Art
Skill 3   Modify Picture Shapes, Borders, and Effects
Skill 4   Insert, Size, and Move Shapes
Skill 5   Add Text to Shapes and Insert Text Boxes
Skill 6   Apply Gradient Fills and Group and Align Graphics
Skill 7   Convert Text to SmartArt Graphics and Add Shapes
Skill 8   Modify Smartart Layouts, Colors, and Styles
Skill 9   Insert Video Files
Skill 10 Apply Video Styles and Adjust Videos

MORE SKILLS

Skill 11 Compress Pictures
Skill 12 Save Groups as Picture Files
Skill 13 Change Object Order
Skill 14 Design Presentations Using Appropriate Graphics

► Presentation slides can be shared using the Reuse Slides command so that frequently used content does not need to be recreated.

1. **Start** PowerPoint to display a new blank presentation. In the title placeholder, type Aspen Falls Employee Alliance and then in the subtitle placeholder, type Join the Club!

2. On the **Themes tab**, in the **Theme Options group**, click the **Background** button, and then click **Style 3**. Compare your slide with **Figure 1**. ──────

3. On the **Standard toolbar**, click **Save**. Navigate to the location where you are saving your files, create a folder named PowerPoint Chapter 3 and then using your own name, save the document as Lastname_Firstname_p03_Alliance

4. Display the **Home tab**. In the **Slides group**, click the **New Slide button arrow**, and then in the **Office Theme** gallery, click **Two Content**. In the title place-holder, type Employee Fitness Events

5. In the left placeholder, type Team sports and then press ⌷return⌷. Press ⌷tab⌷ to increase the list level. Type Soccer and then press ⌷return⌷. Type Basketball and then press ⌷return⌷.

6. Press ⌷shift⌷ + ⌷tab⌷ to decrease the list level. Type Weekly classes and then press ⌷return⌷. Press ⌷tab⌷. Type Kickboxing and then press ⌷return⌷. Type Boot camp and then press ⌷return⌷. Type Water aerobics Compare your slide with **Figure 2**. ──────

■ **Continue to the next page to complete the skill**

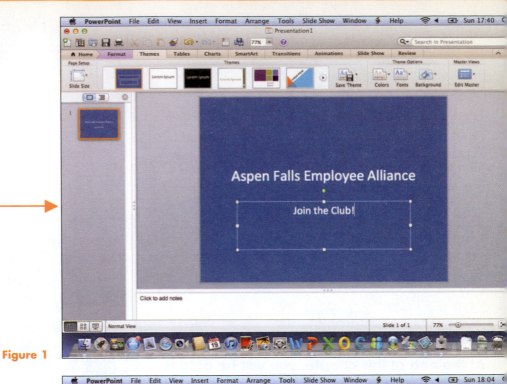

Figure 1

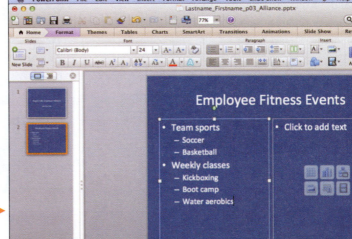

Figure 2

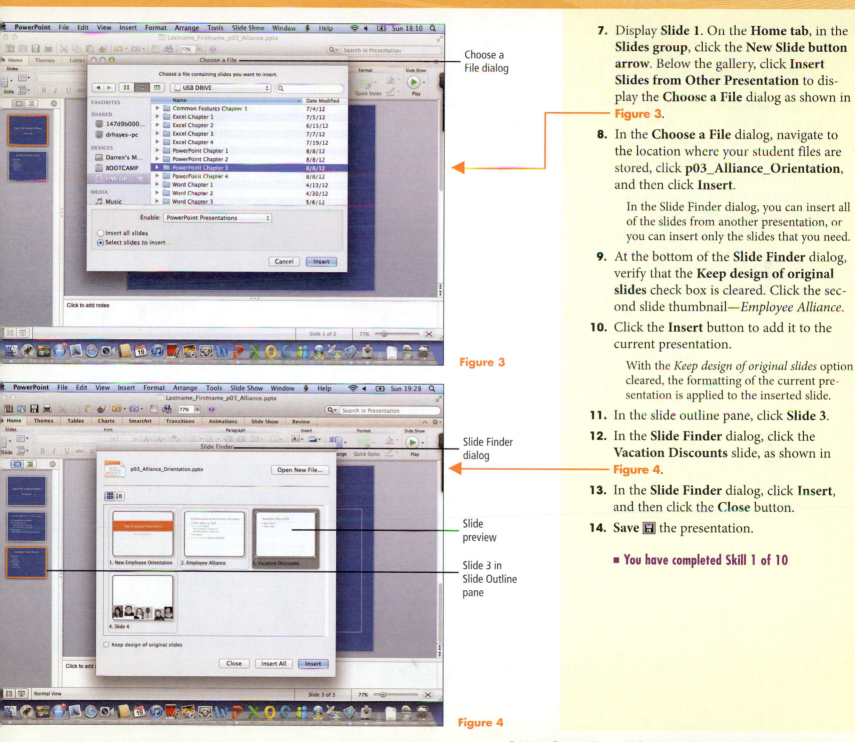

Choose a File dialog

Figure 3

Slide Finder dialog

Slide preview

Slide 3 in Slide Outline pane

Figure 4

7. Display **Slide 1**. On the **Home tab**, in the **Slides group**, click the **New Slide button arrow**. Below the gallery, click **Insert Slides from Other Presentation** to display the **Choose a File** dialog as shown in **Figure 3**.

8. In the **Choose a File** dialog, navigate to the location where your student files are stored, click **p03_Alliance_Orientation**, and then click **Insert**.

> In the Slide Finder dialog, you can insert all of the slides from another presentation, or you can insert only the slides that you need.

9. At the bottom of the **Slide Finder** dialog, verify that the **Keep design of original slides** check box is cleared. Click the second slide thumbnail—*Employee Alliance*.

10. Click the **Insert** button to add it to the current presentation.

> With the *Keep design of original slides* option cleared, the formatting of the current presentation is applied to the inserted slide.

11. In the slide outline pane, click **Slide 3**.

12. In the **Slide Finder** dialog, click the **Vacation Discounts** slide, as shown in **Figure 4**.

13. In the **Slide Finder** dialog, click **Insert**, and then click the **Close** button.

14. **Save** 💾 the presentation.

■ **You have completed Skill 1 of 10**

► Recall that clip art refers to images included with Microsoft Office, whereas pictures are images that are saved as a file with an extension such as .jpg, .bmp, or .tif.

1. Display **Slide 3**. In the placeholder on the right, click the **Clip Art Browser** button to display the Clip Art pane.

2. In the **Media** pane, click the **All Images** box arrow, and then click **People**.

3. Scroll down, and then click the soccer player image, as shown in **Figure 1**.

4. Drag the image to the slide placeholder on the right, and then when the pointer displays release the mouse button.

5. In the **Media** pane, click **Close**, and then compare your screen with **Figure 2**.

   ■ **Continue to the next page to complete the skill**

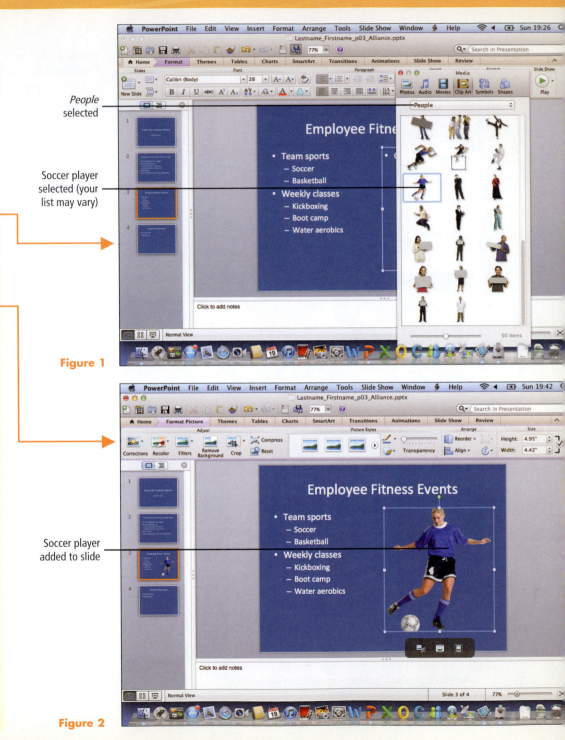

People selected

Soccer player selected (your list may vary)

Figure 1

Soccer player added to slide

Figure 2

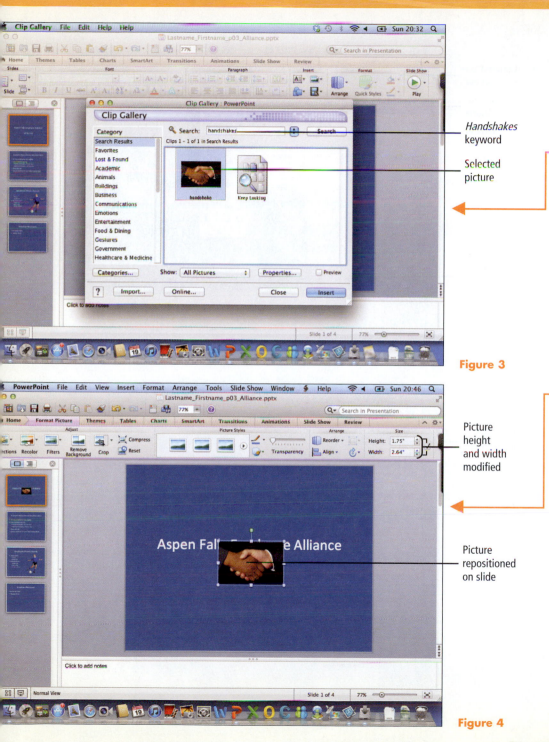

Handshakes keyword

Selected picture

Figure 3

Picture height and width modified

Picture repositioned on slide

Figure 4

6. Display **Slide 1**. On the **Home tab**, in the **Insert group**, click the **Insert a picture or clip art** button, and then click **Clip Art Gallery**. In the **Clip Gallery** dialog, in the **Search** box, replace the existing text with handshakes

7. Click the **Search** button, and then locate and click the picture shown in **Figure 3**. If you are unable to locate the same picture, choose a similar picture. Click **Insert**.

8. Click to select the picture. On the **Format Picture tab**, in the **Size group**, double-click in the **Height** box ⌗Height: 5.09"⌗ to select its displayed number. Type 1.75 and then press ⎌return⎌.

> When you change the height of a picture in this manner, the width is adjusted proportionately.

9. Point to the picture to display the ✧ pointer. Drag the picture to the center of the slide so that the subtitle and part of the title are covered as shown in **Figure 4**.

10. **Save** 🖫 the presentation.

■ **You have completed Skill 2 of 10**

▶ Inserted pictures are usually rectangular, but they can be changed to a number of different shapes available in PowerPoint.

▶ *Picture effects* are picture styles that include shadows, reflections, glows, soft edges, bevels, and 3-D rotations.

1. On **Slide 1**, if necessary, select the picture.

2. On the **Format Picture tab**, in the **Adjust group**, click the *right* part of the **Crop** button—the **Crop button arrow**. Point to **Mask to Shape**, then point to **Basic Shapes**, and then compare your screen with **Figure 1**.

3. Under **Basic Shapes**, click the first shape—**Oval**—to change the shape of the picture from a rectangle to an oval.

4. In the **Picture Styles group**, click the **Effects** button. Point to **Shadow**, and then click **Shadow Options**.

5. On the left side of **Format Picture** dialog, click **Glow & Soft Edges**. In the **Soft Edges** box, type 25 as shown in **Figure 2**.

6. Click **OK**.

7. Display **Slide 3**, and then select the picture. On the **Format Picture tab**, in the **Picture Styles group**, click the **Effects** button. Point to **Shadow**, and then point to, but do not click, several of the options to view the shadow available effects.

■ **Continue to the next page to complete the skill** ➤

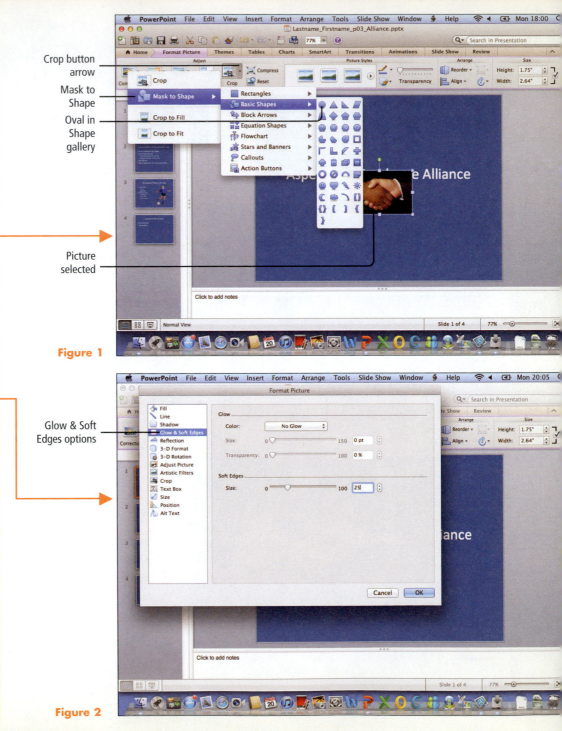

Crop button arrow

Mask to Shape

Oval in Shape gallery

Picture selected

Figure 1

Glow & Soft Edges options

Figure 2

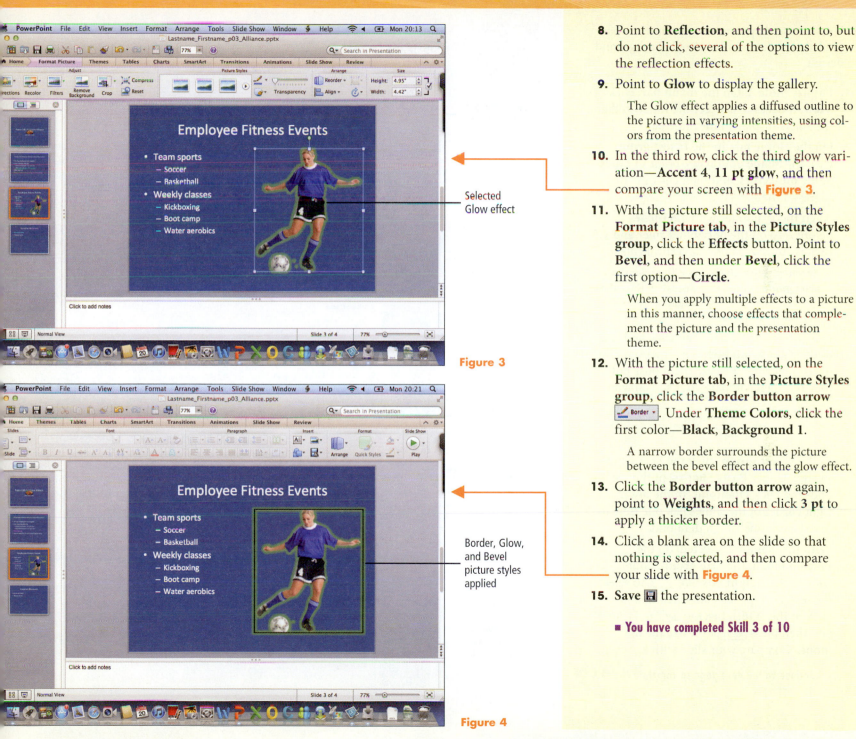

Selected Glow effect

Figure 3

Border, Glow, and Bevel picture styles applied

Figure 4

8. Point to **Reflection**, and then point to, but do not click, several of the options to view the reflection effects.

9. Point to **Glow** to display the gallery.

The Glow effect applies a diffused outline to the picture in varying intensities, using colors from the presentation theme.

10. In the third row, click the third glow variation—**Accent 4**, **11 pt glow**, and then compare your screen with **Figure 3**.

11. With the picture still selected, on the **Format Picture tab**, in the **Picture Styles group**, click the **Effects** button. Point to **Bevel**, and then under **Bevel**, click the first option—**Circle**.

When you apply multiple effects to a picture in this manner, choose effects that complement the picture and the presentation theme.

12. With the picture still selected, on the **Format Picture tab**, in the **Picture Styles group**, click the **Border button arrow** **✎ Border ▾**. Under **Theme Colors**, click the first color—**Black**, **Background 1**.

A narrow border surrounds the picture between the bevel effect and the glow effect.

13. Click the **Border button arrow** again, point to **Weights**, and then click **3 pt** to apply a thicker border.

14. Click a blank area on the slide so that nothing is selected, and then compare your slide with **Figure 4**.

15. Save **🖫** the presentation.

■ **You have completed Skill 3 of 10**

▶ You can use shapes as design elements, particularly on slides with a simple background design.

1. Display **Slide 2**. On the **menu bar**, click **View**, if necessary, select the Ruler so that the rulers display in the Slide pane.

2. On the **Home tab**, in the **Insert group**, click the **Shape** button 🔲, point to **Lines and Connectors**, and then click the first shape—**Line**.

3. Align the ⊕ pointer with **4.5 inches** before zero on the horizontal ruler and **2.5 inches** above zero on the vertical ruler.

   As you position the pointer, the ruler displays *guides*—lines that display in the rulers to give you a visual indication of where the pointer is positioned.

4. Hold down ⎵shift⎵, and then click and drag to the right to **4.5 inches** after zero on the horizontal ruler. Release the mouse button, and then compare your screen with **Figure 1**.

   To draw a straight line, press ⎵shift⎵ while dragging.

5. In the **Insert group**, click the **Shape** button 🔲. Under **Basic Shapes**, in the second row, click **Diamond**. In the lower right corner of the slide, click one time to insert a one-inch-high diamond.

6. With the diamond selected, on the **Format tab**, in the **Size group**, double-click in the **Height** box `Height: 5.09"` to select the text *1"*. Type 0.25 and then double-click in the **Width** box `Width: 5.07"`. Type 0.4 and then press ⎵return⎵ to resize the diamond. Compare your slide with **Figure 2**.

   ■ **Continue to the next page to complete the skill** ➤

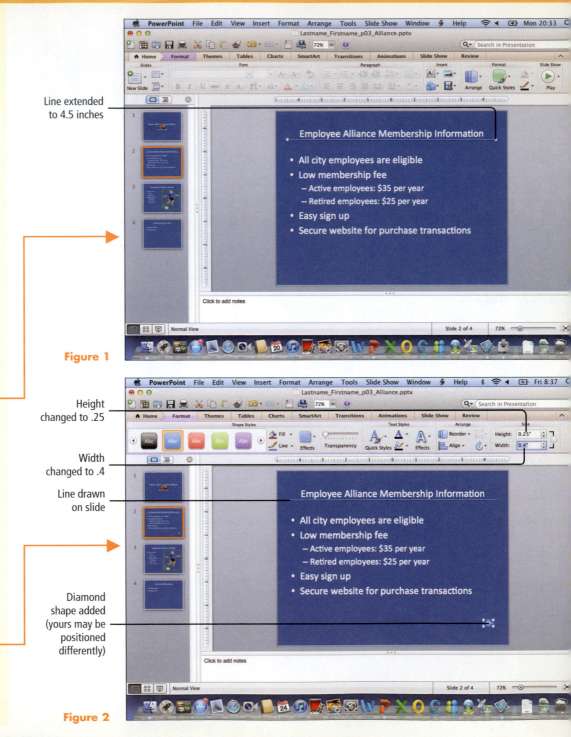

Line extended to 4.5 inches

Figure 1

Height changed to .25

Width changed to .4

Line drawn on slide

Diamond shape added (yours may be positioned differently)

Figure 2

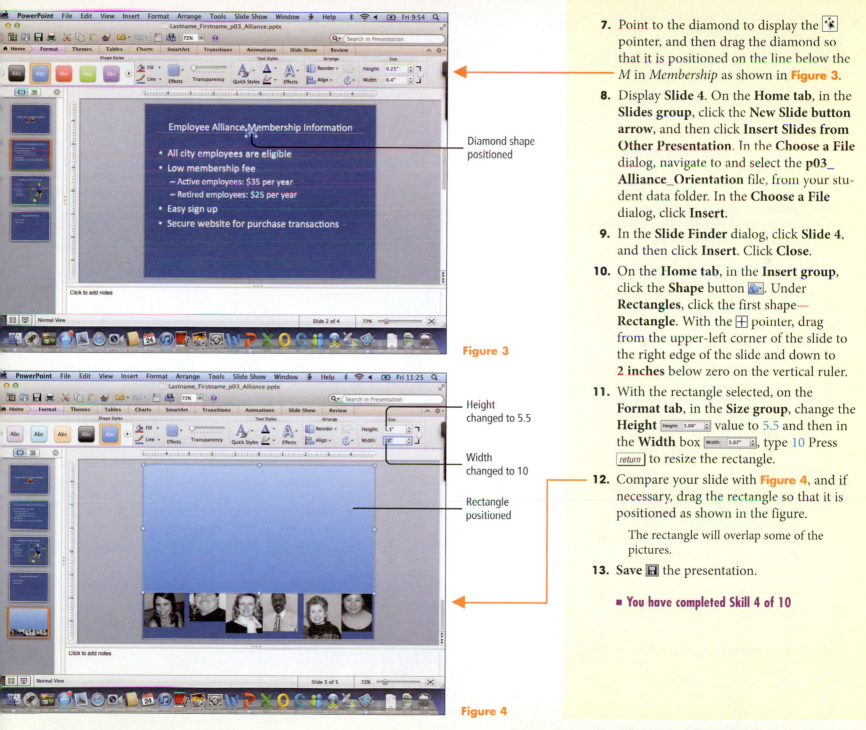

Figure 3

Figure 4

7. Point to the diamond to display the ✛ pointer, and then drag the diamond so that it is positioned on the line below the *M* in *Membership* as shown in **Figure 3**.

8. Display **Slide 4**. On the **Home tab**, in the **Slides group**, click the **New Slide button arrow**, and then click **Insert Slides from Other Presentation**. In the **Choose a File** dialog, navigate to and select the **p03_Alliance_Orientation** file, from your student data folder. In the **Choose a File** dialog, click **Insert**.

9. In the **Slide Finder** dialog, click **Slide 4**, and then click **Insert**. Click **Close**.

10. On the **Home tab**, in the **Insert group**, click the **Shape** button ⬛. Under **Rectangles**, click the first shape— **Rectangle**. With the ✛ pointer, drag from the upper-left corner of the slide to the right edge of the slide and down to **2 inches** below zero on the vertical ruler.

11. With the rectangle selected, on the **Format tab**, in the **Size group**, change the **Height** [Height: 5.09"] value to **5.5** and then in the **Width** box [Width: 5.07"], type **10** Press [return] to resize the rectangle.

12. Compare your slide with **Figure 4**, and if necessary, drag the rectangle so that it is positioned as shown in the figure.

The rectangle will overlap some of the pictures.

13. Save 🖫 the presentation.

■ **You have completed Skill 4 of 10**

Diamond shape positioned

Height changed to 5.5

Width changed to 10

Rectangle positioned

▶ A *text box* is an object used to position text anywhere on a slide.

▶ In addition to being used as design elements, shapes can be used as containers for text.

1. On **Slide 5**, if necessary, select the rectangle.

   To insert text in a shape, select the shape, and then begin to type.

2. Type Questions? Press return , and then type Contact an Employee Alliance Associate Press return , type (805) 555-1087 and then compare your slide with **Figure 1**.

   When you type text in a shape, it is centered both horizontally and vertically within the shape.

3. Select the three lines of text, and then change the **Font Size** to **40**.

4. With the three lines of text still selected, on the **Format tab**, in the **Text Styles group**, click the **Quick Styles More** button. Under **Applies to All Text in the Shape**, click the third thumbnail in the first row—**Fill - Red**, **Accent 2**, **Warm Matte Bevel**.

5. In the **Text Styles group**, click the **Text Fill button arrow** 🅰 · to display the gallery. Under **Theme Colors**, in the second column, click the first color—**White**, **Text 1**. Click in the grey area outside the slide so that nothing is selected, and then compare your slide with **Figure 2**.

   WordArt styles can be applied to the text in a shape.

   ■ Continue to the next page to complete the skill

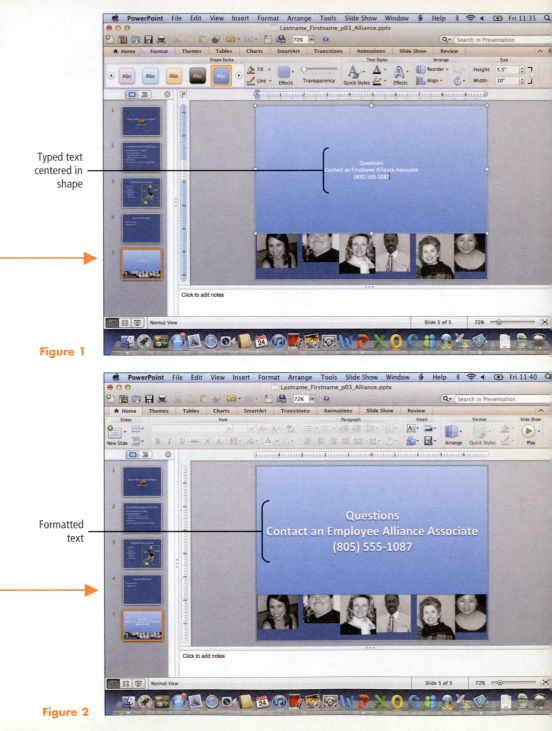

Typed text centered in shape

Figure 1

Formatted text

Figure 2

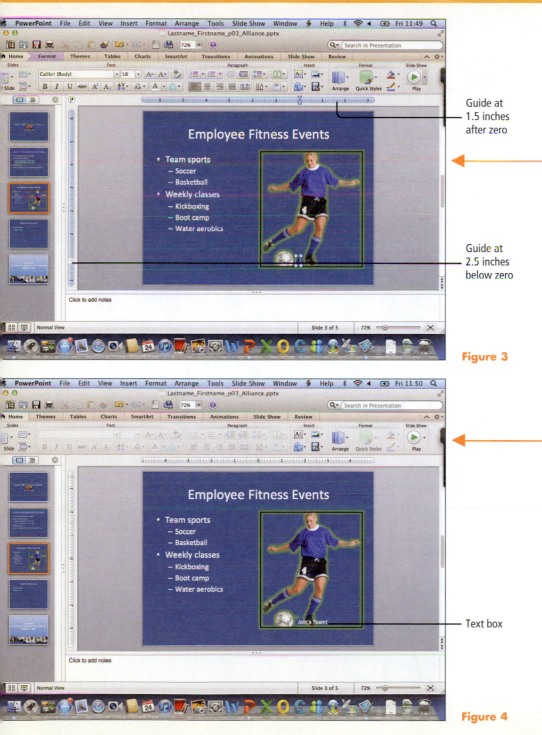

Guide at
1.5 inches
after zero

Guide at
2.5 inches
below zero

Figure 3

Text box

Figure 4

6. Display **Slide 3**. On the **Home tab**, in the **Insert group**, click the **Text** button [A], and then click **Text Box**. Position the pointer on the slide, aligned at **1.5 inches** after zero on the horizontal ruler and at **2.5 inches** below zero on the vertical ruler.

7. Without moving the pointer, click one time to insert a text box, as shown in **Figure 3**. Type Join a Team! If the text box displays one character at a time in a vertical line, on the Standard toolbar, click Undo, and then repeat Steps 6 and 7.

8. Click anywhere on the slide so that the text box is not selected.

   Unlike shapes, when a text box is inserted, it does not include borders or fill colors. Text inserted in a text box appears to be floating on the slide and is formatted in the same font as the body font used in content placeholders.

9. Compare your slide with **Figure 4**. If your text box is not positioned as shown in the figure, select the text box and then use the [▲], [▼], [◄], or [►] keys on your keyboard to *nudge*—move an object in small increments using the directional arrow keys— the text box so that it is positioned as shown.

10. **Save** [💾] the presentation.

   ■ **You have completed Skill 5 of 10**

▶ A *group* is a collection of multiple objects treated as one unit that can be copied, moved, or formatted.

1. Display **Slide 5**, and then select the rectangle. On the **Format tab**, in the **Text Styles group**, click the **Effects** button. Point to **Bevel**, and then click the second-to-last bevel—**Hard Edge**.

2. In the **Shape Styles group**, click the **Fill button arrow**, and then click **Fill Effects**. In the **Format Shape** dialog, click the **Gradient tab**, and then under **Styles and direction**, click the **Style** button, and then click **Radial**, as shown in **Figure 1** to apply a gradient fill to the shape. Click **OK**.

   A *gradient fill* is a gradual progression of colors and shades, usually from one color to another, or from one shade to another shade of the same color, to add a fill to a shape.

3. Display **Slide 2**. Select the diamond. Hold down shift, and then click the line so that both objects are selected as shown in **Figure 2**. If you selected one of the placeholders, click anywhere on the slide to deselect the objects, and then try again.

4. On the **Format tab**, in the **Arrange group**, click the **Align** button, and then click **Align Center**. In the **Arrange group**, click the **Align** button, and then click **Align Middle** to align the shapes.

   The line and the diamond move so that their center points are aligned.

5. With the objects selected, on the **Format tab**, in the **Arrange group**, click the **Group** button 🔲, and then click **Group**.

   Sizing handles enclose the objects as one unit.

■ **Continue to the next page to complete the skill**

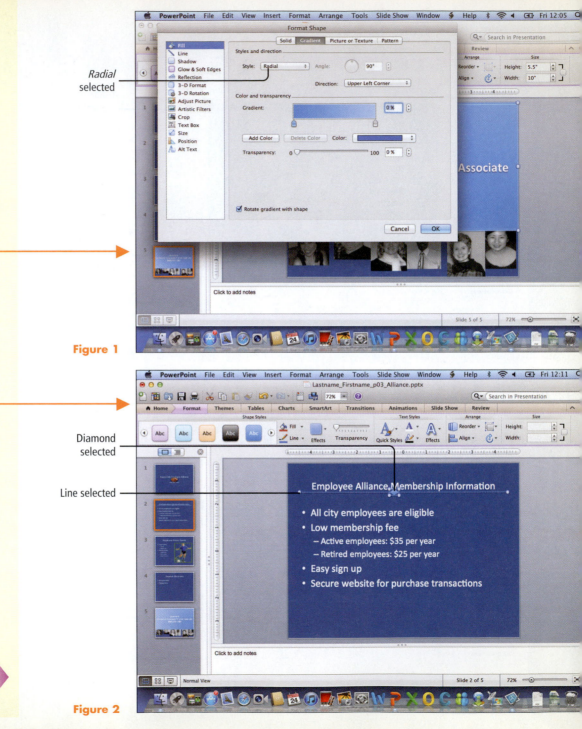

Radial selected

Figure 1

Diamond selected

Line selected

Figure 2

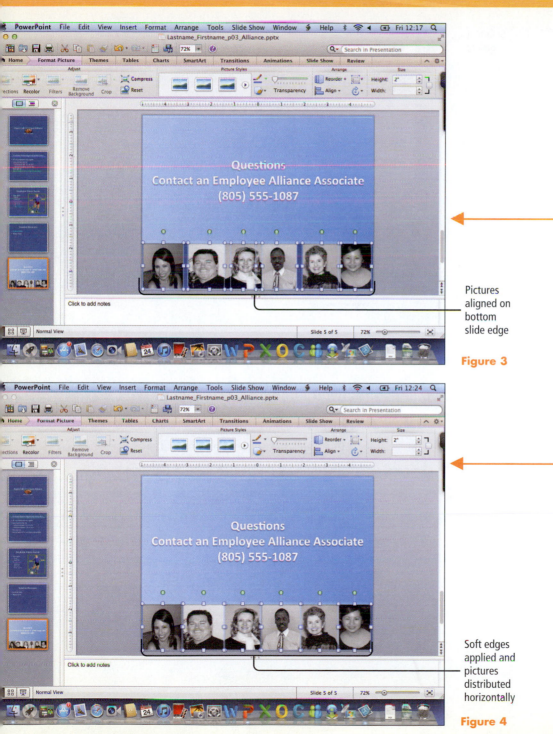

Pictures aligned on bottom slide edge

Figure 3

Soft edges applied and pictures distributed horizontally

Figure 4

6. Display **Slide 5**. Hold down shift, and then click each picture at the bottom of the slide so that all six of the pictures are selected. If you selected the rectangle, hold down shift, and then click the rectangle so that it is not selected.

7. On the **Format Picture tab**, in the **Arrange group**, click the **Align** button, and then click **Align to Slide**. Click the **Align** button, and then click **Align Bottom**. Compare your slide with **Figure 3**.

   The combination of the Align to Slide and Align Bottom options aligns the selected objects along the bottom of the slide.

8. With the pictures selected, on the **Format Picture tab**, in the **Picture Styles group**, click the **Effects** button. Point to **Shadow**, and then under **Outer**, click **Outside Bottom Right**.

9. With the pictures selected, on the **Format Picture tab**, in the **Arrange group**, click the **Align** button. Click **Align Selected Objects**. Click the **Align** button, and then click **Distribute Horizontally**. Compare your slide with **Figure 4**.

   With Align Selected Objects selected, the pictures distribute evenly between the left edge of the left picture and the right edge of the right picture.

10. With the pictures selected, in the **Arrange group**, click the **Group** button, and then click **Group**. In the **Arrange group**, click the **Align** button. Click **Align Center** to center the group on the slide.

11. **Save** the presentation.

   ■ **You have completed Skill 6 of 10**

▶ A *SmartArt graphic* is a designer-quality visual representation of information that you can use to communicate your message or ideas effectively.

▶ You can include text and pictures in a SmartArt graphic, and you can apply colors, effects, and styles that coordinate with the presentation theme.

▶ You can convert text that you have already typed—such as a list—into a SmartArt graphic.

1. Display **Slide 4**, and then click anywhere in the bulleted list. On the **SmartArt tab**, in the **Insert SmartArt group**, click the **List** button, and then compare your screen with **Figure 1**.

   A gallery displays with a large selection of SmartArt graphics.

2. Scroll down and review each of the SmartArt graphics.

   The eight types of SmartArt layouts are summarized in **Figure 2**.

   ■ **Continue to the next page to complete the skill**

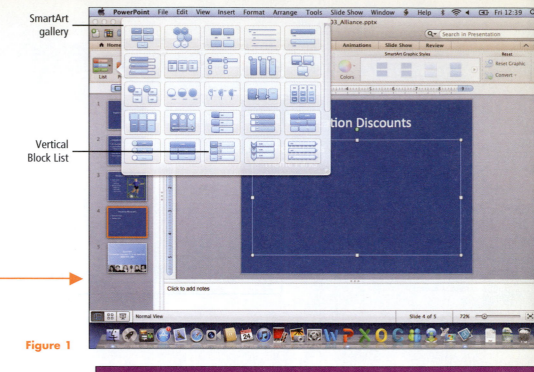

SmartArt gallery

Vertical Block List

Figure 1

Figure 2

Microsoft PowerPoint SmartArt Layout Types	
Type	**Purpose**
List	Illustrates nonsequential information.
Process	Illustrates steps in a process or timeline.
Cycle	Illustrates a continual process.
Hierarchy	Illustrates a decision tree or creates an organization chart.
Relationship	Illustrates connections.
Matrix	Illustrates how parts relate to a whole.
Pyramid	Illustrates proportional relationships, with the largest component on the top or bottom.
Picture	Communicates messages and ideas using pictures in each layout.

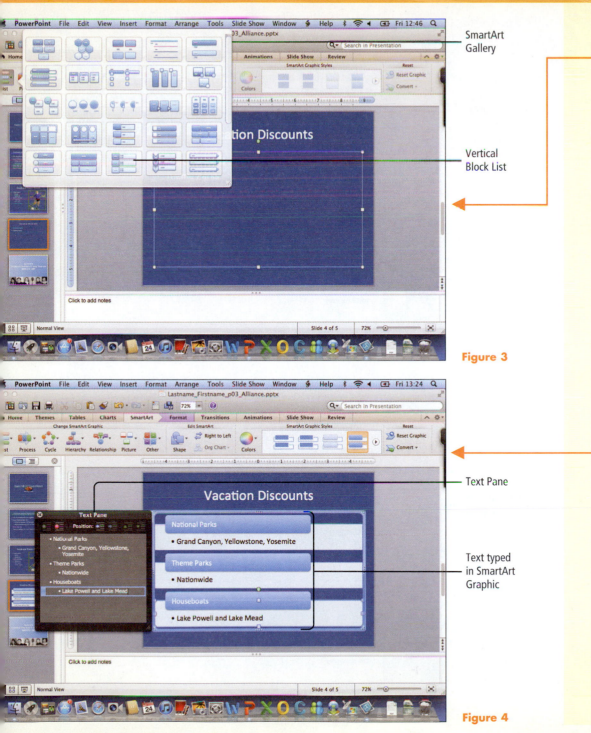

SmartArt Gallery

Vertical Block List

Figure 3

Text Pane

Text typed in SmartArt Graphic

Figure 4

3. Use the ScreenTips to locate **Vertical Block List**. Compare your screen with **Figure 3**.

4. Click the **Vertical Block List** thumbnail to convert the bulleted list to a SmartArt graphic.

   The Text Pane displays to the left of the SmartArt graphic.

5. If necessary, in the Text Pane, click to the right of the text *National Parks,* click the **Add Bullet** button to insert a shape below *National Parks.* Type Grand Canyon, Yellowstone, Yosemite In the **Text Pane**, click the **Position Right** button.

6. In the **Text Pane**, click to the right of the text *Theme Parks,* and then click the **Add Bullet** button. Click the **Position Right** button, and then type Nationwide.

7. With the insertion point after Nationwide, press return. Click the **Position Left** button.

8. Type Houseboats and then press return. Click the **Position Right** button and then type Lake Powell and Lake Mead

9. Compare your screen with **Figure 4**, and then **Save** the presentation.

   ■ **You have completed Skill 7 of 10**

► When you create a SmartArt graphic, choose a layout that provides the best visual representation of your information.

► The colors that you apply to a SmartArt graphic are coordinated with the presentation color theme.

► SmartArt styles include gradient fills and 3-D effects.

1. On **Slide 4**, if necessary, select the SmartArt graphic. On the **SmartArt tab**, in the **Change SmartArt Graphic group**, click **Picture**. Point to **Captioned Pictures** as shown in **Figure 1**.

2. Click the **Captioned Pictures** thumbnail to convert the SmartArt to the Captioned Pictures layout.

3. In the SmartArt, in the first rectangle, click the **Insert Picture from File** button [icon]. Navigate to the location where your student files are stored, click **p03_Alliance_Canyon**, and then click **Insert**.

4. In the middle rectangle, use the technique just practiced to insert **p03_Alliance_Park**, and then in the last rectangle, insert **p03_Alliance_Boat**. Compare your slide with **Figure 2**. If you moved the mouse when you clicked the Insert Picture from File button, the shape may have moved. If this happened, click Undo to reposition the shape, and then try again.

   ■ **Continue to the next page to complete the skill**

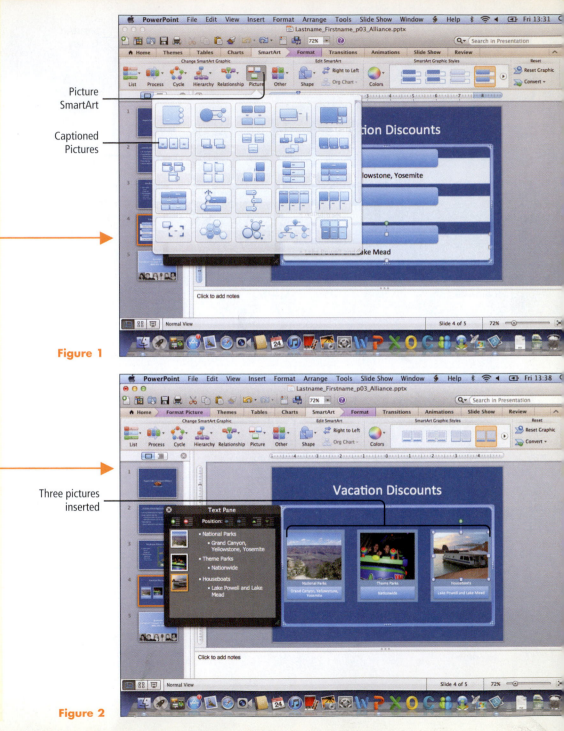

Picture SmartArt

Captioned Pictures

Figure 1

Three pictures inserted

Figure 2

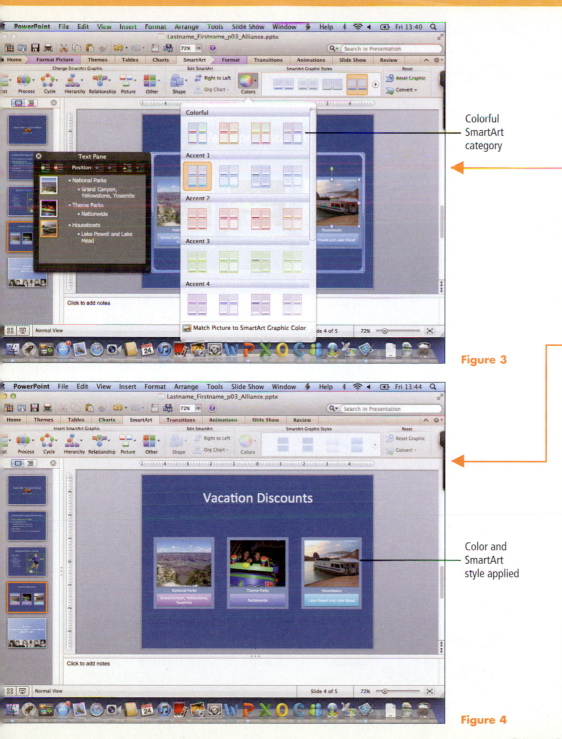

Figure 3

Figure 4

5. In the **SmartArt Graphic Styles group**, click the **Colors** button to display the **Color** gallery.

> The colors that display in the gallery coordinate with the color theme.

6. Point to several of the color options. Then, under **Colorful**, point to the fourth style—**Colorful Range - Accent Colors 4 to 5**—as shown in **Figure 3**.

7. Click **Colorful Range - Accent Colors 4 to 5** to apply the color change to the SmartArt graphic.

8. On the **SmartArt tab**, in the **SmartArt Graphic Styles group**, click the **More** button to display the **SmartArt Styles** gallery. Point to several of the styles. Click the fourth style—**Moderate Effect**. Click in a blank area of the slide, and then compare your screen with **Figure 4**.

9. Save the presentation.

■ **You have completed Skill 8 of 10**

Colorful SmartArt category

Color and SmartArt style applied

► You can insert, size, and move video files in a presentation, and you can control when the video will begin to play during a slide show.

1. Display **Slide 1**, and then insert a **New Slide** with the **Title and Content** layout. In the title placeholder, type Justin Tamari, AFEA Director

2. In the content placeholder, click the **Insert Movie from File** button ▣, and then navigate to the location where your student files are stored. Click **p03_Alliance_ Director**, and then click **Insert**. Alternately, on the Standard toolbar, click Insert, point to Movie, and then click Movie from File. Compare your screen with **Figure 1**.

   The video displays in the center of the slide, and playback and volume controls display in the video controller below the video. Video formatting and editing tools display on the Ribbon.

3. Be sure that the speakers are on, or insert headphones into the computer. On the video controller below the video, point to the **Play/Pause** button ▶ so that it is highlighted.

4. Click the **Play/Pause** button ▶ to view the video, and then compare your screen with **Figure 2**. If necessary, on your keyboard, click the Mute/Unmute button to adjust the volume on your system.

   As the video plays, the video controller displays the time that has elapsed since the start of the video.

   ■ **Continue to the next page to complete the skill** ➤

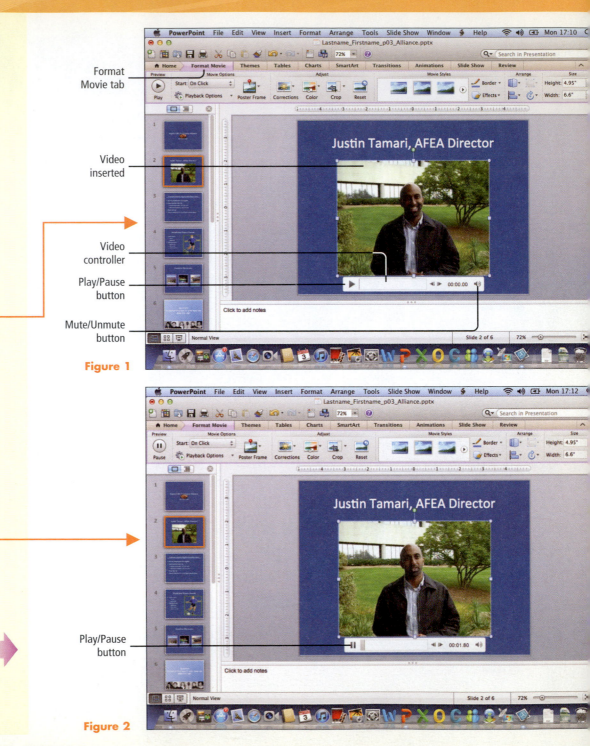

Format Movie tab

Video inserted

Video controller

Play/Pause button

Mute/Unmute button

Figure 1

Play/Pause button

Figure 2

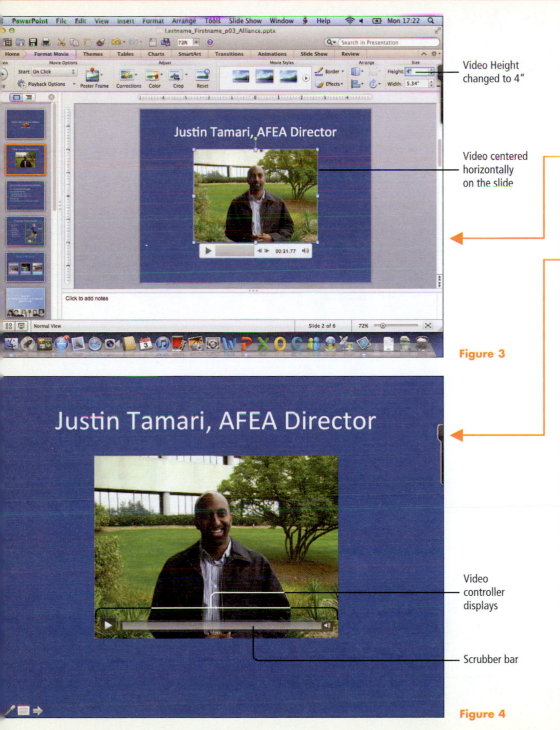

Video Height changed to 4″

Video centered horizontally on the slide

Figure 3

Justin Tamari, AFEA Director

Video controller displays

Scrubber bar

Figure 4

5. On the **Format Movie tab**, in the **Size group**, click in the **Height** box ▭. Type 4 and then press ⎕. Notice that the video width adjusts proportionately. On the **Format Movie tab**, in the **Arrange group**, click the **Align** button ▭, and then click **Align Center** to center the video horizontally on the slide. Compare your screen with **Figure 3**.

6. On the left side of the status bar, in the **View** buttons, click the **Slide Show** button ▭ to display **Slide 2** in the slide show. Point to the video to display the ▭ pointer, and then compare your screen with **Figure 4**.

   When you point to the video during the slide show, the video controller displays.

7. With the ▭ pointer displayed, click the mouse button to view the video. When the video is finished, press ⎕ to exit the slide show.

8. If necessary, select the video. On the **Format Movie tab**, in the **Movie Options group**, click the **Start arrow**, and then click **Automatically**. In the **View** buttons, click the **Slide Show** button ▭ to display **Slide 2** in the slide show. When the video is finished, press ⎕ to exit the slide show.

   The Start Automatically option begins the video when the slide displays in the slide show. You can use this option if you want the video to begin playing without clicking the mouse button.

9. **Save** ▭ the presentation.

   ■ **You have completed Skill 9 of 10**

▶ You can apply styles and effects to a video and change the video shape and border.

▶ You can recolor a video so that it coordinates with the presentation theme.

1. On **Slide 2**, if necessary, select the video. On the **Format Movie tab**, in the **Movie Styles group**, click the **More** button 🔽. In the **Movie Styles** gallery, under **Moderate**, click the seventh style—**Snip Diagonal Corner**, **Gradient**. Click on a blank area of the slide, and then compare your screen with **Figure 1**.

2. Select the video. On the **Format Movie tab**, in the **Movie Styles group**, click the **Effects** button. Point to **Shadow**, and then if necessary, scroll down to display the **Perspective** options.

3. Under **Perspective**, click the second thumbnail—**Perspective Upper Right**.

4. With the video selected, on the **Format Movie tab**, in the **Adjust group**, click the **Color** button.

   The Recolor gallery displays colors from the presentation theme that you can apply to the video.

5. Point to several of the thumbnails to view the color change, and then click the second thumbnail—**Grayscale**—to change the color of the video. Compare your slide with **Figure 2**.

6. On the **Format Movie tab**, in the **Adjust group**, click the **Color** button, and then click the first thumbnail—**No Recolor**—to change the video color back to the original.

   ■ **Continue to the next page to complete the skill**

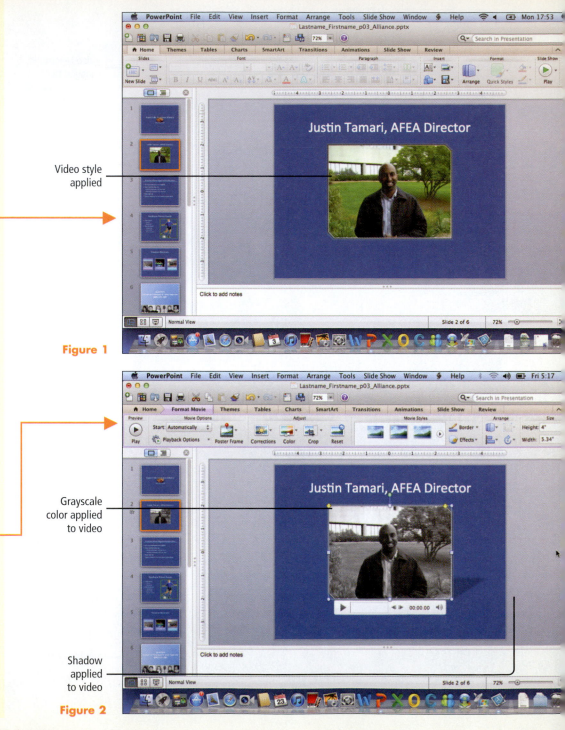

Video style applied

Figure 1

Grayscale color applied to video

Shadow applied to video

Figure 2

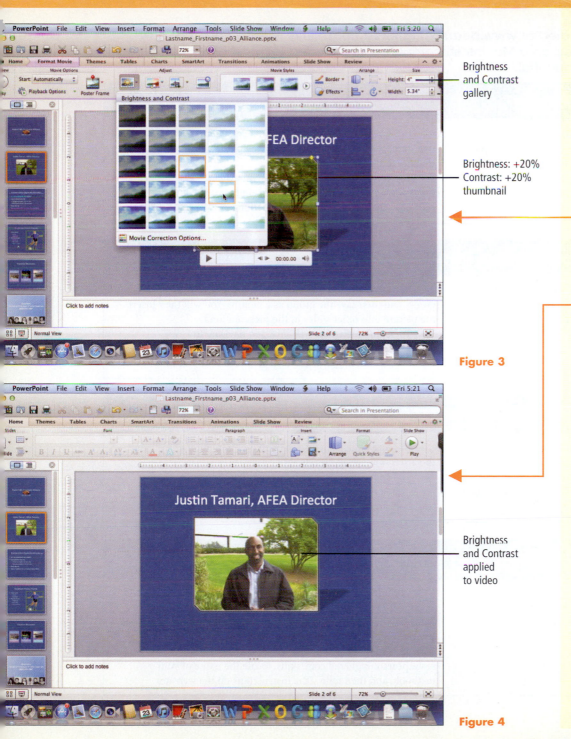

Brightness and Contrast gallery

Brightness: +20% Contrast: +20% thumbnail

Figure 3

Brightness and Contrast applied to video

Figure 4

7. With the video selected, on the **Format Movie tab**, in the **Adjust group**, click the **Corrections** button to display the **Brightness and Contrast** gallery.

 The Brightness and Contrast gallery displays combinations of brightness and contrast adjustments that you can apply to a video to improve color and visibility.

8. In the fourth row, point to the fourth thumbnail to display the ScreenTip **Brightness: +20% Contrast: +20%** as shown in **Figure 3**.

9. Click **Brightness: +20% Contrast: +20%** to apply the correction to the video, and then click anywhere on the slide so that the video is not selected. Compare your screen with **Figure 4**.

10. On the **Transitions tab**, in the **Transition to This Slide group**, click the **More** button ⬇. Under **Exciting**, click **Switch**. In the **Apply To group**, click **All Slides**. On the **Slide Show tab**, in the **Play Slide Show group**, click **From Start**, and then click the mouse button to advance the presentation. At the end, click one more time to return to your slides.

11. Insert a **Header & Footer** on the **Notes and Handouts** that includes the **Date and time**, a **Page number**, and, using your own name, the **Footer** Lastname_Firstname_p03_Alliance

12. **Save** 🖫 the presentation. Print or submit the file as directed by your instructor. **Quit** PowerPoint.

 Done! You have completed Skill 10 of 10, and your presentation is complete!

The following More Skills are located at **www.pearsonhighered.com/skills.** Please note that only More Skills that can be performed on a Macintosh computer are included in this section; therefore, the numbering is not always sequential.

More Skills Compress Pictures

The large file sizes of pictures from digital cameras or scanners can slow the delivery of a presentation and make your presentation files large. You can compress the presentation pictures so that the file size is smaller.

In More Skills 11, you will open a presentation, view the file size, compress the pictures in the presentation, and then view the changes to the file size.

To begin, open your web browser, navigate to www.pearsonhighered.com/skills, locate the name of your textbook, and then follow the instructions on the website.

More Skills Save Groups as Picture Files

A group can be saved as a picture file so that you can insert it on another slide, insert it in another presentation, or use it in other programs. In this way, saving a group as a picture facilitates easy sharing among presentations and applications.

In More Skills 12, you will open a presentation, create a group, and then save the group as a picture. You will then insert the picture into other slides in the presentation.

To begin, open your web browser, navigate to www.pearsonhighered.com/skills, locate the name of your textbook, and then follow the instructions on the website.

More Skills Change Object Order

When objects such as shapes and pictures are inserted on a slide, they often overlap. The first object inserted is positioned at the bottom of the stack, and the next object inserted is above the first object. You can change the order in which objects overlap by moving them backward and forward in the stack.

In More Skills 13, you will open a presentation and change the order of inserted objects.

To begin, open your web browser, navigate to www.pearsonhighered.com/skills, locate the name of your textbook, and then follow the instructions on the website.

More Skills Design Presentations Using Appropriate Graphics

When you are creating a presentation, the graphics that you choose affect how your message is perceived by your audience. Thus, it is important to choose appropriate graphics for every presentation that you create.

In More Skills 14, you will review design principles that will assist you in choosing appropriate graphics for your slides. You will view two slides and compare the different messages conveyed when different graphics are used.

To begin, open your web browser, navigate to www.pearsonhighered.com/skills, locate the name of your textbook, and then follow the instructions on the website.

Key Terms

Gradient fill 360

Group 360

Guides 356

Nudge 359

Picture effects 354

SmartArt graphic 362

Text box 358

Online Help Skills

1. **Start** Safari or another web browser. In the **address bar**, type microsoft.com/ mac/how-to and then press return to display the home page for Microsoft Office Mac.

   This website provides you with helpful links to get started, find out what is new, and tutorials about Office 2011.

2. Under **Product Help**, click **PowerPoint 2011**.

3. Under **PowerPoint Help**, click the **Movies and Audio** link.

4. Click **Set the play options for a movie in your presentation**, and then compare your screen with **Figure 1**.

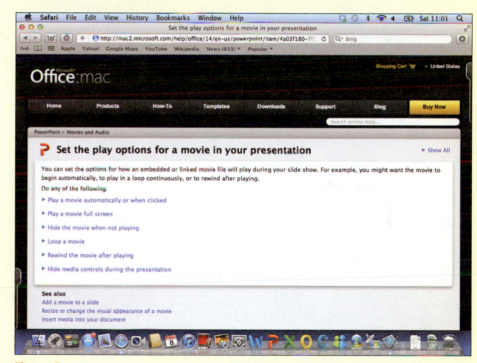

Figure 1

5. Read the displayed content under each link, and then answer the following questions. How can you set a slide to automatically play a movie? What does it mean to *loop a movie*? How do you hide media controls during a slide show?

Matching

Match each term in the second column with its correct definition in the first column by writing the letter of the term on the blank line in front of the correct definition.

___ **1.** A command used to insert slides from another presentation into an existing presentation so that content does not need to be recreated.

___ **2.** Formatting options applied to pictures that include shadows, reflections, glows, soft edges, bevels, and 3-D rotations.

___ **3.** Lines that display in the rulers to give you a visual indication of where the pointer is positioned.

___ **4.** Objects such as lines and circles that can be used as design elements on a slide.

___ **5.** An object used to position text anywhere on a slide.

___ **6.** The action of moving an object in small increments by using the directional arrow keys.

___ **7.** Multiple objects treated as one unit that can be copied, moved, or formatted.

___ **8.** A fill effect in which one color fades into another.

___ **9.** A designer-quality visual representation of information that you can use to communicate your message or ideas effectively by choosing from among many different layouts.

___ **10.** A command used to change a list into a SmartArt graphic.

A Convert to SmartArt Graphic

B Gradient fill

C Group

D Guides

E Nudge

F Picture effects

G Reuse Slides

H Shapes

I SmartArt graphic

J Text box

Multiple Choice

Choose the correct answer.

1. The task pane that is used to insert slides from another presentation.
   - A. Insert Slides
   - B. Browse Slides
   - C. Reuse Slides

2. The name of the box in which the height of a picture can be changed.
   - A. Height Size
   - B. Shape Height
   - C. Crop Height

3. The default alignment applied to text typed in a shape.
   - A. Left
   - B. Center
   - C. Right

4. A SmartArt layout type that illustrates non-sequential information.
   - A. Process
   - B. Cycle
   - C. List

5. A SmartArt layout type that illustrates a continual process.
   - A. Hierarchy
   - B. Cycle
   - C. Process

6. A SmartArt layout type that illustrates a decision tree or creates an organization chart.
   - A. Relationship
   - B. Hierarchy
   - C. Pyramid

7. A SmartArt layout type that illustrates connections.
   - A. Relationship
   - B. Hierarchy
   - C. Pyramid

8. The tab in which video Start options are found.
   - A. Format Movie
   - B. Playback
   - C. Design

9. The button that displays video Brightness and Contrast options.
   - A. Color
   - B. Design
   - C. Corrections

10. The button that displays the video Recolor gallery.
    - A. Color
    - B. Design
    - C. Corrections

Topics for Discussion

1. Some PowerPoint presenters advocate using slides that consist of a single statement and a graphic so that the presentation reads like a story. Other presenters advocate using slides that combine the "single statement and graphics" approach with slides that include detail in the form of bullet points, diagrams, and pictures. What is the advantage of each of these approaches? Which approach would you prefer to use?

2. Sharing presentation slides among employees in an organization is a common practice. What types of information and objects do you think should be included on slides that are shared within an organization?

Skill Check

To complete this presentation, you will need the following files:

- p03_Fitness
- p03_Fitness_Classes
- p03_Fitness_Information

You will save your presentations as:

- **Lastname_Firstname_p03_Fitness**
- **Lastname_Firstname_p03_Fitness2**
- **Lastname_Firstname_p03_Fitness3**
- **Lastname_Firstname_p03_Fitness4**

1. **Start** PowerPoint, open **p03_Fitness**, and then display **Slide 3**. On the **Home tab**, in the **Slides group**, click the **New Slide button arrow**. Click **Insert Slides from Other Presentation**.

2. In the **Choose a File** dialog, navigate to your student files, click **p03_Fitness_Classes**, and then click **Insert**. In the **Slide Finder** dialog, click **Slide 2**, click **Insert**, and then **Close** the pane. **Save** your presentation in your **PowerPoint Chapter 3** folder, using your own name, as Lastname_Firstname_p03_Fitness

3. Display **Slide 2**. In the content placeholder, click the **Clip Art Browser** button. In the **Media** task pane, click the **All Images arrow**, and then click **People**. Scroll down, and then drag the image of the athlete—**rbs1_00** to the slide. **Close** the task pane. Compare your screen with **Figure 1**.

4. With the picture selected, on the **Format Picture tab**, in the **Size group**, change the **Height** to 3.75 and then press return. Drag the picture to center it within the blue rectangle on the right side of the slide.

5. On the **Format Picture tab**, in the **Adjust group**, click the **Crop button arrow**, and then click **Mask to Shape**. Point to **Rectangles**, click **Rounded Rectangle**. In the **Picture Styles group**, click the **Picture Effects button**, point to **Bevel**, and then under **Bevel**, click the first effect—**Circle**.

6. On the **Home tab**, in the **Insert group**, click **Insert an Item**, and then click **Text Box**. Align the pointer at **0.5 inches** after zero on the horizontal ruler and at **2 inches** below zero on the vertical ruler, and then click. Type Join a Class! Click in a blank area of the slide, and then compare your slide with **Figure 2**.

7. On **Slide 3**, in the content placeholder, click the **Insert Movie from File** button. From your student files, insert **p03_Fitness_Information**. On the **Format Movie tab**, in the **Size group**, change the **Height** to 3.5 and then drag the video so that it is centered in the dark blue rectangle.

■ **Continue to the next page to complete this Skill Check** ▶

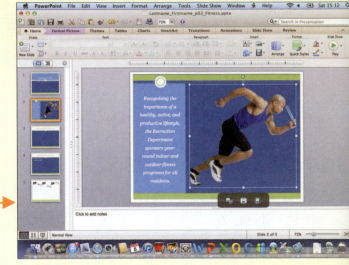

Figure 1

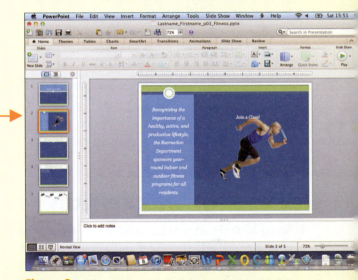

Figure 2

8. On the **Format Movie tab**, in the **Movie Options group**, click the **Start arrow**, and then click **Automatically**. In the **Movie Styles group**, click the **More** button, and then under **Subtle**, select **Glow Rectangle**.

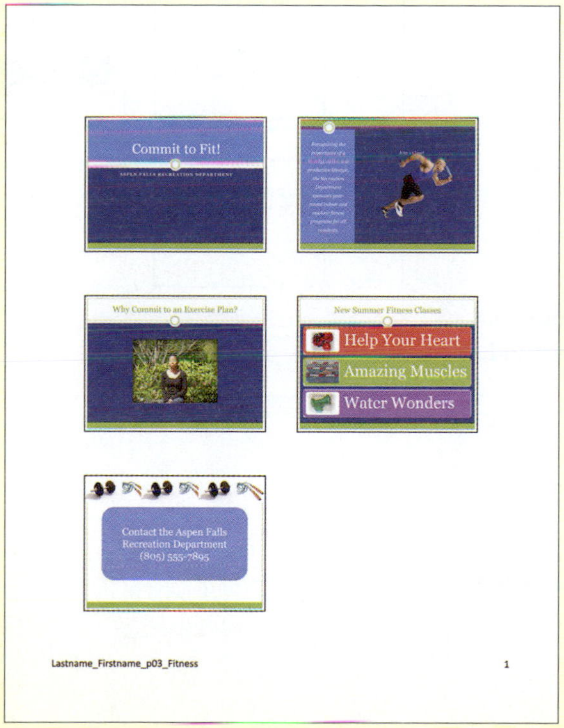

9. On **Slide 4**, click the bulleted list. On the **SmartArt tab**, in the **Insert SmartArt Graphic group**, click **Picture**. Scroll down the gallery, and then locate and click **Vertical Picture List**.

10. On the **Text Pane**, click the **Add Shape** button, and then type Water Wonders

11. In the first shape, click the **Insert Picture from File** button. From your student files, insert **p03_Fitness2**. In the second shape, insert **p03_Fitness3**. In the last shape, insert **p03_Fitness4**.

12. Change the SmartArt colors to **Colorful - Accent Colors**, and then apply the first 3-D SmartArt style **Polished**. Compare your slide with **Figure 3**.

13. Display **Slide 5**. Hold down ⌈ shift ⌉, and then click each picture. On the **Format Picture tab**, in the **Arrange group**, click the **Align** button, and then click **Align to Slide**. Click the **Align** button, and then click **Align Top**.

14. With the pictures selected, click the **Align** button, and then click **Align Selected Objects**. Click the **Align** button, and then click **Distribute Horizontally**.

15. In the **Arrange group**, click the **Group** button, and then click **Group**.

16. On the **Home tab**, in the **Insert group**, click **Shapes**. Under **Rectangles**, click **Rounded Rectangle**. Align the pointer with **4 inches** before zero on the horizontal ruler and with **2 inches** above zero on the vertical ruler. Drag to draw a rectangle that extends to **4 inches** after zero on the horizontal ruler and to **2 inches** below zero on the vertical ruler.

17. In the shape, type Contact the Aspen Falls Recreation Department and then press ⌈ return ⌉. Type (805) 555-7895 and then change the **Font Size** to **40** for all of the text in the shape. Apply the **Flip** transition to all of the slides.

18. View the slide show. Insert a **Header and Footer** on the **Notes and Handouts** with a **Page number** and, using your own name, the **Footer** Lastname_Firstname_p03_Fitness **Save** your presentation, and then compare it with **Figure 4**. Print or submit the file as directed by your instructor.

Done! You have completed the Skill Check

Figure 3

Figure 4

Assess Your Skills 1

To complete this presentation, you will need the following files:

- p03_Vendors
- p03_Vendors_Events

You will save your presentation as:

- Lastname_Firstname_p03_Vendors

1. **Start** PowerPoint, and then from your student files, open **p03_Vendors**. With **Slide 1** displayed, click the **Insert Slides from Other Presentation**, and then insert **Slide 3—Summer Events**—from the student data file **p03_Vendors_Events**. **Save** your presentation in your **PowerPoint Chapter 3** folder, using your own name, as Lastname_Firstname_p03_Vendors

2. On **Slide 2**, convert the text to a SmartArt **Horizontal Bullet List**. Change the SmartArt color to **Colorful Range - Accent Colors 4 to 5**, and then apply the **3-D Cartoon** SmartArt style.

3. On **Slide 4**, insert a **Rectangle** basic shape. Draw the shape so that it extends from **4.5 inches** before zero on the horizontal ruler and **0 inches** on the vertical ruler to **4.5 inches** after zero on the horizontal ruler and **2.5 inches** below zero on the vertical ruler.

4. In the shape, type Summer events in Aspen Falls garner large tourist numbers. During the past five years, overall attendance has increased by 19 percent, and tourist spending has increased by 23 percent.

5. Increase the **Font Size** to **24**, and then change the **Font Color** to **Black, Text 1**. Apply a **Glow** shape effect—**Orange, 18 pt glow, Accent color 5**.

6. On **Slide 1**, insert a **Clip Art** image by selecting the **Photos** category. Insert the picture with the yellow sun, as shown in **Figure 1**. If you cannot locate the picture, choose another appropriate picture.

7. Change the **Height** of the picture to 3.5 Change the **Width** of the picture to 3.5 and then change the shape to a **32-Point Star**—the last shape in the third row under **Stars and Banners**. Using the **Align to Slide** option, change the alignment to **Align Center** and **Align Bottom**.

8. Insert a **Header and Footer** on the **Notes and Handouts** that includes a **Page number** and, using your own name, the **Footer** Lastname_Firstname_p03_Vendors **Save** your presentation, and then compare it with **Figure 1**. Print or submit the file as directed by your instructor.

Done! You have completed Assess Your Skills 1

Figure 1

Assess Your Skills 3 and 4 can be found at **www.pearsonhighered.com/skills**.

Assess Your Skills 2

To complete this presentation, you will need the following files:

- p03_Paths
- p03_Paths_Greenway

You will save your presentation as:

- Lastname_Firstname_p03_Paths

Lastname_Firstname_p03_Paths   1

Figure 1

1. **Start** PowerPoint, and then from your student files, open **p03_Paths**. Save your presentation in your **PowerPoint Chapter 3** folder, using your own name, as Lastname_Firstname_p03_Paths

2. Display **Slide 2**, and then change the picture shape to the last shape under **Rectangles—Rounded Diagonal Corner Rectangle**. Apply the first **Bevel** effect—**Circle**—and then apply an **Accent 2, 8 pt glow** picture effect.

3. Insert a **Text Box** positioned just below the lower left corner of the picture. Type View from Hacienda Point and then change the **Font Size** to **24** and the **Font Color** to **Light Yellow, Text 2**. Select the slide title, the picture, and the text box, and then align the selected objects using the **Align Center** option.

4. Display **Slide 3**, and then in the content placeholder, from your student files, insert the video **p03_Paths_Greenway**. Apply the **Intense, Reflected Perspective Right** video style, and then change the **Video Options** so that the video starts **Automatically** during the slide show.

5. **Adjust** the video by changing the **Corrections** option to **Brightness: 0% (Normal) Contrast: +20%**.

6. Display **Slide 4**, and then convert the bulleted list to a SmartArt Graphic with the

Alternating Flow layout located in the **Process** types. Change the SmartArt color to **Colored Fill - Accent 3**, and then apply the 3-D **Inset** SmartArt style.

7. On **Slide 5**, insert a **Wave** Stars and Banners shape that extends from **4 inches** before zero on the horizontal ruler and **2 inches** above zero on the vertical ruler to **4 inches** after zero on the horizontal ruler and **0** on the vertical ruler. Type Grand Opening on March 20 and then change the **Font Size** to **40**.

8. Apply a **Bevel** shape effect—**Angle**.

9. Display **Slide 6**, and then align the four pictures by using the **Align Bottom** option. With the **Align to Slide** option selected, distribute the pictures horizontally. Apply a **Soft Edge Rectangle** effect, and then **Group** the pictures. View the slide show from the beginning.

10. Insert a **Header and Footer** on the **Notes and Handouts** that includes a **Page number** and, using your own name, the **Footer** Lastname_Firstname_p03_Paths

11. Compare your completed presentation with **Figure 1**. **Save** the presentation, and then print or submit the file as directed by your instructor.

Done! You have completed Assess Your Skills 2

Assess Your Skills Visually

To complete this presentation, you will need the following file:

- p03_Process

You will save your presentation as:

- Lastname_Firstname_p03_Process

Start PowerPoint, and then from your student files, open **p03_Process**. Format and edit the slide as shown in **Figure 1**. **Save** the file, using your own name, as Lastname_Firstname_p03_Process in your **PowerPoint Chapter 3** folder.

To complete this slide, apply the **Civic** theme and apply the **Solstice** theme colors. The content placeholder text is sized at **22** points. For the SmartArt graphic, use the **Repeating Bending Process** layout. After you create the SmartArt, drag the *Improve* shape so that it is centered as shown in **Figure 1**. Add a **Footer** to the **Notes and Handouts** with the file name and page number, and then print or submit the file as directed by your instructor.

Done! You have completed Assess Your Skills Visually

Figure 1

Skills in Context

To complete this presentation, you will need the following file:

- New blank PowerPoint presentation

You will save your presentation as:

- Lastname_Firstname_p03_Programs

Using the following information, create a presentation with an appropriate theme, and then create four slides that describe new programs offered to city employees. The presentation will be part of a larger presentation on employee benefits. On one slide, convert the text to a SmartArt graphic describing the programs, and then format the SmartArt appropriately. Insert and format at least one Clip Art image illustrating the programs.

To improve employee health and productivity, the City of Aspen Falls is offering several voluntary programs to city employees. The first program—*A City in Motion*—offers a free pedometer so that employees can record the number of steps taken each day. Human Resources will provide maps of walking routes adjacent to various city offices for those who want to walk with colleagues before or

after work or during lunch. The second program is *Fit in Aspen Falls*. All city employees are eligible to receive discounts on individual and family memberships at local fitness centers. The third program—*Wellness through the Week*—is a series of classes held during lunch hours or immediately after work, including yoga, preventive health care, stress reduction, health and nutrition, and more.

Save the presentation, using your own name, as Lastname_Firstname_p03_Programs Add a **Footer** to the **Notes and Handouts** with the file name and page number, and then print or submit the file as directed by your instructor.

Done! You have completed Skills in Context

Skills and You

To complete this presentation, you will need the following file:

- New blank PowerPoint presentation

You will save your presentation as:

- Lastname_Firstname_p03_Careers

Using the skills you have practiced in this chapter, create a presentation with an appropriate theme that includes four to six slides describing a career in which you are interested. On one slide, convert the text to a SmartArt graphic that either lists the credentials that you need or demonstrates the process that you must follow to be successful in this career. Insert and format pictures on at least two slides that illustrate people who have chosen this career.

Save the presentation, using your own name, as Lastname_Firstname_p03_Careers Add a **Footer** to the **Notes and Handouts** with the file name and page number, and then check spelling in the presentation. Print or submit the file as directed by your instructor.

Done! You have completed Skills and You

CHAPTER 4

Present Data Using Tables, Charts, and Animation

- ▶ Tables and charts are used to present information in an organized manner that enables the audience to understand important data with ease.

- ▶ When possible, use charts to display numeric data, particularly when making comparisons between data.

- ▶ Use chart and table styles to apply formatting in a manner that complements the presentation theme.

- ▶ Animation effects enhance a presentation by drawing attention to important slide elements, particularly when the timing of animation effects is precisely controlled during a slide show.

- ▶ Use animation in a manner that focuses audience attention on important slide information.

©Surpasspro | Dreamstime.com

Aspen Falls City Hall

In this chapter, you will create documents for the Aspen Falls City Hall, which provides essential services for the citizens and visitors of Aspen Falls, California. In this project, you will edit a presentation that summarizes the City of Aspen Falls Retirement fund and membership. You will insert and format a table, pie chart, and column chart, and you will apply and modify entrance and effects.

Time to complete all
10 skills – 60 to 75 minutes

Student data file needed for this chapter:

p04_Fund

Outcome

Using the skills in this chapter, you will be able to work with PowerPoint presentations like this:

You will save your presentation as:

Lastname_Firstname_p04_Fund

SKILLS

Skills 1-10 Training

At the end of this chapter you will be able to:

Skill 1 Insert Tables
Skill 2 Modify Table Layouts
Skill 3 Apply Table Styles
Skill 4 Insert Column Charts
Skill 5 Edit and Format Charts
Skill 6 Insert Pie Charts
Skill 7 Apply Animation Entrance and Emphasis Effects
Skill 8 Modify Animation Timing and Use Animation Painter
Skill 9 Remove Animation and Modify Duration
Skill 10 Navigate Slide Shows

MORE SKILLS

Skill 12 Insert Hyperlinks in a Presentation
Skill 14 Design Presentations with Appropriate Animation

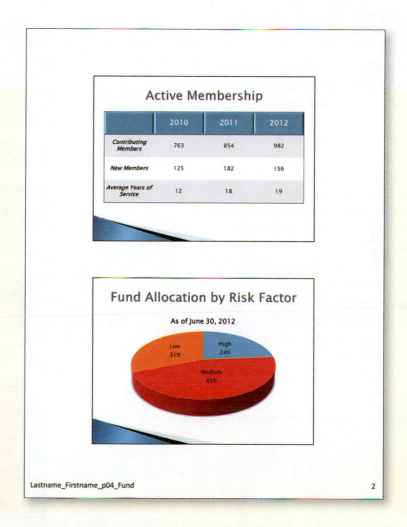

► In a presentation, a **table** is used to organize and present information in columns and rows.

► In tables, text is typed into a **cell**—the intersection of a column and row.

1. **Start** PowerPoint. From your student files, open **p04_Fund**. On the **menu bar**, click **File**, and then click **Save As**. Navigate to the location where you are saving your files, create a folder named PowerPoint Chapter 4 and then, using your own name, **Save** the presentation as Lastname_Firstname_p04_Fund

2. Display **Slide 2**, and then insert a **New Slide** with the **Title and Content** layout. In the title placeholder, type Active Membership and then **Center** 🔳 the title.

3. In the content placeholder, click the **Insert Table** button 🔲.

4. In the **Insert Table** dialog, in the **Number of columns** box, type 3 and then press `tab`. In the **Number of rows** box, type 2 and then compare your screen with **Figure 1**. ────

5. Click **OK** to create a table with three columns and two rows.

6. In the first row, click in the second cell. Type 2011 and then press `tab`.

   Pressing `tab` moves the insertion point to the next cell in the same row.

7. Type 2012 and then compare your table with **Figure 2**. ────

   ■ **Continue to the next page to complete the skill** ➤

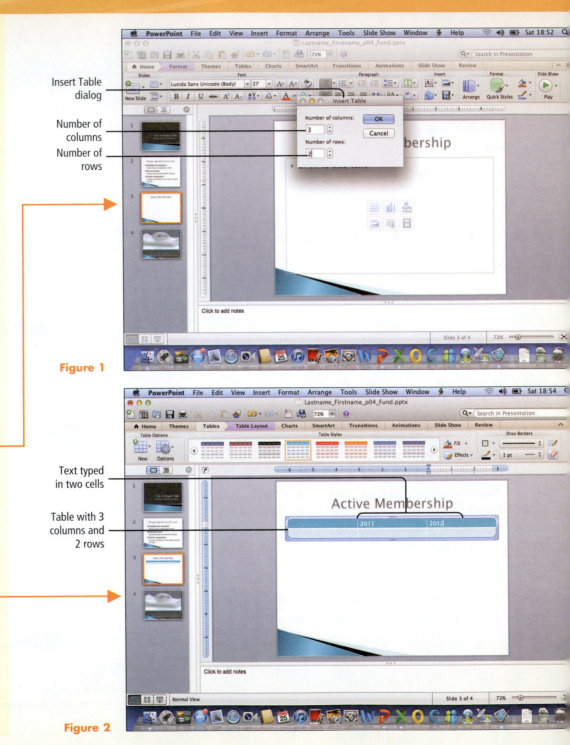

Insert Table dialog

Number of columns

Number of rows

Figure 1

Text typed in two cells

Table with 3 columns and 2 rows

Figure 2

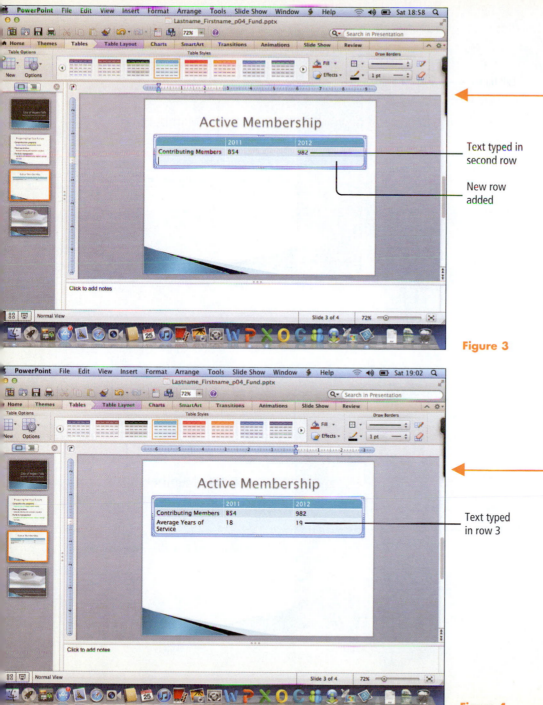

Figure 3

Figure 4

8. Press `tab` to move the insertion point to the first cell in the second row. With the insertion point positioned in the first cell of the second row, type Contributing Members and then press `tab`. Type 854 and then press `tab`. Type 982 and then press `tab` to insert a new blank row. Compare your table with **Figure 3**.

> When the insertion point is positioned in the last cell of a table, pressing `tab` inserts a new blank row at the bottom of the table.

9. In the first cell of the third row, type Average Years of Service and then press `tab`. Type 18 and then press `tab`. Type 19 and then compare your screen with **Figure 4**. If you inadvertently inserted a blank row in the table by pressing `tab`, on the Standard toolbar you can click Undo to remove it.

10. Save 🖫 the presentation.

■ **You have completed Skill 1 of 10**

▶ You can modify the layout of a table by inserting or deleting rows and columns and by changing the height and width of rows and columns.

▶ The height and width of the entire table can also be modified.

1. Click in any cell in the second column, and then click the **Table Layout tab**. In the **Rows & Columns group**, click the **Left** button.

   A new second column is inserted and the width of every column is adjusted so that all four columns are the same width.

2. Click in the first cell in the second column. Type 2010 and then click in the second cell in the second column. Type 763 and then click in the last cell in the second column. Type 12 and then compare your table with **Figure 1**.

3. With the insertion point positioned in any cell of the third row, on the **Table Layout tab**, in the **Rows & Columns group**, click the **Above** button to insert a new third row.

4. In the first cell of the row you just inserted, type New Members and then press [tab]. Type the remaining three entries, pressing [tab] to move from cell to cell: 125 and 182 and 156 Compare your slide with **Figure 2**.

   When you need to delete a row or column, click in the row or column that you want to delete, and then in the Rows & Columns group, click Delete. A list will display with the option to delete columns, rows, or the entire table.

   ■ **Continue to the next page to complete the skill** ➡

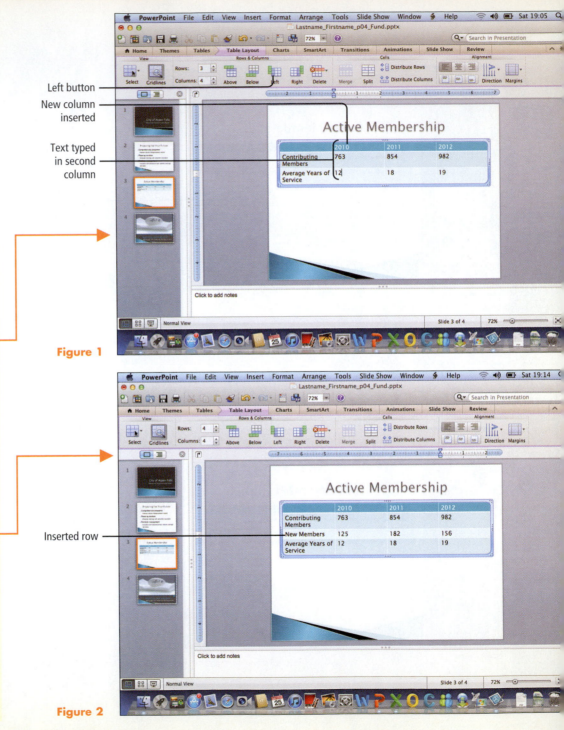

Left button
New column inserted
Text typed in second column

Figure 1

Inserted row

Figure 2

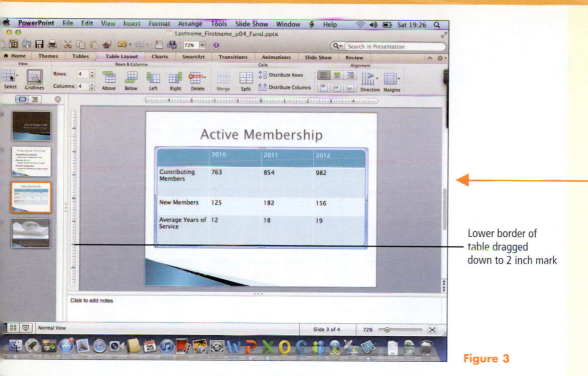

Lower border of table dragged down to 2 inch mark

Figure 3

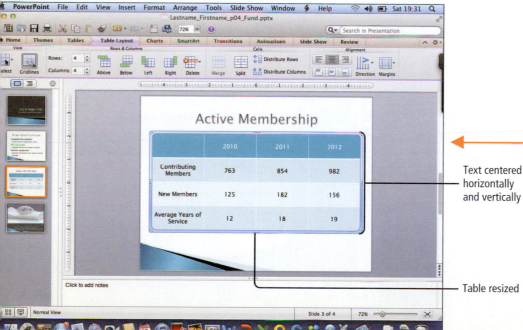

Text centered horizontally and vertically

Table resized

Figure 4

5. At the center of the lower border surrounding the table, point to the four dots—the sizing handle—to display the ⊞ pointer.

6. With the ⬍ pointer, drag down until the lower edge of the table extends to the **2 inches** mark below zero on the vertical ruler, and then release the mouse button to size the table. Compare your screen with **Figure 3**.

7. Click in the first cell of the table. On the **Table Layout tab**, in the **Cells group**, click the **Distribute Rows** button.

   The Distribute Rows button adjusts the height of the rows in the table so that they are equal. If you do not select any rows, all of the table rows are adjusted. When you want to distribute certain table rows equally, select only the rows that you want to distribute. To distribute the width of columns equally, use the Distribute Columns button.

8. On the **Table Layout tab**, in the **View group**, click the **Select** button, and then click **Select Table**. In the **Alignment group**, click the **Center Text** button ▤, and then click the **Align Text Middle** button ▥.

   All of the text in the table is centered horizontally and vertically within the cells.

9. Compare your table with **Figure 4**, and then **Save** 🖫 your presentation.

   ■ **You have completed Skill 2 of 10**

► A *table style* applies borders and fill colors to the entire table in a manner consistent with the presentation theme.

► Four color categories exist within the table styles—Best Match for Document, Light, Medium, and Dark.

1. Click in any cell in the table. On the **Tables tab**, in the **Table Styles group**, click the **More** button ⬇. In the **Table Styles** gallery, point to each of the styles.

2. Under **Medium**, in the third row, point to the second style—**Medium Style 3 - Accent 1**—as shown in **Figure 1**.

3. Click **Medium Style 3 - Accent 1**.

   The cells in the first table row are filled with a blue color. In the remaining rows, the fill color alternates between white and light gray.

4. On the **Tables tab**, in the **Table Options group**, click **Options**, and then click **Banded Rows** to remove the checkmark.

   The Table Options group controls where table style formatting is applied. For example, when the Banded Rows option is cleared, the alternating fill colors are cleared from the table rows, and only the header row contains a fill color.

5. In the **Table Options group**, click **Options**, and then click **Banded Rows** to reapply the light gray fill color to alternating rows. Compare your slide with **Figure 2**.

   ■ **Continue to the next page to complete the skill**

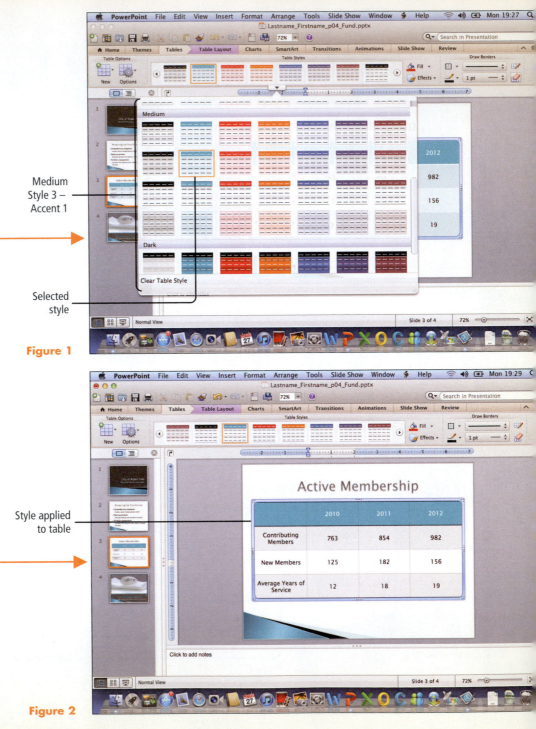

Medium Style 3 – Accent 1

Selected style

Figure 1

Style applied to table

Figure 2

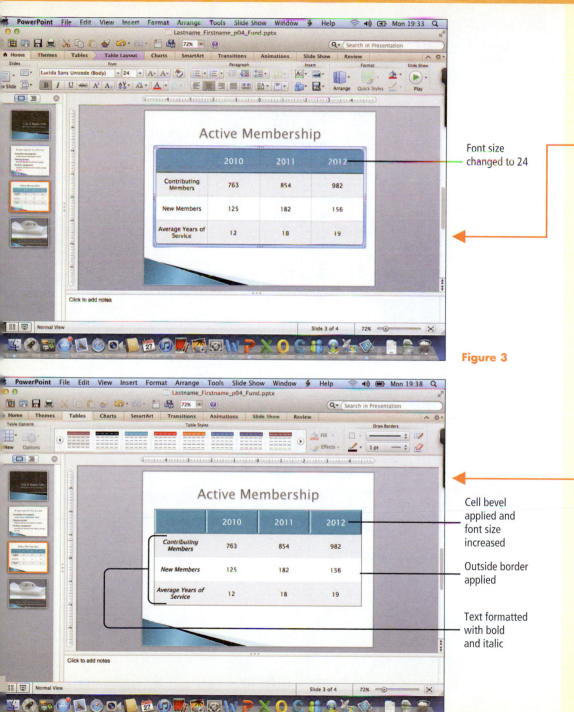

Figure 3

Font size
changed to 24

Cell bevel
applied and
font size
increased

Outside border
applied

Text formatted
with bold
and italic

Figure 4

6. Move the pointer to the left of the first row in the table to display the **Select Row** ➡ pointer, and then click the mouse button to select the row.

7. With the first row in the table selected, on the **Home tab**, in the **Font group**, change the **Font Size** to **24**. Compare as shown in **Figure 3**.

8. With the first row still selected, on the **Tables tab**, in the **Table Styles group**, click the **Effects** button. Point to **Cell Bevel**, and then under **Bevel**, click the first bevel—**Circle**—to apply the effect to the first table row.

9. In the first column, drag to select the second, third, and fourth cells. On the **Home tab**, in the **Font group**, apply **Bold**, and then apply **Italic**.

10. On the **Table Layout tab**, in the **View group**, click **Select**, and then click **Select Table**. On the **Tables tab**, in the **Draw Borders group**, click the **Borders button arrow**, and then click **Outside Borders**.

11. Click in a blank area of the slide, and then verify that a thin border displays on the outside edges of the table as shown in **Figure 4**. **Save** the presentation.

■ **You have completed Skill 3 of 10**

► A *chart* is a graphic representation of numeric data.

► A *column chart* is useful for illustrating comparisons among related categories.

1. With **Slide 3** displayed, on the **Home tab**, insert a **New Slide** with the **Title and Content** layout. In the title placeholder, type Fund Rate of Return by Risk Factor and then change the **Font Size** 18 ▾ to **36**. **Center** ≡ the title.

2. In the content placeholder, click the **Insert Chart** button ▮. On the **Charts tab**, in the **Insert Chart group**, click **Column**, as shown in **Figure 1**. ───

3. Under **2-D Column**, click the first chart— **Clustered Column**—and then compare your screen with **Figure 2**. ───

The Excel application starts. On your screen, an Excel worksheet displays columns and rows that intersect to form cells. A cell is identified by its column letter and row number.

The worksheet contains sample data in a data range outlined in blue, from which the chart in the PowerPoint window is generated. The column headings—*Series 1, Series 2,* and *Series 3*—display in the chart *legend*, which identifies the patterns or colors that are assigned to the data in the chart. The row headings—*Category 1, Category 2, Category 3,* and *Category 4*—display along the left side of the chart as *category labels*— labels that identify the categories of data in a chart.

■ **Continue to the next page to complete the skill** ➤

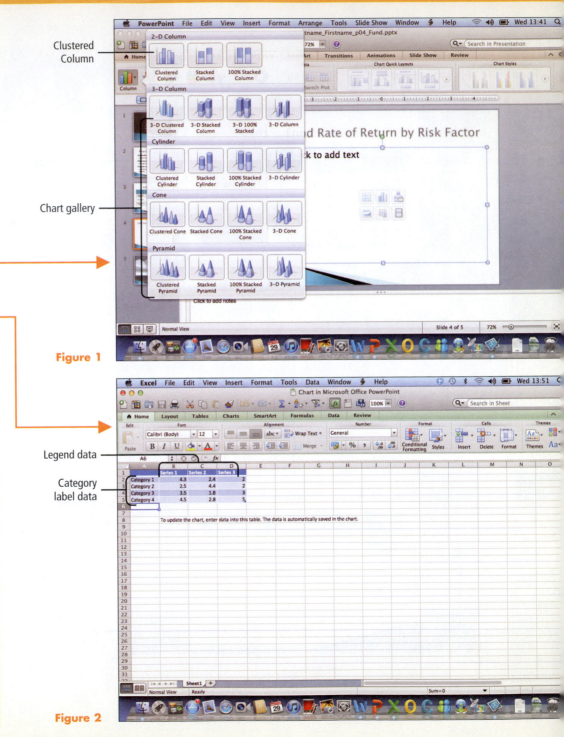

Clustered Column

Chart gallery

Figure 1

Legend data

Category label data

Figure 2

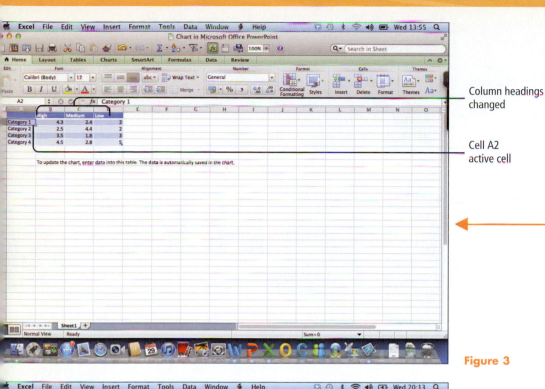

Column headings changed

Cell A2 active cell

Figure 3

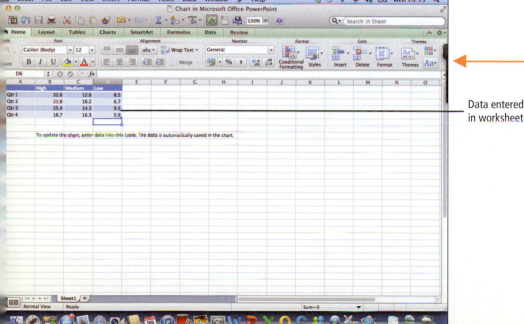

Data entered in worksheet

Figure 4

4. In the **Excel** window, click in cell **B1**. Type High and then press [tab] to move to cell **C1**. In the PowerPoint window, the chart legend is updated to reflect the change in the Excel worksheet.

5. In cell **C1**, type Medium and then press [tab]. In cell **D1**, type Low and then press [tab]. Compare your screen with **Figure 3**, and verify that cell A2 is selected.

   When the rightmost cell in a blue, outlined range of data is selected, pressing [tab] makes the first cell in the next row active.

6. Beginning in cell **A2**, type the following data, pressing [tab] to move from cell to cell:

	High	Medium	Low
Qtr 1	22.6	12.6	8.5
Qtr 2	21.8	16.2	6.7
Qtr 3	25.4	14.3	9.5
Qtr 4	18.7	16.3	5.9

7. In cell **D5**, which contains the number 5, type 5.9 and then press [return]. Compare your screen with **Figure 4**. If you have made any typing errors, click in the cell that you want to change, and then retype the data.

8. On the **menu bar**, click **Excel**, and then click **Quit Excel**.

   You are not prompted to save the Excel worksheet because the worksheet data is part of the PowerPoint presentation. When you save the presentation, the Excel data is saved with it.

9. **Save** 🖫 the presentation.

   ■ **You have completed Skill 4 of 10**

▶ After a chart is created, you can edit the data values in the Excel worksheet. Changes made in the Excel worksheet immediately display in the PowerPoint chart.

▶ Charts are formatted by applying predefined styles and by modifying chart elements.

1. On Slide 4, if necessary, click the chart so that it is selected. On the **Charts tab**, in the **Data group**, click **Edit** to display the Excel worksheet.

   Each of the twelve cells containing the numeric data that you entered are *data points*—individual data plotted in a chart. Each data point is represented in the chart by a *data marker*—a column, bar, or other symbol that represents a single data point. Related data points form a *data series* and are assigned a unique color or pattern represented in the chart legend. Here there is a data series for *High,* one for *Medium,* and one for *Low.*

2. In the **Excel** worksheet, click cell **B2**, which contains the value *22.6.* Type 18.5 and press ⎆return⎆, return to PowerPoint, and then notice the chart change. Compare your screen with **Figure 1**.

   In the chart, the first data marker in Qtr 1 is decreased to reflect the change to the data.

3. In the **Excel** worksheet, click cell **D5**, which contains the value *5.9.* Type 7.2 and then press ⎆return⎆. Compare your screen with **Figure 2**.

4. On the **menu bar**, click **Excel**, and then click **Quit Excel**.

   ■ **Continue to the next page to complete the skill**

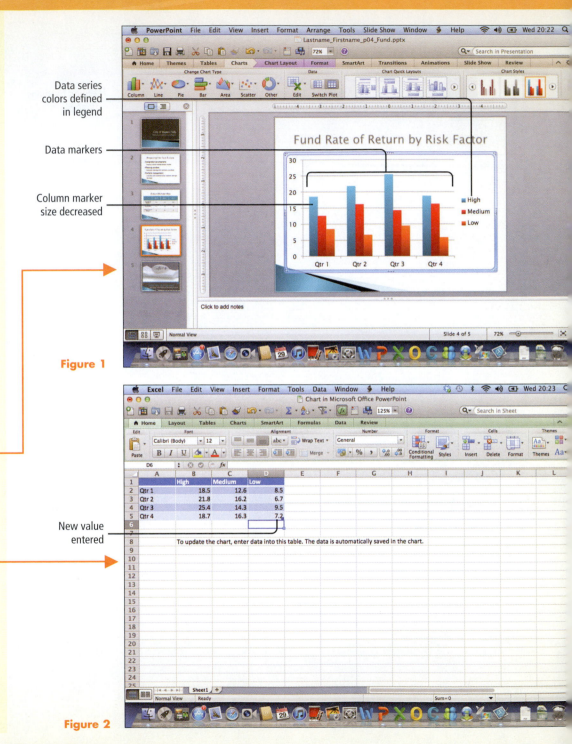

Data series colors defined in legend

Data markers

Column marker size decreased

Figure 1

New value entered

Figure 2

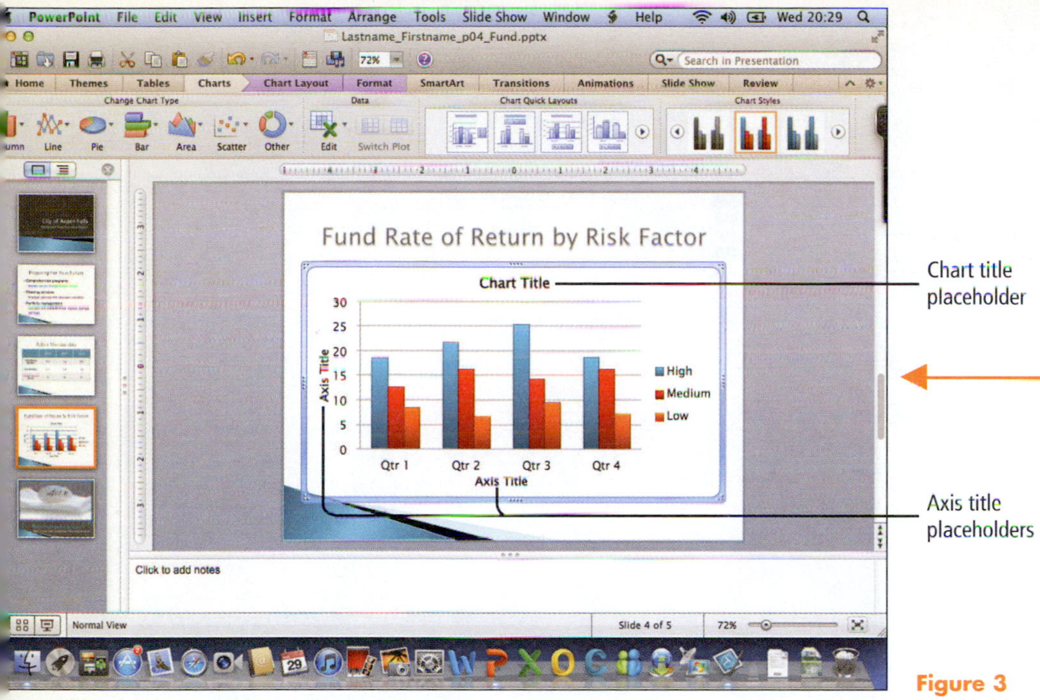

Figure 3

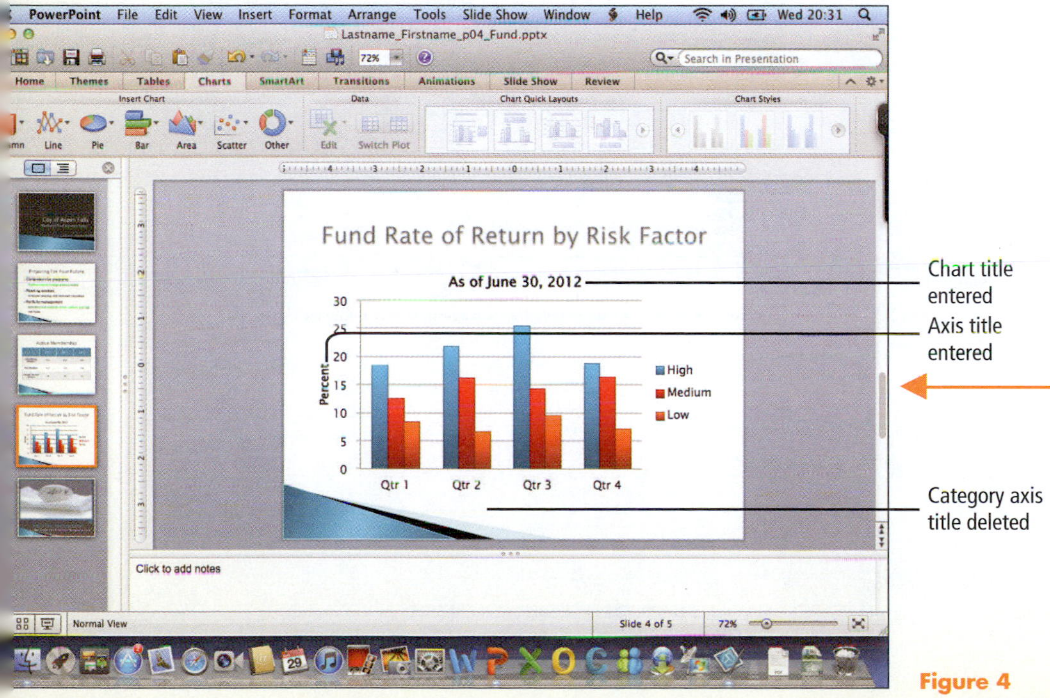

Figure 4

5. With the chart selected, on the **Charts tab**, in the **Chart Styles group**, click the **More** button to display the **Chart Styles** gallery.

   A ***chart style*** is a prebuilt set of effects, colors, and backgrounds designed to work with the presentation theme. For example, you can have flat or beveled columns, colors that are solid or transparent, and backgrounds that are dark or light.

6. The thumbnails in the **Chart Style** gallery are numbered sequentially. In the second column, in the fourth row locate and click **Style 26**.

7. On the **Charts tab**, in the **Chart Quick Layouts group**, click the **More** button to display the **Chart Quick Layouts** gallery, which provides options for adding and positioning chart elements such as titles. Click the ninth layout—**Layout 9**—and then compare your slide with **Figure 3**.

   Placeholders for the chart title and axis titles display.

8. Click the **Chart Title** placeholder, and then type As of June 30, 2012 Below the chart, click the **Axis Title** placeholder, and then press delete to remove the category axis title. To the left of the chart, click the **Axis Title** placeholder. Type Percent and then click on a blank area of the slide so that the chart is not selected. Compare your slide with **Figure 4**.

9. **Save** the presentation.

■ **You have completed Skill 5 of 10**

▶ A *pie chart* is used to illustrate percentages or proportions and includes only one data series.

▶ When creating a chart, you may need to delete unwanted data from the Excel worksheet so that it does not display in the chart.

1. Display **Slide 3**, and then add a **New Slide** with the **Title and Content** layout. In the title placeholder, type Fund Allocation by Risk Factor and then **Center** ≡ the title.

2. In the content placeholder, click the **Insert Chart** button ▥. On the **Charts tab**, in the **Insert Chart group**, click **Pie**. Under **3-D Pie**, click first chart—**3-D Pie**.

3. In the displayed **Excel** worksheet, click cell **B1**, which contains the word *Sales*. Type Amount and then press `tab`. Type High and then press `tab`. Type 293 and then press `tab`. Type Medium and then press `tab`. Type 562 and then press `tab`. Type Low and then press `tab`. Type 388 and then press `tab`. Compare your screen with **Figure 1**.

   The sample data in the worksheet contains two columns and five rows as defined by the blue style in the worksheet. In this chart, the 4th Qtr data in row 5 is unnecessary.

4. In the **Excel** worksheet, position the pointer over the row heading **5** so that the ➡ pointer displays. With the ➡ pointer displayed, click to select the row, as shown in **Figure 2**.

   ■ **Continue to the next page to complete the skill**

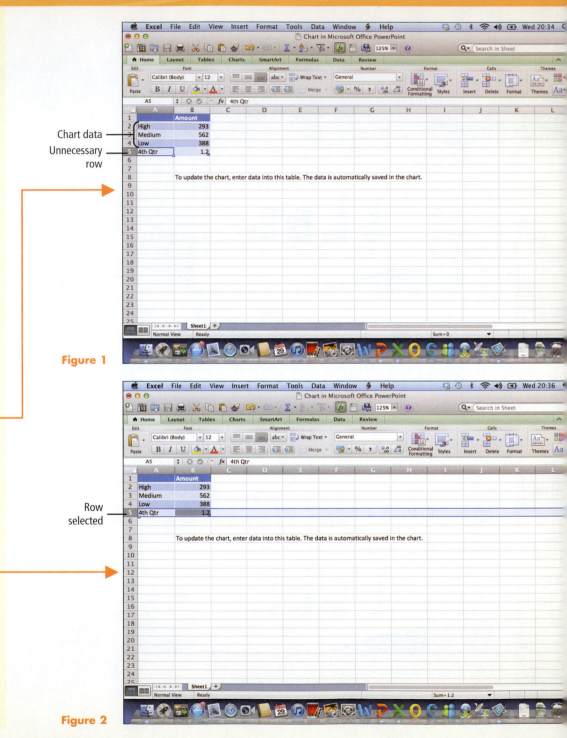

Chart data

Unnecessary row

Figure 1

Row selected

Figure 2

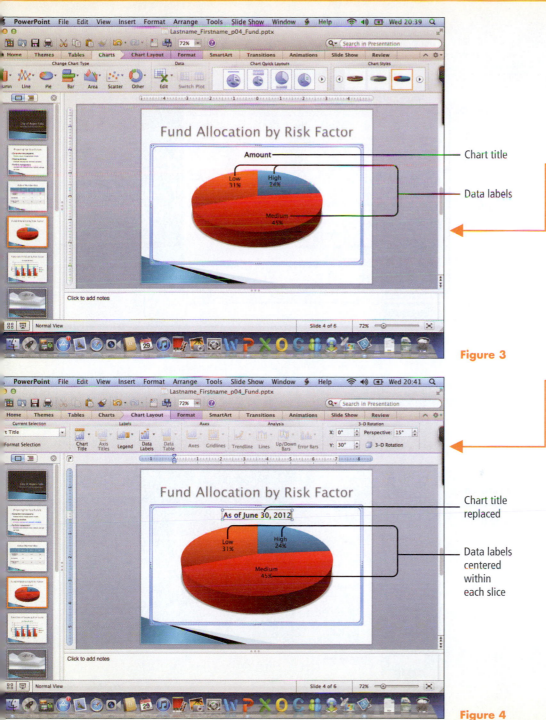

Figure 3

Figure 4

5. On the **Home tab**, in the **Cells group**, click **Delete** to delete the extra row from the worksheet.

6. On the **menu bar**, click **Excel**, and then click **Quit Excel**.

7. In PowerPoint, on the **Charts tab**, in the **Chart Quick Layouts group**, click the first layout—**Layout 1**. Compare your screen with **Figure 3**.

> Recall that a pie chart includes one data series. Thus, the legend is usually omitted and *data labels*—text that identifies data markers—are positioned on or outside of the pie slices. Layout 1 displays a title and the category names and the percentage that each slice represents of the total.

8. Click anywhere in the chart title—*Amount*—so that the title is selected. Type As of June 30, 2012 to replace the title.

9. On the **Chart Layout tab**, in the **Labels group**, click **Data Labels**, and then click **Center**. Compare your slide with **Figure 4**.

> The data labels are centered within each pie slice.

10. On the **Charts tab**, in the **Chart Styles group**, click the **More** button. In the second column, second row, click **Style 10**, and then **Save** the presentation.

■ **You have completed Skill 6 of 10**

Chart title

Data labels

Chart title replaced

Data labels centered within each slice

► *Animation* adds a special visual or sound effect to an object on a slide.

1. Display **Slide 1**. On the **Transitions tab**, in the **Transition to This Slide group**, click **Wipe**, and then in the **Apply To group**, click the **All Slides** button.

2. Click in the title. On the **Animations tab**, in the **Entrance Effects group**, click the **More** button ⬇ to display the **Entrance Effects** gallery. Compare your screen with **Figure 1**.

   An *Entrance Effect* is an animation that brings an object or text onto the screen. An *Emphasis Effect* is an animation that emphasizes an object or text that is already displayed. An *Exit Effect* is an animation that moves an object or text off the screen.

3. Under the **Basic** category, click **Split** to apply the effect. Compare your screen with **Figure 2**.

   The number 1 displays to the left of the title placeholder, indicating that the title is the first object in the slide animation sequence. The number will not display during the slide show.

4. On the **Animations tab**, in the **Animation Options group**, click the **Effect Options** button, and then click **Vertical Out**.

   The Effect Options control the direction and sequence in which the animation displays.

   ■ **Continue to the next page to complete the skill**

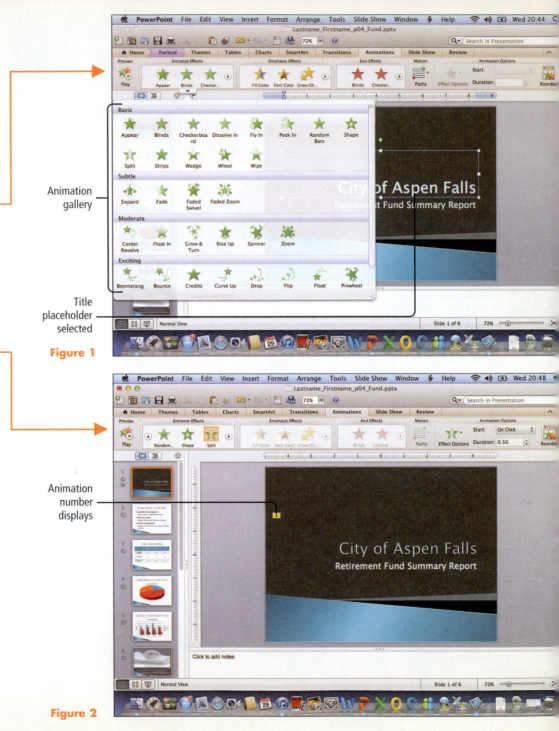

Animation gallery

Title placeholder selected

Figure 1

Animation number displays

Figure 2

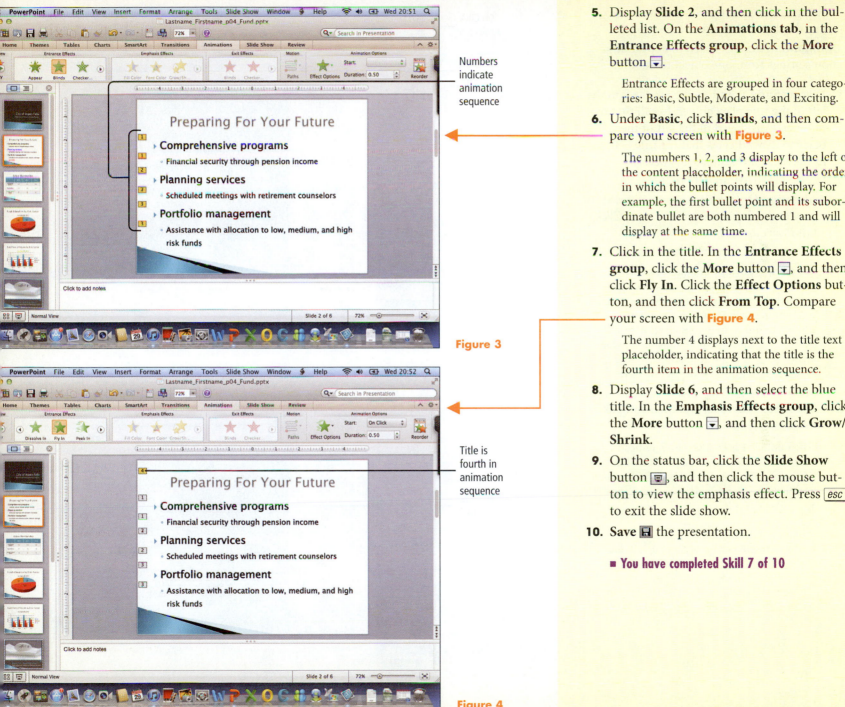

Numbers indicate animation sequence

Figure 3

Title is fourth in animation sequence

Figure 4

5. Display **Slide 2**, and then click in the bulleted list. On the **Animations tab**, in the **Entrance Effects group**, click the **More** button.

   Entrance Effects are grouped in four categories: Basic, Subtle, Moderate, and Exciting.

6. Under **Basic**, click **Blinds**, and then compare your screen with **Figure 3**.

   The numbers 1, 2, and 3 display to the left of the content placeholder, indicating the order in which the bullet points will display. For example, the first bullet point and its subordinate bullet are both numbered 1 and will display at the same time.

7. Click in the title. In the **Entrance Effects group**, click the **More** button, and then click **Fly In**. Click the **Effect Options** button, and then click **From Top**. Compare your screen with **Figure 4**.

   The number 4 displays next to the title text placeholder, indicating that the title is the fourth item in the animation sequence.

8. Display **Slide 6**, and then select the blue title. In the **Emphasis Effects group**, click the **More** button, and then click **Grow/ Shrink**.

9. On the status bar, click the **Slide Show** button, and then click the mouse button to view the emphasis effect. Press ⎋ esc to exit the slide show.

10. **Save** the presentation.

   ■ **You have completed Skill 7 of 10**

► Timing options control when animated items display in the animation sequence.

► *Animation Painter* is used to copy animation settings from one object to another.

1. Display **Slide 1**, and then click the *1* to the left of the title placeholder. Recall that the number 1 displayed to the left of the placeholder indicates that the title is first in the slide animation sequence.

2. On the **Animations tab**, in the **Animation Options group**, click the **Start** arrow to display three options—*On Click, With Previous,* and *After Previous.* Compare your screen with **Figure 1**.

   On Click begins the animation sequence when the mouse button is clicked or the [spacebar] is pressed. **With Previous** begins the animation sequence at the same time as any animation preceding it or, if it is the first animation, with the slide transition. **After Previous** begins the animation sequence immediately after the completion of the previous animation.

3. Click **After Previous**, and then compare your screen with **Figure 2**.

   The number 1 is changed to 0, indicating that the animation will begin immediately after the slide transition; the presenter need not click the mouse button or press [spacebar] to display the title.

■ **Continue to the next page to complete the skill**

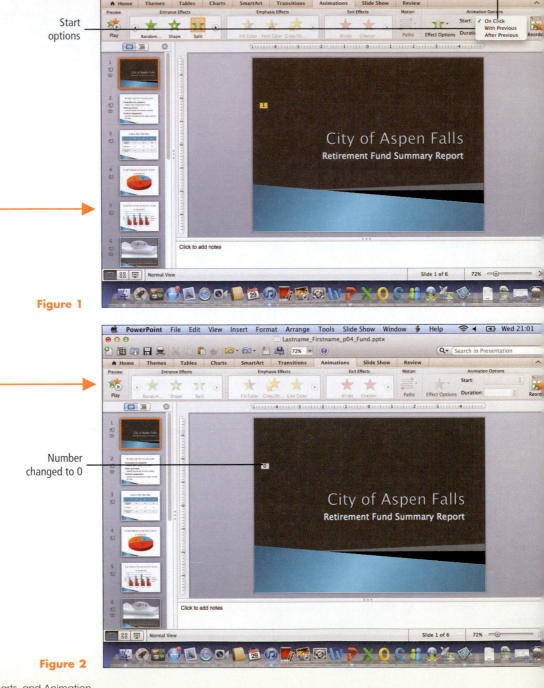

On Click selected

Start options

Figure 1

Number changed to 0

Figure 2

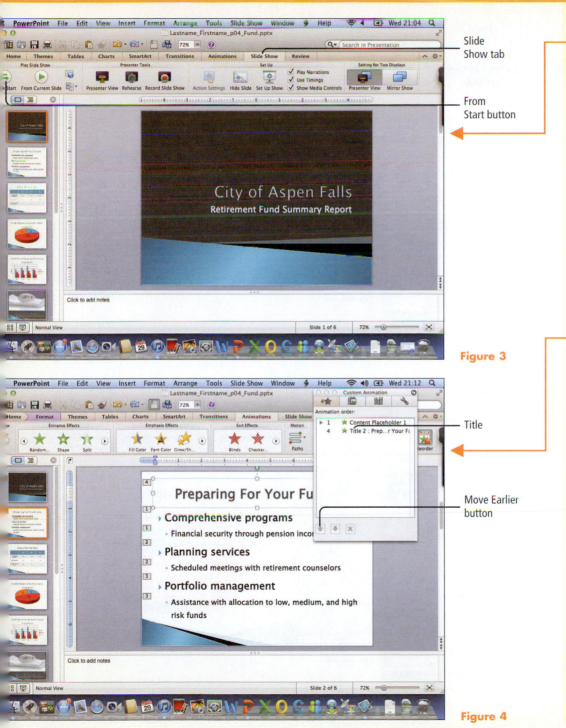

Slide Show tab

From Start button

Figure 3

Title

Move Earlier button

Figure 4

4. Click the **Slide Show tab**, and then compare your screen with **Figure 3**.

> The title and the subtitle display zeroes, indicating that each begins immediately upon completion of the previous animation.

5. On the **Slide Show tab**, in the **Play Slide Show group**, click **From Start**. Notice that the title displays immediately after the slide transition.

6. Select **Slide 2**. Continue to click to display each of the first-level points and their associated second-level points. Click one more time and notice that the title displays after the list text. Press ⏎ esc ⏎ to return to Normal view.

7. On **Slide 2**, click the **Animations tab**, in the **Animation Options group**, click the **Reorder** button, and then compare your screen with **Figure 4**.

> The title animation number changes to 1, indicating that it is the first animated object on the slide. You can use the Move Earlier and Move Later buttons to change the animation order of selected objects.

8. In the **Custom Animation** dialog, click the *Title 2*. Click the **Up** button ⬆ so that the title displays first. **Close** ❌ the **Custom Animation** dialog. Notice that the number for the title changes to *1*.

9. **Save** 💾 the presentation.

■ **You have completed Skill 8 of 10**

▶ You can change the duration of an animation effect by making it longer or shorter.

▶ When an animation effect interferes with the flow of the presentation, you can remove the effect.

1. Display **Slide 3**. Click anywhere in the table to select it. On the **Animations tab**, in the **Entrance Effects group**, click the **More** button ⬇, and then click **Fade** to apply the animation to the table. Compare your screen with **Figure 1**.

2. Display **Slide 4**, and then select the pie chart. On the **Animations tab**, in the **Entrance Effects group**, click the **More** button ⬇, and then under **Basic**, click **Wipe** to apply the animation to the chart. In the **Animation Options group**, click the **Effect Options** button, and then under **Direction**, click **From Top**.

3. At the left of the **Animations tab**, in the **Preview group**, click the **Play** button, and notice that the Wipe effect is a rapid animation. In the **Animation Options group**, click the **Duration up spin arrow** five times to increase the **Duration** to **01.00**—1 second. Compare your screen with **Figure 2**.

    You can set the duration of an animation by typing a value in the Duration box, or you can use the up and down spin arrows to increase and decrease the duration in increments.

    ■ **Continue to the next page to complete the skill** ▶

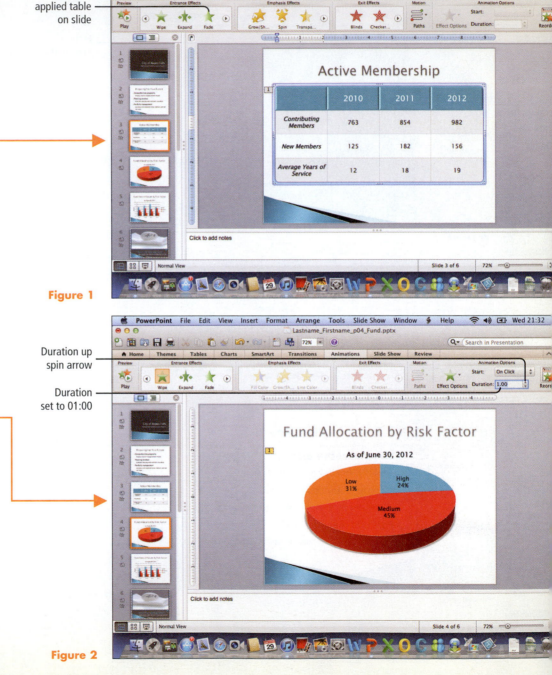

Fade effect applied table on slide

Figure 1

Duration up spin arrow

Duration set to 01:00

Figure 2

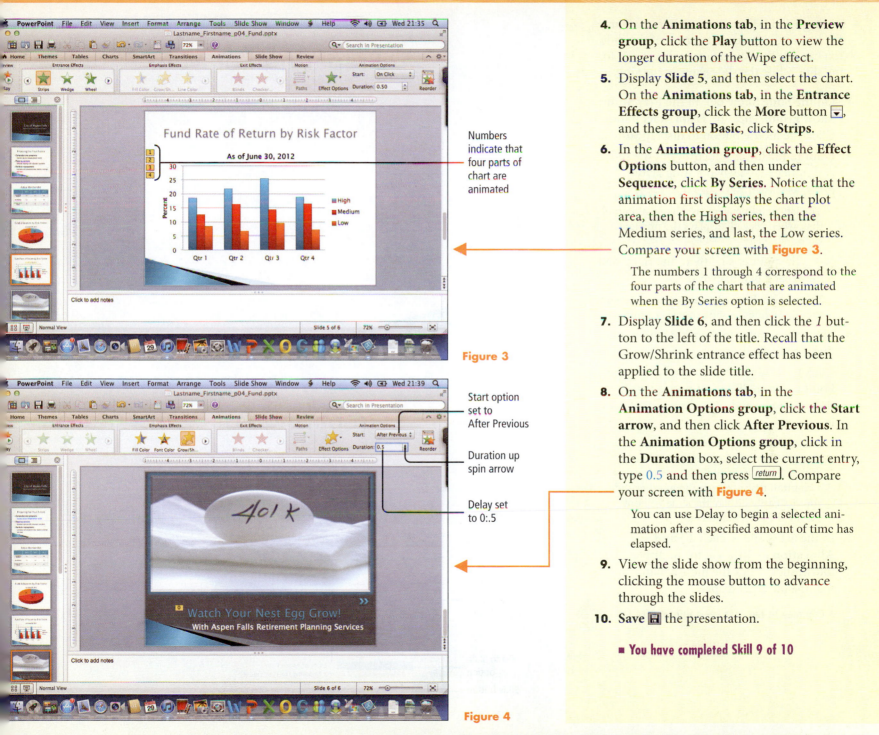

Numbers indicate that four parts of chart are animated

Figure 3

Start option set to After Previous

Duration up spin arrow

Delay set to 0:.5

Figure 4

4. On the **Animations tab**, in the **Preview group**, click the **Play** button to view the longer duration of the Wipe effect.

5. Display **Slide 5**, and then select the chart. On the **Animations tab**, in the **Entrance Effects group**, click the **More** button ⬇, and then under **Basic**, click **Strips**.

6. In the **Animation group**, click the **Effect Options** button, and then under **Sequence**, click **By Series**. Notice that the animation first displays the chart plot area, then the High series, then the Medium series, and last, the Low series. Compare your screen with **Figure 3**.

   The numbers 1 through 4 correspond to the four parts of the chart that are animated when the By Series option is selected.

7. Display **Slide 6**, and then click the *1* button to the left of the title. Recall that the Grow/Shrink entrance effect has been applied to the slide title.

8. On the **Animations tab**, in the **Animation Options group**, click the **Start arrow**, and then click **After Previous**. In the **Animation Options group**, click in the **Duration** box, select the current entry, type **0.5** and then press ⏎. Compare your screen with **Figure 4**.

   You can use Delay to begin a selected animation after a specified amount of time has elapsed.

9. View the slide show from the beginning, clicking the mouse button to advance through the slides.

10. Save 🖫 the presentation.

   ■ **You have completed Skill 9 of 10**

► During a slide show, a *navigation toolbar* displays in the lower-left corner of the slide. You can use the navigation toolbar to go to any slide while the slide show is running.

1. On the **Slide Show tab**, in the **Play Slide Show group**, click the **From Start** button. Click the mouse button to display **Slide 2**.

2. Point to the lower-left corner of the slide and notice that a left-pointing arrow displays, as shown in **Figure 1**.

   The left-pointing arrow is a navigation tool that, when clicked, displays the previous slide.

3. Move the pointer slightly to the right, and notice that a pen displays.

   The pen can be used to *annotate*—write on the slide while the slide show is running.

4. Move the pointer to the right, and notice that a slide displays.

5. Click the **Slide** button to display a menu. Point to **Go to Slide** and notice that the slide numbers and titles display as shown in **Figure 2**.

   You can navigate to any slide in the presentation by using the Go to Slide option. Thus, if an audience member has a question that is relevant to another slide, you can easily display the slide without exiting the presentation.

6. In the list of slides, click **4 Fund Allocation by Risk Factor** to display the fourth slide. Click the mouse button so that the pie chart displays.

   ■ **Continue to the next page to complete the skill**

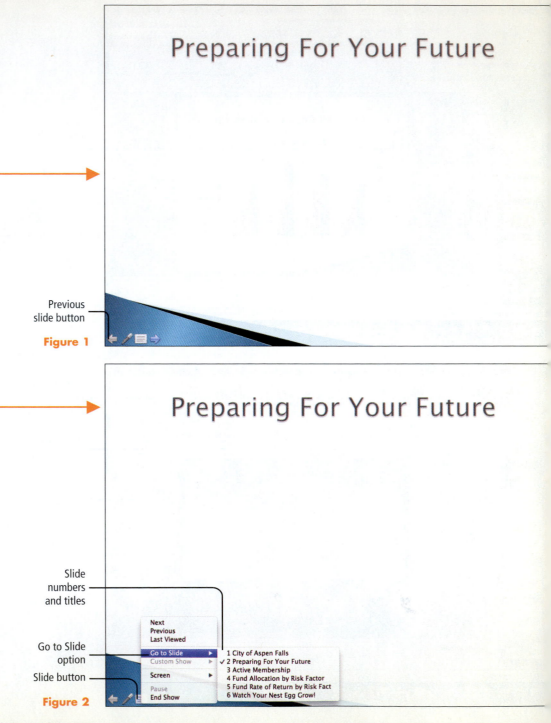

Previous slide button

Figure 1

Slide numbers and titles

Go to Slide option

Slide button

Figure 2

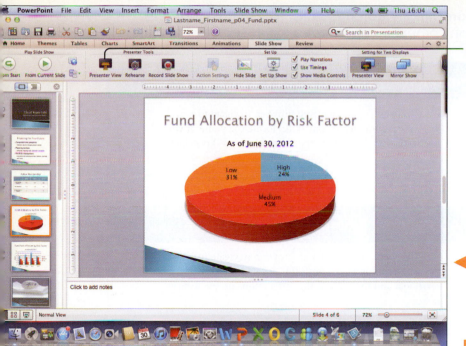

Figure 3

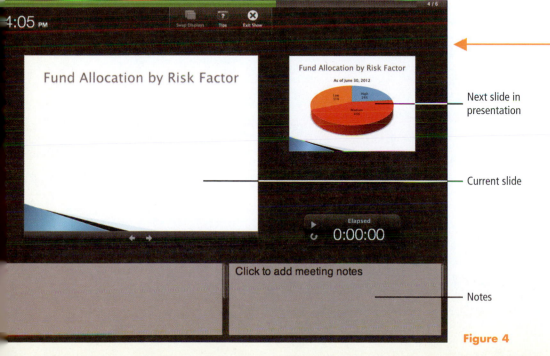

Next slide in presentation

Current slide

Notes

Figure 4

7. On your keyboard, press [B].

   The [B] key is a toggle key that displays a black screen. During a slide show, it may be desirable to pause a presentation so that a discussion can be held without the distraction of the presentation visuals. Rather than turning off the projection system or ending the slide show, you can display the slide as a black screen and then redisplay the same slide when you are ready to resume the presentation.

8. On your keyboard, press [B] to redisplay **Slide 4**. Press [esc] to end the slide show.

9. On the **Slide Show tab**, in the **Presenter Tools group**, locate the **Presenter View** button, as shown in **Figure 3**.

   Recall that you can use Presenter View to display a presentation in a manner similar to a slide show, except that the taskbar, title bar, and status bar remain available in the presentation window. This view is useful when you are making a presentation during a web conference.

10. Click the **Presenter View** button, and then compare your screen with **Figure 4**.

11. Press [esc] to return to Normal view, and then insert a **Header and Footer** on the **Notes and Handouts**. Include the **Page number** in the **Footer** Lastname_Firstname_p04_Fund (use your own name).

12. **Save** 🖫 the presentation. Print or submit the file as directed by your instructor. **Quit** PowerPoint.

   Done! You have completed Skill 10 of 10, and your presentation is complete!

The following More Skills are located at **www.pearsonhighered.com/skills.** Please note that only More Skills that can be performed on a Macintosh computer are included in this section; therefore, the numbering is not always sequential.

More Skills Insert Hyperlinks in a Presentation

Hyperlinks include text, buttons, and images that when clicked during a slide show activate another slide or a website.

In More Skills 12, you will open a presentation and insert a hyperlink to a website.

To begin, open your web browser, navigate to www.pearsonhighered.com/skills, locate the name of your textbook, and then follow the instructions on the website.

More Skills Design Presentations with Appropriate Animation

Animation effects, when used properly, can emphasize important presentation information and provide a method for improving presentation pace and timing.

In More Skills 14, you will review design concepts for applying appropriate animation in a presentation.

To begin, open your web browser, navigate to www.pearsonhighered.com/skills, locate the name of your textbook, and then follow the instructions on the website.

Key Terms

After Previous.............. 396

Animation.................. 394

Animation Painter.......... 396

Annotate 400

Category label............. 388

Cell...................... 382

Chart 388

Chart style................ 391

Column chart 388

Data label 393

Data marker 390

Data point 390

Data series............... 390

Emphasis Effect 394

Entrance Effect............ 394

Exit Effect 394

Legend 388

Navigation toolbar......... 400

On Click.................. 396

Pie chart................. 392

Table.................... 382

Table style 386

With Previous............. 396

Online Help Skills

1. **Start** Safari or another web browser. In the **address bar**, type microsoft.com/mac/how-to and then press ⏎ return to display the home page for Microsoft Office.

   This website provides you with helpful links to get started, find out what is new, and tutorials about Office 2011.

2. Under **Product Help**, click **PowerPoint 2011**.

3. Under **PowerPoint Help**, click the **Charts** link.

4. Click **Create a combination chart**, and then compare your screen with **Figure 1**.

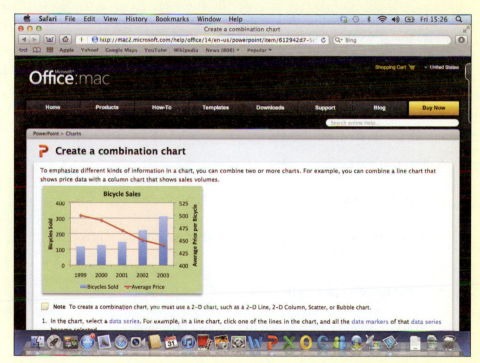

Figure 1

5. In your browser, click the Back button, and then click on each of the links. Read the displayed content under each link, and then answer the following questions. What is a combination chart? What is a secondary axis and why would you add one to a chart? How do you change the rotation or perspective of a 3-D chart?

Matching

Match each term in the second column with its correct definition in the first column by writing the letter of the term on the blank line in front of the correct definition.

____ **1.** In a table or worksheet, the rectangular box formed by the intersection of a column and row.

____ **2.** A format used to organize and present information in columns and rows.

____ **3.** Predefined formatting that applies borders and fill colors to a table so that it is consistent with the presentation theme.

____ **4.** A graphic representation of numeric data.

____ **5.** A chart type useful for illustrating comparisons among related categories.

____ **6.** Text that identifies the categories of data in a chart.

____ **7.** Text that identifies a data marker in a chart.

____ **8.** A column, bar, area, dot, pie slice, or other symbol that represents a single data point.

____ **9.** Individual data plotted in a chart.

____ **10.** Visual or sound effects added to an object on a slide.

A Animation

B Cell

C Chart

D Column chart

E Category label

F Data label

G Data marker

H Data point

I Table

J Table style

Multiple Choice

Choose the correct answer.

1. A prebuilt set of effects, colors, and backgrounds applied to a chart that is designed to work with the presentation theme.
   A. Chart layout
   B. Chart style
   C. Chart effect

2. A group of related data points.
   A. Data series
   B. Data label
   C. Data marker

3. A chart element that identifies the patterns or colors that are assigned to the data in the chart.
   A. Data series
   B. Data label
   C. Legend

4. A type of chart used to illustrate percentages or proportions using only one series of data.
   A. Column chart
   B. Line chart
   C. Pie chart

5. A type of animation that brings a slide element onto the screen.
   A. Entrance Effect
   B. Emphasis Effect
   C. Exit Effect

6. Animation that emphasizes an object or text that is already displayed.
   A. Entrance Effect
   B. Emphasis Effect
   C. Exit Effect

7. Animation that moves an object or text off the screen.
   A. Entrance Effect
   B. Emphasis Effect
   C. Exit Effect

8. A feature that copies animation settings from one object to another.
   A. Format Painter
   B. Animation Painter
   C. Copy and Paste

9. The action of writing on a slide while the slide show is running.
   A. Annotate
   B. Edit
   C. Navigation

10. A toolbar used to go to any slide while the slide show is running.
    A. Animation toolbar
    B. Slide Show toolbar
    C. Navigation toolbar

Topics for Discussion

1. When you apply animation to a slide, you can also apply sound effects. Do you think that using sound in a presentation is an effective technique for keeping the audience focused? Why or why not?

2. Recall that a column chart is used to compare data and a pie chart is used to illustrate percentages or proportions. Give examples of the types of data that an organization such as the City of Aspen Falls might use in a column or a pie chart.

Skill Check

You will save your presentation as:

- Lastname_Firstname_p04_Report

Comments
Increased revenue from sales and property tax
Increased facilities capital expenditures
Increased revenue from bond issue

Figure 1

1. **Start** PowerPoint. From your student files, open **p04_Report**. **Save** the presentation, using your own name, in your **PowerPoint Chapter 4** folder as Lastname_Firstname_p04_Report

2. Display **Slide 3**. In the content placeholder, click the **Insert Table** button. In the **Insert Table** dialog, in the **Number of columns** box, type 2 and then click **OK**.

3. In the first table cell, type Month and then press [tab]. Type Ending Cash Balance and then press [tab]. Type January and then press [tab]. Type 33,713,918 and then press [tab] to create a new row. Type February and then press [tab]. Type 28,688,318 and then press [tab]. Type March and then press [tab]. Type 35,987,156

4. With the insertion point positioned in the last column, on the **Table Layout tab**, in the **Rows & Columns group**, click the **Right** button. In the new column, type the text shown in the table in **Figure 1**.

5. Point to the table's bottom-center sizing handle—the four dots. Drag down until the lower edge of the table extends to the **3 inches** mark below zero on the vertical ruler.

6. Click in the table, and then on the **Table Layout tab**, in the **View group**, click **Select**, and then click **Select Table**. In the **Cells group**, click the **Distribute Rows** button. In the **Alignment group**, click the **Center Text** button, and then click the **Align Text Middle** button.

7. On the **Tables tab**, in the **Table Styles group**, click the **More** button. Under **Medium**, in the third row, click **Medium Style 3 - Accent 2**. Select the first table row, and then change the **Font Size** to **24**. Select the remaining table text, and then change the **Font Size** to **20**. Click in a blank area of the slide, and then compare your slide with **Figure 2**.

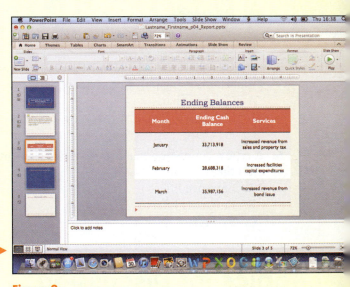

Figure 2

■ **Continue to the next page to complete this Skill Check** ▶

	General	Utilities	Assessments
January	2568700	1698470	1875020
February	3258694	1833241	1221900
March	2794127	2057964	2384005

Figure 3

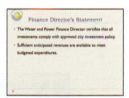

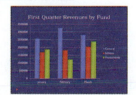
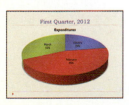

Lastname_Firstname_p04_Report   1

Figure 4

8. Display **Slide 4**. In the content placeholder, click the **Insert Chart** button. Click the first chart—**Clustered Column**. In the **Excel** window, click cell **B1** containing the text *Series 1*. Type General and then type the remaining data shown in **Figure 3**, pressing [tab] to move from cell to cell.

9. In the **Excel** worksheet, click to select row heading **5**, and then on the **Home tab**, in the **Cells group**, click **Delete**. **Quit** Excel.

10. With the chart selected, on the **Charts tab**, in the **Chart Styles group**, click the **More** button. Click **Style 26**.

11. Display **Slide 5**. In the content placeholder, click the **Insert Chart** button. Insert a **3-D Pie**. In the **Excel** worksheet, click cell **B1**. Type Expenditures and then press [tab]. Type January and then press [tab]. Type 2287769 and then press [tab]. Type February and then press [tab]. Type 4589760 and then press [tab]. Type March and then press [tab]. Type 3200336 and then press [tab]. Select heading **5**, and then on the **Home tab**, in the **Cells group**, click **Delete**. **Quit** Excel.

12. On the **Charts tab**, in the **Chart Quick Layouts group**, click **Layout 1**. On the **Chart Layout tab**, in the **Labels group**, click **Data Labels**, and then click **Center**.

13. Display **Slide 2**, and then click the bulleted list. On the **Animations tab**, in the **Entrance Effects group**, click **Fly In**. Click the **Effect Options** button, and then click **From Left**. In the **Animation Options group**, click the **Duration up arrow** to change the duration to **0.80**. Select the title.

14. Display **Slide 4**, and then select the chart. On the **Animations tab**, in the **Emphasis group**, click the **More** button, and then under **Basic**, click **Transparency**. In the **Animation Options group**, click the **Duration up arrow** five times to display **0.50**. Click the **Start arrow**, and then click **With Previous**.

15. Display **Slide 1**, and then click the *1* to the left of the title. On the **Animations tab**, in the **Animation Options group**, click the **Start arrow**. Select **After Previous**. View the slide show from the beginning, and then display the presentation in **Reading View**. Return to **Normal** view.

16. Insert a **Header and Footer** on the **Notes and Handouts**. Include a **Page number** in the **Footer** Lastname_Firstname_p04_Report (use your own name).

17. **Save**, and then compare your presentation with **Figure 4**. Print or submit the file as directed by your instructor. **Quit** PowerPoint.

Done! You have completed the Skill Check

Assess Your Skills 1

To complete this presentation, you will need the following file:

- **p04_City_Hall**

You will save your presentation as:

- **Lastname_Firstname_p04_City_Hall**

1. **Start** PowerPoint. From your student files, open **p04_City_Hall**. **Save** the presentation, using your own name, in your **PowerPoint** Chapter 4 folder as Lastname_Firstname_p04_City_Hall

2. Display **Slide 3**. In the content placeholder, insert a table with 2 columns and 5 rows. In the five cells of the first column, type the following headings:

   Project
   Exterior   Interior
   Parking   Landscape

   In the second column, type the following:

   Percent Complete
   85%   45%
   20%   0%

3. Insert a third column to the right of the *Percent Complete* column. Type the following:

   Completion Date
   November 2013   January 2014
   June 2014   July 2014

   Size the table so that its lower edge aligns at the **3 inches** mark below zero on the vertical ruler. If necessary, distribute the rows, and then apply the **Medium Style 3 - Accent 1** table style. Center the text horizontally and vertically within the cells. Animate the table by applying the **Wipe** Entrance Effect.

4. Display **Slide 4**. Insert a **3-D Pie** chart. In the **Excel** worksheet, in cell **B1**, type Cost Beginning in cell **A2**, enter the following data:

Exterior	1257500
Interior	1258650
Parking	750000

5. In the **Excel** window, delete row **5**, and then **Quit** Excel. Change the chart layout to **Layout 1**, and then delete the chart title. Apply the **Style 10** chart style, and change the **Data Labels** placement to **Center**.

6. Display **Slide 2**, select the content placeholder, and then apply the **Split** Entrance Effect and change the **Effect Options** to **Vertical Out**.

7. Display **Slide 5**, and then apply the **Dissolve In** Entrance Effect to the picture. Change the **Duration** to **0.75**. Apply the **Darken** Emphasis Effect to the caption. For both the caption and the picture, modify the **Start** option to **After Previous**.

8. View the slide show from the beginning and use the navigation toolbar to display **Slide 4** after you display **Slide 1**. Return to **Slide 1**, and then view the presentation in the correct order.

9. Insert a **Header and Footer** on the **Notes and Handouts**. Include a **Page number** in the **Footer** Lastname_Firstname_p04_City_Hall (use your own name).

10. **Save**, and then compare your presentation with **Figure 1**. Print or submit the file as directed by your instructor. **Quit** PowerPoint.

Done! You have completed Assess Your Skills 1

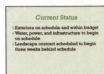

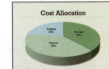

Lastname_Firstname_p04_City_Hall

Figure 1

Assess Your Skills 2

Assess Your Skills 3 and 4 can be found at **www.pearsonhighered.com/skills**.

To complete this presentation, you will need the following file:

- p04_Benefits

You will save your presentation as:

- Lastname_Firstname_p04_Benefits

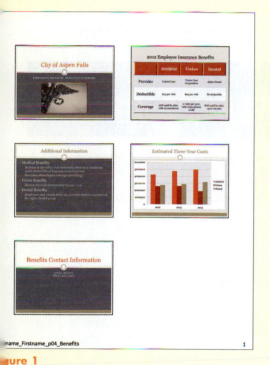

name_Firstname_p04_Benefits 1

Figure 1

1. **Start** PowerPoint. From your student files, open **p04_Benefits**. **Save** the presentation, using your own name, in your **PowerPoint Chapter 4** folder as Lastname_Firstname_p04_Benefits

2. Display **Slide 2**. In the content placeholder, insert a table with 3 columns and 4 rows. In the first row, type the following headings:

   Medical   Vision   Dental

   In the second row, type:

   United Care   Vision Care Corporation
   Alpha Dental

   In the third row, type:

   $15 per visit $25 per visit   No deductible

   In the fourth row, type:

   90% paid by plan, with no maximum
   2 visits per year, with $250 glasses credit
   80% paid by plan, up to $2,000

3. Insert a column to the left of the first column. Beginning in the second row, type the following headings:

   Provider   Deductible   Coverage

4. Size the table so that its lower edge aligns at the **3 inches** mark below zero on the vertical ruler. Distribute the rows, and then apply the **Medium Style 3 - Accent 1** table style. Center the table text horizontally and vertically. Change the first row and first column **Font Size** to **28**, and then apply the **Circle** cell bevel effect to the first row. **Animate** the table by applying the **Wipe** effect.

5. Display **Slide 4**, and then insert a **Clustered Column** chart. In the **Excel** worksheet, in cell **B1**, type Medical In cell **C1** type Vision and in cell **D1** type Dental Beginning in cell **A2** enter the following data:

2012	4228550	2586430	2758490
2013	4752280	2687500	2896430
2014	4967870	1889480	3198560

6. In the **Excel** worksheet, delete row **5**, and then **Quit** Excel. Apply the **Style 34** chart style.

7. Edit the chart data by changing the *2013 Vision* data in cell **C3** to 2622330

8. On **Slide 3**, apply the **Float In** Entrance Effect to the content placeholder.

9. On **Slide 5**, apply the **Fly In** Entrance Effect to the title. Change the **Effect Options** to **From Top**. Use the **Reorder Animation** options to move the title animation earlier so that it displays before the subtitle. Set the title and subtitle animations to start **After Previous**. View the slide show from the beginning.

10. Insert a **Header and Footer** on the **Notes and Handouts**. Include a **Page number** in the **Footer** Lastname_Firstname_p04_Benefits (use your own name).

11. **Save**, and then compare your presentation with **Figure 1**. Print or submit the file as directed by your instructor. **Quit** PowerPoint.

Done! You have completed Assess Your Skills 2

Assess Your Skills Visually

To complete this presentation, you will need the following file:

- New blank PowerPoint presentation

You will save your presentation as:

- Lastname_Firstname_p04_Accounts

Start PowerPoint. Create the table as shown in **Figure 1**. **Save** the file, using your own name, as Lastname_Firstname_p04_Accounts in your **PowerPoint Chapter 4** folder. To complete this presentation, use the **Module** design theme. Type and align the text as shown in the figure and apply the **Light Style 2 - Accent 1** table style. In the first table row, change the **Font Size** to **24**, and apply a **Circle** bevel effect. Add a footer to the **Notes and Handouts** with the file name and page number, and then print or submit the file as directed by your instructor.

Done! You have completed Assess Your Skills Visually

Savings Account Comparison

Account Type	Description	Rate
Savings Account	Traditional account for short-term needs	1%
Savings Certificate	Competitive rates Guaranteed return	1.5% to 3.5%
Money Market Account	Minimum $2,500 balance Unlimited withdrawals	1.25% to 1.75%
Individual Retirement Account	Invest after-tax dollars	2.25% to 4.5%

Figure 1

Skills in Context

To complete this presentation, you will need the following file:

- New blank PowerPoint presentation

You will save your presentation as:

- Lastname_Firstname_p04_Power

Using the information provided, create a presentation in which the first slide title is Aspen Falls Utilities Division and the subtitle is Power Distribution and Usage Apply a design theme. Create two more slides, one with a table and one with a pie chart, that include information about the types of power that the city uses and their distribution to customers. The city's power supply is composed of 52% hydroelectric power, 28% natural gas, 15% renewable energy sources, and 5% coal. On a monthly basis, the average distribution of power in megawatt hours is 705,500 for residential customers, 1,322,600 for commercial customers, and 587,900 for industrial customers.

Format the chart and table with styles and apply animation to each. Insert a footer with the file name on the **Notes and Handouts**. Print or submit the file as directed by your instructor.

Done! You have completed Skills in Context

Skills and You

To complete this presentation, you will need the following file:

- New blank PowerPoint presentation

You will save your presentation as:

- Lastname_Firstname_p04_Cars

Using the skills you have practiced in this chapter, create a presentation with four slides in which you compare three cars that you would be interested in purchasing. Apply an appropriate presentation theme. On one slide, insert a table with three columns that include the vehicle name, price range, and description of important features. On another slide, insert a column chart that compares the prices of the three vehicles. On the last slide, insert a picture of the car that you would like to purchase and include at least three bullet points indicating why you chose the vehicle. Apply animation to the slides and insert an appropriate footer. Print or submit the file as directed by your instructor.

Done! You have completed Skills and You

Glossary

3-D See three-dimensional.

Absolute cell reference A cell reference that remains the same when it is copied or filled to other cells. An absolute cell reference takes the form A1.

Accounting number format A number format that applies comma separators where appropriate, inserts a fixed U.S. dollar sign aligned at the left edge of the cell, applies two decimal places, and leaves a small amount of space at both the right and left edges of the cell to accommodate parentheses for negative numbers.

Active cell The cell outlined in black in which data is entered when you begin typing.

After Previous An animation option that begins the animation sequence immediately after the completion of the previous animation.

Anchor A symbol to the left of a paragraph mark that indicates which paragraph the picture is associated with.

Animation Visual or sound effects added to an object on a slide.

Animation Painter A feature that copies animation settings from one object to another.

Annotate The action of writing on a slide while the slide show is running.

Argument The values that a function uses to perform operations or calculations. The type of argument a function uses is specific to the function. Common arguments include numbers, text, cell references, and names.

Arithmetic operator A symbol that specifies a mathematical operation such as addition or subtraction.

AutoCorrect A feature that corrects common spelling errors as you type; for example, if you type *teh*, Word will automatically correct it to *the*.

AutoFit Automatically changes the column width to accommodate the longest entry.

AVERAGE function A function that adds a group of values, and then divides the result by the number of values in the group.

Axis A line bordering the chart plot area used as a frame of reference for measurement.

Background style A slide background fill variation that combines theme colors in different intensities or patterns.

Bar chart A chart type that illustrates comparisons among individual items.

Bibliography A list of sources referenced in a document and listed on a separate page at the end of the document.

Body font A font applied to all slide text except titles.

Browser Software that is used to view websites and navigate the web.

Bullet point Individual line of bulleted text on a slide.

Bulleted list A list of items with each item introduced by a symbol such as a small circle or checkmark.

Calculated column A column in an Excel table that uses a single formula that adjusts for each row.

Category axis The axis that displays the category labels in a chart.

Category label A label that identifies the categories of data in a chart.

Category label Nonnumeric text that identifies the categories of data.

Cell The box formed by the intersection of a row and column in a table or worksheet.

Cell address The column letter and row number that identify a cell, also called the cell reference.

Cell reference The column letter and row number that identify a cell, also called a cell address.

Cell references The numbers on the left side and the letters across the top of a spreadsheet that address each cell.

Cell style A prebuilt set of formatting characteristics, such as font, font size, font color, cell borders, and cell shading.

Chart A graphic representation of numeric data.

Chart layout A prebuilt set of chart elements that can include a title, legend, or labels.

Chart sheet A workbook sheet that contains only a chart and is useful when you want to view a chart separately from the worksheet data.

Chart style A prebuilt chart format that applies an overall visual look to a chart by modifying its graphic effects, colors, and backgrounds.

Citation A note in the document that refers the reader to a source in the bibliography.

Clip art Graphics and images included with Microsoft Office or obtained from other sources.

Clip art A set of images, drawings, photographs, videos, and sound included with Microsoft Office or accessed from Microsoft Office Online.

Clipboard A temporary storage area that holds text or an object that has been cut or copied.

Clustered bar chart A chart type that is useful when you want to compare values across categories; bar charts organize categories along the vertical axis and the values along the horizontal axis.

Color scales Visual guides that help the user understand data distribution and variation.

Column break An applied column end that forces the text following the break to the top of the next column, but does not automatically create a new page.

Column chart A chart type useful for illustrating comparisons among related numbers.

Column heading The letter that displays at the top of a column in a worksheet.

Comma cell style A cell style that adds commas where appropriate and displays two decimals.

Comment A note that is attached to a cell, separate from other cell content.

Comparison operator Compares two values and returns either TRUE or FALSE.

Conditional formatting A format such as cell shading or font color, which is applied to cells when a specified condition is true.

Content control In a slide template, a placeholder that will contain text, SmartArt, pictures, or other content.

Contents Underlying formulas and data in a cell.

Contextual tool Tools that enable you to perform specific commands related to the selected object.

Contrast The difference in brightness between two elements, such as the difference between text color and its background color.

Copy A command that places a copy of the selected text or object in the Clipboard.

Criteria The condition that you specify in the logical test.

Cut A command that removes the selected text or object and stores it in the Clipboard.

Data bar A visual cue to the reader about the value of a cell relative to other cells. The length of the data bar represents the value in the cell.

Data label Text that identifies a data marker on a chart.

Data marker A column, bar, area, dot, pie slice, or other symbol that represents a single data point.

Data point A chart value that originates in a worksheet cell.

Data point Individual data plotted in a chart.

Data series In a chart, data points that are related to one another.

Data source A mail merge document that contains information, such as names and addresses, that change with each letter or label.

Detail sheet A worksheet with cells referred to by summary sheet formulas.

Dialog Box where you can select multiple settings.

Displayed value Data displayed in a cell.

Document properties Information about a document that can help you identify or organize your files, such as the name of the document author, the file name, and keywords.

Document theme A set of design elements that provides a unified look for colors, fonts, and graphics.

Dot leader A series of evenly spaced dots that precede a tab stop.

Double-spacing The equivalent of a blank line of text displayed between each line of text in a paragraph.

Drag To move the mouse while holding down the mouse button and then to release it at the appropriate time.

Drag and drop A method of moving objects in which you point to the selection, hold down the mouse button, and then drag the object to a new location.

Drop cap The first letter (or letters) of a paragraph, enlarged and either embedded in the text or placed in the left margin.

Edit To insert text, delete text, or replace text in an Office document, spreadsheet, or presentation.

Embedded chart A chart that is placed on the worksheet containing the data. Beneficial when you want to view or print a chart with its source data.

Emphasis Effect Animation that emphasizes an object or text that is already displayed.

Endnote A reference placed at the end of a section or a document.

Entrance Effect Animation that brings an object or text onto the screen.

Error indicator A green triangle that indicates a possible error in a formula.

Error value A message that displays whenever a formula cannot perform the calculations in the formula.

Excel table A series of rows and columns that contains related data. Data in an Excel table is managed independently from the data in other rows and columns in the worksheet.

Exit Effect Animation that moves an object or text off the screen.

Explode Pull out one or more slices of a 3–D Pie chart to emphasize a specific slice or slices in a pie chart.

Field A category of data—such as a file name, a page number, or the current date—that can be inserted into a document.

Field In a PivotTable, a category that summarizes multiple rows of information from the source data.

Fill color The inside color of text or an object.

Fill handle The small black square in the lower right corner of the selection.

Filter A command to display only the rows of a table that meet specified criteria. Filtering temporarily hides rows that do not meet the criteria.

Find and Replace A command that enables you to find and then replace a character or string of characters in a worksheet or in a selected range.

Finder An Apple application that enables the user to find files, folders, applications, and attached devices.

First line indent The location of the beginning of the first line of a paragraph to the left edge of the remainder of the paragraph.

Floating object An object or graphic that can be moved independently of the surrounding text.

Font A set of characters with the same design and shape.

Font style Formatting that includes bold, italic, or underline.

Footer (Word) A reserved area for text, graphics, and fields that display at the bottom (footer) of each page in a document.

Footer (PowerPoint) Text that displays at the bottom of every slide or that prints at the bottom of a sheet of slide handouts.

Footnote A reference placed at the bottom of the page.

Format To change the appearance of the text—for example, changing the text color to red.

Format Painter A command that copies formatting from one selection of text to another.

Formatting marks or nonprinting characters Using characters on a keyboard that do not print, like a `spacebar` or `return`.

Formula An equation that performs mathematical calculations on number values in the worksheet.

Formula AutoComplete Assists in inserting functions.

Formula bar A bar below the Ribbon that displays the value contained in the active cell. It is used to enter or edit values or formulas.

Freeze Panes A command used to keep rows or columns visible when scrolling in a worksheet. The frozen rows and columns become separate panes.

Function A prewritten Excel formula that takes a value or values, performs an operation, and returns a value or values.

Function A prewritten formula that takes input, performs an operation, and returns a value. Functions are used to simplify and shorten formulas.

Future value (Fv) The value of the loan or investment at the end of different time periods. The future value for a loan is usually zero.

Gallery A visual display of choices from which you can choose.

General format The default Excel number format that does not display commas or trailing zeros to the right of a decimal point.

Goal Seek A what–if analysis tool used to find a specific value for a cell by adjusting the value of another cell.

Gradient fill A gradual progression of colors and shades, usually from one color to another, or from one shade to another shade of the same color, to add a fill to a shape.

Grid lines Lines between the cells in a table or spreadsheet.

Group A collection of multiple objects treated as one unit that can be copied, moved, or formatted.

Guides Lines that display in the rulers giving a visual indication of where the pointer is positioned.

Hanging indent The first line of a paragraph extends to the left of the rest of the paragraph.

Header (Word) Reserved area for text, graphics, and fields that display at the top (header) of each page in a document.

Header (PowerPoint) Text that prints at the top of each sheet of slide handouts.

Headings font A font applied to slide titles.

Horizontal alignment The orientation of the left or right edges of the paragraph—for example, flush with the left or right margins.

Hyperlink Text or a graphic that you click to go to a file, a location in a file, or a web page on the World Wide Web or a web page on an organization's intranet.

IF function A function that checks whether criteria is met, and then returns one value when the condition is TRUE, and another value when the condition is FALSE.

Indent The position of paragraph lines in relation to the page margins.

Insertion point A vertical line that indicates where text will be inserted when you start typing.

Interest The charge for borrowing money or the income from loaning money; generally a percentage of the amount borrowed or invested.

Justified Paragraph text is aligned flush with both the left margin and the right margin.

Keyboard shortcut Moves the insertion point to the beginning of the document.

Label Text data in a cell, also called a text value.

Landscape orientation A page orientation in which the printed page is wider than it is tall.

Layout The arrangement of the text and graphic elements or placeholders on a slide.

Layout Gallery A visual representation of several content layouts that you can apply to a slide.

Leader A series of characters that form a solid, dashed, or dotted line that fills the space preceding a tab stop.

Leader character A character such as a dash or a dot that is repeated to fill the space preceding a tab stop.

Legend A box that identifies the patterns or colors that are assigned to the data series or categories in the chart.

Line spacing The vertical distance between lines of text in a paragraph.

List level Levels of text on a slide identified by the indentation, size of text, and bullet assigned to that level.

Logical function A function that applies a logical test to determine if a specific condition is met.

Logical test Any value or expression that can be evaluated as being TRUE or FALSE.

Mail merge A Word feature that creates customized letters or labels by combining a main document with a data source.

Main document In a Word mail merge, the document that contains the merge fields and the text that remains constant.

Manual line break Moves the remainder of the paragraph following the insertion point to a new line while keeping the text in the same paragraph.

Manual page break Forces a page to end at a location you specify.

Manual page break Moves the text following the insertion point to a new page.

Margin The space between the text and the top, bottom, left, and right edges of the paper when you print the document.

MAX function A function that returns the largest value in a range of cells.

Metadata Information and personal data that is stored with your document.

MIN function A function that returns the smallest value in a range of cells.

Name A word that represents a cell or range of cells that can be used as a cell or range reference. Names used in formulas and functions clarify the meaning of the formula and assist navigating large worksheets.

Name Box An area by the formula bar that displays the active cell reference.

Navigation toolbar A toolbar that is used to navigate to any slide while the slide show is running.

Normal view (Excel) A view that maximizes the number of cells visible on the screen.

Normal view (PowerPoint) The view in which the window is divided into three areas—the Slide pane, the pane containing the Slides and Outline tabs, and the Notes pane.

Notes page A printout that contains the slide image in the top half of the page and speaker notes typed in the Notes pane in the lower half of the page.

Notes pane An area of the Normal View window used to type notes that can be printed below a picture of each slide.

NOW function A function that returns the serial number of the current date and time.

Nudge Moving an object in small increments using the directional arrow keys.

Nudge To move an object a little bit at a time by holding down the ctrl key and then pressing one of the arrow keys.

Number format A specific way that Excel displays numbers.

Number value Numeric data in a cell.

Numbered list A list of items with each item introduced by a consecutive number to indicate definite steps, a sequence of actions, or chronological order.

On Click An animation option that begins the animation sequence when the mouse button is clicked or the spacebar is pressed.

Operator precedence The mathematical rules for the order in which calculations are performed within a formula.

Organization chart Graphic that represents the hierarchy of relationships between individuals and groups in an organization.

Outline A Word feature that displays headings and body text, formatted so you can move headings and all associated subheadings and body text along with the heading.

Page Layout view A view where you prepare your document or spreadsheet for printing.

Paragraph spacing The vertical distance above and below each paragraph.

Paste To insert a copy of the text or object stored in the Clipboard. The Paste Options button displays near the pasted text.

Paste area The target destination for data that has been cut or copied.

Picture An image created with a scanner, digital camera, or graphics software that has been saved with a graphic file extension such as .JPEG, .TIFF, or .BMP.

Picture effects Picture styles that include shadows, reflections, glows, soft edges, bevels, and 3–D rotations.

Picture Style A prebuilt set of formatting borders, effects, and layouts applied to a picture.

Pie chart A chart type that illustrates the relationship of parts to a whole.

PivotTable report An interactive, crosstabulated Excel report used to summarize and analyze data.

Placeholder A box with dotted borders that is part of most slide layouts and that holds text or objects such as charts, tables, and pictures.

Placeholder text Reserved space in shapes into which you enter your own text.

PMT function Calculates the payment for a loan based on constant payments and a constant interest rate.

Point Font unit of measurement, with one point equal to 1/72 of an inch.

Point The unit of measurement in which fonts are measured.

Portrait orientation A page orientation in which the printed page is taller than it is wide.

Present value (Pv) The initial amount of the loan; the total amount that a series of future payments is worth today.

Principal The initial amount of the loan; the total amount that a series of future payments is worth today. Also called the present value (Pv) of a loan.

Quick Style A style that can be accessed from a Ribbon gallery of thumbnails.

RAM The computer's temporary memory.

Range Two or more cells on a worksheet that are adjacent.

Range finder An Excel feature that outlines all of the cells referenced in a formula. It is useful for verifying which cells are used in a formula and can be used to edit formulas.

Rate The percentage that is paid for the use of borrowed money.

Relative cell reference Refers to cells based on their position in relation to (relative to) the cell that contains the formula.

Row heading The number that displays at the left of a row.

Safari The default web browser that comes preinstalled on an Apple Macintosh computer.

ScreenTip Informational text that displays when you point to a command or thumbnail on the Ribbon.

Section A portion of a document that can be formatted differently from the rest of the document.

Section break Marks the end of one section and the beginning of another section.

Separator character In a data list, a character such as a comma or tab that separates elements of each column.

Serial number A sequential number often used as an underlying value for dates.

Series A group of things that come one after another in succession. For example, the months January, February, March.

Sheet tabs The labels along the lower border of the workbook window that identify each worksheet or chart sheet.

Shortcut menu A list of commands related to the type of object that you reference.

Single-spacing No extra space is added between lines of text in a paragraph.

Sizing handle A small square or circle at the corner or side of a selected graphic that is dragged to increase or decrease the size of the graphic.

Slide An individual page in a presentation that can contain text, pictures, tables, charts, and other multimedia or graphic objects.

Slide handout Printed images of more than one slide on a sheet of paper.

Slide master The top slide in a hierarchy of slides that stores information about the theme and slide layouts of a presentation, including the background, color, fonts, effects, placeholder sizes, and positioning.

Slide Sorter view The PowerPoint view in which all of the slides in the presentation display as thumbnails.

Slide transition A motion effect that occurs in Slide Show view when you move from one slide to the next during a presentation.

SmartArt graphic A visual representation of information used to communicate your message or ideas effectively by choosing from among many different layouts.

Source data The data that is used to create a PivotTable report.

Sparkline A chart inside a single cell used to show data trends.

Split bar Displays near the middle of the document window and indicates the location of the border between the windows.

Spreadsheet The primary document that you use in Excel to store and work with data, also called a worksheet.

Statistical function A predefined formula that describes a collection of data—for example, totals, counts, and averages.

Style A predefined set of formats that can be applied to text, paragraphs, table cells, or lists.

SUM An Excel function that adds all the numbers in a range of cells.

Summary sheet A worksheet that displays and summarizes totals from other worksheets.

Synonym A word with the same meaning as another.

Tab scrolling buttons The buttons to the left of the sheet tabs used to display Excel sheet tabs that are not in view.

Tab stop A specific location on a line of text, marked on the Word ruler, to which you can move the insertion point by pressing ⌷tab⌷; used to align and indent text.

Table Text or numbers displayed in a row and column format to make the information easier to read and understand.

Table style A prebuilt combination of borders and fill colors applied to the entire table in a manner consistent with the presentation theme.

Template A prebuilt document, workbook, or presentation used as a pattern for creating new documents, workbooks, or presentations. You use a template to build a document without having to start from a blank document.

Text alignment The horizontal placement of text within a placeholder.

Text box A movable, resizable container for text or graphics.

Text box (Access) An object on a form or report that displays the data from a field in a table or query.

Text effect A set of decorative formats, such as outlines, shadows, text glow, and colors that make text stand out in a document.

Text value Character data in a cell, also called a label.

Text wrap A format that displays text on multiple lines within a cell.

Text wrapping Manner in which text displays around an object.

Theme A set of unified design elements that provides a unique look for your documents using colors, fonts, and graphics.

Theme color A set of coordinated colors that are applied to the backgrounds, objects, and text in a document.

Theme font A theme that determines the font applied to two types of slide text—headings and body.

Thesaurus A research tool that lists words that have the same or similar meaning to the word you are looking up.

Three-color scale A color scale that compares a range of cells by using a gradation of three colors; the shades represent higher, middle, or lower values.

Three-dimensional Refers to an image that appears to have all three spatial dimensions: length, width, and depth.

Thumbnail A miniature image of a presentation slide.

Toggle button A button used to turn a feature both on and off. The paragraph mark (¶) indicates the end of a paragraph and will not print.

Top/Bottom Rules Conditional formatting used to emphasize the highest or lowest values in a range of cells.

Total cell style A cell style that applies a single top border, which indicates that calculations were performed on the numbers above, and a double bottom border that indicates the calculations are complete.

Total row A row that displays as the last row in a tab and provides functions in drop-down lists for each column.

Triple-click To click three times fairly quickly withou moving the mouse.

Truncated Cut off.

Two-color scale Conditional formatting that compares a range of cells by using a gradation of two colors; the shade of the color represents high or lower values.

Underlying formula The formula as displayed in th formula bar.

Underlying value Data displayed in the formula bar.

URL An acronym that stands for Uniform Resource Locator and that identifies a web address.

Value Data in a cell.

Value axis The axis that displays the worksheet's numeric data.

Volatile The result of a function that is updated eac time the workbook is opened.

With Previous An animation option that begins the animation sequence at the same time as the animation preceding it or, if it is the first animatio with the slide transition.

WordArt A text style used to create decorative effec in a presentation.

Word wrap When Word determines whether the word you are typing will fit within the established margin. If it does not fit, Word moves the entire word to the beginning of the next line.

Workbook A file that you can use to organize vario kinds of related information.

Worksheet The primary document that you use in Excel to store and work with data, also called a spreadsheet.

X-axis Another name for the horizontal axis of a ch

Y-axis Another name for the vertical axis of a char

Index

Numbers

3-D charts, 198, 200, 202–205
3-D Rotation button, 203

A

Above button, 384
absolute cell references, 192
Accounting number format, 194
active cell, 158
Add Bullet button, 363
addition formulas, 162–163, 232
address labels
    creating, 142–143
    previewing and printing, 144–145
After Previous setting for animation effects, 396
Align button, 360–361, 367
Align Text Left button, 64, 65, 68
Align Text Middle button (Excel), 191, 259
Align Text Middle button (PowerPoint), 385
Align Text Right button, 64, 74, 111
aligning tabs, 100
aligning text. *see also* centering text;
        justifying text
    in columns, 127
    in documents, 64–65, 100–101
    in headers and footers, 74
    in slides, 290–291
    in tables, 109, 111, 112
    in worksheets, 159, 191, 228, 259
All Slides button, 301, 394
anchor symbol, 97
angling worksheet cells, 259
animation, 394
animation effects for presentations
    adding, 394–395
    duration, changing, 398–399
    timing, 396–397
Animation Painter, 396
annotating slide shows, 400
area charts, 199
arguments, function, 254
    commas separating, 261
    text values in, 260
arithmetic operators, 162
    combining several, 232
    on number keypad, 164
    precedence, 232

ascending filter in Excel tables, 269
Auto Fill Options button, 171
AutoComplete, 162, 225
AutoFit button, 105
autofitting
    table contents, 105, 112
    worksheet contents, 190
AutoSum button, 254–255, 256
AVERAGE function, 254–255
axes, chart, 196, 240–241

B

Background button, 322, 324, 326–327, 331, 350
Background gallery, 324
background styles (PowerPoint), 324–325
backgrounds, slide, 326–327
backwards compatibility, 49
banded rows in tables, 386
bar charts (Excel), 199, 240–241
Below button, 108
bevel effect, 141, 203, 207, 355, 360
bibliographies
    citations to, 78–79
    creating, 80–81
Bibliography button, 80
Bibliography gallery, 80
black, 400
black screen, displaying during slide shows, 401
blank documents, creating, 4–5
blank presentations, creating, 7
blank worksheets, creating, 6
body font, 323
Bold button (Excel), 195, 201
Bold button (PowerPoint), 291, 330, 337
Bold button (Word), 39, 62, 106, 110–111, 134
bolding text, 62, 106, 110–111
    in slides, 290–291, 295, 330, 337, 387
    in worksheets, 195, 201
books, citing, 78–79
Border button (Excel), 258
borders
    graphic, 99, 355
    page, 134–135
    paragraph, 134–135
    table, 113, 387
Borders and Shading dialog, 134–135
Borders button (Word), 134

Break button, 128
breaks, 128
    column, 128–129
    line, 67
    page, 36
    section, 126
brightness, video, 369
Brightness and Contrast gallery, 369
bullet points (PowerPoint), 288–289, 333
    adding, 363
    aligning, 363
    converting to SmartArt graphics, 362–363
    formatting, 332–333
    indenting, 289
    levels, changing, 289
    line spacing, 297
Bulleted List button, 19, 72
bulleted lists (Word), 19, 72–73
Bullets gallery, 333
business reports, formatting, 62

C

calculated columns, 268
Captioned Pictures slide layout, 364–365
category axis/label, 196, 388
cell addresses. *see* cell references
cell ranges
    converting Excel tables to, 272–273
    moving, 228
    moving, with functions, 258–259
    selecting, 161, 254
    selecting nonadjacent, 172
cell references, 10, 158
    absolute, 192
    to other worksheets, 238–239
    relative, 170
cell styles, 167, 194–195
Cell Styles gallery, 167
cells, table
    defined, 104, 382
    formatting text in, 110–111
    merging, 112
cells, worksheet, 6
    active, 158
    angling, 259
    borders, 258
    clearing contents and formats, 226–227

colors, applying, 259
conditional formatting, 252, 262–263
contents, 226
copying, 165, 171, 236–237
defined, 6
formatting, 255, 258, 259, 273
merging, 161, 164
moving, 228
orientation, 259
pasting, 237
ranges, 161
referencing in formulas, 192–193
selecting, 160, 172
Center Text button (Excel), 191, 195, 228
Center Text button (PowerPoint), 291, 320–321, 385
Center Text button (Word), 34, 64, 80, 94, 110–112, 130, 132
centering PowerPoint graphics, 361
centering tables, 105
centering text
in documents, 34, 64, 80, 94, 105, 130, 132
in slides, 291, 295, 320–321, 385
tab stops and, 100
in tables, 110–111, 112
in worksheets, 191, 195, 228
centering worksheets, 175
Character Spacing button, 330
character spacing in slide text, 330–331
chart layouts, 198, 200, 240
Chart Quick Layouts gallery, 391
chart sheets, 200–201
Chart Styles gallery, 391
charts, 196, 388
3-D effects, 202–203
bevel effect, 203, 207
clustered bar charts, 240–241
column charts, 196–199
data labels, 201
elements of, 196–197
embedded charts, 196
formatting, 198–203, 240–241
formatting text in, 205
inserting in PowerPoint presentations, 388–389, 392
legends, 197, 199, 241
margins, setting, 209
moving, 200, 240
pie charts, 199–205
printing, 208–209
renaming, 200
rows, inserting, 207

selecting, 204
selecting elements in, 201
shadow effects, 202, 207
sparklines, 263
switching axes, 240
text boxes, inserting, 205, 240
types of, 199
updating, 206–207
WordArt in, 206–207
checking spelling and grammar
adding words to dictionary, 173
in documents, 42–43, 45
in presentations, 292–293
in worksheets, 172–173
Choose a File dialog (PowerPoint), 351
Choose a File dialog (Word), 143
Choose a Picture dialog, 20, 94, 296–297
Choose button (Word), 4
Choose Picture button, 326
citations, 78–81
Citations dialog, 81
Clear Formatting button, 336
clearing
cell contents and formats, 226–227
Excel filters, 271
presentation formatting, 336–337
clip art, 352–353. *see also* **graphics**
in PowerPoint, 296–297
in Word, 40, 136–137
Clip Art Browser button, 352
Clip Art Gallery, 353
Clip Art task pane, 136
Clip Gallery dialog, 353
Clipboard, 16, 334
Close button, 7, 40, 44
closing windows, 16
clustered bar charts, 240–241
Clustered Column chart, 196
Color button, 332, 368
Color gallery, 365
colors
for fonts, 110, 134, 331
for numbered lists, 332
for page borders, 134–135
for paragraph backgrounds, 134–135
for pie charts, 203, 204
for slides, 322–323
for SmartArt graphics, 140, 365
for tables, 110, 386–387
for text, 131
for video files, 368

for WordArt, 329
for workbooks, 223
for worksheet cells, 259
Colors button (Excel), 223
Colors button (PowerPoint), 322, 365
column breaks, 128–129
Column button (Excel), 196, 198
column charts, 196, 388–389
creating, 196–197
formatting, 198–199
column headings, 158, 166
Column Width dialog, 191, 228, 236
columns, document
creating, 126–127
inserting column breaks, 128–129
spacing between, 129
columns, table, 109
columns, worksheet
calculated, 268
freezing and unfreezing, 266–267
hiding, 273
referencing in formulas, 193
width, setting, 166, 191, 228, 236
Columns button, 126–127, 129, 137
Columns dialog, 127, 129, 137
Comma cell style, 194–195, 235, 239, 255, 258
comparison operators, 260
Conditional Formatting button, 262, 263
conditional formatting (Excel), 252, 262–263. *see also* **formatting worksheets**
content placeholders (PowerPoint), 288
Content with Caption slide layout, 295
contents of cells, 226
contextual tools, 296
continuous section breaks, 128
contrast, in slide text, 331
contrast, video, 369
Copy button, 165, 229, 236–237
copying, 16
in Finder, 13
formulas and functions, 170–171
ranges, 229
slide text and graphics, 334–335
text, 16–17
text formatting, 68–69
worksheet cells, 165, 171, 229, 236–237
worksheet formatting, 234–235
worksheets, 267, 269
Corrections button, 369
COUNT function, 271
Create New Source dialog, 78–79

creating documents, 28–50
changing fonts, 38–39
checking spelling and grammar, 42–43
editing text, 32–33
entering text, 30–31
with footers, 46–47
inserting graphics, 40–41
inserting text from other documents, 36–37
proofing options, 44–45
selecting text, 34–35
creating workbooks, 156–178
addition/subtraction formulas, 162–163
copying formulas and functions, 170–171
displaying and printing formulas, 176–177
entering data, 160–161
footers, 174–175
formatting and editing data, 172–173
formatting cells and columns, 166–167
multiplication/division formulas, 164–165
SUM function, 168–169
criteria for logical functions, 260–261
Crop button, 354
cropping pictures, 354
Currency button, 194
currency formatting, 172, 194, 235
Customize Footer button, 241
Cut button, 17
Cut button (PowerPoint), 334
Cut button (Word), 70
cutting text, 17, 70, 334–335

D

data bars, 263
data labels, 205, 393
Data Labels button, 201
data markers, 197, 390
data points, 197, 390
data series, 197, 390
data source (mail merge), 142–143
date and time
in headers and footers, 75, 174–175
in slide handouts, 302, 369
in worksheets, 7, 224–225, 265
Date and Time dialog, 75
decimal tab alignment, 100
decimal value display in Excel, 172, 194
Decrease Decimal button, 194
Decrease Indent button, 289
Delete button, 108, 145
deleting
animation effects, 398–399

cell contents and formats, 226–227
citations, 81
slides, 299
table rows/columns, 108, 145, 384, 393
text, 14, 32
words, 34
descending filter in Excel tables, 269
detail sheets, 238–239
dialogs, 22
diamond shape, inserting in slides, 356
dictionary, adding words to, 173
displayed values (Excel), 160
Distribute Rows button, 385
dividing by zero error, 192
division formulas, 164–165, 232
Dock, 4
Document dialog, 63, 128
Document Elements tab, 46
document fields, 46, 75, 80–81
document headers and footers, 46–47, 74–75
document margins. *see* margins
document statistics, 44–45
document themes, 132–133, 190
documents. *see also* Word 2011
creating, 4–5, 28–50
editing text in, 14–15
enlarging/reducing display of, 141
file formats for, 49
graphics in, 40–41, 94–99
opening, 13
printing, 10–11, 48–49
saving, 8–9, 15, 49
dollar signs in tables, 109
dot leaders, 101
double-spacing text, 66
Downloads folder, 12
dragging and dropping, 17, 228
Draw Borders group, 113
drawing lines in PowerPoint, 356
duration of animation effects, 398
Dynamic Content slide transitions, 300

E

Edit Citation dialog, 79
Edit Source dialog, 79, 81
editing text, 14–15. *see also* formatting text
in documents, 32–33
finding and replacing, 70–71
in presentations, 288–289
undoing, 15, 107, 160, 325
Effect Options button, 300, 394–395

Effects button (Excel), 202–203, 207
Effects button (PowerPoint), 354–355, 361, 387
Effects button (Word), 141
embedded charts, 196
Emphasis Effects, 394–395
emphasis effects for presentations, 394–395
endnotes, 76–77
enlarging document display, 141
entering text, 15
in documents, 5, 30–31, 102–103
in presentations, 288–289
in SmartArt graphics, 139
in tables, 107, 384
in worksheets, 7, 158–159, 160–161
Entrance Effects, 394–395
entrance effects for presentations, 394–395
Error Checking button, 193
error indicators and values, 192
Excel 2011, 6–7. *see also* workbooks; worksheets
Excel Function Library, 252
Excel tables, 268
converting to ranges, 272–273
creating, 268–269
filtering data in, 270–271
sorting, 269
Excel Workbook gallery, 6
Excel Workbook Gallery dialog, 6, 158, 190
Exciting slide transitions, 300
Exit Effects, 394
exit effects for presentations, 394–395
exploding pie chart slices, 204–205

F

fade effect for slides, 398
Field dialog, 47
fields, document, 46, 75, 80–81
file formats, 49
file name in footers, 46–47
files, inserting
in documents, 36
in presentations, 350–351
fill colors, 329
Fill gallery, 329
fill gradients, 360–361
fill handle, 170–171, 233, 235, 238
Filled Square Bullets format, 333
fills, SmartArt, 140
Filter button, 271
filtering data in Excel tables, 270–271
filters, graphic, 99
Find and Replace button, 71

Find and Replace command, 264
Find and Replace dialog, 264
Finder, 9
finding text
    in documents, 70–71
    in worksheets, 264–265
first-line indents, 65, 100
flash drive, saving to, 8–9
floating objects, 97
Font Color gallery, 331
font colors, 110, 134, 331
Font dialog, 22, 133, 290
font sizes
    in documents, 18
    in slides, 295, 320, 387, 388
    in worksheets, 199, 205, 231
font styles, 38
fonts, 38–39, 94, 145, 290–291
    as small caps, 69, 290
    with themes, 323
    in WordArt, 329
Fonts button, 322–323
Footer button, 46
footers
    in documents, 46–47, 74–75
    in presentations, 302–303, 369, 401
    in workbooks, 174, 190
    in worksheets, 239, 241, 255
Footnote and Endnote dialog, 77
Footnote button, 76
footnotes, 76–77
Format Background dialog, 324–327, 331
Format button, 191, 228, 236, 273
Format Cells dialog, 225, 258–259
Format Chart Area dialog, 203
Format Data Labels dialog, 201
Format Data Series dialog, 202
Format Movie tab, 366–367
Format Painter, 68–69, 336–337
Format Painter button (PowerPoint), 336–337
Format Painter button (Word), 68–69
Format Picture dialog (PowerPoint), 354
Format Picture tab, 20, 95
Format Selection button, 203, 204
Format Text dialog (Excel), 199
Format Text dialog (PowerPoint), 290, 330–333
formats, file, 49
formatting, 18
formatting charts, 198–203, 240–241
formatting graphics
    in documents, 98–99

    in presentations, 296
    as SmartArt, 140–141
formatting labels, 145
formatting marks, 5, 30
formatting presentations, 316–338
    background pictures and textures, 326–327
    background styles, 324–325
    bullet points and numbered lists, 332–333
    character spacing, 330–331
    fonts and colors, 322–323
    with Format Painter, 336–337
    themes for, 320–321
    with WordArt, 328–329
formatting rules. see conditional formatting (Excel)
formatting slides
    clearing formatting from, 336
    slide layouts, 294–295
    themes, 320
formatting tables
    in PowerPoint, 384–385
    in Word, 104–105, 112–113
formatting text, 18–19, 34, 60–73, 328–329. see also
        editing text; styles
    aligning, 64–65, 100, 127
    bolding, 62, 106, 110–111, 195, 290
    bulleted and numbered lists, 72–73
    centering, 34, 64, 100, 191, 195, 291, 385
    in charts, 205
    coloring, 110, 131, 331
    in columns, 126–127
    fonts, 18, 38–39, 69, 110
    Format Painter, 68–69
    italicizing, 21, 167, 290, 321
    margins, 62–63
    in slides, 290–291, 295, 321, 323, 330–331, 358
    spacing, 22, 32, 66–67
    in table cells, 110–111, 385
    with text effects, 130–131
    in worksheets, 167, 191
Formatting toolbar, 5
formatting worksheets, 172–173. see also conditional
        formatting (Excel)
    with borders, 258
    with cell styles, 167, 194–195, 235, 239, 255, 258
    with colors, 259
    column and row sizes, 166–167, 191
    in groups, 234–235
    large, 272–273
    with number formats, 194–195
    with themes, 190–191, 223
Formula AutoComplete, 162

Formula Builder, 260–261
Formula Builder task pane, 260–261
formulas, 162. see also functions
    absolute cell references in, 192–193
    addition and subtraction, 162–163
    arithmetic operators, 162, 232
    autocompleting, 162
    constructing, 162
    copying, 170–171
    displaying and printing, 176–177, 258
    error indicators, 192
    moving to new cells, 258–259
    multiplication and division, 164–165
    parentheses in, 233
    range finder, 192
    referencing cells in, 192–193
    referencing other worksheets in, 238–239
Freeze Panes button, 266–267
Freeze Panes command, 266–267
freezing and unfreezing worksheet panes, 266–267
From Start button, 400
functions, 168, 254. see also specific function names
    arguments for, 254, 260–261
    copying, 170–171
    criteria for, 260–261
    defined, 254
    displaying, 258
    inserting, 254–257
    moving to new cells, 258–259

G

galleries, 20
General format, 194
glow effect, 98, 131, 354–355
Go to Slide option, 400
gradient fills, 360–361
grammar checking. see spelling and grammar checking
graphics (Word)
    anchor symbols, 97
    borders for, 99
    clip art, 40, 136–137
    filters for, 99
    formatting, 98–99
    inserting, 40–41, 94–99
    nudging, 99, 137
    resizing and moving, 96–97, 98
    selecting, 20, 137
    SmartArt, 138–139
    special effects for, 98, 111
    styles for, 99
    wrapping text around, 41, 97, 137

grayscale video, 368
grid lines, 10, 175, 199
Gridlines button, 199
Group button, 360–361
grouping
    PowerPoint graphics, 360–361
    worksheets, 230–235, 239
groups, 360
guides, 356

H

handouts, slide, 302–303, 369, 401
hanging indents, 80, 100
Header and Footer dialog, 302–303
headers
    in documents, 46–47, 74–75
    in presentations, 302–303, 369, 401
    in worksheets, 239, 241
headings, document, 5, 18
headings, worksheet
    creating, 158, 166
    printing on each page, 272–273
headings font, 323
Help Center dialog, 45
hiding
    slide background graphics, 327
    worksheet columns and rows, 273
highlighting cells with conditional formatting, 262–263
horizontal alignment, 64

I

IF function, 260–261
ignoring spelling mistakes, 42, 292
images. *see* graphics
Increase Decimal button, 195
Increase Font Size button, 320, 321
Increase Indent button (PowerPoint), 289
Increase Indent button (Word), 19, 72, 73
indenting bullet points, 289
indenting text
    in bulleted and numbered lists, 72–73
    in paragraphs, 64–65, 80, 100–101
indents, 64
inline graphics, 136
Insert button (Excel), 234
Insert button (PowerPoint), 351
Insert button (Word), 37
Insert Chart button, 388, 392
Insert Date button, 174
Insert File dialog, 36–37
Insert File Name button, 174, 201, 241

Insert Movie from File button, 366
Insert Picture from File button, 296–297, 319, 364
Insert Sheet button, 236
Insert Sparklines dialog, 263
Insert Table dialog, 382
Insert Worksheet button, 236
inserting
    graphics, 94–95
    slides, 294–295
    tables, 106–107
    worksheets, 236
insertion point, 5, 32, 288
Italic button (Excel), 167, 191
Italic button (PowerPoint), 291, 321, 337
Italic button (Word), 21, 39
italicizing text
    in documents, 21
    in slides, 290–291, 295, 321, 337, 387
    in worksheets, 167, 191

J

Justify Text button, 127
justifying text, 64, 127

K

keyboard shortcuts, 32

L

labels, 159. *see also* text values (Excel)
    creating, 142–143
    previewing and printing, 144–145
landscape orientation, 63, 176, 239
large worksheets, formatting, 272–273
launching. *see* starting
Layout button, 294, 328
Layout gallery, 294
layouts, slide, 294–295, 362–365
layouts, table, 384–385
leader characters, 101
leaders, 101
Left button, 384
left-aligning text, 64–65, 100
Legend button, 199
legends, chart, 197, 199, 241, 388
line breaks, 67
line charts, 199
line spacing, 22, 32, 66–67
    in bulleted and numbered lists, 72–73
    in paragraphs, 103, 133
    in slide bullet points, 297
    in slide text, 291, 295, 297
Line Spacing button (PowerPoint), 291, 295, 297

Line Spacing button (Word), 30, 72–73, 103, 133
line weight
    for picture borders, 355
    for Word tables, 113
Line Weight button, 113
lines, drawing in PowerPoint, 356. *see also* pictures (PowerPoint)
lines of text, selecting, 15, 34–35
List button (PowerPoint), 362
list levels (PowerPoint), 288–289
lists. *see* bullet points (PowerPoint); bulleted lists; numbered lists
logical functions and tests, 260

M

magnification, 48
mail merge, 142–145
Mail Merge button, 142
Mail Merge Manager, 142
main document (mail merge), 142
Manage button, 78, 80
manual line breaks, 67
manual page breaks, 36, 67
margins
    chart, 209
    document, 62–63
    page, 10
Margins button (Excel), 10, 175, 209
Margins button (Word), 62, 128
Margins gallery, 62
mathematical operations. *see* arithmetic operators
MAX function, 256–257
Merge button (Excel), 161, 231–232, 259
Merge button (Word), 112
merging cells
    in Word tables, 112
    in worksheets, 161, 164
Microsoft Excel 2011. *see* Excel 2011
Microsoft PowerPoint 2011. *see* PowerPoint 2011
Microsoft Word 2011. *see* Word 2011
MIN function, 256–257
minimizing windows, 7
Move Chart dialog, 200, 240
Move or Copy dialog, 267, 269
movie files, in PowerPoint, 366–369
moving
    cell ranges, 228
    charts, 200, 240
    slides, 299
    text, 16
    worksheets, 237

moving around. *see* navigating
multiplication formulas, 164–165, 232
muting/unmuting volume, 366

N

Name Box (Excel), 161
navigating
    presentations, 287
    slide shows, 400–401
    slides, 287
    SmartArt graphics, 139
    tables, 107, 383
    worksheets, 159, 206–207
navigation toolbar (PowerPoint), 400
New Folder button, 8
New Formatting Rule dialog, 262–263
New Slide button, 294, 295, 351
Newsprint texture for slide backgrounds, 327
Next Page section breaks, 128
No Spacing button, 32, 34
nonprinting characters, 5, 30
Normal button, 190
Normal View button, 158, 175
Normal view (Excel), 158, 175, 190
Normal view (PowerPoint), 288–289
Notes Pages, 304–305
Notes pane (PowerPoint), 286, 304–305
NOW function, 264–265
nudging objects, 99, 137, 359
number alignment in tables, 109
number formats (Excel), 172–173, 194–195, 224
number keypad, entering arithmetic operators on, 164
number values (Excel), 159, 171
Numbered List button, 73
numbered lists
    in documents, 72–73
    in slides, 332–333
Numbering button (PowerPoint), 332

O

Object dialog, 95
Office theme, 320
Office Theme gallery, 350
On Click setting for animation effects, 396
Open button, 13
Open dialog, 190
opening
    documents, 13
    Excel 2011, 6–7
    PowerPoint 2011, 6–7, 286
    presentations, 286

Word 2011, 4–5
    workbooks, 190
operator precedence, 232
operators
    arithmetic, 162, 164, 232
    comparison, 260
orientation, 63, 176, 239
Orientation button, 176, 259
Outline tab (PowerPoint), 286

P

page borders, 134–135
page breaks, 36, 67, 128
Page Layout button, 174, 272
Page Layout view (Excel), 10, 174–175, 190
Page Layout view (Word), 10
page numbers in headers and footers, 74–75, 401
page orientation, 63, 176, 239
Page Setup dialog, 175, 209, 241, 272–273
painting formats. *see* Format Painter
Paragraph dialog, 23, 65–67, 72–73, 101, 113, 126
paragraph marks, 5. *see also* nonprinting characters
paragraph spacing, 66, 113
paragraphs. *see also* text
    borders, applying, 134–135
    copying formatting of, 68–69
    indenting, 64–65
    selecting, 22, 34–35
    shading, 134–135
    spacing, 32, 66–67, 103, 291
paste area (Excel), 229
Paste button (Excel), 165, 229, 236–237
Paste button (PowerPoint), 334
Paste button (Word), 17
Paste Options button, 17, 73, 334–335
Paste Special dialog, 237
pasting, 17, 236–237
    files, in Finder, 13
    slide text and graphics, 334–335
    text, 16–17
    worksheet cells, 165, 229, 237
pausing slide shows, 401
pen pointer for slide shows, 400
Percent Style button, 192
percentages in Excel, 165, 172
periodicals, citing, 78–79
Picture Border button, 99
Picture button, 20, 95, 136
picture effects, 98, 353, 354, 360. *see also* graphics (Word); pictures (PowerPoint)
Picture Effects button, 98

picture styles, 297
Picture Styles gallery, 20, 297
pictures (PowerPoint). *see also* graphics (Word)
    aligning, 360
    borders for, 355
    cropping, 354
    cutting, 334–335
    effects, adding, 354–355
    grouping, 360–361
    hiding, 327
    inserting and formatting, 296–297, 364–365
    shapes, changing, 354–355
    sizing and moving, 296, 352–353, 356–357
    SmartArt, 362–365
Pie button, 200
pie charts, 199, 200, 392
    creating, 200–201
    exploding slices of, 204–205
    inserting in PowerPoint presentations, 392–393
    rotating slices of, 202–203
placeholder text, 139
placeholders, slide, 288, 290–291
plastic wrap effect, 99
playing slide shows, 301
playing videos in PowerPoint, 366
points, in font size, 38, 290
portrait orientation, 63, 239
Position Left button, 363
Position Right button, 363
PowerPoint 2011. *see also* presentations
    closing, 7
    screen elements, 286
    starting, 6–7, 286
PowerPoint Presentation Gallery, 7, 318
presentations. *see also* formatting presentations; PowerPoint 2011; slides
    checking spelling in, 292–293
    copying formatting in, 336–337
    creating, 7, 318–319
    editing and replacing text in, 14–15, 288–289
    headers and footers, 302–303
    navigating, 287
    notes pages, 304–305
    opening, 286
    pausing, 401
    printing, 302–303
    saving, 15, 287
    templates for, 286, 318
    themes, 320–323
    transition effects for, 394–395
    video files, adding, 366–369

Presenter Tools group, 401
Presenter View, 401
Presenter View button, 401
Preview button, 176
previewing
    charts, 208
    mail merge labels, 144
    worksheets, 176, 273
Print dialog (Excel), 209
Print dialog (PowerPoint), 303
Print dialog (Word), 10–11, 48–49
Print preview, 10
Printer button, 49
printing, 10–11
    charts, 208–209
    documents, 48–49
    formulas, 176–177
    mail merge labels, 145
    notes pages, 304–305
    presentation handouts, 302–303
    slides, 302–303
    workbooks, 209, 241
    worksheet headings, 272–273
    worksheets, 10–11, 175, 239, 241
Process button, 138
proofing options, 45
proofing underlines, 42
Properties button, 112

Q

Quick Layouts, 240
Quick Styles, 132–133, 207
Quick Styles button, 328

R

RAM (random access memory), 8
range finder, 192
ranges, cell, 161
    converting Excel tables to, 272–273
    copying, 229
    moving, 228
    moving, with functions, 258–259
    selecting, 161, 254
    selecting nonadjacent, 172
rectangles, in PowerPoint, 357. *see also* pictures
        (PowerPoint)
Reference Tools dialog, 44
Reference Tools task pane, 44, 293
references, cell. *see* cell references
References group, 78
reflection effect, 98, 141, 355

relative cell references, 170, 193
renaming
    charts, 200
    Excel tables, 269
    sheet tabs, 267
    worksheets, 175, 222, 267
Replace All button, 264–265
Replace button, 264–265
Replace dialog (Excel), 264
Replace dialog (PowerPoint), 289
replacing text
    in documents, 70–71
    in presentations, 288–289
    in worksheets, 264–265
resizing
    columns, 166
    graphics, 96–98, 296, 353
    PowerPoint shapes, 356–357
    SmartArt graphics, 140
    video files, 367
    Word tables, 112
Review Pane, 71
Review Pane button, 71
Ribbon, 4, 20–21
Right button, 109
right-aligning text
    in documents, 64, 100
    in tables, 111
rotating pie chart slices, 202–203
rotating worksheet cells, 259
row headings, 158, 166
rows, table
    adding and deleting, 108, 145
    selecting, 387
rows, worksheet
    freezing and unfreezing, 266–267
    height, setting, 166, 191
    hiding, 273
    inserting, 171, 234
    referencing in formulas, 193
    total row, 270
rulers, 32
rules. *see* conditional formatting (Excel)

S

Safari, 12
Save As dialog (Excel), 222
Save As dialog (Word), 9
Save As file formats in Word, 49
Save button (Excel), 9
Save button (Word), 8, 15, 23

Save dialog, 8
saving, 8–9, 15
    file formats for, 49
    as new file, 13
    presentations, 287
    in previous version, 49
    workbooks, 190
    worksheets, 159
scaling worksheets, 177, 273
ScreenTips, 20
scroll box, 287
Search button (PowerPoint), 353
search filter in Excel tables, 270–271
searching and replacing. *see* finding text; replacing text
section breaks, 126, 128
sections, document, 126
selecting
    all text, 16
    chart elements, 201
    charts, 204
    graphics, 20, 137
    lines, 15, 34–35
    multiple files, 12
    paragraphs, 22, 34–35
    placeholders, 291
    ranges, 161, 254
    ranges, nonadjacent, 172
    shapes, in PowerPoint, 358
    slides, 298
    SmartArt graphics, 140
    table rows/columns, 387
    tables, 112, 385
    text, 18, 34–35
    words, 14, 34–35
    worksheet cells, 160–161
    worksheets, 230
    worksheets, all, 255
serial numbers, 224
shading paragraphs, 134–135
shadow effects
    for charts, 202, 207
    for graphics, 111, 131, 354, 361
    for video files, 368
Shape button, 356–357
Shape Effects button, 141
Shape Height button, 96
Shape Width button, 96
shapes. *see also* pictures (PowerPoint)
    adding text to, 358–359
    aligning, 360
    grouping, 360–361

inserting, 354–355
selecting, 358
sizing and moving, 356–357
sheet tabs, 206–207, 222–223, 236
copying, 267
grouping indicators, 230
renaming, 267
shortcut menus, 22–23
shortcuts, keyboard, 32
Show all nonprinting characters button, 5
Show Formulas button, 176
Show Toolbox button, 293
single-spacing text, 66
size, font, 18, 320
sizing handles, 96, 296
Slide button, 400
Slide Finder dialog, 351, 357
slide handouts, 302–303, 369, 401
slide layouts, 294–295, 328, 350, 362–365
Slide pane, 286
Slide Show button, 367, 395
slide shows, 300–301, 400–401. *see also*
    presentations
animation effects, 394–399
transition effects, 300–301, 337, 369, 394–397
Slide Sorter view, 298–299
Slide Sorter view button, 297
slides, 286. *see also* **presentations**
aligning objects in, 361
animation effects, 394–399
backgrounds, 324–327
clearing formatting from, 336–337
copying and pasting in, 334–335
copying formatting in, 336–337
deleting, 299
displaying, 287
editing and replacing text in, 288–289
Format Painter with, 337
formatting text in, 290–291, 295,
    330–331, 387
inserting, 294–295
inserting from other presentations, 350–351
moving, 299
navigating, 287
nudging objects on, 359
organizing in Slide Sorter view, 298–299
printing, 302–303
Quick Styles, applying, 358
selecting, 298
text boxes, 358–359
themes, changing, 320–321

thumbnails of, 287
transitions, 300–301, 337, 369, 394–397
Slides tab, 286
small caps fonts, 69, 290
SmartArt graphics, 138–141, 362–365
SmartArt Styles gallery, 365
soft edges effect, 354
Sort & Filter group, 271
sorting Excel tables, 269
Source Manager dialog, 81
sources, 78–81
spacing text
in documents, 22, 32, 66–67, 113
in slides, 291, 297, 330–331
Sparkline button, 263
sparklines, 263
special effects for graphics, 98, 111
spelling and grammar checking
adding words to dictionary, 173
in charts, 209
in documents, 42–43, 45
in presentations, 292–293
in worksheets, 172–173
Spelling and Grammar dialog, 42–43
Spelling button, 173, 209
Spelling dialog (Excel), 173
Spelling dialog (PowerPoint), 293
spreadsheets, 158. *see also* **worksheets**
Standard toolbar (Excel), 158–161, 165, 168, 191, 229,
    239, 254
Standard toolbar (PowerPoint), 293, 319, 325, 334,
    336–337, 350
Standard toolbar (Word), 5, 8, 13, 15–16, 48, 69,
    70, 96, 141
Star Bullets format, 333
starting
Excel 2011, 6–7
PowerPoint 2011, 6–7, 286
Word 2011, 4–5
statistical functions, 254
statistics, document, 44–45
status bar, 286
student data files, working with, 12–13
styles, 132. *see also* Quick Styles
applying, 5, 18
for charts, 198
for graphics, 99, 297, 354–355
for slides, 324–325
for SmartArt graphics, 364–365
for tables, 104–105, 386–387
vs. themes, 133

for video files, 368
for workbooks, 191
for worksheet cells, 167, 172
Styles button, 167, 172–173, 191, 195, 228, 230, 232,
    235, 255
Subtle slide transitions, 300
subtraction formulas, 162–163, 232
Sum button, 168, 235, 239, 254
SUM function, 168–169, 191, 235, 239, 254–255
summary sheets, 238–239
Switch Plot by column button, 240
synonyms, 44, 292–293

T

tab alignment options, 100
tab scrolling buttons, 222
Tab Selector button, 100
tab stops, 100–103
Table Properties dialog, 105, 112
table styles, 386
Table Styles gallery, 386
tables (Excel)
converting to ranges, 272–273
creating, 268–269
filtering data in, 270–271
sorting, 269
tables (PowerPoint), 382
applying borders, 387
applying styles, 386–387
creating, 382–383
formatting, 384–387
navigating, 383
selecting, 385
tables (Word), 104
adding and deleting rows/columns,
    108–109
autofitting contents, 105, 112
borders, adding, 113
creating, 106–107
entering text in, 107
formatting, 104–105, 110, 112–113
formatting text in, 110–111
inserting, 95
as mail merge data source, 142
merging cells in, 112
navigating, 107
number alignment in, 109
resizing, 112
selecting, 112
styles for, 104–105
Tabs dialog, 101, 103

templates
Excel, 6
PowerPoint, 286, 318
Word, 4
text. *see also* editing text; entering text;
formatting text
aligning, 64–65, 74, 100, 127, 290–291
centering, 34, 64, 80, 94, 100, 110–111, 112, 130, 132,
191, 291, 295, 320–321
copying, 16–17
cutting, 17, 70, 334–335
deleting, 14, 32
finding and replacing, 70–71, 264–265
indenting, 64–65, 72–73, 80, 100
inserting from other documents, 36–37
moving, 16
pasting, 16–17
selecting, 18, 34–35
selecting all, 16
text boxes
in charts, 205, 240
in slides, 358–359
Text button, 328, 359
text effects, 130–131, 290
Text Effects button, 130–131
Text Fill button, 140
Text Pane button, 138
Text Shape Add button, 139
Text That Contains dialog, 262
text values (Excel), 159
copying, 165
in function arguments, 260
Text wrap format, 190
text wrapping, 21, 41, 97, 137, 191, 228
Texture gallery, 327
textures, in slide backgrounds, 327
theme colors, 203–204, 322, 325, 329, 332–333,
355, 358
theme fonts, 323
Theme Fonts gallery, 323
themes
for charts, 203
for documents, 132–133, 190
for presentations, 320–323
vs. styles, 133
text colors, 131, 140
for workbooks, 190–191, 223
Themes button (Excel), 191
Themes button (Word), 21
Themes gallery, 21, 320
thesaurus

in PowerPoint, 292–293
in Word, 44
thumbnails, slide, 287, 298–299
Tight character spacing, 330
Tile effect for slide backgrounds, 326
time. *see* date and time
timing animation effects, 396–397
titles, worksheet, 272–273
toggle buttons, 5
Total cell style, 195
total row in worksheets, 270
transitions, slide, 300–301
effects for, 337, 369, 394–395
timing, 396–397
Transitions gallery, 300
transparency, in slide backgrounds, 326
triple-clicking, 22
truncated text in worksheets, 160
Two Content slide layout, 294, 319, 350
typefaces. *see* fonts
typing text. *see* entering text

U

underlying formulas, 164
underlying values (Excel), 160
Undo button (Excel), 160
Undo button (PowerPoint), 325
Undo button (Word), 96, 107
undoing edits, 15, 107, 160, 325
updating charts, 206–207
updating fields, 81
USB flash drive, saving to, 8–9

V

value axis, 197
values (Excel), 159, 160
Vertical Process graphic, 138
video files, in PowerPoint, 366–369
View buttons (PowerPoint), 286
View Merged Data button, 144
volatile functions, 265

W

wavy red or green lines. *see* spelling and grammar
checking
Web browser, 12
windows
closing, 16
minimizing, 7
Wipe transition, 337

With Previous setting for animation
effects, 396
Word 2011, 4–5. *see also* documents
word count, 44
Word Count button, 44
Word Count dialog, 45
Word Document Gallery, 4, 13
Word documents. *see* documents
word wrap, 30–31. *see also* wrapping text
WordArt
in charts, 206–207
in PowerPoint shapes, 358
in slides, 328–329
words. *see also* text
deleting, 34
selecting, 14, 34–35
workbooks, 158. *see also* creating workbooks; Excel
2011; worksheets
creating, 158
formatting, 190–191, 223
opening, 190
printing, 209, 241
saving, 8–9, 190
worksheets, 158. *see also* Excel 2011;
workbooks
aligning text in, 159, 191, 259
angling cells in, 259
borders in, 258
checking spelling in, 172–173
clearing cells contents and formats,
226–227
column/row width, setting, 166, 191,
228, 236
conditional formatting, 252, 262–263
copying, 267, 269
copying and pasting in, 165, 229, 236–237
creating, 6–7, 158
date and time in, 7, 224–225, 265
deleting rows/columns from, 393
editing text in, 14–15
entering data, 158–159, 160–161
filtering, 270–271
finding and replacing in, 264–265
formatting data in, 172–173, 191, 195,
199, 228
freezing and unfreezing panes, 266–267
grid lines, 10
grouping, 230–235, 239
headers and footers, 174–175, 239, 241, 255
hiding columns and rows in, 273
inserting, 236

inserting columns and rows, 171, 234
large, formatting, 272–273
merging cells in, 161, 164
moving, 237
navigating, 159, 206–207
page orientation, 176–177
previewing, 176, 273
printing, 10–11, 175, 239, 241
renaming, 175, 222, 267
saving, 8–9, 15, 159

scaling, 177, 273
scrolling in, 266
selecting all, 230, 255
sheet tabs, 206–207, 222–223
tab colors, 222–223, 237
truncated text in, 160
wrapping text in, 191
Wrap Text button (Excel), 191, 228
Wrap Text button (Word),
    21, 97, 137

wrapping text, 21
   around graphics, 41, 97, 137
   in worksheets, 191, 228

Y

y-axis, 197

Z

zooming in and out, 48, 141